The Right
To Be
Different

Deviance and Enforced Therapy

Nicholas N. Kittrie

Foreword by Thurman Arnold

Penguin Books Inc
Baltimore · Maryland

Penguin Books Inc
7110 Ambassador Road
Baltimore, Maryland 21207

First published by The Johns Hopkins Press 1971
Published in Pelican Books 1973

Printed in the United States of America by
Kingsport Press Inc., Kingsport, Tennessee

For the memory of my grandfather,
a man of God and law
who lost to tyranny his life but not his faith

CONTENTS

Foreword

The administration of criminal law to be respected and accepted by the public must represent to the average citizen his ideal of justice. As late as a half century ago the public consensus was that a man who committed a crime should get the punishment he "deserved." That and only that was justice. The defense of insanity was recognized. A criminal penalty ought not to be imposed unless it could be shown there was moral guilt. Moral guilt, of course, meant the consciousness of wrong doing.

It was generally conceived that there were two little men in the top of every individual's head. One was called Reason, the other Emotion or Impulse. Everyone had, to a greater or less extent, evil impulses. It was the duty of the little man called Reason to keep his foot on the neck of the little man called Impulse to prevent him from having his way. If Reason did not succeed in doing so the man was a criminal. Only if an individual lacked the capacity to reason could he be excused of his crime on the ground of insanity.

Within the last half century these simple ideas so satisfying to a former generation have become confused. According to the modern science of psychiatry, of which the public was unaware a half century ago, thinking is a form of behavior—there is no little man in the top of anyone's head called Reason who is separate from or in control of another little man called Impulse. The right and wrong test was judicially repudiated in some states led by the decision in the *Durham* case in the District of Columbia.

Yet the Durham Rule, logical as it may seem from a scientific point of view, has led to confusion and curiously contradictory results. If a criminal defendant is convicted in the District of Columbia he is sent to St. Elizabeths for therapeutic treatment. The net result has been in some cases to keep him incarcerated at the whim of the board of psychiatrists for a much longer time than would have been possible had he not been acquitted on the ground of insanity.

For example, in a case in my office the accused had been caught with a small arsenal of guns and ammunition in the back of his car. The maximum penalty for the crime was six months. Unfortunately for the defendant, he was acquitted on the ground of insanity and sent to St. Elizabeths. Since his offense involved dangerous weapons the psychiatrist at St. Elizabeths refused to take the responsibility of releasing him. He brought habeas corpus; there was the usual conflict of psychiatric testimony. The case went up to the Court of Appeals on denial of habeas corpus by the lower court. The lower court's ruling was affirmed. The case came up the second time. Habeas corpus was then granted on a narrow procedural ground. The net result was that the defendant was incarcerated for over four years.

It is this sort of conflict between modern humanitarian ideals and practical results in the administration of criminal law which the author discusses in this book. He asserts, and I think correctly, that among intellectuals and reformers in criminal law a new ideal has become dominant, which the author describes as the ideal of the therapeutic state. He says:

> The implications of the therapeutic state for the treatment of crime and criminals are dramatic, representing a departure from the moral-religious concept that crime and other antisocial behavior are manifestations of "evil" and should therefore be suppressed and punished as a means of purging the evildoer as well as society.... As the moral-religious preoccupation with moral guilt (as manifested to this day in the concept of *mens rea*) now gives way to the concept of sanctions mainly as a tool of social defense, the door is also opened to new experiments with the treatment of offenders.

The book contains a brilliant analysis of the practical difficulties and conflicts which are created by the acceptance of the ideal of a therapeutic state. The problems raised by alcoholism and drugs and juvenile delinquency are treated in depth. The procedural safeguards necessary to prevent the ideal of a therapeutic state from lodging uninhibited power in psychiatric boards are carefully analyzed. There is an elaborate discussion of methods of meeting the population explosion which conform to due process. The book comes to no doctrinaire conclusion. It is fully aware of the difficulties, both ideological and practical. The author's prediction is as follows:

... For a long time to come, both the system of criminal justice and the therapeutic state are likely to coexist as dual modes of social control. Increasingly, however, the therapeutic state will receive those offenders and deviates with whom society is willing to experiment through newer programs of rehabilitation and therapy. The therapeutic state is therefore likely to show the road toward more effective treatment techniques.

Some time, in an uncertain future, both modes are destined to merge into a unified system of social sanctions where individual guilt will be relatively irrelevant.

The author deserves the congratulations of all persons interested in this complex field. It is in my view by far the best treatment of the problem of the therapeutic state that has yet appeared.

THURMAN ARNOLD

PREFACE: The Dynamics of the Therapeutic State

Like the five blind men, each grasping a different part of the fabled elephant and each describing a different beast, so the perceivers of the therapeutic state have seen in it diverse realities. Some have viewed it as a humanistic boon. Other have portrayed it as the first rational endeavor for the scientific control of deviant behavior. Still others have compared it to the infamous Star Chamber proceeding—the royal Tudor court that dispensed arbitrary punishments without proper regard for the safeguards that the law usually provided for the liberty of the subject.[1]

Widely diverse elements in society—psychologists and sociologists, psychiatrists and social workers, lawyers and law enforcement experts, humanitarians, social reformers, and pragmatic politicians—have joined together under the therapeutic banner for an allegedly joint endeavor. While all subscribe academically to the overall non-penal philosophy, each has some particular aims it seeks to accomplish, ranging from greater tolerance of deviation and the deviant to the institution of more stringent societal controls for social defense. How the therapeutic state has grown and how it operates in present-day America is reported later; but the reader should preliminarily be

[1] C. L. Scofield, *Court of Star Chamber* (1900).

aware of the complex forces that have molded the therapeutic state and how each segment sees within this framework the means to accommodate its own primary purposes.

THE VISION OF THE PRAGMATIC POLITICIAN

On June 18, 1969, three black assemblymen from Harlem and the South Bronx, along with sympathetic white colleagues, were considering reviving a proposal that the state set up "health camps" for narcotic addicts to curb soaring crime rates by "getting them off the streets."[2] One of these leaders, the Reverend Oberia D. Dempsey, described narcotic addiction as a national problem which assumes the proportions of an epidemic. "If we can draft our young men and send them to camps in Vietnam, we can draft our addicts and send them to therapeutic communities in health camps for 10 years, 20 years—as long as it takes to cure them of the drug habit," he said.

Two years earlier, similar voices were heard in the New York legislature during debates on a proposed law providing that addicts be involuntarily committed to special institutions until cured. Speaker after speaker voiced frustration at the failure of both criminal law and medical science to find a cure for narcotic addiction. Then Max Turshen, Democrat of Brooklyn, expressed the feelings of colleagues on both sides of the aisle when he said: "We haven't got the medical answer. So we got to do the next best thing. We've got to keep these people off the streets." Responding in opposition Albert Blumenthal, a Reform Democrat, asked rhetorically: "Perhaps we should tell the public that we're faced with a threat as great as bubonic plague—and until we find a cure we're going to set up a concentration camp in every community."[3]

THE VISION OF THE IRREPRESSIBLE THERAPIST

Designating undesirable conduct, a condition, or even views, as illness rather than crime has been a major earmark of this century's therapeutic state. The measure of the transition from a penal to a therapeutic model is dramatically illustrated by a recent interim report of The National Institute of Mental Health's Joint Commission on Mental Health of Children, which concluded that racism is the

[2] Lissner, "Harlem Leaders Weighing Plan for Camps to Restrain Addicts," *New York Times*, July 18, 1969, p. 36.

[3] *Ibid.*, March 31, 1966, pp. 1 and 28.

number one public health problem facing America today.[4] Traditionally, the commission noted, a public health problem is defined as a problem (1) that threatens a large number of people, (2) that costs a large sum of money, (3) that is impossible to treat on an individual basis, and (4) that could cause chronic sustained disability. On all of these counts racism was found by the commission to be a most compelling health hazard. But what is to be done to remedy this problem? Does the remedy lie primarily in educational campaigns to produce more racial understanding, or in the outpouring of resources, both financial and human, to ameliorate grievances? And if racism is a contagious illness, should its most dominant carriers be isolated for individual treatment so as to stop the spread of the epidemic?[5]

THE VISION OF THE APPREHENSIVE PATIENT

The clients of the therapeutic state increasingly recognize it as a two-edged sword. They fear that the label of treatment engenders in the public as much suspicion and hostility toward the one who is being treated as does the criminal label; they fear that in the name of therapy society seeks to impose controls over people and behavior that should be free of societal intervention; and they fear, finally, that the therapeutic state possesses tools of human control that far exceed in their threat to individual liberty the sanctions possessed by the criminal model.

Peter Hutt, a District of Columbia attorney specializing in alcoholism law and seeking a test case in order to challenge the local law which made public intoxication a crime, soon discovered that chronic alcoholics were as fearful of therapeutic labels as they were of criminal sanctions. To alcoholics his proposed argument that they were ill and should not be punished had many undesirable implications. Reports Hutt: "Every person, of 50 I talked with, said, 'You aren't going to call me insane?' I said, 'No.' They said, 'I'm a chronic alcoholic, but no one is going to put me in the looney business. I'm perfectly alright in appearance, but I just like to drink.' "[6]

---

[4] *Washington Free Press*, no. 48, January 16–31, 1969, p. 8.

[5] Significant in this connection is a statement attributed to United States Deputy Attorney General Richard Kleindienst: "If people demonstrated in a manner to interfere with others, they should be rounded up and put in a detention camp." Evans and Novak, "U.S. Seeking to Retain Authority for Detention Camps in Wartime," *Washington Post*, October 16, 1969, p. A21.

[6] Hutt, "Comments," *S.C. L. Rev.* 347 (1967).

Speaking one evening in November 1967, at an American University symposium on The Homosexual and the Law, Dr. Franklin F. Kamney, past president of The Mattachine Society, reported his organization's work for improving the status of the homosexual in America. Complaining of discriminatory employment practices and the oppressive criminal law which makes homosexuality a crime, Dr. Kamney was urging greater social understanding and acceptance of his group's needs and right to be different. Upon the completion of the formal papers—in which the viewpoints of medicine, religion and the law were presented—questions and comments were entertained from the student audience. A young man stood up and earnestly expressed support for Dr. Kamney: "Yes, I agree that homosexuality between consenting adults should not be a crime. These people lack the power to change their behavior. What they need is medical and psychiatric treatment, not punishment." There were flashes of color and anger in Dr. Kamney's face as he vehemently responded to the sympathetic youth. "No, this is not my view! No, it is not proper for society to substitute forced therapy for criminal punishment! Merely because someone deviates sexually from majority norms does not make him 'ill,' anymore than deviation from the majority's religion would justify such designation. Society must permit deviation unless it poses an actual threat to somebody else's life or safety." As the moderator of that evening's symposium, this author for the first time fully realized that to some members of society the dangers of the therapeutic response to deviation appear more real than the hazards of the traditional criminal process. The Mattachine Society, in this case, was well aware that due to changing social and police attitudes criminal sanctions are rarely invoked for homosexual violations, unless the offense is publicly committed or involves youthful participants. On the other hand, the new possibility of a designation of mental illness and compulsory therapeutic measures loomed much more ominously.

THE VISION OF THE UNBELIEVERS

As each of the blind men had a different concept of the elephant's esthetics, similarly today's society is certainly short of consensus regarding what an illness is, who should determine its criteria, and how we are to measure its adverse public effects.[7]

[7] A recent Harris Survey of a cross section of 1895 American households to determine what nonconforming behavior is considered most harmful to American life disclosed that 67 percent viewed prostitutes as harmful and 63 percent so

On station WNBC-TV, in a program titled "For Women Only," moderator Aline Saarinen one morning in March of 1969 interviewed a group of practicing homosexuals.[8] The following exchange took place on the program.

Woman (in audience): "Do homosexuals want to be cured?"

Female homosexual: "Well, most of us do not want to be cured because we don't regard our activities as disease. If I enjoy going to bed with another woman, and this is pleasurable and does not debilitate me in any way, if I can fulfill my functions on my job, and enjoy myself, and subjectively feel that I am having a good time, I don't see where the disease is. . . ."

THE VISION OF REALITY

Recent interviews of 100 persons, including physicians, various other professionals, judges, lawyers, former addicts, and members of the newly heralded New York State Narcotic Addiction Control Board, disclosed the overwhelming opinion that the therapeutic programs instituted under the board were more like prison confinement than rehabilitation.[9] When these programs were first proposed in the New York state legislature, state Senator Manfred Orenstein likened the proposed program to "establishing a leper colony—just to isolate these people from society." After two years of watching the commission's work, he concluded, however, that "it is worse than a leper colony—at least leper colonies try to cure."

These, then, are some dimensions of the dynamics of our particular elephant—the therapeutic state.

The study of human deviation and deviants has increasingly become popular in the psychological and sociological circles. There has in fact been for some time now a sharp competition for predominance in this arena by the various behavioral and social sciences.

Yet despite the fact that the law offers the framework of controls and sanctions within which the other disciplines frequently must work,

---

viewed homosexuals. At the same time 69 percent considered atheists harmful, 8 percent considered "bookworms" harmful, 59 percent viewed Vietnam protesters harmful, and 46 percent similarly viewed working mothers. *Washington Post*, October 20, 1969, p. A4.

[8] Kent, "For Women Only?" *New York Times*, March 30, 1969, p. D21.

[9] Severo, "Narcotic Unit Assailed," *ibid.*, April 22, 1969, p. 43.

the legal literature on the control of deviation has reflected limited critical evaluation and assessment of new developments and has often shied away from the major policy issues. This volume is intended to fill the existing gap by synthesizing diverse interdisciplinary approaches and subjecting them to the scrutiny of current legal and constitutional standards. It is intended, however, that this book will not only enlighten the legally trained reader but will further communicate the legal approach to members of the other disciplines concerned with social controls.

My interest in the therapeutic state dates back some fifteen years. While directing, from 1955 to 1958, a national research project on the rights of the mentally ill, under the auspices of the American Bar Foundation, I became aware of the need for a critical review of the legal standards and safeguards applicable to the various borderline territories of social control lodged between civil and criminal law. Subsequently, with the influence of Professor Francis A. Allen of Chicago University, now Dean at the University of Michigan, I became aware of the issues in three related areas—psychopathy, addiction, and juvenile delinquency—and discovered a common trend in the social plan for all four groups, as well as a similarity of legal problems in the relationship between the rehabilitative ideal and due process.

Reflected throughout this study is the lawyer's traditional concern with the excesses of power, in this case the conformity-enforcing zeal of the "therapeutic state." (Clearly, my major purpose has been not to *block* the rehabilitative ideal but to *blend* its unbridled power.) But as this volume neared completion, the fear of societal excesses, which still remains very real, is somewhat dulled by yet another and opposite surge toward a "permissive society," where even fundamental needs of social order and organization fail to achieve broad public consensus and support.

Of particular interest to the reader may be three amicus curiae briefs which were side-products of this study and which cast additional light upon the questions here discussed. The first amicus brief (*Horton* v. *United States of America*, nos. 17,261 and 17,540, U.S. Court of Appeals for the District of Columbia Circuit, 1963, reported in 317 F.2d 595) dealt with the treatment of drug addicts and was prepared by me as counsel for Drs. Leo H. Bartemeier, Francis J. Braceland, Lawrence Kolb, William C. Menninger, Herbert Modlin, Winfred Overholser, Leon Salzman, and Joseph Satten. The second amicus brief (*Kent* v. *United States of America*, misc. 824, October term, 1965, Supreme Court of the United States, reported in 383

U.S. 541) dealt with procedural safeguards for juvenile offenders and was prepared by me as counsel for Messers. Thurman Arnold, Gary Bellow, Elyce Zenoff Ferster, Steven P. Frankino, Robert Edward Goostree, Rufus King, Dr. Verl Lewis, Vernon X. Miller, James E. Starrs, B. J. Tennery, and Arnold Trebach. The third amicus brief (*in re* Gault, Supreme Court of the United States, no. 116, October Term, 1966, reported in 387 U.S. 1) was filed by me on behalf of the American Parents Committee and again concerns the issue of due process in juvenile proceedings.

To Dean Kenneth Pye of the Duke University Law School, Professor Chester J. Antieau of Georgetown University, Judge Orman Ketcham of the District of Columbia Juvenile Court, and Professor Sam Dash, Director of the Georgetown Institute of Criminology, many thanks are due for thorough critiques of the whole work. I was especially fortunate to have the friendship and counsel of Professor Norval Morris of the University of Chicago, who graciously served as an intellectual midwife throughout this study.

This preface would be lacking unless I also expressed my appreciation to my other friends, colleagues, and students who contributed to this study, usually through advice and consultation, sometimes through forebearance and understanding. Among these should be counted: Dean Paul Dean of the Georgetown Law Center; Dean B. J. Tennery, Professor Robert Goostree, and the late Dean John S. Myers of The American University, Professor Richard Arens of McGill University; Professor Arthur Keeffe of Catholic University; Dr. Saleem Shah of N.I.M.H.; Professor Hermann Blei of the University of Berlin; and many others. To Molly P. Rzesutek, Pat Cook, and Sally Maitland I am indebted for secretarial assistance.

Painstaking and able research assistance was furnished by my students: William C. Gardner, Ralph N. Albright, Jr., Philip B. Sklover, Edward J. Black, and Christine Schanes. Leslie L. Gladstone contributed to the updating of the materials and has searched out many of the interesting case illustrations. Eldon D. Wedlock, Jr., now Assistant Professor of Law at the University of South Carolina, was responsible not only for overall rewriting and editorial contributions but also for much of the material on addiction and the modification of man. To Hugh Craig I express my thanks for a thorough editorial review, and Diane Neustadter requires special mention for insisting not only upon a more readable but also upon a more cohesive manuscript. Some assistance for this study came from the Council on Education in Professional Responsibility of the Association of American

Law Schools, under the direction of Dean Howard R. Sacks, and from the National Defender Project of the American Bar Association of General Charles L. Decker.

My wife and six-year-old son Orde, three-year-old daughter Norda Nicole, and two-year-old Zachary McNair, who passed too many evenings and weekends without the family head, certainly deserve final recognition.

The Right To Be Different

1

The Divestment of Criminal Justice and the Coming of the Therapeutic State

Social groups create deviance by making the rules whose infraction constitutes deviance and by applying those rules to particular people and labeling them as outsiders. From this point of view, deviance is not a quality of the act the person commits, but rather a consequence of the application by others of rules and sanctions to an "offender." The deviant is one to whom that label has successfully been applied: deviant behavior is behavior that people so label.—H. S. Becker, *Outsiders: Studies in the Sociology of Deviance* 9 (1963)

Punishments are not remedies which were devised by man's reason, but concession to sub-human instincts which stir in him.... But in the Future, when the Courts convict a prisoner, he will not merely disappear from view, to undergo a senseless, indiscriminating punishment. He will not, in fact, be punished more than any other patient; but he may have to undergo a course of treatment varied according to his special need, which may, or may not, be painful in its operation. The difference between the cut of the surgeon and the stab of the assassin lies mainly in the motive which made the wound. They will inflict no moment of unnecessary suffering; if they have to give any pain, there will be purpose in it, and a friendly purpose.—G. Ives, *A History of Penal Methods* 266, 335 (1914)

If you are to punish a man . . . you [must] injure him.

If you are to reform . . . [a man] you must improve him,
and men are not improved by injuries.—G. B. Shaw, Preface
to S. and B. Webb, *English Prisons under Local Government*
xiv--xv (1922)

THE DEVIANTS

Who are the deviants? They are by no means a homogeneous group,
and the symptoms which mark them for societal attention are not
simple to classify. The earmarks of some are predominantly medical—
the schizophrenic, the manic-depressive, the senile. Others may
manifest their deviance through intellectual, chronological, social,
economic, sexual, or doctrinal nonconformity: the mentally retarded
who requires supportive surroundings, the rebellious youth, the unmarried mother, the skid-row alcoholic, the adult homosexual, and
the radicalized marijuana smoker. Probably the characteristics many
deviants share most commonly are poverty and alienation.

Contemporary America may have a reasonably broad consensus regarding some of those labeled deviant: the violent sex offender or the
psychiatrically disturbed juvenile delinquent. Social agreement may be
increasingly tenuous regarding the many others who are labeled
deviants for less hazardous social behavior and for lesser personal
deviance—the truant child, the excessive drinker, and the promiscuous
welfare recipient.

Some deviants, while socially maladjusted or psychologically abnormal, might be comparatively innocuous: the senile old lady who
nightly roams the streets without apparent aim, followed by a retinue
of cats; the school dropout; the vagrant; the homosexual; the school-
age girl who runs away from home to live in a psychedelic haven.
Others are more troublesome: the teenage boy who telephones his
spinster neighbor to make risqué suggestions, the neighborhood
painter who regularly goes on alcoholic binges while his family
languishes for lack of means, the Peeping Tom, the physician who
frequently injects his own veins with narcotics to counter the anxieties
of daily life. Still others are a major menace to society: the habitual
molester of children, the narcotics pusher exploiting the curiosity and
inadequacies of the urban ghetto dwellers, the psychopathic mass-
killer.

All of the above are the subjects of this book. Some may be universally designated as antisocial; some may be more properly described as asocial; and with regard to the conduct of a few there
may be no current social consensus. What they all have in common,

however, is that their behavior is proscribed or controlled by law. They also share the distinction of being increasingly sought out for "treatment" instead of "punishment." While hitherto no comprehensive term has been coined to encompass these diverse groups who are frequently viewed as patients and are subjected to therapeutic controls, we shall call them "deviants" in order to differentiate them from "criminals," who remain subject to the traditional criminal sanctions.

Every society has its rules. These may range from the prohibitions of murder and theft contained in the Ten Commandments to Elizabethan and Victorian proscriptions of vagrancy, alcoholism, and illicit sexual intercourse. In most societies, it is expected that a majority of the citizenry will conform to these rules a great portion of the time. But every society also has its nonconformists who need to be dealt with through the law. While the law is usually viewed as an instrument for curbing nonconformity, we must recognize from the outset that the law also functions to create and define criminality and deviation. The amount of crime and deviance in any given society will greatly depend on the range of conduct sought to be controlled.

Traditionally, the criminal law has been the major tool of the state—as contrasted with the church, family, and peer-groups—for enforcing conformity upon those who refused or were unable to abide. The criminal law in its origins failed to differentiate the various classes of nonconformists. To be poor, to beg in public, or to be mentally distracted was as much an offense as to commit a violent crime. And whether poor, diseased, or delinquent, all those charged with deviant status or acts were grouped together for equal treatment in the criminal process.

In its quest for social order, criminal law has functioned primarily as a system for assessing individual blame, and for meting out criminal penalties that fit the severity of the offense and the degree of guilt. In recent years, however, America has seen a departure from criminal sanctions and a concomitant utilization of a different system or model of social controls, described as "civil," "therapeutic," or *"parens patriae"* (a term derived from the English concept of the King's role as father of the country). Within this system, little or no emphasis is placed upon an individual's guilt of a particular crime; but much weight is given to his physical, mental, or social shortcomings. In dealing with the deviant, under the new system, society is said to be acting in a parental role *(parens patriae)*—seeking not to punish but to change or socialize the nonconformist through treatment and therapy.

The need for safeguards that would protect the individual against police excesses has long been recognized in the Anglo-American experience with criminal justice. The United States Constitution's Eighth Amendment prohibition of cruel and unusual punishment, the Fifth and Fourteenth Amendment mandates of due process, and the procedural guarantees secured by the Fourth, Fifth, and Sixth Amendments—all are examples of the necessary safeguards against the abuse of liberty in the alleged name of criminal justice.

At the inception of the therapeutic revolution, it was thought that the individual required no protection against the state acting in his behalf as *parens patriae*. Yet the complaints of abuses, as well as a growing suspicion of government's big-brother role and the social pressures for conformity, now make it necessary to explore the history and workings of the therapeutic state, which is steadily acquiring the tools for the control and, indeed, the modification of man.

In setting out to evaluate the accomplishments of the therapeutic state and to determine what new safeguards American law must build against its abuses, it is not my intention to convey even the slightest nostalgia for the bygone days of the harsh and mechanistic criminal law. To that system there is no return. The therapeutic state proclaims more humane attitudes and promises greater skills for the control of antisocial conduct. This work, however, is dedicated to the proposition that proper and timely guarantees against therapeutic excesses will better enable our society, which was founded on concepts of liberty and individualism, to benefit from the fruits of the new age.

THE MEANING OF DIVESTMENT

The criminal law in the United States has been undergoing a process of divestment—a relinquishing of its jurisdiction over many of its traditional subjects and areas. Many classes of criminal offenders are no longer subject to its sanctions: the mentally ill, the juvenile, and, at times, the alcoholic, the drug addict, and the psychopath. Similarly, various types of proscribed conduct are no longer designated as criminal; it is no longer a crime, for example, to be addicted to drugs or for a chronic alcoholic, in Maryland, Virginia, and Washington, D.C., to be publicly intoxicated.

In 1967, of a total national population numbering 197.8 million persons, nearly 71 million were under the age of 18 and usually not subject to criminal jurisdiction. An estimated 24 million people suffered from some form of mental illness or mental defect; with these should be considered an additional group of some 8 million chronic alcoholics, chronic drug addicts, and psychopaths. To many of these groups the criminal law is no longer applicable, thus leaving possibly only 46 out of every 100 Americans subject to the sanctions of the criminal process.[1] Significantly, the divestment process and its broader concepts of mental abnormality have thrust into the background the more restricted function of the insanity defense in relieving persons of criminal responsibility under the law.[2]

This process of divestment has not been motivated, on the whole, by societal willingness to begin tolerating the conduct or condition previously designated as criminal. Instead, divestment has most frequently indicated a shift from criminal sanctions to a different system of social controls. Thus divestment, carried out in the name of the new social emphasis upon therapy, rehabilitation, and prevention—as contrasted with criminal law's emphasis upon retribution, incapacitation, and deterrence[3]—has produced new types of borderland proceedings and sanctions, lodged between the civil and criminal law.

Historically, the therapeutic ideal is traceable to the common law concept of the benevolent role of the sovereign as the guardian of his people. "The king, as *parens patriae*, has the general superintendence of all charities," said Blackstone.[4] Yet while the declared purpose of the newly designed programs is radically different from those of

[1] Based on the assumption that these mental, medical, and age disabilities are sufficient to constitute a defense under the applicable insanity tests, the juvenile court exemptions, and the recent federal holdings abolishing the offense of drug and alcoholic addiction. *See* U.S. Bureau of the Census, *Current Population Reports: Population Estimates*, Series P-25, no. 321 (November 30, 1965); National Committee Against Mental Illness, Inc., "What Are the Facts about Mental Illness?" (1964); National Association of Retarded Children, telephone inquiry; Library of Congress, Legislative Reference Service, memorandum to Senator Thomas H. Kuchel, May 19, 1966; U.S. Bureau of the Census, *Statistical Abstract of the United States* 25 (1968).

[2] L. Radzinowicz, *Ideology and Crime* 113 (1966); A. S. Goldstein, *The Insanity Defense* (1967).

[3] The sanctions of criminal justice have been invested, in the criminological literature of the last century and a half, with the following rational objectives: (1) Society's innate need for retribution or social condemnation; (2) the need for social defense through the incapacitation and disarming of the wrongdoer; (3) the psychological impact of sanctions as deterrents upon both past and prospective criminals; and (4) the rehabilitation of the offender, in order to prevent further antisocial acts and influence. *See* P. W. Tappan, "Objectives and Methods in Correction," in *Contemporary Correction* 3–16 (P. W. Tappan ed. 1951).

[4] 3 W. Blackstone, *Commentaries* 427 (1783).

traditional criminal law, the social sanctions utilized often remain as severe as those applied by the criminal process.[5] The subject of these proceedings is not punished or burdened with a criminal record, but he may be incarcerated for a long and often indeterminate period. In addition, his return to society from a nonpenal institution is not necessarily any easier, and frequently is less predictable, than return from prison. Nor is the treatment accorded in civil or therapeutic institutions always better or more effective than in prisons.

The growth of new controls in the areas of mental health, alcoholism, drug addiction, psychopathy, and juvenile delinquency has become a national preoccupation, if not a passion. In great part this growth has been the product of a continuing search for less judicially cumbersome and more individualized and informal programs of social control. Accordingly, the new programs often dispense with the typical criminal law adversary procedures and resort to informal interdisciplinary and administrative processes.

Although the Supreme Court of the United States has in recent years directed its attention to criminal law[6] (3.7% of the court decisions in 1929 dealt with criminal law, whereas 32% of the decisions in 1966 were in this area), and keeps vigorously adding pickets to the fence protecting due process and the rights of those accused of crime, this book suggests that the more challenging questions of individual liberty and societal controls in America are and will be posed elsewhere. The new arena is not that of criminal law but that of the therapeutic *parens patriae* law. In criminal law the state assumes the role of accuser and penalizer; in the *parens patriae* field the state functions in a paternal and therapeutic role. Nevertheless, those incarcerated under the state's *parens patriae* powers already far outnumber those imprisoned under the state's criminal sanctions.[7] For

[5] F. A. Allen, *The Borderland of Criminal Justice* 34–35 (1964).

[6] During the 1966 term, the Supreme Court rendered opinions in 119 cases, of which 38 were in the criminal law area; compare this with 1949 when, out of 98 opinions, 16 were of criminal implication; 1937 when, out of 152 opinions, 23 were in the criminal area; and 1929 when, out of 134 opinions, 10 involved criminal actions. *See* the table on p. 7.

[7] In 1966, a total of 77,851 persons were sentenced to federal and state prisons. During the previous year, some 384,948 people were committed to institutional care as mentally ill. A total of 39,500 children were sent to training schools and detention homes in 1964. In 1966, the total number of persons in state and federal prisons was 210,895. The total number of patients in mental institutions during 1965 was 487,904, and the number of persons in juvenile training schools and detention homes was 56,516. *See* U.S. Bureau of the Census, *Statistical Abstract of the United States* 75, 158, 159 (1968); U.S. Department of Health, Education, and Welfare, *Statistics on Public Institutions for Delinquent Children: 1964* Table A 20–25 (1965).

every criminal sent to prison, more than four persons are subjected to noncriminal incarceration.

The *parens patriae* approach, typifies some of our social experiments in crime prevention as compared with crime management. In criminal law we deal with the offender after the overt act; the *parens*

The Supreme Court and Criminal Law
(A Tabulation of Supreme Court Opinions Dealing with Criminal Law)

Year	Total Cases w/Full Opinions	Total Criminal Cases	% Criminal
1815	45	1	2.2
1825	27	0	0
1835	38	3	7.9
1845	44	2	4.5
1856	121	0	0
1865	156	5	3.2
1875	462	4	.9
1885	675	13	1.9
1894	234	38	16.2
1805	262	54	20.6
1896	220	37	16.8
1905	166	22	13.3
1915	230	22	9.6
1925	209	20	9.6
1929	134	10	7.5
1933	158	16	10.1
1937	152	21	13.8
1940	166	17	10.2
1943	138	20	14.5
1945	135	25	18.5
1948	124	24	19.4
1949	98	16	16.3
1950	98	15	15.3
1951	90	24	26.7
1952	110	23	20.9
1953	78	14	17.9
1954	81	22	27.2
1955	94	17	18.1
1956	113	33	29.2
1957	119	34	28.6
1958	112	29	25.9
1959	105	20	21.9
1960	118	32	27.1
1961	96	25	26.0
1962	117	27	23.1
1963	127	33	25.9
1964	114	31	27.2
1965	107	38	35.5
1966	119	38	31.9

patriae sanctions are often concerned with the prevention of criminal acts by dealing with those showing a proclivity toward antisocial conduct. Consequently, the *parens patriae* approach is likely to present an ever-expanding territory as our society continues to shift further from crime repression and management to crime prevention.

To date, we have warded off the most searching constitutional law questions in these new areas by resorting to a semantic double-talk which differentiates between "criminal" and "noncriminal" proceedings and sanctions[8]—a distinction not carefully drawn, not easily defensible, and liable to accelerated legal attack in the future. Consequently, if we are to preserve the opportunity for social experimentation in the crime and delinquency prevention area, we must seriously and expeditiously consider the question: What should be the role and applicability of the traditional constitutional guarantees, designed and developed in conjunction with criminal law, in the "civil" borderlands of criminal justice?

THE *PARENS PATRIAE* POWER

The divestment of criminal law is only an adjunct to or part of a broader transition toward the public welfare state and its most recent incarnation, the therapeutic state.[9] Recent developments within the criminal law itself are also symptomatic of this very movement.

The post-medieval state in which the common law and the traditional criminal process flourished was primarily a Hobbesian, selfish, individualistic, cruel, law-and-order–oriented institution, offering few welfare services.[10] Repression and police power were the major tools of that society's search for social order and tranquility. The history of the subsequent Anglo-American legal institutions, including the United States Constitution, has, therefore, been primarily a recital of the attempts to curb and refine the exercise of the police power.

---

[8] Allen, *Borderland of Criminal Justice* 14.

[9] For a colorful but alarmist account of the therapeutic state, T. Szasz's *Law, Liberty and Psychiatry* (1963) is highly recommended. His study is limited to the area of mental illness and commitment to mental institutions and does not touch on the other topics dealt with in this volume.

[10] *See* C. K. Allen, *The Queen's Peace* (1953), esp. ch. 1, "Royal Peace"; *see also* Thomas Hobbes, *The Leviathan* (M. Oakeshott ed. 1946). According to Hobbes, were it not for civil government, life would consist of the ruthless competition of unmoral men for desirable things and would be "solitary, poor, nasty, brutish and short." It is the main duty of the state, therefore, to protect this natural unmoral man against himself and his fellows; T. F. T. Plucknett, *A Concise History of the Common Law* 61–62 (1956).

The role of the sovereign as *parens patriae* was rather limited in the common-law tradition.[11] Social institutions for the care of the ill and disabled were either within the ecclesiastical dominion or the responsibility of the local feudal lord. Continuing the Roman legal tradition,[12] however, the English sovereign also assumed the functions of protecting certain incompetent subjects. Suggestions of the sovereign's role as *parens patriae* are evident in the early eleventh-century enactments of the Anglo-Saxon King Aethelred II (nicknamed "the Unready"), a prolific lawgiver though a weak king. In *VIII Aethelred 33* it was decreed: "If an attempt is made to deprive any wise man in orders or a stranger of either his goods or his life, the king shall act as his kinsman and protector . . . unless he has some other." Another early manifestation of the *parens patriae* role in English law was the recognition by Edward II in the fourteenth century of the sovereign's responsibility towards the property and later the person of the insane.[13]

In medieval England the mentally disordered were first the responsibility of the church and the lord of the manor. When a national law of guardianship developed, its emphasis was proprietary, to protect the feudal succession and the heirs against the dissipation of assets.[14] The original guardianships dealt with children and the mentally defective only, but by the middle of the fourteenth century they were extended to the mentally ill and were made a duty of the Crown. From this modest beginning, followed by the slow process of welfare functions shifting from the feudal lords, the medieval guilds, and the church to the state in the seventeenth, eighteenth, and nineteenth centuries, the *parens patriae* state of present day came into full bloom.

In the political and economic forums, some of the manifestations of

[11] 1 *English Historical Documents* (D. C. Douglas ed. 1955); F. L. Attenborough, *Laws of the Earliest English Kings* (1922).

[12] In ancient Roman law, the head of the family had the power (*potestas*) and supervision over sons and daughters of any age. Consequently, it was only the mental disability of the head of the family which was of concern to the state. Later Roman law provided for the appointment of guardians (curators) by the magistrates. *Corpus Juris Civilis* (Krueger, Mommsen, Schoell, and Kroll eds.), vol. II, *Codes* (Berolini; Weidmannos, 1893–1929), code 5.70.6.

[13] *De Praerogative Regis*, 17 Edw. 2, c. 9 and 10 (1324); 2 L. Shelford, *A Practical Treatise on the Law Concerning Lunatics, Idiots, and Persons of Unsound Mind* 7 (1833).

[14] Feudal interests often prevailed over family ties. "The orphaned infant was treated as an adjunct to his lands; if he had lands held by several lords, the wardship of his body went to the lord of the oldest tenure." Plucknett, *History of the Common Law* 545.

the new *parens patriae* state, popularly known as "the welfare state," have been both welcomed and damned since the turn of the century.[15] There is little doubt of the public demand for and acceptance of increasing governmental social welfare services. Beginning with aid for the poor and public education and extending to housing, retirement benefits, medical care, and possibly a guaranteed general subsistence,[16] the state has assumed a growing responsibility for both its needy and less needy populace.

Traditionally scrutinized from the perspectives of political and economic philosophy, the growth of the welfare state has been viewed in terms of conservatism versus liberalism, free enterprise versus planned economy, totalitarianism versus individualism. Although the questions sometimes extended to the legal arena, the debate was usually limited to general concepts of public law, including such issues as judicial review, constitutional limitations of government, and the state-federal relationship. It is only recently that the new structures and the changed social balances produced by the *parens patriae* state, including questions of the welfare recipient's rights in relation to the power of the beneficent state, have received scrutiny from the viewpoint of individual liberties.[17] Recent observations by Yale law professor Charles Reich with regard to welfare recipients are applicable to the beneficiaries of rehabilitative treatment under other *parens patriae* programs:

> The law of social welfare grew up on the theory that welfare is a "gratuity" furnished by the state, and thus may be made subject to whatever conditions the state sees fit to impose. A corollary legal theory holds that since all forms of welfare represent the expenditure of public funds, the public may properly interest itself in these funds even after they have reached the hands of beneficiaries. With these justifications at hand, recipients have been subjected to many forms of procedure and control not

[15] For a significant conservative critique *see, e.g.,* F. A. Hayek, *The Road to Serfdom* (1956). Indeed, T. Szasz's *Law, Liberty and Psychiatry* and *Psychiatric Justice* (1965) appear to manifest in the realm of psychiatry the same conservative concern.

[16] *The Guaranteed Income: The Next Step in Economic Evolution?* (R. Theobald ed. 1966).

[17] Reich, "Individual Rights and Social Welfare: The Emerging Legal Issues," 74 *Yale L. J.* 1245 (1965); Wickenden, *Memorandum: Poverty and the Law: The Constitutional Rights of Assistance Recipients* (National Social Welfare Assembly, March 25, 1965); Burrus and Fessler, "Constitutional Due Process Hearing Requirements in the Administration of Public Assistance: The District of Columbia Experience," 16 *Am. U. L. Rev.* 199 (1967).

imposed on other citizens. No one will deny that fair and reasonable eligibility standards and effective protection against fraud are
necessary when benefits are handed out. But the poor are all too
easily regulated. They are an irresistible temptation to moralists,
who want not only to assist but to "improve" by imposing virtue.
They are subject to social workers' urges to prescribe "what is
best." And they are necessarily caught up in the workings of large
organizations which by their nature are rigid and dehumanizing.[18]

Even a brief survey of the expanded public welfare functions of the
state discloses a host of legal issues that cut deeply into the areas of
individual liberties and governmental powers: May the state seek to
impose standards of moral behavior upon beneficiaries by cutting off
aid to needy children if the mother gives birth to an illegitimate child
after accepting welfare payments? May the state invade the recipient's
privacy by raiding a residence to see if there is an able-bodied man in
the house or to evaluate the manner by which the aid is spent?[19]
May the recipient be compelled to work in order to qualify for
assistance?

Even more complex and hazardous are the issues of individual
liberty that come to the fore as society progresses from public welfare activities for voluntary recipients to more drastic therapeutic
programs directed toward unwilling and uncooperative clients. Because the *parens patriae* state cannot long remain satisfied with the
passive role of humane support for what already exists, it has embarked on and will naturally and progressively explore active programs designed not only to relieve but to prevent crime, delinquency,
and poverty. As Professor Reich suggests, society cannot be long
content in "assisting." Soon enough it wants also to "improve" the disadvantaged and social delinquents through the imposition and instill-
ing of virtue.[20] With the merger of the newly broadened public welfare role of the state with the reforming drive of the social and
behavioral sciences, the therapeutic state has been launched. Its primary
aim is defined as rehabilitation and prevention. But how are these to
be attained and at what cost to individual liberty?

[18] Reich, "Individual Rights" 1245–46.
[19] *See* Parrish v. Civil Service Commission of County of Alameda, 425 P.2d
223 (1967), which severely limits the right of the county to conduct early morning
raids to determine welfare eligibility. Very significant also is the recent application of constitutional safeguards to the noncriminal searches and inspections by
welfare departments. Camara v. Municipal Court of City & County of San
Francisco, 87 S. Ct. 1727 (1967); See v. City of Seattle, 87 S. Ct. 1737 (1967).
[20] Reich, "Individual Rights."

THE CRIMINAL JUSTICE BACKGROUND

The divestment of criminal law is a product of both popular and scholarly dissatisfaction with the concepts and workings of the criminal system and must be observed vis-à-vis the historical background and the recent development of criminal law. Both the divestment movement and recent progress within criminal law itself are closely connected with the advances of the *parens patriae* concept and the modern growth of the social and behavioral sciences.

Criminal law is a tool of social order, utilizing whatever means society considers adequate and proper to produce the desired social behavior or, more specifically, social conformity. "The purpose of every system of criminal law, and of every prison and correctional program is the protection of the order and security of society. The true test of the value of the methods by which criminals are apprehended, prosecuted and punished is the extent to which the methods followed succeed in actually protecting society."[21] Yet efficiency is not the only measure of success. In assessing the effectiveness of a system of justice, one must not lose sight of the totality of social values and individual liberties that might be affected by the tools that are selected.

Throughout early history, the response to crime was primarily an individual or familial affair rather than a societal or state responsibility.[22] Retaliation, or punishment in kind (*lex talionis*), was evidently the most symbolic and exact system of penalties to administer. But even its classical manifestation of the biblical *schedule* of "an eye for an eye and a tooth for a tooth" reflects a restraint upon the avenging relative, to exact no greater punishment than the harm that was done, and testifies to the replacement of primitive and boundless bloodthirst[23] with a more rationally applied scale of justice.

Private feuds officially continued in European practice throughout the Middle Ages. Anglo-Saxon King Edmund, in the middle of the

[21] F. Bergan, "The Sentencing Power in Criminal Cases," 13 *Albany L. Rev.* 1 (1949).

[22] "The penal law of ancient communities is not a law of crimes; it is a law of wrongs, or, to use the English technical word, of torts. The person injured proceeds against the wrongdoer by an ordinary civil action. . . ." H. J. S. Maine, *Ancient Law* 379 (1931).

[23] "The human being, like the animal, when struck, instinctively gives back blow for blow . . . the animal wounded by a stone or arrow seeks vengeance of the stone or arrow. It considers it responsible for its wound." Hamon, "The Illusion of Free Will," 13 *Univ. Magazine* (London, 1899).

tenth century, and Canute, just before the Norman conquest, were still establishing rules for the feud.[24] Half a century after the conquest, the law of England still provided: "If anyone kill another in revenge . . . let him not take any of the goods of the slain, neither his horse nor his helmet, nor his sword nor his money; but in the customary way let him lay out the body of the slain, his head to the west and feet to the east, upon his shield, if he has it. . . . Then let him go to the nearest vill and declare it to the first one he meets . . . thus he may have proof and defend himself against the slain's kin and friends."[25]

Religion provided the theory for the transition from the private to the public outlook on crime;[26] the Crown's self-interest provided the pragmatic justification. Early in the history of human organization is found a common acceptance of the primitive notion that crime calls for the pacification of society and its gods. Writing of primitive societies, Saleilles, the French comparative law professor, observed: "The evidence points to the fact that in the primitive period . . . crimes within the fold, among members of the same social group were extremely uncommon. . . . They aroused a feeling of astonishment and pity. . . . For this reason, when the response appeared, it was likely at first to assume a religious and later a legal aspect."[27] Explaining primitive punishment, Saleilles continues: "The culprit is appraised in terms of his crime. . . . But his punishment is referred to a higher source and ascribed to an outraged divinity. He is delivered to the vengeance not of the people but of the gods; it is they who demand an expiation, and the people offer it. Primitive punishment is thus a composite of religious observances and legal forms, and not primarily a measure of protection."[28]

In church-imbued medieval Europe, crime and sin continued to be inextricably merged. Punishment not only gave vent to the retributive need of the offended's kin and community but was often considered a surrogate for Hell or purgatory if the sinner repented his offense. From the foggy interface of state and church in this period evolved the concept that certain acts were punishable as crimes if they offended the temporal regimes of God represented by the Prince. Indeed, criminal law as a state sanctioned system was not known in

[24] II Edmund 1.7 (941–946); I Canute 5a(2b) (1020).
[25] *Leges Henrici Primi* 83 (6).
[26] N. Marshall, *Penitential Discipline of the Primitive Church* 49, 190 (1844).
[27] R. Saleilles, *The Individualization of Punishment* 28, n. 2 (1911).
[28] *Ibid.* 30.

England until the reign of Canute (1016–35). It was then that pleas of the Crown, encompassing various criminal offenses, were first formulated, thus creating a distinction between the established civil and the new criminal law.[29]

The strengthening of central governments toward the end of the Middle Ages made the sovereign's intervention in the criminal arena both possible and desirable as a tool for the consolidation of central authority. Earlier the princes and feudal lords had discovered that intervention in the control of crime could be profitable. During the pre-conquest period of private feuds and monetary compensation, the local lords often demanded that along with the *wergild* payable to the injured party, an additional fine, the *wite*, be paid to them for the disturbance of the peace.[30] As the king's role became more secure in the twelfth century, the heavy fines imposed on individuals and groups,[31] as well as the forfeiture of all property of people convicted of felonies, became an important source of revenue to the Crown and the local lords.

The facility with which the sovereign's armies could be turned into police insured that thereafter offenders and punishments would be handled by the state. This transfer of functions, however, reflected little change in the public attitude that "God's will" was served by present and earthly punishment, a belief that provided both executioner and spectator with the feeling that they were directly participating in the "Lord's work."

Making criminal law the responsibility of the state rather than clan or church effected little change in the major sanctions of the process. Societal emphasis tended even more toward repressive measures combining terror with retributive revenge. The extinction of the life of the offender long remained a major tool of criminal justice. But death too came in different measures. Under a 1530 English law[32] all poisoners were to be boiled alive, and burning was the penalty appointed for heresy and treason until 1790.[33] The ceremonial spectacle of public execution as a religio-educational tool continued in England until 1868 and in the United States until 1936.[34] Abandoned long be-

[29] II Canute 12–15; Plucknett, *History of the Common Law* 426–27.

[30] G. Ives, *A History of Penal Methods* 8 (1914).

[31] As a form of collective responsibility, the hundreds (a unit in English local government intermediate between the village and the shire) were liable to be fined for undetected murders. T. Maddox, *History and Antiquities of the Exchequer* 539 (1769).

[32] Hen. 8, c. 9.

[33] J. F. Stephen, *A History of the Criminal Law of England* 477 (1883).

[34] The last public execution in the United States took place in Kentucky, August 1936. *Encyclopedia Britannica* (1967 ed.), s.v. "Hanging."

fore that were such sixteenth-, seventeenth-, and eighteenth-century practices as drawing and quartering and the public gibbeting (hanging in chains) of offenders who were left to perish as a warning to would-be evildoers.

Another common approach to the requiting of offenders was corporal punishment—flagellation, pillorying, or mutilation. Mutilation was often directed against the erring limb—the thief's hand, the rapist's sex organ.[35] While the punishment of the "guilty" limb displays a primitive concept of fragmentized responsibility, the practice also conveys a pragmatism of specific deterrence. Mutilation further served the useful purpose of "branding" the individual on the theory that by his very appearance the condemned man would warn society of errant ways.[36]

One will seek in vain for a documentation of the popular belief that modern man has tended more than his ancestors to temper his sense of revenge-deterrence with more humane criminal sanctions. History, instead, reveals an uneven pattern in which no single society nor any given age can lay claim to freedom from blood-thirsty extremes. While the disciples of Marxist materialism claim to find in each economy the total explanation for its penal preferences ("each society punishes through the deprivation of that which it considers most valuable: property, life or liberty"), a more eclectic history of sanctions does not always succeed in matching the highest values of given societies with their penal methods.

Exile, the least retributive of the ancient penal methods and a measure designed for both social defense and for giving the offender a "second chance," was well recognized in biblical Israel.[37] It is illustrated not only by the poetic account of Adam and Eve's expulsion from the Garden of Eden but also by the later establishment of "shelter cities" to which accidental killers could voluntarily exile themselves as a protection against the "avengers of blood." The Roman law similarly required that a person charged with treason, arson, or poisoning be denied fire and water, thus forcing his de-

[35] A dispatch from Saudi Arabia reported that no thief has had his hand severed from his arm for more than a year. *New York Times*, May 31, 1960, p. 3. Up to the reign of Henry III, poaching in the King's forest was punished with the loss of eyesight. *Carta de Foresta*, 2 Hen. 3.

[36] The biblical story of Cain's mark well illustrates the ancient antecedents of this mode of thinking; *see* Gen. 4:15. In ancient Anglo-Saxon law a man charged with illegal coining might forfeit his hand and have it nailed over the mint; a woman might lose her nose and ears if she committed adultery. Ives, *History of Penal Methods* 8.

[37] Gen. 3:23; Deut. 19:2–12.

parture from Rome. Later it allowed any citizen condemned to death to escape the penalty through voluntary exile.[38]

Exile, accompanied by forced hard labor, continued as a common penal tool in modern times. Motivated more by economic than by humane considerations, exile may nevertheless be viewed as a constructive penal sanction: it permitted criminals to become pioneers in new worlds. The English Vagrancy Act of 1597 was the first statutory authorization in Great Britain to banish offenders to lands beyond the sea.[39] Under it, large-scale exile to the American colonies continued until 1776. Subsequently, Australia became the major recipient of this cheap labor and only in 1855 and 1857 did the Penal Servitude Acts abolish transportation.[40]

Another economically exploitative form of banishment was the sentencing of criminals to galley labor. In 1602 Queen Elizabeth appointed a commission to encourage the practice of commuting death penalties to galley labor, so that offenders might be "In such sort corrected and punished that even in their punishment they may yield more profitable service to the Commonwealth."[41] Service in the growing imperial fleets (and sometimes the army), if not terminated by disease, exhaustion, or death in the course of naval warfare, often resulted in the felon's rehabilitation. But in the way that transportation was curtailed with the closing of the American market after independence,[42] so galley service was slowly reduced with the introduction of sailing ships which supplanted boats moved with oars.[43]

A most interesting phenomenon has been the reliance of various societies upon monetary compensation as a penal method. Viewed initially as a substitute for retaliation, compensation dates back to early history and has a religious parallel in the sacrificial offering of goods to expiate sins. In early law because there was no distinction between civil and criminal offenses, the offering of "blood money" (the Anglo-Saxon *wergild*, which defined the value of a man's life) to

---

[38] Anyone had the right to execute a person who broke his exile. H. F. Jolowicz, *Historical Introduction to the Study of Roman Law* (1939).

[39] 39 Eliz., c. 4.

[40] France abolished transportation in 1938; in Siberia the Soviet practice was continued until the end of the Stalin regime. G. Ives, *History of Penal Methods* 202.

[41] See E. C. Wines, *State of Prisons and Child-saving Institutions in the Civilized World* 10–11 (1880); Ives, *History of Penal Methods* 104.

[42] This development caused a great upsurge in the importation of slaves into the United States to meet the needs of the depleted labor market. J. C. Ballagh, *White Servitude* 38 (1895).

[43] Ives, *History of Penal Methods* 106.

the injured person or his relatives was an accepted social remedy.[44] In some societies this method of compensation extended to all offenses. Indeed, one of the main purposes of the Anglo-Saxon legal system prior to the Norman conquest was to control and mitigate personal revenge by providing a system of compensation through monetary payment. While it was the task of the courts to fix this price, the enforcement of its payment was originally left to the victim's family.[45] Viewed in this light, the recent drive for compensation to victims of crime[46] (as distinguished from criminal punishment) can be easily traced to ancient origins.[47]

Imprisonment is a relatively new penal sanction; in ancient Israel, Greece, and Rome, incarceration was unknown. Gaols were erected only as temporary warehouses for those en route to trial. Personal liberty was not then viewed sufficiently valuable to render its denial a punishment.

The end of the Middle Ages marked the introduction of incarceration as an alternative to the earlier, physically brutal penal sanctions. The idea of imprisonment was apparently conceived and developed in the monastic system of the early Christian church.[48] It was a natural progression from the church's emphasis on solitude as a condition of penitence to the idea that solitary confinement for criminals would afford a proper environment for their redemption. The earliest known prisons were the Bridwell house of correction set up in London in 1553 for the detention and reformation of the poor, the Rasp Huis built by the Protestants in Amsterdam in 1593 for women who were to be reformed by work and religious exercises, and the St. Michel prison for young offenders built by Pope Clement XI in 1703.[49]

[44] By the time of Ranulf de Glanvill (d. 1190), reputed author of the first treatise on the common law, the old scheme of *wer* had vanished and state-sanctioned criminal penalties had taken its place.

[45] While the freemen in Anglo-Saxon society at that time atoned for their transgressions with fines when possible, slavery, mutilation and death were accepted substitutes if the wrongdoers could not pay. Ives, *History of Penal Methods* 7.

[46] Samuels, "Compensation for Criminal Injuries in Britain," 17 *U. Toronto L. J.* 20 (1967); Note, "State Statute to Provide Compensation for Innocent Victims of Violent Crimes," 4 *Harv. J. Legis.* 127 (1966); "Symposium, Compensation to Victims of Crimes of Personal Violence—An Examination of the Scope of the Problem," 50 *Minn. L. Rev.* 211 (1965); Foulkes, "Compensating Victims of Violence," 52 *A.B.A.J.* 237 (1966).

[47] Saleilles, *Individualization of Punishment* 23.

[48] The church had early developed imprisonment as a means of punishment. In 1229, for example, the Council of Toulouse ordered that recanted heretics should be saved from execution and should instead be imprisoned for life. H. C. Lea, *History of the Inquisition in the Middle Ages* 321, 484 (1955).

[49] See S. and B. Webb, *English Prisons under Local Government* 12–17 (1922).

In several European principalities systematic confinement was first imposed as a preventive measure, under *lettres de cachet*,[50] upon persons considered *potentially* dangerous to the court rather than upon convicted criminals. The 1670 French code of laws still contained no mention of imprisonment as a criminal penalty.

The first uses of general prisons for the punishment and correction of those convicted of crimes were implemented in 1681 and 1682 in the American Quaker colonies of West Jersey and Pennsylvania, but the humanitarian alternative to brutal corporal punishments was abandoned under the pressure of the British authorities. It was not until 1790 that the State of Pennsylvania reintroduced imprisonment in Philadelphia's Walnut Street jail as a regular method for punishing criminals.[51]

The discovery and occasional adoption of less retributive penal methods made little impact upon the total picture of criminal law in Europe in the seventeenth and eighteenth centuries. The social turmoil caused by the termination of the feudal system, mass migration, urban growth, and industrial development produced political regimes with little patience for humane or rational experiments in crime control. As the Crown demanded and gained the primary role in the administration of criminal law, the protection of civil order was advanced as the reason for criminal sanctions. The earlier church concern for the reformation of the sinner-criminal was no longer a factor. The surplus of labor cheapened the value of human life; repressive and brutal punishment became so common that many later English criminologists have come to regard the system as "criminal law by terrorism."[52] The number of offenses for which capital punishment was prescribed consistently grew until it reached 350 in 1780 (it dropped to 17 by 1839).[53] The mood of the times is graphically illustrated by George Ives, the English historian of penology:

> The bodies of criminals were not infrequently burned immediately after hanging, and the ordinary penalty for treason in England was that the person convicted should be drawn feet fore-

---

[50] F. Funck-Bretano, "Les Lettres de Cachet d'apres des Documents Inedits," *Revue des Deux Mondes* (1892); A. Chassaigne, *Des Lettres de Cachet Soux l'Ancien Régime* (1903); K. L. von Bar, *A History of Continental Criminal Law* 191 (1916).

[51] *Encyclopedia Britannica* (1955 ed.), s.v. "Prison"; H. E. Barnes, *A History of the Penal, Reformatory and Correctional Institutions of New Jersey* (1918).

[52] Bergan, "Sentencing Power in Criminal Cases" 2.

[53] E. H. Sutherland and D. R. Cressey, *Principles of Criminology* 262 (1955).

most upon a hurdle to the place of execution, where he was hanged from a noose to exhibit him as a felon, between heaven and earth as being worthy of neither. He was promptly cut down and, whilst still living, mutilated, eviscerated, and had his heart cut out and thrown into a fire. The head was then cut off and the body was quartered and carried away to be parboiled to preserve it; afterwards the head and the members were distributed in different places and hung up to the public gaze.[54]

If the severity of this period in the history of European and English criminal law is not disputed (more than twenty years after the French Revolution, men and women were being executed in England for thefts of more than 40 shillings in value),[55] its inefficiency is equally certain. A favorite target of pickpockets was a crowd gathered to witness a public execution—perhaps of one of their fellows. Much earlier the Venetian ambassador to Rome under Clement VII (1478–1534) wrote: "The severity of justice is such that the executioner has difficulty in attending to it.... And a strange thing is that it is said that this severity has only caused the increase of brigandage."[56]

Punishments were both barbarous and inherently arbitrary and unequal in application. The nobility was exempt from some of the most painful penalties. The "benefit of clergy," a relief from punishment applicable to anybody who was tonsured or who could read, exempted the better educated from such sanctions.[57] Frequently, the punishment was not decreed by law but was determined by local custom or left entirely to the judge's discretion.

Brutal and unjust punishments, however, are only the most startling evidence that the criminal justice system of the period had not only failed to consider carefully the complexities of crime but had also overlooked those concepts of individual rights now considered basic to the fair exercise of governmental power. Crimes were ill defined and both the Crown and judges exercised arbitrary discretion to convict ex post facto for acts not previously prohibited; procedural safeguards were nonexistent; no assistance of counsel was allowed; police would keep individuals in custody indefinitely on unknown charges and had the further powers of judgment and sentence; witnesses were secretly examined; and torture was employed to wrench

---

[54] Ives, *History of Penal Methods* 263.
[55] *Encyclopedia Britannica* (1955 ed.), s.v. "Prison."
[56] A. Dubarry, *Le Brigandage en Italie* 105, 114 (1875).
[57] D. Rock, *The Church of Our Fathers* i, 144 (1903).

confessions from the accused.[58] Some of these practices were derived
from the absolute and tyrannical powers of the medieval princes; others
appear to be holdovers from the earlier period of ecclesiastical justice,
in which the assumption of Godly oversight was thought sufficient to
remedy earthly inequities.

THE EMERGENCE OF CLASSICAL CRIMINOLOGY

During the eighteenth century's Enlightenment, or Age of Reason,[59]
new theories about the relationship of man to society were articu-
lated. No longer content to accept the stewardship of God and traditional authority, the philosophers sought to discover rational and
scientific principles governing humans and human society. From their
attempts was born a new regard for the place of the individual in
society, and an acknowledgment of basic rights and liberties to which
the individual was deemed entitled against the corporate needs and
machinations of the state.

Although Montesquieu, Rousseau, and Voltaire, among others, had
directed their attention to the problems of criminal justice, it was
Cesare di Beccaria who promulgated the first comprehensive theory
of criminal justice founded upon the principles of human dignity
developed by his predecessors. In 1764, his work, *On Crimes and
Punishments*, became the lodestone of what is now considered the
liberal or classical school of criminology. Beccaria's precepts of
criminal justice were denounced for sedition and heresy, and the
author would have been persecuted but for the sanctuary granted by
Count Firmian, the liberal representative of Maria Theresa who ruled
that part of Italy. Today, these concepts are considered axiomatic by
most of society.

First, Beccaria departed from the older and abstract concept that
crime is punished to protect "the state," and instead postulated that a
crime should be punished because it infringes upon specific rights and
liberties of the citizens of the society. The criminal is punished because he is a man whose free will makes him responsible for his acts;
if his acts infringe upon the rights of others, he should pay.

Second, Beccaria described when the criminal law should be invoked. Crime could best be prevented by punishing certain overt acts

[58] A. Esmein, *A History of Continental Criminal Procedure with Special Reference to France* 183–350 (1914).

[59] For an assessment, *see* A. Cobban, *In Search of Humanity: The Role of the
Enlightenment in Modern History* (1960).

rather than by attempting to administer vague standards of moral virtue. Crimes and their punishments should be prescribed in advance of the time that they become effective. Since it is repressive, the criminal law should be used sparingly and directed only toward activities that would infringe upon the rights and liberties of other members of the citizenry. Prohibiting activities unnecessarily would simply increase rather than decrease crime.

Third, punishment should be proportionate to the crime committed and must not become excessive. In assessing punishment, neither an individual's idiosyncrasies nor his wealth or birth should be in issue, but only his acts. The criminal penalty should be measured by whether it suffices as a punishment, not by whether it succeeds at reformation. Yet punishment should be sufficient to serve as a specific future deterrent to the particular offender as well as a general deterrent to other potential criminals.

Fourth, Beccaria announced guidelines for the administration of the criminal law. An individual's rights and liberties should at all times be protected by strict rules of procedure. A presumption of innocence should prevail, for it would be better that some guilty persons be freed than that one innocent man be punished.

Fifth, punishment should swiftly follow the commission of the acts, both to impress the causal connection between crime and punishment and to protect the accused from unreasonable pretrial incarceration. The nature as well as the extent of punishment should correspond to the offense: theft should be punished with fines, acts of violence with corporal punishment. Still, imprisonment should generally be substituted for corporal punishment since it would allow delicate adjustments in the severity of punishment and would equalize the effect of punishment on men of different stations.

After the initial shock, Beccaria's principles quickly gained a wide following. Moved by the popular response, most of the enlightened despots of Europe adopted at least parts of the new criminology. Some of these principles found their way into the American Declaration of Independence and the United States Constitution.

The most direct recognition of the new criminology was provided by the results of the French Revolution. The Declaration of the Rights of Man (August 26, 1789) spells out the principle of classical penology as well as the principle of revolutionary equality: "No person shall be punished except by virtue of a law enacted and promulgated previous to the crime and applicable according to its terms. Offenses of the same nature shall be punished by the same kind of penalties whatever the rank and the station of the offender." In 1791 the Constituent Assembly declared that "penalties should be proportioned to the crimes for which they are inflicted and . . . they are intended not merely to punish but to reform the culprit."[60]

Yet the classical school was later to discover the faults of its emphasis upon punishments that are proportionate to the crimes. In seeking a rational and equal system of penalties, the individual traits of the particular offender were thus overlooked. The impact of this classical philosophy, musically recorded by Gilbert and Sullivan in "The Mikado," is still manifested in several sentencing statutes that prescribe unbending schedules of punishments that, in the legislative opinion, fit the crime and from which judges may not deviate.[61]

While liberal trends were influencing Europe, parallel thinking and developments were evolving in England. A contemporary of Beccaria, John Howard (1726–90), advocated the establishment of a national penitentiary in lieu of transporting convicted criminals from England to the colonies. He believed in educational training, congregate work in ships, religious inculcation, and after-care upon release.[62] Some of these proposed reforms were motivated by increased interest in humanitarianism; many were motivated by Jeremy Bentham's (1748–1832) pragmatic enlightenment. Bentham's proposed Panopticon was envisioned as a prison that would give the community maximum security against escape with a minimum expenditure for staff. His detailed plan consisted of a pragmatic formula for offender classification and education followed by supervision for the discharged prisoner. Overall, crime was to be prevented by the recognition and removal of its causes.[63]

The modern, progressive study of crime and criminals, which began with Cesare di Beccaria, John Howard, and Jeremy Bentham, in the form of classical criminology, remained a dominant force in Europe until the middle of the nineteenth century. Drawing on the tradition of eighteenth-century liberalism, which espoused a belief in the free will of man and his responsibility to his fellow citizens under the

[60] Von Bar, *Continental Criminal Law* 320–24.

[61] An example of such an effort may be cited in a law enacted by the United States Congress in the 1930s which prescribed a mandatory 25-year sentence for all defendants convicted of armed postal robbery. 62 Stat. 797 (1948), 188 U.S.C. §2114 (1964).

[62] J. Howard, *The State of Prisons in England and Wales, with Preliminary Observations, and an Account of Some Foreign Prisons* (1780). Part of Howard's knowledge was derived from his own experience after being captured by a French privateer and interned in a dungeon in Brest.

[63] C. Philipson, *Three Criminal Law Reformers* (1923).

"social contract," the classicists were hedonistic in orientation. Combining Bentham's pragmatism with Beccaria's systematism, they argued that men choose between the anticipated pleasures of criminal acts and the pains imposed by society upon such behavior. Thus, a fitting and certain schedule of penalties would effectively serve to limit temptations.[64] "Pleasure and pain," held Beccaria, "are the only springs of actions in beings endowed with sensibility."[65] It therefore followed logically that punishment should be "not less in any case than what is sufficient to outweigh . . . the profit of the offense."[66]

If man has an unfettered free will to elect between several possible courses of action, the fact that one chooses a prohibited action then becomes sufficient justification to punish him. Without this free will, however, punishment would be unfair and ineffective. This reasoning was especially evident in the classicists' vigorous efforts to abolish the punishment of insane persons under the criminal law. The efforts were not totally new since insane and youthful offenders had early been recognized as exempt from criminal sanctions.[67] Still, the classicists saw their reward in the systematization of the insanity defense in England by the M'Naughten rule[68] and on the Continent by analogous code provisions. To be exempt from criminal punishment, M'Naughten required that "at the time of the committing of the act, the party accused [must be] labouring under such a defect of reason, from disease of the mind, as not to know the nature and quality of the act he was doing; or if he did know it, that he did not know he was doing what was wrong."[69] All the operative elements of this rule pertain to one's ability to choose the proper course of action, thus underscoring the central role of free will, and the function of punishment as a manipulator of this will, in classical criminology.

---

[64] J. Bentham, *An Introduction of the Principles of Morals and Legislation* (1907); C. B. Beccaria, *On Crimes and Punishments* (1764; Paolucci trans. 1963); Sutherland and Cressey, *Principles of Criminology* 52–53.

[65] C. B. Beccaria, *An Essay on Crime and Punishments* 12 (Ingraham trans. 1819).

[66] Bentham, *Morals and Legislation* 179.

[67] Historically, the exemption of those lacking evil intent had not been consistent, however. Frequently, the immaturity and mental condition of offenders went totally unrecognized. Primitive retribution often exacted punishment even from wrong-doing animals. "Accused animals would occasionally receive a 'poetic punishment' like the sow at Falaise, which, in the year 1386, was convicted of having bitten the face and leg of a child. She was dressed up in human clothing, and mutilated in the head and hind leg, before being hanged before the crowd in the market place." Ives, *History of Penal Methods* 257.

[68] Daniel M'Naughten's case, House of Lords, 8 Eng. Rep. (1843).

[69] *Ibid.* 718.

THE THERAPEUTIC STATE'S FOUNDATIONS
IN DETERMINISTIC CRIMINOLOGY

Classical criminology's free-will, egalitarian, yet mechanistic approach to the administration of criminal justice finally, and ironically, came under attack both for its denial of individualism and its pragmatic defects. The new challenge stemmed from a growing scientific awareness of the multiplicity of the social causes of crime and the diversity of criminal types; pragmatically, it was the result of the realization that punishment alone, however severe, is impotent to deter or prevent crime.

Seeking the sources of criminal behavior and the means for its prevention, scientific criminology directed its attention to two major, and possibly controllable, elements: crime as an expression of conditions surrounding man and crime as a product of man's constitution (colorfully and homonymously contrasted as "nurture" and "nature"). Soon, classical criminology's assumption of free will was replaced by two schools of determinism—social determinism, on one hand, and bio-psychological determinism, on the other. Among students of criminal behavior definite preferences have been manifested over the years either for the exclusive or at least predominant role of "nurture"[70] or, in contrast, for the predominance of "nature."[71] Only in more recent times has a mixture of both been put forward in the form of a multi-factor approach.[72]

In the 1830s, two Frenchmen—Lambert Adolphe-Jacques Quetet, an astronomer, and Andre-Michel Guerry, a lawyer—postulated that crime was a phenomenon of social organization and that, as such, it was susceptible to scientific measurement and prediction. Although they proceeded separately and jealously, their work was largely complementary. Utilizing newly introduced criminal statistics, both men investigated the rate of crime for various demographic sets, relating its incidence to age, sex, education, climate, and race. From these studies emerged two patterns: first, the rate of crime and its types in a given group were approximately constant; and second, the various segments of the population (for example, the young, the urban, the

---

[70] "We cannot indeed expect to alter human nature; but we *can* alter the eliciting surroundings." Ives, *History of Penal Methods* 333.

[71] For a highly readable account of the various schools of criminology, see Radzinowicz, *Ideology and Crime.*

[72] Sutherland and Cressey, *Principles of Criminology* 59–62.

poor) contributed to the crime rate approximately the same propor-tion from year to year.

Recognition of the social conditions within which criminals and crime are bred is present in many nineteenth-century writings. A British Royal Commission inquiring into the problems of crime re-ported in 1863: "The number of crimes committed . . . is probably less affected by the system of punishment which may be in use than by various other circumstances, such as the greater or lesser welfare of the population, the demand for work, etc."[73] Karl Marx was one of the first to predict that the elimination of capitalistic exploitation would result not only in the dissolution of the political state but in the disappearance of crime as well.[74]

The partisans of social determinism have ranged in interpretations from Marx's and Bonger's[75] dialectical materialism through Suther-land's[76] "differential association" and on to Merton's[77] "anomie." Wil-liam Adrian Bonger, a Dutch professor of sociology, proposed in 1916 the theory that the capitalistic economic system forces the poorer classes disproportionately into crime through poverty, unemployment, bad housing, slack upbringing due to working mothers, lack of educa-tion, and lack of opportunities. The capitalistic society, according to Bonger, nourishes the bad seeds of crime. While an altruistic society would prevent its members from inclining to egoistic manifestations, capitalism's mode of production based on private property and in-dividual profit is inimical to the development of social consciousness and reciprocity. With the interest of its members in eternal competi-tion and conflict, men under capitalism tend to be more egoistic and "more capable of crime."[78]

Edwin H. Sutherland, an American sociologist writing some twenty years after Bonger, represents a different school of social determinism, which owed its origins to the French social psychologist Gabriel Tarde[79] and postulated the social transmittability of patterns of crime. Hypothesizing that persons acquire patterns of criminal behavior in the same way they acquire lawful patterns, Sutherland concluded that a person becomes a delinquent because of an excess of social

[73] Report, Royal Commission 23 (1863) in Ives, *History of Penal Methods* 200.
[74] K. Marx, *The Poverty of Philosophy* (1847; Eng. trans. 1935).
[75] W. A. Bonger, *Criminology and Economic Conditions* (Horton trans. 1916).
[76] Sutherland and Creesey, *Principles of Criminology* 74–81.
[77] R. K. Merton, *Social Theory and Social Structure* 161–94 (1957).
[78] Radzinowicz, *Ideology and Crime* 43.
[79] G. de Tarde, *Penal Philosophy* (1890; Howell trans. 1912).

associations favorable to law violation, and attributed high-crime incidence among groups—young adults, ghetto dwellers—to the absence of anticriminalistic traditions.

A modern emphasis on social factors is stressed by Robert K. Merton who sees in crime a manifestation of the conflict between society's placement of emphasis upon success goals—such as wealth and prosperity—and the inaccessibility of these goals to a considerable part of the population. The criminal, then, is a person who accepts society's success values but is denied the legitimate means to attain them—for him crime is the only means for achieving the socially desired successes.

The emphasis on man's biology or psychology rather than his social condition as the key to crime has been more formally described as constitutional determinism. As much as social determinism owes its origins to Marx, constitutional determinism is heavily linked to the ideas of Darwin.

In the 1860s, the Italian criminologist Cesare Lombroso developed a theory for the scientific analysis of crime and criminals. Unlike the social determinists, this new school (called positivist from its reliance on experimental methods of analysis) postulated that criminals are born as such rather than led by their environment into lives of crime. From this thesis sprang the concept that an individual's proclivity toward crime was predetermined by his lineage and could be predicted by various physiological or psychological anomalies.

As with social determinism, constitutional deterministic theories cover a broad spectrum ranging from Lombroso's theory of the criminal type and Lange's claims for inherited criminality[80] to psychiatric and psychoanalytical determinism and even Sheldon and Eleanor Glueck's multi-factor formula for criminological prediction.[81] Lombroso[82] emphasized that criminals are by birth of a distinct biological type, identified by a long lower jaw, flat nose, sparse beard, and low sensitivity to pain. He believed these anatomical characteristics to be an atavism, a throwback to a pre-human type. Drawing from Darwin's teachings, he believed that the evolution of man from lower animals implied the possibility of organic and moral regression to the standards of primitive man. Lange sought to establish through

[80] J. Lange, *Crime and Destiny* (1930).

[81] S. and E. Glueck, *Predicting Delinquency and Crime* (1959) and *Unraveling Juvenile Delinquency* (1950).

[82] G. Lombroso Ferrero, *Criminal Man According to the Classification of Cesare Lombroso* (1911).

his study of one-egg twins as contrasted with two-egg twins that criminality is inherited. The most recent illustration of biological determinism is contained in the current scientific debate regarding the effect of the XYY chromosomal irregularity upon deviant behavior.[83]

Psychiatric determinism was expounded first by the mid-nineteenth-century psychiatrists—such as J. C. Prichard and H. Maudsley—who explained crime as moral insanity.[84] Later studies, of which Goddard's[85] is typical, suggested that nearly all criminals and delinquents are of low-grade mentality and constitute an inferior mental type. The psychoanalysts—long the step-children of psychiatry—have emphasized, on the other hand, the effects of repressed unconscious conflicts and early traumatic experiences (especially sexual) upon criminal behavior.[86] To this day faith in constitutional determinism combining both biological and psychological factors, is manifested in the emphasis upon psychometric studies of the delinquent's personality[87] and the numerous attempts to construct delinquency prediction tables.

The social determinist and the positivist or constitutional determinist schools of criminology need not maintain mutually exclusive theories. Historically each school felt that it alone had provided the true prescription for the genesis of crime. Despite their scholastic jealousies, however, both the positivists and the social determinists reached a common philosophical position that distinguished them from the classical school of criminology by postulating that free will could never provide the foundation for a system of criminal justice. Either persons were born with criminal behavior patterns, or their social climate induced criminal tendencies: individuals exercised little control over these forces. Thus the purpose of classical punishment—deterrence through retribution—held little credence with the newer schools of criminology, for retribution was unlikely to change the predisposing factors of environment or individual nature.

About this rallying point, Italian Criminal Law Professor Enrico Ferri in the late nineteenth century gathered adherents from both the positivists and the social determinist school. Ferri attempted to con-

---

[83] Marinello, Berkson, Edwards, and Bannerman, "A Study of the XYY Syndrome in Tall Men and Juvenile Delinquents," 208 *J.A.M.A.* 321 (1969); Note, "The XYY Chromosome," 57 *Georgetown L. J.* 892 (1969).

[84] Radzinowicz, *Ideology and Crime* 46.

[85] H. H. Goddard, *Human Efficiency and Levels of Intelligence* 73–74 (1920).

[86] Hakeem, "A Critique of the Psychiatric Approach to Crime and Delinquency," 23 *Law & Contemp. Prob.* 650–82 (1958).

[87] K. F. Schuessler and D. R. Creesey, "Personality Characteristics of Criminals," 55 *Amer. J. Sociol.* 476–84 (1950).

struct a complete foundation not only for the understanding of crime but also for its prevention through social and economic change. As Ferri graphically stated: "Certain discreet shelters arranged in convenient places contribute more to the cleanliness of cities than fines and arrests."[88] While Ferri believed that with the coming of social justice "penal justice as an establishment of violent repression and class domination is destined to disappear," his earlier exposure to Lombroso's biological determinism and to Herbert Spencer's philosophical law that neither physical nor social homogeneity can be permanently retained, conditioned him against predicting that social reform would bring the total end of crime. "Even Socialism," Ferri concluded, "which looks forward to a fundamental transformation of future society on the basis of brotherhood and social justice, cannot elevate itself to the absolute and naive faith that criminality, insanity and suicide can ever fully disappear from the earth."[89]

Scientific evidence indicated to Ferri that man and not just the conditions about him must be explored and treated in order to have effective crime prevention.

> If you regard the general condition of misery as a sole source of criminality, then you cannot get around the difficulty that out of one thousand individuals living in misery from the day of their birth to that of their death, only one hundred or two hundred become criminals, while the other nine hundred or eight hundred either sink into biological weakness or become harmless maniacs or commit suicide without perpetrating any crime. If poverty were the sole determining cause, one thousand out of one thousand poor ought to become criminals. If only two hundred become criminals, while one hundred commit suicide, one hundred end as maniacs, and the other six hundred remain honest in their social condition, then poverty alone is not sufficient to explain criminality. We must add the anthropological and telluric factor.[90]

It was Ferri's eclecticism that allowed both the social determinists and the positivists to see him as their champion. Adherents to the determinist schools gathered strength to attack the classical concepts of free will, egalitarianism, retribution, and deterrence as the proper foundations for criminal justice. Led by Ferri, the insurgents proposed abolishing criminal responsibility and moral guilt as the founda-

[88] E. Ferri, *Criminal Sociology* 242 (Kelly and Lisle trans. 1917).
[89] E. Ferri, *The Positive School of Criminology* 119 (Kelly and Lisle trans. 1906).
[90] *Ibid.* 60.

tion of criminal justice and replacing them with principles of social defense. They proposed that when an individual has been found to have committed an act harmful to society, the law should not be concerned with questions of guilt and its degrees nor with measuring a fit punishment, but should humanely apply whatever measures are necessary to protect society from further transgressions by the same individual. In applying these measures, the law should take particular account of the offender's heredity and the environmental factors that caused his antisocial behavior. "Punishment should fit the individual, not the offense."[91]

The temporal continuity between Ferri's recognition that even under the most favorable social conditions sporadic cases of criminality may arise (due to traumatic factors or to bio-psychological pathology)[92] and the early blossoming of psychology and psychiatry gave impetus to the claims of the behavioral scientists that the cause of crime and other antisocial behavior lies within their discipline. The emphasis in the search for the control of crime and delinquency shifted from socioeconomic and hereditary factors to the internal psychological makeup of the individual offender. The criminal is thus described as "carrying out in his actions his natural unbridled instinctual drives; he acts as the child would act if it only could."[93] Criminal behavior, according to the psychiatric thesis, must be viewed as an expression of certain personality disturbances, developed quite apart from the socioeconomic culture. Often, these disturbances are said to reflect the delinquent's relations with his parents. "We may say that the causes of a child's delinquent behavior may be traced to his parents, particularly to his mother's emotional attitude toward his early instinctual manifestations."[94]

A recent statement of the psychoanalytical viewpoint will well illustrate the changed approach:

The criminal commits his specific crime for two reasons; he is confronted with an unconscious conflict (variable factor) and solves his conflict by commiting a herostratic [Herostratos, in 346 B.C., burned the famous temple of Artemis in Ephonos in order to gain fame] motor act (constant factor), motivated by an infantile pre-oedipal pattern, also unconscious. It is, therefore, not

[91] Ferri, *Criminal Sociology.*
[92] *Ibid.* 568.
[93] F. G. Alexander and H. Staub, *The Criminal, the Judge and the Public* 30 (Zilboorg trans. 1956).
[94] D. Abrahamsen, *Who Are the Guilty?* 27 (1952).

true that everyone is a potential criminal. Criminality presupposes specific childhood conflicts and their insolubility. By the same token it is not true that unfavorable social factors alone can explain criminality. In many instances the social factor in criminal action is either an excuse or a rationalization for hidden unconscious motives. The focal point of the criminal act is the repetition of injustices experienced in reality or fantasy in the child-mother (later, father) relationship, projected and perpetuated masochistically upon society.[95]

The psychoanalytical literature frequently interprets specific features of crimes in terms of their presumed unconscious significance for the criminal. The victim may thus be viewed as a stand-in for the murderer's wife or father, and a stolen automobile may be said to symbolically stand for the offender's mother.[96] While this type of permutation does not represent the consensus of psychiatric thinking about antisocial behavior, its focus upon individual-centered explanations of crime is typical,[97] and today it exerts an increasing influence upon the emerging penal and correctional system.

Surveying the dramatic change in criminological thought and its bearings upon administering criminal justice, one recent writer concluded:

> But by the beginning of the 20th Century a realization of the inefficiency of this system of deterrence by long penal servitude as an effective means of protecting society against crime began to be felt and became demonstrable. It was known to be especially wasteful of human values and of human resources. Reformation of the offender was no part of it.
>
> The last 50 years have witnessed a critical evaluation of the utility to society of these successive systems. The conclusion that they have not succeeded in their purpose has been widespread in all countries. There has evolved from this experience the thesis that a more workable way to protect society is to fit the treatment to the individual; not the punishment to the crime; to attempt to learn the causes of his offense by skillful and experienced study and judgment, by reeducation where that is possible so that his skills and talents can be utilized in the interests of society instead of toward its destruction, with the purpose that as a result of the treatment he receives he may become useful to society.

95 *Criminal Psychology* 6–7 (R. W. Nice ed. 1962).
96 Abrahamsen, *Who Are the Guilty?* 23.
97 *Legal and Criminal Psychology* 207 (H. Toch ed. 1961); P. Q. Roche, *The Criminal Mind* 14–29 (1958).

The concept of "treatment" has replaced the concept of "punishment."[98]

This evolution is couched in highly pragmatic terms. It suggests that the recent attitudes toward treatment of offenders spring from an objective determination that brutality, terror, and mechanistic rules do not serve the primary goals of our penal system—social defense. In this modern search for social defense, determinism continues as an underlying philosophy, and the traditional techniques for accomplishing order and conformity—retribution, deterrence, incapacitation, and rehabilitation—assume new perspectives. "Retribution is no longer the dominant objective of criminal law. Reformation and rehabilitation of offenders have become the important goals of criminal jurisprudence."[99] With this dictum, Supreme Court justice Hugo Black summarized the direction of penology in the past thousand years.

Even more forceful and far-reaching is the new concern not only with rehabilitation of offenders but with the very prevention of criminality. Significant and typical of the new concern are the observations of Edwin J. Lukas, formerly executive director of the Society for the Prevention of Crime:

> . . . It is a melancholy fact that nearly every society has underestimated the depth and scope of crime, especially in its context as the symptom of complex aggressive and acquisitive motivations. Now, as in the past, we seem more preoccupied with a desultory nibbling at the thin edges of the difficult problems involved in "prevention," than in coping with their more substantial and, to be sure, complicated essence. . . .
>
> Let us state the proposition in the form of two searching questions, and thus come quickly to the core of this discussion: In the name of prevention, are we content to continue only to repress crime? Shouldn't our efforts instead be concentrated upon preventing the development of individual predisposition to crime? . . . To dwell preponderantly on the former (as we do) is to deal with the problem opportunistically. To shift emphasis more to the latter is to deal with it realistically and enduringly. In brief, we can prevent crime most effectively by learning when and how to prevent individual criminals.[100]

This is clearly a new social manifesto. It proclaims a transition from

[98] Bergan, "Sentencing Power in Criminal Cases" 3.
[99] Williams v. New York, 337 U.S. 241, 248 (1949).
[100] E. J. Lukas, "Crime Prevention: A Confusion in Goal," in *Contemporary Correction* 398 (P. W. Tappan ed. 1951).

a system of sanctions that deals with individuals after an offense has occurred to a social program that seeks a much earlier social intervention—to prevent initially the creation of offenders.

If indeed the psychiatric or the psychosocial analyses of crime and the criminal are correct, their significance to the new social program of prevention is overwhelming. They suggest that external conditions, while contributing to criminal developments, are not controlling, but that an inner imbalance is a prerequisite to crime. It follows that potential criminals could possibly be identified in advance of any offensive act and treated to correct the imbalance. Furthermore, as long as inner conflict remains unresolved, the past or potential criminal will continue being a threat to society.

In the face of these new concepts of criminality, the traditional tools of criminal law, basically forged in the fires of classical criminology, appear patently inadequate while the newer sociopsychiatric or biological tools of the *parens patriae* state assume a greater appeal to those concerned with the control of deviation.

CAUSES FOR THE DIVESTMENT OF CRIMINAL LAW

The increased public acceptance of the state's *parens patriae* role, combined with the promises of modern social and behavioral science in the areas of correction and rehabilitation, have nearly revolutionized criminal justice. Its boundaries have been redefined and, through a process of divestment, noncriminal controls and procedures have usurped areas previously claimed by criminal law. The historical roots of divestment can be traced back to fourteenth century England's exemption of insane murderers from criminal responsibility. But the more meaningful manifestation of this process began with the early nineteenth-century realization that the institutionalization of the nonviolent insane should be distinguished, both physically and conceptually, from the incarceration of criminals.[101]

The growing agitation of the positivists in the late nineteenth

---

[101] The first institution in America designed exclusively for the mentally ill was authorized in New York in 1697. This was to be a one-man asylum and whether it was constructed is not clear. In 1751 the provisional Assembly of Pennsylvania, in response to a petition drawn by Benjamin Franklin, passed an act to encourage the construction of a hospital to serve the insane as well as the physically ill. The hospital opened in 1756. The very first asylum erected exclusively for the mentally ill was opened in 1773 in Williamsburg. The second exclusive institution was not built until 1817 in Frankford, Pennsylvania. *See* A. Deutsch, *The Mentally Ill in America* 42, 95 (1937).

century, and their argument that the crime control activities of the state should fit the offender rather than the crime, accelerated the process of divestment. These cries for reform fell upon receptive ears not only regarding the broader exemption of insane offenders—resulting in the M'Naughten rule—but also in the treatment accorded to juvenile offenders.

At the end of the nineteenth century, juveniles were formally exempted from traditional criminal sanctions and proceedings.[102] A special court was born on July 1, 1899, under an Illinois law that established a juvenile court in the City of Chicago.[103] Through subsequent legislative and judicial actions, psychopaths (in the 1930s),[104] drug addicts (in 1962),[105] and alcoholics (in 1966)[106] were similarly removed from the jurisdiction of the criminal law.

What were the specific reasons for the divestment of criminal law and what social needs does it fulfill? What have been the major reasons for dissatisfaction with criminal law that have resulted in the divestment process?

Social Reform and Humanism

As much as the new criminological theories weakened the philosophic foundations of classical law, it was the economic revolution marking the industrialization of Great Britain and the United States that provided the impetus to change the existing legal system. With the "popularization" of government, new classes obtained a voice by which they could proclaim their dissatisfaction with long prison sentences and the harsh treatment of the past. Individualized treatment (which seeks to relieve the offender's shortcomings) was seized upon as being more humane as well as more effective in controlling crime. Thus socioeconomic pressures for humanization and individual-

---

[102] C. B. Vedder, *Juvenile Offenders* 143, 144 (1963).

[103] 78 *Ill. Laws of 1899* 131.

[104] In 1938, Illinois became the first state to enact a sexual psychopath statute. *Ill. Rev. Stat.* ch. 38, §§820.01 to 825 (1957). Earlier, in 1911, Massachusetts provided for the special treatment of the "defective delinquent." *Mass. Acts and Resolves* ch. 595, §§1–12 (1911); *Mass. Gen. Laws* ch. 123, §§113–24 (1958). A broader approach, not limited to sexual offenders as in Illinois or to mentally deficient offenders as in Massachusetts, is manifested by the Maryland law which encompasses all psychopaths. *Md. Code Ann.* 31B–5 (1957).

[105] Robinson v. California, 370 U.S. 66 (1962).

[106] Driver v. Hinnant, 356 F.2d 761 (4th Cir. 1966); Easter v. District of Columbia, 261 F.2d 50 (D.C. Cir. 1966).

ization[107] as well as the new theories contributed to the movement for the reformation of criminal justice.

The Absence of Moral Guilt

Canon Law based punishment on moral guilt.[108] Derived from this philosophy was the requirement of *mens rea* (literally "evil mind" or awareness of wrongdoing) in the common law of crimes. Without a capacity for *mens rea*, punishment was inappropriate and useless. The recognition that certain classes of offenders were incapable of guilt because of defective mentality resulted in the exemption of criminal lunatics and idiots from criminal sanctions as early as the beginning of the fourteenth century.[109] Children, equally presumed by the common law to lack mental capacity and, therefore, *mens rea*, were likewise exempted from criminal penalties.[110] Originally, the incapacity sufficient to constitute an absence of *mens rea* and an exemption from criminal sanctions required a condition of total delusion or immaturity.

In recent years these standards have been liberalized, in great part due to the more widely accepted determinist philosophy. As scientific evidence increases, we are more willing to believe that man in many instances cannot control his own behavior through free will. Unwilling to embrace totally determinism and its awful denial of man's mastery over his destiny, society accommodates and balances determinism with the classical notion that the absence of *mens rea* exempts one from the criminal law. As evidence mounts that certain people are unable to restrain themselves from acts which may constitute criminal offenses, those individuals are declared to be devoid of *mens rea* and are exempted from the criminal law.

The defense of insanity has been liberalized to encompass a broader

[107] Saleilles, *Individualization of Punishment.*

[108] *See* W. L. Clark and W. L. Marshall, *A Treatise on the Law of Crimes* 11, 12 (1958).

[109] Some writers claim that the insane have been exempt from criminal liability in the Anglo-American legal system since the reign of Edward III (1326–77). *See* J. Biggs, *The Guilty Mind: Psychiatry and the Law of Homicide* 83 (1955). One of the earliest tests of insanity (the knowledge of good and evil) is contained in a volume first printed in 1582: W. Lambard, *Eirenarchia: Or of the Office of the Justice of Peace,* ch. 21.218. *See also* Clark and Marshall, *Law of Crimes* 339.

[110] The exemption under common law was automatic for children under the age of seven. For those aged seven and over, responsibility was a jury question, with a presumption of no responsibility until the age of fourteen and a presumption of capability after fourteen. Clark and Marshall, *Law of Crimes* 391–95.

segment of the mentally affected offenders.[111] Recent judicial findings have held that the drug addict and the alcoholic are devoid of *mens rea* when caught in the grip of their addiction.[112] Two different United States Courts of Appeals recently found that the chronic alcoholic cannot be convicted of public intoxication because his presence in public "is not his act, for he did not will it."[113] Without the necessary "evil intent" or "a consciousness of wrong doing," criminal sanctions cannot be used.[114]

The Inappropriateness of Punishment

The next factor in the divestment process is the absence within classical criminology of defenses against antisocial behavior by persons who cannot or may not be punished. Because punishment is the only sanction utilized by the criminal law, any attempt at quarantining, through the criminal law, those who are ill and dangerous to society immediately runs into humane and moral objections against "punishing" the ill and immature. As more groups of people are exempted from the criminal law because they are too sick or young to possess a *mens rea*, the less effective the criminal law is in providing society with protection through isolation or treatment of dangerous individuals. The therapeutic state in these areas provides the necessary alternatives.

The trend toward the differentiation between the ill and the criminal and the liberation of the former from punishment was institutionalized by the recent expansion of the applications of the Eighth Amendment to the United States Constitution, which proscribes "cruel and unusual punishment." Originally directed against physically cruel methods of punishment of criminals, this protection has lately been construed not only to prohibit punishment disproportionate to the offense but also to proscribe the use of traditional criminal sanctions

[111] For current tests of insanity, *see The Mentally Disabled and the Law* 330–47 (F. T. Lindman and D. M. McIntyre eds. 1961). A raging debate continues about whether those deprived of social judgment and adaptability (the sociopath) should be accorded the same exemptions from criminal sanctions as the mentally ill and defective. *See* United States v. Currens, 290 F.2d 751 (3d Cir. 1961); ALI, *Model Penal Code* §4.01 (Mental Disease or Defect Excluding Responsibility), draft no. 4 (1955).

[112] Robinson v. California, 370 U.S. 66 (1962); Driver v. Hinnant, 356 F.2d 761 (4th Cir. 1966); Easter v. District of Columbia, 261 F.2d 50 (D.C. Cir. 1966).

[113] Driver v. Hinnant, 356 F.2d 764 (4th Cir. 1966); Easter v. District of Columbia, 261 F.2d 50 (D.C. Cir. 1966).

[114] *Ibid.*

against the ill. This line of attack on society's traditional penal formula for the drug addict, supported by a plea for a therapeutic approach, was upheld in 1962 by the United States Supreme Court in the *Robinson* case.[115] Said the court: "It is unlikely that any State at this moment in history would attempt to make it a criminal offense for a person to be mentally ill, or a leper, or to be afflicted with a venereal disease.... Even one day in prison would be a cruel and unusual punishment for the 'crime' of having a common cold."[116]

The *Robinson* court's holding that a state law that criminally imprisons one for a status which is medically recognized to be an illness constitutes "cruel and unusual punishment" in violation of the Constitution[117] was a breakthrough for the divestment movement. The effect of the *Robinson* decision remained limited, however, since the court predicted its decision against the California law upon the fact that it unduly penalized the mere status of addiction rather than an act connected or resulting from it. The therapeutic approach is therefore not imperative in the case of addicts charged with such conduct as the possession or sale of narcotics.[118] Still, the utilization of the Eighth Amendment guarantees as a means for divesting the criminal law did not stop with the *Robinson* case. New efforts were directed to test the validity of laws prescribing criminal sanctions for chronic alcoholics. These challenges met with considerable success.[119]

The Inadequacy of Criminal Sanctions

Beginning with religious and humanitarian considerations against the application of harsh criminal sanctions to the unfortunate and immature, the process of divestment continued under the momentum generated by the growing disillusionment with the determinate sentence utilized by the criminal law. In 1917 Ferri wrote:

[To the] criminalists of the traditional school ... [t]he application of a conditional sentence ... remains offensive to the principle of metaphysical justice ... but it is a wise concession to practical

[115] Robinson v. California, 370 U.S. 66 (1962).

[116] *Ibid.* 666–67.

[117] *Ibid.* 666, 667.

[118] In his dissent Justice White clearly warns against future extensions of the therapeutic view: "If it is 'cruel and unusual punishment' to convict appellant for addiction, it is difficult to understand why it would be any less offensive to the Fourteenth Amendment to convict him for use...." *Ibid.* 668.

[119] Driver v. Hinnant, 356 U.S. 66 (1962); Easter v. District of Columbia, 261 F.2d 50 (D.C. Cir. 1966); Powell v. Texas, 392 U.S. 514 (1968).

utility, being in perfect theoretical accord with the doctrines of anthropology and of criminal sociology. The reclusion of dangerous criminals for an indeterminate time is a proposal of the positivist criminal school, since it would be as absurd to say that a murderer should remain in prison twenty years rather than fifteen or thirty as it would to say in advance that a sick person should stay in a hospital ten days rather than twenty or fifty. As the sick person is kept in the hospital just as long a time as is necessary for his cure, and as the insane patient remains in the asylum all of his life unless cured and leaves it when he is cured, so it should be with the delinquent. . . .[120]

The traditional standard of criminal law has been to fit the punishment to the crime, rather than to the criminal. Society, acting through the modern legislature, continues to set criminal penalties that respond to the severity of the crime. But the severity of the crime provides no meaningful measure for the time or methods required to deal with a particular offender. The conduct of an alcoholic charged with disturbing the peace is not extremely offensive and, consequently, the penalties prescribed for him are not severe. Yet, the reformation of a chronic alcoholic may require more time and facilities than the rehabilitation of the one time passion murderer whose conduct (arousing a greater urge for social condemnation) traditionally results in more severe criminal sanctions. As long as the emphasis was upon the retributive punishment of the offender and the deterrence of others, a punishment fitting the crime was logically sound. Once the emphasis shifted to the rehabilitation of the offender and his return to society, the traditional system of penalties appeared totally inappropriate.

The positivists have long agitated to remove offenders from the "punishment that fits the crime" orbit and to entrust their management to a noncriminal *parens patriae* system in which the period of detention and the applicable sanctions would respond to the therapeutic needs of the delinquent rather than the nature of his offense. The movement for the divestment of criminal justice allows for the replacement of penal facilities with therapeutically oriented institutions; through this transformation society is able to establish new experimental programs in hospitals rather than in prisons for selected offenders and others posing a threat to social tranquility.

The shift from a penal or punitive orientation to a therapeutic one is regarded by behavioral scientists as inducing a better rehabilitative

[120] Ferri, *Criminal Sociology* xlii–xliii.

atmosphere and potential. The concept of "double-expectancy" as described by Danish psychiatrist George Stürup is relevant in this connection.[121] According to Stürup, offenders react according to their perception of what society expects of them. The offender who is labeled "criminal" responds to the negative social expectation that he perceives; his recovery is accordingly inadequate. The deviant believed to be ill is likely to respond to the perception of a more positive social expectation and his recovery might be more satisfactory.

The new noncriminal proceedings have dispensed with some of the cumbersome formalism and procedural requirements of criminal law: counsel, adversary hearing, jury, nonhearsay evidence. The courts have repeatedly emphasized the civil or noncriminal nature of these new proceedings and the inapplicability of the criminal law standards. With reference to sexual psychopathy commitments, the Missouri court stated: "The purpose of a criminal proceeding is to punish. But this Act is but a civil inquiry to determine a status. It is curative and remedial in nature instead of punitive. . . . Proceedings under the Act have none of the elements of a criminal proceeding."[122] The noncriminal process professes the laudatory desire and policy of removing the criminal stigma from those either too young or too deficient medically or mentally to be forever branded.

Prevention in Lieu of Suppression

The divestment of criminal law and the substitution of civil proceedings also permits a drastic departure from the precepts of criminal law, allowing the treatment of a socially hazardous general condition or status prior to the commission of a prohibited overt act. Criminal law is a system designed to deal with criminals *after* an offense. While

---

[121] G. Stürup (Superintendent of Herstedvester Institution, Denmark), "A Situational Approach to Behavior Disorders," reprinted from the *Leeds Symposium on Behavior Disorders* 25–27 (March 1965).

[122] State *ex rel.* Sweezer v. Green, 360 Mo. 1249, 232 S.W. 2d 897, 900 (1950). Of similar effect is Minnesota *ex rel.* Pearson v. Probate Court of Ramsey County, 309 U.S. 270 (1940). Regarding the noncriminal nature of juvenile proceedings, *see* State v. Monahan, 15 N.J. 34, 104 A. 2d 21 (1954); Commonwealth v. Fisher, 213 Pa. 48, 62 A. 198, 200 (1905), to the effect that a juvenile proceeding is not a "trial of a child charged with a crime. . ."; and esp. *in re* Joseph Holmes, 379 Pa. 599, 109 A. 2d 523, 525 (1954), *cert. denied*, 348 U.S. 973 (1954), where the court states: ". . . [s]ince as pointed out, Juvenile Courts *are not criminal courts*, the constitutional rights granted to persons accused of *crime* are not applicable to children brought before them. . ." (109 A. 2d 525).

the public's awareness of criminal sanctions is expected to exert a deterring influence and to curb prohibited conduct, the actual sanctions of criminal law do not, generally, come into use until after a criminal act has in fact been committed or attempted. Noncriminal procedures, on the other hand, have been utilized as a means of preventive control for prospective offenders: the mentally ill person likely to become dangerous to himself or to others, the psychopath with a propensity to commit sexual offenses, the mental defective likely to produce defective offspring, the child exposed to dangerous influences. In being directed toward crime prevention the noncriminal proceedings have appealed and will undoubtedly demonstrate an increasing appeal to those seeking new tools for society's struggle against crime and delinquency.[123]

CHARACTERISTICS OF THE THERAPEUTIC STATE

A new scientific awareness of the causes of human behavior clearly coincides with the advent of the therapeutic state. What are the basic assumptions of this state and what are its characteristics?

In the first place, the therapeutic state builds its foundation on science rather than faith. It therefore speaks not in terms of moral judgment (it abhors such concepts as *"mens rea,"* "free will," "good," "evil") but in concepts reputed to be descriptive and scientific ("mentally ill," "socially delinquent," "psychopathic," etc.).

The implications of the therapeutic state for the treatment of crime and criminals are dramatic, representing a departure from the moral-religious concept that crime and other antisocial behavior are manifestations of "evil" and should therefore be suppressed and punished as a means of purging the evildoer as well as society. Crime is viewed as a natural feature of the social landscape. Criminals are no longer "bad," though they must be dealt with because they are injurious to society. As the moral-religious preoccupation with moral guilt (as manifested to this day in the concept of *mens rea*) now gives way to the concept of sanctions mainly as a tool of social defense, the door is opened to new experiments with the treatment of offenders.[124]

---

[123] *See, e.g.,* M. Guttmacher, "The Psychiatric Approach to Crime and Correction," 23 *Law & Contemp. Prob.* 633, 646 (1958): "There are certain principles in regard to the treatment of criminals upon which there would be general agreement among psychiatrists. The value of prevention over treatment of criminality should be emphasized."

[124] *See* Ferri, *Criminal Sociology,* esp. ch. 5.

The growing acceptance of the deterministic view of crime however, has not totally replaced the classical penal system in actual practice. Instead, deterministic concepts and solutions have been grafted onto the old classical model through the development of social controls over people without *mens rea*—as if pear branches were grafted to an apple tree. But as yet, and probably for some time to come, the hybrid system will have characteristics of both the classical and deterministic schools—just as our tree will bear both pears and apples.

In the new hybrid system of social controls—which is here designated the therapeutic state—the heaviest emphasis has been placed upon the treatment and rehabilitation of offenders. Yet the treatment concept was at best only one of the principles of positivist-deterministic criminology, which laid its total emphasis on social defense. Although treatment was considered a major method for achieving social order in certain cases, the determinists did not completely abandon the concept of quarantine or even execution as effective means of social defense. The humanitarian objections to the latter sanctions were noted; yet these sanctions were not precluded, as a last resort, by the determinist school.

When the concepts of determinism are grafted onto the classical model of criminal justice, two important shifts occur that cause the role of treatment to ascend in the hierarchy of sanctions. First, since the deterministic theory is selectively adapted to offenders who are considered to lack *mens rea*, those who benefit thereby are designated ill, immature, unbalanced, or in some other way deficient. This designation was unnecessary in a pure determinist system of social defense—but it was mandatory to facilitate the hybridization of the criminal system. Second, logically following the thesis of "illness," came the notion that the only proper thing to do with those deficiencies is to treat and hope to cure them. This ascension of treatment and cure as the primary goals of the state in those areas in which the determinist theory was acknowledged has been one of the main factors in the development of the therapeutic state.

One notes in this connection the growing social acceptance of an orientation that views crime and delinquency not as moral problems but medical ones. As asserted by spokesmen for the new regime: "... The whole problem of criminality or criminology is in the field of human behavior psychopathology, the understanding of which requires medical and psychiatric training."[125] And since it is similarly

---

[125] Selinger, "Criminal Hygiene," 10 *Fed. Prob.* 16–19 (1946).

alleged that "the 'normal' offender is a myth, . . ."[126] it would seem to follow that what the criminal needs from society is therapy, not condemnation. Consequently, the therapeutic society is willing to subdue the more primitive pressures for vindictiveness and temper its sanctions with scientific considerations of social effectiveness. Divorcing itself from religious foundations and from the belief in the earthly destiny of a continuous, eternal struggle between right and wrong, the therapeutic state believes in the curative power of science and in the duty of society to use science for the prevention and treatment of its ills.[127]

The second germinating factor of the therapeutic state is the earlier discussed *parens patriae* power and the state responsibility for public welfare. Thus the need for social defense against those who exert little free will of their own, combined with the belief in scientific cure and with the state's traditional right and duty to exercise *parens patriae* functions, have merged to form the new therapeutic state, which has assumed jurisdiction to compel treatment of the unpunishables under the *parens patriae* power.

The therapeutic state differs from its more established sister, the public welfare state, in that the latter offers its services to the voluntary recipient while the former seeks to impose its "beneficial" services compulsorily (since the recipient is held to be incompetent). Under the public welfare, the citizen is faced, at least theoretically, with the final choice either to accept or reject the offered public assistance and any concomitant governmental scrutiny and demands, but the state's therapeutic function is often authoritarian and may be exercised on a deviant individual for the asserted public interest with little or no consideration of his own choice.

The operations of the therapeutic state are in a condition of constant growth. This book surveys some of the more obvious areas—compulsory institutionalization and the involuntary commitment and treatment of the mentally ill and mentally defective, epileptics, alcoholics and drug addicts, juvenile delinquents, and psychopaths. But the therapeutic state does not always rely on institutionalization alone. Its objectives are well accomplished through therapeutic programs that are independent of institutional care, and included in this book is one of the more extreme of the treatment programs serving the therapeutic state: involuntary sterilization.

[126] Abrahamsen, *Who Are the Guilty?* 125.
[127] For a survey of new correctional developments, *see* Guttmacher, "The Psychiatric Approach" 633.

In all of its areas the therapeutic state is tinged with a lingering desire to defend society by isolating and controlling socially dangerous persons. This remnant of its deterministic progenitor is incongruous with the therapeutic state's avowed selfless concern with the sick individual, an avowal that has allowed it to escape the scrutiny of civil libertarians. Asserting its *parens patriae* prerogatives the therapeutic state has resorted to a noncriminal arena, free from the traditional safeguards imposed upon the exercise of coercive powers under the criminal law.

The therapeutic state, not merely as a benevolent father but as a very authoritarian one, is not limited to the areas covered in this volume; its manifestations are evident elsewhere. Can compulsory medical treatment (for example, blood transfusion) be given to adult patients or to children against their or their parents' religious beliefs?[128] Can a trial court refuse to accept in a criminal case the guilty plea of a defendant suspected of mental illness?[129]

In 1962, the courts of the District of Columbia took a large step toward substituting compulsory treatment for punishment, even against the wishes of the offender.[130] In so doing, the defense of insanity, which traditionally served as a shield for the accused, was turned into a possible sword to be used against him.

For the last three centuries criminal justice has struggled with the question of the insane offender. How insane is insane? How deranged must a person be before we relieve him of both moral and legal responsibility? During this time the insanity defense has painfully grown from the primitive "wild beast"[131] and the M'Naghten knowing of "right and wrong"[132] tests of the eighteenth and nineteenth

---

[128] Application of President of Georgetown College, Inc., 311 F.2d 1000 (D.C. Cir. 1964), *cert. denied*, 377 U.S. 978 (1964). This case involves blood transfusion to an objecting adult. *See* Hegland, "Unauthorized Rendition of Lifesaving Medical Treatment," 53 *Calif. L. Rev.* 860 (1965). Under the power of *parens patriae* several courts have ordered medical treatment over the objections of a child's parents. *Examine, e.g.,* State v. Perricone, 37 N.J. 463, 181 A.2d 751 (1962); People *ex rel.* Wallace v. Labrenz, 411 Ill. 618, 104 N.E. 2d 769 (1952).

[129] *See* Overholser v. Lynch, 288 F.2d 388 (D.C. Cir. 1961); *rev'd*, 369 U.S. 705 (1962).

[130] Overholser v. Lynch, 288 F.2d 388 (D.C. Cir. 1961).

[131] An accused could escape punishment if he "doth not know what he is doing, no more than . . . a wild beast;" Judge Tracy's test in Rex v. Arnold, 16 How. St. Tr. 684, 764 (1724).

[132] M'Naghten's case, 10 Cl. and Fin. 200, 8 Eng. Rep. 718, 722 (1843): ". . . to establish a defense on the ground of insanity it must be clearly proved . . . the party accused was harboring under such a defect of reason, from disease of the mind, as not to know the nature or quality of the act he was doing; or, if he did know it, that he did not know he was doing what was wrong."

centuries to the more sophisticated and more liberal "product" formula in *Durham*[133] or the lack of "substantial capacity to conform... [one's] conduct to the requirements of the law" test in *Currens* and the Model Penal Code.[134] Indeed, the expansion of the definitions of criminal insanity could itself be viewed as a divestment of criminal jurisdiction by the social decision to remove a growing class of offenders from criminal sanctions, by reason of their mental condition, and to subject them to hospitalization instead. Still, throughout the history of the insanity defense, society merely displayed a tolerant acceptance of mental disease as a defense to criminal responsibility. The *Lynch* holding, however, takes a bold step toward therapeutic protectionism and authoritarianism, asserting the responsibility and indeed the duty of society to require an offender to undergo therapeutic rather than penal treatment once a mental aberration is demonstrated.

Frederick C. Lynch was charged in the District of Columbia Municipal Court with passing bad checks.[135] Despite Lynch's assertions of his mental responsibility at the time the offenses were committed, the court found him not guilty by reason of insanity and confined him to a mental hospital. Addressing itself to society's duty in seeing that a defendant needing hospital care does not go to prison, the United States Court of Appeals for the District of Columbia said: "... we clearly [have] stated that imprisonment was *wrong* in the case of a mentally ill person, as well as a remedy which could not possibly secure the community against repetition of the offense."[136]

"... [W]e are convinced that criminal insanity is a matter of grave public concern, particularly with respect to the problem of rehabilitation.... In this context the only issue is whether the defendant will go to jail for punishment or to a hospital for treatment...."[137]

---

[133] Durham v. United States, 214 F.2d 862, 874–75 (D.C. Cir. 1954). "The rule ... is simply that an accused is not criminally responsible if his unlawful act was the product of mental disease or mental defect."

[134] United States v. Currens, 290 F.2d 751, 774 (3d Cir. 1961). To constitute a defense, "[t]he jury must be satisfied that at the time of committing the prohibited act the defendant, as a result of mental disease or defect, lacked substantial capacity to conform his conduct to the requirements of the law which he is alleged to have violated." The Model Penal Code of the American Law Institute states: "A person is not responsible for criminal conduct if at the time of such conduct as a result of mental disease or defect he lacks substantial capacity either to appreciate the criminality of his conduct or to conform his conduct to the requirements of law."

[135] Overholser v. Lynch, 109 U.S. App. D.C. 404 (1959).

[136] Overholser v. Lynch, 288 F.2d, 393 (D.C. Cir. 1961). *See* Williams v. United States, 250 F.2d 19, 26 (1957).

[137] Overholser v. Lynch, 288 F.2d, 393 (D.C. Cir. 1961).

"By its very nature, a jail sentence is for a specified period of time, while by its very nature hospitalization, to be effective, must be initially for an indeterminate period. . . ."[138]

"The length of his hospitalization must depend solely on his need (or lack of it) for further treatment. It is true that he may be hospitalized for a longer time than the maximum jail sentence provided by statute. It is equally true that he may be released in a shorter time than the minimum sentence. Hospitalization, in this respect, bears no relation to a jail sentence. A jail sentence is punitive and is to be imposed by the judge within the limits set by the legislature. Hospitalization is remedial and its limits are determined by the condition to be treated."[139]

The Supreme Court reviewed and reversed the *Lynch* case.[140] But in the reversal it did not disturb the circuit court's concept of society's stake in demanding "that a defendant who needs hospital care does not go to prison."[141] The Supreme Court dealt only with the interpretation of the District of Columbia statutory requirement for the automatic mandatory hospitalization of persons found not guilty by reason of insanity.[142] This provision, the court held, was not applicable to persons who had refused to raise the insanity defense. Consequently, a person found not guilty by reason of insanity but who refused to plead this defense may not be automatically committed. If such person requires confinement, he may be hospitalized only through the usual and independent civil procedure.[143]

Frederick Lynch, on his bad check charge, could have been sentenced to a maximum of 12 months in jail.[144] The more likely probability would have been probation. His commitment to a mental institution, on the other hand, was for an indeterminate period of time. Harassed, branded, and tired, Lynch committed suicide.[145]

---

[138] *Ibid.*

[139] *Ibid.* 394.

[140] Overholser v. Lynch, 288 F.2d 388 (D.C. Cir. 1961), *rev'd,* 369 U.S. 705 (1962).

[141] Overholser v. Lynch, 288 F.2d, 393 (D.C. Cir. 1961).

[142] *D.C. Code* §24–301(d) (1967).

[143] *See* Whalem v. United States, 346 F.2d 812 (D.C. Cir. 1965). This principle was more clearly and broadly stated in Bolton v. Harris, 395 F.2d 642 (1968).

[144] *D.C. Code* §22–1410 (1967). The statutory penalty under the Bad Check Law is imprisonment not exceeding one year, or a fine of not more than $1,000, or both.

[145] Arens, "Due Process and the Rights of the Mentally Ill: The Strange Case of Frederick Lynch," 13 *Catholic U. L. Rev.* 3 (1964).

(PRELIMINARY QUESTIONS REGARDING DUE
PROCESS IN THE THERAPEUTIC STATE

Noncriminal *parens patriae* proceedings, designed to replace criminal sanctions, may have great promise for the new social aims of therapy and crime prevention. The Third United Nations Congress on Crime and the Treatment of Offenders held in 1965 made special reference to "the large marginal categories of social misfits (alcoholics, drug addicts, vagrants, sexual deviates) . . . and their effect on the problem of recidivism."[146] It also preliminarily explored the civil commitment of these groups of habitual offenders as a new tool in the fight against recidivism. Since the greatest portion of the repeating offenders in metropolitan America consists of alcoholics and drug addicts, the civil commitment and treatment of this group of offenders has gained greater appeal than the present ineffective criminal process.[147]

If society is to shift from crime management and control to a more aggressive role of crime prevention, therapeutic and preventive commitments naturally suggest themselves. If one's propensity for criminality or delinquency can be determined by means of new scientific formulae (in the form of psychiatric observations, psychological testing, sociological evaluations, chromosomal testing, or a combination of any of these and others, not overlooking the Glueck delinquency prediction tables recently claimed to be perfected),[148] then the therapeutic and preventive proceedings may more frequently be invoked as likely successors to the traditional criminal sanctions.

The increasing function of the state in the *parens patriae* and therapeutic role appears to be derived from scientific progress and the newer concepts of public welfare; its advent has been warmly welcomed by the progressive spokesmen in society. The creation of the juvenile court to deal with the delinquent and neglected child was thus hailed by Dean Roscoe Pound as "one of the most significant

146 *See* U.N. Document MCPC, 1965, 4 GE. 65–9490, p. 8.
147 *See Washington Post*, April 20, 1966: "The House Judiciary Committee yesterday approved legislation that would give narcotic addicts a voluntary chance to avoid prison. The bill, backed by the Administration, would permit addicts charged with Federal crimes to request commitment for medical treatment and rehabilitation instead of standing trial. . . . The proposed program is similar to those being operated in several states."
148 E. T. Glueck, "Spotting Potential Delinquents: Can It Be Done?" 20 *Fed. Prob.* 7 (1956); Monaschesi, "Prediction of Criminal Behavior," in *Encyclopedia of Criminology* 324 (V. C. Branham and S. B. Kutash eds. 1949).

advances in the administration of justice since the Magna Carta."[149] A similar reception was given to eugenic sterilization and special legislation dealing with psychopaths. A few years ago the *Durham*[150] test of insanity, which significantly expanded the class of those exempted from criminal sanctions by reason of mental illness, was similarly greeted as a liberal and progressive omen[151] and was followed by the expansion of the state's *parens patriae* powers into the areas of drug addiction and alcoholism.

More recent and more searching scrutiny raises serious questions regarding both the conceptual framework of the therapeutic state and the procedural safeguards that apply to the exercise of the state's *parens patriae* powers. Clearly, the assumption of a broad *parens patriae* role also necessitates the exercise of comprehensive responsibility and extensive powers. Some of the resultant hazards have been dramatically noted by Dr. Thomas Szasz, a pronounced critic of his own psychiatric fraternity: "The impediment I want to consider here is restraint on persons exercised by psychiatrists by virtue of the powers vested in them by law. For those oppressed by psychiatrists, liberty means freedom from psychiatric coercion."[152]

Another potentially undesirable product of the therapeutic state is the hastening of the erosion of society's reliance upon the concept of personal responsibility.[153] While the determinists found no scientific justification for classical criminal law's insistence upon the institution of free will and sought to abolish the concept of personal guilt, the modern engineers of social organization cannot overlook the utility of these concepts—even if recognized to be only fictional and ritualistic—in the promotion of socially desired behavior. Granting that mental patients, juveniles, addicts, and psychopaths (as well as the rest of the populace) may in fact never exercise total free will in their social conduct, cannot society's endorsement of the free-will concept still work towards the enhancement of whatever self-restraint the diverse members of these groups might be able to generate?

By emphasizing the therapeutic function of the state and by giving sympathetic consideration to mental and other aberrations, our society accelerates the divestment of criminal justice in the name of bene-

---

[149] S. Glueck, *Roscoe Pound and Criminal Justice* 38 (1965).
[150] Durham v. United States, 214 F.2d 862 (D.C. Cir. 1954).
[151] Fortas, "Implications of Durham's Case," 113 *Amer. J. Psychiatry* 577 (1957).
[152] Szasz, *Law, Liberty and Psychiatry* 67.
[153] J. Hall, "Responsibility and Law: In Defense of the M'Naghten Rules," 42 *A.B.A.J.* 917 (1956).

ficence. Yet this divestment, which increasingly frees persons from criminal responsibility, is not the only goal in the process of the therapeutic state.

Underneath the shibboleths lies the need for social defense. Public protection does not permit the complete release of the proved or potential delinquent. The therapeutic state is programmed to serve this public need as well as that of treatment and cure.

The goals of social defense, however, may be in opposition to the interests or desires of the accused man: the noncriminal incarceration and treatment, involuntary or even coercive—often imposed without traditional protections against abuses of power by the state—quite possibly result in even more objectionable deprivations of liberty than those possible under the criminal process.

The comparatively new areas of noncriminal or therapeutic treatment raise several legal and nonlegal questions. Foremost is the question of the basic balance between society's right to protect and improve itself in its members through preventive measures, and the individual's right to be left alone. How much of a social hazard must be demonstrated before society may step in and subject a deviant to therapy? May society seek to remedy one's status or personality over one's objections? This is in essence the question of substantive due process relating to the criteria justifying state intervention, as contrasted with the required procedural safeguards. The traditional approach of Anglo-American society has been for the state to act only after an antisocial act has been committed or once "clear and present danger"[154] has been demonstrated. In the past, society generally sought to control not a status or condition but an act.[155] Karl Llewellyn has clearly described this attitude:

> Angel or devil, a man has a claim to a fair trial, not of his general social desirability, but of his guilt of the *specific offense* charged against him. . . . General social desirability of others, through most of history, has meant to men in power such attitudes and actions and opinions as do not threaten their own con-

[154] Schenck v. United States, 249 U.S. 47 (1919) (Holmes J.).
[155] See Z. Chafee, *Free Speech in the United States* 81 (1946). Chafee, in connection with the deportation and exclusion of anarchists, likewise warns against legislation directed against people rather than action. Says he: "The war power should, I have endeavored to show, be used against utterances only to ward off dangerous acts, but this power over immigration is primarily directed to dangerous persons. It is concerned less with what men do than with what they are— whether they are diseased, crippled, of psychopathic inferiority, liable to become a public charge." *Ibid.* 235–36.

tinuance in power. Our forefathers learned it again when York and Lancaster were warring, learned it yet again from the early Stuarts and the later. Their learning left its mark upon our law. It is not for the official to judge whether an accused is socially undesirable. Only the legislature passes on that point, and the legislature must pass upon it not for single men, nor after the event, but for whole classes, and for whole classes in advance. . . . So the job of police and prosecutor is to bring subjects to book. The job of court and jury is to see *whether* the suspect has committed the particular offense. . . .[156]

Yet in the therapeutic *parens patriae* realm we often ignore the question of whether a particular offense has been committed and instead are moved to exercise therapeutic sanctions by a finding of the general social undesirability of one's condition or status.

Beyond the substantive questions regarding the exercise of therapeutic sanctions looms the question of procedural due process. Assuming that a noncriminal program is utilized to accomplish a therapeutic social aim, what procedural safeguards must be established in order to protect the rights of the person allegedly requiring treatment? How carefully should the disabling physical or mental status be defined by law? Should there be a requirement of proof of previous antisocial behavior? Should there be a right to a hearing and counsel? Does an administrative confinement or one based on a medical certificate, without a prior independent hearing, satisfy the elements of due process? Should the state be required to disclose the medical record upon which it proceeds against an individual? Should the term of the therapeutic treatment be determinate or indeterminate? Should the social sanctions depend on the availability of treatment? Should the individual against whom sanctions are exercised have the legal right to demand effective treatment?

In the face of the growing trend toward therapy and prevention, it is essential that we examine the record established in those areas where these very methods have been utilized in the past: the treatment of the mentally ill, the alcoholics and drug addicts, the juvenile delinquents, and the psychopaths. Have fundamental individual rights been protected? Can the successes and failures of the noncriminal procedures be gauged in terms of the aims professed for them? Are the people who are exposed to noncriminal sanctions effectively treated and "cured" or do they merely remain in indeterminate

---

[156] Llewellyn, "The Sacco-Vanzetti Case," in *Cases and Materials on the Legal Profession* 232 (E. E. Cheatham ed. 1955).

custody? Do persons subjected to noncriminal sanctions respond better to treatment in the absence of the criminal label? Is society's acceptance of the person released from noncriminal treatment more favorable than it is of the "criminal"?

Only after these questions have been satisfactorily answered may society safely proceed with further experiments and programs in the therapeutic *parens patriae* arena—in search for more effective tools for the attainment of improved social order and tranquility. What Professor Norval Morris of the University of Chicago recently demanded with regard to the criminal system is even more appropriate to the *parens patriae* or therapeutic process: ". . . practices must cease to rest on surmise and good intentions; they must be based on facts."[157]

[157] N. Morris, "Impediments to Penal Reform," 33 *U. Chicago L. Rev.* 627, 638 (1966).

2

The Mentally Ill: Serenity in a Disordered World

Nowhere (except in some monastic institutions) is diversity of taste entirely unrecognized; a person may, without blame either like or dislike rowing, or smoking, or music or athletic exercises or chess or cards, or study, because both those who like each of these things and those who dislike them are too numerous to be put down. But the man . . . who can be accused either of doing "what nobody does," or of not doing "what everybody does," is the subject of as much depreciatory remark as if he or she had committed some grave moral delinquency. Persons are required to possess a title, or some other badge of rank . . . to be able to indulge somewhat in the luxury of doing as they like. . . . To indulge somewhat, I repeat; for whoever allow themselves much of that indulgence . . . are in peril of a commission *de lunatico*. . . .—J. S. Mill, *On Liberty* 83 (1930)

In the Sixteenth Century the deranged were expelled, shipped off, or executed;
In the Seventeenth Century the insane were locked up in jails and houses of correction;
In the Eighteenth Century madmen were confined in madhouses;
In the Nineteenth Century lunatics were sent to asylums;
In the Twentieth Century the mentally ill are committed to hospitals;
In the Twenty-first Century . . . .—Adapted from K. Jones, *Lunacy, Law, and Conscience* ix (1955)

In former days, when it was proposed to burn atheists, charitable people used to suggest putting them in the madhouse instead; it would be nothing surprising nowadays were we to see this done, and the doers applauding themselves, because . . . they had adopted so humane . . . a mode of treating these unfortunates, not without a silent satisfaction of their [the atheists] having thereby obtained their deserts.—J. S. Mill, *On Liberty* 84 (1930)

Pinel immediately led Couthon to the section for the deranged, where the sight of the cells made a painful impression on him. Couthon asked to interrogate all the patients. From most, he received only insults and obscene apostrophes. It was useless to prolong the interview. Turning to Pinel Couthon said: "Now, citizen, are you mad yourself to seek to unchain such beasts?" Pinel replied calmly: "Citizen, I am convinced that these madmen are so intractable only because they have been deprived of air and liberty."—S. Pinel, *Traité Complet du Régime Sanitaire des Aliénes* 56 (1836)

THE SANE AND THE INSANE

Individuals described as mentally disordered are often at variance with the conventions and mores of society. The very symptoms of what we commonly define as mental illness, being primarily behavioral rather than physiological, mark those afflicted by it as socially deviant. Frequently, however, such deviation will be manifested not by violent antisocial or criminal conduct but by eccentric activities and asocial withdrawal from common daily functions and responsibilities.

In 1907 a fragile yet determined old lady, who claimed to have founded a new religion, was battling for her liberty from commitment to a mental institution in Pleasant View, New Hampshire. Her proclamation of new religious tenets in the modern scientific age was asserted as proof of her mental derangement. Yet Mary Baker Eddy won her battle and the Christian Science Church now occupies a respectable place among America's more traditional creeds.

In 1956 a John Patler distributed violently racist and anti-Jewish leaflets in New York City. The distribution effort landed him in Bellevue Hospital for a 30-day psychiatric observation.[1] A year later he entered the Marine Corps, where he earned an expert rifleman's badge. Upon discharge he became a ranking officer in the American Nazi party, but internal party dissension followed; in 1967, he was

[1] *Washington Post*, August 26, 1967, p. A7.

accused of assassinating George Lincoln Rockwell, America's Nazi Fuehrer. Despite the interlude of respectable and conforming military service, Patler's history disclosed constant manifestations of deviant behavior, and society was not able to curb the growing menace successfully.

In 1959 the controversial governor of an American state was removed from office and placed in a mental asylum after being subjected to a psychiatric examination that certified him insane. Describing himself as a political prisoner, he succeeded in asserting his gubernatorial power from within the hospital, and by firing the institution's superintendent and appointing a new one, he obtained a speedy discharge. Earl Long soon re-assumed his office as Louisiana's governor. Responding to these bizarre occurrences, one newspaper editorial raised some very searching questions: "It may, of course, be true that Earl Long has been the real victim of an almost macabre plot and, to use his own words, that he has 'never been insane a second in my life.' If so, there should be some... better law to protect sane governors. And if not, there must be some better way... to protect the public welfare in a state of three million people."[2]

Enumerating these adventures is intended to do nothing more than suggest that mental illness is not easily defined or determined; that those kept out of mental institutions may later exhibit varying degrees of social adaptability and even success; that society is not always successful in diagnosing and treating those posing a threat to its safety; and, finally, that the degree of deviation sufficient to land one in a mental asylum is not uniformly and scientifically determinable. Mental illness is not as readily discernible as physical illness; furthermore, different societies may have different degrees of tolerance for mental deviation. Quite relevantly, it has been noted that some of history's most illustrious figures have been prey to what may now be called insane delusions, manic depressive states, or paranoia. Hegel, the philosopher, believed himself a god; Saul, the first Israelite king, suffered from extreme depression; Martin Luther thought himself under attack from tangible devils; Goethe and Dante entertained irrational dislikes of their mother countries; and Mozart believed that the Italians were planning to poison him.[3]

The fundamental problem of current American society in deciding who is mentally disordered and who should be committed to mental

[2] *Washington Post*, July 13, 1959, p. A13.
[3] Comment, "Civil Insanity in the Law of Alabama," 18 *Ala. L. Rev.*, 340–42 (1966).

institutions and pursuant to what procedural safeguards is poignantly illustrated by the case of Mary Kimbrough Jones.[4] Miss Jones was a secretary to Battle Hales, an employee of the U.S. Department of Agriculture. In April 1962, Hales had been investigating the favoritism shown to Texas financier Billie Sol Estes by certain employees of the Department of Agriculture. Hales had made appointments for April 20 to see both Secretary of Agriculture Freeman and an FBI representative in this connection. Arriving at his office that day, Hales found that he had been locked out. He also discovered that he had been transferred to another section of the Department of Agriculture and was being denied all access to his former files. Miss Jones, who had an outstanding record of 25 years' service in government, was worried about the classified files accumulated by her former boss. She expressed her concern to fellow employees.

On April 25, 1962, at the request of the Chief of the Health Division of the Personnel Office of the Department of Agriculture, Miss Jones was picked up by Private Robert Selby of the District of Columbia Metropolitan Police and taken in a police patrol wagon to the District of Columbia General Hospital. At the Hospital, Private Selby signed a printed petition stating that he "observed Miss Jones in a confused state of mind." Later he explained that Miss Jones had walked several times from a desk to a closed window and leaned over the sill to look out. A petition for indeterminate commitment was filed in United States District Court on April 26. Two days after Miss Jones' original confinement, a certificate signed by two psychiatrists recommending treatment was attached to the petition. On that very day the court, without a hearing, entered an order that the "patient" be detained in General Hospital for 30 days unless earlier release was ordered.

On May 7, 1962, ten days later, the Mental Health Commission, which screens commitment cases prior to a final court hearing, held a closed session which lasted one hour and twenty minutes. Miss Jones was refused permission to have the proceedings transcribed, though her counsel offered to pay the cost. At the hearing, one doctor alleged that Miss Jones had declined some meals at the hospital because she believed the food to be poisoned. Miss Jones responded that she "did not eat a couple of meals when she first arrived . . . because the confinement upset her," and that she was "placed in a ward with many people who were sick, was stripped of her clothes, and caused to sleep

---

[4] 108 *Cong. Rec.* 8717–22 (1962) (reported by Sen. John J. Williams).

on a mattress on the floor, and these things caused her to lose her appetite. . . ."[5] No person from the Department of Agriculture appeared at the hearing. All witnesses admitted at the hearing that none knew of any acts, deeds, or facts to indicate that Miss Jones was dangerous to herself or others.

The commission ordered the discharge of the 51-year-old secretary, stating that she was "of sound mind."[6] Ten days later, on May 16, the commission chairman avowed that he had not released Miss Jones as "of sound mind" but rather "we felt that if we could get her under the care of a private doctor, a good psychiatrist, there was no place like home for her."[7]

The Mental Health Commission apparently never determined for certain whether Miss Jones was sane or insane; at any rate, it did not consider her dangerous. But despite existing procedural prerequisites and safeguards, Miss Jones spent some two weeks in a mental institution on the basis of questionable evidence. A psychiatric history will now be included in her work and health record.

The Jones affair clearly shows the natural conflict between individual liberty and the defenders of the public safety, health, and welfare, and it demonstrates the potential hazards of using compulsion even for assertedly therapeutic aims. Moreover, it raises the question of whether our present system for committing patients to mental institutions is compatible, from the viewpoint of both criteria and procedures, with modern social philosophy and scientific experience.

A MEASURE OF THE PROBLEM

Mental disorder is often cited as one of this country's most severe medical and social problems. An estimated 16 percent of the total population of America suffers from some form of mental disability or disturbance[8] and tranquilizers sell here at a rate of 95 billion pills per year.[9] More than half of all our hospital beds are occupied by mental patients; the economic and human resource losses caused by mental illness are immeasurable. Of the approximately 11,400 children born each day in this country, 340, or one out of every 33, are mentally

[5] William Pace, attorney for Mary K. Jones, to Senator Williams, May 17, 1962, in 108 *Cong. Rec.* 8718 (1962).

[6] *Washington Evening Star*, May 7, 1962, *ibid.*, 8717.

[7] *Ibid.*, May 16, 1962, *ibid.*

[8] *See* pp. 4–5 above.

[9] I. Friedelson, Office of Education and Information, HEW, to Senator Thomas H. Kuchel (R., Calif.), January 30, 1967.

deficient. One out of every twelve Americans will require hospitalization for mental illness at some time in his life. There are approximately 3,000,000 people in the United States suffering from acute mental illness, 5,000,000 who are mentally deficient, and some 15,000,000 with other serious personality disturbances.[10] It is estimated that 5,000,000 Americans suffer from chronic alcoholism, a million and a half are epileptics, and 200,000 are addicted to drugs. In most states the epileptic, the drug addict, and the alcoholic are subject to hospital commitments much like the mental patient.

Not all who require mental treatment obtain it, but the population statistics of mental hospitals are nevertheless imposing. Twenty-six persons out of every 10,000 Americans are found in public mental hospitals.[11] Over 350,000 new commitments to mental institutions are made each year, more than three and a half times the number sentenced to state and federal prisons. Over one million patients are on the books of the mental institutions, more than five times the number imprisoned.[12] These ratios would be even higher if the existing laws providing for the commitment of alcoholics, drug addicts, and epileptics were fully utilized.[13]

The question of how mental health can be promoted while protecting individual rights is especially important because, despite increasing public enlightenment concerning mental illness, as many as four-fifths of those entering public mental hospitals in America are still involuntarily committed.[14] By comparison, only one-fifth of all admissions to mental hospitals in England are involuntary.[15]

[10] See pp. 4-5 above. Of the 4,800,000 men aged 18 to 37 who were rejected for military service during World War II (out of approximately 15,000,000 examined), a total of 1,767,000 were turned down for neuropsychiatric or other mental deficiencies. Thus, about 17 percent of those young Americans were deemed unfit for military service on mental grounds. During World War II, there were approximately one million patients with neuropsychiatric disorders admitted to army hospitals. This represented a rate of 45 admissions per 1,000 troops per year. More than 500,000 men were discharged from the army for neuropsychiatric and other personality disorders, representing 39 percent of all medical discharges. A. Deutsch, *The Mentally Ill in America* 464-67 (1949).

[11] American Psychiatric Association and National Association for Mental Health, *Fifteen Indices* 4 (1964).

[12] U.S. Bureau of the Census, *Statistical Abstract of the United States* 76-77 (1966).

[13] See pp. 69-70 below.

[14] U.S. Congress, Senate, Committee on the Judiciary, Subcommittee on Constitutional Rights, *Hearings*, 88th Cong., 1st sess., 1963, p. 61.

[15] "Informal Way on Mentally Ill," *Daily Telegraph* (London), September 13, 1967, p. 11.

Commitment to mental hospitals is assertedly a civil, not a criminal, procedure. Directed toward persons suffering from an illness rather than those charged with a crime, its purpose is therapy, not punishment. But when mental hospitalization continues in large measure as a coercive process, one must ask: What professed social needs and aims will justify this involuntary commitment? What precise condition of mental derangement or defect should be demonstrated to invoke this exercise of social control? Who should make the final determination of the necessity for commitment—a jury, a judicial officer, a medical or other board, or the mental institution itself? What procedural safeguards are necessary in the commitment process to protect the liberty of the individual without unduly undercutting the therapist's program? To what extent are the constitutional limitations on the criminal process applicable to "civil" or "noncriminal" commitment procedures?

HISTORICAL FOUNDATIONS

Antiquity records the deviations of the insane, both benign and raving. The contrasting images of the friendly village fool, on the one hand, and the violent demoniac, on the other, are deeply embedded in the folk literatures of all people. Madness and the madmen have long conveyed ambiguous images of both mockery and menace.[16] The classical writings thus convey not only the stories of the far-famed oracles at Delphi, often recruited from the ranks of the mild-mannered insane possessed by religious delusions,[17] but also the violent seizures of Hercules, whose murderous rampage resulted in the slaying of his own and his brother's children. The ancients saw in insanity an intervention of the gods, brought on by human sin and failings. Yet the illness was not considered beyond human cure, and the Bible reports an early instance of therapy in the tale of the evil spirit which was visited upon King Saul and which departed upon David's playing the harp.

Some ancient societies displayed considerable tolerance toward their mentally disordered members.[18] The cohesive tribal systems in

[16] M. Foucault, *Madness and Civilization* 13 (1965).

[17] The insane were frequently considered to be in the special guardianship of the gods. 2 E. B. Tylor, *Primitive Culture* 117 (1924).

[18] For the treatment of the insane in Egypt, Greece, and Rome *see* I. E. Westermarck, *The Origin and Development of Moral Ideas* 269–70 (1906–8); G. Ives, *A History of Penal Methods* 77–96 (1914).

primitive societies permitted continued communal care for the disabled and even a partial utilization of their skills and limited contributions. Only the violent insane required strict supervision. Similarly, the early Christians tended the insane in their churches, in which they stood in a special part, often being provided there with food and shelter.[19]

The Middle Ages exhibited a great intolerance for deviation. Widespread poverty, disease, mass movement of populations, and religious fanaticism made intolerable the lot of the mentally ill, who were thought to be possessed by devils. Stricter controls were imposed not only upon the raving insane, to prevent them from doing harm but also upon the great mass of other incompetents. Unable to subsist without begging or becoming public charges, the wretched, the infirm, the retarded, the senile, and the lazy were all regarded as minor delinquents.

In Europe, the mad were often executed as witches, chained, or thrown into gatehouses and prisons, where they might furnish horrible diversion for the other prisoners.[20] Those more fortunate were driven out of the city enclosures and forced to roam over distant fields. In northern Europe, two modes of ritual exclusion were developed: the "Ship of Fools" (*das Narrenschiff*) and pilgrimages to holy places. Entire ships were chartered and insane persons were entrusted to seamen to be dropped off in uninhabited places. Special shrines to which the mad were taken on pilgrimages in the hope of recovery were created.

Whereas the Middle Ages drove out the insane, the Renaissance confined them. Some historians see this change not as a chance development. Many cloisters and monasteries began to be abandoned by their former occupants, and the drastic abatement of leprosy brought about the vacating of the more than 19,000 leprosaria, the special medieval institutions in which lepers were committed. The vacated institutions provided the space and facilities for the next step in the treatment of the socially unfit in Europe: confinement.

Until modern times, Western society for the most part refused to differentiate among the common criminal, the vagrant, the indigent, and the insane. All were subject to the criminal law and the traditional criminal sanctions—execution, bondage, transportation, and later confinement—applied equally to the sound and to the insane, to the

---

[19] I. J. Bingham, *Antiquities of the Christian Church* 322–23 (1843–45).
[20] Ives, *History of Penal Methods* 83.

violent criminal offenders, and to the meek social misfits whose only crime was indigency and an inability to care for themselves. As late as 1750 Robert François Damiens, a palpably insane man who pricked Louis XV of France with a penknife as the king was leaving the palace, was exposed to an incredibly barbaric execution: his flesh was torn with red-hot pincers, the hand that wielded the knife was burned off with lighted sulphur, his tongue was torn out at the root, and finally he was drawn and quartered.

Sources of State Responsibility for the Mentally Ill In England

The authority for the state's exercise of great power over the person of the insane[21] may be traced to three distinct conceptual sources fundamental to the Anglo-American political system. The state as protector of the peace may exercise its general policing powers in all cases where public order is disturbed or threatened. This power of the state to protect the peace and the public welfare (commonly referred to as the "police power")[22] by necessity included the right to restrain the violent and was recognized as one of the inherent rights of the sovereign.[23] One of the first collisions between the state and the mentally ill was therefore the confining of "furiously mad" individuals in order to stop or prevent acts of violence.[24] This police power over the violently deranged was subsequently amplified by specific commitment laws, but the general police power in fact still serves as

[21] State control over mentally ill persons, as typified by commitment to asylums, should be distinguished initially from the ancient power of guardianship. Legal guardianship is an old institution which functions through the appointment of special guardians to protect the proprietary assets of the mentally ill, minors, and other incompetents. Only secondary is the protection of the afflicted or immature person. Significantly, Western civilization from Rome until recent history has shown greater concern for the protection of the property of the mentally ill than for his person. This emphasis was prevalent also in England and in the colonies, where legislation designed to guard the estate of the insane was enacted long before these governments became concerned with the personal welfare of the mentally ill. For a history and survey of guardianship *see The Mentally Disabled and the Law* 218–62 (F. T. Lindman and D. M. McIntyre eds. 1961); *see also Deutsch, Mentally Ill in America* 40.

[22] The reference here is to the police power in the strict or narrow sense. In a broader sense, the term could encompass all state actions. *See* P. A. Freund, *Police Power* 242 (1904); 16 *Am. Jur.* 2d, "Constitutional Law" §262 (1964).

[23] Eubank v. City of Richmond, 226 U.S. 137 (1912); Drysdale v. Prudden, 195 N.C. 722, 143 S.E. 530, 536 (1928); 29 *Am. Jur.*, "Insane Persons" §34 (1960). Even the United States Constitution grants implied recognition to the prior existence of the police power in the states. *U.S. Const.*, amend. X; 16 *Am. Jur.* 2d, "Constitutional Law" §259 (1964).

[24] For one of the first laws of this kind in this country *see New York Laws of 1788*, ch. 31.

authority for the control of the mentally ill when special legislation is lacking.

A second source for the state authority was contained in the recognition of the sovereign's position as *parens patriae*.[25] The guardianship of the person and control of the property of the legally disabled in medieval England was originally a role performed by the feudal lord of the manor on which the lunatic resided. This function, however, was assumed by the king after the Crown's consolidation in England in the thirteenth century. As *parens patriae* the sovereign functioned as the protector of the proprietary and personal interests of his subjects. "The King," says an early legal commentator, "as the political father and guardian of his kingdom, has the protection of all his subjects, and of their lands and goods; and he is bound, in a more peculiar manner to take care of those who, by reason of their imbecility and want of understanding, are incapable of taking care of themselves."[26]

Traditional historians claim that the guardianship of incompetents was assumed by the royal house in order to end the abuses inherent in the decentralized arrangements, by which the local lords were able to dispose of the estates of incompetents without any supervision from the Crown.[27] A more critical assessment of this undertaking by the Crown must not ignore the resultant political and economic advantages. The assumption of the new function not only permitted the king to supervise the management and transfer of the property of the insane but also allowed him to reap the profits of the estates under his guardianship.[28]

The power asserted by the Crown over the indigent insane as members of the pauper community is the third source of state authority. Until the beginning of the sixteenth century, the church was responsible for relieving the needs of the poor.[29] The ancient English kings had ordained that "the poor should be sustained by parsons, rectors of the church, and by parishioners, so that none of them die for want of sustenance."[30] The Reformation and the subsequent dissolution of monasteries, however, weakened the church's capability for

[25] 3 W. Blackstone, *Commentaries* 427 (1783).

[26] 2 L. Shelford, *A Practical Treatise on the Law Concerning Lunatics, Idiots, and Persons of Unsound Mind* 9 (1833).

[27] *Ibid.* 10; 2 J. Reeves, *History of the English Law* 307 (1814).

[28] 1 Blackstone, *Commentaries* 303.

[29] Under common law, matters of charity were thought more appropriate for the church. 41 *Am. Jur.*, "Poor and Poor Laws" §2 (1960).

[30] Cerro Gordo County v. Boone County, 152 Iowa 692, 133 N.W. 132, 134 (1911).

the task. In addition, the economic changes of that time enlarged the pauper class. The conversion of cultivated lands into enclosed pastures for sheep farming in connection with England's wool industry caused unemployment. Price levels kept rising to keep pace with the increased wealth from the influx of New World treasures. Aggravated by the monetary debasement under Henry VIII and Edward VI and by the collapse of the medieval rural economy which came with the rise of wool and other industries, the English economy suddenly became susceptible to booms and slumps. The church could not meet the new welfare demands with its weakened resources, and the civil authorities were forced to assume responsibility for a large uprooted population. In 1536, at the time of Henry VIII, the law first made paupers a charge on the local municipalities, cities, towns, and parishes. But in 1601 the overall responsibility was shifted from the local to the national authorities by the famous Poor Law of Queen Elizabeth.[31]

Pursuant to the various programs for dealing with the poor, the destitute insane were generally accorded the same treatment as paupers and both were exposed to the same experiments in public welfare. These included the payment of doles to the poor and also their hiring out to farmers and other contractors who provided for them in return for labor.[32] Relief was granted primarily to settled or permanent residents, and recipients were required to wear a large red or blue "P" on their garments. Claims of abuses (that dole payments were made to undeserving persons and that hiring out provided farmers with cheap labor while their wards were not humanely treated) finally brought an end to the practices of providing relief outside institutions. Well-regulated workhouses were finally recognized as the only proper forms for the care of the poor.[33]

Utilizing the recently abandoned monasteries and leprosaria (in the middle of the twelfth century, England and Scotland had 220 leprosaria serving a national population totaling a million and a half inhabitants) soon permitted the development of internment programs for the growing number of common paupers and other social misfits. Leprosy had disappeared and the leper almost vanished from memory. The structures, however, remained. "Often, in these same places, the formulas of exclusion would be repeated . . . [p]oor vagabonds . . . and 'deranged minds' [taking] the part played by the leper. . . ."[34]

[31] 43 Eliz., c. 2.

[32] T. Mackay, *A History of the English Poor Law* (1899).

[33] *See*, generally, 1 S. and B. Webb, *English Poor Law History: The Old Poor Law* 1–100 (1927).

[34] Foucault, *Madness and Civilization* 7.

Society's recognition of the special character of the insane came in two stages. The violent criminal offenders rather than the docile insane were first exempted from the criminal process. This divestment started in the English common law during the thirteenth and fourteenth centuries when those charged with homicides were first accorded the benefit of royal pardons for insanity and subsequently were allowed to plead insanity as a defense.[35]

Although serious criminal offenders were increasingly allowed to plead insanity in order to exempt themselves from the criminal process, the relatively harmless yet indigent and hopeless insane, charged with nothing more than lunacy, continued to be thrown into jails and workhouses together with other lesser criminals, such as idlers, drunkards, and beggars. Only the growth in the number of special institutions for the care of mental patients during the first quarter of the nineteenth century led to the second stage in divesting the criminal process of authority over the insane. Combining various features of the workhouse and the public hospital, the mental asylum grew out of these earlier institutions.[36] The special hospitalization of the insane may thus be viewed as the institutional progeny of the seventeenth and eighteenth centuries. "[I]n the history of unreason, it marked a decisive event. the moment when madness was perceived on the social horizon of poverty, of incapacity for work, of inability to integrate with the group, the moment when madness began to rank among the problems of the city."[37]

But the new institutional model was also compulsory and, like imprisonment, stood for total social exclusion.[38] As long as therapeutic science and skills remained undeveloped, confinement in the name of *parens patriae* was almost certainly more a preventive detention measure for the benefit of society than an individually oriented program of treatment.

[35] J. Biggs, *The Guilty Mind* 81–84 (1955). Even to this day, however, the criteria which should be employed in drawing the line between the "evil" offender and the "ill" one is undetermined: the M'Naghten test, the Durham test, the Currens test, and the American Law Institute test present differing formulas. *See* above, pp. 12 43 and nn. 132–34.

[36] A Halliday, *A General View of the Present State of Lunatics and Lunatic Asylums* 10 (1828).

[37] Foucault, *Madness and Civilization* 64.

[38] The mad, nevertheless, were reckoned among the local "sights" until the end of the eighteenth century. The public paid to go around in the asylums and inmates would be given grass to eat for the amusement of visitors. Some mental institutions became notorious for the inmate plays presented, with much sound and fury, for public spectators. H. W. Carter, *A Short Account of Some Principal Hospitals* 42 (1819).

The Early American Experience

Although a few special institutions for the mentally ill existed in America in the latter part of the eighteenth century, widespread involuntary commitment practices were not instituted until the first quarter of the nineteenth century. Still, the mentally ill, violent and otherwise, came in contact with various phases of the law long before that, usually in connection with the general criminal law or the poor laws.

Those who offended the criminal law or were predisposed to violence were detained in jails or similar facilities. Under the common law the insane offender was exempted from criminal punishment, but he was often committed to the care of the magistrate who confined him in the local jail as a means of protecting the public.[39] An early method of controlling the dangerous madman is described in the 1689 records of York County, Virginia. John Stock kept "running about the neighborhood day and night in a sad distracted condition to the great disturbance of the people. . . ."[40] Consequently, the sheriff was ordered to take hold of Stock and to keep him safely "in some close roome" to prevent his "doing any further mischiefe."[41] A similar procedure is reported in the annals of New York City. In 1725 the town marshal was paid two shillings six pence a week by the churchwardens in order "to subsist Robert Bullman a Madman in Prison."[42] Albert Deutsch, a leading historian of the treatment of the mentally ill in America, concludes: "Not infrequently the unfortunate person spent decades incarcerated like a common criminal."[43]

The nonviolent and merely indigent insane were given the same treatment as other paupers. Some communities provided them with food and shelter; others persecuted them. According to Deutsch: "The [harmless insane] . . . were hardly more fortunate than the . . . [violent insane] . . . for in colonial times and long after pauperism was looked upon as merely a lesser type of crime."[44] Carefully following the patterns of the famous Elizabethan Poor Law Act of 1601, the American colonies' welfare programs emphasized repression rather than relief.

[39] Deutsch, *Mentally Ill in America* 50, 51; E. B. O'Callaghan, *Documents Relative to the Colonial History of the State of New York* 689–90 (1853–87); 2 *Public Records of the Colony of Connecticut* 313, 590 (1759).

[40] W. B. Blanton, *Medicine in Virginia in the Seventeenth Century* 131 (1930).

[41] *Ibid.*

[42] Deutsch, *Mentally Ill in America* 42.

[43] *Ibid.*

[44] *Ibid.*

Harsh settlement requirements were imposed to withhold relief from poor strangers, including indigent insane. Newcomers who were prospective public charges were unceremoniously "warned out" by being informed that imprisonment was to be expected unless they expeditiously left town.[45]

Society's utilization of the tools of repression, correction, and therapy with regard to the insane and other deviants was initially intermingled. When houses of correction were first built they were intended to hold the criminal, the indigent, and the insane. Connecticut's first house of correction, authorized in 1727, provided for the incarceration of "all rogues, vagabonds and idle persons going about in town or country begging, or persons ... feigning themselves to have knowledge in physiognomy, palmistry, or pretending that they can tell fortunes ... common drunkards, common nightwalkers, pilferers, wanton and lascivious persons ... and also persons under distraction and unfit to go at large, whose friends do not take care for their safe confinement."[46] Similarly, until the middle of the nineteenth century almshouses were heavily used as a dumping ground for the neglected sick, aged, infirm, young, insane, feeble-minded, vagrant, and the like.[47]

Neither the procedures applicable to the "violent" insane nor those applicable to the "harmless" ones recognized the mentally ill as a distinct class. Since the first hospital intended exclusively for the mentally ill was not constructed until 1773 in Williamsburg, Virginia, and the second not until 1824 in Lexington, Kentucky,[48] any special programs for the insane were impossible before the middle of the nineteenth century. It was at that time that the nation adopted civil commitment laws.

THE SHIFT TO PROCEDURAL FORMALISM

Before the spread of insane asylums, when the restraint of the dangerous mentally ill was viewed primarily as part of the police power, incarceration at some public facility was usually limited to the duration of violent behavior. Designed merely as supplements to police power, these early laws were typified by the New York statute of

---

[45] S. Drake, *Town of Roxbury* 383 (1878).

[46] H. W. Capen, *Historical Development of the Poor Law of Connecticut* 63 (1905).

[47] *See* J. L. Gillin, *Poverty and Dependence* (1926); A. P. Miles, *Introduction to Public Welfare* (1949); *Encyclopedia Britannica* (1962 ed.), s.v. "Poor Law."

[48] Deutsch, *Mentally Ill in America* 71.

1788: "Whereas, there are sometimes persons who by lunacy or otherwise are furiously mad, or are so disordered in their senses that they may be dangerous to be permitted to go abroad; therefore, Be it enacted, that it shall and may be lawful for any two or more justices of the peace to cause such person to be apprehended and kept safely locked up in some secure place, and if such justices shall find it necessary, to be there chained. . . ."[49]

After the growth of insane asylums around the middle of the last century, long-term commitments to these special institutions became the major public program for dealing with the insane deviate. Early commitment procedures were highly informal both here and in England. Commitment was viewed strictly as an administrative procedure. An order of a public official (such as the overseer of the poor) or the police authorities was sufficient to place an indigent insane in the available institution: poorhouse, prison, or hospital.[50] This procedure is illustrated by an authorization for admission issued by Benjamin Rush, one of the pioneers of American psychiatry. Scrawled on a chance scrap of paper was the cryptic conclusion: "James Sproul is a proper patient for the Pennsylvania Hospital. . . ."[51] Even when the states began to formulate special commitment procedures for their newly established mental institutions, the rules were extremely sketchy. The 1851 Illinois commitment statute, for example, provided that married women and infants who, in the judgment of the medical superintendents of the state asylum at Jacksonville, are evidently insane or distracted "may be entered or detained at the request of the husband or the guardian of the infant, without the evidence in other cases."[52]

In fact, the reason behind the procedural requirements of the early period was not so much to prevent the improper commitment of unwilling innocent people as to exclude paupers and vagabonds who were only too willing to be admitted to the institutional benefits.[53] But the growth of mental institutions and the concomitant increase in the number of commitments finally resulted in complaints of abuses and the institution of several suits alleging illegal commitment.

A consequence of these developments was the adoption of the elaborate procedural details for present-day commitments. The most

[49] *New York Laws of 1788*, ch. 31.
[50] Deutsch, *Mentally Ill in America* 420, 421.
[51] *Ibid.* 422.
[52] *Ill. Laws of 1851*, §10, pp. 96, 98.
[53] Royal Commission of the Law Relating to Mental Illness and Mental Deficiency, *Report 68* (1957).

famous crusader for tightening commitment laws in this country was Mrs. Dorothy Packard, an ex-patient who set out in the 1860s to arouse public concern in order to make "railroading" to lunatic asylums impossible.[54] Her exposés resulted in the introduction of many formal guarantees of due process into commitment procedures, including a hearing and a jury trial for determining a person's insanity. The new procedures not only served to protect patients but also protected institutional officials against claims of malfeasance and wrongful detention.[55]

Strict commitment procedures remained unopposed by the medical profession. Only in the middle of the twentieth century has modern psychiatry generated sufficient support for the introduction of more informal commitment practices and broader commitment criteria.

PRESENT FRAMEWORK

Who Is Subject to Commitment?

Who is mentally ill? "Some say all of us. A few say none."[56] Yet all states have formulated criteria which designate certain people as mentally disordered and subject to commitment. Commitment describes the removal of a person, judged to be mentally ill, from his usual surroundings to a hospital authorized to detain him. In modern reality the mental hospital is a conglomerate, multi-purpose institution: a jail, a hospital, poorhouse, and an old people's home. It protects society from the dangerously insane, provides shelter and food to the feeble-minded and senile, treats all who can improve, and custodializes those who cannot.[57]

A majority of mental patients are institutionalized through the exercise of the state's compulsory power.[58] Although there is little

[54] Curran, "Hospitalization of the Mentally Ill," 31 *N.C. L. Rev.* 274, 276 (1953). At about the same time Charles Reade's *Hard Cash* (1964) became a best seller in this country. The story concerned the illegal commitment of the young hero due to the machinations of his business associates who sought to separate him from his fortune.

[55] Deutsch, *Mentally Ill in America* 423.

[56] Association of the Bar of New York City, Special Committee to Study Commitment Procedures, *Mental Illness and Due Process* 17 (1962).

[57] Since the disappearance of the poorhouses and the multi-generation family structure, mental institutions have received a new influx of homeless patients. Clausen, "Mental Disorders," in *Contemporary Social Problems* 135–36 (R. K. Merton and R. A. Nisbet eds. 1961).

[58] Up to 59 percent of all mental hospital patients in Texas, for example, are involuntary. Cohen, "The Function of the Attorney and the Commitment of the Mentally Ill," 44 *Tex. L. Rev.* 424, 436 (1966).

recognition of the departure from the common law police power concept which limited compulsory restraint only to the dangerously insane, present commitment criteria are much broader. The exercise of
state compulsion now extends to those who are homeless and helpless[59] and, oftentimes, in the name of therapy to those incompetents
who are completely harmless.[60] This expansion of affected classes has
never been given appropriate scrutiny or attention.[61] Allegedly, the
liberalization was first given judicial endorsement by Chief Justice
Shaw of Massachusetts as early as 1845[62] in a case that, according to
Deutsch, "was one of the most important decisions affecting the civil
insane in the history of American jurisprudence. It defined the justifications and limitations implicit in the common law concerning restraint of the insane. Moreover, Chief Justice Shaw ruled that restraint
of the insane was legally justified not only by regard for public or
personal safety, but by consideration of remedial treatment. This was
probably the first time that the therapeutic justification for restraint
was explicitly stated in a decision handed down by an American
court."[63] If this analysis is correct, the cornerstone of the full-fledged
modern therapeutic state was laid in 1845.

A progressive broadening of the criteria for commitment, has occurred
during the last century. This expansion is manifested not only by
commitment practices but also by the language of the various state
laws.[64] In many states, the commitment laws now specify that the
prospective patient's "need for treatment" is a condition sufficient to

[59] Certification of Anon. 1–12, 138 N.Y.S.2d 30 (1954).

[60] *E.g.*, Pennsylvania provides for the commitment of those "in need of care
and treatment by reason of mental disability." Purdon's *Penn. Stat.* tit. 50, §4406
(1954).

[61] Such scrutiny is further hampered by states, such as Kansas, which refuse to
disclose the records adjudicating persons mentally ill even to abstractors. Cobean,
"New Kansas Philosophy about Care or Treatment of the Mentally Ill," 6 *Washburn L. J.* 448 (1967).

[62] *In re* Josiah Oakes, 8 Law Rep. 122 (Mass. 1845).

[63] Deutsch, *Mentally Ill in America* 423. Yet the cited case contains no clear
expression of such a proposition. The paucity of legal critiques in the *parens
patriae* area is well illustrated by the continued reliance upon this lone and ambiguous case as a landmark decision in the growth of therapeutic commitment
powers. *See also* Curran, "Hospitalization" 274, 291.

[64] *E.g.*, 1966 *Del. Code Ann.* §1–302. The current state laws are as follows:
Alabama—*Ala. Code* §45.205 (1959); Arizona—*Ariz. Rev. Stat.* §36–501.5 (Supp.
1959); Alaska—*Alaska Stat.* §§47.30.20, 47.30.030, 47.30.040 (1962); Arkansas—
Ark. Stat. Ann. §59–232 (Supp. 1967); California—*Cal. Wel. & Inst. Code* §5550
(West 1968); Colorado—*Colo. Rev. Stat. Ann.* §71–1–1(b) (1963); Connecticut—
Conn. Gen. Stat. §17–176 (Supp. 1965); Delaware—*Del. Code Ann.* §1–302
(Supp. 1966); Florida—*F.S.A.* §1.01(5) (1961); Georgia—*Ga. Code Ann.* §88.401
(Supp. 1963); Hawaii—*Hawaii Rev. Laws* §§81–21, 81–31 (Supp. 1965); Idaho—
Idaho Code §66.317(b) (Supp. 1967); Illinois—*Ill. Ann. Stat.* ch. 91½, §§1–8,

justify commitment.[65] In these states the old requirement of dangerousness no longer limits the powers of the state. Some states have even
made the welfare needs of persons other than the patient, such as
members of his family, a sufficient criterion for commitment.[66] Only
five states continue to use the term "dangerous" or require a likelihood of injury in all their definitions of committable persons.[67] Seven
states base a person's commitment exclusively on his need for care,
and twelve jurisdictions have established the need for care or dangerousness as alternate criteria. The test in seven other states is that
of the patient's own welfare or the welfare of others. Several states
merely require that the committed person be "mentally ill."[68] A 1951
Pennsylvania statute permits the commitment of anyone who suffers
from a mental illness which "lessens the capacity of a person to use
his customary self-control, judgment and discretion in the conduct of
his affairs and social relations."[69] The Draft Act for the Hospitalization
of the Mentally Ill,[70] proposed as a model for the states, similarly pro-

---

1–18 (Smith-Hurd 1966); Indiana—*Ind. Stat. Ann.* §22.1301–1 (Burns 1964);
Iowa—*Iowa Code* §4.1(6), 229.40 (1966); Kansas—59 *Kan. Stat. Ann.* §2903(1)
(Supp. 1967); Kentucky—*Ky. Rev. Stat. Ann.* §202.010(2) (1968); Louisiana—*La.
Rev. Stat.* §28.2(3) (1950); Maine—34 *M.R.S.A.* §2251(5) (1964); Maryland—
Md. Code Ann. art. 59, §31 (1968); Massachusetts—*Mass. Ann. Laws* 123–1 (1965);
Michigan—*Mich. Stat. Ann.* §14.844 (Supp. 1968); Minnesota—*M.S.A.* §253A.02(3)
(Supp. 1967); Mississippi—*Miss. Code Ann.* §698 (1942); Missouri—*Mo. Rev. Stat.*
§202.780(5) (Supp. 1959); Montana—*Mont. Rev. Code* §§38–401, 38–402 (1947);
Nebraska—*Neb. Rev. Stat.* §83–306(3) (1958); Nevada—*Nev. Rev. Stat.* §433.655
(1967); New Hampshire—*N.H. Rev. Stat. Ann.* §135:21 (1964); New Jersey—
N.J.S.A. §30:4–23 (Supp. 1967); New Mexico—*N.M. Stat. Ann.* §34–2–1(a)
(1953); New York—*N.Y. Mental Hygiene Law* §2.8 (McKinney 1959); North Carolina—*N.C. Gen. Stat. Ann.* §122–36(d) (1964); North Dakota—*N.D. Century Code*
§25–0101(1) (1960); Ohio—*Ohio Rev. Code Ann.* §5122.01(a) (Page's Supp.
1967); Oklahoma—*Okla. Stat.* §43A–3(c) (Supp. 1967); Oregon—*Ore. Rev. Stat.*
§426.120 (1968); Pennsylvania—59 *P.S.* §1072(11) (1954); Rhode Island—*R.I.
Gen. Laws* §43–3–7 (1956); South Carolina—*S.C. Code of Laws* §32–911(1)
(1962); South Dakota—*S.D. Code* §27.7 (1967); Tennessee—*Tenn. Code Ann.*
§§33–1201(a), 33–604 (Supp. 1900); Texas—*Tex. Stat.* §5547–4(K) (Vernon
Supp. 1968); Utah—*Utah Code Ann.* §64–7–28(a) (1968); Vermont—*Vt. Stat.
Ann.* §18.3602(f) (Supp. 1967); Virginia—*Va. Code* §37.1–1(15) (Supp. 1968);
Washington—*Wash. Rev. Code* §71.02.010 (1958); West Virginia—*W.Va. Code
Ann.* §27–1–2 (1966); Wisconsin—*Wis. Stat.* §990.01(16) (1965); Wyoming—
Wyo. Stat. Ann. §25–49 (1967); District of Columbia—*D.C. Code* §§49–207, 21–
521, 21–541 (1967).

[65] *E.g., Colo. Rev. Stat. Ann.* §71–1–1(b) (1963).
[66] *E.g., Ill. Ann. Stat.* (Smith-Hurd 1966).
[67] *D.C. Code* §21–521 (1967).
[68] *E.g., Del. Code Ann.* §1–302 (1966).
[69] *Pennsylvania Mental Health Act of 1951* §102(11).
[70] U.S. Department of Health, Education, and Welfare, National Institute of
Mental Health, Federal Security Agency, *A Draft Act Governing Hospitalization
of the Mentally Ill* §9(g)(3) (Public Health Service Pub. no. 51, 1952).

vides for the commitment of those who are "in need of care or treatment" and lack sufficient capacity to evaluate such need responsibly.

While most commitment statutes emphasize the protective and curative benefits that are to accrue to the patient or to society, some have embarked on expeditions which are potentially more hazardous. Massachusetts provides for the involuntary hospitalization of any person subject to a "character disorder" which renders him so deficient in "judgment or emotional control" that he is likely to conduct himself in a manner which "clearly violates the established . . . conventions of the community."[71] By this standard, any social nonconformity could well be grounds for commitment.

The standards for commitment in the District of Columbia metropolitan area are not uniform. Maryland's standards that the person be *"non compos mentis"* (literally, not of sound mind) and that confinement be "necessary and proper"[72] are among the least precise criteria in the nation. Virginia utilizes society's benign concern for the incompetent's safety and conditions of life. The statute specifies that grounds for commitment exist whenever "it would be for . . . [the mentally ill person's] safety and benefit to receive care and treatment."[73] The District of Columbia, on the other hand, emphasizes the likelihood of danger concept. Commitment is predicated upon the existence of a "psychosis or other disease which substantially impairs the mental health of a person"[74] and renders him "likely to injure himself or other persons if allowed to remain at liberty."[75]

How the statutory criteria are applied in reality cannot be readily ascertained, because juries, judges, and physicians may interpret the legal terminology in diverse manners. In the District of Columbia, where the "likelihood" of danger is an element of major significance in the law, the instructions given to juries hearing commitment cases have liberally defined injury to others as "intentional or unintentional acts which result in harm to others, or cause *trouble* or *inconvenience* to others."[76] The Utah law requires, similarly, that no person alleged to be mentally ill be detained pending a medical examination and a hearing unless the commitment application avers that the proposed patient is dangerous to himself and others. But a recent survey disclosed that the Utah courts have established a presumption of danger

---

[71] *Mass. Ann. Laws* ch. 123, §1 (1965).
[72] *Md. Ann. Code* art. 16, §144 (replacement vol. 1966).
[73] *Va. Code*, §37–1–1(1) (Supp. 1966).
[74] *D.C. Code*, §21–501 (1967).
[75] *Ibid.* §21–541(a)(1).
[76] Comment, "Liberty and Required Mental Health Treatment," 114 *U. Pa. L. Rev.* 1067, 1070 (1965) (emphasis added).

in virtually all cases, and they routinely order the individual's apprehension following the initial application. This approach accounted, at least in part, for the fact that as many as forty-six percent of those detained pending the initial examination were discharged at the subsequent hearings.[77]

The mentally ill are not the only objects of commitment. The mentally deficient or defective, whose mental growth is arrested due to cogenital conditions, have also been inmates of mental institutions. Commitment statutes in all but eight states provide for the compulsory hospitalization of mentally deficient persons.[78] The criteria for the commitment of this class range from the vague Maryland requirements that the person be *"non compos mentis"* and that it be "necessary and proper"[79] to confine him to the District of Columbia formula requiring a "mental defectiveness from birth, or often early age," which is so pronounced that the person is "incapable of managing himself," necessitating hospitalization "for his own welfare, or the welfare of others, or for the welfare of the community."[80] While some statutes continue to rely on dated terminology such as "feeble-minded, idiot and imbecile," other states have utilized modern definitions. Massachusetts, for example, defines a mentally deficient person as one "whose intellectual functioning has been abnormally retarded, or has demonstrably failed, the deficiency being manifested by psychological signs."[81] Still, very few of the states place major reliance on modern testing tools.[82] Not a single statute requires psychological or intelligence testing or provides for the utilization of test scores in determining whether the mental deficiency is sufficiently severe to justify commitment.

Alcoholics are also subject to involuntary commitment as part of the mental illness laws in thirty-six states.[83] Again, there is no uniform statutory definition of the degree of alcoholism sufficient to justify commitment. In thirty-four states drug addicts may likewise be committed to mental institutions.[84] The statutes, however, are hazy with regard to the degree of addiction sufficient for involuntary hospitaliza-

---

[77] Comment, "Hospitalization of the Mentally Ill in Utah: A Practical and Legal Analysis," *Utah L. Rev.* 223, 228 (1966).
[78] *Mentally Disabled* 18 (Lindman and McIntyre eds.).
[79] *Md. Code Ann.* art. 16, §§132, 144 (1957).
[80] *D.C. Code* §32–603 (1967).
[81] *Mass. Ann. Laws* ch. 123, §1 (1965).
[82] *Mentally Disabled* 18 (Lindman and McIntyre eds.).
[83] *Ibid.*
[84] *Ibid.*

tion. Similarly, epileptics are subject to involuntary commitment to mental hospitals in some eighteen states,[85] despite strong medical opinion that epilepsy is not properly classified as a mental illness.

What legal limitations are there on the state power to adopt and apply ill-defined and uncertain commitment criteria? The Fourteenth Amendment to the United States Constitution protects American citizens against infringements upon liberty without "due process of law." This requirement is not only a guarantee against administrative and procedural arbitrariness but also a guard against substantive abuse—vague and improperly motivated legislative policies. The common law insures against laws that are "void for vagueness."[86] Both requirements, however, have been applied almost exclusively in criminal matters, insisting in the name of fundamental fairness that no man be held criminally liable for conduct that he could not have reasonably believed to be prohibited by the state.[87] The standards of substantive due process required in noncriminal statutes, on the other hand, have not been equally stringent. Since mental commitments have been considered a civil procedure, often taking place without even the benefit of counsel, commitment criteria have rarely been challenged for their vagueness, and when challenged have been summarily upheld.[88]

Procedures for Involuntary Commitment

Until the end of the nineteenth century, the law did not permit voluntary hospitalization in public mental institutions in this country. The fear of high welfare costs accounted for this policy that kept out of institutions all but the most acute patients. Massachusetts in 1881 enacted the first voluntary admission law, but this was limited to paying patients only.[89]

By the 1920s, as the modern mental health movement began to emphasize the need for early diagnosis and treatment, twenty-eight states permitted voluntary admissions.[90] At present all states include provisions for voluntary hospitalization. Under these laws, either the

[85] *Ibid.* 87, 88.

[86] 21 *Am. Jur.* 2d, "Criminal Law" §17 (1965).

[87] People v. Munoz, 9 N.Y.2d 51, 172 N.E.2d 535 (1961); People v. Johnson, 6 N.Y.2d 549, 161 N.E.2d (1959).

[88] *See, e.g.,* Prochaska v. Brinegar, 251 Iowa 834, 102 N.W.2d 870 (1960).

[89] *Mass. Acts of 1881,* ch. 272.

[90] Overholser, "The Voluntary Admission Law: Certain Legal and Psychiatric Aspects," 3 *Amer. J. Psychiatry* 475 (1924).

patient himself or his parent or guardian may apply directly to a public hospital for admission. In many states neither supporting certification by independent physicians nor a judicial hearing is required. Once admitted, however, the voluntary patient is not a completely free man. In several states all patients in public institutions are considered civilly incompetent and their property becomes subject to management by court-appointed guardians. Similarly, one's freedom in the institutions may be severely curtailed by restrictions on visitation, correspondence, and release.[91]

Many hospital administrators have not favored the admission of voluntary patients, who, because of their freedom to come and go, impose an unsettling influence upon formal institutional processes. Often, authorities have exercised their discretion to refuse admission to such patients. The state legislatures, concerned about the premature return of unrecovered patients to the community, similarly have discouraged voluntary admissions by imposing restrictions upon the patient's right to be released at will.[92] Lack of proper community education regarding the nature of mental illness and the improving medical facilities for its treatment further accounted for the limited number of voluntary admissions to public institutions and the predominance of involuntary commitments in this country. In 1949 only slightly more than ten percent of the 138,253 admissions to state mental hospitals were voluntary.[93] In 1963 nearly 450,000 mental patients were voluntarily treated in private hospitals and outpatient psychiatric clinics; but of the 283,591 patients admitted to public mental hospitals the overwhelming majority continued to be involuntary. A 1964–65 sample of fourteen states showed that voluntary admissions still averaged only 32.5 percent of all hospital entries.[94] Thus, while the more privileged have increasingly found access to voluntary treatment either through informal admission to private clinics or by means of private psychiatric care, this choice has not usually been available to the indigent.

The term "involuntary commitment" does not always imply actual

[91] *Mentally Disabled* 107–22 (Lindman and McIntyre eds.).
[92] *Ibid.* 112–14.
[93] World Health Organization, *Hospitalization of Mental Patients* 15 (1955).
[94] In 1960–61, voluntary admissions ranged from only 2.3 percent of all admissions to public mental hospitals in Florida to 60 percent of all admissions in Alaska. Council of State Governments, Interstate Clearing House on Mental Health, *Action in the States in the Fields of Mental Health, Mental Retardation and Related Areas* 7 (1963). The ratio of voluntary admissions, however, has been growing in recent years.

compulsion. Any case in which the request for hospitalization does not originate with the patient is an involuntary commitment.[95] Although it does not necessarily signify that the person was actively opposed to the attempt to hospitalize him, an involuntary commitment does imply a lack of volition on the part of the patient. The term thus encompasses unresisted hospitalization as well as that accomplished against the active will of the patient. This dual meaning must be kept in mind when evaluating the commitment process and the adequacy of the procedural safeguards provided in conjunction with them.

Involuntary commitment legislation since Mrs. Packard's campaign in the middle of the last century has generally emphasized the traditional criminal law safeguards, including notice to the patient of the pending petition for commitment, a fair hearing, and the right to a jury trial. Yet these would clearly have a different meaning and value for the lucid individual actively opposing his commitment than for the passive patient who is not cognizant of what is happening. Only in the last two decades has this emphasis upon formalism been reversed. Many of the newer commitment statutes thus exhibit a considerable departure from past procedures, primarily by permitting hospitalization of emergency and nonprotesting patients without a judicial hearing or any attendant formalities other than a medical certificate.[96]

Because commitment procedures are governed by state legislation, their development has not followed a uniform pattern throughout the country, though occasionally the states have copied each other's commitment procedures. The provisions of the Draft Act for the Hospitalization of the Mentally Ill (proposed in 1952 by the Federal government as a model for state adoption) has provided a basis for the law of six states,[97] but in general the unifying influences have been weak and the commitment procedures vary widely in the several states. Some require a formal judicial hearing and a finding of mental illness prior to hospitalization. Others leave the question of admission to an institution's medical staff whose determination is subject to judicial review only on appeal. A majority of states, moreover, have

[95] U.S. Department of Health, Education, and Welfare, *A Draft Act Governing Hospitalization of the Mentally Ill*, §5, p. 22.

[96] *See, e.g.,* the Pennsylvania provisions for a 10-day emergency detention pursuant to a medical certificate. Purdon's *Pa. Stat. Ann.* tit. 50, §4405 (Supp. 1967).

[97] U.S. Department of Health, Education, and Welfare, *A Draft Act Governing Hospitalization of the Mentally Ill.*

not one exclusive commitment law but authorize hospitalization under a variety of different procedures, the formality of each depending on the patient's lucidity and cooperation and the term for which commitment is sought.

Despite the diversity, involuntary hospitalization procedures may be divided into three major patterns according to the type of agency—court, administrative tribunal, or the hospital itself—which has the power to commit.[98] Thirty-seven states have a judicial procedure, with a hearing before a judge who may issue an order for commitment. In thirteen of these states, the law specifically provides for a jury trial if demanded by the patient or if ordered by the judge.

Commitments through nonjudicial procedures are permitted in thirty-one states; in twelve of these no judicial procedures are available. Of the nonjudicial jurisdictions, a minority provide for a pre-commitment hearing before special administrative tribunals consisting of legal, medical, and sometimes lay representatives. These mixed tribunals can be a panel of municipal officers, as in Maine,[99] or a board consisting of the clerk of the district court, a physician, and an attorney, as in Iowa.[100]

In nineteen states commitment may be effected without a prior hearing before an independent tribunal. These states require only that an application for commitment be prepared by a relative or a public official, that it be accompanied by a medical certificate, and that these be submitted to the hospital authorities at the time the patient is presented. On the basis of these documents the mental institution may hold the patient indeterminately. The patient will be accorded a hearing and review subsequent to his commitment if he specifically requests them.

Although there is no uniform commitment process, certain procedural elements are common. Even the recent statutes permitting commitment without a hearing have adopted the same preliminaries required by the more formal commitment laws. Proceedings are usually begun with a sworn petition of relatives, friends, certain officials, or any interested citizen, accompanied by a physician's certificate stating the person is mentally ill and in need of commitment. In states which permit commitment without a preliminary hearing, the formal procedure ends at this point; the alleged mentally ill per-

---

[98] The following analyses of the commitment procedures are derived from *Mentally Disabled* 16–38 (Lindman and McIntyre eds.).

[99] *Maine Rev. Stat.* §27–104 (1954).

[100] *Iowa Code Ann.* §228.2 (Supp. 1966).

son may be lawfully admitted and restrained in any available institution. In the other states, the person involved must be notified of the proceedings, and his presence is usually required at a hearing. In many states, the court or special tribunal appoints physicians to examine the alleged patient. This examination is usually informal and conducted prior to the final hearing. In several states, the alleged mentally ill person may also demand a jury determination of his sanity. Following the hearing, the judge or special tribunal must make a formal order of commitment if the evidence supports such action.[101]

The most common involuntary commitments in this country are for an indeterminate time, meaning that a patient is not automatically released upon the expiration of a specified term. Release depends on the decision of the hospital administrators that the patient no longer requires detention and that adequate outside facilities are available for him. Various procedural safeguards are available to secure the discharge of the patient who needs no further hospitalization: periodic review of his condition by hospital authorities might be required by law; he may demand a hearing on his condition by the hospital administration; he may appeal to the courts for relief.

Although the traditional commitment to mental institutions has been for an indeterminate time, the last twenty years have witnessed a trend toward temporary or observational hospitalization.[102] These short-term commitments (a widespread practice in Europe and the United Kingdom) are conducted with a minimum of legal formalities and may be obtained on medical certification only. Sixteen of our states permit this type of hospitalization.

Still limited in use, temporary hospitalization for observation has been widely recommended. In the opinion of the Council of State Governments: "[It] offers an opportunity for prompt and effective observation—when it may do the most good—without the delay that accompanies formal admission for an indefinite period. [It] . . . should be authorized by all states, with specific legal recourse being provided in cases where there is any doubt of the need for hospitalization, and with a specific limit being placed on the length of hospitalization under such admission."[103] In most cases, the patient must be released at the conclusion of the specific observation period, unless procedures for indeterminate commitment have been commenced by the authorities.

[101] M. Guttmacher and H. Weihofen, *Psychiatry and the Law* 291 (1952).

[102] *Mentally Disabled* 37–38 (Lindman and McIntyre eds.).

[103] Council of State Governments, *The Mental Health Programs of the Forty-Eight States* 5–6 (1950).

Observational commitment has also been utilized in conjunction with the more formal procedures for indeterminate hospitalization. Twenty-three states allow the court in pending commitment cases to order the diagnostic hospitalization of the alleged mentally ill person. In Texas, commencement of proceedings for indeterminate judicial commitment is prohibited unless the alleged patient has previously been in a mental hospital for sixty days under an observational order.[104]

Apart from short-term hospitalization for observation and diagnosis, the laws of all but thirteen states also permit the emergency detention of the mentally ill in situations where public safety demands the person's immediate confinement.[105] Such special statutes have been instrumental in providing better facilities for those detained. While patients detained under the general police functions are often kept in jail, the special statutes frequently require transferral to a hospital. Without special authority, police detentions under the common law are often restricted to dangerous persons found at large and are strictly limited to the danger period,[106] while detention statutes authorize the taking into custody of mental patients from private homes and provide for confinement periods ranging from forty-eight hours to thirty days.[107]

HOW BROAD A COMMITMENT POLICY?

How disturbed or deviant need one be to merit confinement as insane? Consider the following press account:

Sanity Tests for General Are Rejected

A petition to place retired Army Brig. Gen. Herbert C. Holdridge under mental observation was dismissed yesterday by an Arlington mental commission.

The petition for psychiatric examination of the 73-year old West Point graduate was brought by his wife, Julie Austin of Los Angeles, former actress.

She said her husband, who heads a group called the Constitutional Provisional Government of the United States, suffers from delusions of grandeur and a persecution complex.

---

[104] *Texas Mental Health Code* art. 5547–40 (Supp. 1958).
[105] *Mentally Disabled* 38–40 (Lindman and McIntyre eds.).
[106] *See* Jillson v. Caprio, 181 F.2d 523 (D.C. Cir. 1950), to the effect that a patient could not be taken into custody from a private home without a warrant.
[107] *Mentally Disabled* (Lindman and McIntyre eds.).

Her statement indicated also the Secret Service encouraged her to seek the commitment for her husband. A service spokesman said later his agency is aware of Holdridge.

The Commission yesterday was conducted by Associate County Judge L. Jackson Embrey and Dr. Gerhard Cotts, an Arlington psychiatrist. Embrey said later it was decided there was insufficient evidence to show that Holdridge is dangerous to himself and to others because of any possible mental condition.[108]

This account supplies an up-to-date American illustration of the perils of deviance envisioned by John Stuart Mill. A retired general is reported to have delusions. A governmental official reputedly encourages the general's wife to seek his commitment to a mental hospital. The general may be an eccentric, but should he be committed against his will? A special mental commission examines the case. What should be their criterion: His need for treatment? His wife's unwillingness or inability to care for him? The fact that he may be dangerous? The news story from Arlington, Virginia, clearly pits individuality against the need to protect and promote public safety, health, and welfare.

Broadened commitment standards are generally recommended by psychiatrists as a means of reaching the mentally ill in the early stages of their illnesses, but they have been viewed with alarm by others who challenge the very designation of mental illness as a disease rather than as a phenomenon of social nonconformity.[109] Fearing an improper extension of the state power, the critics point out that under some of the new statutes neurotics, political deviants, and those suffering from personality disorders may be subject to indeterminate hospitalization against their will, even when no immediate likelihood of "danger" has been shown. Thus a young adult who neglects his personal hygiene and refuses to study or earn a living may be diagnosed as "schizophrenic" or as suffering from a "functional psychosis" and be involuntarily hospitalized.[110]

Those opposed to broader commitment policies assert that neither public safety nor public welfare is sufficient to support a deprivation of liberty in cases lacking an *immediate* threat to life or property.[111]

[108] *Washington Post*, May 29, 1965.

[109] Szasz, "Whither Psychiatry?" 33 *Social Research* 439 (1966); *see*, generally, T. J. Scheff, *Being Mentally Ill* (1966).

[110] D. K. Henderson and I. R. C. Batchelor, *Textbook of Psychiatry*, ch. 11 (1962); Alexander and Szasz, "Mental Illness as an Excuse for Civil Wrongs," 43 *Notre Dame Lawyer* 24–25 (1967).

[111] Curran, "Hospitalization" 291.

Even if the patient, due to his illness, may himself lack insight or capacity to seek treatment, the state should not compel therapy unless the public safety is directly endangered by the unremedied mental condition.

A number of persons with cancer or heart disease do not possess sufficient appreciation of their illness to understand that hospitalization, proper medical treatment, and appropriate living conditions would be best for them. Some do have such knowledge but still refuse to follow medical advice that would prolong their lives or improve their health. Should society undertake to cure these groups by involuntary methods, in the manner applied to the mentally ill? To the critics of liberalized commitments it is clear that

> the citizen's right to his personal behavior and beliefs cannot be infringed upon where his behavior injures neither himself nor others. Social nonconformity is often called mental illness. Hasn't an individual the right to believe, act or seek cures according to his own ideas? Hasn't he the right to refuse medical judgments and treatments on the grounds of individual choice?[112]

In 1859 John Stuart Mill similarly urged that

> the only purpose for which power can rightfully be exercised over any member of a civilized community against his will is to prevent harm to others. . . . His own good either physical or moral is not a sufficient warrant. He cannot rightfully be compelled to do or forebear because it will be better for him to do so, because it will make him happier, because in the opinion of others, to do so would be wise, or even right.[113]

The psychiatrists and related professions contend that to wait until a mentally ill person becomes dangerous is to delay the needed treatment improperly. Concepts of preventive medicine and prompt care warn against lost time between the first diagnosis of mental illness and its treatment. Because mental illness differs from all other illnesses in that it affects a person's ability to recognize his need, it is society's duty to provide treatment over the patient's opposition.

The Medical Criteria of Mental Illness

The degree of mental illness sufficient to justify society's substitution of the patient's judgment has been neither suggested by the medi-

[112] Memorandum submitted by Mrs. Margaret Seeger to the American Bar Foundation, February 12, 1957.
[113] J. S. Mill, *On Liberty* 11 (1930).

cal profession nor adequately defined in law.[114] Modern psychiatry has
not been conspicuously successful or consistent in its definition and
classification of mental illness, and the uniform international nomenclature proposed by the World Health Organization has never been
generally adopted in this country.[115] The criteria of our commitment
laws fail to mention or reflect even the most traditional medical group-
ings and classifications of mental disorders. The *psychoses* are the most
severe, involving a major personality disintegration, and include both
the "organic" disorders of old age (senile dementia and psychosis
with cerebral arteriosclerosis) and the "functional" disorders (such as
schizophrenia, manic-depressive reactions, and involutional melan-
cholia), which are without a clearly defined organic cause. The *psycho-
neuroses* are characterized by anxiety and personality disturbances
which impair one's ability to carry out one's normal activities yet
are considered benign because they do not entail a sharp break with
reality. The *psychosomatic* disorders are often induced by emotional
factors and are characterized by very real organic symptoms and malfunctioning, ranging from headaches and transitory skin rashes during
periods of stress to the more severe cases of ulcerative colitis, hyper-
tension, and chronic vomiting. *Personality disorders*, finally, are characterized by developmental defects or pathological trends in personality structure which result in social incompatibility, poor judgment,
lack of stamina, and ineptness,[116] but produce minimal subjective
anxiety and distress in the patient himself.

While such medical classifications are totally ignored, commitment
laws invariably utilize such general standards as "insanity" or "mental
illness," or, more frequently, combine them with such additional and
broad social criteria as the patient's danger to himself or others, his
inability to manage his affairs, or the potential benefit to be derived
from treatment.

The criteria for commitment—not purely medical, social, or legal—
have become a matter of cordial understanding between psychiatric
experts and committing tribunals. The single most important element
in the commitment decision is whether, in the judgment of the particu-

[114] One author recently suggested that compulsory treatment be sanctioned
only when the eventual benefit to the ill person resulting from treatment out-
weighs the limitations on him necessary for the therapy. Comment, "Liberty"
1067. Interesting as a general principle, this standard remains subject to ambiguity and contrasting interpretations.
[115] American Psychiatric Association, *Diagnostic and Statistical Manual: Mental
Disorders* (1952); *Contemporary Social Problems* 131 (Merton and Nisbet eds.).
[116] Merck, *Manual of Diagnosis and Therapy* 1264–1328 (C. E. Lyght ed., 9th
ed., 1956).

lar tribunal, the alleged mentally ill person can no longer be expected to meet in a reasonable manner the standards of the outside world without becoming an undue burden on his family or the community.

It is only natural that the broadness and latitudes of our commitment criteria should be reflected in the populations of mental institutions. Contrary to popular belief, those suffering from psychoses do not constitute the major portion of those committed. The aged, the neurotic, and others without particularly serious mental disorders account for the majority of all admissions. Statistical tabulations of first admissions to public mental hospitals demonstrate that, with the exception of older patients (those over 64 years of age), patients classified under the various categories of psychoses account for less than half of all admissions.[117] Of a reported 135,476 first admissions in 1965, the following are the major classifications:[118] psychotic disorders, 32,971; acute brain syndromes, 4,900; chronic brain syndromes, 30,952; psychoneurotic reactions, 14,869; personality disorders, 33,662 (including 2,988 with personality pattern disturbance, 4,973 with personality trait disturbance, 1,811 with antisocial reaction, 14,242 with alcoholism, and 514 with dyssocial reaction); transient situational personality disturbances, 4,957; mental disorder undiagnosed, 7,544; and without mental disorder, 1,747. Similar evidence led a recent investigator to conclude that

... there is a large proportion of the patient population, 43 per cent, whose presence in the hospital cannot readily be explained in terms of their psychiatric condition. Their presence suggests the putative character of the societal reaction to deviance, and that for at least a near majority of the patients, their status is largely ascribed rather than achieved.[119]

DUE PROCESS FOR THE MENTALLY DISORDERED?

"Due process" is a guarantee offered the American citizen by the Constitution, a safeguard against arbitrary government and officialdom.[120] Historically, due process was derived from the colonists' ex-

---

[117] *Contemporary Social Problems* 133 (Merton and Nisbet eds.).

[118] U.S. Department of Health, Education, and Welfare, *Patients in Mental Institutions*, pt. 2, p. 21 (1965).

[119] Scheff, *Being Mentally Ill* 168.

[120] The Fifth Amendment to the United States Constitution, which applies to the federal government, provides: "No person shall ... be deprived of life, liberty, or property, without due process of law." The Fourteenth Amendment, applicable to the various states, has identical language.

perience with oppressive European governments, in whose hands the citizen was a helpless pawn. The requirement of due process assures the citizen protection in his efforts to defend himself against the overwhelming governmental apparatus. It requires that the fate of the citizen's life, liberty, or property not be decided in closed chambers, that he be advised of the specific charges against him and have an opportunity to challenge adverse evidence, that he be permitted to introduce his own witnesses, and that the necessary assistance of counsel be afforded for his defense. Nowhere does the Constitution limit the requirement of due process to criminal procedures only; indeed, it specifically applies in all situations where a person might be deprived of life, liberty, or property. Yet, traditionally, the greatest insistence upon due process has been in the criminal realm, on the assumption that the citizen requires less protection against noncriminal governmental controls and intervention.

What is the public purpose behind mental commitments? The state statutes, statistics of commitments to hospitals, and observations within the institutions continue to demonstrate that the mental hospital is neither exclusively a tool of community defense against the dangerously insane nor primarily a dispenser of therapy for those who require it. Commitment serves to prevent breaches of the peace and harm to persons or property but also to provide treatment and cure, to relieve the family of the burden of a disabled member, and to provide care and custody for the miscellaneous groups of problematic and maladjusted indigent misfits.[121] A Texas report claims that ". . . seventy percent of all the patients don't need to be in a mental hospital. . . . They could be treated at home, in clinics, or other institutions."[122] It is obvious, therefore, that involuntary commitments not only serve multiple purposes but are frequently utilized where lesser social controls and sanctions would suffice.

To translate into reality the prevailing but erroneous belief that compulsory hospitalization is a noncriminal social program serving a reasonable therapeutic function for the patient, the law must formulate procedures that protect the individual from arbitrary commitment for nontherapeutic reasons. It is not sufficient to accept hospitalization

[121] I. Belknap, *Human Problems of a State Mental Hospital* 32 (1956).

[122] Gainfort, "How Texas is Reforming Its Mental Hospitals," *The Reporter* 19 (November 29, 1956). It has been asserted that as many as 50 percent of the patients who in years past were subject to long-term commitment could, with the aid of new drugs, be placed in out-patient facilities. Bleicher, "Compulsory Community Care for the Mentally Ill," 16 *Clev.-Mar. L. Rev.* 93, 94 (1967).

as serving the needs of both the individual and society. The two needs are not always the same. If commitment is occasionally utilized for the protection of society rather than for treatment, should not pre-commitment procedures be constitutionally circumscribed? Even if the main purpose of commitment is the patient's own welfare, by what logic does the prospect of treatment justify expediting commitment by stripping the individual of his constitutional protections against the excesses and errors of the state? Since lesser sanctions than commitment could in many instances meet both society's and the individual's needs, would not the opportunity for a fair hearing best help determine other treatment alternatives?

In spite of the logical support for the maintenance of due process protections, recent world-wide developments have been in the other direction. In England, for example, after 100 years of agitation and three Royal Commissions, the British Parliament in 1958 adopted a new Mental Health Act[123] authorizing the compulsory hospitalization of persons suffering from three types of mental disorders—mental illness, mental subnormality, and psychopathic disorder. The first classification, mental illness, is never defined. The second is described as "a state of arrested or incomplete development of mind which includes subnormality of intelligence and is of such a nature or degree that the patient is incapable of living an independent life." Psychopathic disorder is defined as "a persistent disorder or disability of mind . . . which results in abnormally aggressive or seriously irresponsible conduct . . . and requires or is susceptible to medical treatment."[124] Although the language of the bill is qualified by the assertion that nothing in the act is to be construed as implying that a person may be treated as mentally disordered "by reason only of promiscuity or other immoral conduct,"[125] it provides that an alleged mentally disordered person may be hospitalized indefinitely on the recommendation of two private physicians, without prior requirement of a court or other hearing. Most European countries have long permitted involuntary mental admissions without prior legal safeguards.[126]

The adoption of the English Mental Health Act with its broad grant of power to medical administrators follows an accelerated general trend in Anglo-American law away from a strict judicial process to

---

[123] Mental Health Act, 7 and 8 Eliz. 2, c. 72 (1958).
[124] *Ibid.* c. 72, pt. I, §4(4).
[125] *Ibid.* pt. I, §4(5).
[126] Roener, "Hospitalization Under European Laws," in Association of the Bar of New York City, *Mental Illness and Due Process* 275.

a more informal administrative procedure.[127] The transition, motivated
by promises of more effective, more specialized, and speedier dispositions, has been widely endorsed by social reformers who argue that
anachronistic legal formalism needlessly imposes requirements and
sanctions on people who require psychiatric assistance, not legal aid.

The new emphasis on loosening the judicial control over commitment proceedings represents the swing away from the nineteenth-
century legal and social reforms that sought strict statutory regulations for the confinement of the mentally ill. Campaigning against the
absence of independent controls over the admission and treatment of
mental patients in public hospitals, crusaders for tightening commitment laws succeeded in cloaking the statutes in the elaborate procedural details that present-day reformers are trying so hard to shed.

The discontent with existing commitment procedures because they
do not meet fully modern needs[128] comes from many camps. Psychiatrists have argued that the requirements of due process have stigmatized the patient, have made treatment less accessible to those needing
it, and have retarded the abatement of mental illness.[129] They assert
that commitment procedures resembling criminal proceedings adversely traumatize the patient, and the resultant taint of criminality is
partially responsible for the adverse public attitude toward mental
illness. It is felt that the medical question of hospitalization is improperly delegated to judicial officers who are either inadequately
informed or too busy to devote the necessary time. Altogether, the
traditional admission procedures are said to be cumbersome and an
impediment to speedy and timely treatment. "It is necessary for
lawyers to recognize that commitment to a mental institution involves
peculiar considerations not present in ordinary legal cases,"[130] noted
the authors of a leading text on law and psychiatry.

Aiming for more efficient and less time-consuming methods for
treating the mentally ill, the Group for the Advancement of Psychiatry
views the requirements of due process—public hearing, well-defined

[127] Kadish, "A Case Study in the Signification of Procedural Due Process," 2
Western Pol. Q. 93 (1956).
[128] This discontent becomes especially interesting juxtaposed with the current
reverse trend in Soviet law, where the demand for greater individual liberty is
resulting in the restoration of many of the traditional concepts of "due process"
originally discarded as bourgeois nonsense. Recent dispatches from the Soviet
Union in the daily and periodical press. *See*, generally, *Soviet Criminal Law and
Procedure* (H. J. Berman ed. 1966).
[129] Guttmacher and Weihofen, *Psychiatry and the Law* 290.
[130] *Ibid.*

standards for judgment, notice, confrontation, a reasonable deliberation aided by advocates—not only as heartless but as a serious hind-
rance.

The worst aspects of contemporary commitment laws are: Legal
service and notice to the patient; insistence on personal appearance in court; exposure of patient as public spectacle and the
public record of such; emphasis on lay judgment as in trial by
jury; identification of mental illness and criminality by similarity
of procedure (and)...use of anachronistic terminology....[131]

In this country, however, attempts to replace the "last ditch stands
of archaic legal prerogatives"[132] with less formal proceedings have not
been totally successful. With no viable alternative plan for an effective check upon involuntary hospitalization, procedural formalities
guarantee at least some measure of personal attention for the patient
and some safeguard against abuse of power by the state. The position
of the American Bar Association has therefore remained unequivocal:
"Any person, before he is committed to a mental hospital, or otherwise deprived of his liberty, should be served with notice and given a
full opportunity to be heard."[133]

The trend and pressures for adopting new procedures will continue.
Most states have attempted reforms to reflect the advances medicine
has made in the field of mental illness. Lacking the necessary physical
and professional resources and suffering from constant medical-legal
disagreements, these efforts have been only partially effective. The
consequence has been that while the proponents of greater informality
remain dissatisfied with the progress made to date, the libertarians
have become alarmed by the abolition of the early procedural safeguards.

THE EARMARKS OF DUE PROCESS

Mrs. Anna Duzynski was a recent Polish emigrant; neither she nor
her husband had learned to speak English. They were living on the
northwest side of Chicago when on October 5, 1960, Mrs. Duzynski
discovered that $380 in cash was missing from their apartment. Sus-

---

[131] Group for the Advancement of Psychiatry, *Commitment Procedures*, Report
no. 4 (April 1949).
[132] Kansas Legislative Council, *Survey of Psychiatric Facilities in Kansas*, Pub.
no. 143, 5 (1946).
[133] 72 *Reports of the American Bar Association* 295 (1947); *see also Mentally
Disabled* 41 (Lindman and McIntyre eds.).

pecting that the money had been stolen by the janitor, who was in possession of a spare key, Mrs. Duzynski rushed to his flat and demanded the return of the stolen money. The janitor called the police, complaining that both Mr. and Mrs. Duzynski were insane and should be put in a mental institution. Without further examination, the police seized both Anna and her husband, Michael, and took them in handcuffs to the Cook County Mental Health Clinic. At the clinic the Duzynskis were unable to answer any of the questions directed to them in English. Pursuant to lax commitment procedures, the Duzynskis were pronounced mentally ill and were committed to the Chicago State Hospital. Six weeks later, Michael Duzynski still knew less about why he had been denied his freedom than he had when thrown into a Nazi concentration camp in World War II. Finally, in complete desperation, he hanged himself. The very next day, the hospital officials released Anna Duzynski.[134]

The Supreme Court of the United States, in an attempt to define the scope of due process, noted in 1883: "In all cases, that kind of procedure is due process of law which is suitable and proper to the nature of the case...."[135] The proper procedural requisites for commitment must therefore be related to the nature of this process. Commitment consists of the removal of a mentally ill person from society to an institution. Since the twin aims of commitment are the protection of society and the treatment of the illness, procedural safeguards must serve as a means for exploring and balancing the numerous social and medical considerations involved in each case. The patient may want to challenge the mental illness diagnosis, deny his being a public danger or his inability to manage in a noninstitutional setting; he may seek to question the adequacy of treatment within the institution; or he may wish to explore available treatment within the community. To follow any of these courses, a person requires time to prepare his case, an opportunity to be heard, and adequate professional counsel.

Time to Prepare

The United States Supreme Court has never determined whether an alleged mentally ill person is constitutionally entitled to prior notice of the proceedings initiated for his commitment. The state

---

[134] Wille, "Why Refugee Asked for Ticket to Russia," *Chicago Daily News*, March 29, 1962, p. 10; Kutner, "The Illusion of Due Process in Commitment Proceedings," 57 *Nw. U. L. Rev.* 383, 384 (1962).

[135] *Ex parte* Wall, 107 U.S. 265, 289 (1883).

courts are in disagreement.[136] About one-half of the states requiring judicial action prior to commitment specifically require that notice be given to the patient. Most other statutes either ignore the question or provide that no hearing should be held if it would be injurious to the patient's condition. Sixteen states further require that notice of the proceedings be given to the immediate relatives of the ill person, and four states require notice to his guardian. The nonjudicial commitment statutes usually make no reference to notice. Even though the traditional role of notice is to afford a person an opportunity for the preparation of his defense, most statutes fail to specify how far in advance of the hearing such notice must be given. Twenty-four hours' notice, the minimum in some states, greatly diminishes the value of this opportunity.[137]

Psychiatrists have decried the traumatic effect of personal notice on a person who is mentally ill.[138] Legal papers, they say, produce only anxiety and confusion in a sick mind; they are not merely medically harmful but often useless in protecting the rights of the disturbed individual. These arguments have received the support of some leading legal writers who feel that "where the person is mentally incapable of understanding the nature of the proceeding or preparing therefore, or is so deranged that notice would do him harm, the purpose of protecting his interest can be more effectively accomplished in some other way than by serving him with legal papers."[139]

In answer to the therapist's plea for the abolition of notice, proponents of legal safeguards argue that the traumatic effect could not possibly be any worse than the trauma of finding oneself detained in a mental institution without any prior warning. To decide that a person is too deranged to benefit from notice, moreover, is effectively to prejudge his competency. Said the Kansas Court of Appeals: "It will not do to say it is useless to serve notice upon an insane person; that it would avail nothing because of his inability to take advantage of it. His sanity is the very thing to be tried."[140]

Although personal notification may not be an indispensable element

---

[136] Porter v. Ritch, 70 Conn. 235, 39 Atl. 169 (1898); Olsen v. MacFeely, 202 Ga. 140, 42 S.E.2d 366 (1947); Georgia Railroad Bank & Trust Co. v. Liberty National Bank, 180 Ga. 4, 177 S.E. 803 (1934); Maxwell v. Maxwell, 189 Iowa 7, 177 N.W. 541 (1902); *in re* Masters, 216 Minn. 553, 13 N.W.2d 482 (1944); Brayman v. Grant, 130 App. Div. 242, 114 N.Y. 336 (1909); Hammon v. Hill, 228 F. 999 (W.D. Pa. 1915); Payne v. Arkebauer, 190 Ark. 614, 80 S.W.2d 76 (1935); Hiatt v. Soucek, 240 Iowa 300, 36 N.W.2d 432 (1949).

[137] *Mentally Disabled* 49–51 (Lindman and McIntyre eds.).

[138] Group for the Advancement of Psychiatry, *Commitment Procedures.*

[139] Guttmacher and Weihofen, *Psychiatry and the Law* 295–96.

[140] *In re* Wellman, 3 Kan. App. 100, 103, 45 P. 726, 727 (1896).

in a proper legal process, some contend that its abolition would affect the very validity of the commitment procedures.[141] Substituted notice to the patient's family or guardian has been used extensively in this country since the beginning of the nineteenth century, and many feel that it can properly be used in lieu of notifying the patient himself.[142] But substituted notice remains suspect because it is often the very people who are required to be given notice that are actively seeking to accomplish the patient's commitment. To assume that the family's and patient's interests are always, or nearly always, compatible is to ignore the realities of family strife. At times it is one's family against which one needs the most protection.

An Opportunity To Be Heard

Since the statutory extension in the last century of due process requirements to commitment proceedings, it has been recognized that the alleged mentally ill person is entitled, prior to his involuntary hospitalization, to a hearing and to the right to be present at it.[143] Recently, however, there has been considerable departure from this standard. Of the thirty-seven states which provide for judicial commitment, all but six make the hearing mandatory. Of the latter, one state leaves it to the discretion of the judge; the others condition it upon the patient's demand.[144] When nonjudicial procedures are utilized, hearings are not always required, and in the case of commitments by medical certification they are nonexistent. While the failure of many states to accord a hearing is drawing only slight criticism, the pressure to abolish traditional hearings is continuing. Guttmacher and Weihofen, a leading team consisting of a psychiatrist and a lawyer, claim that "the enforcement of this 'right' may do more harm than good. In many cases of mental illness . . . the patient is already suffering from the feeling that people dislike him, and from delusions of persecution. Requiring him to sit in a courtroom and listen to his trusted physician and his nearest and dearest relatives testify to the facts regarding his mental condition is likely to confirm his worst

---

[141] Curran, "Hospitalization" 274, 281.

[142] Comment, "Veto of the Illinois Mental Health Bill," 36 *Ill. L. Rev.* 747 (1942); Comment, "Three Controversial Aspects of New Illinois Mental Health Legislation," 47 *Nw. U. L. Rev.* 100 (1952).

[143] *In re* Lambert, 134 Cal. 626, 66 P. 851 (1901); appeal of Sleeper, 147 Me. 302, 84 A.2d 115 (1952); *ex parte* Allen, 82 Va. 365, 73 A. 1078 (1909).

[144] *Mentally Disabled* 56–59 (Lindman and McIntyre eds.).

suspicions. The result may be dangerous to them as well as injurious to him."[145]

Generally, the arguments made for and against the requirement of a hearing are similar to those regarding notice. The psychiatric profession argues that hospital admissions are primarily medical questions and that therefore commitments to mental hospitals should resemble the informal administrative procedures of general hospitals, performed speedily and effectively by qualified medical experts.

The legal opposition to such summary commitments, however, is still militant. A Special Committee on the Rights of the Mentally Ill of the American Bar Association concluded that proper notification and a full opportunity to be heard are prerequisites for any mental commitment: "On this we, the committee, insist as a constitutional requirement."[146] Similarly, the British Civil Liberties Council contends than since the decision to confine an individual is not primarily a medical decision but rather a social one, medical experts should give evidence, but the decision must be based on social criteria and made by a judicial officer as a "representative of society deputed for the purpose."[147]

Only recently has growing attention been directed to the social rather than medical implications of mental illness and health. While social scientists focus increasingly upon mental illness as a social phenomenon, one author recently pointed out with concern that the image of mental health corresponds to a well-adjusted, middle-class person, whereas the "symptoms" that the medical profession associates with mental illness are often typical of the everyday life in urban slums.[148]

The importance of nonmedical and nonpsychiatric factors in the decision to commit an individual has been recognized by leading medical commentators. Henderson and Gillespie, authors of a leading English text on psychiatry, state:

Apart from the medical side, the social and economic circumstances are often decidedly factors for and against certification [to a hospital]. Certification is desirable where no adequate ac-

[145] Guttmacher and Weihofen, *Psychiatry and the Law* 298.

[146] 72 *Reports of the American Bar Association* 295.

[147] National Council for Civil Liberties, *Submissions to the Minister of Health on Recommendations of the Royal Commission on the Law Relating to Mental Illness and Mental Deficiency* 5 (1957).

[148] Bleicher, "Compulsory Community Care" 98; *see also* Scheff, "Social Conditions for Rationality: How Urban and Rural Courts Deal with the Mentally Ill," 7 *Amer. Behav. Sci.* 21 (1964).

commodation at home or in [a] special nursing home is available or where money is a consideration. Certification is unnecessary where adequate arrangements for treatment can be made outside of mental hospitals, and undesirable where the patient occupies an important public position. . . .[149]

If no independent hearing regarding the need for confinement is available, commitments may often be based on medical criteria exclusively or else may be motivated by socioeconomic factors only. No doubt physicians are best qualified to prescribe medical treatment, but it is questionable whether they should be granted the power to compel compliance. The delegation of commitment powers to the medical expert, furthermore, has been viewed as adverse to the physician's therapeutic role vis-à-vis the patient. The therapist, argues psychiatrist T. Szasz, a critic of his own profession, would betray this role if he were vested by the state with the power to coerce and restrain unwilling patients.[150]

The courts divide on the question of whether a pre-hospitalization judicial or other independent hearing is a requirement of due process. There are followers[151] of the 1896 Kansas Court of Appeals' philosophy that "[n]otice and opportunity to be heard lie at the foundation of all judicial procedure. They are fundamental principles of justice which cannot be ignored."[152] More recently, considerable force was added to the opposition to summary commitment procedures by the Missouri Supreme Court's decision that only during an emergency may an involuntary patient be held without a hearing.[153] If an emergency does not exist or the hospitalization extends beyond the emergency, a hearing becomes a constitutional requisite. In the Missouri court's opinion, even though a post-hospitalization hearing could be demanded and habeas corpus is formally available as a remedy for the patient, the indeterminate commitment is unconstitutional without a prior hearing. This 1954 decision is nationally significant because it declared unconstitutional those provisions which had been adopted from the Draft Act prepared by the Federal Security Agency, a pre-

[149] D. K. Henderson and R. D. Gillespie, *Textbook of Psychiatry* 684 (7th ed. 1950).

[150] T. Szasz, *Law, Liberty and Psychiatry* 5, 7, 51 (1963).

[151] *In re* Lambert, 134 Cal. 626, 66 P. 851 (1901); State *ex rel.* Blaisdell v. Billings, 55 Minn. 467, 57 N.W. 794 (1894); People *ex rel.* Sullivan v. Wendel, 33 Misc. 496, 68 N.Y. 948 (1900). *See also* Comment, "Veto of the Illinois Mental Health Bill."

[152] *In re* Wellman, 3 Kan. App. 100, 103, 45 P. 726, 727 (1896).

[153] Missouri *ex rel.* Fuller v. Mullinax, 364 Mo. 858, 269 S.W.2d 72 (1954).

cursor of the National Institutes of Health, as a model for the de-formalization of the commitment procedures.

Some courts have held that a hearing is not a prerequisite to commitment and that involuntary hospitalization is lawful without a prior hearing. In these states, however, the patient must be accorded the unqualified right, either through a post-hospitalization hearing or through habeas corpus,[154] to contest his restraint at a judicial hearing.[155]

Even the creation of a statutory requirement for a hearing and for the patient's right to be present may be of little avail. A recent study of commitment proceedings in Travis County, Texas, where a hearing is mandatory and open to the patient, disclosed that out of forty proposed patients only two appeared at the hearing. The others had apparently either not been advised or had not insisted upon their right.[156] Whether the patient is present or absent, the hearings may still often amount to little more than assembly-line justice. In Texas, a total of seventy-five minutes was devoted to the hearing of forty cases (or 1.8 minutes per patient).[157] What permits such hasty disposition of commitment cases is the willingness of many judges and attorneys to rely exclusively on medical examinations and conclusions reached before trial. In the commitment hearing, concluded a recent critic, the real decision-making process is hidden from view and the "observer is limited to results of decisions that have been made within the internal administrative structure of the hospital."[158]

Trial by One's Peers

Does the right to a hearing include the right to a trial by jury? The jury first appeared in commitment procedures almost a century ago and has been under attack ever since. "The use of a lay jury to determine such a highly technical medical question has been compared to

[154] Habeas corpus petitions have not, however, been effective as a release procedure, because the patients, in the face of hospital opposition, usually cannot meet the burden of proving that they are no longer in need of hospitalization. Comment, "Hospitalization of the Mentally Disabled in Pennsylvania," 71 *Dick. L. Rev.* 300, 319 (1967).

[155] Hammon v. Hill, 228 F. 999 (W.D. Pa. 1915); Payne v. Arktebauer, 190 Ark. 614, 80 S.W.2d 76 (1935); Hiatt v. Soucek, 240 Ia. 300, 36, N.W.2d 432 (1949); *in re* Dowdell, 169 Mass. 387, 47 N.E. 1033 (1897); *in re* Crosswell's petition, 28 R.I. 137, 66 A. 55 (1907).

[156] Cohen, "Function of the Attorney" 429.

[157] *Ibid.* 430.

[158] *Ibid.* 433.

calling in the neighbors to diagnose meningitis or scarlet fever. The strong flavor of a criminal trial lent to the proceedings by the use of a jury is most unfortunate for the person concerned," one legal writer noted.[159]

Originally, a jury trial was viewed as the primary preventive against improper commitments. Recently, critics have argued that the lay jury has not demonstrated any particular aptitude in this regard, and with the generally decreasing role of the jury in judicial proceedings, its survival in the commitment arena is viewed as anachronistic. The rebuttal to these arguments is that the jury's role is not to diagnose the illness but rather to help make the social judgment of whether the patient can manage at large or whether he should be involuntarily hospitalized.[160]

Thirteen states provide for the use of juries in commitment hearings.[161] In most of these jurisdictions, the jury trial must be demanded by the patient, although it is often within the discretion of the judge to grant or refuse the request. A few states employ specialized juries for commitment cases—either six-juror panels or a requirement that at least one juror be a physician.

Whether a trial by jury in commitment cases is guaranteed by the federal or state constitutions is still another question. The right to trial by jury in civil cases guaranteed by the Seventh Amendment applies to federal courts and is not judicially recognized as applicable to proceedings in state courts.[162] Since commitment proceedings are typically state practices, only the general requirements of the Fourteenth Amendment that no person be deprived of liberty without due process can presently provide a uniform standard for state commitment procedures.[163]

The constitutions of the majority of the states recognize the right

[159] Curran, "Hospitalization" 283.
[160] *Mentally Disabled* 18 (Lindman and McIntyre eds.).
[161] *Ibid.* 56–59.
[162] Only recently did the United States Supreme Court hold that the right to jury trial in federal criminal cases, as contained in the Sixth Amendment, applied also to state criminal procedures. Duncan v. Louisiana, 88 S. Ct. 1444 (1968). The states' freedom to retain or abolish juries in civil cases is discussed in Walker v. Sauvinet, 92 U.S. 90 (1875); N.Y. Central R.R. Co. v. White, 243 U.S. 188, 208 (1917); Snyder v. Massachusetts, 291 U.S. 97, 105 (1934).
[163] Even some proceedings in the District of Columbia courts do not come within the federal jury standards established by the Sixth and Seventh Amendments, for these standards apply only to proceedings which are based on the federal government's general judicial power under Article III of the Constitution. The Seventh Amendment guarantee of a jury trial is therefore not binding upon commitment proceedings in the District of Columbia as long as the power to

to jury trials for both criminal and civil actions. Yet the undefined *parens patriae* character of commitment proceedings excludes them not only from criminal trial requirements but also from the applicable requirements for civil cases. Often, in deciding whether the right to a jury trial in commitment cases exists, state courts have determined the question by reference to whether such a right existed in common law. Although common law commitments were in fact utterly informal, some state rulings nevertheless held that the insane were entitled to a jury trial in common law and that therefore the state sought to preserve such a right.[164] Other courts have insisted that the absence of recognition of this right at common law is not controlling: as long as the right was recognized in the state or territory before the adoption of the present constitution, it was preserved by the constitutional guarantees of a jury trial.[165]

Assistance of Counsel

Persons charged with serious crimes in the United States are guaranteed legal representation before they may be tried and convicted.[166] There is no such protection for mentally ill patients, though both groups are liable to a curtailment of their liberty through institutional confinement, and the mentally ill are open to even more far-reaching interference with their property rights. If a distinction is to be drawn between the two groups, the mentally ill are in need of more extensive procedural safeguards; they are less likely than felons to comprehend the nature of the proceedings and their consequences or to be able to represent their own interests.

Forty-two states recognize an individual's right to be represented

---

commit individuals is held not to be part of the general judicial power of the United States but is considered a domestic enactment for the district. Article III reads: "Section 1. The judicial power of the United States, shall be vested in one supreme court, and in such inferior courts as the Congress may from time to time ordain and establish." Jacob v. New York City, 315 U.S. 752 (1941); Campbell v. St. Louis Union Trust Co., 346 Mo. 200, 139 S.W.2d 935 (1940).

[164] Shumway v. Shumway, 2 Conn. 339 (1829); *in re* McLaughlin, 87 N.J. Eq. 138, 102 A. 439 (1917); White v. White, 108 Tex. 570, 196 S.W. 508 (1917); Warker v. Warker, 100 N.J. Eq. 499, 151 A. 274 (1930).

[165] State *ex rel.* Peper v. Holtcamp, 235 Mo. 242, 138 S.W. 521 (1911); Warrick v. Moore County, 291 S.W. 950 (Tex. Civ. App. 1927); *in re* Moynihan, 332 Mo. 1022, 62 S.W.2d 410 (1933).

[166] In Gideon v. Wainwright, 272 U.S. 335 (1963), the Supreme Court held that the Fourteenth Amendment requirement of due process made the Sixth Amendment's guarantee of right of counsel obligatory upon the states in criminal cases.

by his own counsel at the commitment hearings. If the patient has no counsel, twenty-two states provide that counsel must be appointed for the indigent or unrepresented patient, and six other states require such appointment upon the patient's request.[167] Only in jurisdictions requiring judicial or other independent hearings is counsel actually accorded an opportunity to function properly. Without the hearing, the counsel is like an actor without a stage.

The effectiveness of counsel's role in commitment proceedings for the indigent mentally ill is subject to further doubt because of the inadequate provisions for his compensation. Only twenty-two states provide for county or state compensation of indigent's counsel, the maximum fees ranging from ten dollars to twenty-five dollars. In most states which require that counsel be appointed at the patient's request, no funds are available for counsel's compensation. An inordinate number of cases are referred to a single staff attorney assigned by the local legal aid agency, or else inexperienced private attorneys may be appointed at random—all resulting in superficial and at times totally inadequate legal representation. A 1966 observer in Travis County, Texas, reported as follows:

> The attorney, in accordance with the normal practice, had been appointed to represent all the patients whose hearings were scheduled that day. While awaiting the opening of the hearings, the writer asked the attorney how many cases were to be heard that day. "Forty, I believe." "Have you contacted any of the proposed patients?" "No, I haven't but I did receive letters from two of them. I may get a chance to consult with them before we get underway." That opportunity did not materialize.[168]

What should be the function of counsel in a mental commitment proceeding? A 1961 American Bar Foundation report notes[169] that counsel must guard not only against scheming relatives but also against incompetent and lax medical judgment and the improper extension of involuntary commitments to borderline cases.[170] He must

---

[167] Cohen, "Function of the Attorney" 460–66.

[168] *Ibid.* 428.

[169] *Mentally Disabled* 29 (Lindman and McIntyre eds.).

[170] Many states require an independent medical examination prior to involuntary hospitalization. A recent news story from Baltimore describes the examination of one patient, a Miss Anderson:

> The two doctors who examined her are paid $4 apiece for everyone they look at. They're elderly gentlemen, both over 70; neither is a psychiatrist. Dr. Ogden, one of the two physicians, says he can't recall Miss Anderson's case, which isn't surprising since he and his partner see about 10 patients a

make certain that a patient's need for treatment not be denied merely because of his inability to pay for hospitalization. Counsel's role extends not only to the protection of the patient's liberty but also to the safeguarding of his property. The court may need to be alerted to the advisability of declaring a patient incompetent and appointing a guardian to protect real and personal property. Counsel can help the patient meet the legal-economic problems that might arise as a consequence of institutionalization, such as family support, overdue installment payments, and possible property foreclosures. Counsel can effectively contribute to a reduction in the use of involuntary commitments by making certain that other community alternatives are fully explored and utilized and by persuading patients who require hospital care to choose voluntary institutionalization over compulsory treatment.

Perhaps the main task of legal counsel, in this as in the other realms of the therapeutic state, is the "individualizing function"—insistence upon careful, fair, and personalized assessment of every case in the face of depersonalized people-processing bureaucracies. One recent commentator thus portrays the attorney as the possible possessor of the key for unlocking the "closed circuitry of decision making" in the modern therapeutic state.[171]

Dramatic insight into counsel's recent role in commitment cases is contained in a brief filed in 1966 with the United States Supreme Court in *Baxstrom* v. *Herold*.[172] The statistics contained in this brief[173] revealed that when counsel had been assigned to those alleged to be mentally ill, commitment was successfully resisted in about twenty percent of the cases. The Public Defender of Cook County, Illinois, in the one-year period from December 1, 1963, to November 30, 1964, handled 6,174 applications for commitment, of which 951 were dis-

---

day by their estimate. The police estimate they see about 15, usually in about 30 minutes.

Dr. Ogden explains that no attempt is made to do a refined examination and that about all they look for is "exaggerated behavior." Miss Anderson says they never entered her cell but just looked at her through the bars. The doctor agrees such may have been the case, but, as he points out, at such wagon you're not going to get a fully pedigreed shrink to get in his car and drive to two jails, men's and women s, every day of the week to make a thorough set of tests. Von Hoffman, "A Trap," *Washington Post*, January 26, 1970, p. B1.

[171] Cohen, "Function of the Attorney" 437.

[172] 383 U.S. 107 (1966).

[173] Brief for Petitioner, App. B, United States Supreme Court, no. 219, Baxstrom v. Herold, 383 U.S. 107 (1966).

missed. In 1964, the Legal Aid Agency for the District of Columbia successfully resisted commitments in 223 of 639 cases. Of ten cases handled by the Atlanta Legal Aid Society, commitment was successfully resisted in seven. Similarly, the Public Defender of San Francisco handled 101 commitment cases, of which 40 resulted in a denial of commitment. These statistics by no means demonstrate that all those kept from being committed indeed were afflicted with no mental problems. They do indicate, however, that presence of counsel may guarantee more careful attention to the question of whether commitment is the appropriate social solution in a given case.

Due to the narrow issues raised in the *Baxstrom* case, the Supreme Court did not resolve in its decision the broad question of the right of counsel in a commitment proceeding.[174] But its recent pronouncements extending the right in criminal and juvenile cases (the *Gideon, Escobedo, Miranda,* and *Gault* cases)[175] augur a greater reliance upon counsel for the protection of individual rights.

Yet while the aid of counsel is being sought increasingly, not only in criminal justice but also in its therapeutic borderlands, recent observations of lawyers' conduct in mental commitment as well as in other *parens patriae* proceedings raise critical questions regarding counsel's competence in these new arenas. In the allegedly nonadversary climate of these proceedings, where the patient's and the state's interest are supposed to coincide, attorneys trained for the traditional adversary conflict often find themselves "roleless." "[U]nless the proceeding is adversary in nature . . . the attorney does not engage in any preparation and does not effectively participate in the hearing. . . . The consequence is the allocation of effective decision-making to the medical, more particularly the psychiatric, profession with the legal process and the attorney assuming a ceremonial function."[176] Increasingly, it thus becomes apparent that to challenge the thoroughness of the medical testimony effectively, to seek out background community information, and to help determine the alternatives to commitment,

[174] Baxstrom, a convicted criminal with a long history of arrests, was committed to a mental institution pursuant to a special New York procedure authorizing the commitment to mental institutions of felons found to be insane at the completion of their criminal sentence. The Supreme Court held that Baxstrom was denied equal protection of the law because of the failure of the special procedure to satisfy the usual state commitment laws: the right to a jury review and a judicial finding "that he is dangerously mentally ill." *Ibid.* 110.

[175] Gideon v. Wainwright, 372 U.S. 335 (1963); Escobedo v. Illinois, 378 U.S. 478 (1964); Miranda v. Arizona, 384 U.S. 436 (1966); *in re* Gault, 87 S. Ct. 1428 (1967).

[176] Cohen, "Function of the Attorney" 424–25.

judge and counsel must be taught to understand sociopsychological data and to assume a newly critical role for which they had not hitherto been prepared.

FROM CUSTODIAL WAREHOUSES . . .

Regardless of the law-book standards for involuntary hospitalization of mental patients, the day-to-day practices reflect a greater response to the social realities than to legal formulae. Mental hospitals are class institutions, and commitment is a selective practice, separating the poor from the privileged.[177] A mental patient who is well cared for in a home or a private facility will not be exposed to the sanctions of a public commitment.[178] Only when family resources do not permit private care or when the family no longer considers itself adequate for the undertaking does institutional commitment provide the answer.

The recognition of this socioeconomic reality is also manifested in the release practices of the public mental institutions. Irrespective of the patient's progress and recovery prognosis and with little regard to his degree of social danger, most hospitals will release a committed patient if private care is available. A patient who has a home or family to receive him is almost at total liberty to leave. Otherwise, little initiative is displayed by the institutions toward the discharge of chronic patients.[179] Commitment and discharge are often dictated less by the patient's mental condition than by his socioeconomic status.

Our state mental hospitals, long the major public instrument for the control and treatment of mental illness, have played an unhappy historical role. As conglomerate entities, these institutions have filled a host of diverse social needs. Some patients have been hospitalized merely because nobody else will care for them; others are committed because they are a potential threat to the public peace. Treating both alike has contributed to the prison image of the public mental institution. No effective programs of therapy can originate or be properly pursued in the unsettling milieu of an institution catering to such diverse social needs.

Built in geographically isolated locations, mental institutions were denied public interest and support. Even the more recent interest in mental health has found American psychiatrists oriented toward the

[177] A. Hollingshead and F. Redlich, *Social Class and Mental Illness* (1958).
[178] Note, "Commitment of the Mentally Ill—Superior Court of Los Angeles County," 36 *S. Cal. L. Rev.* 109, 115 (1962).
[179] A. L. Strauss *et al.*, *Psychiatric Ideologies and Institutions* 116 (1964).

more lucrative private practice, involving neurotic rather than psychotic patients, while state hospitals rely primarily on lay staffs whose main function is custodial, not therapeutic. Two research psychologists who recently arranged to be admitted to Pennsylvania's largest mental institution, the Philadelphia State Hospital, reported that life inside the hospital was characterized by an overwhelming sense of boredom and betrayal. Due to the shortage of attendants—three to every 85 patients—the patients learned early that they can get little favors, such as coffee, cigarettes, and access to the sunlit dayroom, if they "learn to be sick" and cooperate with the staff. Responding to the findings of this unusual yet not unexpected report, a hospital spokesman dryly noted: ". . . the time has come when state hospitals are turning from custody to care, and the time has come to decide what kind of care it will be."[180]

Only a small segment of admitted patients have the advantage of proper classification, treatment, and early release. Says a recent report: "At the diagnostic center . . . the initial allocation of a patient is in the hands of an important 'fate maker.' The odds appear to be against most patients who are sent to the back wards. At this, as at most state hospitals, unfortunately no machinery is available for moving patients from chronic to treatment status. . . ."[181] For a great number of patients, therefore, the mental hospital serves merely as a custodial depository—the end of the road.[182] The annual death rate in public mental hospitals is staggering: it amounts to 10 percent of the total patient population and compares with a national death rate of 9.4 per thousand population. In 1963, public mental institutions reported 49,052 patient deaths, contrasted with a total of 283,591 new admissions.[183]

Doubt has been cast on the ability of an isolated and regimented "total" institution to provide an environment within which meaningful therapeutic progress can be made. Most psychiatric therapy focuses on improving the patient's ability to view himself realistically in relation to other people and to function effectively in an open community. Traditional mental hospitals obviously fail, therefore, to provide the necessary milieu in which a patient can progress toward independent living.[184] The very institutional system, being first con-

[180] *New York Times*, January 14, 1969, p. 10.

[181] Strauss, *Psychiatric Ideologies* 105, 110.

[182] M. Greenblatt, *et al.*, *The Patient and the Mental Hospital* (1957).

[183] U.S. Bureau of the Census, *Statistical Abstract of the United States* 77 (1966).

[184] G. Caplan, *Principles of Preventive Psychiatry* 110 (1964). On the advantages of community care over traditional commitments *see* Ozarin and Brown,

cerned with the maintenance of order, may block the mobilization of effective therapeutic action.[185]

In the face of the realities of commitment and treatment, it is clear that a major portion of the institutional populations, who are brought there under legal compulsion and assertedly for therapy, would be more appropriately placed in old people's homes, temporary public shelters, or under other less compulsory forms of public health and welfare care.

It is questionable whether involuntary commitment is an appropriate tool for bringing treatment even to those for whom therapy is available. Aside from philosophical and constitutional objections, placing the therapist in the role of a guard has corrupted the rehabilitative role of the mental hospital and has adversely affected both patient and therapist, as Dr. Szasz has argued convincingly.[186] Reaching this same conclusion, British psychiatry has increasingly stressed that ". . . no true doctor-patient or nurse-patient relationship can develop so long as one party is a prisoner of the other and legally inferior to the other. When the doors are open and legal disability has been removed, the staff can use their personalities to deal with psychiatric crises and to help the patient to solve his problems of adjustment."[187]

. . . TO THERAPEUTIC CENTERS

Assuming custodial, curative, or social defense roles, mental institutions are obviously filling an existing social vacuum. But the question recurs: In the face of democracy's commitment to individuals and diversity, may compulsion and legal sanctions properly be used to accomplish diverse social aims not connected with the prevention of actual danger to life or property?[188] Even if the more traditional legal questions regarding compulsory commitment for the sole purpose of

---

"New Directions in Community Mental Health Programs," 35 *Amer. J. of Orthopsychiatry* 10, 13 (1965); McMahon, "The Working Class Psychiatric Patient," in *Mental Health of the Poor* 283 (F. Riessman *et al.* eds. 1964).

[185] H. W. Dunham and S. K. Weinberg, *The Culture of the State Mental Hospital* (1960); Belknap, *Human Problems.*

[186] Szasz, *Law Liberty and Psychiatry.*

[187] MacMillan, "Community Treatment of Mental Illness," *The Lancet* 202 (July 26, 1958).

[188] This same question is now smoldering in the realm of criminal control of sexual morality and deviant conduct. *See* E. Schur, *Crimes without Victims* (1964); *see also* Devlin, "The Enforcement of Morals" (Maccabaian Lecture of the British Academy, 1959), in *Criminal Law and Its Process* 8 (M. G. Paulsen and S. H. Kadish eds. 1962); Hart, "Immorality and Treason," 62 *Listener* 162–63 (July 15, 1956).

cure or custody could be satisfactorily answered, there still remains the basic question of the propriety of such commitments under present hospital conditions.

If the theory of curative commitment is constitutionally valid, then its validity must further depend on the committed person's receiving as much effective care and treatment as modern medicine has at its disposal.[189] In the average mental hospital ward in 1961, a mental patient experienced person-to-person contact with a physician for about fifteen minutes every month.[190] In 1966 in Pennsylvania, the existing psychiatrist-patient ratio in the state mental institutions could guarantee the average patient not more than a fifteen-minute psychiatric interview once every ten days.[191] Despite the average national ratio of one psychiatrist for every 1,300 persons,[192] less than a third of these psychiatrists are involved in mental hospital work even on a part-time basis. Many people who require mental care, as noted by the District of Columbia Mental Health Commission in the case of Mary K. Jones, may do better at home or at other community-based facilities.

How can the law remedy the defects of the system? Perhaps an insistence on the traditional formalities of due process is not the most effective method for protecting both society and those suffering from mental illness. This clearly is an area where new and unorthodox procedures may provide better protection than hurried, legally correct, traditional court hearings. Community investigations by social workers, as an aid to the courts, are already required in some places.[193] A short-term observational detention, permitting a careful diagnosis of

---

[189] Birnbaum, "The Right to Treatment," 46 *A.B.A.J.* 499 (1960).

[190] U.S. Congress, Senate, Committee on the Judiciary, Subcommittee on Constitutional Rights, *Hearings on Constitutional Rights of the Mentally Ill*, 87th Cong., 1st sess., 1961, pt. 1, pp. 43–44.

[191] In June 1966, the state's 18 mental hospitals had an average daily census of 34,900 patients. These institutions were served by 106 treating psychiatrists, producing a psychiatrist-patient ratio of 1 to 324. Assuming that psychiatrists were able to work 8 hours daily, seeing patients at 15-minute intervals, not more than 32 patients could be seen by a psychiatrist per day. Such an overworked psychiatrist would need more than ten days to complete one interview cycle for his quota of 324 patients. Comment, "Mentally Disabled in Pennsylvania" 300, 334.

[192] A survey completed in 1965 ascertained that there were at that time 15,140 psychiatrists in the United States plus about 3,600 in residence training programs. Of this 18,740 total, approximately 5,800, or 31 percent, spent at least some time in public and private mental hospitals. American Psychiatric Association and National Association for Mental Health, *Fifteen Indices* 18.

[193] State v. Merrick, 2 Ohio 2d 13, 205 N.W.2d 924 (1965).

the patient's condition, must in some states precede all regular indeterminate commitments. Counseling to encourage voluntary hospitalization must be increasingly utilized.[194]

To safeguard against abuse, a central state agency might be made responsible for the review of all new commitments to guarantee conformity with the law.[195] The commitment order of every patient should be automatically reviewed at regular intervals to prevent neglect. Regular inspections of mental institutions and their inmates should be undertaken by independent experts. And inmates should be accorded the affirmative "right to treatment"—that is, the right to insist upon treatment as a *quid pro quo* for commitment. The recognition that the therapeutic state's compulsory power is conditioned upon its duty and ability to treat may in the long run serve as a major tool in the overhaul of present institutions into centers of therapy.[196]

Some drafters for legal reform have called for a system "containing more of the elements of a scientific determination, with as little resort to adversary process as possible."[197] Such an arrangement would require that the decision to commit be made by medical or some other experts, based on impartial investigations of the individual and his surroundings. Supposedly, the major safeguard would not be notice, a hearing, and the like, but an exhaustive investigation of all relevant facts necessary for those properly qualified to make a correct decision. This plea for the rule of experts, rather than judges, has been heard from time to time in other legal fields as well and will have to be answered beyond the boundaries of commitment proceedings. However, fear of unchecked power by biased administrators, coupled with our traditional preference for the judicial process as a guarantee for liberty, does not indicate that the path of reform will be in that direction.

In America it appears that the judicial process, with its adversary nature and right to counsel, will continue to be the major tool for protecting individual liberty and for guarding against administrative

---

[194] California, until recently, made provision for counselors in mental health for this purpose. Note, "Commitment of the Mentally Ill" 114–15.

[195] The recent Mental Hygiene Law in New York vests such authority in the Mental Health Information Service and its neighborhood service centers. Comment, "Incarceration of the Mentally Ill—New York's New Law," 17 *Syracuse L. Rev.* 671 (1966).

[196] On the role of the "right to treatment" in the therapeutic state *see* Chapter 8 of this book.

[197] Note, "Controversial Aspects of New Illinois Mental Health Legislation."

zeal or neglect. Legal scrutiny has been moving away from the old preoccupation with "railroading" (unjust commitments by scheming relatives) to a broader concern with the efficacy of the overall mental illness treatment system. Both judge and counsel have recently claimed the right to know whether other and less restrictive social measures might suffice in a given case, and similarly to inquire into the nature of treatment accorded to committed patients.[198] In this new role the legal process may well become instrumental in forcing an overhaul of the traditional mental institutions and in producing a new and expanded allocation of therapeutic and welfare services.

Because the therapeutic state in its programs for the mentally disabled has long relied on a drastic exclusion process, not much more humane than imprisonment, a dichotomy has developed in the mental health arena between the public interest and individual rights. Some people have been deprived of their liberties in the state's attempt to give them psychiatric care. Others have been deprived of psychiatric care in their desire to guard their liberty.[199]

The search must continue for a better balance between individual and public rights, not only through an emphasis upon procedural properties, which serve to guarantee an individualized process, but also through reasonably and clearly defined criteria for state intervention.[200] Neither new quests for societal conformity nor the resurgence of past beliefs in the value and indispensability of psychiatry and its allied sciences must be allowed to dictate an oppressive resort to compulsory therapy. A pluralistic society must learn to live with a great degree of mental and behavioral deviation.

Ultimately, however, it is not cumbersome procedures that retard progress and prevent necessary mental treatment. What is lacking is a climate of confidence in mental institutions and in the public therapy system, as well as a demonstration of the results of therapy, which relies upon more cooperation and less compulsion. To attain greater public acceptance, the prophets of mental health will have to forego some of their evangelical zeal. Cure is at best difficult with an unwilling patient. Compulsory process must be reserved only for those who pose a likelihood of danger to life or property. Although the need for

[198] Lake v. Cameron, 364 F.2d 657 (1966); Rouse v. Cameron, 373 F.2d 451 (1966), *aff'd* on rehearing, 387 F.2d 241 (1967). These judicial developments will be discussed in greater detail in the concluding chapter of this book.

[199] Bleicher, "Compulsory Community Care" 93.

[200] "District of Columbia Hospitalization of the Mentally Ill Act," Pub. L. 88–597 (September 15, 1964), *D.C. Code Ann.* §§21–231 to 21–357 (Supp. IV 1965).

early treatment, before an individual becomes a source of danger, is acknowledged, such treatment should be accomplished through the encouragement of truly voluntary hospitalization or ambulatory treatment in community clinics. The greatest step toward a general acceptance of treatment, as well as toward more meaningful protection for the patient's rights, will be made not so much through an insistence on legal formalities as through a fundamental change in the character of institutional care. Centers for short-term therapy, special day or night clinics, which permit patients to continue operating within the community, and halfway houses, which cushion the return to society, are major parts of the answer.[201] "The minimum dislocation from normal environment is the duty of the state under *parens patriae*."[202] There must be a total retooling of the nation's therapeutic system—from custodial storehouses which suppress the skills of independent living into free therapeutic centers operating in the community and offering treatment to those who voluntarily seek it.

[201] Federal impetus in this direction was given by the 1963 Community Mental Health Centers Act, Pub. L. 88–164 (October 31, 1963), 42 *U.S.C.* §2681 *et al*. The act makes provisions for matching grants to the states for the construction of such centers, authorized to provide inpatient, outpatient, partial hospitalization, emergency, consultation, and education services. By the end of the 1967–68 fiscal year, it was expected that 286 centers, in territories encompassing a total population of 47 million, would have been funded. 6 *U.S. Cong. & Ad. News* 1900 (1967). Yet the progress remains insufficient. An estimated two million Americans sought psychiatric treatment at community clinics in 1966 but were turned away because of lack of personnel or facilities. "For most of the more than 300,000 children seen in mental health outpatient clinics last year (1966), the 'treatment' was a single diagnostic interview followed by the admission that there were no facilities in the particular area for prolonged treatment." U.S. Congress, Senate, Labor and Public Welfare Committee, *Report no. 294*, 90th Cong., 1st sess., 1967, in 6 *U.S. Cong. & Ad. News* 1098, 1100 (1967).

[202] Bleicher, "Compulsory Community Care" 102.

3

Delinquent Youths: Rebels With Cause and Without

By being delinquent, many juveniles already are protesting against
the way adults are building their world for them.—Lopez-Rey,
"Present Approaches to the Problem of Juvenile
Delinquency," 23 *Fed. Prob.* 24, 27 (1959)

Juvenile delinquency can be viewed as a term used by
communities to give focus to their generalized concerns about
[youthful] deviation and deviant behavior.— W. E. Rhodes,
"Delinquency and Community Action," in *Juvenile Delinquency*
209 (H. C. Quay ed. 1965)

[The establishment of the juvenile courts is] one of the most
significant advances in the administration of justice since the
Magna Carta.—R. Pound, quoted in National Probation and
Parole Association, *Guides for Juvenile Court Judges* 127 (1957)

The court does not confine its attention to just the particular offense
which brought the child to its notice. For example, a boy who
comes to court for such trifle as failing to wear his badge
when selling papers may be held on probation for months because
of difficulties at school; and a boy who comes in for playing ball
on the street may . . . be committed to a reform school because
he is found to have habits of loafing, stealing or gambling which
cannot be corrected outside.—H. H. Baker, "Procedure of the
Boston Juvenile Court," 24 *Survey* 649 (1910)

NOT SO MUCH TO PUNISH AS TO REFORM

Deviation from societal norms is not an exclusively adult predilection. The deviations of youth are generally called juvenile delinquency and include a broad range of activity: rebellion against the educational system, protest against the parental role, inability to get along with one's peers, unwillingness to prepare for the awaiting labor market, rejection of acceptable sexual mores, and violation of adult rules regarding personal grooming and modes of conduct. Delinquency, obviously, includes more serious types of behavior that threaten the life, safety, and property of others.

In England in 1801 a child aged thirteen was hanged for stealing a spoon. In 1808 a girl of seven was publicly hanged at Lynn. In 1831 a boy of nine was hanged in Chelmsford for setting fire to a house, and as late as 1833, a boy aged nine was sentenced to death for stealing a printer's color valued at two pence.[1] But at the beginning of the next century most children in America were no longer subject to criminal punishment.

The divestment of traditional criminal justice, and its replacement by the new rehabilitative ideal and therapeutic controls, is nowhere more dramatic than in the treatment of offending juveniles. Juveniles between the ages of 10 and 18 numbered 35 million in 1965 and accounted for 18 percent of the American population.[2] They also comprised 21 percent of all police arrests and 48 percent of the arrests for serious offenses.[3] In 1967, more youngsters under 11 were arrested for murder, robbery, assault, burgarly, larceny, and auto theft than were adults 50 years and over.[4] Yet the arrested juvenile is not subject to adult criminal tribunals but to disposition by juvenile courts; these, purportedly, do not dispense criminal justice but offer the offending juvenile regenerative treatment.

In fact, however, the asserted exemption of the delinquent juvenile

[1] T. Grygier, "The Concept of the 'State of Delinquency' and Its Consequences for Treatment of Young Offenders," 11 *Wayne L. Rev.* 627 (1965); A. Koestler and C. H. Ralph, *Hanged by the Neck* (1961).

[2] U.S. Bureau of the Census, *Statistical Abstract of the United States* 8 (1968).

[3] FDI, *Uniform Crime Reports* 114 (1965); U.S. Bureau of the Census, *Current Population Reports: Population Estimates*, Series P-25, no. 321, November 30, 1965; statement of J. Edgar Hoover, *Cong. Rec.* 23073–23074 (daily ed. September 27, 1966).

[4] Clayton, "F.B.I. Study Blames Juveniles, Prisons for Rise in Crime," *Washington Post*, September 1, 1968, p. A1. Six out of every ten juveniles arrested for violent crimes (murder, rape, robbery, and assault) are Negro and seven out of ten arrested for property crimes (burglary, larceny, and auto theft) are white.

from the severity of traditional criminal justice has also provided the rationale for stripping him of the historical protections against the arbitrary and excessive police powers of the state. He was not accorded the right to bail, to counsel, or the right to confront his accusers. The youthful deviations made subject to control by the juvenile authorities have not been as precisely or carefully defined as the conduct prohibited under adult criminal laws. Being disagreeable to one's family or coming from certain deprived socioeconomic backgrounds are often sufficient evidence of delinquency. The juvenile is expected to be as well-behaved as his senior, and more, or else the sanctions of the juvenile court can apply. The adult may be quarrelsome and may refuse to improve himself, but the child must be "governable" and "education-bound." The adult may associate with whomever he wishes, but the child may not, since undesirable juvenile deviations are more amorphous than adult misconduct—because of society's desire to undertake earlier social prophylactics—it is easier to be adjudicated delinquent than criminal. Consequently, despite the exemption of juveniles from criminal punishment, more than 564,000 youths under 15 years of age (including some 80,000 no older than age 10) were arrested in 1968, nearly a third on such exclusively juvenile deviations as violating curfew, having inappropriate associations, and being "runaways."[5]

Asserting its *parens patriae* role, society claims the privilege for an early and precipitous intervention in a juvenile's life. What is the nature of the special social programs—purported to reform and rehabilitate—that these juveniles are exposed to? In November 1968, Dave M. White, aged 13, hanged himself in the county jail at Breckenridge, Minnesota, where he had been held for 41 days awaiting a hearing on a delinquency petition. "It should have been recognized that 41 days in jail, usually in virtual isolation from other human beings, might drive even an average adult to take his own life," commented the executive director of the Minnesota Correctional Service.[6] It is not uncommon to find juveniles wasting away in detention homes, often no better equipped than the jail which held Dave White, for as long as 600 days, awaiting some form of disposition.[7] The new juvenile justice has certainly not been swift in dealing with its wards; nor have its techniques always differed from traditional penology. Reporting recently to a United States Senate subcommittee, former

5 FBI, *Uniform Crime Reports* 115 (1968).
6 *New York Times*, March 6, 1969, p. 27.
7 Irving, "Juvenile Justice—One Year Later," 8 *J. Fam. L.* 1, 2–3 (1968).

Governor Hulett C. Smith of West Virginia recounted how his home state locks young offender girls alone in a room with a copy of the Bible for the first 30 days of detention, in the hope they will "repent."[8] Based on the inspection of juvenile institutions in several states, Joseph R. Rowan, director of the John Howard Association of Illinois, reported that he saw more brutality in juvenile facilities than in adult prisons.[9] Increasingly, the suspicion is growing that the *parens patriae* state, originally created to provide the wayward youth with rehabilitation rather than punishment, has for the most part served society only as an old-fashioned jailor.

THE TWO-EDGED SWORD

The defendant, John Palmiere, was 11 years old. The charge was truancy—he had been absent from school for 100 days in 1967. The sentence, handed down in New York City Juvenile Court by Judge Phillip B. Thurston, was 18 months in an institution catering mainly to incorrigibles.

Heard in October 1968, the case came to light when the boy's mother, Mrs. Vincent Palmiere, spoke to a reporter. "I begged the judge," she related. "I said, 'How can you give him 18 months for not going to school?' But he said, 'The case is closed.'"[10]

As a result of the publicity the case was reopened. An appellate judge ordered the city to show cause why John should not be released from the institution pending an appeal.

Consider another instance. The police are investigating the larceny of 90 cases of liquor from a liquor store. An informer directs them to two juvenile brothers who were allegedly seen in the "getaway" car. At about 5:30 in the morning the police officers enter the apartment house where the juveniles and their mother live and, as is customary in juvenile cases, take the brothers into custody without a warrant. When an attorney is contacted, he is uncertain whether the constitutional safeguards against unreasonable search and seizure, which specify no age differentiations, extend also to juvenile suspects.[11]

---

[8] *Ibid.*

[9] "Our field attracts sadistic people, who like to beat kids around," Rowan noted. See Downie, "Institutions for Delinquents Deplored," *Washington Post*, March 7, 1969, p. A11.

[10] *New York Times*, September 22, 1968, p. E7.

[11] See J. Ketcham, *in re* of Two Brothers and a Case of Liquor, Docket 66-2652-J and 66-2253-J, Juvenile Court for the District of Columbia (1966). Here the protections of the Fourth Amendment were extended to juvenile court.

In the face of these inequities, civil libertarians have been seeking a greater measure of due process for children. But the public, while contemplating the wisdom and propriety of according juveniles full measure of adult protections, is equally disturbed by assertions that juvenile courts are too "soft" on delinquents and not sufficiently concerned to protect the public. "Maybe there ought to be a harsher, sterner, more severe look by the judge sitting on dispositions," said Chief Judge Morris Miller of the District of Columbia Juvenile Court.[12] Judge Miller was calling attention to the fact that 33 percent of the juveniles referred to his court in 1967 had previously been involved in delinquent acts, yet most had been allowed to remain in the custody of their parents. Perhaps judges should "be a little more concerned with the safety of the community instead of the rehabilitative features exclusively," concluded Judge Miller.

Professing a dedication to the rehabilitative ideal, the juvenile court system was born in America in 1899.[13] In the search for a total break with the discredited adult penal system, the juvenile process was conceived more as a system for the diagnosis and treatment of social diseases than as a measure of social defense; in the new scheme the offending juvenile was viewed as incapacitated and requiring compassion and salvation rather than rights and punishments. With the passage of years, however, observers began noting with alarm that the juvenile court was not fulfilling its lifesaving promise. "There is evidence, in fact, that there may be grounds for concern that the child received the worst of both worlds: that he gets neither the protections afforded to adults nor the solicitous care and regenerative treatment postulated for children," asserted Justice Fortas in 1966.[14] In the view of some critics, the original promise is incapable of fulfillment. Others believe that a rethinking of juvenile justice is necessary because "some children who are old enough to realize they are exempted from the laws that both govern and protect adult citizens of the United States, might feel that the law generally does not apply to them, and, therefore, it does not need to be respected. For this segment of our youth, there is literally no meaning to the concept of citizenship as a two-edged sword. For them, the sword's twin-cutting edges of rights and responsibilities have been dulled."[15]

[12] "Judge Backs Stronger Penalties for District's Juvenile Repeaters," *Washington Post*, September 29, 1967, p. B6.

[13] *Laws of Ill. of 1899* 131–37, §§1–21.

[14] Kent v. United States, 383 U.S. 541, 556 (1966).

[15] B. D. McGarry, "The Two Edged Sword: Constitutional Rights of American Children" 1, 2 (unpublished manuscript in Washington College of Law Library,

Today the evolution of the special juvenile process gives rise, therefore, to some important questions: Have the safeguards provided by the juvenile system been effective in protecting the child against abuse? Has the supplanting of traditional criminal proceedings by a "benevolent" therapy-oriented process adequately fulfilled society's need for protection? What is the effect, upon both juvenile offender and society, of a system of controls that substantially differs from that applicable to adult offenders? What have been the comparative rehabilitative and preventive successes of the juvenile process as compared with the adult system?

Recent statistics indicate not only the size but also the complexity of the special system of justice designed for juveniles. In 1968 the FBI reported nearly one and a half million arrests of children under 18 years of age.[16] From 1960 to 1968, juvenile arrests for serious offenses increased 78 percent, whereas the number of persons in that age group increased only 25 percent.[17]

Youths also account for a large portion of institutional incarcerations. A total of 87,578 adults were sentenced to federal and state prisons and reformatories in 1964, while 39,511 youths were committed to custodial juvenile institutions.[18] In 1960 a total of 229,306 inmates were held in federal and state prisons, while 56,516 youths were in the custody of training schools and detention homes.[19]

Delinquency touches a much larger segment of the juvenile popu-

1966). The President's Commission on Law Enforcement and the Administration of Justice similarly pointed out in 1967 that there is "... increasing evidence that the informal procedures, contrary to the original expectation, may themselves constitute a further obstacle to effective treatment of the delinquent to the extent that they engender in the child a sense of injustice provoked by seemingly all-powerful and challengeless exercise of authority by judges and probation officers." *The Challenge of Crime in a Free Society* 85 (1967).

[16] FBI, *Uniform Crime Reports* 115 (1968). These statistics in no way reflect the size of "hidden delinquency" in this country. Several investigators indicate that the extent of misbehavior among adolescents is much greater than that reflected in official records. Wirt and Briggs, "The Meaning of Delinquency," in *Juvenile Delinquency* 3 (H. C. Quay ed. 1965).

[17] FBI, *Uniform Crime Reports* 1 (1968). In the District of Columbia, arrests of juveniles for serious offenses increased 63 percent between 1960 and 1965. In contrast, adult arrests decreased 11 percent during the same period. U.S., President's Commission on Crime in the District of Columbia, *Report* 773 (1966).

[18] U.S. Bureau of the Census, *Statistical Abstract of the United States* 161 (1966); U.S. Department of Health, Education, and Welfare, *Statistics on Public Institutions for Delinquent Children*, Table A, 20–25 (1964).

[19] U.S. Bureau of the Census, *Statistical Abstract of the United States* 156 (1968).

lation than is usually acknowledged. In a recent statement, J. Edgar Hoover noted that, despite the increase in juvenile offenses, only 4 percent of the nation's youth population are involved in delinquency problems.[20] Yet, this is merely an annual figure. When the rate of delinquency is computed on the basis of the total juvenile population in the vulnerable eight years from age 10 through 17, "the chances are that about 11% of these children, including boys and girls, will be referred to the juvenile court for delinquent behavior (excluding traffic)."[21] When boys alone are considered, it is estimated that one boy in every six will face the court at one time or another in his juvenile career.

HISTORICAL INVOCATIONS

The historical origins of the juvenile court have been compared to "the chaplain's prayer that opens a political convention, graceful and altogether unexceptional, but hardly determinative of subsequent proceedings."[22] As in the case of other beneficient invocations, the early champions of the juvenile court and its special programs for youthful offenders never foresaw the complexity of the issues that were to follow nor the difficulties in achieving their aspirations.

Although there are pleadings for special and kindly treatment of juveniles as far back as Biblical and classical antiquity, the more relevant historical antecedents of our system are found in the English common law of the past three centuries. Children under the age of seven have been totally exempted from criminal sanctions under common law since the thirteenth century.[23] While children between seven and fourteen continued to benefit theoretically from a presumed lack of criminal capacity, unless a mental maturity was proved, those over the age of fourteen were presumed criminally responsible unless their incapacity was proved.[24] Despite this recognition of criminal incapacity by reason of extreme immaturity, both English and American court records report the execution of children between the ages of

[20] *Cong. Rec.* 23073–74 (daily ed. September 27, 1966).

[21] U.S. Congress, Senate, Labor and Public Welfare Committee, Subcommittee to Investigate Juvenile Delinquency, *Report no. 1664*, 89th Cong., 2d sess., 1966, p. 2.

[22] Cohen, *Law and the Social Order* 192 (1933), cited in Ludwig, "Rationale of Responsibility for Young Offenders," 29 *Neb. L. Rev.* 521, 522 (1950).

[23] R. M. Perkins, *Criminal Law* 729–33 (1957); Woldale's Case (1218–19) in 56 *Selden Society* 415, pl. 1134 (1937).

[24] W. L. Clark and W. L. Marshall, *A Treatise on the Law of Crimes* 391–95 (1958).

eight and twelve for serious offenses, such as murder and arson, until the middle of the nineteenth century.[25] More prevalent was the incarceration of offending children in ordinary penal institutions.[26]

In matters other than criminal law, the court of chancery was recognized as early as the fourteenth century to have jurisdiction over the affairs of children. "The power of the court of chancery to interfere with and control not only the estates but the persons of all minors within the limits of its jurisdiction, is of very ancient origin and cannot now be questioned."[27] This power over minors was the outgrowth of the proposition that the king (in his capacity as *parens patriae*) through his chancellor (the keeper of the king's conscience) was responsible for the protection of all those unable to care for themselves because of either youth or mental defect.[28] This English doctrine was followed in the colonies.

In conjunction with the social and penal reform movements,[29] it was argued in the early nineteenth century that offending juveniles who are still susceptible to moral education and character reform should be separated from the influence of hardened adult offenders and be afforded special treatment. Although this humanitarian striving for a completely separate juvenile process was not readily accepted, special institutions for juveniles did predate the establishment of the juvenile court in this country. The New York City House of Refuge, the first institution for children convicted of crime, was established in 1824 and by 1900 when the juvenile court originated, there were some 65 reformatories for children in the United States,[30] exemplifying the ideal of providing specialized facilities for juvenile offenders.[31]

[25] Godfrey v. State, 31 Ala. 323 (1958); State v. Guild, 10 N.J.L. 163 (1828); Perkins, *Criminal Law* 730.

[26] For a detailed discussion of the treatment of juveniles in eighteenth- and nineteenth-century criminal law *see* A. Platt, "The Child Savers" (unpublished manuscript, Center for the Study of Law and Society, University of California, 1966). There has been some recent questioning of the derivation of the *parens patriae* power, with the suggestion that its origins go back no earlier than the eighteenth century. Note, "The *Parens Patriae* Theory and Its Effect on the Constitutional Limits of Juvenile Court Powers," 27 *U. Pitt. L. Rev.* 894, 899 (1966).

[27] Cowles v. Cowles, 3 Gilman 435 (1946), cited in Mack, "The Juvenile Court," 23 *Harv. L. Rev.* 104 (1909). A full treatment of juvenile cases arising in chancery may be found in Nicholas, "History, Philosophy, and Procedures of Juvenile Courts," 1 *J. Fam. L.* 151 (1961).

[28] Nicholas, "Juvenile Courts" 152.

[29] Outlined in Chapter 1, pp. 32–44, of this volume.

[30] Tappan, "Approach to Children with Problems," in *Justice for the Child* 149, 169 (M. K. Rosenheim ed. 1962).

[31] Rosenheim, "Perennial Problems in the Juvenile Court," *ibid.* 2.

Purporting to impose upon the child a "correctional" experience, while at the same time isolating him from the horrors of prison life, these special houses received juveniles not only from ordinary criminal courts but also from various social agencies and public officials.

Despite the noble aspirations of the experiment, many suits were filed at the time to discharge the detained children on the ground that they had been unconstitutionally deprived of the right to a jury trial.[32] An early Pennsylvania decision, rich with implications for the yet unborn juvenile court movement, met the constitutional issue squarely. "The House of Refuge is not a prison, but a school, where reformation, and not punishment, is the end. It may indeed be used as a prison for juvenile convicts who would else be committed to a common gaol; and in respect to these, the constitutionality of the act which incorporated it, stands clear of controversy."[33]

Following the model of the houses of refuge, communities began to create diverse types of specialized treatment for child offenders. A probation service in Massachusetts in 1869 provided for the presence of an agent of the State Board of Charities at criminal trials involving juveniles.[34] Although separate courts for juveniles had not yet been established, such a service at least indicated a degree of civic concern coincident with the efforts of the new breed of social worker typified by Chicago's Jane Addams.[35] For the most part, however, juveniles were treated as if they were adults during the greater part of the nineteenth century, and not until 1899 in Chicago was the juvenile court process, as we know it today, implemented.[36]

The drive toward the establishment of the first juvenile court in Cook County, Illinois, not only grew out of vague humanitarian aspirations but also out of a commitment to deterministic philosophies and a rejection of the classical criminal law's preoccupation with criminal conduct rather than with the criminal himself.[37] Where sanctions pre-

---

[32] Nicholas, "Juvenile Courts" 155.

[33] *Ex parte* Crouse, 4 Wharton 9 (1839), cited in *ibid.*

[34] Rosenheim, "Perennial Problems" 3. A more complete history may be found in H. H. Lou, *Juvenile Courts in the United States* (1927).

[35] R. Lubove, *The Professional Altruist: The Emergence of Social Work as a Career, 1880–1930* (1965).

[36] *Laws of Ill. of 1899* 157.

[37] "The child savers subscribed to the positivist image of man in three crucial respects: (1) they emphasized the primacy of the criminal actor rather than the criminal law as the major point of departure in the construction of etiological explanations of delinquency; (2) they rigidly adhered to a deterministic model of human behavior; and (3) they generally demonstrated interest in only the *abnormal* features of delinquent behavior." Platt, "The Child Savers" 296.

viously had been measured primarily by the state's need for protection, the new movement advocated an emphasis on the shortcomings of the child and the need to treat him with individualized care rather than with penal exactitude. A leading juvenile court judge wrote in 1909: "The problem for determination . . . is not, 'Has this boy or girl committed a specific wrong,' but 'What is he, how has he become what he is, and what had best be done in his interest and in the interest of the state to save him for a downward career?'"[38]

Since juvenile offenders were not to be punished but treated as helpless children in need of care and attention, the ultimate goals of the juvenile court were viewed as being completely different from those of the traditional criminal procedure. The juvenile offender was conceived as "the product of social conditions that were no fault of his own and it was therefore the responsibility of the court to aid the child in his claim against society."[39]

The juvenile court, assuming a parental role, was to tailor the juvenile's treatment to the eradication of the behavior or of those traits in his character that led him toward his antisocial conduct. The emphasis was shifted from an attempt to deter through punishment to an intensified effort to uplift the juvenile's moral and spiritual well-being to the point where he would later take his place in society as a worthy citizen. At no time, however, was agreement reached among the various disciplines as to the etiology of delinquency or the specific programs for its treatment. Since the determinants of delinquency were variously described—spiritual degeneration or malevolence, biological disorders (including genetic and neurologic imbalances), experimental deficiencies (including inappropriate learning and psychopathogenic factors), and social inadequacies (including cultural, sociological, and economic factors)—the proposed remedies for delinquency were also appropriately varied.[40]

Although the original statute[41] enacted in 1899 affected only juveniles who violated specific laws and ordinances, it was soon broadened to cover those thought to be on the brink of delinquency. In 1905 the Illinois definition of delinquency was extended to encompass not only those charged with a violation of the adult laws, but also the incor-

[38] Mack, "The Juvenile Court" 104.

[39] Flexner, "The Juvenile Court as a Social Institution," 23 *Survey* 607 (1909).

[40] Wirt and Briggs, "The Meaning of Delinquency" 12–16; Briggs and Wirt, "Prediction," in *Juvenile Delinquency* 172–75 (H. C. Quay ed. 1965).

[41] *Laws of Ill. of 1899* 157.

rigibles, those exposed to undesirable associates, and "the ungovernable, dissolute and reckless—in short, all children whose conduct did not conform to a model of wholesome youthful activity."[42] Significantly, a key issue in those early days of the juvenile court movement is still a thorny problem: Should "delinquency" be ". . . [d]efined so as to comprehend the noncriminal but nonetheless harmful conduct of children?"[43]

The early juvenile court acts raised most of the significant legal issues that challenge juvenile court proceedings today. One of the first problems was replacing the constitutionally guaranteed procedures of the criminal law with the more informal processes of the juvenile court.[44] A 1905 landmark case illustrates the early preoccupation with this question, and the answer it provided long stood undisturbed:

> [T]he action is not for the trial of a child charged with a crime, but is mercifully to save it from such an ordeal, with the prison or penitentiary in its wake, if the child's own good and the best interests of the state justify such salvation. Whether the child deserves to be saved by the state is no more a question for a jury than whether the father, if able to save it, ought to save it. No constitutional right is violated.[45]

The juvenile court obviously was not created in a social and legal vacuum. The ancient precedent of the state's *parens patriae* role, the penal reform movement, the advent of deterministic criminology, and the establishment of special institutions for juveniles augured the change in the manner of processing young offenders. The time was ripe and the Chicago court soon became the prototype for similar legal tribunals. The concept of a special system of juvenile justice spread quickly, and by 1932 all but two states had enacted special juvenile laws.[46]

Despite the natural growth of juvenile courts, their precise role in the overall social program for the control of delinquency has continued to be a subject of disagreement. To this day it remains uncertain to what extent the juvenile court, rather than, for example, a less formal welfare-type youth agency, should serve as the first point of

---

[42] Rosenheim, "Perennial Problems" 9.

[43] *Ibid.* 12.

[44] *Ibid.* 7.

[45] Commonwealth v. Fisher, 213 Pa. 48, 62 A. 198, 200 (1905).

[46] Dunham, "The Juvenile Court: Contradictory Orientation in Processing Offenders," 23 *Law & Contemp. Prob.* 508, 509 (1958).

contact for juvenile problems and as the nexus of community services for children in trouble.

Similarly undefined is the role of the court with regard to the agencies responsible for the administration of juvenile services and facilities. Courts, probation services, and juvenile institutions are frequently independent totalities. Rarely does the court visit or concern itself with the institutionalized "case." Neither does the juvenile institution usually have the means for following the progress of its ward after his release.[47] Without comprehensive provisions for coordination, the result has been fragmented juvenile programs in which little case accountability and follow-through is possible and where evidence of failure or success cannot be readily measured.[48]

For a proper assessment of the juvenile process, its structure must be recognized not as a monolithic unity but rather as a fluid and diverse institution. There are varying degrees of competence among those who serve in the juvenile court, and there are still widely differing views about the function of courts as social tools—and their responsibilities and aims in relation to individual offenders. A prominent British commentator appropriately concluded: "This means that there tends to be no such thing as a juvenile court system . . . but rather a broad legal framework within which each court develops its own individuality, its social climate, its ethos."[49]

The result is that in the juvenile arena we have largely abandoned the certainties of a rigid legal system without yet being able to substitute another kind of well-formed and defined process. It is for this reason that the juvenile system presents not only many dilemmas but also grave dangers in view of the unique characteristic of judicial power—the fact that society entrusts to courts the ultimate sanction of compulsion.

INADEQUACIES OF THE JUVENILE PROCESS

Individualized Justice and Constitutional Limits

Whether the therapeutic goals of the juvenile process truly justify dispensing with constitutional safeguards would be a moot question

[47] A. J. Kahn, *A Court for Children* 229–33 (1953).

[48] For a criticism of the lack of coordination among the various juvenile services in the District of Columbia *see* President's Commission on Crime in the District of Columbia, *Report* 777. State services are similarly fragmented and little statewide planning, reporting, or follow-up exists. Irving, "Juvenile Justice" 3.

[49] E. L. Younghusband, "The Dilemma of the Juvenile Court," 33 *Soc. Serv. Rev.* 11–12 (1958).

if the new process were directed to willing juveniles only. The use of society's authority over unwilling recipients, however, changes the nature of the juvenile court's "civil-therapeutic" procedures from a purely beneficial treatment program to a social sanction.

In an oft-cited 1955 case, *in re* Poff,[50] the District Court for the District of Columbia expressed the following broad policy regarding juvenile rights:

> The original Juvenile Court Act enacted in the District of Columbia . . . was devised to afford the juvenile protections in addition to those he already possessed under the Federal Constitution. Before this legislative enactment, the juvenile was subject to the same punishment for an offense as an adult. It follows logically that in the absence of such legislation, the juvenile would be entitled to the same constitutional guarantees and safeguards as an adult. If this be true, then the only possible reason for the Juvenile Court Act was to afford the juvenile safeguards *in addition to those* he already possessed. The legislative intent was to enlarge, *not to diminish*, these protections.[51]

This language remains, however, an announcement of desired policy, not a statement of fact.

In the juvenile area, as in other areas of the therapeutic state, the individual's major safeguards are contained in the constitutional requirements of due process, substantive and procedural. Although much attention in recent years has been directed toward the lack of procedural safeguards in juvenile courts, equally pressing questions surround the substantive criteria of delinquency. What type of conduct or condition must a juvenile exhibit in order to come under the coercive powers of the juvenile court? And how strictly must the criteria for delinquency be framed?

There is a wide area of juvenile court jurisdiction over delinquent juveniles[52] whose general status or particular conduct society may find offensive, but which nonetheless fall short of being criminal by adult standards. What power should society exercise over juveniles who drop out of school, leave home, form undesirable associations, and

50 135 F. Supp. 224 (C.C.C. 1955).
51 *Ibid.* 225.
52 This study is limited to delinquency and will not encompass the criteria or procedures concerning "neglected" and "dependent" children. These include children on whose behalf social intervention is required primarily because of the failure or inability of parents to provide necessary care. For a detailed discussion *see* Paulsen, "The Delinquency, Neglect and Dependency Jurisdiction of the Juvenile Court," in *Justice for the Child* 44–81 (M. K. Rosenheim ed. 1962).

appear to progress towards crime, yet are short of it? When may society take preventive measures, and to what extent should social intervention depend on the availability of adequate treatment facilities?

The hazy area is rapidly expanding. It encompasses the juvenile who lets his whiskers grow contrary to parental wishes, who spends his time in pool halls, who absents himself from school or hitchhikes across country, who fails to come home to sleep, or who associates with bad company. Indeed, as parental discipline and religious influences diminish, significant questions arise about how the responsibility for "misbehaving" juveniles should be shifted from the home and church to the coercive powers of the police and juvenile court.

Broad social questions are involved in determining the limits of the expanding "definition" of delinquency. Since in the legal tradition the statutory criteria are supposed to establish with exactitude whether a juvenile's behavior is sufficient to subject him to the jurisdiction of the court,[53] current definitions are often criticized as being too "vague," of being inadequate to apprise a juvenile of prohibited conduct. But the juvenile courts were designed not only to reform delinquents but also to prevent delinquency, to deal with general modes and conditions of juvenile life as well as with specific acts. How is this mission to be discharged unless the court is allowed to intervene at an early stage of the juvenile's personal growth and malfunctioning, a stage which is incapable of strict definition?

Most critics, however, have attacked not issues of criteria but the juvenile court procedures that permit the denial of traditional constitutional safeguards to the child. They ask why a youth charged with delinquency—and his parents—are not afforded protection against unreasonable search and seizure, or accorded the right to be released on bail pending trial, the right to a timely notice of the charges, the right to counsel, the right to confrontation and cross-examination of witnesses, the privilege against self-incrimination, and the right to a court transcript and appellate review. These questions have remained unanswered throughout the seventy-year history of the juvenile court. Only recently, in the Supreme Court decision in the *Gault* case, was significant light cast upon the subject [54]

[53] This depends, however, on an overwhelming amount of discretion on the part of the police, the social services making the preliminary investigation, and the court itself, as discussed on pp. 125–28.

[54] *In re* Gault, 387 U.S. 1 (1967). For a full discussion *see* pp. 122 and 138–48 of this volume.

The propriety of procedural rights in juvenile court is a question, much like the substantive issues cited earlier, that touches upon the basic philosophy of the court itself. Ostensibly, the constitutional protections usually applicable to criminal cases would not appear necessary in view of the asserted civil and therapeutic nature of the juvenile proceeding. But it has increasingly been observed that regardless of the designation of the proceeding, the final adjudication may well operate to deprive a juvenile of his liberty and the juvenile's family of his companionship. A growing realization of the burdens imposed by purportedly therapeutic sanctions has therefore produced a marked recent trend toward vesting juveniles with more of the procedural rights available to an adult in a criminal trial.[55]

The early critics of the juvenile court procedures were motivated by fear of abuse; they based their plea for procedural safeguards primarily on the grounds that the therapeutic aim of the court was scant reason for dispensing with the presumption of innocence and the ordinary requirements of due process in proving the child's involvement.[56] These would appear to be fundamental and inescapable requirements, for delinquency is a fact that must be established before the court may impose its therapeutic disposition. To hold otherwise would place, at the outset, the burden of proving innocence upon the child and his parents.[57]

But this earlier emphasis upon procedural propriety as a safeguard against unsubstantiated findings of delinquency was followed by a recognition of other uses of due process: Is not an orderly court proceeding, in itself, a requisite first step in the rehabilitative process? How can the judge give his most sympathetic consideration to the question of disposition unless the charged child has an opportunity to present the most favorable aspects of his case? How can the most fitting social solution be reached if the judge relies only on an unchallenged social report by the court staff? How else, in an increasingly impersonal society, are we to prevent undue haste, neglect, and abuse in juvenile court.

Judge Moylan of the Baltimore Juvenile Court asks: "Can a proper balance be struck between the basic philosophy of the juvenile court and its underlying informality, and the maintenance of procedural

---

[55] *See, e.g., in re* Contreras, 109 Cal. App. 2d 787, 241 P.2d 631 (1952); *in re* Holmes, 379 Pa. 599, 109 A.2d 523 (1954) (Musmanno, J., dissenting), *cert. denied,* 348 U.S. 973 (1955); Kent v. United States, 386 U.S. 545 (1966); *in re* Winship, 396 U.S. 885, 90 S. Ct. 1068 (1970).

[56] *In re* Holmes, 379 Pa. 599, 109 A.2d 523 (1954) (Musmanno, J., dissenting).

[57] *Cf.* Gideon v. Wainwright, 372 U.S. 335, 344 (1963).

safeguards of due process, guaranteeing fundamental fairness in all hearings, criminal or civil?"[58]

The Substantive Problem: Overly Broad Criteria for Compulsory Intervention

The Standard Juvenile Court Act,[59] proposed by the National Council on Crime and Delinquency and designed to serve as a voluntary model for the various states, exemplifies the problem of broad and uncertain criteria.

[T]he court shall have exclusive original jurisdiction in proceedings: 1. Concerning any child who is alleged to have violated any federal, state or local law or municipal ordinance, regardless of where the violation occurred. . . . 2. Concerning any child . . . (b) whose environment is injurious to his welfare, or whose behavior is injurious to his own or others' welfare; or (c) who is beyond the control of his parent or other custodian.[60]

While the first clause seeks specificity, the second part uncovers wide areas over which the juvenile court judge is given nearly unlimited discretion. If an adult, for example, were arrested by the police in a public street in the early hours of the morning, he would be hastily released in the absence of any criminal charges. If a juvenile is apprehended under similar circumstances, he can be committed to an institution for being in an unsuitable environment and beyond the control of his parents. This well illustrates the perplexing possibility under the juvenile court system whereby a person can lose his liberty not for something he *does* but for something he *is*.

Statistics from the United States Children's Bureau substantiate these observations. Charges against youths brought before the juvenile court may consist of such serious offenses as murder, robbery, and rape, but poverty offenses are most typical, with auto theft accounting for 10 percent of all cases, larceny 15 percent, breaking and entering 11 percent, and vandalism 3.5 percent. Yet another 26.8 percent of all delinquency charges involve behavioral offenses that only juveniles can commit, such as truancy, running away, curfew violations, or being ungovernable.[61] Furthermore, 70 percent of all girls and 25 per-

[58] Moylan, "Comments on the Juvenile Court," 25 *Md. L. Rev.* 310, 313 (1965).

[59] Standard Juvenile Court Act (6th ed. 1959).

[60] *Ibid.* §8.

[61] U.S. Department of Health, Education, and Welfare, Children's Bureau, *1964 Juvenile Court Statistics* 10 (1965).

cent of all boys in institutions are committed for indiscretions which do not constitute adult offenses: running away, being truant, being ungovernable.[62]

A recent sample of 20 training institutions for delinquent children demonstrated that some 30 percent of their inmates were children committed for conduct that would not have been criminal had they been adults. Of the children detained pending a juvenile hearing, 48 percent of those held in special detention facilities and 40 percent of those actually detained in jails were not charged with adult criminal acts.[63] In 1964 "running away" and "ungovernability" each constituted 8 percent of the cases referred to juvenile courts.[64] One out of every six youths in juvenile court was there for noncriminal behavior.

The fact that a child is ungovernable brings him within the definition of delinquency. But what behavior is ungovernable? How do the police and the court decide when a child has acted in such a way? On the basis of whose values should this decision be made?[65] Is governability not a relative term, depending on whether or not there is a living father, a working mother, a permissive grandmother or a strict disciplinarian grandfather? With such broad definitions, apprehension and adjudication too often depend upon the child's socioeconomic background or upon the personal values of the police, the judge, or the court's social service staff. The broad discretion under the law means also that the number of reported delinquencies may greatly vary from community to community and from one social class to another, because many minor and even serious juvenile problems may be handled by referral to other community agencies without further resort to police or court action.[66]

Exact and certain criteria are an indispensable condition of individual justice. Valid throughout the law, this maxim requires "greater clarity in the definition of the jurisdiction of the juvenile courts."[67] Nothing manifests the truth of this assertion more than a mere list of the diverse acts or conditions which constitute delinquency

[62] *Ibid.* 20.

[63] Sheridan, "Juveniles Who Commit Noncriminal Acts: Why Treat in Correctional Systems?" 31 *Fed. Prob.* 26, 27 (1967).

[64] U.S. Department of Health, Education, and Welfare, *1964 Juvenile Court Statistics* 10.

[65] Diana, "The Rights of Juvenile Delinquents: An Appraisal of Juvenile Court Procedures," 47 *J. Crim. L.C. & P.S.* 561 (1956–57).

[66] Perlman, "Reporting Juvenile Delinquency," 3 *J. Nat. Prob. & Parole Assoc.* 243–49 (1957).

[67] Allen, "The Borderland of Criminal Law: Problems of Socializing Criminal Justice," 32 *Soc. Serv. Rev.* 107 (1958).

under various state laws. Professor Sussman[68] compiled the following delinquency definitions:

1. [A juvenile who] violates any law or ordinance;
2. [Who is] habitually truant;
3. [Knowingly] associates with thieves, vicious or immoral persons;
4. Incorrigible;
5. Beyond control of parent or guardian;
6. Growing up in idleness or crime;
7. So deports self as to injure self or others;
8. Absents self from home [without just cause] without consent;
9. Immoral or indecent conduct;
10. [Habitually] uses vile, obscene, or vulgar language [in public places];
11. [Knowingly] enters, visits house of ill repute;
12. Patronizes, visits policy shop or gaming place;
13. [Habitually] wanders about railroad yards or tracks;
14. Jumps train or enters car or engine without authority;
15. Patronizes saloon or dram house where intoxicating liquor is sold;
16. Wanders streets at night, not on lawful business;
17. Patronizes public poolroom or bucket shop;
18. Immoral conduct around school (or in public place);
19. Engages in illegal occupation;
20. In occupation or situation dangerous or injurious to self or others;
21. Smokes cigarettes (or uses tobacco in any form);
22. Frequents place the existence of which violates the law;
23. Is found [in place for permitting of which] adult may be punished;
24. Addicted to drugs;
25. Disorderly;
26. Begging;
27. Uses intoxicating liquor;
28. Makes indecent proposal;
29. Loiters, sleeps in alleys, vagrant;
30. Runs away from state or charity institution;
31. Found on premises occupied or used for illegal purposes;
32. Operates motor vehicle dangerously while under the influence of liquor;
33. Attempts to marry without consent, in violation of law;
34. Given to sexual irregularities.

[68] F. B. Sussman, *Law of Juvenile Delinquency* 21 (1959).

Of course the rationale of such broad standards is that the juvenile court, to act in the child's interest, should not be hampered by narrowly and technically constructed limitations upon its authority. If the court perceives conduct tending to the criminal or exposure to a dangerous environment, it should have the power to act as a father would to correct the situation. Granting this broad power in the form of ambiguous criteria and unbounded dispositional discretion presupposes that the juvenile courts and their officers will use the power exclusively in the interests of the child—never otherwise.

But unchecked discretion, much like other power, has its corrupting influence. Abuses of the unlimited discretion given to juvenile courts by the uncertain standards of "delinquency" are recorded in several appellate cases. In a Nebraska case[69] only the intervention of the state Supreme Court and its propounding a parallel to the animal world maxim that "every dog is entitled to his first bite" saved a young man from a juvenile record. Sanders, seventeen years old, slapped another boy, Stewart, in return for an alleged insult. No serious damage resulted and the two never saw each other again. Soon afterward, Stewart was set upon by several other youths and his jaw was broken. Sanders was apprehended. He had an unblemished record, stable home situation, satisfactory scholastic conduct, and no truancy violations. The district court, nevertheless, made a finding of delinquency. The appellate court reversed the finding and suggested that, even had Sanders been "involved" as charged, a conclusion of delinquency would still be unwarranted. Said the court: "There was no previous misconduct of appellant claimed or shown. A single violation of a law of the state by a minor does not always permit of a conclusion that the transgressor is a juvenile delinquent."[70] A practical appellate court sought to require more than a first offense before affirming an adjudication of delinquency. Would the court have held otherwise had the alleged delinquent's home background or school record been less than exemplary?

Several studies of delinquency in the United States have demonstrated that Negro children are committed to juvenile institutions at a younger age, for less serious offenses, with a lesser past juvenile record than white children.[71] There is little in the law of most states to guarantee that a boy having an altercation in or out of school

[69] *In re* Sanders, 168 Neb. 458, 96 N.W.2d 218 (1959).

[70] *Ibid.* 222.

[71] Under loose standards, it is often the child's background rather than his specific deed which determines the disposition of his case. Axelrod, "Negro and

would not be subject to sanctions unwarranted by the gravity of the offense.

In the face of indefinite criteria, the courts must constantly guard against excessive "therapeutic" zeal. A youth of fourteen found access to an unoccupied house and with two friends of the same age proceeded to build a "clubhouse." Their offense was in entering the garage attached to the house and removing a flashlight and three fuses.[72] They were detected when the clubhouse caught fire. The parents made immediate restitution, amounting to $14. The juvenile court had found the youths delinquent even in the face of their clean records, regular attendance at school and Sunday school, and favorable recommendations by a minister and deputy sheriff. In reversing the decision, the Appellate Court of Illinois stated, "it is apparent that the deputy sheriff had a better understanding of the word delinquent than the State's Attorney, who seems to have regarded the Family Court Act as a criminal statute designed for punishment of petty offenders."[73] The court was satisfied that the boys committed a wrong but held that the juvenile law was not intended to prescribe punishment for an isolated misdemeanor; neither was the State's Attorney justified in his haste to exercise the extreme remedy of taking a child away from his parents and placing him under state supervision.[74]

A California legislative commission's[75] evaluation of a similarly broad delinquency law demonstrated the effects of inexact substantive standards.

There is an absence of well-defined empirically derived standards and norms to guide juvenile court judges, probation, and law enforcement officials in their decision making. Consequently, instead of a uniform system of justice, varied systems based upon divergent policies and value scales are in evidence. Actually, whether or not a juvenile is arrested, placed in detention, or referred to the probation department, and whether or not the petition is dismissed, probation is granted, or a ... commitment is ordered by the juvenile court, seems to depend more upon the community in which the offense is committed than upon the intrinsic merits of the individual case. Basic legal rights are neither

White Institutionalized Delinquents," 57 *Amer. J. Sociol.* 569–74 (1952); Rhodes, "Delinquency and Community Action," in *Juvenile Delinquency* 250 (H. C. Quay ed. 1965).
[72] *In re* Johnson, 30 Ill. App. 2d 439, 174 N.E.2d 907 (1961).
[73] *Ibid.* 910.
[74] *Ibid.* 908.
[75] *Cal. Wel. & Inst. Code* §700(b), (f), (i), (k) (1956).

being uniformly nor adequately protected under present juvenile court provisions and procedures.[76]

The width of the schism between the ideal and the reality of *parens patriae* is illustrated by a recent West Virginia case.[77] Mills, a fourteen-year-old boy with no previous record of any misconduct, phoned the local school and falsely reported the presence of a bomb. Under the state statute, a person molesting or disturbing any free school is guilty of a misdemeanor and can be jailed up to thirty days.[78] But Mills, not subject to the criminal law because of his age, came under the jurisdiction of the juvenile court which determined Mills a delinquent and accordingly committed him to the state training school until he attained the age of twenty-one. On review, the West Virginia Supreme Court of Appeals affirmed the youth's seven-year commitment for an act which, if committed by an adult, would carry a maximum jail sentence of thirty days.[79]

Similar facts gave rise to *in re Gault*,[80] the first juvenile case decided by the United States Supreme Court. Gerald Gault, a child of fifteen, was arrested and charged with making lewd telephone calls to a neighboring woman. (The actual communication consisted of the following questions: "Do you give any?" "Are your cherries ripe today?" "Do you have big bombers?") The juvenile court committed Gault to the State Industrial School until adulthood. No particular grounds were specified by the judge for the finding of delinquency. At a subsequent procedure for the child's release on habeas corpus, the judge volunteered the explanation that Gerald was "habitually involved in immoral matters."[81] On another occasion the judge stated that he thought the telephone calls amounted "to disturbing the peace."[82] Under the Arizona laws, the maximum penalty for an adult convicted of using obscene language over the telephone cannot exceed a two-month jail term.[83]

Widespread abuses made possible by vague standards are also

---

[76] California, Governor's Special Study Commission on Juvenile Justice, *A Study of the Administration of Juvenile Justice in California*, pt. 1, p. 12 (1960).

[77] State v. Mills, 144 W. Va. 257, 107 S.E.2d 772 (1959).

[78] *W. Va. Code* §6040(14) (1961).

[79] State v. Mills, 144 W. Va. 257, 107 S.E.2d 772 (1959).

[80] 387 U.S. 1 (1967). The Supreme Court's holding in this case is discussed beginning on p. 138.

[81] Application of Gault, 99 Ariz. 181, 407 P.2d 760 (1965).

[82] Brief for the American Parents Committee (Nicholas N. Kittrie, counsel) as Amicus Curiae, 6–7, *in re* Gault, October Term, no. 116, U.S. Supreme Court (1966).

[83] *Ariz. Rev. Stat.* §13–377 (1956).

described by criminal law professor Starrs in a recent account of youthful civil rights demonstrators brought before juvenile courts in the South:

> ... the Juvenile Court, like other legal processes in the South, may be no more than another arm of segregation. It can ... intimidate civil rights demonstrators and their parents by long periods of inhuman confinement without recourse to bail. . . . It can, with telling impact, browbeat them into disbelief or uncertainty in the rightness of their cause. And it can in ominous tones, threaten to invoke its continuing jurisdiction to recall and redetermine the case of any juvenile upon his breach of elaborate and obscure probationary conditions. . . . On occasion, children have been adjudged delinquent when their parents, not they, were active civil rights workers.[84]

Similarly, the United States Civil Rights Commission recently reported how juvenile courts utilize "the latitude permitted in juvenile proceedings to curtail or penalize participation in constitutionally protected activities."[85]

The importance of these reported cases is not that a particular individual was maltreated under a vague standard of delinquency (although that is certainly important enough), but rather that the juvenile judiciary has failed to limit effectively the use of its wide powers. Although appellate courts in some of these cases rectified the specific injustice, the fact remained that due to the unavailability of attorneys in the juvenile courts very few juvenile cases reached the appellate level. The first and only substantial line of defense against abuses of broad criteria is the juvenile court judges themselves. This line is none too secure, because of the inadequate training of juvenile court judges and the haste with which the cases are heard.

If the need for reform is accepted, the question of how juvenile delinquency could be more adequately defined remains. Whether noncriminal misbehavior should provide a ground for juvenile court action continues as one of the most difficult issues.[86] Suggestions for a more precise listing of juvenile offenses in the statutes proper have similarly met strong opposition as contrary to the broader protective and preventive philosophy of the juvenile court.

---

[84] Starrs, "A Sense of Irony in Southern Juvenile Courts," 1 *Harv. Civil Liberties–Civil Rights L. Rev.* 129 (1966).
[85] U.S. Commission on Civil Rights, *Report* 174 (1965).
[86] Paulsen, "Jurisdiction of the Juvenile Court" 50.

Professor Frank Remington,[87] of the University of Wisconsin Law School believes that narrowly defined criteria cannot be legislatively established: ". . . [t]here is, particularly in the juvenile field, bound to be an ambiguity in regard to what conduct can properly be used as a basis for subjecting a person to the juvenile justice process."[88] Although delinquency could be somewhat more precisely defined, there can never be a definition capable of mechanical application. Remington's solution is a resignation to some ambiguity in the inevitable statutes and a corresponding insistence upon administrative self-restraint, whereby ". . . law enforcement and social work agencies assume responsibility for the development of sensible and fair policies for operating within the outer limits of the legislation."[89]

But can we rely upon the discretion of the police, social workers, and juvenile judges to cope with the hazards contained in vague standards? There is the example of the police chief in Madison, Wisconsin, who announced that he would not enforce a juvenile curfew ordinance literally but only where the circumstances indicated that the youth was abroad for no legitimate reason.[90] Contrary to the criticism by a local newspaper, Professor Remington argues that this is a good "common sense" solution to a problem created by impossibility of drafting a law without ambiguity and indefiniteness. Such common sense, contends Remington, is an essential element of due process. But is not this situation the very one which is open to abuse when administered by a different police chief?

"Yonder's Wall" was a Washington, D.C., store specializing in psychedelic posters, beads, clothes, and other paraphernalia, and as such served as a legitimate mecca for the young. In January 1968, the police conducted a narcotics raid, which uncovered marijuana in an upper story of the building. More than half of the juveniles arrested were apprehended as they walked in off the street during normal business hours for the shop. Adults who similarly entered the store were not arrested. According to the Acting Chief of the Metropolitan Police Narcotics Squad, the reason for the difference in treatment was that in order to arrest an adult "you really have to get a violation of law."[91]

Without a massive change in attitude among those entrusted with

[87] Remington, "Due Process in Juvenile Proceedings," 11 *Wayne L. Rev.* 688 (1965).
[88] *Ibid.* 692.
[89] *Ibid.* 693.
[90] *Ibid.*
[91] *Washington Post*, January 23, 1968, p. A6.

administering our police and juvenile court systems, the current indefinite standards harbor much potential abuse.[92] Furthermore, when the authorities themselves betray the protective philosophy of the juvenile courts, arguments that strict legislative standards are inconsistent with that philosophy become meaningless, even disingenuous.

The Procedural Problem: Individual Safeguards in the Process of Justice

An assessment of the juvenile court's function as an individualized system of social control must consider carefully the adequacy of procedural safeguards accorded the accused delinquent, both in and out of court. Court procedures cannot be isolated from the rest of the juvenile process. The whole range of practices from the initial apprehension of a juvenile to the final disposition of his case must be examined.

How is a juvenile first brought to the attention of the juvenile court? The Standard Juvenile Court Act (a voluntary model formulated by juvenile court leaders and proposed for state adoption) provides that ". . . [w]henever the court is informed by any person that a child is within the purview of this Act, it shall make a preliminary investigation to determine whether the interests of the public or of the child require that further action be taken."[93] The District of Columbia similarly provides[94] that any person may report a child to the juvenile court. The Director of Social Work, a juvenile court officer, then decides whether to file a petition asking for an official court hearing and disposition.

Usually a complaint to the juvenile court follows an initial involvement by the police.[95] Judge Ketcham of the District of Columbia

[92] Vague standards foster abuses. In 1965 the police reported 5,073 arrests of children age 10 and under for disorderly conduct. Another 1,089 were arrested on the charge of "suspicion," with no particular offense listed. FBI, *Uniform Crime Reports* 112 (1965). Without strict legislative criteria, the courts will have to guard actively against such excesses. An interesting light on the criteria problem is shed in an article by Westbrook, "*Mens Rea* in the Juvenile Court," 5 *J. Fam. L.* 121 (1965). He contends that the criminal law requirement of no conviction without a *mens rea* can be used to advantage by judges in expressing clearer and more readily ascertainable limits upon the juvenile process.

[93] Standard Juvenile Court Act §12; 5 *J. Nat. Prob. & Parole Assoc.* 351 (1959).

[94] *D.C. Code Ann.* §16–2302 (1966 Supp.). The Virginia law is contained in *Va. Code* §16.1–164 (1950). The Maryland law is contained in *Md. Code Ann.* art. 26, §86(a) (1957).

[95] The 1964 figures for Chicago illustrate this situation: 98.4 percent of the juvenile court cases were referred by law enforcement agencies. Note, "Juvenile

Juvenile Court observes the "great majority of juvenile proceedings are instituted by police officers, although most statutes provide that any interested party may file a petition."[96] The role of the police is important not only because of their arrest power but also because of their screening function in juvenile cases, well demonstrated by the statistics of the Chicago Youth Division: Of over 40,000 juvenile offenses recorded in 1964, some 27,000 were adjusted at the police station level and some 13,000 were referred to the court.[97] Of some 1,400,000 youths arrested annually in this country,[98] more than one-half are released by the police without court referral.[99]

These initial stages are of inestimable significance because they represent the first confrontation between the youth and the juvenile authorities. Furthermore, they determine whether the youth will be subjected to an "informal adjustment"[100] by the police or the court's staff, or whether he merits a more formal disposition through filing a petition and receiving a hearing before the judge.

Few communities have a special police force to engage in juvenile work. The arrested juvenile, consequently, is often exposed to the typical adult police procedures: he is photographed and his fingerprints are taken.[101] Still, in compliance with the therapeutic goals of the juvenile process, police departments usually refer to the apprehension of a youth as a "taking into custody" rather than an arrest or "booking," thus striving to avoid the stigmatizing labels of the standard criminal proceeding.[102] But the very fact that the police custody of a juvenile is not considered an arrest gives the police even greater dis-

---

Delinquents: The Police, State Courts and Individualized Justice," 79 *Harv. L. Rev.* 775, 776, n.5 (1966).

[96] Ketcham, "The Unfulfilled Promise of the Juvenile Court," in *Justice for the Child* 33 (M. K. Rosenheim ed. 1962). Judge Ketcham's article originally appeared in 7 *Crime and Delinquency* 97 (1961).

[97] Chicago, Citizens Committee on the Family Court, *Bulletin no. 4* (April 1965); Chicago, Police Department, Youth Division, *Annual Report* (1964).

[98] U.S. Senate, Subcommittee to Investigate Juvenile Delinquency, *Report no. 1664* 2.

[99] FBI, *Uniform Crime Reports* 104 (1965), in which 53 percent of a sample of juveniles arrested are reported to have been released by police without court referral.

[100] Standard Juvenile Court Act §12.

[101] U.S. Department of Health, Education, and Welfare, Children's Bureau, *Police Services for Children* 27–31 (1954).

[102] The procedure at the District of Columbia Metropolitan Police Department, Youth Aid Division, is an excellent example. *See* Note, "District of Columbia Juvenile Delinquency Proceedings: Apprehension to Disposition," 49 *Geo. L. J.* 322 (1960).

cretion. In traditional criminal arrests the detained person may not be released upon the police's own discretion. This authority is vested in an independent magistrate as a safeguard against police arbitrariness and abuses—since the police may at times use the arrest power as a harassment technique. Since the juvenile suspect is not arrested, he need not, therefore, be formally released by a magistrate. Given this freedom from judicial scrutiny, the police power with regard to juvenile apprehension and release is practically uncurbed.[103]

The process of informal screening and dispositions by the police, including referral to community agencies, is usually a power assumed by them and not one established by juvenile statutes. The Standard Juvenile Court Act merely provides that if a child is not released from custody in a reasonable time, the officer or other person in charge shall promptly notify the court of his intention to file a complaint.[104] The District of Columbia statutory provision[105] quite clearly denies the police such screening discretion by providing that when an officer has apprehended a youth, he must immediately report the fact to the court.

In light of the absence of any statutory foundation for police discretion in determining the "seriousness" of offenses, the police department's extension into the dispositional arena merits careful empirical examination and evaluation not hitherto undertaken.[106] Since nearly half of all arrested juveniles are released by the police without court referral, the effect of the confrontation with the police assumes great importance. What is the nature and impact of the police intervention in these cases? What conditions are exacted by the police for the favor of the release? What image of law and order does the released juvenile carry away with him?

Because the constitutional right to bail is not usually applicable to juveniles,[107] the police are also entrusted with broad discretion as to whether an arrested child is to be kept in detention pending the hearing of his case in juvenile court. A common complaint is the excessive

[103] This fact undoubtedly contributed to the attitude demonstrated in the "Yonder's Wall" incident.

[104] Standard Juvenile Court Act §16.

[105] *D.C. Code Ann.* §11–912 (1961).

[106] These police screenings, although admitted to be of questionable legality, are defended and fully described (as they occur in the District of Columbia) in Note, "District of Columbia Juvenile Proceedings" 322, 329.

[107] *Mass. Gen. Laws Ann.* ch. 119, §67 (1958), is unusual in that it makes bail available in juvenile cases. *See also* Fulwood v. Stone, 394 F.2d 939 (D.C. Cir. 1967).

detention of children on minor charges.[108] The problem is further aggravated by the shortage of special detention facilities for children. Most state laws prohibit the confinement of children in jails and police stations; still, the lack of other facilities results in the detention of substantial numbers of children each year in adult institutions.[109] Even the detention centers specially designed for juveniles do not differ significantly from jails and it is not uncommon to find children locked up in these places for periods ranging from a few weeks to as long as 20 months awaiting a hearing and disposition.[110]

If the juvenile is not released after the initial police screening, he will be given, in most metropolitan areas, the benefit of a second screening by the juvenile court social staff, the members of which are usually referred to as "intake" officers.[111] In many states a delinquency petition may not be formally filed with the court until after an informal investigation by the court's social "intake" staff. By deciding against a formal delinquency petition, or by referring the child to other social agencies, a "capable intake service, given the support and confidence of the judge, can very properly handle up to 50 percent of all incoming cases without referring them to court."[112] In fact, nationwide, 54 percent of all cases reaching the juvenile courts are disposed of informally by the staff without any hearing by the judge.[113]

---

[108] Elson, "Juvenile Courts and Due Process," in *Justice for the Child* 101 (M. K. Rosenheim ed. 1962).

[109] Sussman, *Juvenile Delinquency* 41; California, Governor's Commission on Juvenile Justice, *Administration of Juvenile Justice in California*, pt. 1, pp. 41–42, and pt. 2, pp. 78–79; Ketcham, "Unfulfilled Promise" 36–37.

[110] "Children are still to be found in some county jails, lost in red tape and waiting for months for the opportunity to be admitted to juvenile correctional institutions." Note, "The *Parens Patriae* Theory" 894, 903.

[111] In a recent study 82 percent of the reporting 1,200 juvenile courts stated that they had no "intake" unit or workers to discharge this function. Sheridan, "Juveniles Who Commit Noncriminal Acts" 26, 30.

[112] Keve, "Administration of Juvenile Court Services," in *Justice for the Child* 188 (M. K. Rosenheim ed. 1962).

[113] Of 686,000 cases reaching the juvenile court staff, 353,000 were released informally by the court's staff and 333,000 were disposed of judicially. U.S. Department of Health, Education, and Welfare, *1964 Juvenile Court Statistics* 11. These figures do not include traffic or neglect cases. *Ibid.* 13. Still, this type of informal disposition must also be carefully guarded against prejudice, laziness, and abuse. The comment at §12 of the Standard Juvenile Court Act discusses this "unofficial casework" or "nonjudicial handling of cases." In most jurisdictions, of which Maryland and Virginia are typical, the judge himself is required to determine whether the situation merits the official exercise of court powers. On the other hand, the District of Columbia procedure is illustrative of the practice in areas large enough to support a staff of social workers attached to the juvenile court. *Md. Code Ann.* art. 26, §§53–54 (1957), and *Va. Code* §16.1–164 (1950).

Upon a youth's referral by the police, the juvenile court's Director of Social Work conducts a fact-finding investigation into the juvenile's history. At this time most of the background material and "evidence" is gathered which later will constitute a report to the judge. Much of what will be considered by the judge enters the youth's file at this point, but procedural safeguards are notably absent. There is no guarantee that hearsay and irrelevant information will be excluded. There is no opportunity for the youth or his family to challenge the truth of the material placed in his file. The presence of an attorney at this point is not guaranteed, though it has been asserted to be a necessity for the favorable and articulate presentation of the youth's position in a hearing.[114]

If it is determined, after the preliminary social investigations and conferences with the youth and his family have been conducted, that judicial action is required (this is usually the case if the youth denies the charges or if the offense is serious), a formal petition is filed with the court. This petition asserting a youth's delinquency is a highly important document, analogous to the information or indictment filed in criminal court. Yet as all other phases of the juvenile process, this too suffers from indefiniteness. The basic standards of pleading and due process in both criminal and civil proceedings require an accurate statement of the alleged wrong. The Standard Juvenile Court Act accordingly requires that the petition be verified by the filer and that it set forth plainly "the facts which bring the child within the purview of this Act."[115] Most juvenile courts, however, because of the informal and noncriminal nature of the proceedings, have been reluctant to require that the petition conform with strict tests of specificity in listing the charges against a youth. "It is not necessary that the petition be drawn by one learned in the law. But it should show in plain and clear language the facts or situation which reveal dependency, neglect or delinquency. An intelligent layman should be able to do that."[116] The majority of juvenile courts thus merely require that the allegations of the petition be "reasonably definite."[117] Obviously, unless the peti-

Virginia allows the judge to proceed informally as he sees fit and to make such adjustment as is practicable without a petition. *D.C. Code Ann.* §16-2302 (Supp. 1966).

[114] Handler, "The Juvenile Court and the Adversary System: Problems of Function and Form," 7 *Wis. L. Rev.* (1965).

[115] Standard Juvenile Court Act §12.

[116] State *in re* Graham, 110 Utah 159, 170 P.2d 172, 177 (1946).

[117] *E.g.*, People v. Lewis, 260 N.Y. 171, 183 N.E. 353 (1932); State v. Allaman, 154 Ohio 296, 95 N.E.2d 753 (1950).

tion states the charge in definite terms, the youth or his family are in no position to respond to it effectively. Many parents of low socio-economic background therefore find themselves completely puzzled and silenced by the *parens patriae* process.

The most ritualistic stage in a juvenile court procedure is the hearing before the judge. The child, his parents, his lawyer (if one is available to the family or provided by the court) and local public welfare officials are all allowed to be present at this informal hearing conducted to determine both the youth's complicity, if any, and the required disposition of the case. If the youth does not deny the charges, the hearing is usually directed toward disposition only.

Most statutes regulating the judicial hearing follow the general outline of the Standard Juvenile Court Act, which provides that juvenile cases are to be heard by the court without a jury and separate from adult cases. "Such hearings shall be conducted in an informal manner and the general public shall be excluded."[118] In keeping with the non-criminal informality of the proceeding, the Standard Act has little more to say on the conduct of the hearing.

The central figure is the judge. He conducts the hearing and poses the questions. No prosecuting attorney is present and frequently there is no defense counsel. The hearing clearly departs from the typical courtroom procedure in the United States—where the attorneys ask the questions and witnesses are cross-examined—and resembles the nonadversary trials in European civil law countries.

Contrary to the traditions of American criminal law,[119] the accused child need not be present during the hearing. According to the Standard Act: "The child may be excluded from the hearing at any time at the discretion of the judge."[120] Similarly, the Children's Bureau of the federal government states:

A fair hearing does not mean that the child, in particular, or that both parents need to be present while all the evidence is being presented. The child, however, in delinquency cases would be permitted to be present whenever there is a right of confrontation particularly in the first part of the hearing where a determination is being made as to the allegations in the petition. The court may exclude the child (but not his counsel) from the hear-

[118] Standard Juvenile Court Act §19. For a typical law *see Utah Code Ann.* §55–10–94 (Supp. 1965).

[119] *U.S. Const.*, amend. VI: "In all criminal prosecutions, the accused shall enjoy the right . . . to be informed of the nature and cause of the accusation; to be confronted with the witnesses against him. . . ."

[120] Standard Juvenile Court Act §19.

ing at any time that he thinks proper and should do so, especially when the evidence is considered not fit for him to hear or when it may damage his confidence in his parents.[121]

Thus the child may have no opportunity to respond personally to the adverse evidence and its sources. And because few juvenile cases are appealed, "there has not been developed a body of precedent to guide and control" the judge[122] in this discretion to exclude the major party to the process. In a similar effort to differentiate between the criminal and juvenile hearing, the laws in most jurisdictions completely abolish jury trials in juvenile court.[123]

Before the court can make a disposition, it must first decide the issue of the child's delinquency or "involvement." Since the cases reaching the court are usually the more serious and may result in the child's commitment to an institution, what degree of evidence or "burden of proof" should be required to establish a child's complicity? Because of the civil nature of the proceedings, some judges only required a preponderance of the evidence (the burden to be established in a civil case) in order to establish a child's delinquency.[124] Others demand a more exacting measure of the juvenile's delinquency, insisting on proof beyond a reasonable doubt (the criminal law standard).[125] The Supreme Court of the United States, after some hesitation in deciding the issue,[126] recently resolved the conflict in favor of the standard requirement of proof beyond a reasonable doubt.[127]

Equally significant is the question of the type of evidence that may be properly considered by the court. Many commentators urge that, in deciding complicity or involvement, a juvenile's past record should

[121] U.S. Department of Health, Education, and Welfare, Children's Bureau, *Standards for Juvenile and Family Courts* 75 (1966).

[122] Elson, "Juvenile Courts and Due Process" 98.

[123] The state laws are collected in 67 *A.L.R.* 1082 (1930); *see also* Paulsen, "Fairness to the Juvenile Offender," 41 *Minn. L. Rev.* 547 (1957). Professor Paulsen says: "A jury trial would inevitably bring a good deal more formality to the juvenile court without giving a youngster a demonstrably better fact-finding process than trial before a judge." *Ibid.* 559. Maryland goes so far as to specifically exclude jury trials. *Md. Code Ann.* art. 26, §83(a) (1957).

[124] People vs. Lewis, 260 N.Y. 171, 183 N.E. 353 (1932), is the outstanding case on this position. *See also* Note, "Juvenile Delinquents" 775, 795 (1966).

[125] Jones v. Commonwealth, 185 Va. 335, 38 S.E.2d 444 (1946), is the leading case on this position. *See also in re* Urbasek, 38 Ill. 2d 535, 232 N.E. 716 (1967); United States v. Costanzo, 395 F.2d 441 (4th Cir. 1968).

[126] *In re* Whittington, 391 U.S. 341 (1968), which raised the issue of standard of proof in a juvenile case, was remanded without opinion on the merits to the state court.

[127] *In re* Winship, 396 U.S. 885, 90 S. Ct. 1068 (1970).

not be considered; otherwise the court will be inclined to treat him not for what he did but for what he "is." Only at final disposition, the argument continues, should the juvenile's record be assessed in order to determine the future course of action. For these reasons it is urged that the hearing concerned with the determination of complicity should be totally separate from the hearing concerned with the disposition. "A two-step hearing seems essential to discourage the merging of jurisdictional facts, proof, and social data at the hearing. Separating the determination of jurisdiction and the truth of the allegations of the petition from a decision as to treatment makes somewhat easier the requirement of strict proof as to the former."[128] Yet a majority of courts do not observe these requirements.

Before making the disposition, the judge must determine the sufficiency of the allegations in the petition and be convinced of the youth's complicity beyond a reasonable doubt. Although juvenile judges do not pronounce a youth guilty, as is the case in criminal trials, a finding of "involvement"[129] is usually made. In most states—to stress the juvenile courts emphasis upon the delinquent rather than on his act—there is only a general finding of delinquency without specification of the particular misconduct. Some states, seeking to avoid criminal-type labeling, go even further in requiring that the court merely find that the child "is subject to its jurisdiction,"[130] without noting whether the child is delinquent, neglected, or dependent. But a California appellate court has raised a fundamental question about whether such semantic differentiations, allegedly intended to protect the child's reputation, have a true meaning in fact: "While the juvenile court law provides that adjudication of a minor to be a ward of the court shall not be deemed to be a conviction of crime, nevertheless, for all practical purposes, this is a legal fiction, presenting a challenge to credulity and doing violence to reason."[131]

The Ultimate Problem: Lack of Effective Dispositional Alternatives

The juvenile court judge is vested with broad discretion in disposing of cases since the juvenile statutes neither classify delinquent con-

---

[128] Elson, "Juvenile Courts and Due Process" 105–6.

[129] *See* National Council on Crime and Delinquency, Advisory Council of Judges, *Procedure and Evidence in the Juvenile Court* (1962).

[130] The recent District of Columbia Crime Commission recommends distinguishing between delinquent and other children. President's Commission on Crime in the District of Columbia, *Report* 687.

[131] *In re* Contreras, 109 Cal. App. 2d 787, 789, 241 P.2d 631, 633 (1962).

duct nor ascribe to it degrees of severity and specific dispositions, as is typical in criminal laws. The juvenile disposition, it was long ago postulated, must fit the child's needs, not his offense.

There are four principal methods of disposition in delinquency cases: dismissal, probation, foster-home placement, and commitment to a training school or similar juvenile institution.[132] Other sanctions are also possible, such as imposing fines and ordering the juvenile to make restitution of property or reparation for damages,[133] and other alternatives are available to judges, even in the absence of definite statutory provisions, within their broad authority to make any lawful disposition they deem necessary for the child's welfare. Some judges, allegedly for the purpose of avoiding the creation of juvenile records, also utilize the practice of so-called "unofficial case handling." The accused child in these cases is often released provisionally subject to informal court supervision. After the conclusion of the informal probationary period, the case will be officially dropped. But since the juvenile process was designed in the first place to relieve juveniles of a formal record and criminal identification, the very creation of this secondary informal system amounts to an admission of the juvenile court's failure to remove the criminal stigma from juvenile cases.[134]

More than half the juveniles brought to the attention of the nation's juvenile courts are disposed of informally, either by the intake staff or by the judge himself without a formal hearing. Of these, 8.2 percent are dismissed as not involved, 44 percent are released after being given a warning, 16 percent are placed under informal supervision, and the remaining 31 percent are exposed to a variety of other informal remedies. Of those whose cases receive formal judicial hearing, the following dispositions are reported: 8.2 percent dismissed as not involved, 10.8 percent released after a warning, 49 percent placed on probation, 20.8 percent committed to institutions, and 11.2 percent disposed of otherwise (including foster-home placement).[135]

In the case of minor first offenders, a warning and release are the usual disposition. Probation is more typically used for the second-time offenders or when the offense is more serious. Probation is the most common disposition when the court decides a disruption of the juvenile's home atmosphere or routine would serve no valid rehabilitative

---

[132] Sussman, *Juvenile Delinquency* 45; *see also* Standard Juvenile Court Act §4.

[133] Fradkin, "Disposition Dilemmas of American Juvenile Courts," in *Justice for the Child* 129–30 (M. K. Rosenheim ed. 1962).

[134] For a discussion of unofficial handling and the inherent dangers of abuse *see ibid.* 123–25.

[135] U.S. Department of Health, Education, and Welfare, *1964 Juvenile Court Statistics* 11.

purpose. It usually entails counseling visits to the child's home or the juvenile's reporting to a social worker assigned to supervise his rehabilitative progress. Foster-home placement is utilized mostly when the court determines that commitment to a special institution is too drastic a remedy, but decides nevertheless that the juvenile's home life is too disruptive and tends to jeopardize his chances for rehabilitation.[136] Foster home placement is especially common with children who are also found to be neglected and dependent. Institutional commitment, on the other hand, is described as reserved for the recidivists and hard-core offenders whose response to milder treatments is predictably unfavorable.[137]

The court is not precluded from informally amending or modifying its disposition at any time. The District of Columbia law thus authorizes the court "to make such further disposition of the child as may be provided by law and as the court deems to be for the best interests of the child."[138] A court may usually release a child from institutional custody to probationary status without a hearing. A more questionable practice, however, is that of committing to an institution, without a new hearing, a youth who had previously been placed on probation.

The only reasonable justifications for revoking a child's probationary status are that he has violated the terms of his probation, that new evidence has come to the attention of the court regarding his complicity in the original offense, or that the environment surrounding the child on probation has changed so that probation is no longer a viable disposition. In each of these situations a hearing before the court should be necessary to establish the alleged facts and to allow the child to challenge their truth. To commit a child who is on probation to an institution in the absence of such a hearing opens many possible avenues to abuse and error. The termination of probation, for example, may be founded upon a caseworker's report that the father has left the home environment and the child is therefore without strong male control—a requisite for his probation. But this report may be founded upon hearsay, or the absence may be only temporary. Similarly, if it is alleged that a child has violated the terms of his probation or was more deeply involved in the offense than shown at his adjudication, he should be allowed to challenge these new factual

[136] In the recent District of Columbia crime report, foster-home care in the community was strongly recommended over institutionalization. President's Commission on Crime in the District of Columbia, *Report* 731.

[137] An exhaustive compendium of avenues of disposition open to the courts, and their implications, may be found in U.S. Department of Health, Education, and Welfare, *Standards for Juvenile and Family Courts* 84–100.

[138] *D.C. Code Ann.* §16–2308(a)(3) (1966 Supp.).

findings before he is removed from probationary status and committed to an institution. In many states, this opportunity is often lacking, leaving the juvenile unable to protect himself against ill-founded or untrue allegations regarding his behavior and environment.

The most striking difference between most state laws and the provisions of the Standard Act concerns the length of commitment. Juveniles in the District of Columbia may be committed to a juvenile institution for an indeterminate period, but not beyond maturity. A youth fourteen years old who is formally committed to the National Training School for Boys can be held until age twenty-one, regardless of his particular offense. Since the commitment is expected to be responsive to the child's need rather than the severity of the offense, it is possible for a child to be committed and "treated" for several years for a minor offense. In the landmark *Gault* case, which will be discussed later, Gerald Gault was ordered committed until maturity on a charge of making lewd telephone calls, for which adults could be punished by a maximum of two months in jail.[139] To guard against such therapeutic excesses, the Standard Act provides that a commitment order is to remain in effect for no longer than three years, unless a petition is filed to extend it.[140] This approach thus seeks to impose some regular formula for timely review of commitment orders.

The juvenile court has never been the exclusive judicial tribunal for dealing with youthful offenders. A child may be subjected to the sanctions of the criminal law in lieu of the juvenile process by the juvenile court's waiver of jurisdiction. The great majority of states permit such a waiver if the youth is in the upper age brackets and charged with a grave offense; once jurisdiction is waived, he faces trial in criminal court as if he were an adult.[141] Many states have enacted waiver provisions similar to those of the Standard Juvenile Court Act. Under the Standard Act, a juvenile sixteen years of age or older charged with an act that would be a felony if committed by an adult may be certified for trial by the criminal court if after full investigation and a hearing the juvenile judge determines that the best interest of the child or the public requires such certification. No child under sixteen at the time of his alleged offense may be so certified.[142]

Waiver is a social reaction to the "bad seeds" among delinquent

---

[139] *In re* Gault, 387 U.S. 1 (1967).

[140] Standard Juvenile Court Act §24.

[141] Some states, including Colorado, even permit the juvenile court itself to commit a child over a certain age to any adult institution if his delinquency is chronic or amounts to the commission of a felony. *Colo. Rev. Stat.* §105–1–7 and §105–2–27 (1953).

[142] Standard Juvenile Court Act §13.

juveniles. It is a regression to the retributive motives of criminal law, an admission of the failure of therapeutic programs; often it is the ill and disturbed children, those in greatest need of special treatment, who are thus waived to the adult courts. Both the logic and criteria employed by many courts in determining whether jurisdiction over a juvenile should be waived are in conflict with the juvenile court philosophy.[143] Waiver can serve as a tool of repression:

> At first glance previous failure seems a reasonable ground for transfer, but it, too, is in conflict with juvenile court purposes and philosophy, since in effect it means that the court rejects any further attempt to treat the child. Such rejection implies either inadequacy of resources, for which the child is thus made to suffer, or a desire on the part of the court to avoid recording another failure....
>
> If the juvenile court feels powerless to help ... is the criminal court in a better position? .... It has been held [therefore] that the juvenile court is not justified in transferring a case, no matter how serious, to the criminal court unless the child's own good and the best interests of the state cannot be obtained by retention of jurisdiction....
>
> An illustration of transfer as punishment for a child's attitude came from a study in one state which found that "three counties engaged in the questionable practice of remanding youth to the criminal court for trial when the youth denies the allegations of the petition.... The threat of certification to the criminal court is also used in some instances to prevent a youth from asserting his rights."[144]

Because the process of waiver is so susceptible to abuses of due process, waiver was the first phase of the juvenile process to be scrutinized by the United States Supreme Court. In 1966 the court in *Kent* v. *United States*[145] specified that the due process clause of the Fifth Amendment and the Juvenile Court Act of the District of Columbia required that the juvenile court hold a hearing and state the basis for its decision prior to waiving jurisdiction. At the hearing the youth must be represented by counsel who is to have full access to the social files and all other records upon which the judge will base his decision. Implied in the court's opinion is the recognition that a youth faced

[143] National Council on Crime and Delinquency, "Transfer of Cases between Juvenile and Criminal Court: A Policy Statement by the Advisory Council of Judges," 8 *Crime and Delinquency* (1962).

[144] *Ibid.* 6, 7.

[145] 383 U.S. 541 (1966).

with waiver stands precariously between two entirely different systems of justice and that procedural safeguards are indispensable tools in seeking a disposition which is required by law to be best for the individual delinquent as well as for society.

As if to reassure all doubters of its nonpenal character, the Standard Act, as most other juvenile statutes, makes a final provision that no adjudication of delinquency, dependency, or neglect in juvenile court may operate to attach any criminal stigma to the juvenile's record. For this reason, restrictions are usually imposed upon public and media access to both juvenile court hearings and records.[146] How effective these provisions are in warding off inquiries about a juvenile's past is a question of grave importance. The understandable interests of the armed services, future employers, and law enforcement agencies are in direct conflict with the fundamental purpose of protecting the immature from social prejudgment based on past antisocial behavior. A 1953 study of the New York City Children's Court reported that representatives of the FBI, the Civil Service, the Army, the Red Cross, the Traveler's Aid Society, the Hack License Bureau, the Department of Public Welfare, and various other social agencies had free access to the court's legal records despite the usual statutory prohibition.[147] Legislation is needed that will require the expunging of juvenile records after a certain period of good behavior. Such procedure would not only be compatible with the fundamental philosophy of the juvenile court but would provide an additional incentive in the rehabilitation effort.

THE SUPREME COURT AND THE JUVENILE

In the 1966 *Kent* decision, in a case only tangentially touching the major problems of the juvenile process, the Supreme Court served notice that it was aware of the shortcomings of juvenile justice.[148]

While there can be no doubt of the original laudable purpose of juvenile courts, studies and critiques in recent years raise serious questions as to whether actual performance measures well enough against theoretical purpose to make tolerable the immunity of the process from the reach of constitutional guarantees applicable to

---

[146] Although access to juvenile court records has been restricted, the police still have complete discretion regarding their own release of juvenile information and the destruction of arrest records. Note, "Juvenile Delinquents" 775, 785.

[147] Kahn, *A Court for Children* 59–60.

[148] Kent v. United States, 383 U.S. 541 (1966).

adults. There is much evidence that some juvenile courts . . . lack the personnel, facilities, and techniques to perform adequately as representatives of the State in a *parens patriae* capacity, at least with respect to children charged with law violations.[149]

Following the notice of concern, the court, in the next term delineated in the *in re* Gault decision several minimum requirements of due process to be followed by juvenile courts.[150]

This milestone pronouncement resulted from the indeterminate incarceration in the Arizona State Industrial School of a fifteen-year-old youth charged with making a lewd phone call, an offense carrying a maximum penalty of a $50 fine or two months imprisonment for adults. On June 8, 1964, while on probation for being in the company of another juvenile who had stolen a wallet, Gerald Gault was taken into custody upon the verbal complaint of a neighbor that he had made an obscene telephone call. The authorities never advised Gault's parents of his "arrest." Upon learning of their son's detention from a neighbor, his mother inquired at the detention home and was cursorily advised of the charge by a probation officer named Flagg and was notified of the hearing to commence the next day. Since Arizona has no formal intake procedure, Probation Officer Flagg filed a petition reciting that "said minor is under the age of 18, and is in need of the protection of [the] Honorable Court; [and that] said minor is a delinquent minor."[151] This petition was never served upon Gault's parents, nor did it refer to any factual basis for the intervention of the court. At the initial hearing, in the judge's chambers, the complaining witness was not present; no record, transcript, or memorandum of the proceedings was made; nor was there any sworn testimony offered. There was, however, at this hearing a testimonial conflict as to whether Gault had made the alleged phone call. While the judge took the case under advisement, Gerald was kept in confinement for two or three days. On the day he was released, a note from Probation Officer Flagg, written upon plain paper, was received by Mrs. Gault: "Judge McGhee has set Monday, June 15, 1964, at 11:00 a.m. as the date and time for further Hearings on Gerald's delinquency."[152]

At the second hearing, the complaining witness was not present. When Mrs. Gault specifically requested the witness's presence, the judge informed her that it was not necessary. The judge himself had

[149] *Ibid.* 555–56.
[150] *In re* Gault, 387 U.S. 1 (1967).
[151] *Ibid.* 5.
[152] *Ibid.* 6.

never spoken to the complaining witness and the only communication with her was her telephoned complaint to Probation Officer Flagg. At the hearing a "referral report," in part authored by Probation Officer Flagg, was received by the court, although its existence was not made known to Gault or his parents. Upon this basis, Gerald was committed to the State Industrial School.

Gault's parents challenged the legality of his confinement and sought his release by a petition for a writ of habeas corpus, but the Superior Court of Arizona denied the writ, and the denial was affirmed by the Supreme Court of Arizona. Reversing the Arizona courts, the United States Supreme Court's opinion was expressly limited to the adjudicatory stage of the Arizona juvenile court process[153] in which the juvenile was found "involved" as charged—and did not consider any questions raised by the arrest, detention, and disposition of Gerald Gault.

The Right to Notice

The Supreme Court held that the notice given to Gerald and his parents was insufficient to comport with the minimal standards of due process. Specifically the court stated:

> Notice to comply with due process requirements must be given sufficiently in advance of scheduled court proceedings so that reasonable opportunity to prepare will be afforded, and it must "set forth the alleged misconduct with particularity."[154]

The aim of this notice requirement is to apprise the accused of the nature of the charge with sufficient particularity to enable him to prepare an adequate defense in subsequent court proceedings. The court further stated that written notice of either the specific charge or an allegation of facts supporting a charge would be sufficient.[155] If the grounds of the charge are the violation of a criminal statute or ordinance, then clearly the petition must set out either the specific offense charged or the facts that underlie the charge. This holding would apparently invalidate petitions alleging simply "delinquency," but it does not establish the substance of the notice required when the petition is grounded in those nebulous behavior patterns not tolerated in juveniles—"ungovernability," "incorrigibility," or "habitual immorality." From the court's opinion it would seem that a petition which "spe-

[153] *Ibid.* 13.
[154] *Ibid.* 33.
[155] *Ibid.*

cifically" alleges one of these inexact charges of conduct upon which a finding of delinquency could be based would meet the standard set out in *Gault*.

But does such a petition give adequate notice? Where there is a formal intake apparatus—for example, a staff conference with parents and child—the notice contained in the petition may be superfluous, since the specific facts involved have been made known to the parents. On the other hand, where there is no social work intake staff, a petition charging "ungovernability," although possibly comporting with the *Gault* standard, is not likely to give the parents or child sufficient notice upon which to build a defense.

The Right to Counsel

Until the *Gault* decision, the role of the attorney in juvenile court was at most precarious. Availability of counsel benefited from the general recognition that as notice is required for the preparation of a defense, so the right to counsel is necessary to effect that defense.[156] Since the prerogative of being defended in court by a skilled advocate has been identified with the need for protection from a prosecuting adversary and the juvenile court procedures were conceived to be therapeutic, nonadversary, and informal—there appeared to be no need for protection and, therefore, no need for a lawyer in the juvenile process.[157] Even where the right to counsel was acknowledged, the courts were not clear on the question of whether the right was constitutional or dependent upon statutory authority,[158] whether a juvenile had to be advised of this right, and whether counsel had to be provided if the youth lacked means to employ one.

In some states, however, the juvenile's need for counsel was recognized although unevenly satisfied by liberal courts. In a widely cited District of Columbia case,[159] the court concluded in 1956 that a juvenile could not intelligently exercise the protections granted by the

---

[156] *See* Gideon v. Wainwright, 372 U.S. 335 (1963).

[157] *In re* Custody of a Minor, 102 U.S. App. D.C. 94, 250 F.2d 419 (1957), a dependency proceeding in which the court held that since such a hearing was not "any kind of proceeding *against* the child," the right to counsel did not exist. Collateral to this right to counsel is the right of parents to be represented where there exists the threat that their child may be taken from their custody either in delinquency cases or in dependency or neglect hearings.

[158] Algase, "The Right to a Fair Trial in Juvenile Court," 3 *J. Fam. L.* 292, 302 (1963). A few states specifically recognized the right to counsel in juvenile court. *See, e.g., Ark. Stat. Ann.* §45–217 (1947); *Utah Code Ann.* §17–18–1(4) (1953). The Standard Juvenile Court Act is silent, as are the statutes of Maryland, Virginia, and the District of Columbia.

[159] Shioutakon v. District of Columbia, 236 F.2d 666 (D.C. Cir. 1956).

local statute (which specified the right to notice, a hearing, and jury trial) unless he was represented by counsel. By holding that the right to counsel was implied in the statute, the court avoided the question whether counsel was required by the Constitution.[160]

New York and California, the nation's two most populous states, similarly granted the right to counsel in juvenile court,[161] either on the basis of statutory interpretation or on the ground that a denial of counsel would preclude a fair trial. And while legal writers were in almost unanimous agreement that the right to counsel was an indispensable element of due process,[162] most states continued before *Gault* either to ignore the need or to resist it actively.

In *Gault* the Supreme Court held that the due process clause of the Fourteenth Amendment required that,

> . . . in respect of proceedings to determine delinquency which may result in commitment to an institution in which the juvenile's freedom is curtailed, the child and his parents must be notified of the child's right to be represented by counsel retained by them, or if they are unable to afford counsel, that counsel will be appointed to represent the child.[163]

Undeniably the right to counsel has been extended to the juvenile process, but to what extent? The finding of the right to counsel in *Gault* was conditioned upon "proceedings to determine delinquency which may result in commitment to an institution. . . ." Thus counsel is apparently not required in informal dispositions by the court's staff or in judicial cases which do not result in an institutional commitment. At what stage of the juvenile process the right commences, and by what manner a juvenile judge can predetermine a juvenile's forthcoming disposition in order to decide whether counsel's presence is required, are questions not illuminated by the *Gault* decision. The court no doubt was responding to the *parens patriae* foundation of the juvenile court which disavowed formalism and adversary contest in favor of individualized remedies for the immature.[164] The court's limited formulation of the right to counsel suggests, however, that when juvenile courts resort to institutionalization as the means to implement justice, their *parens patriae* motives become suspect in light

---

[160] *Ibid.* 667.

[161] People v. Dotson, 46 Cal. 2d 891, 299 P.2d 875 (1956); People v. James, 9 N.Y.2d 28, 172 N.E.2d 552, 211 N.Y.S.2d 170 (1961).

[162] *See, e.g.,* P. W. Tappan, *Juvenile Delinquency* (1949); Paulsen, "Fairness to the Juvenile Offender" 547; B. Fine, *1,000,000 Delinquents* (1955); Ketcham, "Legal Renaissance in Juvenile Court," 60 *Nw. U. L. Rev.* 590–98 (1965).

[163] *In re* Gault, 387 U.S. 41 (1967).

[164] *Ibid.* 14–15.

of the present incapacity of institutions to formulate individualized rehabilitative techniques.[165] *Gault*, therefore, extends counsel's protection to those proceedings where a special proclivity to subvert the *parens patriae* concept has been shown.

In attempting to project the effect of *Gault* upon the future presence of counsel in the juvenile court process, past patterns must not be overlooked. Although the right to counsel has been previously accorded juveniles in many of our large cities, attorneys have appeared only in an estimated five percent of all juvenile court cases.[166] This may be due, in part, to the general attitude of distrust toward attorneys by juvenile court judges.[167] Even among juvenile court judges who professed to welcome counsel, "their practice sometimes belied their words," a survey found.[168] This resistance to the attorney's presence in juvenile court may reasonably be expected to continue.[169] Since under the *Gault* holding counsel must be present at the adjudicatory stage of proceeding which may result in a commitment, it is likely that to justify absence of counsel courts will reach informal determinations not to commit a child prior to the adjudicatory stage. The *Gault* court was undoubtedly seeking to compel the juvenile judge to make an open, deliberate, and individualized assessment of the child's need for institutionalization as opposed to the other remedies available to the court:

> Under traditional notions, one would assume that in a case like that of Gerald Gault, where the juvenile appears to have a home, a working mother and father, and an older brother, the Juvenile

[165] *Ibid.* 27.

[166] Based on a survey of judges in the 75 largest cities in the United States. Note, "Juvenile Delinquents" 775, 796.

[167] A 1960 survey of California juvenile court judges disclosed judicial ambivalence regarding the contribution of counsel to the juvenile process and uncertainty as to whether juveniles and their parents should be advised of their right to consult with attorneys. On the value of attorneys in juvenile court, the judges' comments ranged from "[they] help families to understand procedures. Excellent go-between for parents and court" to "A few attorneys may help but generally they do not know anything about the juvenile court and mess things up." On the question of advising parents of the right to counsel, comments ran from "It is my practice to inform parents of the right" to "It is not necessary. Those who are interested trust the court; those who are hostile bring an attorney." California, Governor's Commission on Juvenile Justice, "Judges' Attitude toward Presence of Counsel," *Administration of Juvenile Justice in California*, pt. 2, p. 12 (1960).

[168] Note, "Juvenile Delinquents" 797.

[169] As of November 1967, however, approximately 50 percent of the children appearing before D.C. Juvenile Court requested and received representation by counsel. Haines, "Gault and the District of Columbia," 17 *Amer. U. L. Rev.* 153, 158 (1968).

Judge would have made a careful inquiry and judgment as to the possibility that the boy could be disciplined and dealt with at home, despite his previous transgressions.[170]

The final outcome, which calls practically for a predetermination of dispositions, may bring about even greater juvenile court reliance upon the child's social record than his present misdeed and a drawing of more formal lines in the juvenile process between serious delinquents and minor ones.

The Right to Confrontation

If counsel is the motivating force behind the effective exercise of constitutional safeguards, the rights of confrontation and cross-examination are his principal tools. Relying upon the juvenile court's professed paternal purpose, judges have often been reluctant to conduct the proceedings in a manner similar to regular trials requiring adherence to evidentiary standards such as sworn testimony, the prohibition of hearsay, confrontation of witnesses, etc. And, generally, courts have been free to adopt any procedure they consider desirable because they usually operate under broad statutory language which merely provides that the hearing is to be conducted in an informal manner.[171]

Those who support informality argue that "the hearing in the Juvenile Court may, in order to accomplish the purposes for which juvenile court legislation is designed, avoid many of the legalistic features of the rules of evidence. . . ."[172] Yet, the dangers engendered by the admission of hearsay and unsworn testimony in juvenile court are readily apparent.

An apprehended youth may attempt to relieve himself of responsibility by falsely ascribing blame to another. There may be inaccuracies in the offhand remarks of neighbors, teachers, and others who are asked to comment upon a youth's background and character to a case worker but who are not called upon to give sworn testimony subject to cross-examination before the court. The conclusion is therefore inescapable that "[h]earsay, opinion, gossip, bias, prejudice, trends of hostile neighborhood feelings, the hopes and fears of social workers,

---

[170] *In re* Gault, 387 U.S. 28 (1967).

[171] Standard Juvenile Court Act §19: "The hearings shall be conducted in an informal manner and may be adjourned from time to time."

[172] *In re* Holmes, 279 Pa. 599, 109 A.2d 523 (1954); *see*, however, Musmanno, J., dissenting.

are all sources of error and have no more place in children's courts than in any other court."[173]

Where the juvenile court employs the services of an intake staff, it is often their assessment, in the form of a social service record of the juvenile, that becomes the primary source of information at the time of the hearing. With the overwhelming caseload of most juvenile courts, the temptation is to accept the statements contained in this report as conclusive, without verifying or testing in court what may have been only arbitrary opinions. This temptation is made even more attractive in those jurisdictions which view the social service report as the court's property and withhold it from the scrutiny of child, family, or counsel.

Undertaking to cure some of these evidentiary defects, *Gault* held that, in the absence of a valid confession, a determination of delinquency and an order of commitment to a state institution cannot be sustained in the absence of sworn testimony subjected to the opportunity for cross-examination.[174]

The use of hearsay and unsworn testimony was not completely precluded. The court did not expressly hold that such testimony could not be considered by the judge in reaching his determination but only that there need be sufficient sworn testimony subject to cross-examination to support a determination of delinquency.[175] Thus the juvenile judge may continue using social service reports or other unsworn testimony as long as a minimum of constitutionally sanctioned evidence is properly before him.

Privilege against Self-incrimination

Because the Supreme Court has held that the rights of confrontation and cross-examination are conditioned upon the "absence of a valid confession," the juvenile court's ability to rely upon a juvenile's confession assumes major significance. A confession of involvement permits the court to proceed directly to the dispositional stage; the absence of such a confession requires an adjudicatory stage to deter-

[173] Paulsen, "Fairness to the Juvenile Offender" 547, 562; People v. Lewis, 260 N.Y. 171, 183 N.E. 353 (1932); Paulsen, "Jurisdiction of the Juvenile Court" 55. The leading case in the District of Columbia which upholds the minor's right to oppose introduction on hearsay or privileged evidence is *in re* Sippy, 97 A.2d 455 (D.C. Mun. Ct. App. 1953).

[174] *In re* Gault, 387 U.S. 1, 57 (1967).

[175] In administrative law a similar concept called the "residuum" rule has developed following the result of Carroll v. Knickerbocker Ice Co., 218 N.Y. 435, 113 N.E. 507 (1916).

mine delinquency, and the attachment of right to counsel, confrontation, and cross-examination as long as the threat of commitment exists.

The validity of confessions can be seriously affected, however, by the provisions of the constitutional privilege against self-incrimination.[176] As with other guarantees, the place of this privilege in the juvenile process has been ambiguous,[177] leaving uncertain two of its major manifestations.

Are confessions or other statements given by a youth without benefit of counsel competent in an adjudication of delinquency? Despite criticisms, the courts have usually been reluctant to exclude such self-incriminating statements, on the grounds that such an exclusionary rule would defeat the informal nature of juvenile court hearings.[178]

A second question goes to the crux of the self-incrimination clause: Should a juvenile in a delinquency hearing be required to testify against himself? Here again it has been argued that, since the aim of the court is rehabilitative and the objective of the proceeding is to ascertain all relevant information, there should be no harm in requiring the youth to testify if he is assured immunity from criminal prosecution for offenses revealed by his statements.[179] Accordingly, 38 states have specifically prohibited the use of a youth's juvenile court testimony in other tribunals.[180] Without such immunity, several cases have emphatically upheld the juvenile's privilege against self-incrimination. In *in re* Tahbel,[181] the court issued a writ of habeas corpus to a juvenile held in contempt for failing to answer a question on the basis that his constitutional right against self-incrimination had been vio-

---

[176] *U.S. Const.*, amend. V: "No person . . . shall be compelled in any criminal case to be a witness against himself. . . ."

[177] Algase, "Right to a Fair Trial" 298.

[178] The leading example is *in re* Holmes, 379 Pa. 599, 104 A.2d 523 (1954), the famous Pennsylvania case in which the court refused to reverse the juvenile court's finding, despite the fact that the youth was implicated largely by hearsay testimony. Most jurisdictions, such as California with *in re* Contreras, 109 Ca. App. 2d 787, 241 P.2d 631 (1952), hold that admission of hearsay and self-incriminating testimony operates unfairly against the accused. Accord: *in re* Mantell, 157 Neb. 900, 62 N.W.2d 308 (1954); *in re* Ballard, 192 S.W.2d 329 (Tex. Civ. App., 1946); *in re* Barkus, 168 Neb. 257, 95 N.W.2d 674 (1954).

[179] Paulsen, "Fairness to the Juvenile Offender" 547, 562.

[180] Sussman, *Juvenile Delinquency*. The District of Columbia, D.C. *Code Ann.* §16–2308 (1966 Supp.), and Maryland, *Md. Code Ann.* art. 26, §83(e) (1957), are included. Virginia has no specific statutory rule, but Kiracofe v. Commonwealth, 198 Va. 833, 97 S.E.2d 14 (1957), interpreted the Virginia statute, *Va. Code* §16.1–179 (1950), as having the same effect.

[181] 46 Cal. App. 755, 189 P. 804 (1920). Accord: People v. Lewis, 260 N.Y. 171, 183 N.E. 353 (1932). *See also* Dendy v. Wilson, 142 Tex. 460, 179 S.W. 2d 269 (1944).

lated. Until *Gault*, nevertheless, incriminating statements could generally be elicited and used in juvenile court proper so long as the juvenile was totally immune from later criminal prosecutions based upon such incriminating revelations. The Supreme Court, however, subscribed to the theory that, because juvenile commitment was so akin to penal sanctions, the Constitution demanded the assurance of the privilege whenever the child faced the possibility of commitment:

> ... Juvenile proceedings to determine "delinquency," which may lead to commitment to a state institution, must be regarded as "criminal" for purposes of the privilege against self-incrimination. ... For this purpose, at least, commitment is a deprivation of liberty. It is incarceration against one's will, whether it is called "criminal" or "civil." And our Constitution guarantees that no person shall be compelled to be a witness against himself when he is threatened with deprivation of his liberty. . . .[182]

Prohibiting the compulsory testimony of children, *Gault* does not require the presence of counsel to guarantee that a confession is voluntary.[183] But it makes clear that coerced confession obtained from a child who is not aware of his right to keep silent or acts out of suggestion, fright, or despair will be inadmissible in court. The greatest care must therefore be taken to assure that confessions obtained from juveniles are voluntary and not given by those ignorant of their rights.[184]

The Limits of Gault

Important as the *Gault* case is, it cannot be regarded as a panacea for the ills of the juvenile court. Indeed, it is significant that some of the fundamental guarantees of *Gault* are already being eroded. There has been in several states a rush to develop waiver forms whereby juveniles before the court are asked to waive the right to counsel, the right to be informed of the charges, the right to remain silent, the right to face and cross-examine his accusers, and the right to receive

---

[182] *In re* Gault, 387 U.S. 1, 49–50 (1967).

[183] In *Gault* the court was obviously seeking to be less restrictive upon the means for protecting the privilege against self-incrimination than it was in Miranda v. Arizona, 384 U.S. 436, 444 (1966). In *Miranda* the court relied almost exclusively upon counsel's presence during interrogations. Judge Ketcham of the District of Columbia Juvenile Court, however, predicts that the *Miranda* doctrine will be used to guarantee the propriety of a juvenile's confession. Ketcham, "Guidelines from Gault: Revolutionary Requirements and Reappraisal," 53 *Va. L. Rev.* 1700 (1967).

[184] *In re* Gault, 387 U.S. 1, 55 (1967).

due notice of the court hearing.[185] Legally, the validity of such waivers by an immature child is highly questionable unless sufficient mental capacity and a total lack of compulsion are demonstrated. What is especially appalling, however, is the very attempt to take away safeguards which were only recently recognized by the United States Supreme Court as requisites for the proper functioning of juvenile justice.

The *Gault* decision itself is circumscribed by severe internal limitations. First, the newly recognized safeguards are applicable only to the court's adjudicatory proceeding and only when a determination of delinquency may result in commitment. Thus, the right to notice, to counsel, to confrontation, and to cross-examination do not apply in either the intake or dispositional stages. But because it is often the intake officers who determine whether a child should be brought before the court for an adjudicatory hearing, developments significant to the child may occur at the intake stage without his being afforded the necessary safeguards.[186]

Similarly, once the child has been adjudicated delinquent, the rights guaranteed him by the Supreme Court are inapplicable. In the hearing to decide his disposition, there is no restriction upon the use of hearsay, no requirement of sworn testimony, no right to counsel. Yet in this dispositional stage the future of the juvenile is most vulnerable to an ill-considered exercise of judicial powers.

> The disposition can range from an admonition followed by a reunion with parents, to commitment in an institution not greatly different from a prison. Surely, the information on which such a decision is taken ought to be carefully gathered and dispassionately evaluated. The process of disposition in the juvenile court must meet a standard of fairness, and that standard requires as a minimum that casework reports be made available to the child's lawyer upon request.... How can we insure fairness in disposition without some way of testing the basis for decision, and how can we test without knowing what ought to be tested? Can we be content by trusting the professional discipline of the social worker alone?[187]

---

[185] Irving, "Juvenile Justice" 1, 8.

[186] In some jurisdictions intake officers have limited powers to adjust cases informally. *See* N.Y. Fam. Ct. Act §734(a) (ii) (McKinney 1963), implemented by N.Y. Fam. Ct. Rule 7.3 (McKinney 1963). Insofar as these adjustments are evidence of offensive behavior, they may be considered as adjudications. Still, the guarantees accorded in *Gault* apparently do not apply.

[187] Paulsen, "Fairness to the Juvenile Offender" 567.

Unquestionably, the *Gault* limitation of procedural rights to the adjudicatory phase severely inhibits their protective nature.[188] The limitation results from the Supreme Court's striking a conciliatory posture between the protagonists and the antagonists of the existing juvenile court system. The ultimate argument of the critics had been that commitment without traditional due process is unconscionable. The supporters countered by arguing that formalities required by due process would adulterate the therapeutic nature of the court.

The Supreme Court has attempted to satisfy both sides. It has invalidated commitments in cases where due process was not accorded in the adjudicatory stage, but it has left the juvenile court free to order other dispositions without traditional procedural safeguards.[189] In so doing, the Court has chosen the deprivation of liberty characteristic of commitment as the fulcrum upon which the diverse interests are to be balanced. In reality, however, institutional commitment is fast falling from favor in the therapeutic state. Instead, more emphasis is being placed upon extra-institutional supervisory techniques allowing an individual to acclimate himself gradually to the demands of social responsibility. Thus, the Court's choice of commitment and deprivation of liberty as the focal points of traditional due process is at least a tacit approval of these other dispositional avenues available to juvenile courts. If the decision acts to reduce the attractiveness of commitment as an efficient social remedy, the use of the protections availed in *Gault* should correspondingly decrease, leaving the juvenile process virtually unscathed by its encounter with the Constitution.

The "Unavailable" Rights

In its search for an accommodation between the informal discretion of the *parens patriae* process and the recognized safeguards required when denial of liberty is involved, the *Gault* decision has left numerous constitutional questions unanswered. Several guarantees accorded to adults facing criminal prosecution consequently remain unavailable to juveniles.

[188] Judge Ketcham suggests a total and significant bifurcation of the adjudicatory and dispositional stages. In the latter, he would allow counsel to examine the data collected by the social service staff and to explore alternative dispositional avenues. Ketcham, "Guidelines from Gault" 1717.

[189] One recent exception has been the requirement that a juvenile's involvement in all cases be established beyond a reasonable doubt. *In re* Winship, 396 U.S. 885, 90 S. Ct. 1068 (1970).

The right to be released on bail pending a determination of delinquency is one of these.[190] Juveniles are often detained prior to a hearing of their case without benefit of bond, even though "[i]t would be unthinkable to urge that a legislature could circumvent the constitutional right to bail where it exists by the simple expedient of labelling the proceedings 'non-criminal,' and yet this is, in effect, what the courts are permitting in denying the applicability of the constitutional bail clauses to children incarcerated by juvenile authorities in advance of their hearings."[191]

There is no statutory provision governing bail for children in any jurisdiction, despite judicial assertions that the laws which create juvenile courts cannot operate to take away a child's constitutional right to bail.[192]

Although a small number of courts recognize the constitutional right to bail, the weight of judicial opinion remains opposed to the strict availability of the right in juvenile courts.[193] In a recent decision, *Fulwood* v. *Stone*,[194] the Court of Appeals for the District of Columbia held it unnecessary, however, to determine whether there is a constitutional right to bail in juvenile proceedings, finding that an adequate substitute for bail was provided by the Juvenile Court Act, which allows the pre-adjudicatory release of a child upon the written promise of the parent, guardian, or custodian to bring the child to the court at the designated time. When such assurance is lacking, the act requires that the court secure for the child "custody, care, and discipline as nearly as possible equivalent to that which should have been given him by his parents."[195] The D.C. Receiving Home where the youngsters are detained was characterized in a recent study as hardly equivalent to the ordinary home environment.[196]

Another flagrant exception to the trend of according juveniles greater safeguards—comparable to the rights accorded adults in crimi-

[190] *U.S. Const.*, amend. VIII.

[191] Antieau, "Constitutional Rights in Juvenile Courts," 46 *Cornell L. Q.* 387 (1961).

[192] "Tribunals of this nature were established with the view of showing more consideration to the juvenile and were not designed to deprive him of any of his constitutional rights." State v. Franklin, 202 La. 439, 12 S.2d 211 (1943).

[193] *Ex parte* Espinosa v. Price, 144 Tex. 121, 188 S.W.2d 576 (1945); *in re* Magnuson, 110 Cal. App. 2d 73, 242 P.2d 362 (1952); State v. Fullmer, 76 Ohio App. 335, 62 N.E.2d 268 (1945); Rubin, "Protecting the Child in the Juvenile Court," 43 *J. Crim. L.C. & P.S.* 425, 443 (1952).

[194] 394 F.2d 939 (1967).

[195] *D.C. Code Ann.* §16–2316 (1967).

[196] President's Commission on Crime in the District of Columbia, *Report* 665–76.

nal trials[197]—involves the constitutional protection against double jeopardy, prohibiting a second prosecution or punishment for the same offense.[198] "[W]ith the discussion of double jeopardy in juvenile courts, we plunge back into one of the gloomiest topics in the whole field of juvenile court law."[199] Often this important constitutional protection is circumvented in cases involving juveniles. A juvenile may thus be adjudicated delinquent in juvenile court and committed to a juvenile facility; he may then be tried in criminal court for the same offense, or a related one.[200] *In re* Smith[201] involved a youth adjudged delinquent for repeated acts of sexual intercourse and committed to a state juvenile institution. Subsequently brought before the criminal court for the same offense, he was sentenced to 60 days in the workhouse. After serving this sentence he was recommitted to the juvenile institution. A plea of double jeopardy was rejected by the court, which reasoned that Smith had been punished only once, since his time in the juvenile institution was therapeutic and not punitive.[202]

Maryland's leading case of double jeopardy[203] concerned a youth who could not "adjust" to the institution to which the juvenile court had committed him. As a result, he was taken before the adult criminal court to stand trial again for the offense upon which his delinquency commitment was predicated. The court's elusive logic: because the juvenile court was not a criminal court, the youth could not be "jeopardized" by the proceeding in juvenile court. A similar North Dakota case concerns a youth who was tried several times in juvenile court for the same offense.[204]

The late Judge Holtzoff declared in *United States* v. *Dickerson*:[205]

Ineluctable logic leads to the conclusion that the constitutional protection against double jeopardy ... is applicable to all proceedings, irrespective of whether they are denominated criminally

[197] *See, e.g., in re* Contreras, 109 Cal. App. 2d 787, 241 P.2d 631 (1952).

[198] *U.S. Const.*, amend. V: ". . . nor shall any person be subject for the same offense to be twice put in jeopardy of life or limb."

[199] Algase, "Right to a Fair Trial" 315.

[200] People v. Silverstein, 121 Cal. App. 2d 140, 262 P.2d 656 (1953); *in re* Dearing v. State, 151 Tex. Crim. App. 6, 204 S.W.2d 983 (1947). (A 16-year-old boy committed murder. He was "kept on ice" in a reformatory on a prior burglary charge until he was old enough to be indicted in criminal court for murder.)

[201] 114 N.Y.S.2d 673 (1952).

[202] But *cf.* an account of the squalid, nonrehabilitative conditions prevalent in the facilities in the District of Columbia in *Washington Post*, July 26, 1966.

[203] Moquin v. State, 216 Md. 524, 140 A.2d 914 (1958).

[204] State v. Smith, 75 N.D. 29, 25 N.W.2d 270 (1946).

[205] 168 F. Supp. 899 (D.D.C. 1958).

or civil, if the outcome may be deprivation of liberty of the person. Previous constitutional rights cannot be diminished or whittled away by the device of changing names of tribunals or modifying the nomenclature of legal proceedings. The test must be the nature and the essence of the proceeding rather than its title. If the result may be a loss of personal liberty, the constitutional safeguards apply.[206]

Unfortunately, this decision was reversed on technical grounds,[207] and the denial of the protection against double jeopardy in juvenile court remains another sad commentary on the supremacy of labels over substance in the juvenile court process.[208]

The recent Ohio case of *in re* Whittington demonstrates how waiver provisions, permitting juvenile courts to relinquish jurisdiction over certain serious cases, can place a juvenile in jeopardy in both the juvenile court and the criminal court. Whittington was arrested and brought before the juvenile court on a charge of murdering a neighbor. After a hearing which raised constitutional questions about the standard of proof to be carried by the state (whether the civil requisite of "preponderance of evidence" or the criminal standard of "beyond a reasonable doubt"), he was adjudged a delinquent. After the state appellate courts upheld this finding,[209] the juvenile court disposed of the case by turning Whittington over to the adult criminal court, and a grand jury indicted him for first degree murder. Having been found delinquent by the juvenile court, and subject to its sanctions, Whittington was also to be tried as an adult. Would he still be a delinquent child and subject to treatment by the juvenile court if the criminal court acquitted him of the charge?

The questions raised in the *Whittington* case will not soon be authoritatively answered, due to another flaw in the juvenile court system—the lack of standards to govern appeals from orders of juvenile courts. Few jurisdictions prescribe clear procedures and rules for this. Whittington appealed from the initial delinquency order to the state appellate courts which found that the order was final and appealable; they also affirmed the order on the merits.[210] Whittington then appealed to the United States Supreme Court through a petition for

---

[206] *Ibid.* 901.

[207] United States v. Dickerson, 271 F.2d 487 (D.C. Cir. 1959).

[208] Sheridan, "Double Jeopardy and Waiver in Juvenile Delinquency Proceedings," 23 *Fed. Prob.* 43 (1959).

[209] *In re* Whittington, 13 Ohio App. 2d 11, 233 N.E.2d 333 (1967).

[210] *Ibid.*

certiorari; the petition was granted.[211] Before the case was heard by the Supreme Court, the juvenile court entered its disposition order waiving Whittington to the criminal court. Learning of this development and uncertain of the effect the disposition order had on the issues before it, the Supreme Court remanded the case to the state courts for a further ruling.[212] In a complete reversal, the Ohio Court of Appeals held that a delinquency finding without a disposition order was not final and therefore not appealable.[213] The waste of resources and time, together with the effect that such a mire of procedural uncertainty can have on a juvenile, urgently require that the conditions surrounding appellate procedures be defined carefully[214] and that the right to appeal be given equal attention with the other rights not available to juveniles.

Now that the Supreme Court of the United States in *Kent*, in *Gault*, and in *Winship* has addressed itself three times in as many years to the constitutional issues raised by the juvenile process, the prospects for the future are becoming clearer. The differentiation between criminal and juvenile process will no longer hold off the extension of adult safeguards to juvenile proceedings. But today both the *Kent* and *Gault* decisions remain restricted in application. *Kent* deals exclusively with waivers to adult courts and *Gault* is limited to the youth's rights at the adjudicatory hearing and only in those cases where commitment may result. *In re* Winship deals exclusively with the burden of proof to be applied. Unaffected is the whole range of the juvenile process prior and subsequent to the judicial stage. Unresolved are the substantive questions about vagueness of criteria governing juvenile offenses,[215] about the standards of arrest and search for juveniles, the right to bail, to grand jury indictment, and to jury trial.[216] Equally

[211] *Ibid.* 389 U.S. 819 (1967).

[212] *Ibid.* 391 U.S. 341 (1968).

[213] To conserve judicial effort, the Ohio court consolidated the remand from the Supreme Court with an appeal from the disposition order of the juvenile court. It held that the disposition could not be supported by the facts brought out in the hearing and remanded all phases of the case to the juvenile court for further proceedings. *In re* Whittington, 13 Ohio App. 2d 164, 245 N.E.2d 364 (1969).

[214] *See* Ketcham, "What Happened to Whittington?" 37 *Geo. Wash. L. Rev.* 324, 331–32 (1968). Ketcham also argues that *Whittington* demonstrates the impracticality of according rights at one stage of the proceedings but denying them at others. *Ibid.* 332.

[215] The Supreme Court was to address these questions in Matiello v. Connecticut, 395 U.S. 209 (1968).

[216] The Supreme Court recently held that the Sixth Amendment does not require trial by jury in state juvenile delinquency proceedings. McKeiver v. Pennsylvania, 9 Cr. L. 3234 (June 21, 1971).

uncertain is whether a juvenile is entitled to protection against double jeopardy, to assistance of counsel during a police interrogation, and to access and opportunity to respond to all incriminating evidence. To the degree that the denial of any traditional rights increases the hazards of the juvenile's exposure to dispositions and sanctions that are substantially criminal, the future extension of adult safeguards by our courts can be predicted.

IS THERE A SUBSTITUTE FOR DUE PROCESS?

The juvenile court was heralded 71 years ago as an experiment for the reformation of offenders: emphasizing rehabilitation rather than punishment for youthful delinquents and relying on procedures radically different from those of the criminal process. Today this early model of *parens patriae*—by virtue of its previous successes and failures—might well aid in assessing the future promise of new and untried therapeutic programs; but any realistic assessment cannot escape the fact that while the juvenile process attempts to employ increasing community resources and a greater number of sociopsychological aids to remedy delinquency at its roots, the public, in large part, continues to look to this and to any other innovative programs primarily for a more effective accomplishment of the traditional aims of criminal justice—protection for the community.

The juvenile court process has long suffered from an irresolvable ambivalence of the two postures available to it. Either the administering tribunal is a "court" with a "judge," legal procedures, legal safeguards, and legal solutions, or it is a board of social assistance which dispenses economic, educational, sociological, and psychological remedies apart from any legal compulsion. Our juvenile courts are torn by the desire to achieve much of the latter posture while having to operate within the framework of the former. Dean Paulsen of the University of Virginia urges that the juvenile court "is not in point of fact a clinic, a school, or a studio. It is a court operated by legal rules and legal standards. This statement will surprise no one, but it deserves to be underscored. The juvenile court, whatever its aims may be, exists as a law court with all the connotations appropriate to such an institution."[217] This reassertion of the court's legal role is especially relevant

[217] Paulsen, "The Juvenile Court and the Whole of the Law," 11 *Wayne L. Rev.* 597, 598 (1965).

in the light of the growing recognition that considerations of public protection weigh heavily in the juvenile court determination vis-à-vis the rehabilitative ideal. "Despite the emphasis on *parens patriae* aims, the juvenile court possesses the power to deprive a youth of his liberty and to separate child and family; there is in fact a stigma attached to a juvenile court adjudication of delinquency."[218]

Even so, the juvenile court's role is not generally conceived as merely or typically legal. The juvenile court is not only the tribunal to which serious delinquency cases are referred but often the central clearing house for all juvenile problems in the community. With communities lacking specialized youth welfare services, both the police and the juvenile court participate in a host of situations involving education, welfare, and home discipline, along with strict delinquency questions.

The court's operation as a welfare institution, however, has never been evaluated in detail. Writers are usually content to theorize that "juvenile justice should be a mixture of adequate legal disposition and advanced social welfare practice."[219] Grygier, a Canadian criminologist, has formulated a more penetrating analysis of the nature of the juvenile court:

> Despite its chancery procedure, the juvenile court is not *just* a welfare agency, and it is a criminal rather than a civil court. At the same time, it is more a welfare agency than is any other court, although all criminal and civil courts have some welfare functions. The question is not whether the juvenile court is a court, but whether the aspects of criminal procedure or the aspects of the administration of welfare should prevail, to what extent they should prevail, and under what circumstances.[220]

Legal standards and social welfare precepts are not always compatible. Because offender rehabilitation is purportedly the primary aim of the juvenile system, each youth must be treated according to his particular needs. Yet traditional legal process has emphasized "equal protection" and equal justice.

Two boys attempt a theft from a five and ten.[221] They are apprehended. One boy comes from a stable home and has no previous record; the other has a record of similar offenses and comes from an unstable home. Both boys have committed the same act. Should they

---

[218] Jones v. Commonwealth 185 Va. 335, 38 S.E.2d 444, 447 (1946).

[219] Yablonsky, "The Role of Law and Social Science in the Juvenile Court," 53 *J. Crim. L.C. & P.S.* 426–36 (1962).

[220] Grygier, "Concept of the 'State of Delinquency' " 627, 637.

[221] Paulsen, "The Juvenile Court" 601.

be accorded equal justice under the law or is society better served by nonequal treatment? The purely legal solution would nullify the rehabilitative nature of the juvenile process either by imposing social sanctions upon one who does not require them, or by withholding treatment from one who needs it.[222]

Admitting the need for inequality of treatment and broad discretion on the part of the juvenile court, the question of how we are to safeguard against abuses becomes even more pressing. Abuses may result from a court's assigning greater weight to considerations of public protection than to the child's rehabilitation, excessive therapeutic zeal, the inability of families to assume their legitimate burdens, and from a corresponding willingness to abdicate their responsibility in favor of the state. Because juvenile facilities and treatment may differ from adult penalties in nomenclature only, different dispositions may be in fact nothing more than unjust and disparate sentences.

In challenging the need for due process in the juvenile system, it will not suffice to assert that within the therapy-oriented juvenile proceedings the interests of the individual and of society will harmonize. The Michigan statute typically postulates that the law shall be liberally construed to advance "... the child's welfare and the best interest of the state...."[223] Dean Francis Allen of the University of Michigan cogently questions this statutory invocation:

> Are these objectives in all cases the same? Are there instances in which the best interests of the community, if not inconsistent with the welfare of the child, are at least to some degree separate and distinct? Is it possible that the traditional view of the court as exclusively or largely a therapeutic or rehabilitative agency has obstructed identification of areas of legitimate community interest that the court may properly be expected to serve?[224]

To Professor Joel Handler of the University of Wisconsin the conflict between child and society is unreal:

> The delinquent ... is not the enemy of society. He is society's child, and, therefore, the interests of the state and the child do not conflict but coincide. Since the interests coincide there is no need for the criminal adversary adjudicatory procedure. The juvenile court, as a parent, is only concerned with trying to find out what can be done on the adolescent's behalf. The issues are

[222] Considerations of the rehabilitative need are becoming more important in the exercise of the judge's sentencing power in the adult criminal process as well.
[223] *Mich. Stat. Ann.* §27.3178 (598.1) (1962).
[224] Allen, "The Juvenile Courts and the Limits of Juvenile Justice," 11 *Wayne L. Rev.* 676, 680 (1965), reprinted from Allen, *Borderland of Criminal Justice.*

not criminal responsibility, guilt and punishment, but understanding, guidance and protection.[225]

But even Professor Handler recognizes the need for constructive reform in the fact-finding phase of the juvenile process. Despite his belief that the disposition of the child should be free from adversary conflict, he asserts that it is appropriate for the decision-maker to remain uncommitted until both the state and juvenile have presented their stories. He advocates, therefore, the imposition of adversary procedures at the pre-disposition stages, with the court dividing into three types of services and staff: investigation, defense, and hearing.[226] This diversification would release the juvenile court staff, which has often been compelled to present both sides of a case, of their multifunctional burdens. Furthermore, careful separation of the various phases of the juvenile process, and the resulting division of responsibility for these phases, would alleviate abuses caused by the overconcentration of power in a single administrative staff.

A similarly motivated proposal has been advanced by Professor Remington of the University of Wisconsin.[227] For the nonjudicial phases of the juvenile process, he recommends a "self-imposed administrative due process" as a workable alternative to reliance upon traditional safeguards which may interfere with the desired administrative flexibility. His proposal is deeply rooted in the premise that only through the upgrading of the quality and quantity of personnel in the juvenile area and the facilitation of self-imposed standards might we avoid the sterility that would result from inflexible legislatively imposed controls.[228]

The Fear of Undue Due Process

Some of the most dedicated supporters of the juvenile court continue to see the concern for the absence of traditional safeguards as

---

[225] Handler, "The Juvenile Court and the Adversary System" 7, 10.

[226] *Ibid.* 41–44. The adverse effects of nondifferentiated responsibilities by the same administrative staff are described by Elson, "Juvenile Courts and Due Process" 95.

[227] Remington, "Due Process" 688. Interesting sidelights to this question are to be found in Sloane, "The Juvenile Court: An Uneasy Partnership of Law and Social Work," 5 *J. Fam. L.* 170, 177 (1965). Sloane questions the "court and/or Agency" status of the present-day juvenile court, finds the problem totally unresolved, and suggests examining the experience of other countries. He quotes Dean Roscoe Pound as advocating the juvenile court's role as a judicial tribunal rather than as an administrative agency.

[228] Remington, "Due Process" 696.

misplaced. Judge Paul Alexander of Ohio, one of the foremost leaders in the juvenile area, views much of the constitutional Bill of Rights as not readily fitting in the picture of the juvenile courts.[229] He pleads instead for the "supra-constitutional" rights of children—those social, moral, economic, and other needs which are fundamental and "natural" for a child's healthy growth.

> The moment we insist upon affording children, whether in home, school, civic and legal matters, or court, all constitutional liberties, rights and safeguards afforded to adults, we open the door to a number of undesirable and potentially dangerous factors; so that, instead of protecting the child, as is our honest intention, we may be doing him a disservice, an injustice. Justice to a child must be more than due process of law and fair legal treatment. No abstract right can be as sacred as a human child.[230]

However well intentioned this view may be, to grant every juvenile court the discretion to disregard constitutional guarantees and to substitute instead the judge's and staff's personal concepts of "natural rights" could produce much uncertainty if not conscious abuse. Inescapably, as long as the court possesses the power of compulsion and remains "permeated by the philosophy of criminal law and criminal prosecution," the juvenile court must also accept and live with most of the traditional safeguards of due process.[231]

The growing introduction of procedural safeguards has increased

---

[229] Alexander, "Constitutional Rights in Juvenile Court," 46 *A.B.A.J.* 1206, 1207 (1960).

[230] *Ibid.* 1210.

[231] An *amicus curiae* brief filed with the United States Supreme Court in the *Gault* case urged that:

1. No system of social sanctions, however designated, which is authorized to deprive a person of his freedom and to separate him from his family can be exempt from constitutional safeguards.

2. Our constitutional precepts do not allow for the existence of two systems for dispensing justice: one legal and the other extra-legal.

3. The adversary system of justice, however criticized and modified, still remains the best guaranty for maintaining the necessary balance between societal and individual interests, and continues to afford the best protection against inequity and the abuse of discretion.

4. The absence of counsel deprives the child of needed protection while equally removing from society, which pays the bill, an important auditing and scrutiny device to protect against inadequate and socially wasteful dispositions.

5. Depriving children of legal safeguards available to adults is not only objectionable from a constitutional point of view, but tends also to adversely affect their development toward responsible adult citizenship.

6. Our concept of justice has traditionally emphasized procedural guaranties over human discretion, adversary process over inquisitorial justice. While the

the fear of a return to old-fashioned criminal justice. To some the new reforms are threatening to turn the juvenile court into a legalistic circus in which legal counsel, utilizing the techniques of the criminal defense, advises his juvenile client: "Don't admit a thing, let them prove it against you!" Certainly the court's rehabilitative aims will gravely suffer if the youthful offender is given the impression early in life that he can "beat the rap" of social responsibility with the aid of his counsel's technical skills and the newly accorded procedural rights. Today's youthful offender, several criminological studies indicate, is often tomorrow's criminal.[232] Thus, those seeking to expand the availability of legal services in the juvenile court must shoulder a dual burden: to accord the child his constitutional safeguards while guarding against a diminution of the child's sense of social responsibility, so that the child who requires treatment in his own and in society's interest is not merely turned loose to become the eventual victim of Pyrrhic courtroom victories.[233]

It has been noted that the delinquent child often manifests a lack of respect for law because he fails to comprehend or identify with the values it represents.[234] The attorney in the juvenile process, therefore, may have a broader role than merely being the juvenile's courtroom representative. Counsel, because he might be "the first law figure who has performed a helpful function"[235] for the youth, may also be able to help reform his client's view of the legal system and to affect the juvenile's future conduct. Learning from the preventive rather than the adversary role previously developed by lawyers working in the planning of corporate activities, there is no reason why juvenile counsel could not similarly help his client avoid future controversies through legal counseling.[236] This calls for a restructuring of the at-

---

institution of additional safeguards in the juvenile court will require more staff and the expenditure of time—these are the expected costs of American justice. Brief for the American Parents Committee as Amicus Curiae 8, 9; *in re* Gault, 387 U.S. 1 (1967).

[232] Fifty-one percent of the convicted adult offenders in the United States District Court for the District of Columbia had prior criminal records, including 72 percent of the robbers, 69 percent of the rapists, and 70 percent of the auto thieves. President's Commission on Crime in the District of Columbia, *Report* 138.

[233] Alexander, "Constitutional Rights" 89.

[234] Holton, "Prevention of Delinquency through Legal Counseling: A Proposal for Improved Juvenile Representation," 68 *Colo. L. Rev.* 1080, 1082 (1968).

[235] Paulsen, "The Expanding Horizons of Legal Services II," 67 *W. Va. L. Rev.* 267, 276 (1965).

[236] It has been suggested that counsel could play a positive rehabilitative role by providing friendly advice to the juvenile on the demands and imperatives of the law and suggesting voluntary rehabilitative efforts by parents through private or public community institutions. Holton, "Prevention of Delinquency" 1080.

torney's function and the acquisition of new skills and sensitivities. Such efforts toward the development of new roles for counsel laboring in the *parens patriae* realms might certainly advance the reformation of juvenile justice.[237] If the judge can be viewed as fulfilling a paternal role, is it not possible to expand counsel's brotherly function?

The Unfulfilled Promise of "Treatment"

Important as they are in safeguarding against abuse, the reforms of the juvenile court criteria and procedures will be of little avail in making the rehabilitative promise come true as long as the means, the personnel, the talents, and public support necessary to accomplish the regeneration of delinquent juveniles remain lacking.

By their very nature, the powers exercised by the juvenile court process from intake to disposition are negative powers. Although they can effect a change in a juvenile's life by severing him from his roots, they cannot guarantee that he will receive the treatment and community reception that he allegedly needs. Unfortunately, courts "have very little positive power to give damaged young people what they really need—to be wanted in a happy home, to find socially acceptable satisfaction in the neighborhood, to get along well in school and work and to have friends."[238]

The juvenile judge, without special training, is not necessarily competent to mete out the social and therapeutic programs for a child's rehabilitation. Recommendations have been advanced for specialized interdisciplinary boards that will assume responsibility for disposition once the judicial finding of involvement has been made. "It is ... argued that courts can serve best by functioning in their traditional role, that of determining whether or not the state under the doctrine of *parens patriae* should assume protective jurisdiction.... [Once this happens] youngsters could ... be referred to functionally autonomous treatment centers with power to render the full range of disposition decisions, including probation."[239] The concept and practice of placing disposition in the hands of behavioral science experts is neither new nor unique.[240] This country continues to exhibit, however, an accep-

---

[237] There is a definite need for a reassessment of counsel's role in all the *parens patriae* type proceedings. Disagreement has been growing between judges and lawyers as to how much of the attorney's adversary role should be allowed in the juvenile process. 17 *Juvenile Judges Journal* 125 (1967).

[238] Younghusband, "Dilemma of the Juvenile Court," 10, 18.

[239] Fradkin, "Disposition Dilemmas" 135.

[240] The drafters of the Model Youth Correction Authority Act, originally adopted by the five states, assumed that while guilt or innocence should be

tance of judicial sentencing, even though almost one-fourth of the nation's 2,800 juvenile court judges are not trained in the *law* and more than half devote less than one-fourth of their time to juvenile and family matters.[241]

If the child has a discernible problem and is truly in need of help, he could be in the worst straits of all. The inefficacy of the rehabilitative promise is illustrated by a recent five-month study of juvenile cases in affluent suburbs of Washington, D.C.:[242]

A 15-year-old girl who had threatened suicide several times and was judged in need of hospitalization at the age of 9, hanged herself in Arlington Jail after the court there had made several unsuccessful attempts to place her in a hospital.

An unmarried pregnant 15-year-old was placed with delinquents in the Bon Air School for Girls, the Virginia training school, after the juvenile court refused her request to get married instead.

A 9-year-old with a history of arson and emotional trouble and in need of psychiatric care was sent to stay with his grandparents in New York when psychiatric care could not be found for him in suburban Virginia.

A 14-year-old chronic runaway, who lived with his aunt and uncle because his mother was dead and father in the state hospital, was returned to training school after seven months at home, because the judge had no place else to send him.

For the juvenile delinquent without a fitting home, the training school exists as the major treatment facility. But commitment frequently serves the community's social defense needs more than the child's therapeutic requirements.[243] Many training schools are little more than crowded detention centers.[244] A recent report by the executive director of the National Council of Juvenile Court Judges noted:

The juvenile justice system includes so-called "state training

---

determined by due process of law, the question of what to do to deter the offender from future misbehavior should be left in the hands of persons qualified in the sciences of human behavior. B. M. Beck, *Five States: A Study of the Youth Authority Program as Promulgated by the American Law Institute* 79 (1951).

[241] George Washington University Center for Behavioral Science, *Biographical Data Survey of Juvenile Court Judges* 10, 11 (1964). On the recent efforts to provide special training for juvenile court judges, see Ketcham, "Summer College for Juvenile Court Judges," 51 *J. Amer. Jud. Soc'y*. 330 (1968).

[242] Brockett, "Troubled Kids are Waifs in Suburbia," *Washington Post*, p. H1.

[243] N. T. Teeters and J. O. Reinman, *The Challenge of Delinquency: Causation Treatment and Prevention of Juvenile Delinquency* 228 (1950).

[244] S. Wheeler and L. S. Cottrell, *Juvenile Delinquency: Its Prevention and Control* 32 (1966).

schools" which have been defined as places of "cold storage" in which there is frequently very little training. One could have seen children sleeping in tents in St. Louis County, Missouri, last summer because there was no place for them in the adjoining detention home. In the city of brotherly love, Philadelphia, children have been sleeping on the floor of the gymnasium in the youth center. In West Virginia children are housed on the top floor of a building whose fire escape has long ago been condemned.[245]

These "correction centers"[246] undoubtedly tend to advance the criminal training of both minor offenders and merely neglected children by grouping them with the seriously maladjusted and hard-core delinquents.[247] In some states estimates of mentally retarded juveniles in the training school populace run as high as 30 percent.[248]

Many of the juvenile institutions are operated on a custodial "obedience and conformity" model. Facilities for the child's individual and social development, re-education, and treatment are limited. Recent researchers have exploded the contradictions between the goals and requirements of confinement and custody, on the one hand, and the goals of rehabilitation and change, on the other, concluding that the latter aims cannot be accommodated in institutions patterned after the former.[249] Grave doubt has been cast, in fact, upon the propriety of training in total institutions offering compulsory, comprehensive life programs as a meaningful preparation for life on the outside. While the institutions that emphasize development and re-education at least preserve the personal skills and emotional controls needed after release, those patterned on obedience and conformity reportedly produce results which are "clearly negative . . . for the experience of being dominated cannot be expected to produce positive personality changes or to increase one's capability for legal conformity in an open, individualistic and achievement-oriented society."[250] The brief time

---

[245] Irving, "Juvenile Justice" 2, 3.

[246] The director of the New York State youth programs recently told a United States Senate Judiciary Subcommittee that it might be better if juveniles who break the law were never arrested or sent to training schools. Similarly, Joseph R. Rowan, director of the John Howard Association of Illinois, referred to juvenile institutions as "crime hatcheries" and recited how teenagers, 14 and older, in Chicago's Cook County Jail were sexually molested, tortured, beaten, and murdered by other prisoners. Downie, "Institutions for Delinquents Deplored," *Washington Post*, March 7, 1969, p. A11.

[247] President's Commission on Crime in the District of Columbia, *Report* 700.

[248] Irving, "Juvenile Justice" 1, 2.

[249] Ferdinand, "Some Inherent Limitations in Rehabilitating Juvenile Delinquents in Training Schools," 31 *Fed. Prob.* 30 (1967).

[250] Street, Vinter, and Perrow, *Organization for Treatment* 281 (1966).

that therapists are given (the average commitment is 8.2 months for boys, 10.7 months for girls) to reverse the complex behavioral and personal ills of infancy, childhood, and adolescence extinguishes any hope for meaningful rehabilitation.[251]

When an offender is spared commitment and is left within the community, the probation services available to the juvenile courts are even less able to supervise and guide his life effectively.[252] It has been claimed that "[b]ased on actual performance over a term of years, a good juvenile court and probation service, operating in a community with adequate social resources and utilizing them fully, can put as high as 90 percent of its juvenile delinquents on probation the first time around and 50 to 75 percent the second or third time around, and get as high as 75 to 80 percent successes."[253] Probation is often a farce.

Supervised by the court and subject to patronage, probation officers are poorly trained (only one in ten has a specialized training), underpaid and overworked.[254] Moreover, half of the 3,000 counties in this country are without any juvenile probation services whatsoever.[255] The "contact time" between the probation officer and the child is a key ingredient, yet observers report that probation officers "spent no more than fifteen minutes with their probationers during office visits and, on the average, saw their clients no more frequently than once a month."[256] Conditions of probation can sometimes be satisfied by occasional telephone calls to the probation officer advising him that all is in order, although the juvenile in fact may be becoming progressively

[251] In 1964 there were 44,100 children in public training schools for delinquent children, of whom three-fourths were boys and one-fourth were girls. Of the children committed in 1964, 28 percent had been previously admitted to juvenile institutions. U.S. Department of Health, Education, and Welfare, Children's Bureau, *1964 Statistics on Public Institutions for Delinquent Children* 1, 3 (1965).

[252] Fifty-four percent of the juveniles referred by the police to the District of Columbia Juvenile Court in 1966 were already under the court jurisdiction at the time or had been so during the preceding 12 months. President's Commission on Crime in the District of Columbia, *Report* 140.

[253] MacCormick, "The Community and the Correctional Process," 27 *Focus* 88 (1948).

[254] A 1966 survey showed that 75 percent of the juvenile courts had no in-service training for their probation officers and that the officers' maximum annual salaries were less than $5,000. Sheridan, "Juveniles Who Commit Noncriminal Acts" 20, 30.

[255] Ketcham, "Unfulfilled Promise" 31–32; U.S. Department of Health, Education, and Welfare, Office of Program Analysis, Committee on Juvenile Delinquency, *Programs and Services in the Field of Juvenile Delinquency* 4 (1958).

[256] Fradkin, "Disposition Dilemmas" 128.

involved in crime. No wonder recent studies of probation indicate failure rates during supervision ranging from 15 percent to 22 percent and post-probation failures have been reported to be as high as 43 percent.[257]

The frequent choice between poorly supervised probation, on one hand, and last-resort commitment, on the other, is much too narrow.[258] There is a need for dispositions less drastic than commitment yet more meaningful than probation, which can at the same time afford juvenile authorities an effective scrutiny of the youth's rehabilitative progress. In some cities the police, through their informal dispositions, have shown considerable innovation. With parental consent, they impose restrictions of varying severity upon offending juveniles, and many of these are reported to be highly effective. Kansas City, Missouri, utilizes a program called "grounding." A typical "grounded" youth must attend school regularly, may leave the house only if accompanied by a parent, must dress conventionally, must cut his hair in a reasonable manner, and must study at home for a minimum prescribed period each day. After this schedule is enforced for a month, the conditions are gradually relaxed.[259]

Individualized justice requires greater experimentation with diverse forms of restitution by the delinquent who will be allowed to remain at large but will be required to make cash payments out of his allowance or earnings. More utilization could be made of various forms of service on part-time and weekend work crews.[260] Fines deducted over several weeks from a youth's salary or pocket money are proper for developing a sense of social accountability, and can afford the court a better "installment" system for observing the delinquent's progress than is now available. Similarly, weekend or short-term confinement in juvenile detention centers (long utilized both in Britain and Germany), while manifesting a deliberately punitive character, may nevertheless provide the "short sharp shock" which is acceptable from a therapeutic point of view.[261] Attendance centers, where juveniles are ordered to take part in off-hours citizenship training programs, while continuing to attend school or hold a job, furnish another ac-

[257] Schreiber, "How Effective Are Services for the Treatment of Delinquents" 8, 9, in *Juvenile Delinquency* 240, 241 (H. C. Quay ed. 1965).

[258] For a recent evaluation of dispositional alternatives *see* T. Rubin and J. F. Smith, *The Future of the Juvenile Court* 31–42 (1968).

[259] Note, "Juvenile Delinquents" 775, 784.

[260] Fradkin, "Disposition Dilemmas" 129.

[261] Rhodes, "Delinquency and Community Action" 218; Grunhut, "Juvenile Delinquents under Punitive Detention," 3 *Brit. J. Delinq.* 191–209 (1955).

ceptable pattern.[262] Most significant are various types of "half-way" hostels and probation homes where the juvenile remains under continuing supervision while able at the same time to work and attend school outside.[263]

There is no doubt that in the juvenile delinquency process, as much as in the mental illness system, there will be in the coming years a drastic departure from primary reliance upon institutional treatment in remote locations and a growing emphasis, instead, on community-centered diagnostic and treatment facilities—where social resources will be brought to bear upon the child in his family and community context.[264] A special incentive for this development might possibly be provided by the newly recognized "right to treatment," which stresses the duty of the *parens patriae* state to provide adequate, fitting, and the least interventive services for those over which it exercises its controls. The right to treatment is thus advanced as the *quid pro quo* that must be accorded the individual for any deprivation of liberty under therapeutic auspices.[265]

CURING THE ILLS OF THE JUVENILE COURT PROCESS

The American system of juvenile justice was ushered in with much pomp and promise; today its temples lack trained and devoted servants. It has become "a big brother system in which . . . big brother is often tired, overworked, and frequently demoralized and underpaid."[266] The judge barely has an opportunity to learn the juvenile's problem, much less supervise his progress after disposition. There are too few judges: the District of Columbia's full complement is three juvenile court judges, only two of whom are usually serving at any given time, one always being promoted to a more "important" career. West Berlin, with a population three times that of Washington, has 18 juvenile court judges.[267] Warsaw, with a population less than twice

[262] Maglio, "The Citizenship Training Program of the Boston Juvenile Court," in *The Problem of Delinquency* (S. Glueck ed. 1959).

[263] Spencer and Grygier, "The Probation Hostel in England," *ibid.*; Rhodes, "Delinquency and Community Action" 218.

[264] Fradkin, "Disposition Dilemmas" 134–39. A recent Federal effort toward the promotion of community-based services for delinquent and pre-delinquent youths is contained in the Juvenile Delinquency Prevention and Control Act of 1968, Pub. L. 90–445, 88 Stat. 462 (July 31, 1968).

[265] Kittrie, "Can the Right to Treatment Remedy the Ills of the Juvenile Process?" 57 *Geo. L. J.* 848 (1969). For a more detailed discussion of the right to treatment *see* pp. 10–11 and 402–4 of this volume.

[266] Irving, "Juvenile Justice" 1, 2.

[267] Logan and Kleeman, "Berlin Report: Juvenile Delinquency Before the Wall and Afterward," *Wash. U. L. Q.* 296, 302 (1963).

that of Washington, has 12 full-time juvenile judges. The American judge who has 20 to 30 juvenile cases scheduled each morning cannot be expected to perform effectively the postulated functions of the *parens patriae* power.

Despite the promise that the juvenile process would emphasize individualized justice, "[o]ne hears judges, for example, asking whether we in effect dispense what might be called mathematical justice—the first time a juvenile appears in court he receives a warning; the second time he is put on probation; and for the third appearance he is committed."[268] Committing him to an understaffed traditional institution totally contradicts current knowledge about means for effective behavioral change.[269]

By default of the modern family, church, school, and community, the role of principal guardian of social order and conformity devolves increasingly on the police and the courts. This burden is too heavy for the machinery of justice to assume all by itself. The process of juvenile justice is burdened with responsibilities that should be vested elsewhere; as it presently exists the juvenile court system cannot discharge its diverse roles and develop more individualized services and programs. The concept of "delinquency" has been stretched too far.[270] The juvenile court should serve as a last-resort service, employed only when questions of restraint and compulsion arise. Its business, usually, should be limited to juveniles whose conduct would constitute a violation of the law if committed by an adult.[271]

It should not be the province of the juvenile court to serve as a family and child welfare agency or to rehabilitate children who run away from home, smoke, drink, who are truants, and who are other-

[268] Irving, "Juvenile Justice" 1, 2.

[269] The role of the newly recognized "right to treatment" as a possible vehicle for the reformation of existing treatment programs in discussed in detail in Chapter 8. *See* Creek v. Stone, 126 U.S. App. D.C. 329, 379 F.2d 106 (1967), and *in re* Elmore, 127 U.S. App. D.C. 176, 382 F.2d 125 (1967), discussed in Kittrie, "Right to Treatment" 848.

[270] For an interesting account of the hazardous dynamics of labelling *see* Grygier, "The Concept of 'The State of Delinquency'—An Obituary," 18 *J. Legal Educ.* 131 (1966). Grygier notes that children labelled in derogatory terms tend to conform to our worst expectations, and, as a result, we have to do a lot of running, like the Red Queen, in order to stand still.

[271] Somewhat in this direction, New York, California, Colorado, and Illinois have limited the application of the delinquency designation to only those who have violated adult criminal laws. Truant and ungovernable youth brought before the court are designated as minors "in need of supervision." Rubin and Smith, *Future of the Juvenile Court* 8. "Maladjustment and delinquency are not interchangeable terms. Consequently, delinquent juveniles should be considered as constituting, sociologically, a separate problem from that raised by juveniles who are in need of assistance or protection through general social, mental health and

wise "incorrigible." For these deviations other appropriate remedies must be found in existing or new social welfare agencies. Let the schools deal with truancy. Let the family deal with drinking, smoking, and incorrigibility.[272] A record of delinquency should not be based upon this type of conduct alone. It is significant that in many of these situations the fault is often not that of the juvenile but of his school, his neighborhood, or his parents.[273] Here we are frequently dealing not with delinquency but with inadequate environmental exposure, inadequate schools,[274] and family neglect.[275] What is required is not so much the reformation of the child as the reformation of his school,[276] his home condition, and his family life. Remedies that produce changes in a delinquent's school or family would often be more appropriate than those directed to the child himself.

What is the road ahead? If the juvenile court movement is not to be "swept away by the tide of legal history," we must seek a host of urgent reforms. Judge Ketcham of the District of Columbia Juvenile Court has outlined some:[277]

---

other types of welfare services. . . . By 'juvenile delinquency' should be understood the commission of an act which, if committed by an adult, would be considered a crime." Secretariat, Second United Nations Congress on the Prevention of Crime and the Treatment of Offenders, *New Forms of Juvenile Delinquency: Their Origin, Prevention and Treatment* 51–52 (London, August 8–20, 1960, A/Conf. 7).

[272] Several cases and authors have dealt with the rights of parents over their children, concluding that a parent must be shown to be incapable of care and guidance before a child may be removed to an institution. Mill v. Brown, 31 Utah 473, 88 P. 609 (1907). Note, *"Parens Patriae Theory"* 894, 905.

[273] Only 47 percent of the juvenile offenders lived with two parents at the time of their first referral to the juvenile court. President's Commission on Crime in the District of Columbia, *Report* 122.

[274] Over one-fifth of the juvenile offenders referred to the juvenile court in the District of Columbia had dropped out of school. *Ibid.* 127.

[275] Research has amply demonstrated that parents frequently fail to exercise proper control and thus contribute directly to juvenile delinquency. Glueck, "Toward Improving the Identification of Delinquents," 53 *J. Crim. L.C. & P.S.* 164 (1962). Yet the juvenile court rarely directs its sanctions to parents. Grygier, "Concept of the 'State of Delinquency' and Its Consequences" 648. For a contrasting account of how Israel deals with parental responsibility *see* Reifen, "The Implications of Laws and Procedures in the Juvenile Court in Israel," 3 *Brit. J. Crim.* 130 (1962).

[276] Some investigators believe schools help cause juvenile delinquency by placing improper academic demands on children. Eichorn, "Delinquency and the Educational System," in *Juvenile Delinquency* 332 (H. C. Quay ed. 1965). Unless the slow learner is given a simplified academic program with some out-of-school experience, revolt and truancy are unavoidable. Havinghurst, "Dealing with Problem Youth," in *Exceptional Children* (J. F. Magary and J. R. Eichorn ed. 1960).

[277] Ketcham, "Unfulfilled Promise" 38–39.

1. That legislatures provide juvenile courts with sufficient trained judges and adequate professional staff to dispose patiently yet expeditiously of all cases referred to them;
2. That juvenile court procedures that afford due process and fair treatment for the child and his parent and prevent the unwarranted intervention of over-zealous representatives of the state in the private lives of such individuals be formulated . . . ;
3. That procedures for assessing the needs of children coming before these courts be developed by behavioral scientists; and
4. That the state appropriate sufficient funds for the prompt construction and adequate staffing of institutions truly designed to provide delinquent and dependent juveniles the care, guidance and discipline that should have been provided by their parents.

These reforms involving adequate and fair procedures, are important not only to guard against the abuse of individual rights but also to guarantee that juvenile programs remain in the public eye and do not become corrupt in the darkness of public apathy. The juvenile court, revitalized through the injection of procedural reforms and the stripping of its public welfare appendices, should be better able to direct itself to its primary function: the control and reformation of serious juvenile deviation. This society, its legislatures, and its courts must curb their therapeutic over-zealousness and acquire a greater degree of tolerance for lesser deviations, whether of the rich or of the poor.

At the same time, a juvenile court operating with broader procedural safeguards would be much less reluctant to apply more severe sanctions when the circumstances and offender case histories so dictate. Several recent commentators have noted the juvenile court's inadequacy in dealing with serious older offenders and have noted the need to focus more effectively on the problems and attitudes of the youth in the period between childhood and maturity. One writer concludes that

[c]ommunity leaders who are considering the possibility of basic reorganization of the juvenile court would do well to listen to the clients who speak of their juvenile court experiences in tones of contempt and boredom. In the eyes of these clients, adults are over-lenient (or stupid or both) and do not expect the adolescent to assume even appropriate responsibility for his own behavior, and the court is just one more adult institution to be endured and manipulated.[278]

[278] E. Studt, "The Client's Image," in *Justice for the Child* 209, 210 (M. K. Rosenheim ed. 1962).

Finally, no juvenile court, any more than a criminal court, can alone constitute society's main protection against antisocial deviation. Dealing only with a relatively small sampling of the actual offending community, the juvenile court remains in great part a ritual of justice rather than comprehensive justice. And this indeed it must remain, if we do not wish to create a police state. Juvenile courts can share in the campaign for deterrence and the prevention of delinquency. But the major efforts must be made within the community itself and must be directed toward the contributing factors: poverty, unfit parents, broken homes, inadequate schools, improper vocational training, and lack of opportunities. The problem of delinquency as a whole is not likely to be answered by severer penalties, nor by kindly treatment, or individual psychotherapy. It requires epidemiological approaches— addressed to the social causes and settings of delinquency rather than solely to the affected juvenile himself.[279]

[279] Chess, "The Social Factors in Delinquency," 23 *Amer. J. Orthopsychiat.* 5 (1953).

4

The Psychopaths: Quarantine for the Criminally Inclined

"[T]here's the King's Messenger," said the Queen. "He's in prison now, being punished; and the trial doesn't even begin till next Wednesday; and of course the crime comes last of all."

"Suppose he never commits the crime?" said Alice.

"That would be all the better, wouldn't it?" the Queen said, as she turned the plaster round her finger with a bit of ribbon.

Alice felt there was no denying *that*. "Of course it would be all the better," she said, "but it wouldn't be all the better his being punished."

"You're wrong *there*, at any rate," said the Queen. "Were you ever punished?"

"Only for faults," said Alice.

"And you were all the better for it, I know!" the Queen said triumphantly.

"Yes, but then I *had* done the things I was punished for," said Alice, "that makes all the difference."

"But if you hadn't done them," the Queen said, "that would have been better still; better, and better, and better!"—L. Carroll, *Through the Looking Glass* 254–55 (1966)

The creation of a non-medically determinable category of persons who may be confined for indeterminate periods by a civil proceeding is so serious a departure from traditional concepts of justice that it deserves a critical analysis of the broadest terms. . . .—Sas v. Maryland, 334 F.2d 506, 517 (4th Cir. 1964)

The [sexual psychopathy law] raises the problem of how far legislation should move toward equating crime with mental illness. The possibility of treating most criminals as mental patients is provocative. The Committee thoroughly appreciates the potentialities of this approach, but at the present time sufficient research has not been completed to enable the Committee to endorse such sweeping legislation.—Michigan, Governor's Study Commission on Sex Deviates, *Report* 132 (1951)

A CAPACITY FOR EVIL

"Even within psychiatry," psychiatrist Seymour Halleck noted recently, "there is widespread disagreement as to whether psychopathy is a form of mental illness, a form of evil or a form of fiction."[1] Yet the law provides an elaborate system for the control of diverse types of deviants defined as psychopaths or defective delinquents.

"Psychopath" is one of the most criticized words in the psychiatric vocabulary. Its etymological definition is "a sick mind," although in medical usage it connotes not psychosis, neurosis, or mental defect, but rather a moral or social inadequacy. Some forty years ago Dr. William A. White, an early leader in the field of criminal psychiatry, declared that psychopathy had become a wastebasket diagnosis. The American Psychiatric Association has defined the psychopath as "a person whose behavior is predominantly amoral or antisocial and characterized by impulsive irresponsible actions satisfying only immediate or narcissistic interest . . . accompanied by minimal outward evidence of anxiety or guilt."[2] Notwithstanding this impressive battery of scientific language, the association notes that the term is considered poor and inexact by many members.

Some psychiatrists strongly assert that the concept, as well as the term, is devoid of meaning. "[T]he term 'psychopathic personality' is no longer regarded by psychiatry as meaningful; yet it will probably remain embalmed for some time to come in the statutes of several states where the pursuit of demons disguised as sexual psychopaths

[1] S. Halleck, *Psychiatry and the Dilemmas of Crime* 99 (1967).
[2] *Psychiatric Glossary* 38 (1957).

affords a glimpse of a 16th Century approach to mental illness,"[3] commented one prominent psychiatrist. But Dr. Cleckley,[4] an intensive researcher of psychopathic case histories, establishes an effective case for the psychopathic denomination and lists sixteen characteristics common to the class, including such desirable character traits as unusual charm and absence of irrational delusions but also such personality defects as unreliability, lack of remorse, pathological egocentricity, and poor interpersonal relations. The psychopath is thus seen as one who suffers not from a particular identifiable defect but as a person whose thinking, feeling, and acting are impaired by a disability of social interaction and responsibility.[5]

On November 19, 1964, Charles H. Lomax was brought before the District of Columbia Court of General Sessions.[6] At the hearing, a female witness, aged 26, testified that on August 1, 1964, she observed Lomax standing in a doorway in the 4400 block of Wisconsin Avenue, Northwest. She testified also that he was naked from his waist down, that his private parts were exposed, and that her feelings were injured by this sight. Evidence was submitted that once before, some sixteen years earlier, Lomax had been convicted of a similar act of indecent exposure. An examining psychiatrist testified further that Lomax had admitted to him other instances of exposure and that he found these impulses very hard to control. Although Lomax's conduct was offensive to others, the psychiatrist stated that Lomax was not so dangerous as to attack anyone. Upon the conclusion of this testimony, the court found Lomax to be a psychopath and ordered him civilly committed for an indeterminate period of confinement and treatment at St. Elizabeths Hospital in Washington, D.C.[7]

Edward C. Cowman was found guilty in the Criminal Court of Baltimore, on January 8, 1958, on a charge of burglarizing his employer's warehouse and safe.[8] Forty-eight years of age, Cowman had two previous convictions, the first of which was in California in 1946 on charges of grand larceny. After one year in jail he was granted

---

[3] P. Roche, *The Criminal Mind* 25 (1958).

[4] H. M. Cleckley, *The Mask of Sanity* 355–56 (1970).

[5] Caldwell, "Constitutional Psychopathic State," 3 *J. Crim. Psychopath.* 171–72 (1941).

[6] Lomax v. District of Columbia, 211 A.2d 772–75 (1965).

[7] In a Michigan case of indecent exposure, a misdemeanor with maximum imprisonment of one year, the defendant was found to be a psychopath and after seven years of confinement was still trying in vain to secure his release. *In re* Kemmerer, 309 Mich. 818, 5 N.W.2d 652 (1944); Kemmerer v. Benson, 165 F.2d 702 (6th Cir. 1948).

[8] Cowman v. State, 151 A.2d 903 (1959).

probation on condition that he make restitution in the value of the stolen property, some $4,000. After drinking heavily and failing to make the agreed payments, Cowman's probation was revoked and he was returned to jail for another eighteen months. Moving to Maryland upon his release, he was there convicted in July 1955 on charges of larceny after trust and was sentenced to one year in the House of Correction. After the third conviction in 1958, Cowman was ordered to undergo psychiatric examinations. The case history disclosed that Cowman had the equivalent of two and one-half years of college credit and had worked as a bank teller for eight years and as an airline cost accountant for an equal number of years. The medical reports described him, however, as "basically a cold, hostile person who has only superficial relationships with other people." The reports noted, similarly, that he tended to use his "excellent intelligence" to flout the law. Describing him as a demanding infant who becomes angry with the world when it does not fulfill his demands, the medical testimony indicated that Cowman's heavy drinking tended to emphasize his emotional instability. Citing the medical conclusion that Cowman was "a predatory, unmoral, emotionally unstable man, who is likely to continue to violate laws," the court found him to be a "defective delinquent" and ordered his civil commitment for an indeterminate period to Maryland's Patuxent Institution.

A man, Chapman, was charged in 1942 with committing a homosexual act with a consenting adult male.[9] The medical report concluded that if left free he would continue his homosexual activity. Consequently, Chapman was confined for treatment "until fully and permanently recovered."

William Barnes, Jr., was charged in 1957 with the unauthorized use of a vehicle.[10] As a result of lengthy medical observations he was described as intellectually deficient and emotionally unbalanced. The medical observers concluded that Barnes had "demonstrated a persistent aggravated anti-social behavior" and that he would constitute "an actual danger to society" unless confined and treated. On the basis of this evidence the jury recommended that he be civilly committed for indeterminate confinement and treatment.

Patient C–930,[11] a single white male forty-five years old, was committed to the psychopathic institution in 1962 after being charged with assault and maiming. His record disclosed that he attended school

[9] People v. Chapman, 301 Mich. 584, 4 N.W.2d 18 (1942).

[10] Barnes v. Director of the Patuxent Institution, 175 A.2d 20 (1961).

[11] J. Finn, "Criminal Justice and the Violent Sex Offender" 31 (unpublished paper in Washington College of Law Library, 1966).

through the seventh grade and had an I.Q. of 104. His health record was normal. The patient's father was divorced from his mother, whom the patient did not remember. The father remarried and the step-mother beat the children. The patient went to live with his grand-mother when he was fifteen. He stressed that he first learned of differ-ences in the sexes when he was sixteen. His first sexual intercourse was in the house of a prostitute when he was eighteen. He denied any homosexual conduct or pedophilia. Patient C–930 had a bad conduct discharge from the army and a previous criminal record. The first offense was a minor assault and the second was the theft of a bear. The bear incident was recorded in the patient's own words:

> I didn't steal it. I used to feed the bear candy bars and one day the chain broke and he followed me, and me and the bear were down on Broadway getting drunk. He could drink more than me. They picked us up and they sent the bear back and they gave me 30 days.

The offense which resulted in his commitment as a psychopath was rather spectacular. He met the victim in Cumberland and took her to his home, allegedly to visit his invalid aunt. The woman went will-ingly, but upon discovering that he had no whiskey, wanted to depart. When she tried to leave, he took her to the basement, tied her up, and cut her body. He used a small knife, and the cuts did not produce permanent scars. After making the incisions, the patient took the vic-tim to a bedroom, placed her on a bed, and went away. He left town but surrendered to the police in another jurisdiction. He said that he was sorry he had hurt the woman. The woman testified that he had given her a drink after the incident. The patient was not sentenced for the offense, but instead was indeterminately committed for treat-ment and rehabilitation. In 1966, after four years in a psychopathic institution, patient C–930 sought release. The reviewing physician on the staff of the institution responded negatively: "If released, with his lack of insight, he would probably continue a nomadic existence and would be dangerous to others in the environment." The decision was made, therefore, by the institution's director to continue the commit-ment of patient C–930 for a further indeterminate period.

Writing in 1884 against classical criminology's occupation with guilt and its adherence to punishments which respond to the severity of crimes, Enrico Ferri, the father of positivist criminology, asserted:

> [To the] criminalists of the traditional school . . . the application of a conditional sentence . . . remains offensive to the principle of metaphysical justice . . . but it is a wise concession to practical

utility, being in perfect theoretical accord with the doctrines of
anthropology and criminal sociology. The reclusion of dangerous
criminals for an indeterminate time is a proposal of the positivist
criminal school, since it would be as absurd to say that a murderer
should remain in prison twenty years rather than fifteen or thirty
as it would be to say in advance that a sick person should stay in
a hospital ten days rather than twenty or fifty. As the sick person
is kept in the hospital just as long a time as is necessary for his
cure, and as the insane patient remains in the asylum all of his
life unless cured and leaves it when he is cured, so it should be
with the delinquent. . . .[12]

Positivist criminology never saw the full fruition of its doctrines in
America: that delinquents be treated as sick persons and reclused
until cured. But in the psychopathy programs, and to a lesser extent
in the other arenas of the therapeutic state, the deterministic philosophies of Ferri came close to realization.

The designations "psychopathy," in the older medical texts, or "so-
ciopathy" and "defective delinquency" in the newer writings have
served as classifications for diverse groups of deviants, considered
socially immature and behaviorally ill-controlled and selected for
therapeutic sanctions under the programs originally propounded by
positivist criminology. Psychopaths are not afflicted with any particular physical illnesses; neither do their mental aberrations come within
the traditional psychiatric definitions of mental illness. A psychopath
is neither psychotic nor neurotic. Psychopaths, instead, are "ill primarily in terms of conformity with the prevailing cultural milieu."[13]
More simply stated, psychopathy encompasses diverse groups of
habitual or potential offenders, persons with a propensity to criminal
behavior or other nonconforming conduct. What brings them together
is their social insensitivity, an uncontrollable impulse for unacceptable
forms of personal gratification, and a resultant inclination to get in
trouble with the law.

The divestment of criminal justice, as seen in the case of the mentally ill and the juvenile, was generally motivated by sincerely charitable beliefs that those affected by the shift are entitled to relief from
the severity of the traditional criminal process. Even so, divestment is
rarely an end in itself, for those relieved from criminal sanctions still
require social controls and assistance. The criminal process has thus

[12] E. Ferri, *Criminal Sociology* xlii (1917).
[13] Merck, *Manual of Diagnosis and Therapy* 1327–28 (C. E. Lyght ed., 9th ed.,
1956); *see also ibid.* 1143 (11th ed. 1966).

been displaced by another involuntary system of controls which forms the basis of the therapeutic state. In some areas of the therapeutic model, however, it becomes difficult to ascertain whether the therapeutic program is introduced primarily to serve as a humane shield for the protection of deviants or whether it is offered as a pragmatic and drastic sword to be used against them. Especially in the case of psychopaths, or defective delinquents, doubts have been raised that their removal from the criminal process is due to sympathetic considerations, such as existed in the case of the insane and the young; it is perhaps attributable primarily to society's fear of their special capacity for evil.

THE ILLUSIVE PSYCHOPATH

A random group of defective delinquents committed for treatment in Maryland[14] reveals divergent personality patterns: ages range from 25 to 47; intelligence quotients vary from 72 to 104; maximum educational accomplishments run from fifth grade to college degree; no ethnic background predominates; some are married and others not; some are parents and others childless; some are deeply religious and others totally lack any religious convictions. What all these Maryland inmates do have in common is a record of repetitive conflicts with the law. The conflicts themselves, however, do not establish a uniform pattern of deviant behavior for all inmates, although the records show that many inmates have committed similar offenses—that is, homosexuality, exhibitionism, and assaults on small children. Other histories demonstrate a variegation of offensive behavior stretching from unauthorized absence from military base to larceny, armed robbery, assault, incest, or sodomy. From this analysis, the general (legally used) definition of a psychopath or defective delinquent may be derived: A recidivist with a propensity to habitual crime (with emphasis upon sexual offenses).

This habitual pattern has caused society to view the psychopath as more than an ordinary criminal. The sensationalization of certain crimes ascribed to "a psychopath" by the news media, together with a popular notion that psychopaths commit progressively more heinous and ghoulish crimes, has contributed to the branding of the psychopath as a leading public enemy.[15]

---

[14] Finn, "Criminal Justice and the Violent Sex Offender."
[15] *See,* generally, C. T. Duffy and A. Hirshberg, *Sex and Crime* (1967).

Sexual crimes have been primarily responsible for the formation of this public conception. People can easily identify with one whose wife, child, or friend has been a victim of a vicious sexual assault. For example, Albert Fish, described as a "meek and innocuous 65-year-old man, gentle and benevolent, friendly and polite," was credited with eighteen different acts of perversion involving sexual crimes upon at least one hundred children and the murder of five after he became impotent. To the examining psychiatrist he also admitted cannibalism, involving several of his victims.[16] The strong public reaction to the cruelty and violence of these acts has activated a search for programs that would insulate society from the sexual and other habitual offenders. Conventional criminal procedures, which mold the sanction to the particular crime with little regard for the nature of the criminal, have been considered inadequate to deal with the habitual, progressively dangerous offender. How will society be protected from a psychopath whose exhibitionism or voyeurism merit only a thirty-day jail sentence, but whose next offense may be a violent attack on an innocent woman or child? There have been two answers to this search for additional social protection. One has been stiffer criminal penalties for habitual offenders;[17] the other has been the enactment of psychopathy or defective delinquency commitment laws.

In 1957 two young boys were sexually assaulted and killed in a park south of Boston, Massachusetts. The person charged with the crime had only months before been released from prison after serving a sentence for another sexual offense. The Massachusetts Legislature immediately reacted by enacting a Sexually Dangerous Law which is still in effect. Under this statute, persons convicted of sexual offenses may be committed for indeterminate treatment, from one day to life, to a "hospital," in lieu of a criminal proceeding and incarceration.[18]

The majority of these psychopathy laws have been enacted during the past thirty years and, like other state laws, do not have much uniformity. The procedures differ, the types of offenders included are varied. Generally, however, an emphasis upon the sexual offender is evident: an emphasis attributable to the fact that psychopathy legisla-

[16] Mihm, "A Re-examination of the Validity of our Sex Psychopath Statutes in the Light of Recent Appeal Cases and Experience," 44 *J. Crim. L.C. & P.S.* 716, 717 (1954).

[17] For a discussion of the special criminal law provisions dealing with habitual offenders and the applicable requirements of due process *see* Chandler v. Fretag, 348 U.S. 3 (1954); Oyler v. Boles, 368 U.S. 448 (1962).

[18] Cohen and Kozol, "Evaluation for Parole at a Sex Offender Treatment Center," 30 *Fed. Prob.* 50 (1966).

tion is often the result of similar public reactions to sensationally pub-
licized sex crimes.[19] The treatment programs provided vary, but all
share a provision that prescribes an involuntary and continuous term
of commitment until a cure (or at least a marked improvement) is
achieved.[20]

Two common denominators of the psychopathy laws are their asserted noncriminal nature and the illusive nature of their subject—a
habitual delinquent not considered mentally ill, yet believed to suffer
from a *personality* disorder because of his inability to conform his
behavior to the minimum demands of society. Dr. Benjamin Rush,
described as the father of American psychiatry, first recognized this
group of delinquents at the end of the eighteenth century and characterized their disorder as a congenital defect of the moral sense, in
conjunction with normal or even superior intellect.[21] He coined the
term "anomia" (from the Greek *anomos*, meaning "lawless") to describe
this personality deficiency. While the term "anomia" has been generally
replaced by "psychopathy," the primary identifying characteristic of
the habitual delinquent is not a mental disorder or defect but an
incapacity to conduct himself "with decency and propriety in the business of life."[22]

Despite the amorphous definition of psychopathy, the social evils
perpetrated by psychopaths have been extensively cited as a justification for the creation of special experimental treatment programs for
this group of troublesome recidivists. The selection of the candidates
for these experimental programs depends upon a cooperative legal-
medical effort. The psychopathy statutes usually list the legal criteria

[19] *The Mentally Disabled and the Law* 298 (F. T. Lindman and D. M. Mc-
Intyre eds. 1961).

[20] Because of a general lack of guilt feelings or concern for the future, most
psychopaths do not experience their illness in terms of psychic pain, and very
few ever seek psychiatric aid on a voluntary basis. Note, " 'Psychopathic Personality' and 'Sexual Deviation': Medical Terms or Legal Catch-alls; Analysis of the
Status of Homosexual Alien," 40 *Temp. L. Q.* 328, 331 (1967).

[21] M. Guttmacher and H. Weihofen, *Psychiatry and the Law* 87 (1952).

[22] *Ibid.* Illustrating the psychopath's intellectual and moral incongruity and
remarkable ability to be charmer and devil at the same time is the oft-told
anecdote about the fire in a French theater. As panic was spreading and the
spectators were turning from an audience into a mob, a huge bearded man leaped
through the orchestra onto the stage. He raised his hand with an imperious
gesture and cried "Que chacun ragagne sa place." Such was the authority of his
voice and bearing that everyone obeyed him. As a result, they were all burned
to death, while the bearded man walked quietly out through the wings to the
stage door, took a cab which was waiting for someone else, and went home to
bed. McDonald, "The Prompt Diagnosis of Psychopathic Personality," 122 *Amer.
J. Psychiatry* 48 (1966).

for this special class, consisting in most part of previous criminal or deviate behavior. The statutes further require evidence of behavioral abnormality and criminal propensities. These must be medically demonstrated. The representatives of the medical disciplines, on the other hand, view the statutory requisite as primarily legal.[23] Out of this medico-legal labyrinth a prediction of the alleged psychopath's future conduct is finally reached, which may lead to his commitment to an institution for an indeterminate portion of his life.

The Legislative History

The first psychopathy legislation was enacted by the Massachusetts legislature in 1911.[24] Known as the Briggs Act, it created a distinct class of habitual criminal offenders, denominated by "defective delinquents," and directed their commitment to special and purportedly noncriminal institutional programs. Redrafted in 1921 and amended several times, the tenor of the original act remains essentially unchanged. The law allows commitment of a defective delinquent on a first offense if the court is of the opinion that the convicted offender has a tendency to recidivism of a serious type. The term of commitment is indefinite and proceedings may be initiated by a variety of civil servants: district attorneys, probation officers, officers of the department of correction, public welfare officers, and officers of the department of mental diseases.

Conviction of a particular offense is required in Massachusetts before a finding of defective delinquency. The other prerequisite is the filing with the judge of a certificate by two qualified physicians that the individual is "mentally defective." Although the law fails to define the term "mental defective," the actual practice has accepted an "intelligence quotient of 75–i.e., a mental age of 12 years–as the dividing line between normal and subnormal."[25] The Massachusetts law[26]

---

[23] In 1950 the Committee on Forensic Psychiatry of the Group for the Advancement of Psychiatry suggested: "In statutes the use of technical psychiatric terms should be avoided whenever possible. Psychiatric knowledge and terminology are in a state of flux. Once having become a part of the public law such a term attains a fixity unresponsive to newer scientific knowledge and application." Group for the Advancement of Psychiatry, Committee on Forensic Psychiatry, *Psychiatrically Deviated Sex Offenders*, Report no. 9, p. 1 (1950). *See also* Comment, "Criteria for Commitment under the Wisconsin Sex Crimes Act," *Wis. L. Rev.* 980 (1967).

[24] *Mass. Acts and Resolves* ch. 595, §§1–12 (1911).

[25] Robinson, "Institution for Defective Delinquents," 24 *J. Crim. L.C. & P.S.* 352, 371 (1933).

[26] *Mass. Ann. Laws* ch. 123A, §§1–11 (Supp. 1965).

was substantively copied by other states.[27] The New York version provided for the commitment of "any mental defective over 16 years of age convicted of a criminal offense."[28] Originally the act provided for commitment either before or after conviction. But claims that feeble-minded persons were being committed on trumped-up charges for the purpose of relieving relatives and friends of support resulted in making prior conviction a prerequisite for confinement. The defective delinquent statutes usually make no distinctions between the types of crimes committed by the habitual offenders (whether sexual or non-sexual), but their applicability is restricted to those delinquents suffering from some intellectual deficiency.

The second flood of legislation commenced in the late thirties and crested in the following decade. These laws were primarily directed toward the sexual offender. In passing the first sex offender act in 1937,[29] Michigan sought to single out the person who had been convicted of a specified sex crime and, although not insane, appeared to be a sex degenerate or pervert or to suffer from a mental disorder with marked sex deviation and tendencies dangerous to the public safety. It provided that the court could, before pronouncing sentence, conduct an examination of such person with the assistance of two or more physicians and, upon a finding of psychopathy, could order his commitment to a state hospital for an indeterminate time. Michigan's attempt at psychopathy legislation was ill-fated, however. One year later the Michigan Supreme Court declared the statute invalid on the ground that as a criminal proceeding it failed to observe the right to jury trial and the protection against double jeopardy guaranteed to the accused under the Michigan constitution.[30] The court based its conclusion that the Michigan law was a criminal proceeding on two main premises—that it appeared in the criminal procedure code and that the indefinite confinement was an added penalty for the overt crime.

Illinois, in 1938, successfully legislated the first sexual psychopath law[31] after Michigan's attempt was declared unconstitutional.[32] To avoid the objections raised in Michigan, the new law endeavored to

[27] Guttmacher and Weihofen, *Psychiatry and the Law* 193, 194.

[28] 34 *N.Y. Consol. Law* (McKinney Supp. 1938), "Mental Deficiency Law," §§124–26.

[29] *Mich. Pub. Acts of 1937*, no. 196.

[30] People v. Frontczak, 286 Mich. 51, 281 N.W. 534 (1938).

[31] *Ill. Rev. Stat.* ch. 38, §§820.01 to 825 (1957).

[32] *Mich. Pub. Acts of 1937*, no. 196, p. 305; People v. Frontczak, 286 Mich. 51, 281 N.W. 534 (1938).

make the confinement more analogous to an insanity commitment than
to a criminal sentence by removing the psychopathy provisions from
the penal code and providing for the psychopath's commitment without the requirement that he be convicted first.

Under the Illinois law, a finding of psychopathy had to be made
prior to the criminal trial. Upon the offender's commitment to the
Department of Public Welfare, the criminal charge was held in abeyance, to be reinstituted upon the patient's release from his psychopathic confinement.[33] The sexual psychopath was identified by his
inability to control his sexual habits or perversions and the resultant
propensity to unlawful sexual behavior. He was "not mentally ill or
feebleminded to an exent making him criminally irresponsible,"[34] but
nevertheless one predisposed to the "commission of sexual offenses,"
utterly lacking in "power to control his sexual impulses," and potentially "dangerous to others."[35] In some states the sexual psychopath
statutes were superimposed upon earlier "defective delinquent" laws,
producing legal and medical confusion over the criteria and procedures applicable in a given case.[36]

The latest development stage in psychopathy legislation, typified by
the 1951 Maryland statute,[37] eliminates the emphasis on the sexual
offender and once more emphasizes habitual offenders generally.
Some of these laws, like the Maryland statute, even return to the
earlier "defective delinquency" terminology. The Maryland law boldly
attempts to carve out a broad new program of social controls not only
for sex offenders or the mentally retarded but for recidivists generally.
It defines the defective delinquent as an individual who

> by the demonstration of persistent aggravated antisocial or crimi-
> nal behavior, evidences a propensity toward criminal activity,
> and who is found to have either such intellectual deficiency or
> emotional unbalance, or both, as to clearly demonstrate an actual
> danger to society so as to require ... confinement and treatment.[38]

[33] Because the psychopathic confinement was not considered a criminal penalty,
the U.S. constitutional prohibition of double jeopardy was not regarded as applicable. Amend. V: ". . . nor shall any person be subject for the same offense to
be twice put in jeopardy of life or limb. . . ."

[34] *Ala. Code* tit. 15, §434 (Supp. 1963).

[35] *Cal. Wel. & Inst. Code* §5500 (1966); *Iowa Code Ann.* 225A.1 (1966
Supp.).

[36] Group for the Advancement of Psychiatry, *Psychiatrically Deviated Sex Offenders* 4; New Jersey, Commission on the Habitual Sex Offender, *The Habitual
Sex Offender* 68 (1950).

[37] *Md. Code Ann.* art. 31B, cn. 476 (1951).

[38] *Ibid.* art. 31B, §5 (1957).

Designed particularly for the treatment of the more offensive recidivists, the terminology of the Maryland law extends, nevertheless, to all persons convicted of felonies, sex crimes, or crimes of violence, and to those with two or more convictions for any lesser offense which is punishable by imprisonment.

Consequently, the Maryland law is virtually unlimited in its application to all convicted felons and many of the misdemeanants, with the exception of those charged with trivial offenses, such as intoxication and disorderly conduct.[39] Even individuals of abnormally high intelligence may be committed if they have shown "emotional imbalance."[40]

THE PERSON, THE PROCESS, AND THE PROGRAM

The Person

At present twenty-nine states and the District of Columbia have some special legislation for the treatment of the defective delinquent or psychopathic offender.[41] Fewer than half of the statutes agree on the nomenclature for the individual subject to these special programs.[42] Various state statutes make reference to "Sexually Dangerous Persons,"[43] "Mentally Disturbed Sex Offenders,"[44] "Psychopathic Of-

[39] Cowman v. State, 220 Md. 207, 151 A.2d 903, 906 (1959).

[40] Palmer v. State, 137 A.2d 119 (1957).

[41] The applicable laws are as follows: *Ala. Code* tit. 15, §§434–42 (1959) and (Supp. 1965); *Cal. Wel. & Inst. Code* §§5500–22 (1966); *Colo. Rev. Stat. Ann.* §§39–19–1 to 10 (1963); *Conn. Gen. Stat. Ann.* §§17–244 to 257 (1958); *D.C. Code Ann.* §§22–3501 to 3511 (1967); *Fla. Stat. Ann.* §917.12 (Supp. 1964); *Ill. Ann. Stat.* ch. 38, §§105–1.01 to 12 (Smith-Hurd 1964); *Ind. Ann. Stat.* §§9–3401 to 3412 (repl. vol. 1956); *Iowa Code Ann.* §§225A.1 to 15 (Supp. 1966); *Kan. Gen. Stat. Ann.* §§62–1534 to 1537 (1964); *Md. Code Ann.* art. 31B, §§5–11 (1957); *Mass. Ann. Laws* ch. 123A, §§1–11 (1965); *Mich. Stat. Ann.* §§28.967(1) to (9) (1954); *Minn. Stat. Ann.* §§526.09 to 11 (1945); *Mo. Ann. Stat.* §§202.700 to 770 (1959); *Neb. Rev. Stat.* §§29–2901 to 2907 (repl. vol. 1964); *N.H. Rev. Stat. Ann.* §§173.1 to 16 (repl. vol. 1964); *N.J. Stat. Ann.* §§2A.164–3 to 13 (1953) and (Supp. 1966); *Ohio Rev. Code Ann.* §§2947.24 to 20 (Page Supp. 1964); *Ore. Rev. Stat.* §§137.111 to 119 (Supp. 1963); *Pa. Stat. Ann.* tit. 19, §§1166–74 (1964); *S.D. Code* §13.1727 (Supp. 1960); *Tenn. Code Ann.* §§33–1301 to 1305 (Supp. 1966); *Utah Code Ann.* §§77–49–1 (Supp. 1965); *Va. Code Ann.* §§53–278.2 to 3 (repl. vol. 1958); *Vt. Stat. Ann.* tit. 18, §§2811–16 (1959); *Wash. Rev. Code Ann.* §§71.06.010 to 260 (1962); *W. Va. Code Ann.* §§2666 (1), (2) (1961); *Wis. Stat. Ann.* §§959.15(1), (2) (1958); *Wyo. Stat. Ann.* ch. 7, §348–57 (1957).

[42] Note, "The Plight of the Sexual Psychopath: A Legislative Blunder and Judicial Acquiescence," 41 *Notre Dame Lawyer* 527, 528–29 (1966).

[43] *Ill. Ann. Stat.* ch. 38, §§105–1 to 12 (1964).

[44] *Cal. Wel. & Inst. Code* §§5500–522 (1962).

fenders"[45] and "Defective Delinquents." In twelve jurisdictions, he is some type of "psychopath,"[46] and seventeen jurisdictions include a sex element in their definition.[47] Most commonly, a person subjected to these special laws must have been brought to the attention of the authorities by a prior charge of specified offense, frequently a sexual offense. This offense, however, may range from a passive act of genital exhibitionism or consenting homosexuality to forcible rape. Another element of psychopathy is a behavioral irregularity, primarily a propensity to repeat the prohibited behavior,[48] which may be demonstrated either through a positive finding of potential threat to the community,[49] or through evidence of an individual's "lack of power to control his sexual impulses...."[50] Although some form of mental abnormality is usually required to establish psychopathy, many statutes state that the affected person does not have to be mentally ill,[51] failing to specify, however, which test of insanity, criminal or civil, will negate psychopathy. Only a few states include mentally ill persons within their special psychopathy programs.[52]

Usually, the laws define the psychopath as one who has committed and been convicted of certain specified crimes.[53] In some states, however, the law may be invoked against a person merely *charged* with variously enumerated sexual offenses.[54]

While most states limit the psychopathy process to those involved with sexual crimes, some states extend it also to persons convicted of

[45] *Ohio Rev. Code Ann.* §§2947.24(n) to 28 (Page Supp. 1954).

[46] The twelve jurisdictions are: Alabama, District of Columbia, Florida, Indiana, Iowa, Michigan, Missouri, Nebraska, New Hampshire, Washington, Ohio, and Vermont; *see* note 41 above.

[47] The seventeen jurisdictions are: Alabama, California, Colorado, District of Columbia, Florida, Illinois, Indiana, Iowa, Massachusetts, Michigan, Missouri, Nebraska, New Hampshire, New Jersey, Pennsylvania, Tennessee, and Washington; *see* note 41 above.

[48] Note, "Plight of the Sexual Psychopath" 529.

[49] *See, e.g., Kan. Gen. Stat. Ann.* §62–1536 (1964).

[50] *D.C. Code Ann.* §22–3503 (1967).

[51] *Iowa Code Ann.* §225A.1 (1966); *D.C. Code Ann.* §22–3503 (Supp. V, 1966).

[52] *Colo. Rev. Stat. Ann.* §§39–19–1 to 10 (1963); *Pa. Stat. Ann.* tit. 19, §§1166–74 (1964).

[53] The psychopath is so defined in Connecticut, Kansas, Oregon, South Dakota, Utah, Virginia, West Virginia, Wisconsin, and Wyoming. *See* note 41 above for citations.

[54] Two such states are New Hampshire and Washington; *see* note 41 above for citations. *See also* Note, "Plight of Sexual Psychopath" 531. Illinois recently reversed a commitment where it was shown that no criminal charges were pending. People v. Harris, 77 Ill. App. 2d 300, 222 N.E.2d 107 (1966).

other criminal offenses that may appear to be sexually motivated.[55] At least eight states, however, do not restrict the operation of the psychopathy laws to sexual offenders but encompass persons with a propensity to commit crimes of any sort.[56]

A panorama of psychopathy programs is provided by the District of Columbia metropolitan area. The Virginia law is the simplest and narrowest, limited to persons who have been convicted of a criminal offense that indicates "sexual abnormality."[57] No requirement regarding the offender's mental condition or propensity toward similar conduct is included. The District of Columbia does not require a prior criminal charge or conviction as a prerequisite for a finding of psychopathy. The sexual psychopath is defined as a person "who by course of repeated misconduct in sexual matters has evidenced such lack of power to control his sexual impulses as to be dangerous to other persons. . . ."[58] Such previous misconduct apparently need not be criminal in character; the possibility that some injury, loss, pain, or other evil may occur is sufficient to invoke the law.[59] The Maryland "defective delinquent" law[60] is the broadest in the area. Its application is not restricted to the sexual offender but extends to all offenders who show either an intellectual deficiency or an emotional imbalance. Although embracing any individual "who, by the demonstration of persistent aggravated antisocial or criminal behavior, evidences a propensity toward criminal activity...,"[61] the Maryland law is restricted to offenders who have prior convictions.

The Process

A court finding is required before a person may be adjudicated a psychopath. There is no uniformity among the states, however, as to the prerequisites for such judicial action. In a majority of the states, after conviction of certain offenses, a hearing may be held to determine if the defendant is a psychopath. Either the prosecution or the

[55] *E.g.*, California and Wisconsin; *see* note 41 above for citations. For an example of sexually motivated crime *see* note 131 below.

[56] Maryland's defective delinquent law includes persons charged with property crimes. Cowman v. State, 220 Md. 207, 151 A.2d 903 (1959).

[57] *Va. Code Ann.* §53–278.2 (1958).

[58] *D.C. Code Ann.* §22–3503 (1967).

[59] The likelihood that an exhibitionist would cause psychological injury to an adult viewer was held sufficient to invoke the District of Columbia statute. Carras v. District of Columbia, 183 A.2d 393, 395 (1962).

[60] *Md. Code Ann.* art. 31B (1957).

[61] *Ibid.* §5.

defendant may petition the court for such a hearing, or the court may convene one *suo sponte*[62]—on its own behalf. These "post-conviction" states rely on the criminal conviction to establish their power over an individual, utilizing the psychopathy hearing and decision as a sentencing or disposition procedure.[63] In several states, one may be adjudicated a psychopath *before* any determination of guilt or innocence of a specific crime. In these "pre-conviction" states, a petition for a psychopathy hearing may be filed either prior to or during the criminal trial, and, when granted, the criminal procedure is stayed, sometimes even if the trial has begun.[64] Notably, all but one of the preconviction commitment statutes were enacted prior to 1950.[65] Apparently, the recent trend is toward post-conviction commitments, guaranteeing against abuse by prosecuting attorneys who may resort to the lesser evidentiary requirement of this civil procedure when they lack evidence to obtain a criminal conviction.[66]

A survey of the psychopathy procedures in the District of Columbia metropolitan area again provides an illustration of the existing diversity. Virginia provides for the determination of psychopathy after conviction but before sentencing.[67] Maryland, on the other hand, permits applications for commitment as a defective delinquent only after the offender's conviction and sentencing.[68] In the District of Columbia a person may be committed as a psychopath either after being charged with or after being convicted of one of the specified crimes.[69] Furthermore, a person may also be civilly committed in the District of Co-

---

[62] *See* Note, "Plight of the Sexual Psychopath" n. 27. Fifteen states specifically permit a petition alleging sexual psychopathy or a similar related condition to be filed upon the *conviction* of the defendant of certain sexual offenses.

[63] *Mentally Disabled and the Law* 300 (Lindman and McIntyre eds.). Such post-conviction commitment proceedings are authorized in Alabama, California, Indiana, Kansas, Massachusetts, Michigan, Nebraska, New Jersey, Ohio, Oregon, Pennsylvania, Tennessee, Utah, Vermont, Virginia, Washington, Wisconsin, Wyoming, and the District of Columbia. *Ibid.* 319–29, Table X–B.

[64] *Ibid.* 300. Ten jurisdictions permit such pre-conviction psychopathy commitments: Florida, Illinois, Indiana, Iowa, Michigan, Minnesota, Missouri, New Hampshire, Washington, and the District of Columbia. *Ibid.* 319–29.

[65] J. B. Robitscher, *Pursuit of Agreement: Psychiatry and the Law* 162, 163 (1966); *See also Mentally Disabled and the Law* 300 (Lindman and McIntyre eds.).

[66] Burrick, "An Analysis of the Illinois Sexually Dangerous Act," 59 *J. Crim. L.C. & P.S.* 254, 256, n. 24 (1968). Some abuses of post-conviction psychopathy laws are also claimed by inmates who report that the threat of psychopathy referral often prompts a guilty plea to the criminal charge. Author's interview with inmate, Patuxent Institution, Laurel, Maryland, 1969.

[67] *Va. Code Ann.* §53–278.2 (1958).

[68] *Md. Code Ann.* art. 31B, §6(c) (1957).

[69] *D.C. Code Ann.* §22–3504(d) (1967).

lumbia merely upon evidence of psychopathy without first being charged with any crime whatever. When the proceeding involves a person charged with a crime, the psychopathy hearing must be ordered either before trial or after conviction. In the latter case, however, the completion of the probation period bars a psychopathy proceeding.

Whenever a psychopathy inquiry is begun, a medical examination of the individual is required.[70] A few statutes require that a psychiatric examination be made by a physician who has limited his practice "exclusively to the diagnosis and treatment of mental and nervous disorders for a period of not less than three years."[71] Other statutes merely specify that the examiner be a physician, or they leave the sufficiency of his qualifications to the discretion of the court.[72] The medical inquiry is usually conducted by a panel of at least two court-appointed physicians.[73] One or two interviews with an individual by the medical examiners is sufficient in some states, but others require a person to undergo temporary observational hospitalization ranging from thirty to ninety days. In Maryland a suspected defective delinquent may be indeterminately held at the psychopathic institution upon court order for medical examination even though his criminal sentence may have expired in the interim.[74] In addition, the laws may sometimes authorize an independent psychiatric examination by experts selected by the delinquent.[75] By threatening a contempt citation for refusing to answer, some states coerce persons to respond to the diagnostic questions asked by the court-appointed medical examiners.[76] The safeguards of the fifth amendment protection against self-incrimination are circumvented by characterizing the examination and resultant commitment as a civil proceeding not requiring the traditional safeguards of the criminal law.[77]

Following the medical examination, the judicial evaluation and determination of psychopathy are rendered. Five states require no formal hearing prior to the judicial order, leaving the decision within

[70] *Mentally Disabled and the Law* 301 (Lindman and McIntyre eds.).

[71] *Ala. Code* tit. 15, §434 (1958).

[72] *Iowa Code Ann.* §225A.4 (Supp. 1964). *See*, generally, Note, "Plight of the Sexual Psychopath" 532–34.

[73] *See, e.g., Ind. Ann. Stat.* §9–3404(d) (Supp. 1965).

[74] State v. Musgrove, 241 Md. 521, 217 A.2d 247 (1966).

[75] *See, e.g., Md. Code Ann.* art. 31B, §7(b) (1957).

[76] *Mentally Disabled and the Law* 301 (Lindman and McIntyre eds.).

[77] *In re* Moulton, 77 A.2d 26 (N.H. 1950); Malone v. Overholzer, 93 F. Supp. 647 (Dist. Ct., D.C. 1950); People v. Sims, 382 Ill. 472, 47 N.E.2d 704 (1943); State v. Madary, 178 Neb. 383, 133 N.W.2d 583 (1965); Eggleston v. State 209 Md. 504, 121 A.2d 698 (1956).

the discretion of the court after it reviews the medical evidence submitted.[78] Most states provide for a hearing, but the degree of procedural formality varies. Some states not only specifically require a
hearing but guarantee the right to a jury trial.[79] Only a few, however,
provide for the appointment of counsel if defendant cannot secure
one.[80]

The Legal Status of an Adjudged Psychopath

Once adjudged a psychopath, an individual finds himself subject to
indeterminate confinement; to secure release, he must prove that he is
cured. Such confinement is not considered a criminal sentence, and its
term as well as its conditions therefore lack the constitutional safeguards applicable to criminal sentences.

Although a patient may contest his confinement as a psychopath
through a habeas corpus proceeding,[81] release is normally achieved
through favorable medical recommendations to the committing court.
The effectiveness of habeas corpus proceedings is hampered by the
fact that the petitioning patient must prove that he is ready for release. Many committing institutions refuse to permit their patients to
see outside psychiatrists even if such psychiatrists are willing to visit
the institution, on the ground that such visits would be disruptive to
the institutional programs.[82] It is practically impossible, therefore, for
a patient to be released from a psychopathic institution without staff
approval. Specifically, release is predicated upon an institutional determination that the patient is cured or, more frequently, that he is
sufficiently recovered to pose no threat to others.[83] Normally, the
patient cannot obtain full freedom until he has served a period as a
parolee.[84] If the conditions of this probationary release are violated,

---

[78] Kansas, Pennsylvania, and Utah leave the decision to the sole discretion of
the court, while Colorado leaves it up to the parole board. Wisconsin provides
for a hearing *on application for release*. *Kan. Gen. Stat. Ann.* §62–1536 (1964); *Pa.
Stat. Ann. tit.* 19, §1170(a) (1964); *Utah Code Ann.* §77–49–4 (1953); *Colo.
Rev. Stat. Ann.* §39–19–5(1) (1963); *Vt. Stat. Ann.* tit. 18, §2814 (1959).

[79] *Cf.* Indiana and New Hampshire, which specifically *deny* the right to a jury.

[80] Iowa, Minnesota, and Nebraska. *See Mentally Disabled and the Law* 301
(Lindman and McIntyre eds.).

[81] In a habeas corpus proceeding, the court will order that a detained person
be brought before it in order to determine the legality of the detention.

[82] Sas v. Maryland, no. 14808, U.S. Dist. Ct., January 15, 1969.

[83] Note, "Plight of the Sexual Psychopath" 527, 535–36. *See, e.g., Ill. Ann. Stat.*
ch. 38, §105–9 (Smith-Hurd 1964).

[84] *See, e.g., Pa. Stat. Ann.* tit. 19, §1173 (1964).

either through criminal involvement or because of a violation of administrative regulations, the patient is subject to recommitment.[85]

In the states that allow pre-conviction commitment, the cured or improved psychopath is not a free man.[86] Since the psychopathy process is generally considered therapeutic and nonpenal, it presents no bar to a later criminal trial and penal sentence for the offense which triggered the initial psychopathy commitment,[87] though the state will often make a concession by allowing the period of incarceration in the psychopathic institution to count toward any subsequent criminal sentence for the precipitating offense.[88]

In states that hold post-conviction psychopathy proceedings, commitment to a psychopathic institution will often but not always serve in lieu of the applicable criminal sentence.[89] A California study of released psychopaths indicates that some are subsequently subjected to criminal penalties. "While most judges, in imposing sentence, take into consideration the prolonged enforced hospitalization, a strong minority of them feel that after the patient has been cured he still has to 'pay his debt to society' to the full extent. . . ."[90]

The Program: Maryland Model

One of the newer, most active, and most widely studied state programs for psychopaths operates in Maryland—it well typifies the good and bad aspects of the new trend. Housed in a five-million-dollar physical plant at Patuxent, the Maryland defective delinquent pro-

[85] *Mass. Ann. Laws* ch. 123A, §9 (1965), provides in part: "The violation by the holder of a parole permit to be at liberty of any of the terms or conditions of such permit, or of any law of the commonwealth, shall render such permit void."

[86] On the inapplicability of double jeopardy to psychopathy commitments *see* Application of Keddy, 105 Cal. App. 2d 215, 233 P.2d 159 (1951); Eggleston v. State, 209 Md. 504, 121 A.2d 698 (1956).

[87] People v. Levy, 151 Cal. App. 2d 460, 311 P.2d 897 (1957); People v. Redlich, 401 Ill. 270, 83 N.E.2d 736 (1949). The released psychopath is therefore remanded to the custody of the criminal court for disposition of the suspended criminal charges according to what, in the court's discretion, "justice and the welfare of society may dictate." *Colo. Rev. Stat. Ann.* ch. 39–19–7 (1963); *Kan. Gen. Stat. Ann.* §62–1537 (1968); *contra Fla. Stat. Ann.* §917.12(3) (Supp. 1964), which requires that any pending criminal proceedings be recommenced. At least one jurisdiction expressly provides that a finding of psychopathy will bar subsequent prosecutions upon the original charge, 24 A.L.R. 2d 352.

[88] *Mentally Disabled and the Law* 302 (Lindman and McIntyre eds.).

[89] *Ind. Ann. Stat.* §9–3409 (repl. vol. 1956); *Mich. Stat. Ann.* §28.967(8) (1954). *See also Mentally Disabled and the Law* 302 (Lindman and McIntyre eds.).

[90] Hacker and Frym, "A Sexual Psychopath Act in Practice: A Critical Discussion," 43 *Calif. L. Rev.* 766 (1955).

gram costs $5,000 per patient per year. For 480 patients in 1966, the institution's professional staff, as distinct from custodial personnel, included 11 psychiatrists, 9 psychologists, and 14 social workers. According to Dr. Harold M. Boslow, Director of the Patuxent Institute, psychopathy therapy, unlike the typical mental health program, cannot be limited solely to the improvement of the patient's emotional or mental status.[91] A psychopathy program has to consider many other factors that might affect the probability that a released patient will commit any further antisocial or criminal acts. Although the Maryland defective delinquent law is premised upon the belief that the criminal misconduct of the institutionalized client is caused by emotional immaturity or disturbance, improvement in a patient's emotional status alone has not been sufficient to guarantee his lawful conduct upon return to society. The majority of defective delinquents have little formal schooling and few marketable skills; these deficiencies are often as much an obstacle to social adjustment as the patient's emotional disabilities. The resultant treatment directed "towards the total rehabilitation of the total person" combines, therefore, educational, vocational, and psychotherapeutic programs.

The aim of the Patuxent Institution is to create a "total therapeutic milieu" in which all of its activities, whether custodial, social, or recreational, take place. This means that the system is based on the hypothesis that rewarding socially desirable and personally beneficial inmate behavior will increase the frequency of such behavior and reduce an inmate's tendency to be hostile or to express undesirable attitudes.

To implement this concept, the institution classifies and houses its inmates in one of four tiers, or privilege groups. Depending on this group classification, a patient is allowed more or fewer privileges regarding lights-out time, commissary purchases, job assignment, freedom of movement among inmates and within the institution, and other responsibilities involving personal discretion and liberty. To cope with uncooperative inmates the institution resorts also to "negative rewards." An inmate who declines to cooperate, by not talking with the physicians or failing to perform his duties, may find himself restricted to the "receiving tier" with no therapy and no privileges until he conforms. Such sanctions have been exercised for periods of four or five years and have even been applied to individuals who are

---

[91] Boslow, "Maryland's Approach to the Dangerous Offender" 3–4 (unpublished paper in the Washington College of Law Library, 1967).

at the institution for examination only.[92] "Patients must work their way up to higher . . . [privilege] levels," says Dr. Boslow, "by demonstrating cooperation with the goals of the institution and interest in their own self-government and self-improvement."[93] After an inmate has shown the requisite improvement within the institution, he is granted holiday leaves, then progresses to monthly leaves, and finally to a carefully supervised parole, utilizing an outpatient clinic.

The Maryland program had grown from an average number of 186 patients in 1956 to 434 patients in 1963[94] and nearly 500 in 1968.[95] In the ten-year period from 1955 to 1965, Maryland's Patuxent Institution admitted 1,483 persons for diagnosis. Of these, 826 were recommended for commitment by the medical staff, but only 581, or 82 percent, were found commitable as defective delinquents by the court or jury. During this same period, 143 patients were paroled. Of this group, 62, or 43 percent, were returned as violators; but only 44, or 31 percent, of the parolees violated their parole by commiting new *criminal* offenses. Of those who were granted final release by the superintendent, only 8 percent returned to criminal behavior; of those who were freed from the institution by court action, against the advice of the medical staff, 54 percent had subsequent records of criminal conduct.[96]

SOCIAL FUNCTION AND UTILITY

The psychopathy laws symbolize a contraction of the concept of free will upon which the criminal law is predicated and a reciprocal expansion of the more deterministic approach to social controls. Traditionally, the criminal law has recognized only two classes of offenders—the sane and the insane. Those not criminally insane were presumed to have willed their offensive activity and were held personally responsible. The determinists, emphasizing either environmental or hereditary factors, have, however, made considerable inroads against the philosophy that man is sole master of his destiny. Modern psychological studies have similarly indicated that criminal acts are motivated by factors other than a malevolent will. The psychopathy laws

---

[92] Writ of habeas corpus of Lawrence H. McKenzie, criminal trials nos. 4854 and 4855, law no. 39,033, filed December 13, 1968, in the Circuit Court for Prince Georges County, Md.

[93] Boslow, "Maryland's Approach to the Dangerous Offender" 14.

[94] *Maryland Manual*, 1957 through 1964.

[95] Author's observations, December 1968.

[96] Boslow, "Maryland's Approach to the Dangerous Offender" 22.

assert recognition of man's limited freedom by exempting from criminal sanctions a group of offenders whose antisocial activities are attributable to such nonvolitional factors. The psychopathy laws are sometimes regarded, therefore, as an extension of the criminal defense of insanity, relieving from criminal sanctions a group of social deviants who do not properly fall within the boundaries of normalcy.[97] More significantly, the psychopathy laws recognize the inefficacy of criminal sentences and institutions in dealing with most such offenders, whether mentally or morally deviated.[98] Consequently, special treatment in psychopathic institutions is designed, at least in theory, to meet the progressive and rehabilitative objectives of society rather than the traditional retributive-deterrent aims of the criminal system; the new programs thus find important support in the humanist ranks.

The appeal of the new system of noncriminal social controls also responds to the pragmatic desire of the public to provide for long-term protection against those with a propensity toward crime. As summarily reported by the American Bar Foundation:

> The aim of these statutes is twofold: (1) to protect society by providing for indeterminate confinement of sexually deviated offenders, and (2) during confinement, to provide medical treatment for the cure of their abnormality.[99]

It is this combination of the medical-scientific label and social pragmatism, in addition to past legislative and judicial willingness to exempt the exertion of these powers from the traditional safeguards applicable to the criminal process, that has disturbed many observers. From the skeptics' viewpoint, the function of the new therapeutic controls may therefore harbor a new threat to individual freedom.

To their critics, such special programs are merely "Star Chamber procedure[s]" embellished with diagnostic and treatment facilities.[100] The four-tier system is characterized as a convenient device for withholding privileges from and repressing those inmates who are con-

[97] Mihm, "Sex Psychopath Statutes" 716–17; Maryland Legislative Council, *An Intermediate Sentence Law for Defective Delinquents*, Research Report no. 29, p. 2 (1954); *in re* Mundy, 97 N.H. 239, 85 A.2d 371, 374 (1952).

[98] Glueck has called the indeterminate sentence "indispensable" to modern penology because it makes possible "treatment . . . individualized to meet the specific causes [of each offender's] misconduct." Glueck, "Indeterminate Sentence and Parole in the Federal System," 21 *B. U. L. Rev.* 20, 23–24 (1941).

[99] *Mentally Disabled and the Law* 300 (Lindman and McIntyre eds.).

[100] New Jersey, Commission on the Habitual Sex Offender, *The Habitual Sex Offender* 35.

sidered resistant or unresponsive to rehabilitative efforts. These are kept under maximum security and are, in effect, the forgotten man.[101]

Critics assert that there has not been one full, complete cure in the history of the psychopathic institutions. They complain that the public's view of such programs as panaceas has resulted in serious overcrowding and spotty treatment schedules, with few inmates experiencing any direct regular contact with the medical staff. It is alleged that paroles are often granted merely to relieve the overcrowding. A study of Nebraska practices similarly reported the release of psychopaths whose records showed a prognosis of "poor" and "hopeless."[102] Once released on parole, the psychopath is without clear directives.

> The parolees are kept on a "yo-yo" and thus under constant pressure and concern that they may be recalled at any time. The nature of the sentence, in that it is indefinite and thus able to and does extend beyond the period of criminal incarceration, leaves the defective delinquent in a very precarious position in that he has to meet certain unknown criteria in order to be judged cured and thus declared suitable to re-enter society.[103]

Like a Kafka-esque character, the psychopath is a man to whom no clear-cut social standards are applicable. He suffers from a disputed mental disorder. He is indefinitely committed for an offense, often unproved, that would impose only a mild sentence on others. To secure release, he must be cured of a condition that is not clearly definable and that some say is not treatable. Finally, his return to society depends upon ambiguous conditions.

Despite a constant battle against a growing number of critics, the overall utilization of psychopathy laws has been increasing. Before 1958, only California and Michigan had regularly used their special psychopathy statutes.[104] Despite continuing criticism and outright condemnation, twenty states and the District of Columbia have since utilized these procedures.[105] Wisconsin, Maryland, California, and Michigan still remain the major proponents of the psychopathy laws.

---

[101] Hamill, "Maryland's Defective Delinquent Act" 26 (unpublished manuscript in Washington College of Law Library, 1965).

[102] Comment, "Sexual Psychopathy A Legal Labyrinth of Medicine, Moral and Mythology," 36 *Neb. L. Rev.* 320, 347 (1957).

[103] Hamill, "Maryland's Defective Delinquent Act" 27.

[104] *Mentally Disabled and the Law* 303 (Lindman and McIntyre eds.).

[105] They are: California, Colorado, Connecticut, District of Columbia, Florida, Illinois, Indiana, Kansas, Maryland, Massachusetts, Michigan, Minnesota, Missouri, Nebraska, New Hampshire, New Jersey, New York, Ohio, Pennsylvania, Vermont, Wisconsin.

Much less certain is the degree of success of these programs in achieving the double goals enunciated by the American Bar Foundation: social defense and individual cure.

California reports that during 1958–62 some 800 to 900 persons were annually admitted for observation as sexual psychopaths. Of these, approximately half were subsequently committed each year for treatment.[106] The average period of confinement after a psychopathy commitment in California is about eighteen months. Michigan, another psychopathy innovator, reports a total of 1,051 commitments in 1954–64. Of these patients, 344 were still confined at the end of the period, 242 had been released, 325 were on probation or parole, 75 had been readmitted, 26 had escaped, 29 were at large as violators, and 83 had died.[107] Similarly, Wisconsin reports that, from 1951 to 1960, 1,605 offenders were admitted for preliminary observation. One-half were determined to be psychopaths. Of this group, 146 were placed on probation by the court, and 632 were committed for treatment. Of those committed, 475 were later granted parole, 17 percent of the parolees being later recommitted for parole violations. Of the 414 who were finally completely discharged, only 7 percent had committed any new offenses as of the time of the report.[108] A 1965 survey of the District of Columbia institutions revealed a total of only 46 patients held pursuant to the sexual psychopathy laws.[109]

Summarizing the Maryland experience after its first eleven years, Dr. Harold M. Boslow, Director of the Patuxent Institution, reported the following:

> The first criterion for evaluating the success of any statute relates to the use or practicality of the statute. The Maryland defective delinquent law has been in operation for approximately eleven years. During this period over 1,500 offenders have been referred for evaluation. The usual rate of referral is approximately 125 offenders per year from Baltimore City and all of the twenty-three counties in Maryland. There is no doubt that the Maryland law is in use by the state and is practical.[110]

An independent commission for the valuation of Maryland's Patuxent Institution concluded:

[106] Bowman and Engle, "Sexual Psychopath Laws," in *Sexual Behavior and the Law* 757 (R. Slovenko ed. 1965).

[107] *Ibid.* 762.

[108] *Ibid.*

[109] Saint Elizabeths Hospital Records, 1965.

[110] Boslow, "Maryland's Approach to the Dangerous Offender" 3–4.

We are convinced on the evidence before us that, if it were not for the indeterminate sentence imposed on persons found to be defective delinquents, many of these people would, if they had been released on the expiration of fixed sentences, have committed other and serious crimes against the personal safety of our citizens.... Not all Defective Delinquents can be apprehended or committed to Patuxent. Unfortunately, despite the operation of the law and Patuxent's part therein, heinous crimes will be perpetrated in the future as they have been in the past. In our opinion, however, without the law, these crimes would be substantially greater in number and tragic results.[111]

A MEDICAL AND SCIENTIFIC CRITIQUE

The medical and behavioral disciplines have never been certain just whom the state legislatures have singled out for treatment for psychopathy. "Much of the difficulty in definition arises out of the fact that psychiatrists themselves are in wide disagreement as to the connotation of the term psychopath."[112] Accordingly, a 1950 New Jersey report cited twenty-nine different definitions of the condition by twenty-nine medical authorities.[113]

Generally, the term appears to be an open-ended concept of convenience, drawn to accommodate social and administrative purposes, and used to group together disparate types of deviants identifiable only by their nonconformity with the standards of conduct established by a given community at a given historical period—the psychiatric purse seine for any person who indulges in antisocial conduct.[114] Accordingly, some commentators have questioned the very utility of this amorphous concept and have insisted that we should "rather deal with symptomatology and its social implications,"[115] meaning that we should concern ourselves less with comprehensive terminology and should concentrate more upon the identity and control of the particular offender.

Because of the popular concern with crimes involving sexual behavior, the sexual deviant is more likely than any other offender to

[111] Maryland, Commission to Study and Re-evaluate Patuxent Institution, *Report* (1961).
[112] New Jersey, Commission on the Habitual Sex Offender, *The Habitual Sex Offender* 37.
[113] *Ibid.* 40–42.
[114] Arieff and Rotman, "Psychopathic Personality," 39 *J. Crim. L.C. & P.S.* 158 (1948).
[115] L. C. Kolb, M.D., quoted in Berstein, "Sexual Psychopath Laws" 14 (unpublished manuscript in Washington College of Law Library, 1965).

be designated a psychopath. The emphasis placed upon the sexual
offender by the psychopathy laws is especially questionable and un-
reasoned. To justify this emphasis the following propositions are
advanced: sex offenders comprise a separate and homogenous group
of criminals; sex offenders regularly progress from minor offenses
such as exhibitionism to major offenses such as forcible rape; the sex
deviate is more dangerous than other types of criminals; and a higher
degree of recidivism exists among sex deviates than among other
criminals.[116] These propositions, however, are said to bear little relation to clinical experience and statistics. "There is available a relatively large body of material that challenges the underlying assumptions of the sex deviate laws."[117]

The evidence indicates that those who commit sexual offenses do
not constitute a homogenous group. Because of the variegated sex
crimes, sexual offenders in America may range from adult married
partners who voluntarily practice cunnilingus or fellatio, or adult
homosexuals who privately and voluntarily engage in their deviations,
to the active pedophiliacs or sadomasochistic rapists. Sexual psychopathy laws, which do not clearly distinguish between the violent and
the meek sex offenders or between voluntary and involuntary deviations, are criticized for lack of discrimination and for being out of
touch with American reality.[118] The Kinsey studies indicated that 73
percent of all American males have had some homosexual experience
and that 59 percent had participated in oral sodomy, conduct which
brings them within the psychopathy criteria established by many
states.[119] Broad and imprecise sexual psychopathy laws tend to confuse the distinction between the personal sin and the public crime;
they fail to distinguish between nuisance and danger.[120]

[116] Guttmacher and Weihofen, "Sex Offenses," 43 *J. Crim. L.C. & P.S.* 153,
154 (1952).
[117] *Mentally Disabled and the Law* 304 (Lindman and McIntyre eds.).
[118] The Michigan Governor's Study Commission on Sex Deviates recommended
in 1951 that sentences from one day to life be permitted for psychopaths charged
with the following crimes: rape; sodomy; assault with intent to commit rape or
sodomy, or to take indecent liberties with a child; indecent exposure; gross indecency between males; gross indecency between females; gross indeceny between male and female; incest; window peeping. The proposal, patterned after
the New York law, was not adopted. Michigan, Governor's Study Commission on
Sex Deviates, *Report* 125 (1951). A single dissent noted that to make window
peeping punishable by a sentence of one day to life "and delegating the duration
of the sentence to a psychiatrist or a judge, is not in my opinion a step forward
but is a step far back into antiquity, ante-dating Calpernius Piso." *Ibid.* 168.
[119] Kinsey, *Concepts of Normalcy and Abnormalcy in Sexual Behavior* 28
(1949).
[120] M. Ploscowe, *Sex and the Law* 237 (1951).

The asserted relationship between minor sexual transgressions and truly dangerous conduct has at best been overemphasized.[121] Of a group of thirty rapists studied by the late forensic psychiatrist, Dr. Manfred Guttmacher, only one had previously been convicted of any type of sex offense, whereas ten had prior convictions for burglary.[122] The popular magazine portrayal of the exhibitionist, transvestite, or voyeur undergoing a lycanthropic metamorphosis to a sadomasochistic rapist is exceptional. The Michigan Governor's Study Commission concluded that it was groundless to assume that sex deviates are oversexed "fiends." "The fact is that many true sex deviates are unaggressive, timid, and inoffensive. Characteristically, they are not apt to be over-sexed. . . . Another fallacy is that sex offenders progress to more and more serious sex crimes. It is an exception when they do so."[123] A study conducted in Illinois concluded that no more than 5 percent of the convicted sex offenders were physically dangerous.[124] Tappan, a leading criminologist, similarly reported: "There are very few aggressive and dangerous sex offenders in the criminal population. Most of the deviates are mild, submissive, more an annoyance than a menace to the community."[125]

The proposition that sexual deviates are highly recidivous has been similarly questioned. A statistical study conducted in New Jersey shows that sex offenders have one of the lowest rates as "repeaters" of all types of criminals. Among serious crimes, homicide alone has a lower rate of recidivism. Studies of large samples of sex criminals show that most of them get into trouble only once. Of those who do repeat, a majority commit some offense other than sex crimes. "Those who recidivate are characteristically minor offenders—such as peepers, exhibitionists, homosexuals—rather than criminals of serious menace."[126] A study conducted in California demonstrated that while 16 percent of all state prisoners had been in prison two or more times previously,

[121] See Frisbie, "Treated Sex Offenders Who Reverted to Sexually Deviant Behavior," 29 *Fed. Prob.* 52 (1965).

[122] Guttmacher and Weihofen, *Psychiatry and the Law* 117.

[123] Michigan, Governor's Study Commission on Sex Deviates, *Report* 4.

[124] Illinois, Commission on Sex Offenders, *Report to the Sixty-Eighth General Assembly of the State of Illinois* 11 (1953).

[125] Tappan, "Sentence for Sex Criminals," 42 *J. Crim. L.C. & P.S.* 332, 336 (1951). Massachusetts has recognized the significance of these studies and has accordingly limited its Sexually Dangerous Persons Act to exclude "nuisance offenders—voyeurs, exhibitionists, transvestites, fetishists, and others with similar aberrant modes of behavior." Kozol, "The Criminally Dangerous Sex Offender," 275 *N. Eng. J. Med.* 81 (1966); *Mass. Ann. Laws* ch. 123A, §§1–11 (1965). See also *Ill. Ann. Stat.* ch. 38, §§105–1 to 12 (1964).

[126] New Jersey, Commission on the Habitual Sex Offender, *The Habitual Sex Offender* 38.

only 7.2 percent of the prisoners charged with sexual offenses had a similar record.[127] Evidence indicates that sex offenders have substantially fewer parole violations than other types of offenders.[128] These statistics have led Tappan to the conclusion that: "[o]ur sex offenders are among the least recidivous of all types of criminals. They do not characteristically repeat as do our burglars, arsonists and thugs."[129]

Other commentators, however, citing the discrepancies among the various statistical studies, claim that no valid conclusions can be drawn about the sexual offender's rate of recidivism due to the fact that the victims of sex crimes are often more reluctant to report to the police than are the victims of other crimes. They note the disparate European reports of recidivism among sexual offenders. A study of 3,000 Danes who had committed sexual offenses between 1929 and 1939 reported that 25 percent had relapsed by 1958. Those with an additional conviction prior to the one studied showed a relapse rate of 35 percent. The report also indicated that the older the offender, the greater the chance of relapse. A similar study conducted in England demonstrated that one out of ten of those with one previous sex offense relapsed, whereas those with a history of two or more offenses had a relapse rate of four in ten. Interestingly, those convicted of heterosexual offenses had more success in adjusting after release than did those convicted of homosexual offenses or indecent exposure.[130]

The paucity of scientific studies and definite knowledge about the behavior and social danger of the sex offender makes it difficult to reach meaningful conclusions regarding the utility of special treatment programs in lieu of traditional criminal punishments. Critics of existing programs do not argue that there are no recidivous sexual offenders, but rather that if recidivism is the evil which these special programs seek to eliminate, then various types of criminals other than sexual offenders are in greater need of such attention.[131] An attempt to answer this criticism has been offered by Guttmacher and Weihofen:

[127] California, Langley Porter Neuropsychiatric Institute, *California Sexual Deviation Research* 21 (1953).

[128] *Ibid.* 20–25.

[129] Tappan, "Sentence for Sex Criminals" 336.

[130] Bowman and Engle, "Sexual Psychopath Laws" 757, 770. For reports on other European studies *see* Stürup, "Sex Offenses: The Scandinavian Experience," 25 *Law & Contemp. Prob.* 361 (1960); Williams, "Sex Offenses: The British Experience," *ibid.* 334.

[131] *Mentally Disabled and the Law* 304 (Lindman and McIntyre eds.). One author illustrates this idea succinctly: ". . . there are nonsexual offenses, such as

Perhaps the only valid justification for separate legislation for sexual psychopaths is a pragmatic one. Such legislation permits experimenting with new procedures in a limited area, procedures which would be considered too radical for more general acceptance. If they prove themselves, they can be extended in scope later.[132]

If limited experimentation is accepted as major justification of these special programs, their utility will never be determined without trained personnel and adequate facilities. State legislatures, however, frequently enact this new type of law without providing for the supportive hospital facilities and services required; instead they place the burden on the already overtaxed mental hospitals and correctional institutions.[133] An experienced observer of the Michigan facilities reported: "The only apparent difference between the regimen of prisoners and that of the sex psychopaths was that the latter were designated 'visitors,' though, like the man who came to dinner, they were apparently there for a long stay. The only treatment provided was an occasional visit by a prison psychiatrist."[134] Even in states where special facilities were made available, not enough qualified personnel were found to administer effective programs.[135]

Another of the problems of the psychopathy programs is the present inability of the medical profession to prescribe a generally effective treatment. Indeed, some authorities doubt altogether the ability of medical science to cure or improve substantially the condition of the vast majority of those designated psychopathic.[136] There are no drugs or specific therapy known that benefit the condition of this morally or

---

arson, kleptomania, burglary, and murder, which have sexually motivating aspects. A nine-year-old boy, for example, was referred for psychiatric examination because he was 'burning up the hills.' After several interviews with this lad and his mother, during which she was advised to get him a bed of his own and not have him continue sleeping with her, the fire-setting behavior ceased. Breaking and entering or burglary by the adolescent is often equated [in psychiatry] with breaking and entering the forbidden area of the female, as in rape.... Contrary to popular notion, it is not the exhibitionist, but the burglar who is more likely to commit rape. This relationship is based not only on clinical observation and psychodynamic formulation, but also on criminal statistics." Sadoff, "Sexually Deviated Offenders," 40 *Temp. L. Q.* 305, 312 (1967).

[132] Guttmacher and Weihofen, *Psychiatry and the Law* 133.

[133] Ploscowe, *Sex and the Law* 235 (1951).

[134] *Ibid.*

[135] In Maryland it was recently decided that individual treatment is not necessary as long as the institution provides "milieu therapy" for all patients. Director of Patuxent Institution v. Daniels 221 A.2d 397, 417 (1966).

[136] Birnbaum, "*Primum Non Nocere*: How to Treat the Criminal Psychopath," 52 *A.B.A.J.* 69 (1966).

socially abnormal person. The only treatment for psychopathy known at present is essentially nonmedical—a long-term program of total re-education[137] similar to the Maryland program described earlier. For many of the psychopaths, however, such re-education comes too late in life to be effective. Their institutional commitment is not therapeutic but simply an act of social defense, designed primarily to insulate the public from them.[138]

The lack of treatment facilities and methods, combined with the impossibility of treating many of these offenders, has served as a major weapon for critics of the psychopathy programs. The policy of committing noncriminals and minor deviates for indeterminate confinement without offering them any therapy was described as "atrocious" by Tappan in 1955.[139] According to the American Bar Foundation in 1961:

> The lack of treatment is a basic condemnation of the sex deviate laws, since the philosophy behind such legislation is that these offenders should be treated rather than punished. Lack of treatment destroys any otherwise valid reason for differential consideration of the sexual psychopath. It would appear that the law is looking to medical knowledge for solutions to problems in this area only to find that such knowledge is as yet nonexistent or imprecise.[140]

Five years later, in 1965, the staff of the Indiana Institute for Sex Research (founded by Dr. Kinsey) reported new results of extensive research with various groups of sexual offenders.[141] After studying the records, backgrounds, and attitudes of both sexual offenders who were sentenced to traditional penal institutions and of those selected for psychopathy programs in California, the Kinsey panel reached several important conclusions. First, it found few fundamental differences in the crimes committed by the two groups. Second, the most apparent difference was that the psychopaths represented a relatively more intelligent, better educated, and younger group of offenders. (This disparity, however, could easily be attributed to the screening process through which the state medical authorities attempted to select the

---

[137] Comment, "Sexual Psychopathy" 320, 342.

[138] Recognizing this fact, at least one state provides that psychopathic patients may be transferred to prisons for the balance of their civil indeterminate commitment term. State v. Braggs (Ohio), 221 N.E.2d 493 (1966).

[139] Tappan, "Some Myths About the Sex Offender," 19 *Fed. Prob.* 7 (1955).

[140] *Mentally Disabled and the Law* 307–8 (Lindman and McIntyre eds.).

[141] P. Gebhard, *Sex Offenders* 845–67 (1965).

most responsive offenders for their special program.[142]) Third, after questioning the validity of this division of sexual offenders, the Kinsey group concluded that the existence of the sexual psychopathy process could be justified and its social purpose better fulfilled if it "winnows out those men with whom the clinicians can work most effectively and comfortably, and with a higher probability of alleviating their problems or at least ameliorating their behavior."[143] From this viewpoint, the psychopaths are those sexual offenders who are most amenable to treatment. But this definition disregards one of the primary social aims of the psychopathy legislation—the segregation of the most dangerous offenders. "[S]ome of the most dangerous men are those rejected as sexual psychopaths merely because they are not amenable to treatment, while some of the least dangerous are retained."[144]

Having originally turned to scientific terminology and the medical profession to effect social policies that legislatures could neither accurately define nor justify within the criminal process, society is now increasingly faced with a redefinition of the policies embodied in the psychopathy legislation—a redefinition necessitated by the acknowledged limitations of medicine and the lack of social support for these specialized programs.

WHAT SAFEGUARDS FOR THE PSYCHOPATH?

Inherent in the philosophy behind defective delinquency or psychopathy statutes is the proposition that once punitive and retributive intentions are disclaimed and therapeutic aims are asserted, society assumes the power to subject selected groups of offenders (or suspected offenders) to controls and experiments free from the safeguards which have evolved around the exercise of its more traditional police power. The courts that first scrutinized the legality of the psychopathy laws centered their attention upon the legislature's terminology and the social intent.

When the Michigan Supreme Court struck down the nation's first sexual psychopath law,[145] it was because the procedure had been in-

---

[142] Comment, "Wisconsin Sex Crime Act" 080, 082. *See Wis. Stat. Ann.* §959.15(6) (1965). Screening is also often necessary because of limited facilities for treatment.

[143] Gebhard, *Sex Offenders* 866.

[144] If those most amenable to treatment are to be the prime objects of the psychopathy programs, the investigators conclude, most confirmed homosexuals should be excluded as untreatable. *Ibid.*

[145] *Mich. Pub. Acts of 1937*, no. 106, p. 305.

corporated into the criminal code, yet did not meet the standards required by the criminal law.[146] To overcome these objections, the Michigan legislature transferred the law to the civil code, which made provision for commitment rather than incarceration, and formulated a more precise definition of "sexual psychopath."[147] After these alterations, the state supreme court found the new legislation free of constitutional objections.[148] Significantly, the court emphasized that the statute "makes sex deviators subject to restraint because of their acts and condition, and not because of conviction and sentence for a criminal offense."[149]

When Minnesota's "psychopathic personality" law[150] was reviewed by the United States Supreme Court in 1940,[151] it was also upheld. Speaking for the court, Justice Hughes commented favorably upon the precision of the statutory criteria defining those subject to law. Without addressing itself to most of the serious constitutional issues presently surrounding the psychopathy laws, the court compared the Minnesota statute to provisions for the civil commitment of mental patients.[152]

A more searching evaluation of the sexual psychopathy law was undertaken by the Missouri Supreme Court in 1950.[153] Allen T. Sweezer was charged on July 2, 1949, with unlawfully assaulting one Charlotte Jane Edens. While the charge was pending in the county court, the prosecuting attorney filed a petition with the court to determine whether the suspect was subject to commitment as a sexual psychopath. Sweezer objected on several grounds, alleging that the psychopathy law violated his right to due process of law and that the required medical examination contravened the Missouri Constitution's provision that "[n]o person shall be compelled to testify against himself in a criminal case."[154]

In a comprehensive commentary on state powers, the Missouri Supreme Court stated that "[u]nder its police power the state may

[146] People v. Frontczak, 286 Mich. 51, 281 N.W. 534 (1938).

[147] Mich. Comp. Laws §780.501 to 509 (1948).

[148] People v. Chapman, 301 Mich. 584, 4 N.W.2d 18 (1942).

[149] Ibid. 26. The Illinois Supreme Court similarly observed that "the state not only has the power but the duty to protect society from persons who are sex criminals and who have not recovered from their criminal propensities...." People ex rel. Elliott v. Jurgens, 95 N.E.2d 602 (Ill. 1950).

[150] Minn. Stat. Ann. §§526.09 to 11 (1947).

[151] Minnesota ex rel. Pearson v. Probate Court, 309 U.S. 270 (1940).

[152] Ibid. 272, 276.

[153] State ex rel. Sweezer v. Green, 360 Mo. 1249, 232 S.W.2d 897 (1950).

[154] Mo. Const., art. I, §19.

also enact a new procedure both curative in purpose and rehabilitating in objective, and which substitutes treatment and care for punishment."[155] Furthermore, under its *parens patriae* powers the state has the sovereign duty of guardianship over persons who are "[n]on sui juris and dangerous to the health, morals and safety of its citizens, and to themselves."[156] The designation of the psychopathy proceeding as civil rather than criminal was regarded by the court as fundamental to the decision of whether constitutional safeguards were necessary. The court reasoned that the purpose of a criminal proceeding is to punish, whereas the psychopath process is "but a civil inquiry to determine a status . . . curative and remedial in nature instead of punitive."[157] Having reached this conclusion, the Missouri court stated that one "of the evident purposes of the act is to prevent persons who suffer from this mental disorder . . . from being punished for crimes they commit during the period of this mental ailment."[158] Insistence upon criminal law safeguards was considered unnecessary.[159]

Similar reasoning has been prevalent throughout the legal literature on the subject. Following its detailed study of the state psychopathy laws, the American Bar Foundation approvingly concluded that: "In determining the constitutionality of the sex psychopath statutes, the crux of our consideration rests upon the judicial determination of whether the proceedings . . . are criminal or civil."[160]

Accepting the assumption that psychopathy laws are civil in nature, nearly all states have failed to accord persons petitioned as psychopaths the same rights granted to those charged as criminals. Of the states which allow pre-conviction commitments of psychopaths, only three specifically grant an individual the right to appeal a commitment order.[161] Only one of these states, Iowa, provides for court-appointed counsel if a person is financially unable to secure legal assistance.[162] Only four states give a person the right to have a jury

---

[155] State *ex rel.* Sweezer v. Green, 360 Mo. 1249, 232 S.W.2d 897, 902 (1950).
[156] *Ibid.*
[157] *Ibid.* 900; *see also in re* Moulton, 96 N.H. 370, 77 A.2d 27 (1951).
[158] State *ex rel.* Sweezer v. Green, 360 Mo. 1249, 232 S.W.2d 897, 902 (1950).
[159] More recently, the courts of Illinois have reasoned that because the psychopathy statute results in a deprivation of liberty, strict construction must be given to its requirements, and procedural safeguards common to the criminal process must be accorded. People v. McDonald, 44 Ill. App. 2d 348, 194 N.E.2d 541 (1963); People v. Turner, 61 Ill. App. 2d 353, 211 N.E.2d 486 (1965).
[160] *Mentally Disabled and the Law* 303 (Lindman and McIntyre eds.).
[161] They are Indiana, Iowa, and Missouri. Robitscher, *Pursuit of Agreement* 163.
[162] *Ibid.*

determine his psychopathy.[163] Procedural safeguards in psychopathy proceedings are less critical in the states where the determination of psychopathy is post-conviction and occurs subsequent to trial for a criminal offense.[164] In these states, a person is at least assured of a judicial determination regarding his involvement in the criminal act which has precipitated the commitment proceeding. Nevertheless, several of these states do not provide an individual with sufficient safeguards during the subsequent procedure to determine psychopathy.[165] In this psychopathy proceeding, a person's Fifth Amendment right to remain silent is unavailable, and he may be required to submit to psychiatric testing and interviewing.[166]

In addition to the discrepancies in procedural guarantees between the criminal process and the psychopathy process, there are differences between the power wielded by the administrators of the penal and the therapeutic institutions. The criminal, in prison or otherwise, is protected by the Eighth Amendment's prohibition against cruel and unusual punishment. With respect to psychopaths, however, investigators report:

> Physical restraints have departed from the prison but are standard equipment in many mental institutions. The overcrowded conditions alleviated in prisons have remained to plague the mental institution. There is doubt about the legality of sterilizing criminals, but sterilization, lobotomy, and electric shock treatment are permissible for sexual psychopaths.[167]

The differentiation between the civil and criminal process in determining constitutional rights is more a preoccupation with labels than with substance. Undoubtedly, the sanctions available under the noncriminal psychopathy process are as severe as those available under the criminal process. The committed psychopath may be deprived of his liberty for an indeterminate period, without any assurance that he will receive active therapy or that there is hope of recovery.[168] The only advantage of the "civil" nature of this process would seem to be that the psychopathy commitment does not create a criminal record. The actual value of this arrangement, however, is highly questionable.

---

[163] Missouri, Indiana, New Hampshire, and Minnesota. *Ibid.*
[164] For a list of such states *see* note 63 above.
[165] *Mentally Disabled and the Law* 309 (Lindman and McIntyre eds.).
[166] *Ibid.* 301.
[167] *Ibid.* 310.
[168] Unfortunately, the psychopath's demand for treatment as a *quid pro quo* for his ˙ idefinite term of confinement has until recently been ignored by the

Is it beneficially persuasive to argue, "I have no criminal record; I have merely been detained as a sexual psychopath for the past several years"? In terms of lost time and post-release employment opportunities it is likely that a psychopathy record may be more damning than the record of an old-fashioned criminal conviction.

The need for constitutional safeguards in the psychopathy process must turn upon the major policies and realities behind the laws and not upon a sophistic distinction between civil and criminal. Are psychopathy commitments primarily a vehicle for protective detention and a means for more effective social defense against criminals, suspected criminals, and various nonconformists? If so, then there is no substantive reason why the panoply of strict constitutional safeguards should be denied to one subjected to this process. If, on the other hand, therapy and rehabilitation are the true underlying goals, public support for this drastic experiment equally requires fundamental procedural fairness, guarantees of actual treatment and meaningful safeguards against the zeal of "experts." All of these propositions make their own argument for support from just men.

The psychopath's freedom from future criminal prosecution is an inconsistency in the structure of the psychopathy programs. If a psychopath is one unable to follow a lawful pattern of life because of personality defects, as the Missouri Supreme Court claimed,[169] the logical conclusion would be to accept psychopathy as a defense to criminal charges. The previously expressed view that the psychopathy laws are designed "to prevent persons suffering from this mental disorder ... from being punished for crimes they commit during the period of this mental ailment"[170] cannot be reconciled with the practice of subjecting the released and purportedly cured psychopath to a trial on the precipitating criminal charges. If psychopathic commitment is proposed as a substitution of nonpenal sanctions for penal ones, upon the grounds that the traditional criminal law concepts of

---

courts. For the failure of the courts to intervene in assuming treatment *see in re* Kemmerer, 309 Mich. 313, 15 N.W.2d 652 (1944), *cert. denied*, 329 U.S. 767 (1946); Kemmerer v. Benson, 165 F.2d 702 (6th Cir. 1948), *cert. denied*, 334 U.S. 840 (1948). See, however, Miller v. Overholser, 206 F.2d 415, 419 (D.C. Cir. 1953), which recognizes the right to treatment. For the view that commitment without treatment violates both the spirit of the Illinois statute and the due process clause of the United States Constitution *see* Burick, "Illinois Sexually Dangerous Act" 254, 258, and Nason v. Superintendent of Bridgewater State Hospital (Mass.), 233 N.E.2d 908, 913 (1968).

[169] State *ex rel.* Sweezer v. Green, 360 Mo. 1249, 232 S.W.2d 897 (1950).
[170] *Ibid.* 900.

guilt and punishment are not proper in the treatment of psychopaths, then the subsequent application of the criminal law concept of personal responsibility to a cured or improved psychopath is illogical.[171]

THE PAST AND THE FUTURE

It is time to admit that the divestment of criminal justice and the concurrent therapeutic expansion to psychopaths has not come from religious and humanitarian considerations or from a sense of wardship toward the disadvantaged—as in the case of the insane or the youthful offender. Divestment here has not served as a means for the humanitarian removal of criminal stigmas from offenders who possess a lessened capacity for culpability. Instead, the psychopathy model was viewed as a pragmatic tool for accomplishing under therapeutic auspices what could not be done in the criminal justice realm. Divestment increasingly serves as the vehicle for bringing into the American scene the formulas advanced in the late nineteenth century by positive criminology: the substitution of an indeterminate commitment that "fits the criminal" for the inadequate determinate sentence that merely "fits the crime;" orienting the process of sanctions toward the offender's total personal deficiency rather than toward the manifestations of the particular offense; placing greater emphasis upon who the deviant *is* and what his propensities are than upon his *overt* and antisocial past *act*; and granting greater discretion to the treatment and correctional arms of the state, often represented by social and behavioral scientists, in formulating programs that might more effectively curb and modify deviant behavior.

The existence of the psychopathy programs cannot be viewed as an expansion of the insanity defense, for a finding of psychopathy does not generally relieve the offender of criminal responsibility. Neither can these programs be viewed as an expansion of the civil laws for the commitment of the mentally ill, for the psychopath cannot usually expect to be fully released upon being cured. The psychopathy laws are an odd admixture of the insanity defense, penal incarceration, and civil commitment, yet they have the advantages of none of these. The psychopathy laws neither free the psychopath of responsibility for outstanding criminal charges nor give him the assurance that once

---

[171] See People v. Pygott, 64 Ill. App. 2d 284, 211 N.E.2d 382 (1965), which declares that, under the Illinois statute, once a patient is cured, he may not be tried for the criminal offense. The *Ohio Rev. Code Ann.* §2947.27 (Page Supp. 1964) makes similar provisions.

he is /cured he will be released. Instead, while the psychopath is denied the right to claim his abnormality as a defense, his condition is asserted to justify the exercise of the state's *parens patriae* power to impose a system of purported civil sanctions on top of the criminal process. The psychopath thus remains both patient and criminal.

Procedural and substantive constitutional safeguards have an appropriate function whenever society undertakes to impose sanctions, criminal or otherwise, which affect life, liberty, or property.[172] Where the beneficent motive of a therapeutic program of controls is a bald fiction, such protections are doubly mandatory. Therefore, before one is committed as a psychopath, sufficient proof of this condition and the public danger stemming from it must be demonstrated. Yet unlike other maladies psychopathy cannot be discovered through a simple physical or medical examination; whether a person is a psychopath can be determined by no meaningful symptoms other than his behavior. Because previous antisocial acts as well as a propensity to commit future crimes are component elements in a finding of psychopathy, and because both elements are subject to proof and disproof in a judicial hearing, the practice of denying the alleged psychopath the full measure of constitutional tools necessary to challenge or scrutinize these elements is unconscionable.

After floundering in semantics for nearly half a century, the courts are finally casting off the false rationale that a noncriminal and nonpunitive label justifies the denial of procedural safeguards.[173] A new critical approach to the content rather than the form of labeling was inaugurated by the 1965 *Brown* case, in which the Supreme Court of the United States asserted that

> [i]t would be archaic to limit the definition of "punishment" [under the Bill of Attainder Clause] to "retribution." Punishment serves several purposes: retributive, rehabilitative, deterrent—and preventive. One of the reasons society imprisons those convicted

---

[172] "Measures which subject individuals to the substantial and involuntary deprivation of their liberty contain an inescapable punitive element, and this reality is not altered by the facts that the motivations that prompt incarceration are to provide therapy or otherwise contribute to the person's well-being or reform. As such, these measures must be closely scrutinized to insure that power is being applied consistently with those values of the community that justify interference with liberty for only the most clear and compelling circumstances." F. A. Allen, *The Borderland of Criminal Justice: Essays in Law and Criminology* 37 (1964).

[173] People v. Turner, 61 Ill. App. 2d 353, 211 N.E.2d 486 (1965).

of crimes is to keep them from inflicting future harm, but that does not make imprisonment any the less punishment.[174]

Shortly thereafter, the Pennsylvania psychopathy law, which authorized the post-conviction indeterminate commitment of dangerous offenders, was attacked because it failed to accord the convicted individual separate opportunity to confront and cross-examine witnesses on the issue of his psychopathy and danger to the public.[175] The United States Court of Appeals for the Third Circuit held Pennsylvania's psychopathy law to be a criminal proceeding and the indeterminate commitment no less a criminal punishment because of its purported beneficial purpose.[176] Concluding that the psychopathy process was an independent proceeding involving issues different from those determined in the trial of the criminal offense, the court recognized that the offender "was entitled to a full judicial hearing before the magnified sentence was imposed. At such a hearing, the requirements of due process cannot be satisfied by partial or niggardly procedural protections."[177]

A further indication that procedural safeguards will be increasingly accorded in psychopathy proceedings was the recent United States Supreme Court decision in *Specht* v. *Patterson*.[178] Reviewing an indeterminate post-conviction commitment under the Colorado Sex Offenders Act,[179] the court held that the procedure, whether denominated civil or criminal, must comport with both the equal protection and the due process clauses of the Fourteenth Amendment.[180] The institution of the psychopathy process, to determine whether the convicted petitioner constituted a special public threat, was characterized by the court as a new charge against him; therefore, "he [must] be present with counsel, have an opportunity to be heard, be confronted with witnesses against him, have the right to cross-examine, and to offer evidence of his own."[181] The extension of procedural rights, however, has been limited to post-conviction commitments. Since these

---

[174] United States v. Brown, 381 U.S. 437, 458 (1965).

[175] *Pa. Stat. Ann.* tit. 19, §§1166–74.

[176] United States *ex rel.* Gerchman v. Maroney, 355 F.2d 302 (3d Cir. 1966). For a holding *contra see* Sas v. Maryland, 295 F.Supp. 389 (4th Cir. 1969), which upheld the "civil" rationale.

[177] Gerchman v. Maroney, 355 F.2d 312 (3d Cir. 1966). A similar conclusion was reached in Huebner v. State, 33 Wis.2d 505, 147 N.W.2d 646 (1967).

[178] 386 U.S. 605 (1967).

[179] *Colo. Rev. Stat. Ann.* §§39–19–1 to 10 (1963).

[180] 386 U.S. 608 (1967).

[181] *Ibid.* 610.

psychopathy commitments are precipitated by criminal convictions, the courts have had few reservations about denominating the whole process as criminal and insisting upon criminal safeguards from indictment to psychopathy commitment. The psychopath subjected to pre-conviction commitment has not yet benefitted from similar court rulings. Since pre-conviction commitment is primarily based upon a finding of future public danger rather than upon a conviction for a past criminal act, it more closely resembles the civil commitment of the mentally disordered and is more resistant to a characterization as a penal sentence.[182] It is only a question of time, we hope, before the veil is fully drawn and all psychopathic commitments are recognized as meriting substantially the same safeguards as the criminal process.[183]

Society's power to indeterminately incarcerate persons who have committed only minor offenses, on the speculative assumption that they pose future danger, is of doubtful moral and legal propriety.[184] This power, originating with the more humane programs for the mentally ill, has developed into a dangerous program of "preventive detention" in the case of the psychopaths. Given existing scientific knowledge and the increased interest in behavioral prediction tables, the threat inherent in this approach is alarming. The ambiguities, uncertainties, and arbitrariness lurking in the utilization of psychopathy formulas for measuring antisocial propensities and predicting potential social "threat" and "menace" would continue to give civil libertarians great cause for concern. The spectre of overzealousness in the name of social defense is foreshadowed by the history of the psychopathy laws which have indiscriminately commingled persons of violent sexual predilections with relatively harmless sexual deviates.[185]

[182] The commitment of insane persons and of psychopaths under pre-conviction proceedings was distinguished from post-conviction commitments in United States *ex rel.* Gerchman v. Maroney, 355 F.2d 302, 310 (3d Cir. 1966).

[183] *See in re* Gault, 387 U.S. 1 (1967); "juvenile proceedings to determine 'delinquency,' which may lead to commitment to a state institution, must be regarded as 'criminal' for purposes of the privilege against self-incrimination." *Ibid.* 49.

[184] "Clearly, protracted confinement of a person for a fear that he may pass checks without adequate funds may not be justified, whereas such confinement of a person likely to kill another may be fully warranted." H. Silving, *Constituent Elements of Crime* 32 (1967).

[185] Hacker and Frym, "A Sexual Psychopath Act" 766, 777. In Illinois, for example, over 50 percent of those committed as psychopaths are nonviolent offenders who pose no more than a psychological affront to the community. P. W. Tappan, *Crime, Justice and Correction* 345, 414 (1960).

Professor Norval R. Morris of the University of Chicago, reacting against the hazards to individual liberty stemming from indeterminate sanctions, urges that society not be permitted to exercise more extreme powers under the therapeutic or preventive system than those utilized under the criminal process.[186] While society should be free to direct a deviant to either a punitive program or a therapeutic one, it should be prevented from taking "power over a criminal's life ... in excess of that which would be taken" under the traditional criminal process.[187] The acceptance of such guidelines would make impossible the imposition of indeterminate commitments upon convicted psychopaths while similar offenders channeled through the usual criminal process are assessed lesser penalties. The recent United States Supreme Court decision in *Specht* v. *Patterson*,[188] which accords the protections of the Fourteenth Amendment to sexual psychopaths, similarly points in this direction. But since no comparable criminal standards would be available to limit indeterminate pre-conviction psychopathy confinements, the continuation of individualized and "unequal" programs for psychopaths could be easily effected through a shift to pre-conviction psychopathy commitments.

The reformation of the psychopathy laws is not a simple task. In searching for progress it is imperative to remember that society's right to defend itself from future evils in no way warrants reckless speculations with human lives and destinies. Therapeutic as well as penal interventions cannot be justified merely by a fear of allegation of prospective danger to society. In the accelerated drive toward preventive remedies against delinquency, heavier reliance should be placed upon demonstrated past antisocial conduct than on predicted and speculative future behavior.[189] If the primary justification for the psychopathy process is experimentation in social controls, such experiments should be fairly limited to those with proved antisocial recklessness. The great majority of the existing psychopathy laws do

---

[186] Morris, "Impediments to Penal Reform," 33 *U. Chi. L. Rev.* 627 (1966).

[187] *Ibid.* 656. While supporting indeterminate commitment for "treatable" psychopaths, another writer suggests that "untreatables" be dealt with through longer maximum criminal sentences for violent sex motivated crimes. This, he believes, would minimize the primary objections to the present psychopathy statutes, that nondangerous offenders are being confined for an indeterminate period of time. Burrick, "Illinois Sexually Dangerous Act" 154, 263–64.

[188] 386 U.S. 605 (1967).

[189] Some writers have suggested that protective measures against potentially dangerous persons are justified only in cases where a past harmful conduct, against the bodily integrity of a human being, is first proved. Silving, *Constituent Elements of Crime* 32.

not meet this requirement. As long as the present shortcomings in the criteria of psychopathy laws remain and the procedural safeguards continue to be inadequate, there is no way to relieve the fear that liberty is being denied by the caprices of pseudo-science.[190]

[190] "We dare not, in the 20th Century, blandly deny our whole legal heritage, unique in the world of oppression and bartered blood, and permit ourselves to be stampeded into the dictates of neoscience." Michigan, Governor's Study Commission on Sex Deviates, *Report* 168.

5 The Addicts: Seekers of Drug Euphoria

That humanity at large will ever be able to dispose with artificial
paradises seems very unlikely. Most men and women lead lives at
the best so monotonous, poor and limited that the urge to escape,
the longing to transcend themselves if only for a few moments,
is and has always been one of the principal appetites of the
soul.—A. Huxley, *The Doors of Perception* 62 (1954)

But by selling himself for a slave he abdicates his liberty; he . . .
therefore defeats, in his own case, the very purpose which is the
justification of allowing him to dispose of himself. . . . The
principle of freedom cannot require that he should be free not
to be free.—J. S. Mill, "On Liberty," in *On Liberty, Representative
Government, the Subjection of Women* 126 (Cumberledge
ed. 1912)

Viewed from almost any standpoint, opiate dependency is agreed
to be but a symptom of psychological disorder (even if its origins
are social or even genetic). To work so hard at symptom
suppression through means which cannot be shown to correct the
offender is dubious. To attend so fixedly to behavior which its,
in some ways, only an incidental criminological concern raises

serious doubts about the economy of our efforts.—Blum, "Mind-Altering Drugs and Dangerous Behavior: Narcotics," in President's Commission on Law Enforcement and the Administration of Justice, *Task Force Report: Narcotics and Drug Abuse* 60 (1967)

THE PURSUIT OF HAPPINESS

The girl who gets drunk at a party, the man who drives a car while intoxicated, the chronic drunk panhandling passers-by for one more drink, the middle-aged alcoholic who spends so much on drink that his family's well-being is affected, the excessive drinker who commits larceny, attempts rape, or stabs a teasing fellow-drinker in the local bar, the drug-pusher who supports his own habit by selling marijuana, the addict who commits robbery to obtain funds for narcotics—should we view them as criminal or as ill? With what words should we appraise them? Disgust, blame, sympathy? Should we condemn, ostracize, punish—or can we, instead, seek to understand, feel responsible, and attempt to cure?[1]

The Bible reports that Noah planted a vineyard after the deluge and became drunk on its wine.[2] Since early times alcohol and drugs have accompanied mankind both in intensifying its joys and in lightening its sorrows. Their beneficiaries, from Omar Khayyam and his jug of wine to DeQuincey the opium eater, have frequently praised them in song. Their victims, on the other hand, have long been recognized as serious burdens to society. But particularly since the onset of the industrial age and the resultant urban concentration have the social evils of addiction become visible.

If the seriousness of a deviation—its adverse effects on both private and public safety and welfare—can be deduced from police statistics, then alcoholism certainly merits top listing in this country. Some two million arrests in 1968—one out of every three arrests in America—were for the offense of public drunkenness or other alcohol violations.[3] About half of those detained in jails and in other short-term correctional facilities are held on charges of alcoholism. Possibly two-thirds of all homicides involve an inebriated offender or victim.

Yet to many, alcohol and drugs are indispensable substances in the quest for even temporary euphoria. Drinking, for the most part, is socially condoned. A few people are teetotallers; most people drink

[1] N. Kessel and H. Walton, *Alcoholism* 15 (1965).
[2] Gen. 9:20–21.
[3] FBI, *Uniform Crime Reports for the United States* 111 (1968).

moderately or even excessively. Only a small percentage of all drinkers are alcoholics—addicted to alcohol—and of those exposed to drugs only a segment permanently joins the community of addicts. Nietzsche described both alcohol and Christianity as the great European narcotics.[4] But despite their palliative effect on human misery and poverty, neither alcohol nor narcotics have been endorsed or tolerated by either church or state in modern times. Indeed, public programs for alcohol and drug control have been increasingly sought by church and state. The disruptive effect of these palliatives upon the family structure, their tendency to encourage economic idleness, and their connection with crime, all account to some extent for their social condemnation.

Society has long sought to control alcoholics and drug addicts through the sanctions of criminal justice. The outcome has been an ineffectual revolving door leading from the street to jail to the street again. Because of the inefficacy of the criminal process in controlling their conduct, alcoholics and drug addicts have become the central core of recidivism in this country. A majority of those arrested for public intoxication have lengthy histories of prior drunkenness arrests. In 1965, fifty-six percent of those arrested for intoxication in the District of Columbia had been arrested five times or more during their lifetime, and twenty-nine percent had been arrested fifty times or more. Only twenty-three percent of those arrested for intoxication in that year had no previous drunkenness arrest records.[5]

It is not surprising, therefore, that the most recent expansion of the therapeutic state has been into the realms of alcoholism and drug addiction. Several dramatic court decisions have prodded this process along. In 1962, the United States Supreme Court decreed that the status of drug addiction, as distinguished from the possession and sale of drugs, is not a criminal offense.[6] In 1966, two United States circuit courts ruled that public intoxication because of chronic alcoholism is not a crime and cannot be punished.[7] Society's option to use criminal sanctions for the suppression of drug and alcohol addiction has steadily been curbed. Developments have been so rapid and the conceptual revolution so far ahead of available facilities, that this country's anti-addiction program is in turmoil.

---

[4] F. W. Nietzsche, *The Twilight of Idols* 2 (Ludovici trans. 1888).

[5] President's Commission on Law Enforcement and the Administration of Justice, *Task Force Report: Drunkenness* 1, 73 (1967).

[6] Robinson v. California, 370 U.S. 660 (1962).

[7] Driver v. Hinnant, 356 F.2d 761 (4th Cir. 1966); Easter v. District of Columbia, 361 F.2d 50 (D.C. Cir. 1966).

Motivated by a positivist conception of human behavior and by the same humanistic and therapeutic aims originally reflected in the changing treatment of the mentally ill and juveniles, a shift is vigorously under way from the use of a terminology and machinery of crime and penology to the control of addiction under the auspices of a therapeutic model.[8]

Still, the transition has been hindered by many unanswered issues: Should society completely replace punishment with treatment in the case of addicts, irrespective of the offense charged, or should treatment be reserved to the lesser offender only? Can treatment be compulsorily imposed, and if so, how effective will it be? What can society do with the addict who refuses treatment? How long may the addict be detained if he cannot be readily cured? How are we to deal with the addict who is likely to relapse when he returns to the old adverse surroundings?

Though many questions still remain unresolved, the new noncriminal programs which were only recently described as far-sighted and constructive are already under attack from both traditionalists and reformers. To the first, the therapeutic emphasis smacks of coddling; to the latter, it is a road paved with grave hazards to individual liberty.

The conservatives, fearing that the newer developments do not effectively protect the public interest and safety, urge a continued reliance upon repression. Relieving alcoholics and drug addicts of criminal sanctions, they argue, is a mere invitation for social irresponsibility and decay. The liberals, on the other hand, fear the even greater threat of the therapeutic approach. The New York Civil Liberties Union thus recently declared that the new state law authorizing hospital commitments for drug addicts violates the fundamental guarantees of the Bill of Rights. Asserting that there is no known cure for addiction and that in any event the treatment now offered by the state is wholly inadequate, the NYCLU asked that the therapeutic program be declared unconstitutional. "It is nothing but a concentration camp program, instituted to sweep the addicts off the streets. The so-called treatment they are getting is valueless. It's nothing new. All of this has been tried in the past and failed."[9]

The inadequacy of available scientific remedies frequently lends credence to the old-line penologists. To them jail continues to be the best and safest depository for all social undesirables. Yet while alco-

---

[8] *See, e.g., N.Y. Mental Hygiene Law* §200 *et seq.* (Supp. 1967).
[9] *New York Times,* November 19, 1967, p. E9.

holics are being steadily removed from jails and workhouses, the therapy-oriented reformers, lacking funds, manpower, and facilities, are able to report only limited success.

There remains in the public mind and mores, and in the legal formulations which reflect them, a certain ambivalence regarding the displacement of the old with the new. While research demonstrates that condemnation and repression will not cure alcoholism and drug addiction, the public still feels little confidence in the new alternatives. While the law is now displaying preference for treatment over imprisonment in the case of the docile addict or the public drunk, the feeling continues that punishment should not be done away with if the same addict, under the influence of drugs or alcohol, had committed a crime—stolen, robbed, raped, or killed. Even though the United States Supreme Court has held that a person can only be treated and not punished for being an addict, that very decision still permits the same person to be imprisoned for the possession of a narcotic dosage required for his daily use. Likewise, in Virginia, Maryland, and the District of Columbia, an intoxicated chronic alcoholic wandering aimlessly cannot be sent to prison; the alcoholic clinic is the only lawful place for his confinement and cure. The same individual charged with disturbing the peace, stealing, breaking a window, or negligently setting his mattress on fire while under the influence of alcohol will go directly to jail.

To survey the medical, social, and legal problems posed by addiction is to become quickly embroiled in the quest for a proper balance between determinism and individual accountability, between public order and individual nonconformity. This arena permits not only one of the most dramatic confrontations between conflicting concepts and contrasting solutions but also a confrontation with direct practical implications for more than five of every one hundred adult Americans—the drug addicts and alcoholics.

THE DRUG DRAGON

Scarcely a family medicine chest in America is without some mood-changing or mind-changing drugs—substances used because of their effect upon the mental state. Some are addicting or habit-forming, others not. While a few (such as pep pills) act as stimulants and will keep a truck driver awake at night, others are depressants that will bring sleep to the insomniac, or tranquilizers that will put the anxious neurotic at peace. Too often the terms "drugs" or "narcotics" are used to encompass these substances, even though they pose varying hazards to the user and to society, and consequently require diverse programs of social control.

One of every four Americans took some mood- or mind-changing drug in 1968,[10] and one of every twelve Americans spent some time in the hospital, where he was frequently given narcotics. The use of narcotic and other mind-changing drugs for recognized medical purposes has become commonplace in this society. "In terms of drug use the rarest or most abnormal behavior is not to take any mind-altering drugs at all."[11] The deviant—be he true addict or experimenting abuser—is therefore merely the *indiscriminate* user, a consumer whose drugs are not medically prescribed and supervised and whose use satisfies personal rather than medical aims.

The chewing, eating, or smoking of mind-changing substances is a practice which dates from antiquity. Of today's surviving tribal and primitive societies, many continue to use such substances for relaxation or even religious purposes.[12] The oldest and most widely known of these drugs are the opiates. The cultivation of the poppy plant was common in ancient Mesopotamia, Persia, Egypt, and Greece.[13] Much of the world traffic in these substances still originates in the Middle East.

Arab traders introduced opiates to China in the tenth century.[14] But beginning with the eighteenth century the European powers trafficked increasingly in the opium poppy and the coca leaf as a source of foreign revenue. In 1767 the East India Company began exporting opium from India to China as a revenue item for the Crown,[15] and

[10] "Mood-Changing Drugs are Studied by N.I.H.," *Washington Post*, February 13, 1968, p. A9.

[11] Blum, "Mind-Altering Drugs and Dangerous Behavior: Dangerous Drugs," in President's Commission on Law Enforcement and the Administration of Justice, *Task Force Report: Narcotics and Drug Abuse* 21, 23 (1967).

[12] Blum, "Mind-Altering Drugs" 41; 111 *Cong. Rec.* 15410, cols. 2 and 3 (House) (daily ed., July 8, 1965). On the religious use of peyote by the California Navajos, *see* People v. Woody, 61 Cal.2d 716, 394 P.2d 813, 817 (1964), in which the court noted: "Although peyote serves as a sacramental symbol similar to bread and wine in certain Christian churches, it is more than a sacrament. Peyote constitutes in itself an object of worship; prayers are directed to it much as prayers are devoted to the Holy Ghost. On the other hand, to use peyote for nonreligious purposes is sacrilegious. Members of the church regard peyote also as a 'teacher' because it induces a feeling of brotherhood with other members; indeed, it enables the participant to experience the Deity."

[13] The Greeks are reputed to have given the product of the poppy plant the name "opion," a derivative of "opos," meaning vegetable juice. T. T. Brown, *The Enigma of Drug Addiction* 6 (1961).

[14] *Ibid.*

[15] Lang, "President's Commission Task Force Report on Narcotics and Drug Abuse: A Critique of the Apologia," 43 *Notre Dame Lawyer* 847, 849 (1968).

even though Warren Hastings, the first British governor general of India, in 1783 pronounced opium to be a pernicious article of luxury which ought not to be permitted, he conceded its utility "for the purpose of foreign commerce only."[16] This imperialism by drugs was not always welcomed by the native regimes. In 1820 China banned the importation of narcotics by foreign traders, and the closing of the legitimate route led to the 1839–42 opium wars between Great Britain and China. The British victory soon resulted in the flooding of the Chinese markets with drugs and during the latter part of the nineteenth century, some 8 million addicts were reported in the country.[17]

Drug abuse and addiction have long been described as the cause of much individual grief as well as public problems. But until recent history, it has not been considered a major health and safety threat.[18] To this day, narcotics and other drug abuse in most countries remain a troubled fact of the human condition and human deviation—present, but not overly threatening. In this country, however, the massive incursion of organized crime into the narcotic traffic, combined with the economic costs of supporting the illicit addiction habit, have given rise to a major national evil. The problem is compounded by industrial alienation, population mobility, and the restlessness of youth. The latter elements have recently been turning addiction from an American malady into a universal evil.[19]

THE TEETH OF THE LAW

Prior to 1914, the narcotics[20] traffic in the United States was not subject to any regulations.[21] Because of its relative physical isolation, America was not in the mainstream of the opium trade; but narcotics soon came to the United States through both immigration and through

---

[16] Brown, *Enigma of Drug Addiction.*

[17] *Encyclopedia Americana* (1952 ed.), s.v. "Opium."

[18] The first international convention against the opium traffic was drawn up at The Hague in 1912. *Encyclopedia Britannica* (1965 ed.), s.v. "Narcotics."

[19] At a recent Bradford University symposium on narcotics addiction, Britain's Home Office chief inspector for narcotics noted that the number of registered addicts could increase from the current 2,000 to some 10,000 by 1972. He stressed that heroin is no longer exclusive to the jazz scene and that many of the newer addicts come from universities and from good backgrounds. Referring to the fact that in Britain registered addicts can obtain narcotics legally, Inspector C. G. Jeffery asserted that a certain amount of overprescribing goes on "but if anything it is better than under-subscription, which could lead to an illegal market." *New York Times,* April 21, 1969, p. 34.

[20] The term "narcotics" may have different meanings in pharmacological literature and in law. In pharmacology it is a general term for substances that produce

war. Opium smoking was first introduced to America by the Chinese immigrants who were brought in the second half of the nineteenth century to help build railroads; yet at present persons of Chinese origin play an insignificant role in the American narcotic traffic.[22] The first significant American involvement in the narcotic picture was a result of the Civil War. In the early 1800's a pharmacist's assistant had separated a substance from opium and had named it "morphium" after the god of dreams, Morpheus. The widespread use of morphine by injection as an analgesic during the war left many soldiers addicts, and morphine addiction was consequently labeled the "army disease." At the time, however, morphine and opium were readily and inexpensively available in patent medicines through regular commercial channels, and the addict had no difficulty supporting his habit.[23] Because the addict's supplier was usually a physician or an apothecary, the general welfare of the addict was at least under nominal professional supervision. Although reliable evidence regarding pre-1914 addiction is difficult to secure, it is reported that the narcotic addict of that time was typically a white, Southern, rural male, whose morphine was usually supplied through medical sources.[24] The number of pre-1914 addicts was estimated to be from 100,000[25] to 264,000[26] in a population of approximately 97,227,000.[27] No significant correlation between crime and narcotic addiction was claimed during that period.

THE EVIL SEED

What is commonly referred to as narcotic drugs consists of a great variety of substances, with different properties and with varying de-

---

lethargy or stupor and the relief of pain. In law it applies to specified yet different classes of drugs that have been grouped together for purposes of legal control. Under the federal laws, narcotics include the opiates and cocaine. Under most state statutes, marijuana is also a narcotic.

[21] Ball, "Two Patterns of Narcotic Drug Addiction in the United States," 56 *J. Crim. L.C. & P.S.* 203 (1965).

[22] A. R. Lindesmith, *The Addict and the Law* 133 (1965). Only 13 persons of Chinese origin were reported in 1957 among 7,000 offenders.

[23] *Ibid.* 130.

[24] Larimore, "Medical Views on the Narcotics Problem," 31 *F.R.D.* 53, 83 (1961).

[25] Finestone, "Narcotics and Criminality," 22 *Law & Contemp. Prob.* 69, 79 (1957).

[26] C. E. Terry and M. Pellens, *The Opium Problem* 41 (1925).

[27] U.S. Bureau of the Census, *Statistical Abstract of the United States* 5 (1960). Estimated pop. in 1913.

grees of habit-forming characteristics.[28] Narcotics are defined in the dictionary as substances that induce sleep, dull the senses, and relieve pain. In law, the president's crime commission recently noted, the term "has been given artificial meaning."[29] It does not refer, as might be expected, to one class of drugs encompassing substances with similar chemical properties or pharmacological effects. It is applied, rather, to a number of different classes of drugs that have been grouped together for convenience and for purposes of legal control. These typically include the opiates, cocaine, and marijuana.

The leading narcotics are the opiates, derived from the several alkaloids of the opium poppy or their synthetic equivalents including opium, morphine, codeine, and heroin. Though most opiates are highly addicting, some of them have great medical value and are often prescribed for the relief of pain and for other medicinal purposes. (During 1963 more than one billion individual doses of opiates were legally prescribed in the United States.)[30] Opiates are also used illicitly. The major problem to law enforcement is posed by heroin, the chief source of addiction in the United States.[31] In 1965, of a total of 57,199 active addicts on the name file maintained by the Federal Bureau of Narcotics, 52,793 were heroin addicts.[32]

Although the effect of any drug depends on many variables, such as the mood and expectation of the taker, the opiates are generally known to act as depressants. Describing heroin, the president's crime commission noted that "it relieves anxiety and tension and diminishes the sex, hunger and other primary drives. It may also produce drowsiness and cause inability to concentrate, apathy and lessened physical activity."[33] The American addict typically injects heroin intravenously with a needle. While repeated and prolonged administration leads to tolerance and physical dependence, many use narcotics illicitly without becoming addicted. Significantly, also, the continued use of a

[28] Brown, *Enigma of Drug Addiction*, chap. 1.

[29] President's Commission on Law Enforcement and the Administration of Justice, *Task Force Report: Narcotics and Drug Abuse* 2.

[30] Blum, "Mind-Altering Drugs" 46.

[31] Heroin occupies a special place in the narcotics laws. It is an illegal drug that may not be lawfully imported or manufactured under any circumstances and is not even available for use in medical practice. 21 *U.S.C.* §§173, 502, 505 (1964).

[32] U.S. Treasury Department, Bureau of Narcotics, *Traffic in Opium and Other Dangerous Drugs* 37–46 (1965).

[33] President's Commission on Law Enforcement and the Administration of Justice, *Task Force Report: Narcotics and Drug Abuse.*

dosage to which a person is tolerant will produce no permanent organic damage.[34]

It is the secondary effects of the opiates that are considered most undesirable socially. A person's preoccupation with the drug may result in personal neglect and malnutrition. Withdrawal from drugs is painful: its symptoms, which reach peak intensity in 24 to 48 hours, include muscle aches, cramps, and nausea.[35] Significantly, however, it has been observed that today "the drug available on the street is generally so far diluted that the typical addict does not develop profound physical dependence, and therefore does not suffer serious withdrawal symptoms."[36] The cost of heroin to the addict easily becomes an economic burden supportable by criminal activity only. The substances purchased by the addict may range in purity from 1 percent to 30 percent, and a single "bag" (one fix) is reported to bring a $5.00 price.

Cocaine, a crystalline alkaloid obtained from the leaves of the coca plant, is completely different from the opiates in that it is an excitant and stimulating drug. Although cocaine is habit-forming, the user does not develop a physical dependence and the withdrawal of the drug does not involve the physical ill effects of heroin.[37] Cocaine is derived from the leaves of the coca plant cultivated in South America. It is no longer the major drug of abuse it once was in this country.

Marijuana, another drug frequently grouped with the narcotics,[38] though not addicting, is derived from the flowering tops of the female hemp plant. The plant is often found growing wild. Most of this country's supply comes from Mexico, where marijuana is cultivated and then cut, dried, and pulverized. Commonly converted into cigarettes, it is consumed by smoking, like its more potent Middle Eastern relative "hashish." Marijuana is a hallucinogen and is not habit-forming. Its danger is said to lie in the fact that it may induce exaltation and hilarity, may release inhibitions, increase suggestibility, impair judg-

[34] Isbell, "Medical Aspects of Opiate Addiction," in *Narcotic Addiction* 62 (J. A. O'Donnel and J. C. Ball eds. 1966).

[35] Eddy, Halbach, Isbell, and Seevers, "Drugs Dependence: Its Significance and Characteristics," 32 *Bull. World Health Org.* 724–25 (1965).

[36] President's Commission on Law Enforcement and the Administration of Justice, *Task Force Report: Narcotics and Drug Abuse* 3.

[37] *Ibid.*

[38] Most state laws group marijuana with narcotics with regard to criminal penalties. *N.Y. Public Health Law* §3301 (1967). Most researchers point out, however, that the effects of marijuana are unlike those of the narcotics and more nearly resemble alcoholic intoxication. Blum, "Mind-Altering Drugs" 22.

ment, and provide an introduction to more addicting narcotics.[39] Recent commentators, on the other hand, point out on the basis of existing evidence that the risks of crime, accidents, and suicide connected with marijuana are not likely to be greater than those associated with alcohol.[40] According to the 1967 president's crime commission, the classification of marijuana as a mild hallucinogen rather than as a narcotic is "as good a description as any." The commission noted further that the adverse effects of marijuana are much less than of the more potent hallucinogen LSD.[41]

Although marijuana use is apparently spread across a larger segment of the general population than opiate use, reliable estimates of the prevalence of marijuana are lacking. Its use is most common in depressed urban areas, on one hand, and in academic and artistic communities, on the other. While there are many recent reports of widespread use on campuses, little verification, other than informal polls, is available for the claim that 20 percent or possibly 40 percent of the college populations have been exposed to it. Marijuana's relative inexpensiveness, compared to heroin, makes it much more easily accessible to large numbers of grownups and youths. According to the Chicago Police Department, the local price for a single cigarette in 1966 ranged between 50 and 75 cents; lower prices are reported nearer to the Mexican border.[42]

The illicit user's apothecary consists not only of these traditional substances but also of a large number of newer mood- and mindchanging products. These are usually not habit-forming, but some, such as the barbiturates, are addictive. Many of these substances were developed for specialized medical purposes but have now found their way into unauthorized usage. Contained in this group of drugs, which can become dangerous if used excessively, are the depressants, including the barbiturates (sleeping pills) and tranquilizers, which are useful because of their sedative or anesthetic action in relieving tension and anxiety; the stimulants, including the amphetamines (benzedrine), which prevent drowsiness and have a capacity to elevate one's mood;[43] and a great number of other hypnotic and peptype pills.

[39] Winick, "Marijuana Use by Young People," in *Drug Addiction in Youth* (E. Harmes ed. 1965).

[40] Blum, "Mind-Altering Drugs" 25.

[41] President's Commission on Law Enforcement and the Administration of Justice, *Task Force Report: Narcotics and Drug Abuse* 13.

[42] *Ibid.* 4.

[43] A 1962 study in the United States showed a production rate of 25 ampheta-

Most prominent in the recent drug-abuse area are the hallucinogenic or psychedelic substances. These are synthetic drugs produced by a chemical process; unlike the barbiturates or amphetamines they have no recognized medical use. Some, such as LSD, are many times more potent than the older hallucinogens, such as the cactus-derived peyote used by American Indians, and even minute amounts are capable of producing extreme effects. Taken orally, either in pill form or as a liquid deposited on sugar cubes, these drugs produce altered states of consciousness, including a sharpening and brightening of the senses, vivid panoramic visual hallucinations,[44] and a sensation of peace and unity with one's own environment. If a large dosage (over 700 mcg., a microgram being one-millionth of a gram) is ingested, the user is increasingly enveloped by a sense of insulation; feelings of paranoia, fear, and delirium will frequently ensue.[45] "During LSD use, repressed material may be unmasked which is difficult for the individual to handle. Duration of the experience is usually four to twelve hours but it may last for days."

Although experimental work with hallucinogenic drugs still continues, a number of cited dangers have already been established. These, significantly, are often derived not from the drug's independent qualities but from its accentuation of the taker's characteristics. The drug may thus activate previously latent psychoses, cause the acting out of character disorders, including homosexual impulses, and give vent to suicidal inclinations.[46] It has been observed, however, that while opiates are drugs of social withdrawal, hallucinogens and the newer substances are drugs of rebellion. Additionally, unlike opiate addiction, the abuse of the nonaddictive "soft drugs" is often a periodic phase rather than a long-term involvement.[47]

To nonaddicts most of the mind-changing drugs (narcotic and otherwise), although hazardous, are available in hospitals and from pharmacies upon medical prescription. Some of the hallucinogens, however, are limited to medical experimental work only. The major

---

mine tablets per person. In 1963, drugstores filled nearly 48 million barbiturate prescriptions and nearly 61 million tranquilizer prescriptions. Blum, "Mind-Altering Drugs" 90.

[44] Some researchers point out that while LSD is classified as a hallucinogen, recent data show that hallucinations are infrequent experiences reported by LSD users. *Ibid.* 22.

[45] *New York Medicine*, May 5, 1966, p. 5.

[46] President's Commission on Law Enforcement and the Administration of Justice, *Task Force Report: Narcotics and Drug Abuse* 5.

[47] Lang, "Critique" 847.

problem of law enforcement is therefore with regard to those substances which find their way into the illicit and drug-abuse market.

THE MALADY OF DRUG USE

The most commonly asserted objections to narcotics are their addictive quality, their disruptive effect upon the addict's social role, and their relationship to crime.

The state of chronic narcotic addiction is characterized by "an overpowering desire and need (compulsion) to continue taking the drug and to obtain it by any means."[48] The physiological changes which addicting drugs create in the body produce an overwhelming need for their continued supply. This physical dependence has been described as "the body's slavery to the continued use of opiates."[49] Three phenomena characterize addiction—physical dependence, dosage tolerance,[50] and psychological or emotional dependence. Physical dependence means that the withdrawal of drugs will most often result in an actual sickness which consists of cramps and nausea. Dosage tolerance means an ever-increasing dosage requirement in order to maintain the drug's euphoric effects. The emotional dependence causes the addict who is without drugs to suffer psychic distresses, extreme anxiety, and an overwhelming sense of inadequacy. When he undertakes to abstain from drugs, these fundamental psychic distresses overcome him and give "rise to an irresistible impulse to return to the use of the drug."[51] Once addiction is established, the motive for using narcotics is reported by some experts to be not pleasure but the avoidance of physical and mental pain.[52] The severity of the symptoms facing an addict who tries to resist dependence can be deduced from the precautions that are usually taken during the medical treatment of addiction. Slow physical withdrawal, supervision by physicians, small doses of other drugs, such as methadone, intravenous injections of glucose and warm baths are all part of the standard treatment to overcome the abstinence syndrome.[53] Improper and abrupt withdrawal procedures can be harmful, dangerous, and even fatal.[54]

---

[48] World Health Organization, Technical Report Ser., no. 21, p. 6 (1950).

[49] L. Kolb, *Drug Addiction* 4 (1962).

[50] *Ibid.*

[51] *Ibid.* 95; MacDonald, "Alcoholism and Drug Addiction," 21 *Ohio St. L. J.* 96, 97 (1960).

[52] Kolb, *Drug Addiction* 94.

[53] American Medical Association, Council on Mental Health, "Reports on Narcotic Addiction," 165 *J.A.M.A.* 1968 (1957).

[54] Kolb and Himmelsbach, "Clinical Studies of Drug Addiction, III: A Critical

Despite the addict's need for greater dosages and the difficulties of withdrawal, some experts do not consider addiction itself extremely harmful socially. Says Professor Alfred Lindesmith of Indiana University:

> The relative normality of the heroin or morphine addict contrasts sharply with the state of the alcoholic, the barbiturate addict, or persons under the influence of marijuana. While the opiate addict suffers more than his share of physical disease and minor troubles such as constipation, lack of sexual desire, and tooth decay, there is no known major tissue pathology associated with heroin and morphine addiction as there is with the abuse of alcohol. . . . There are many examples of drug addicts who have continued to engage in productive work and who have even had positions of eminence while they were using drugs.[55]

The conception of addiction as an unpleasant status is also asserted to be false: "A popular conception is that addiction is a disease and as horrible as the affliction has been painted, there are a great many who are well content with their 'unbreakable' habit."[56] The medical profession, likewise, has found little or no evidence that continued use of narcotics, by itself, causes permanent physiological harm.[57] Some respected authorities regard addiction as the manifestation of a personality disorder which might become more severe and dangerous if the addict were cured of his addiction.[58]

Addiction has been condemned for many reasons, but some of the asserted ills are exaggerated. Drugs are not as damaging to health as alcohol. They do not act as aphrodisiacs. They do not usually stimulate violence. What then is the cause of this society's war not only upon addiction but upon addicts?

The taproot of the nation's abhorrence of narcotics is our puritan and liberal heritage. Puritanism and liberalism, traditionally standing for personal responsibility and the belief in the freedom, ability, and duty of the individual to choose and carve his wordly destinies, saw in addiction the denial of these very values and freedoms. Addiction is a yielding and acceptance of man's dependence upon outside influence and artificial support. Moreover, it is an influence and support that

Review of Withdrawal Treatments with Method of Evaluating Abstinence Syndrome," 94 *Amer. J. Psychiatry* 759 (1938).

[55] Lindesmith, *Addict and the Law* x–xi.

[56] Brown, *Enigma of Drug Addiction* 32.

[57] W. B. Eldridge, *Narcotics and the Law* 16–17 (1962).

[58] P. W. Tappan, *Crime, Justice, and Correction* 185 (1960); Chein, "The Use of Narcotics as a Personal and Social Problem," in *Narcotics* 113 (D. M. Wilner and G. G. Kassebaum eds. 1965).

cannot be easily shed. Worse yet, the uncontrolled desire for drugs will lead men to commit acts detrimental to society's welfare, if necessary to obtain the money needed for drugs. A very challenging discussion of the cultural and personal values that play an important role in the shaping of public policy towards narcotics was presented by Professor Blum to the president's crime commission.[59]

> On religious grounds some people may be unwilling to tamper with whatever God had wrought, even if it is sleeplessness or anxiety. That "not tampering" with nature combines respect for what exists with doubt about what might happen.... On cultural grounds drug use is also the subject of ambivalent feelings. In the Anglo-Saxon value system at least, stoicism under pain and "taking it on the chin" are marks of the man. To use a drug can be a sign of weakness, indeed even going to the doctor ... [need] be resisted lest it be taken as self-indulgence or a sissy's way out. Similarly our culture ... has several contradictory ways of looking at pleasure. In Puritan thinking pleasure itself is suspect and the use of any substance to obtain "kicks" or euphoria is evil.... Dependency itself is another area in which the culture provides us with built-in conflicts within ourselves and among one another. ... "He shouldn't need a crutch," they say, or "why doesn't he stand on his own two feet?"... Ours is a social world in which men earn their way and live amongst other men. We contribute ourselves to one another and ordinarily eschew being hermits, mystics, catatonics, misanthropes, or comatose. Does a man have the right to reverse the order and glorify inner experience and become disinterested in the world of other men?[60]

The addict disregards the rest of mankind and is morally condemned for it. But when the specter of criminality is added to the addict's moral repugnance, the social order reacts with force. There is no doubt that narcotics addiction and crime are today inextricably intertwined. It was not always so, however. Before trafficking in narcotics became subject to governmental regulation, drug addiction was regarded more as a health and moral problem than as a source of criminal activity, and understandably so, for recent research has demonstrated that drug use alone does not usually engender criminal behavior.

Lindesmith reports that opiate-type drugs do not directly lead to

[59] Blum, "Drugs, Dangerous Behavior, and Social Policy," in President's Commission on Law Enforcement and the Administration of Justice, *Task Force Report: Narcotics and Drug Abuse* 64.

[60] *Ibid.* 66, 67.

crime or irresponsible behavior; alcohol does. "They (the opiates) have a sedative, tranquilizing effect and if all other things were held equal would probably inhibit rather than encourage crime."[61] The observations of police authorities are that "Bizarre criminal cases attributable to marijuana and other drugs, while common in newspaper stories, are rather rare in official police files. . . . Seldom is there any connection . . . [between crimes of violence] and drugs."[62] The president's crime commission recently concluded that existing evidence on the causal connection between drug use and crime has not enabled it to make definitive estimates on this issue.[63]

More controversial is the role of *marijuana* as a cause of crimes of violence. Since marijuana, unlike the other substances classified as narcotics, is a stimulant rather than a depressant, its encouragement of antisocial behavior has long been suspected. Some law enforcement agencies have claimed over the years that marijuana users account for a significant portion of the major crimes.[64] On the other hand, the Medical Society of the County of New York has stated that there is no evidence of the causal connection between marijuana use and crimes of violence in this country.[65] Several other responsible authorities make similar claims. The president's crime commission concluded:

. . . [G]iven the accepted tendency of marijuana to release inhibitions, the effect of the drug will depend on the individual and the

---

[61] Lindesmith, *Addict and the Law* xi. The drug addict as addict poses little special threat to public lives or limbs. "The effects of opiates are, in general, exactly the opposite of the effects of alcohol, which tends to reduce normal inhibitions and to release aggressions. . . . The sense of well-being and satisfaction with the world are so strong that, coupled with the depressant action of the drug, the individual is unlikely to commit aggressive or violent crime after he is addicted, even though he professionally or habitually did so previous to addiction. . . . In the words of Kolb, 'Both heroin and morphine in large doses change drunken fighting psychopaths into sober, cowardly, non-aggressive idlers.'" D. Maurer and V. Vogel, *Narcotics and Narcotic Addiction* 215–16 (1954). In an unusual display of interdisciplinary unanimity, several experts on addiction agreed that "crimes of violence are rarely, and sexual crimes almost never, committed by addicts." Joint Committee of the American Bar Association and the American Medical Association on Narcotic Drugs, *Drug Addiction: Crime or Disease?* 165 (1961). The committee concluded that "in terms of the number afflicted and . . . ill effects on others in the community, drug addiction is a problem of far less magnitude than alcoholism."

[62] Brown, *Enigma of Drug Addiction* 62.

[63] President's Commission on Law Enforcement and the Administration of Justice, *Task Force Report: Narcotics and Drug Abuse* 11.

[64] U.S. Congress, House Ways and Means Committee, *Hearings on Taxation of Marijuana*, 75th Cong., 1st sess., 1937, pp. 23–24.

[65] *New York Magazine*, May 5, 1966, p. 3.

circumstances. It might but certainly will not necessarily or inevitably lead to aggressive behavior or crime. The response will depend more on the individual than the drug. This hypothesis is consistent with the evidence that marijuana does not alter the basic personality structure.[66]

The Harrison Act of 1914[67] was America's contribution to an international effort to stop the unlicensed traffic of narcotics. The theory was to prohibit importation, sale, and use of illegally imported drugs. The enactment was additionally designed to curb the nonmedical traffic in narcotics (specifically, opiates and cocaine) and took the form of a revenue measure, with harsh and inflexible provisions. The Harrison Act did not designate addiction a crime but made possession of narcotic drugs criminal unless obtained through lawful channels;[68] since most addicts were at that time under some form of professional supervision, the measure was not considered an outright anti-addiction law.

But in a series of decisions interpreting the Harrison Act, the Supreme Court of the United States soon caused the medical profession to abdicate its prominent role in the field of narcotic distribution. The court first decided that any possession of smuggled drugs was a violation of the law;[69] second, that distribution of narcotics by a doctor to an addict in sufficient dosage to maintain his comfort and customary use was not to be excepted from the Harrison Act prohibitions against sales.[70] By the language of the statute, the prohibition against sales did not necessarily apply to dispensing of narcotic drugs by physicians, in the course of their professional practice.[71] But the court ruling made it illegal for a physician to sustain a narcotic addict's habit.[72] In another case, the doctor was stripped of his defense of good faith.[73] It made no difference that the doctor had prescribed the drugs only in order to treat and cure addicts.

This extreme attitude was modified in 1925 when the court held in the *Linder* case that good faith treatment of addicts with moderate

[66] President's Commission on Law Enforcement and the Administration of Justice, *Task Force Report: Narcotics and Drug Abuse* 13.
[67] Act of December 17, 1914, 38 Stat. 785 (1914), as amended, 26 *U.S.C.* §§ 4701–36 (1964); for the substances covered *see* §4731(a).
[68] Lindesmith, *Addict and the Law* 4.
[69] United States v. Jin Fuey Moy, 241 U.S. 394 (1916).
[70] Webb v. United States, 249 U.S. 96 (1919).
[71] Harrison Act, ch. 1, §2(a), 38 Stat. 785, 786 (1914).
[72] Jin Fuey Moy v. United States, 254 U.S. 189 (1920).
[73] United States v. Behrman, 258 U.S. 280 (1922).

amounts of drugs was not a criminal offense.[74] The distinguishing feature between this last decision and the three previous cases was the amount of narcotics involved. In the early cases, a large amount of narcotics had been distributed, whereas the physician in the last case only prescribed a small dosage.[75] But even though the *Linder* decision modified the prior holdings, the typical physician had by this time abandoned the treatment of addicts.[76] Understandably so, since his professional career could be destroyed if his prescriptions of drugs exceeded the court's vague standard of "moderate amount." The medical reluctance to deal with addiction and with addicts has changed little since.

In addition to the federal Harrison Act, all but two states adopted the Uniform Narcotic Drug Act, drafted in 1932 and patterned after the federal law.[77] The uniform act prohibits the sale, distribution, and possession of narcotics[78] (covering opiates, cocaine, and marijuana) by all persons, including physicians, unless properly authorized under the law.[79] The procedures for authorized possession in the act are complex,[80] but suffice it to say that the typical narcotic addict is not usually an authorized person. The act makes no specific attempt to regulate the individual doctor's treatments but is directed against the commercial traffic of narcotics.[81]

Subsequent federal legislation in the narcotics field has been aimed primarily at easing the burden of proof for the prosecution, imposing increasingly stiffer penalties on offenders (for example, mandatory 10 to 40 years imprisonment for a third offense of narcotic possession),[82] and limiting the sentencing discretion of judges by excluding suspension of sentence, probation, or parole eligibility for narcotic violators.[83]

[74] Linder v. United States, 268 U.S. 5 (1925).

[75] *Ibid.* 18.

[76] Lindesmith, *Addict and the Law* 7.

[77] Uniform Narcotic Drug Act, 9B *Uniform Laws Annotated* 409–10 (Table of States). The states which have not adopted the act are California and Pennsylvania. A tabular summary of state penalties may be found in Eldridge, *Narcotics and the Law* 149–87.

[78] Uniform Narcotic Drug Act §1(14).

[79] *Ibid.* §2.

[80] *Ibid.* §1.

[81] *Ibid.* 410 (see Commissioners' Prefatory Note).

[82] As a consequence of the stiff penalties imposed upon narcotics offenders, some 18 percent of all federal prisoners are incarcerated on drug charges without hope for parole. U.S. Congress, Senate, Committee on Government Operations, Permanent Subcommittee on Investigations, *Hearings*, 88th Cong., 2d sess., 1964, pt. 3, p. 627.

[83] *Int. Rev. Code of 1954* §§4701–36; Lindesmith, *Addict and the Law* 25. Under the federal statutes, unauthorized acquisition of narcotics is punishable by

In 1937, federal legislation, again in the form of a tax measure, was extended to cover marijuana traffic and use in a manner similar to the narcotic controls.[84] The scope of the marijuana laws has been somewhat reduced, however, by the 1969 Supreme Court decision in *Leary v. United States*.[85]

In recent years, increased concern with the adverse effects and abuse of other nonnarcotic but dangerous drugs (such as the amphetamines or pep pills, the barbiturates, and the hallucinogenic or psychedelic drugs)[86] resulted in stricter supervision over their manufacture and sale by the federal Food and Drug Administration.[87] The federal laws encompassing these hazardous but nonnarcotic drugs are directed against illicit trafficking, making the first offense a misdemeanor and the second a felony; but possession or use are not punishable under the federal law. Several states have stepped in to fill this vacuum through modifications of their existing narcotic laws. Most state enactments are directed against both the illicit trafficking and the unauthorized possession or use of these drugs.

A brief look at the various legal tools for the control of addiction in the Washington, D.C., area demonstrates their complexity. Virginia, Maryland, and the District of Columbia have all enacted the Uniform Narcotic Drug Act substantially unchanged. In addition, the antinarcotic programs also utilize specialized narcotic vagrancy statutes. The avowed purpose of the statute in the District of Columbia[88] is to protect the public health, welfare, and safety by curbing the public movements of addicts and by safeguarding the public against contacts

---

a minimum of two and a maximum of ten years for a first offense, and a minimum of ten and a maximum of forty years for a third and subsequent offense. A fine of up to $20,000 may also be imposed for each such offense. 26 *U.S.C.* §7237(a) (Supp. 1965). Unauthorized sale is punished more severely: not less than five nor more than twenty years for the first offense, not less than ten nor more than forty for a second or subsequent offense, as well as a fine of not more than $20,000. If the sale is to a person under eighteen years of age, the minimum is ten years and the maximum is forty years. 26 *U.S.C.* §7237(b) (Supp. 1965). A sale of heroin to a person under eighteen years of age by a person eighteen years or older is punishable for not less than ten years nor more than life, but the jury may direct the imposition of a death penalty. 70 Stat. 571 (1956). 21 *U.S.C.* §176(b) (1964).

[84] 26 *U.S.C.* §§4741–76.

[85] 37 *L.W.* 4397 (May 19, 1969).

[86] Ludwig and Levine, "Patterns of Hallucinogenic Drug Abuse," 191 *J.A.M.A.* 29 (1965).

[87] Drug Abuse Control Amendments of 1965, Pub. L. No. 89–74 (July 15, 1965).

[88] *D.C. Code* §33–416a (1967).

with narcotic drug users. The narcotic vagrant in the District of Columbia is defined as a drug user, or a convicted offender, who has no lawful occupation or visible means of support and who is found under suspicious circumstances without being able to give a good account of himself.[89] The Virginia vagrancy statute, likewise, punishes "idle" persons who consort with idlers, gamblers, bootleggers, prostitutes, narcotic users, narcotic vendors, persons engaged in the operation of any disorderly house or illegal enterprise of any kind, or persons having the reputation of doing the above.[90]

An extreme example of the narcotic vagrancy laws is provided by the Indiana statute. In Indiana it is unlawful for any person addicted to narcotics to "go on, into or upon any street or public highway, alley or public place unless such person can present positive proof that he is under the care of a licensed physician for the treatment of such addiction."[91] An ordinary active addict cannot leave his room for any purpose whatsoever without automatically being in violation of the law.

Some states and municipalities have devised yet other programs for the supervision of narcotic addicts. Addicts are there required to register and carry cards identifying themselves as addicts. A few states have also "needle laws" which make it a punishable offense for addicts to have in their possession the paraphernalia required for the injection of narcotics.[92]

The written law is one thing; its administration is another. In order to evaluate the effect of this complex web of criminal laws on the patterns of narcotics use in the United States, it will be helpful to examine the structure of the narcotics traffic and the records and missions of the agencies charged with the enforcement of the laws.

THE NARCOTIC HIERARCHY AND THE LAW

Those involved in the illicit commerce of narcotics, it is generally agreed, fall into one or more of five categories. First, there is the importer, who brings in large quantities of raw narcotics for distribution. Second, there is the wholesaler, who distributes the drugs from the point of entry to the large centers of addict population. Third, there is the peddler, who supplies the pusher, the fourth category, with

[89] *Ibid.* §33–416a(1)(A).
[90] *Va. Code Ann.* §63–338(9) (1960).
[91] *Ind. Stat. Ann.* §10–3538a (Supp. 1966).
[92] Lindesmith, *Addict and the Law* 33.

sufficient quantities of narcotics to distribute to the addict community.[93] The addict himself is, therefore, the fifth and last link in a
long distribution chain.

Through federal laws which regulate the traffic of narcotics, including importation and distribution, it was originally hoped that the government would be able to dry up the sources of supply to the addict
community. However, of an estimated 1½ tons of raw heroin imported
into the United States annually, only 5 pounds were intercepted by
the Bureau of Customs in 1962 and only 65 pounds in 1966.[94] Obviously, our border policing leaves much to be desired. The reasons
for this poor record lie not with the Bureau of Customs, which is
seriously undermanned, but with the fact that full scrutiny over all
imports is impossible.[95] Even when a find is made by the Bureau of
Customs, rarely is the actual importer apprehended. Importers are not
usually drug addicts themselves and do not expose themselves through
personal possession of narcotics. They operate through henchmen, who
in turn employ international travelers and operants such as sailors and
airlines employees to "get a little something into the country." The
profiteers from the illicit trade remain anonymous. Similarly, the
wholesalers of narcotics are rarely known or apprehended.

The peddlers or large retailers of narcotics are sometimes apprehended, but, by and large, most arrests occur among the pushers.
Pushers are often themselves addicted to the drugs that they purvey
and are engaged in the illicit commerce to support their own habit.
They are, therefore, both the victims and the exploiters of these
drugs.

What makes the enforcement of narcotics law especially difficult is
the fact that "there are no complaining witnesses or victims; there
are only sellers and willing buyers."[96] Arrests usually lead the enforce-

[93] Bailey, "The Case for the Voluntary, Outpatient Method of Handling Narcotic
Addiction," 31 *F.R.D.* 73, 76 (1961).

[94] President's Advisory Commission on Narcotic and Drug Abuse, *Final Report*
37 (1963); Customs Agency Service, *Annual Report to the Commissioner of
Customs for Fiscal 1966* 9.

[95] The Bureau of Customs employed 492 port investigators and customs enforcement officers in 1966. The bureau also employed 276 customs agents for top-
echelon criminal customs investigations. The narcotics traffic within the country is
under the control of the Bureau of Narcotics, which had a force of 278 agents in
1966. These agents supervise some 99,000 vessels, 210,000 aircraft, and 47.6 million foreign mail packages arriving in the United States annually. U.S. Congress,
House, House Appropriations Committee, *Subcommittee Hearings on Treasury
Appropriations for 1967*, 89th Cong., 2d sess., 1966, p. 413; U. S. Treasury Department, *Traffic in Opium* 51.

[96] Blum, "Mind-Altering Drugs" 8.

ment official no higher than the local peddler.[97] When one reads that a "dope ring" has been cracked, it usually means little more than the temporary plugging of one small source of supply. Soon, the customers served by the apprehended peddler through his pushers find another source, and another peddler appears to fill the gap.

James Harold Johnson's recent experiences in Prince George County, Virginia, are illustrative of the enforcement practices against marijuana traffic.[98] Johnson, a not very reputable 18-year-old with previous encounters with the law, had been considered by the police to be a major marijuana dealer. Recruiting another juvenile and supplying him with $200 in marked bills, the police sent him off to buy marijuana from Johnson. Since Johnson lacked the necessary supply, the two went to a road-side stand, where Johnson gave the money to a Stephen Jessup for a paper bag containing marijuana. At that time the police intervened. Johnson received 20 years in prison, half of it suspended, for possessing marijuana. Jessup, the 18-year-old who brought the bag to the rendezvous and took the $200 for it, received a suspended sentence for selling marijuana. The juvenile who aided the police got a job as a police cadet. Questioning the sentence, the *Washington Post* noted: When two youths are involved in the same marijuana transaction and the supplier gets a suspended sentence while the retailer goes to prison for 10 years, one has to wonder about the efficacy of justice.

The main force of the Federal Bureau of Narcotics as well as local police forces seem devoted to this skirmish-line action with narcotic traffic at its terminal stage.[99] The ones upon whom the stiff and unmalleable sentences are imposed are not the importers or wholesalers but rather the miserable addicts and pusher-addicts whom the profiteers exploit.[100]

The ineffectiveness of existing enforcement tactics has raised serious doubt as to whether narcotic addiction has actually decreased as a result of the controls and penalties.[101] Federal narcotics officials have vigorously advanced the view that the number of addicts has declined drastically over the years. From a total estimated at more than 200,000 in 1914 (some exaggerated claims put the figure at 1 million), the number of addicts allegedly diminished to about 60,000 during the

[97] Lindesmith, *Addict and the Law* 52.
[98] "Injustice in Virginia," *Washington Post*, May 30, 1969, Editorial Page.
[99] Lindesmith, *Addict and the Law* 42–43.
[100] Blum, "Mind-Altering Drugs" 8.
[101] Maurer and Vogel, *Narcotics and Narcotic Addiction* 213.

time of World War II. Subsequently, the 1960 United States report to the United Nations Commission on Narcotic Drugs stated the number of addicts to be about 45,000.[102] These numbers, however, are challenged as being self-serving.[103] The claim that actual addiction is much more prevalent is substantiated by such partial indicators as the 1960 California report of some 16,000 persons arrested for narcotic offenses in that state alone, and a total of nearly 33,000 narcotic prosecutions reported in 1962 by states accounting for 65 percent of the nation's population.[104] Since arrests and prosecutions usually represent a small sample of all reported crimes, it is similarly expected that the detected narcotic offenses involve only a small segment of the addict population.

· But whatever the precise size of the American addict population, it is absolutely and proportionately much larger than the addict population of the European countries which afford much more freedom for the medical treatment of addiction by individual physicians. Britain, with a population roughly one-third that of the United States, estimates fewer than 2,000 addicts. Most European countries estimate between 300 and 500 addicts.[105]

Notwithstanding the accuracy of statistics, there is no question that more damage is done and more furor aroused by today's addict than by the addict of fifty years ago. Just as the laws and enforcement techniques in this country are challenged as being ineffective in reducing the incidence of addiction, they are also credited with changing the profile of the addict from a fairly inoffensive individual to a highly dangerous criminal.

Before the Harrison Act and its progeny, addiction and crime were not inseparable, as they generally are today. Addicts were usually able to support their habit through legitimate activities. But shut off from an inexpensive supply of drugs and professional supervision by the abdication of the medical profession, the addict had to turn to illicit sources for his supply. Organized crime, quick to spot a profitable market, stepped into the commercial gap opened by the new laws. With the criminal element now in close propinquity with narcotics, it was inevitable that petty hoodlums and gangsters would be

[102] U.N. Economic and Social Council, Commission on Narcotic Drugs, *Summary of Annual Reports of Governments Relating to Opium and Other Dangerous Drugs* 34 (1961).

[103] A detailed criticism of the accuracy and value of these statistics will be found in Lindesmith, *Addict and the Law* 104–22.

[104] *Ibid.* 102, 107.

[105] *Ibid.*

using the drugs. Next, the lower socioeconomic elements in our urban centers became the target of narcotic exploitation by the criminal element, until today, the pattern of drug addiction in the United State is markedly different from that prior to 1914. The typical drug user still remains a male. But nearly half of the active addicts are in the 21–30 age group[106] and instead of being from the rural white areas, especially the South, the typical addict is now an inhabitant of the slums of our northern urban centers—quite often a member of a minority group, chiefly Negro, Puerto Rican, or Mexican.[107] (Since 1955, however, there has been a steady decline in newly reported cases of Negro addiction and a concomitant rise in addiction among whites. This trend is especially evident in the age group under 21 years, where only 25.2 percent of the addicts are Negro and 74.6 percent are white.)[108] The four states with the most serious narcotics problem are New York, California, Illinois, and Ohio,[109] all with large cities and serious slum conditions. But recent evidence suggests addiction does not respect racial origin or socioeconomic status.

The new addict must support his habit in a different manner from the old-style addict.[110] Living in an urban slum offers little opportunity for employment or legitimate income. The addict's financial problem is further complicated by the inflated cost of narcotics purchased on the black market. New York figures for 1965 reveal that the average daily cost of illicit heroin for the user was $14.34. While the price of drugs is not uniform in time or place, it is never low enough to permit the typical addict to support it by lawful income. So he turns to crime, most commonly to the theft of property,[111] or to

[106] Blum, "Mind-Altering Drugs" 48. After about age 40 a number of addicts cease to be reported as either addicts or criminals. This is described as a "maturing out" process. *Ibid.* 56.

[107] Larimore, "Medical Views on the Narcotics Problem," 31 *Fed. Prob.* 80, 83 (1961). According to Federal Bureau of Narcotics data, 51.5 percent of the identified opiate offenders are Negro, 13 percent are Puerto Rican, and 5.6 percent are Mexican. Blum, "Mind-Altering Drugs" 48.

[108] U.S. Treasury Department, Bureau of Narcotics, *Traffic in Opium* 51–53 (1967).

[109] Eldridge, *Narcotics and the Law* 50. More than half the known heroin addicts are in New York. Most others are in California, Illinois, Michigan, New Jersey, Maryland, Pennsylvania, Texas, and the District of Columbia. U.S. Treasury Department, *Traffic in Opium* 37, 43.

[110] It is noteworthy, however, that in the United States and in Western Europe physicians are said to account for about 15 percent of the addict population, or a rate of 30 times higher than expected from normal population figures. Modlin and Montes, "Narcotic Addiction in Physicians," 121 *Amer. J. Psychiatry* 358–65 (1964).

[111] President's Commission on Law Enforcement and the Administration of Justice, *Task Force Report: Narcotics and Drug Abuse* 10. "[I]t is not narcotic drugs

prostitution if the addict is a woman.[112] Since stolen property cannot be converted at full value, it may require $75 or more of stolen property to produce the $15 daily cost of drugs. Simple mathematics will demonstrate the millions of dollars of property subjected to theft in order to support the drug habits of the active addicts. In New York City the figure is estimated at $200 million every year.[113] The New York City Police, burdened with a heavy concentration of users, reports that 11.1 percent of those arrested in 1965 for felonies connected with property were admitted drug users. The same year 9.8 percent of all arrests for petit larceny involved drug users. (The involvement of admitted drug users in felonies against persons amounted to 2 percent.)[114]

But our system of addict repression creates a double drain upon the nation's resources. The addict costs society dearly in terms of property crimes and enforcement personnel, and because he is unable to finance his habit through legitimate employment, he and his skills (however lessened by addiction) are lost to our labor pool. The intention is not to imply here that narcotics usage has no adverse effect upon the addict's health or social functioning. Quite the contrary, a narcotic drug user will be, in most cases, a less productive and useful member of society than the nonuser. (Interestingly, however, the effect of narcotics upon the physical reactions of the addict are less clearly discernible than in the case of alcoholism. The actions of the opiate addict may appear quite normal: his gait does not falter nor does his tongue thicken when under drug influence.)[115] But addiction may not be the real cause of the addict's nonproductivity, but rather the symptom of an underlying personal malfunctioning. Indeed, addiction often manifests itself in mere psychological rather than physiological reliance upon the drug as a solution to misery. Observations in the narcotic ward of the District of Columbia General Hospital

---

themselves, but rather their exorbitant blackmarket cost that forces most addicts into criminal pursuits. It is significant . . . that those addicts who can afford the high prices usually do not engage in crime and are, thus, unknown to the courts." *See also* Howe, "An Alternative Solution to the Narcotics Problem," 22 *Law and Contemp. Prob.* 132, 133 (1957).

[112] Tappan, *Crime, Justice, and Correction* 166 (1960).

[113] Kuh, "A Prosecutor's Thoughts Concerning Addiction," 52 *J. Crim. L.C. & P.S.* 321, 326 (1961).

[114] New York City, Police Department, Statistical and Recorder Bureau, *Statistical Report of Narcotic Arrests and Arrests of Narcotic Users* (1964, 1965).

[115] Brown, *Enigma of Drug Addiction* 54.

confirm the existence of addicts who are addicted to the physical act of injection rather than to the drug injected.[116] These so-called "needle addicts" obviously suffer from a disorder greater than the mere craving for narcotics. If drugs were not available at all, some other form of abnormal behavior (possibly of a more violent nature) might manifest itself.

"Addiction," says a medical expert, "is caused by human weakness—not by drugs, and is a symptom of a personality maladjustment rather than a disease in its own right.... Emotionally normal, mature individuals practically never become addicted."[117] In the absence of addiction, the same maladjusted individual might turn to barbiturates or alcohol. Or he might "manifest" his maladjustment through open expressions of hostility, sexual aggressiveness, or exhibitionism.[118] Several studies have indicated that as many as 72 percent of the known drug addicts had a record of criminal behavior before drug use. The loss of efficiency or quality of productiveness and citizenship attributed to narcotics usage may be irrecoverable even if the addicted state is cured. But our system makes it impossible for addicts to contribute in any fashion.

THERAPY FOR ADDICTION

To many scholars, the ineffectiveness of our past efforts to control the drug traffic is seen as a failure inherent in the criminal law and process. Narcotic bosses are rarely penalized and the harassment and imprisonment of the addict is unlikely to affect his future behavior or that of other individuals who turn to drugs for escape. To the drug users, a confrontation with the criminal process is a chance worth taking in order to satisfy their physical and psychological needs. Moreover, dependence on drugs clearly weakens the addict's self-

[116] Interview with Maurice Corbin, M.D., Addict Ward, D.C. General Hospital, reported in Mills, "The Problem of Drug Addiction in D.C." 7 (unpublished manuscript in Washington College of Law Library, 1966).

[117] Isbell, "Meeting a Growing Menace—Drug Addiction," 50 *Merck Report* 4 (1951). It has been estimated that between 50 and 75 percent of all adult Americans have been exposed to opiate use in some setting but that only 1 in 1,000 becomes an illicit user. It is thus calculated that the maximum chance of becoming an addict simply on the basis of opiate exposure alone is about 1 in 500. Blum, "Mind-Altering Drugs" 48.

[118] Eldridge, *Narcotics and the Law* 24.

control mechanism,[119] and the threat of punishment cannot be expected to increase significantly his ability to conform.[120]

The failure of the criminal process has led to a research for other methods of curbing drug addiction in the United States. Perhaps it would be more accurate to say that there has been a renewed interest in noncriminal methods of dealing with drug addiction, since many state legislatures as well as the Supreme Court and Congress have propounded the theory, as early as the 1920's, that narcotic addicts were sick individuals and should be committed for treatment rather than punished.

The oldest form of civil commitment for addicts was an adjunct to the laws providing for the commitment of the mentally ill. Thirty-three states make provisions in their mental illness commitment laws for the extension of this procedure to narcotic addicts.[121] Under this procedure, a complaint alleging that commitment is necessary must be filed, a medical examination ensues, and a judicial hearing is usually held to determine whether commitment should be ordered.[122]

[119] One's ability or inability to conform to the requirements of the law must be viewed as a relative rather than an absolute concept. L. L. Fuller, *The Morality of Law* 79 (1964). Yet the law must sharply distinguish between those who are accountable and blameworthy and those who are free from guilt due to mental or physical compulsion.

[120] Frankel, "Narcotic Addiction, Criminal Responsibility, and Civil Commitment," 1966 *Utah L. Rev.* 581, 603.

[121] Most of the state statutes lack a clear definition of the degree of addiction sufficient for involuntary hospitalization. Some states rely primarily on medical standards. Louisiana, for example, defines an addict as any person who habitually uses a narcotic drug "to such extent as to create a tolerance for such drug . . . and who does not have a medical need for the use of such drug. . . ." *La. Rev. Stat.* §28:2(6) (1950). Other states make public safety and welfare the primary test. Oregon, which typifies this approach, will commit a person who habitually uses a habit-forming drug "so as to endanger the public morals, health, safety or welfare." *Ore. Rev. Stat.* 475.610(1) (1957). The District of Columbia metropolitan area again displays the diversity of the national picture. The Maryland standards for narcotics commitment are loose. A person habitually addicted to the use of "opium, cocaine, morphine or other intoxicant" to such a degree that he is deprived "of reasonable self-control" is subject to hospitalization. *Md. Code Ann.* art. 16, §43 (Repl. vol. 1966). The District of Columbia permits the commitment of any person who because of addiction to narcotic drugs has lost his "power of self-control" with regard to such drugs, or whose addiction otherwise endangers the public morals, health or welfare. *D.C. Code* §24–602 (1967). Virginia apparently lacks provisions for the commitment of drug addicts. The previous law, repealed in 1965, applied to addicts who had become dangerous to the public or to themselves and were further unable to care for themselves. *Va. Code* §37–1.1 (15) (Supp. 1966). Acts of 1964, §640, repealed §§37–154 and 37–157 of the previous commitment law.

[122] *See, e.g., Ala. Code* tit. 22, §§249–50 (1958); *Ark. Stat. Ann.* §§82–1051 to 1061 (Supp. 1965); *Del. Code Ann.* tit. 16, §4714 (1953); *D.C. Code Ann.*

The adjudged addict is typically confined to a state mental institution, in the absence of specialized facilities, and there he remains until he is released as cured or substantially improved. The official determination of cure and release are often required to be made by the committing court, but in reality, it is an administrative decision made by the superintendent of the treating facility and conveyed to the court.

A combination of factors has limited the use of this procedure. In most jurisdictions this type of commitment cannot be used for voluntary patients, and only compulsory patients are received by the institutions. Some states have required that commitment be initiated on the petition of relatives,[123] and relatives have often been reluctant to commence such action.[124] To the family, the absence of specialized therapeutic facilities makes resort to this commitment the equivalent of a life sentence. Consequently, even judges and hospital administrators have been reluctant to commit addicted patients unless addiction has produced an advanced stage of mental deterioration—at which stage many of these addicts are viewed as beyond cure.[125] The general utilization of civil commitments is restricted by the fact that most statutes prohibit the use of the procedure for those charged

---

§§24–601 to 615 (1961); *Fla. Stat. Ann.* §349.22 (1900); *Ga. Code Ann.* §42–818 (1957); *Iowa Code Ann.* §§224.1–5 (1949); *La. Rev. Stat. Ann.* §28:53 (Supp. 1966); *Md. Code Ann.* art. 16, §43 (1966); *Mass. Ann. Laws* ch. 123, §62 (1965); *Mich. Stat. Ann.* §14.808 (1956); *Minn. Stat. Ann.* §§254.09–10 (1959); *Mo. Rev. Stat.* §§202.360–390 (1962); *Neb. Rev. Stat.* §§83–701 to 707 (1066); *Nev. Rev. Stat.* §§433.250–280 (Supp. 1901); *N.J. Stat. Ann.* §§30:4–177.14 to 177.16 (1964); *N.M. Stat. Ann.* §54–7–35 to 36 (1953); *N.Y. Sess. Laws* ch. 204, §3, p. 403 (1962); *N.C. Gen. Stat.* §§122–36(c), 122–60 to 65.5 (1964); *Pa. Stat. Ann.* tit. 50, §§2061–69 (1954); *R.I. Gen. Laws Ann.* §§21–28–57 to 58 (1956); *Vt. Stat. Ann.* tit. 18, §§2901–02 (1959); *Wash. Rev. Code Ann.* §§69.32.070, 72.48.030 (1962), *Wis. Stat. Ann.* §51.09 (Supp. 1967). See also Chapter 2, pp. 72–74; and *The Mentally Disabled and the Law* 18 (F. T. Lindman and D. M. McIntyre, eds. 1961).

[123] See, e.g., *Mich. Stat. Ann.* §14.808 (1956) (petition of guardian, spouse, next of kin, or some suitable person designated by the probate court); *N.Y. Sess. Laws* ch. 204, §3, p. 403 (1962) (petition of relative or person with whom addict resides); *Pa. Stat. Ann.* tit. 50, §2063 (1954) (petition of parents or relatives). Under the recently enacted federal statute, a proceeding to commit an addict who is neither charged with nor convicted of crime can only be instituted on the petition of the addict himself, one of his relatives, or a person with whom the addict resides or at whose house he may be. Pub. L. No. 89–793, §§301(i), 302(a) (November 8, 1966).

[124] See Report of the New York State Department of Mental Hygiene to the New York Narcotic Addiction Control Commission, in 112 *Cong. Rec.* 24413, 24415 (daily ed. October 6, 1966); cf. 112 *Cong. Rec.* 26579 (remarks of Senator Dodd; daily ed. October 19, 1966).

[125] Winick, "Narcotic Addiction and Its Treatment," 22 *Law & Contemp. Prob.* 9, 25–26 (1957).

with a crime—whether connected with narcotics or not. Only the addict who manages to keep out of trouble is offered the civil treatment route.[126]

Another early method for compelling addicts to undergo treatment was granting broad disposition powers to the judge in minor criminal and narcotics vagrancy cases. In sentencing such narcotic vagrants, the District of Columbia court, for example, is permitted to order medical and mental examinations, referral to proper welfare authorities, confinement at specially designated facilities, and such punishment, control, and rehabilitation as deemed necessary.[127] In addition, in the case of addicts not criminally charged, recourse may be had to the civil commitment procedures to compel treatment.[128] Under the Virginia law, a judge, in lieu of sentence or fine, is allowed to order persons convicted of narcotic vagrancy to be committed to the control and supervision of the Director of the Department of Welfare[129] for an indeterminate period of not less than three months and not more than three years.[130] The procedure is subject to the judges determination that commitment is necessary for the protection of the public health or safety, or for the promotion of the public welfare through the rehabilitation of the offender.[131] Recommitment by the court for additional periods is possible on the recommendation of the public welfare director. (Vagrancy thus carries a confinement and rehabilitation term three times longer than the twelve-month maximum punishment provided for all other misdemeanors.)[132] Trial judges in Maryland, in lieu of imposing penalties, are likewise authorized to commit any person charged with a criminal offense, and shown to be a chronic alcoholic or narcotics addict, to a state hospital for observation and treatment.[133]

Recognizing this illness philosophy, Congress in 1929 created two facilities for the medical treatment of narcotics addicts.[134] These facilities are located in Lexington, Kentucky, and Fort Worth, Texas.

---

[126] Consequently, in 1952 drug addicts constituted less than 1 percent of all first admissions to state mental institutions and one-tenth of 1 percent of the resident hospital population. U.S. Public Health Service, *Patients in Mental Institutions*, pt. 2, p. 50, Table 17 (1952).

[127] *D.C. Code* §33–416a(h) (1961).

[128] *Ibid.* §24–603(b) and §24–601 (1961).

[129] *Va. Code Ann.* §18.1–200 (Supp. 1966).

[130] *Ibid.*

[131] *Ibid.*

[132] *Ibid.* §18.1–9 (1950).

[133] *Md. Code Ann.* art. 16, §49 (Supp. 1965).

[134] Act of January 19, 1929, 45 Stat. 1085, ch. 82 (1929).

But only a small segment of the nation's addicts[135] have been exposed to these hospitals, and the success of the treatment there has been limited.[136] Structured on a voluntary model, the federal institutions lacked the power to hold the patients, who usually dropped out from treatment as soon as they had been withdrawn from their physical dependence. Ninety to ninety-five percent of the patients returned to drugs within six months after leaving treatment.[137]

The Supreme Court embraced the theory that addiction is an illness as early as 1925,[138] a recognition that was reiterated in 1961 in *Robinson* v. *California*.[139] Robinson was convicted under a California statute that made it a crime to "be addicted to the use of narcotics" and punished such addiction with a minimum confinement of 90 days in jail. The Supreme Court held that addiction is a condition of ill health and penalizing one for being in that status would violate the Eighth and Fourteenth Amendments' prohibition against cruel and unusual punishment.[140] The case has not affected, however, the pun-

---

[135] Since 1935 there have been more than 80,000 admissions to the two hospitals. Although voluntary patients have made up almost one-half of the hospital populations at any given time, most have left against medical advice and before the treatment was completed. While voluntary patients were supposed to stay 5 months, the average stay was about 6 weeks. Maddox, "Hospital Management of the Narcotic Addict," in *Narcotics* 159 (D. M. Wilner and G. G. Kassebaum eds. 1965).

[136] One sample of 453 patients released from Lexington to New York shows that 91 percent relapsed 6 months after release. By the fifth year the abstinence rate in the same group had increased to 25 percent. Cole, "Report on the Treatment of Drug Addiction," in President's Commission on Law Enforcement and the Administration of Justice, *Task Force Report: Narcotics and Drug Abuse* 141.

[137] Durvall, Lock, and Brill, "Follow-up Study of Narcotic Drug Addicts Five Years After Hospitalization," 78 *Pub. Health Rep.* 185, 186, 191 (1963); U.S. Congress, Senate, Committee on the Judiciary, Subcommittee on Criminal Laws and Procedures, *Hearings on S. 2191* (Statement of Dr. Leo J. Gehrig), 89th Cong., 2d sess., 1966, p. 189.

[138] Linder v. United States, 268 U.S. 5, 18 (1925).

[139] 370 U.S. 660 (1962).

[140] In its decision, the majority did not rely upon the effect of addiction on the volition or free will of the offender to conform with societal demands. Instead, the emphasis was placed on the nature of prohibited conduct, and the court here felt that addiction, devoid of an overt act, is merely a status or craving which should not be criminally punished. "It is unlikely that any State at this moment in history would attempt to make it a criminal offense for a person to be mentally ill, or a leper, or to be afflicted with venereal disease. A State might determine that the general health and welfare require that the victims of these and other human afflictions be dealt with by compulsory treatment, involving quarantine, confinement, or sequestration. But . . . a law which made a criminal offense of such a disease would doubtless be universally thought to be an infliction of cruel and unusual punishment." *Ibid.* 666.

ishment of addicts charged with the possession, use, or sale of narcotics, or with other offenses committed while in a state of addiction.[141]

The early attempts to cure addicts were largely restricted to detoxification. It was rapidly discovered, however, that physical withdrawal from narcotics, in the security of an institution, does not guarantee against subsequent relapses upon return to the community.[142] The failure of the early therapeutic programs to "cure" a significant number of addicts has provoked much controversy over the method of treatment employed.[143] Research into the psychology of the addict has revealed him to be immature and psychologically overdependent.[144] Narcotics provide him with the needed support. When the addict has been physiologically detoxified (withdrawn) in an institutional setting, he is surrounded by psychological supports—doctors, nurses, therapists, and others.[145] When he is released, however, to the environment

[141] In 1963, one year after *Robinson*, an attempt was made in the District of Columbia courts to expand the *Robinson* doctrine to the case of an addict charged with the possession and concealment of narcotics. Challenging the conviction of one Frank Horton, a chronic addict, the defense argued that an addict's physiological and psychological dependence on drugs was "merely symptomatic of his illness." The argument, supported by eight of the nation's leading psychiatrists, further stated: "The condition of drug addicts seeking drugs in order to maintain their physical and mental balance constitutes a medical problem and only medical treatment can effectively deal with this affliction. Providing criminal penalties for people suffering from a recognized illness constitutes 'cruel and unusual punishment.'" *See* Brief for Amici Curiae (Nicholas N. Kittrie, counsel for Drs. Bartemeier, Braceland, Kolb, Menninger, Modlin, Overholser, Salzman, and Satten), p. 7, Horton v. United States, 115 U.S. App. D.C. 184 (1963). Deciding against Horton, the D.C. Court of Appeals left the issue of the further divestment of criminal law unresolved. Horton v. United States, 317 F.2d 595 (D.C. Cir. 1963).

[142] U.S. Congress, Senate, Committee on the Judiciary, Subcommittee on Criminal Laws and Procedures, *Hearings on S. 2191* (Statement of Dr. Leo J. Gehrig), 89th Cong., 2d sess., 1966, p. 189. The Federal Narcotics Hospital at Lexington, which prides itself on the most advanced treatment methods and facilities for curing addicts, reports a recidivism rate of from 75 percent to 90 percent. Samuels, "A Visit to Narco," *New York Times Magazine*, April 10, 1966, pp. 32, 40.

[143] Frequently, the few addicts who are committed for treatment find themselves not in special facilities but in common mental asylums with little or no treatment. Vaillant and Rasor, "The Role of Compulsory Supervision in the Treatment of Addiction," 30 *Fed. Prob.* 53 (1966); Aronowitz, "Civil Commitment of Narcotic Addicts," 67 *Colum. L. Rev.* 405, 406 (1967).

[144] Berliner, "The Helping Process in a Hospital for Narcotic Addicts," 26 *Fed. Prob.* 57 (1962).

[145] O'Donnell, "The Lexington Program for Narcotic Addicts," *ibid.* 55; Berliner, "The Helping Process" 57.

from which he emerged, the same forces that originally led to his addiction drive him back to the refuge of drugs.[146] Thus, while physical dependence on drugs can be relieved in a matter of days, the psychological propensity to addiction is at least as intractable as any other personality disorder, with its roots in both environmental and psychological influences. The drug addict therefore requires both social and mental rehabilitation.[147]

These findings have recently led the experts to lean more heavily toward programs in which the addict makes a gradual re-entry into the world outside the institution. Such programs would enable the authorities to maintain contact with the addict, to watch for relapses into drug usage, and also to provide the crutch needed by the addict in crucial moments. (A special narcotics project undertaken by the New York State Division of Parole, utilizing continuous outpatient supervision, reports a rate of rehabilitation ranging from 32 to 42 percent.[148]) Two systems have emerged that embody these principles.

The first is the halfway house.[149] In this situation, the addict, after his initial narcotics withdrawal treatment,[150] is free during the day to work, wander, and rest. At night, however, he is required to return to the halfway house. Frequent tests are made to determine if the addict had suffered a relapse. If one has occurred, the addict might be reinstitutionalized for further treatment, or simply given more intensified counseling at the halfway house. Gradually, the tests for relapse become less frequent, the addict is given weekend passes and furloughs, and eventually he is released to the world with the hope that he will be able to cope with his personal crises without regressing to the use of narcotics.

The second method of gradually readmitting the addict to society

[146] Brown, "Narcotics and Nalline: Six Years of Testing," 27 *Fed. Prob.* 27 (1963).

[147] Note, "Civil Commitment of Narcotic Addicts," 76 *Yale L. J.* 1160, 1162 (1967).

[148] Diskind, "New Horizons in the Treatment of Narcotic Addiction," 24 *Fed. Prob.* 56 (1960); Diskind and Klansky, "A Second Look at the New York State Parole Drug Experiment," 28 *ibid.* 34 (1964).

[149] See Yablonsky, "The Anti-Criminal Society: Synanon," 26 *ibid.* 50 (1962); Shelly and Bassin, "Daytop Lodge. Halfway House for Drug Addicts," 28 *ibid.* 46 (1964).

[150] Interesting experiments have been conducted in the use of maintenance doses of methadone, a synthetic opiate, after heroin is withdrawn. Dole and Nyswander, "A Medical Treatment for Diacetylmorphine (Heroin) Addiction," 193 *J.A.M.A.* 646 (1965).

is less elaborate. It merely entails the close supervision of the addict's life and habits by probation or parole officers.[151] The addict is tested frequently for narcotics use and is counseled if necessary.[152] The probation officer seeks to establish a rapport with the addict so that in time of crisis he will seek out the probation officer rather than the narcotics vendor. Gradually, the probation officer withdraws his support from the addict, forcing him to call increasingly upon his own resources to meet his problems. Ideally, the addict will eventually reach a point at which he will need no extraneous support either from narcotics or from the probation officer. At that time, he will be totally released from supervision.

These two approaches have long been advocated by experts in the rehabilitation field, by sociologists, social workers, probation officers, and psychiatrists. The various experts may disagree on many important points, such as what class of addict should be included in the programs, but most authorities agree on three cardinal principles: (1) After institutional confinement and care, supervision must continue; (2) supervision must be compulsory; and (3) must be long in duration, perhaps indefinite, until it is determined that the addict is reasonably able to cope with the outside world on his own.

This need for long-term supervision in turn has led to a dissatisfaction on the part of the rehabilitation experts with the controls available under the criminal law. They feel that the criminal system, assuring the incarcerated person that at a certain point in time he will be released (regardless of his ability to cope with his dependence upon narcotics) renders ineffective any rehabilitative attempts in prison. They assert that an addict who knows that the only condition for release is a recovery, as determined by the hospital superintendent, is much more receptive to treatment than the person held under criminal sanctions, who knows his release is not conditioned upon any significant cooperation on his part. Furthermore, a therapeutic atmosphere is difficult to maintain when the inmates of the institution are adjudged criminals. Most experts agree both that there must be an initial compulsory confinement in an institution and that the traditional criminal incarcerations are inadequate.

[151] Brown, "Narcotics and Nalline" 27; O'Donnell, "The Lexington Program" 55.

[152] Due to existing probation and parole manpower distribution, the addict may get more individual attention and counseling while on parole than while under "treatment" in a special institution. Vaillant and Rasor, "Compulsory Supervision" 53, 58.

Increasing reliance has been placed within the past few years on indeterminate therapeutic confinement rather than the traditional criminal sanctions. The old forms of commitment were unsatisfactory for the new treatments. Civil commitment patterned after the mental illness model reached few addicts, and the narcotics vagrancy route was too narrow in scope for the ambitious new programs of treatment that were advanced. Broader therapeutic programs, designed for a wider segment of the addict population, were called for.

THE NEW WAVE

Experiments with a different type of therapeutic commitment were begun, both in the federal system[153] and by various states, particularly California, Massachusetts, and New York.[154] Most of the recent programs, except for that in Massachusetts, explicitly permit drug addicts to be committed voluntarily on their own petitions.[155] These laws also permit the involuntary commitment of persons judicially determined to be addicts, even if not accused or convicted of any criminal offense.[156] But one of the basic ideas behind the new laws is that when an addict is brought to court, charged with either a narcotics or non-narcotics violation, he should be compelled to undergo treatment for his addiction, instead of being treated through the criminal process. Since criminality is considered symptomatic of addiction, the objective of these programs is to treat the addict's physical craving as well as his psychological dependence and to supervise his return to society.[157] After institutional treatment the addict is introduced to

[153] Narcotic Addict Rehabilitation Act of 1966, Pub. L. No. 89–793 (November 8, 1966).

[154] *Cal. Wel. & Inst. Code* §§3000–3200 (West 1966); *Mass. Ann. Laws* ch. 111A, §§1–10 (Supp. 1965); *N.Y. Mental Hygiene Law* §§200–217 (McKinney Supp. 1966).

[155] Pub. L. No. 89–793, §302 (November 8, 1966); *Cal. Wel. & Inst. Code* §3100 (West 1966); *N.Y. Mental Hygiene Law* §206(2), as amended (McKinney Supp. 1966) (effective April 1, 1967).

[156] Pub. L. No. 89–793, §§301–16 (November 8, 1966); *Cal. Wel. & Inst. Code* §§3100–111 (West 1966); *Mass. Ann. Laws* ch. 111A, §§3–4 (Supp. 1965); *N.Y. Mental Hygiene Law* §206, as amended (McKinney Supp. 1966) (effective April 1, 1967). A noncriminal addict is subject to commitment under the federal act only if "appropriate state or other facilities are not available to such addict." Pub. L. No. 89–793, §302(b) (November 8, 1966). In New York a person so committed for addiction may be held for a maximum period of three years. Pub. L. No. 89–793, §206(5) (b). In California a person committed for addiction is eligible for release after an initial six-month observation period. *Cal. Wel. & Inst. Code* §§3104, 3105 (West 1966).

[157] Pub. L. No. 89–793, §§101, 201, 301(b) (November 8, 1966); *Cal. Wel. &*

halfway-house living and outpatient care under close parole supervision. Periodic testing for drug use is required when the patient is permitted to live in a halfway house and even when he is released from institutional supervision altogether.[158] A breach of any of the strict conditions imposed upon outpatients results in summary recommitment to the institution.[159] This central concept of substituting therapy for punishment is implemented differently by the various states.

In California the commitment for treatment is post-conviction. When an individual is tried and convicted of lesser crimes,[160] sentencing may be postponed until a determination is made whether the convicted defendant is an "addict" or "in imminent danger of becoming an addict."[161] The statute does not contain a comprehensive definition of these terms.[162] In lieu of being sentenced, those found to be addicted are ordered to a rehabilitation center for a period which may extend from six months to ten years.[163] If the patient is released from the rehabilitation program but not cured, sentence will be then imposed, and the time spent at the rehabilitation center will be ap-

---

Inst. Code §§3001, 3006, 3151 (West 1966); *Mass. Ann. Laws* ch. 111A, §§4–6 (Supp. 1965); N.Y. *Mental Hygiene Law* §200(3), as amended (McKinney Supp. 1966) (effective April 1, 1967).

158 Pub. L. No. 89–793, §§101, 201, 301(b), 307 (November 8, 1966); *Cal. Wel. & Inst. Code* §§3151–53 (West 1966); *Mass. Ann. Laws* ch. 111A, §§4, 6 (Supp. 1965); N.Y. *Mental Hygiene Law* §212, as amended (McKinney Supp. 1966) (effective April 1, 1967).

159 Pub. L. No. 89–793, §§101, 201 (November 8, 1966); *Cal. Wel. & Inst. Code* §3151 (West 1966); *Mass. Ann. Laws* ch. 111A, §4 (Supp. 1965); N.Y. *Mental Hygiene Law* §212, as amended (McKinney Supp. 1966) (effective April 1, 1967). In the case of noncriminal addicts committed under the federal act, reinstitutionalization because of breach of conditions of outpatient status requires an order of the committing court. Pub. L. No. 89–793, §307(b) (November 8, 1966).

160 *Cal. Wel. & Inst. Code* §§3050, 3015 (West 1966).

161 *Ibid.* §§3050–51.

162 The meanings of "addict" and of "imminent danger" thus become matters for judicial interpretation, often heavily dependent upon medical judgment. In a leading case which affirmed the constitutionality of the statute, the California Supreme Court held that the relevant terms are words with commonly understood meanings and are not so vague as to render the law impermissibly indefinite. *In re* De La O, 59 Cal.2d 128, 378 P.2d 393 (1962), *cert. denied*, 374 U.S. 856 (1963). Further interpretation of these terms is contained in People v. Victor, 62 Cal.2d 280, 398 P.2d 391 (1965); People v. O'Neil, 62 Cal.2d 748, 401 P.2d 928 (1965); People v. Bruce, 409 P.2d 943 (1966). In these cases the California court held that addiction to narcotics is a "process" rather than an "event" and is characterized by progressive emotional dependence, increased tolerance, and physical dependence. Addiction, accordingly, does not occur until there is physical dependence.

163 *Cal. Wel. & Inst. Code* §§3050, 3051, 3141, 3201 (West 1966).

plied toward it. If the patient is released as improved, the criminal proceedings may be dropped altogether.[164] Under the California formula, the civilly committed addict, after successfully completing the rehabilitation program in the institution, must submit to outpatient treatment for at least three years.[165] This outpatient status is similar to parole, since the patient must report frequently to an officer for testing and counseling in order to guard against a relapse. Only after the institutional program and the outpatient stage have been completed may the patient be returned to the court for release or for the imposition of sentence for the original conviction.[166]

The maximum period that a person may be compelled to participate in the California rehabilitation program is ten years. After an initial commitment not exceeding seven years, the patient must, however, be returned to the trial court. If the director of the narcotics program advises and the court agrees, the patient may be restrained for another three years.[167] Once a patient is released and again resorts to narcotics and to crime, the whole cycle may be commenced again.

The New York procedure, under the Narcotic Control Act of 1966, is significantly different from the California approach. The New York statute authorizes commitment of narcotic addicts or those in "imminent danger" of addiction[168] after certain criminal charges are brought against them.[169] Prior to the trial a defendant may voluntarily seek civil commitment, but only if he has no prior felony convictions, if the current charge is not punishable by life imprisonment or death, and in felony cases, if the prosecuting attorney consents. The court's granting of civil commitment, for a maximum period of three years, brings about an automatic dismissal of the criminal charges. If voluntary civil commitment is not requested or is not granted and the trial on the criminal charges proceeds, involuntary commitment for therapy may be ordered after conviction if the offense is not punishable by death or life imprisonment. If, after ordering a medical examination, the judge is satisfied that the defendant is a narcotics addict, he

---

[164] *Ibid.* §3200.
[165] *Ibid.*
[166] *Ibid.*
[167] *Ibid.* §3201.
[168] N.Y. *Mental Hygiene Law* §201(2) (McKinney Supp. 1966).
[169] *Ibid.* §208. The statutory definition limits narcotics to drugs of the opium, heroin, or morphine group; *ibid.* §201(2). Maryland has a similar statute, but any criminal charge will invoke the judge's authority to commit. *Md. Code Ann.* §10-3538a (Supp. 1966).

may seek the defendant's admission of such fact and, failing that, may make a finding of such condition on his own. Addicts convicted of misdemeanors, including prostitution, *must*, in lieu of sentence, be committed for treatment for a period of three years; those convicted of felonies may at the court's discretion be committed for a period of up to five years. In both instances the imposition of treatment is deemed a judgment of conviction, but the addict may be discharged earlier if cured. Despite the three-year maximum for misdemeanants and the five-year maximum for felons, a differential which smacks of penal rather than therapeutic aims, release may be made upon the completion of the addict's rehabilitation.[170] If an addict successfully completes the rehabilitation program, the original criminal charges must be dropped.[171] This contrasts with California, where the court may impose a sentence on a convict who has completed the rehabilitation program. Again, the New York three- and five-year maximum periods of commitment are much shorter than the ten-year limit for California.[172] In New York, furthermore, the addict is deemed to have completed the program successfully unless the commissioner administering the program certifies the patient back to the court, as one unfit for treatment. At that point, the patient may be tried on the basis of the criminal charge facing him.[173]

The practice of committing the addict to treatment prior to his trial raises serious problems. Enforcement officials complain that when treatment proves unsuccessful and the case comes to trial, the delay places grave hardships upon them.[174] From the addict's point of view, this procedure poses the danger of long-term therapeutic commitment upon unsubstantiated charges. On the positive side preconviction treatment guards against the creation of a criminal record in case the treatment is successfully completed.

For an addict accused of a federal offense, a different therapeutic

[170] N.Y. *Mental Hygiene Law* §§208(4)(a) and (b), 208(5), 206(5), 210(3) (McKinney Supp. 1966).

[171] *Ibid.* §213(4). "Incorrigibility or nonresponsiveness" to medical treatment can result in the court reactivating the original criminal charges. *Ibid.* §213(6).

[172] *Ibid.*

[173] For a discussion of the New York law *see* Comment, "Commitment of the Narcotic Addict Convicted of Crime," 32 *Albany L. Rev.* 360 (1968); Note, "Compulsory Commitment of Narcotic Addicts in New York State," 43 *N.Y.U. L. Rev.* 1172 (1968).

[174] Curran, "Massachusetts Drug Addiction Act: Legislative History and Comparative Analysis," 1 *Harv. J. Legis.* 89, 101 (1964).

plan was created by Congress in 1966.[175] It consists of a comprehensive system of civil commitments for a great variety of offenders.

Addicts charged with criminal offenses have the option of electing "voluntary commitment" in lieu of a trial.[176] Upon a suspect's appearance before the District Court, the court may in its discretion advise him that the criminal charges will be abated if he elects to undergo an examination to determine addiction.[177] He is further advised that if the examination discloses addiction, he will be confined to an institution for treatment and rehabilitation for a period not exceeding three years, to be followed by outpatient aftercare.[178] If the Surgeon General at any time decides that the addict is "cured," he may be released, and the criminal charges against him will be dropped. If the addict fails to complete the program successfully, the Surgeon General is required to certify him back to the District Court for his criminal trial.[179] The time spent in the rehabilitation institution must, however, be credited to any sentence imposed by the court.[180]

For an addict unwilling to undergo rehabilitation voluntarily, the new federal law allows indeterminate commitment, after conviction, for a maximum of ten years. But in no case is the commitment for treatment to exceed the term of the criminal sentence.[181] In addition, the new law provides for the civil commitment of addicted persons who are not charged with any criminal offense, either upon their own voluntary application or upon the application of a relative.[182] An addict so committed cannot voluntarily withdraw from treatment during a forty-two month period and after release must remain under outpatient supervision for three additional years.[183]

THE DANGERS OF THE THERAPEUTIC STATE

The new federal program has been severely criticized by a minority of legislators as being too light on addicts and providing them with an escape from accrued criminal penalties. To these critics the pro-

---

[175] *Narcotic Addict Rehabilitation Act of 1966*; Pub. L. No. 89–793, 80 Stat. 1438 (1966).
[176] 28 U.S.C. §2902 (1966).
[177] *Ibid.* §2902(a).
[178] *Ibid.* §2903(b).
[179] *Ibid.* §2903(c).
[180] *Ibid.* §2903(d).
[181] 18 U.S.C. §4253(a) (1966).
[182] *Narcotic Addict Rehabilitation Act of 1966* tit. III, §302(a).
[183] *Ibid.* §303.

gram is "a distortion of our concepts of basic justice; it allows the trade of crime for a cure, regardless of whether the defendant's addiction had anything to do with his criminal act."[184]

In reality the new law probably adheres too rigorously to the puritan heritage of our past laws without according the traditional safeguards designed to protect the individual against societal excesses. The law betrays the old attitudes of the traditional antinarcotic establishment, thinly cloaked as a new rehabilitative approach. The new effort is not any more tolerant of deviation than the old one; it is more oriented against the individual addict than against the narcotics traffic; the criminal law traditionalists are once more given their pound of retribution. An addict is not eligible for the treatment program if he is charged with a crime of violence, or if he is charged with the sale of narcotics, or if he has two previous felony convictions. Yet those with prior narcotic or serious criminal histories form the most problematic group and are the most compelling evidence of the failure of repressive enforcement techniques. Thus the therapeutic goals are compromised. The basic motive of the programs is not treatment and cure of the addict but rather repression and removal of the addict-deviant from the national scene—and more efficiently and permanently than in the past. It is simply the old intolerance coupled with a new willingness to resort to pseudoscience for more effective societal controls.

Traditionally, criminal law has enforced society's requirements upon deviant behavior. Thus, in connection with the criminal system, our traditional suspicion of state power has engendered an elaborate system for protecting the rights of the individual and the accused. The exactness of the standards of proof, the presumption of innocence, and the various constitutionally guaranteed procedural rights are designed to place a heavy burden upon the state when it attempts to confine an individual for a violation of society's designated norms. The recent decisions of the United States Supreme Court limiting the latitude of the police is evidence of the continuation of this tradition.[185]

Until recently, America has not wished to abandon these protections in favor of more "efficient" methods of dealing with the deviant

---

[184] U.S. Congress, House, Appropriations Committee, *Narcotic Drug Rehabilitation*, 89th Cong., 2d sess., 1966, H. Rept. 1486, p. 49.

[185] Mapp v. Ohio, 376 U.S. 648 (1961); Escobedo v. Illinois, 378 U.S. 478 (1964); Robinson v. California, 370 U.S. 660 (1962); Miranda v. Arizona, 384 U.S. 436 (1966).

members of our society, but when the criminal process proves ineffective, the growing trend is toward the divestment of criminal justice and a resort to new avenues of social control. With this renunciation of the criminal process, however, often comes a denial of the traditional protections. This is as true in the narcotics field as in others we have studied.

In New York, in order to be subjected to the civil commitment procedures, it is sufficient that an addict be arrested on a criminal charge.[186] There need be no proof of his commission of a crime beyond that required for a finding of probable cause to arrest him. A valid arrest by an officer, even without a warrant, will render an addicted individual subject to civil commitment for a period of three years. While it has been emphasized time and again that this is not a criminal procedure, it remains true that an individual may have his freedom restricted for a lengthy period. Since the procedure is not criminal, few of the constitutional guarantees available to those faced with criminal sanctions are afforded to the addict. Furthermore, the burden of proof to be carried by the state has been lessened considerably. Instead of having to prove before a court of law that a defendant committed the specific acts essential to a certain crime, the state need only show that the individual is a narcotics addict to commit him and restrict his freedom. It is conceivable that law enforcement officials pursuing the aim of "getting suspected addicts off the street and put away" may attempt to circumvent the strict requirements of the criminal law by utilizing the lighter burden of proof and the lesser obstacles of civil commitment procedures.

This hazard is somewhat lessened in California, where a narcotics addict must be convicted of a crime before he may be civilly committed. This crime may be either a misdemeanor or felony and may be totally unrelated to narcotics.[187] The California requirement for a criminal conviction prior to civil commitment is a recognition of the Anglo-American tradition that an overt act must be committed or threatened by an individual before the state can confine him against his will. Even so, a conviction of vagrancy (an offense prevalent among addicts) or of narcotics possession would subject an addict to a confinement that could last as long as ten years. As in New York, this possibility could easily tempt California enforcement officers to disregard the less effective criminal sanctions in favor of the civil proceedings which could have much sharper teeth.

[186] N.Y. *Mental Hygiene Law* §207 (McKinney Supp. 1966).
[187] Cal. *Wel. & Inst. Code* §§3050–51 (West 1966).

Under the new federal program, the defendant in a criminal case may be given the option by the court to have the criminal charges held in abeyance if he submits to treatment for a period not to exceed thirty-six months.[188] If the addict does not successfully complete his rehabilitation, the criminal proceedings may be reinstated. The program also provides for a possible ten-year involuntary commitment following conviction—a provision which partially negates the voluntary provisions allowing the accused himself to elect rehabilitation. In the hands of persuasive prosecutors, the combination of the two provisions could be used to overwhelm the accused into waiving his criminal trial and "choosing" commitment, rather than forcing the prosecution to sustain the burden of proof required by a criminal prosecution. The temptation is strong for a prosecutor to resort to therapeutic commitments when his criminal case is weak.

Troublesome, also, is the authorization of therapeutic commitment periods which exceed the terms of imprisonment applicable to the particular offenses charged. The maximum jail sentence for a misdemeanor in New York is one year, as contrasted with the three-year commitment for treatment, and for certain felonies the maximum sentence is less than the five-year commitment. New York's new Narcotic Control Act thus clearly demonstrates how the therapeutic promise grants the state greater powers than are permitted under the traditional criminal process. The disparity was recently challenged in a series of cases in the State of New York Court of Appeals.[189] Upholding the constitutionality of the new provisions, the court pointed out that the commitment program is intended solely for the addict's benefit and went on to warn:

> The extended period of deprivation of liberty which the statute mandates can only be justified as necessary to fulfill the purposes of the program. . . . If compulsory commitment turns out in fact to be a veneer for an extended jail term and is not a fully developed, comprehensive and effective scheme, it will have lost its claim to be a project devoted solely to curative ends. . . . And the constitutional guarantees applicable to criminal proceedings will apply in full measure.[190]

[188] *Narcotic Addict Rehabilitation Act of 1966* ch. 175, 28 *U.S.C.* §2902(a) (1966).

[189] Fuller v. People, 24 N.Y.2d 292 (1969); *in re* James, 22 N.Y.2d 545 (1968).

[190] Fuller v. People, 24 N.Y.2d 292 (1969). For similar conclusions, *see in re* De La O, 59 Cal.2d 128, 378 P.2d 793 (1963), *cert. denied* 374 U.S. 856 (1963).

Professor Lindesmith of Indiana University, who argues for the ambulatory treatment of addiction and for the lawful distribution of drugs to addicts under medical supervision (as in England),[191] states his case against civil commitment as follows:

> Its current popularity is probably largely due to the fact that it seems to offer advantages to both the police and the medical philosophy of addiction. To the former it offers the continuation of the old practice of locking addicts up and of dodging the constitutional guarantees of the Bill of Rights which are built into the procedures of the criminal law. To the liberals and medically oriented it offers a gesture toward a new and more humanitarian approach and a new vocabulary for old practices. For the addict the situation remains substantially unchanged even if he can qualify as one of the select few eligible for civil commitment, except that he may expect to spend more time in institutions. The price of illicit drugs and the illicit traffic are untouched by this program, and the addict must still commit crimes to maintain himself. He still lives in fear of the police and is still exploited by peddlers. If he seeks to quit his habit voluntarily the only establishments to which he has easy access are jails and their equivalents.[192]

Little light has been shed on the future national policy toward therapeutic commitments by recent crime commissions. The president's commission considered therapeutic programs worthy of national testing but warned against confinement under "the pretense of treatment."[193] In addition to the need to tighten procedural guarantees,

---

[191] "[T]he British control system looks upon drug addiction as a medical problem and keeps it primarily in the hands of the physician. The decision whether to give regular prescriptions to the English user is left to the doctor, usually after consultation with another medical man. He does not have to report addicts under his care, but records must be kept both by him and by the druggists who fill the prescriptions. The British system applies pressure on the doctor to persuade the addict to accept treatment for cure of his addiction but allows doctors to prescribe sustaining doses of narcotics for habitual users. As a result, under the drug act addicts can obtain narcotics by prescription for 14 cents, which takes away practically all incentive to secure drugs from illegal sources." S. J. Holmes, "Medical Profession Seen as Leader in Combatting Narcotics Addiction," in *Papers on Drugs* 45, 46–47 (Alcoholism and Drug Addiction Research Foundation of Ontario 1962).

[192] Lindesmith, *Addict and the Law* 292.

[193] "It is essential that the commitment laws be construed and executed to serve the purpose for which they were intended and by which alone they can be justified. This purpose is treatment in fact and not merely confinement with the pretense of treatment. [T]he Commission believes that involuntary civil commitment offers sufficient promise to warrant a fair test. But it must not become the

such as the alleged addict's right to counsel and a hearing,[194] if civil commitment proceedings are to be increasingly utilized, there is also a serious need for substantive due process in the form of reasonable and clearly defined criteria. Assuming that the suspension of traditional American protections against unreasonable intervention by the the state in one's life is justified in the face of the serious drug problem in the United States, there still remains the problem of determining at what point an individual's deviance justifies this drastic action by society.

This question is impending in the area of the hallucinatory drugs currently popular among a growing proportion of American youth. Conflicting statements concerning the short-term and long-term effects of these drugs have been made. Some have decried these substances as the worst development in the history of drug abuse. Others have described them as proper agents for artistic or religious experience and for humanity's mental emancipation.

At best, the dangers or blessings of these drugs are objectively unknown. But there are probably some personality traits common to all those who have recourse to the hallucinatory drugs. If the criminal sanctions currently being applied to curb the use of these new substances are as unsuccessful as they were in curbing narcotic drug usage, it might be argued that the powers of the therapeutic state ought to be invoked because the users are "addicted" to or prone to use these drugs by reason of their peculiar personality traits.[195] The temptation may grow to alter personalities and to cure deviants of those traits which cause them to be susceptible to drug use, thus pitting the therapeutic state against intellectual and artistic liberty and expression. Extreme caution must therefore be exercised lest in seeking to devolve society's concepts of conformity and acceptable

---

civil equivalent of imprisonment ... and the duration of the commitment ... must be no longer than is reasonably necessary." President's Commission on Law Enforcement and the Administration of Justice, *Task Force Report: Narcotics and Drug Abuse* 16.

[194] *See* Chapter 2.

[195] "Although there is probably no such thing as a typical addict personality, certain people are addiction prone." Alexander, "The Criminal Reponsibility of Alcoholics and Drug Addicts in Canada," 31 *Saskatchewan B. Rev.* 71, 78 (1966). The view of the addict or drug abuser as a therapeutic objective was propounded by the president's crime commission: "And the cause of all this, the drug-prone personality and the drug-taking urge, lay hidden somewhere in the conditions of modern urban life and in the complexities of mental disorder." President's Commission on Law Enforcement and the Administration of Justice, *Task Force Report: Narcotics and Drug Abuse* 1.

norms upon individuals, the therapists may encroach upon the differences that enrich the human experience.[196]

Since the object of the entire civil treatment movement is to "cure" the addict of his maladdiction, the criteria that the program administrators set for one's admission or release from therapeutic controls will determine in great part whether society's intervention is reasonable or excessive. The question of what condition of use or abuse, involving what drugs, is to be designated as "addiction" needs careful study. In both New York and California involuntary commitment may be invoked not only against an addict but also against one in "imminent danger" of becoming dependent on or addicted to drugs.[197] The law here clearly concerns itself with one who still remains a noncompulsive, voluntary user of drugs.[198]

Is this state intervention not premature?[199] "[I]t should be noted," said the president's crime commission, "that psychic or emotional dependence can develop to any substance, not only drugs, that affect consciousness and that people use for escape, adjustment or simple pleasure."[200] Could addiction to cigarettes, television, or pornographic literature be similarly condemned as socially hazardous and those addicted be subjected to compulsory treatment?[201]

The standards of "cure" have changed drastically in the last fifty years and may require restudy and redefinition. At first, it was thought that a "cure" would be effected by physically withdrawing an individual from his habits. This concept was abandoned when it was

---

[196] Professor Blum has provocatively asked: "Are drug risks to have a different base than those in parachute skydiving, cave exploring, or travel in dangerous lands? When a man says it affects himself only but others point out that it is his family which may suffer or the community which must pay for his care, who has the right to decide on weighing risks?" Blum, "Drugs, Dangerous Behavior, and Social Policy" 68.

[197] *N.Y. Mental Hygiene Law* §201(2) (McKinney Supp. 1966).

[198] People v. Victor, 62 Cal.2d 280, 398 P.2d 391 (1965); People v. Bruce, 64 Cal.2d 55, 409 P.2d 943 (1966).

[199] The court in People v. Victor, 398 P.2d 391 (1965), concluded that a constitutional defect might exist if the statute were construed to allow the commitment of persons suffering only from a psychological predisposition to addiction. The proper exercise of the state's police power is usually conditioned upon an actual, rather than a theoretical, danger to the individual or to society. Meyer v. Nebraska, 252 U.S. 390 (1923).

[200] President's Commission on Law Enforcement and the Administration of Justice, *Task Force Report: Narcotics and Drug Abuse* 2.

[201] It is essential that we distinguish between less dangerous and more dangerous behavior and differentiate the phenomena of drug use from that of drug dependency, and dependency from that of becoming an overt troublemaker. Blum, "Drugs, Dangerous Behavior, and Social Policy" 65.

realized that addiction was psychological as well as physiological; treatment was subsequently reinforced with psychotherapy in order to provide the necessary psychological support. Vocational guidance was included to enable the addict to be economically independent and to reduce his feelings of inadequacy. Even these steps proved inadequate to effect a permanent cure because upon release the addict was faced with the same environment that led to his initial addiction. The growing tendency is therefore to extend the initial period of institutional care through long-term, parole-type supervision in the community.[202] To many addicts this new type of treatment appears an even greater interference with liberty; one writer envisions it as a lifetime sentence of subjection to state supervision, punctuated by prolonged periods of complete confinement.[203]

In the final analysis, the criteria for social interference with the narcotic euphoria, and the terms and degree of such interference, must be commensurate with both the "disease" and its "cure."[204] We must be cautious to exert social sanctions only when they are clearly justified by the alleged addict's threat to the social order. The state, under its police power, should not be permitted to institute preventive therapeutic programs against the wishes of a citizen unless his condition poses an actual rather than a speculative danger to himself or to society;[205] neither should the state judgment about his need for treatment be substituted for his own under the *parens patriae* guise unless he is utterly lacking in mental capacity to decide for himself.[206] The exertion of therapeutic sanctions which exceed the terms of criminal punishment is defensible only when effective therapeutic programs are made available as the *quid pro quo* for the loss of liberty.[207] Therefore, before the desire to "cure" all the deviates of our

[202] O'Donnell, "The Lexington Program" 55.

[203] Note, "Commitment of Narcotic Addicts" 1160, 1163.

[204] The president's crime commission interestingly noted that "to think only in terms of 'cure' is not very meaningful in the case of a chronic illness such as addiction." President's Commission on Law Enforcement and the Administration of Justice, *Task Force Report: Narcotics and Drug Abuse* 16.

[205] Meyer v. Nebraska, 262 U.S. 390 (1923).

[206] State *ex rel.* Pearson v. Probate Court, 205 Minn. 545, 287 N.W. 297, *aff'd* 309 U.S. 270 (1940).

[207] The opponents of involuntary civil commitments "contend that at the very least there should be a specific finding that the person to be committed is reasonably likely to commit dangerous acts; that mere proof of addiction is not a sufficient showing that a person is dangerous to himself or others; and that, in any event, the commitment is a subterfuge—it holds out the promise of a known method of treatment, or a reasonable prospect of cure, which does not exist." President's Commission on Law Enforcement and the Administration of Justice, *Task Force Report: Narcotics and Drug Abuse* 17.

society becomes a national preoccupation, it is imperative that we take stock both of this nation's drug ills and of the available therapeutic tools.[208]

The California narcotic rehabilitation program, one of the more ambitious among the recent state therapeutic endeavors, well illustrates the newest trend in treatment. Established in 1961,[209] the main branch of the rehabilitation center, designated as a minimum security facility, is located at Corona, Riverside County, and consists of 91 acres surrounded by a high chain link fence. The facility can accommodate 1,860 men and 400 women. Between 1961 and the middle of 1966 there were 5,624 commitments to the center, 4,789 males and 835 females. Among male residents the median age is 26.5 years, and among female residents, 27.9 years; only slightly over a quarter of all inmates have a ninth-grade education or better. A majority experimented with marijuana and dangerous drugs while in their teens, with opiate use commencing at about age 20. Of the inmate population only 6 percent were committed on charges of addiction only; 73 percent were committed after felony convictions and 21 percent after conviction on misdemeanor charges. Approximately 42 percent of the inmates are white, 45 percent of Mexican descent, and nearly 12 percent Negroes.

As soon as an addict is admitted, he undergoes a variety of tests—including IQ, education achievement, vocation aptitude, and personality evaluations. The addict's social and criminal histories are compiled and a recommended treatment program is developed. Meanwhile, he is assigned to a 60-man residence group where he will remain until he is released to the community.[210] The emphasis is on group or community living. Transfer between residence units is discouraged and individuals are expected to face and work out group living problems as they occur. Large group meetings of residents and staff are held five days a week. Discussions first concentrate on everyday problems of institutional living, including pilfering, informing, and other special problems. The groups then begin to consider relationships with friends, family, and the outside world. Two or three

[208] For a detailed critique of indiscriminate civil commitments *see* Aronowitz, "Civil Commitment of Narcotic Addicts and Sentencing for Narcotic Drug Offenses," in *Task Force Report: Narcotics and Drug Abuse* 148–58; Frankel, "Narcotic Addiction" 581, 605.

[209] Lynch, "The California Narcotic Addict Rehabilitation Law," 12 *N.Y. L. Forum* 369, 379 (1966).

[210] Wood, "Statement Prepared for Judiciary Committee of the United States House of Representatives," quoted in *ibid.* 380–81.

times a week, the 60-man groups separate into 15-man segments for
more intensive group discussions. The rest of the addict's day is devoted to work therapy, vocational training, or elementary and high
school education—all intended to supplant his craving for euphoria.

After a minimum of six months of observation and treatment, the
California law permits an inmate's release on parole. At Corona, the
median time before such release is approximately 15 months for men
and 11 months for women. Released inmates are assigned to case-
workers whose caseload is limited to 30 individuals. The caseworker
meets weekly with his whole group and also with each parolee at his
home or job. Each outpatient is chemically tested for narcotics five
times a month for at least six months. If after the first six months all
indications are satisfactory, the test schedule may be reduced to two
surprise tests monthly. Test failure, heavy drinking, failure to maintain adequate employment, or other parole violations result in return
to the center. Discharge from the program may be attained after
three years of narcotic abstention while on an outpatient status. Persons who have not been discharged within a seven-year period must
either be released or brought back to the court for a three-year extension.

Even after an addict has been discharged from the treatment program he may again be committed for a new ten-year maximum period
if he returns to drugs or to drug-connected crime. A pilot study of
released inmates revealed that only 37 percent of the men and 29
percent of the women were able to remain drug free during their first
year of parole.[211] Only one out of five released patients remained
abstinent for two years or more while under outpatient supervision.[212]
Of a total 3,243 inmates released on parole during the program's
first five years, ended May 31, 1966, only 56 had been totally discharged from the program after completing three drug-free years in
the community.[213] Similar results are reported in New York, where
release from commitment is also followed by intensive parole supervision. Of a total 344 addicts who were returned to the community
under supervision, only 11, or about 3 percent, remained abstinent for
more than two years.[214]

[211] *Ibid.* 384.
[212] Aronowitz, "Civil Commitment of Narcotic Addicts" (*Colum. L. Rev.*)
404, 418.
[213] *Ibid.* 418.
[214] New York State, Division of Parole, *Final Report on an Experiment in the
Supervision of Paroled Offenders Addicted to Narcotic Drugs* 61 (1960).

Since existing evidence seriously challenges not only the utility of voluntary commitments but also the therapeutic effectiveness of long-term institutional confinement for involuntary patients,[215] it appears that mass commitment of addicts to hospitals or other facilities guarantees little more than the removal of the offenders from the streets into preventive detention centers.[216] "Civil commitment thus provides an antiseptic way of doing thoroughly what the criminal law cannot do at all."[217] A recent report from New York clearly illustrates the divergence between the promise of treatment and its fulfillment:

> [Upon petitoner's] . . . arrival at Rikers Island [the new treatment center for addicts], he underwent the same classification procedures as newly arrived non-addict prisoners, and, when sent to the Penitentiary, was assigned a cell with a non-addict inmate. Petitioner's daily routine during the almost one year he has been on Rikers Island is almost identical with that followed by his non-addict cellmates. There is no separate school or work facilities for addict prisoners. Whether the addict goes to school, as relator did, or to work, in the various prison vocational shops, both programs are under the complete control of the regular prison administration.[218]

Long-term incarceration for large numbers of potentially dangerous addicts and near addicts is not only impossible because of lack of

[215] Relapse rates after psychiatric hospitalization exceed 90 percent. Vaillant and Rasor, "Compulsory Supervision" 531. Some evidence suggests, however, a higher rate of abstinence for involuntary patients 30 years old and over, and for patients institutionalized for at least 30 days. More prolonged hospitalization demonstrated no better results. Cole, "Treatment of Drug Addiction" 141.

[216] Comment, "The Narcotic Addict Convicted of Crime" 360, 387. The attitude of the New York Legislature in enacting its civil commitment law for addicts was reported in the press: "most of the debate on the bill concerned a controversial provision under which any addict could be committed against his will for a treatment program lasting up to three years. . . . Speaker after speaker voiced frustration at the failure of medical science to find a cure for narcotics addiction. Max Turshen, Democrat of Brooklyn, expressed the feelings of colleagues on both sides of the aisle when he said: 'We haven't got the medical answer. So we've got to do the next best thing. We've got to keep these people off the streets.' . . . Albert Blumenthal, one of a group of Reform Democrats who sought to delete the compulsory commitment section of the Rockefeller bill, said: 'Perhaps we should tell the public that we're faced with a threat as great as bubonic plague—and until we find a cure we're going to set up a concentration camp in every community.'" *New York Times*, March 31, 1966, pp. 1, 28.

[217] Note, "Commitment of Narcotic Addicts" 1160, 1162.

[218] Blunt v. Narcotic Addiction Control Commission, *N.Y. L. J.* October 16, 1968, p. 17.

appropriate facilities but also contrary to our fundamental concepts of individual liberty.

THE ALTERNATIVES

A far more constructive avenue for social action is through the creation of a relatively free therapeutic climate in America. This can be fostered by the establishment and availability of voluntary detoxification facilities for the use of addicts, without commitment or conviction. The development of more effective therapeutic tools, offering treatment in settings removed from the addict culture (in public as well as private outpatient clinics and halfway houses),[219] and greater reliance upon medical discretion in the treatment of the patient within the community are required for the new climate of therapy. The recent availability of methadone treatment may provide such an opportunity. An inexpensive substitute for opiates, methadone has been used by various governmental and private outpatient clinics for the treatment of addiction. Yet while methadone prescriptions overcome the addict's craving for heroin and enable him to lead a normal life in the community, the treatment nevertheless creates a new type of legally sponsored dependency in place of the original prohibited addiction.

Physicians must be drawn into the process of substituting community treatment for institutional confinement. The Harrison Act formally exempts prescriptions issued by a physician "for legitimate medical uses" and also the distribution of drugs to patients "in the course of his professional practice only."[220] But this exemption has been narrowly construed by the courts and the Bureau of Narcotics. The bureau regulations make it unlawful for a physician to prescribe narcotics "not in the course of professional treatment but for the purpose of providing the user with narcotics sufficient to keep him comfortable by maintaining his customary use."[221] Moreover, the Harrison Act is a criminal statute, so a prescription of drugs that falls outside its medical exemption is not merely a professional mistake on the part of a doctor, it is a prosecutable criminal offense.

The medical freedom to experiment must be supported with more

---

[219] For an interesting discussion of Synanon, a voluntary halfway house run by addicts and former addicts and dedicated to rehabilitation, see Yablonsky, "Synanon" 50–57.

[220] *Int. Rev. Code of 1954* §§4704(b)(1), 4705(c)(1).

[221] *U.S. Treas. Reg.* 151.392.

meaningful efforts for the addict's placement within the community.[222] At present, the addict remains constantly outside the bounds of the law. He "lives in almost perpetual violation of one or several criminal laws, and this gives him a special status not shared by other criminal offenders."[223] The underworld monopoly on narcotics, similar to the underworld monopoly of alcohol during Prohibition, is total. Yet this monopoly must be broken before the rational treatment of addiction becomes possible. The first step here is to give the addict lawful access to medical sources who will decide what form of treatment (including controlled drug maintenance) should be undertaken.[224] Clearly, regulated maintenance doses for addicts are preferable to a system under which their craving for the prohibited substances leads to increasing lawlessness.[225]

All this is not meant as an endorsement for free public trading in addictive or other dangerous substances. Criminal restrictions upon the unlawful manufacturing, importation, and sale of narcotics or other hazardous drugs must be continued; underworld exploitation of narcotics must be harshly dealt with; but our efforts must be directed away from addict persecution. We must reconsider the utility and justification of criminal or even of therapeutic sanctions with regard to the lesser offenses of drug possession[226] and use by addicts.[227] "Some criminal offenses, like some minor contagious diseases, represent harm to others so impalpable, insubstantial, or indirect that it

[222] President's Commission on Law Enforcement and the Administration of Justice, *Task Force Report: Narcotics and Drug Abuse* 18.

[223] *Ibid.* 6.

[224] It is significant that a reputable minority within the medical profession "do[es] not regard withdrawal of the addict from drugs as the first, perhaps not even the ultimate, treatment objective." *Ibid.* 19.

[225] A United States Senate subcommittee rejected this approach with indignation: "Finally, we believe the thought of permanently maintaining drug addiction with 'sustaining' doses of narcotic drugs to be utterly repugnant to the moral principles inherent in our law and the character of our people." U.S. Congress, Senate, Committee on the Judiciary, Subcommittee on Improvements in the Federal Criminal Code, *The Causes, Treatment, and Rehabilitation of Drug Addicts,* 84th Cong., 1st sess., 1955, S. Rep. 1850, p. 13.

[226] Given the present state of the therapeutic art, it would be advisable to require that the treatment period be no longer than the maximum sentence allowed for a criminal conviction. *See,* generally, Aronowitz, "Civil Commitment of Narcotic Addicts" (*Colum. L. Rev.*) 405.

[227] See the recommendations contained in President's Advisory Commission on Narcotics and Drug Abuse, *Final Report* 40–42 (1962). Comparing the arguments for the commitment of addicts to the rationale behind mental health commitments, Aronowitz notes (a) that it is unreasonable to conclude from the fact of addiction alone that an addict is an immediate or probable danger to others; (b) that thousands of addicts and narcotic users never come in contact with the

cannot outweigh a man's liberty.... even if it is not unconstitutional for the state to deny addicts all legal access to narcotics, the state should certainly be estopped from confining addicts for fear of the crimes it obliges them to commit."[228] It would be advisable to limit social sanctions, whether criminal or, preferably, in the form of involuntary therapy, to instances where addicts or drug abusers have committed crimes against persons and property.[229] Drug possession and use would be exempted from sanctions, except when the addict has become so mentally incapacitated that rehabilitative efforts are justified in the name of *parens patriae.*[230] It needs to be recognized also that the desire for artificial euphoria must be combatted on a different level than in the past; we must move from concentration upon symptoms to attention to causes. The new campaign must be fought by means of public education, by the removal of urban poverty and racial ghettos which breed a sense of inadequacy and worthlessness,[231] and by building a society better equipped to provide its members with a sense of individual well-being derived from an honorable and useful social role.

---

law and addicts are no graver hazard to society as perpetrators of property crimes than other recidivists; (c) that the addict's refusal to undergo treatment is not a sufficient justification for societal intervention in the name of *parens patriae* in light of the inadequate present state of the therapeutic arts. He concludes, therefore, that "involuntary civil commitment of noncriminal narcotic addicts is not justified on the basis of existing knowledge about addicts, addiction, or methods of treatment, and ... such programs represent an unreasonable and improper deprivation of liberty." *Ibid.* 405, 411.

[228] Note, "Commitment of Narcotic Addicts" 1160, 1186–87.

[229] This distinction represents a pragmatic compromise. "The addict's situation is such that we should not blame him for what he does to himself even though what he does has indirectly harmful consequences to society. But we cannot excuse him for direct invasions upon the rights of others. The difference is not in terms of the capacity of control in the addict but in the degree of danger to society." Frankel, "Narcotic Addiction" 609. Still, it must be admitted that it is fruitless to debate whether addicts should or should not be treated as criminals. The argument is based upon the old-fashioned attempt to distinguish between the "evil" offender and the "ill" one. Yet, whether classified one way or another, the addict requires the very same social sanctions and continued supervision.

[230] The scale for determining society's right to deprive a person of his freedom must depend both on the dangerousness of his conduct and the measure of his mental incapacity. Blum, "Mind-Altering Drugs" 31.

[231] It has thus been observed that "individual treatment, while essential and important, is a less and less effective procedure—when one is dealing with whole populations at risk of drug dependency—than is prevention." Blum, "Drugs, Dangerous Behavior, and Social Policy" 59.

6   The Alcoholics

It is not for kings . . . to drink wine;
Not for princes strong drink:
Lest they drink, and forget the law, and pervert the judgment. . . .
Give strong drink unto him that is ready to perish,
And wine unto those that be of heavy hearts.
Let him drink, and forget his poverty,
And remember his misery no more.—Proverbs 31:4—7

. . . the pursuit of happiness is a peculiarly human characteristic . . .
and so has been the search for drugs to facilitate this pursuit.
Nearly every society appears to have discovered substances which
powerfully influence the mind, lightening fatigue and the burden
of care, promoting fellow-feeling and at least a temporary sense
of well-being.—N. Kessel and H. Walton, *Alcoholism* 7 (1965)

THE ANATHEMA OF ALCOHOL

Although more generally experienced and socially accepted than
drug use, alcoholism was an early target of both legal and moral con-

trols. Had alcoholism[1] been a condition enjoyed or suffered primarily indoors, there would probably be less public preoccupation with it. But the marks of alcohol are constantly in the public eye, and its imprint upon public welfare and safety is heavily felt. There are an estimated five to six million alcoholics in the United States, of whom 1.25 million are chronically addicted.[2] Roughly 250,000 persons each year join the alcoholic ranks.[3]

Based on the number of deaths reported yearly from cirrhosis of the liver, it is estimated that alcoholics constitute 4 percent of the total United States population 20 years of age and over (the second highest rate in the world).[4] This compares with estimates of less than 1 percent for Italy, over 1 percent for England or Canada and more than 5 percent for France.[5] Others estimate the American alcoholism rate to be even higher. Statistical surveys show that alcoholics constitute about 13.2 percent of all first admissions to hospitals in the United States and 22 percent of male admissions.[6] In 1964, for example, the State of Maryland reported that more patients were ad-

[1] The medical literature provides diverse definitions for alcoholism. Some writers focus on the physically debilitating and antisocial effects of the disease. "Alcoholism is a chronic disease, or disorder of behavior, characterized by the repeated drinking of alcoholic beverages to an extent that exceeds customary dietary use or ordinary compliance with the social drinking customs of the community, and which interferes with the drinker's health, inter-personal relations or economic functioning." Keller, in U.S. Department of Health, Education, and Welafare, *Alcohol and Alcoholism* 6 (1968). Other experts stress the addictive nature of alcoholism. Plaut describes it as "a condition in which an individual has lost control over his alcohol intake in the sense that he is consistently unable to refrain from drinking or to stop drinking before getting intoxicated." T. Plaut, *Alcohol Problems* 39 (1967).

[2] Roche Laboratories, *Aspects of Alcoholism* 9 (1963). It is estimated that two-thirds of the adult population drink and that over 5 percent of the annual average American budget is spent on alcoholic beverages. M. E. Chafetz and H. W. Demone, *Alcoholism and Society* 12 (1962).

[3] 112 *Cong. Rec.* 6973 (remarks of Representative Kupferman, 1966).

[4] Pittman, "Public Intoxication and the Alcoholic Offender in American Society," in President's Commission on Law Enforcement and the Administration of Justice, *Task Force Report: Drunkenness*, 20 (1967).

[5] World Health Organization, Expert Committee on Mental Health, Alcoholism Subcommittee, *First Report*, Technical Report Series, no. 42 (1951), and *Second Report*, Technical Report Series, no. 48 (1952).

[6] U.S. Department of Health, Education, and Welfare, National Clearinghouse for Mental Health Information, *Patients in Mental Institutions, 1964: State and County Mental Hospitals* 21 (1966). Because for an alcoholic a stay in a mental hospital is generally brief, less than 6 percent of all resident patients at any given time have an alcoholic diagnosis. Plaut, "Some Major Issues in Developing Community Services for Persons with Drinking Problems," in President's Commission on Law Enforcement and the Administration of Justice, *Task Force Report: Drunkenness* 121.

mitted to state mental hospitals for treatment of alcoholism than ever before; alcoholism was the leading cause for admission, accounting for 31.2 percent of all admissions (or 40 percent of all male admissions). The second leading cause, schizophrenia, accounted for 24 percent.[7]

Alcoholism is clearly a killing disease: cirrhosis of the liver, malnutrition, road accidents, and suicide all take a heavy toll of alcoholics.[8] "The magnitude and importance of the illness of alcoholism are insufficiently appreciated. It is a grave disorder, often fatal. Its impact falls not only on the alcoholic but on a wide circle of family and friends. Its social reverberations affect accident and crime rates, absenteeism and unemployment."[9] Alcoholism is not only a health problem, it is a police, public safety, and public welfare problem as well. Out of an approximate total of five and a half million arrests for all crimes in the United States in 1968, the FBI reported that nearly 1.5 million were for public drunkenness, over 307,000 for driving while intoxicated, 215,000 for other alcohol violations, and some 593,000 for disorderly conduct.[10] A large number were chronic alcoholics with lengthy arrest histories.[11] Much of the police burden is thus produced by the multiple arrests and punishment of a fairly limited number of chronic skid-row alcoholics.

Certainly, even in terms of mere numbers, for drunkenness to account for one out of every three arrests constitutes an enormous burden on the law enforcement agencies;[12] but the burden does not fall only on the police. After an initial detoxification stay in jail, many alcoholics are further processed through the *courts* and are ultimately committed to *correctional institutions* where their term of stay may range from 30 to 120 days.

[7] J. C. Coleman, *Abnormal Psychology and Modern Life* 399 (1956); *Washington Evening Star*, March 15, 1965, p. B4; State of Maryland, Department of Mental Hygiene, *Statistics Newsletter*, VII–8, August 10, 1965.

[8] In 1959 alcoholism was rated beneath only heart disease and cancer in the nation's list of major health problems. 76 *Science News Letter* 82 (1959).

[9] N. Kessel and H. Walton, *Alcoholism* 12 (1965).

[10] FBI, *Uniform Crime Reports for the United States* 110–11 (1968).

[11] In 1964, in the city of Los Angeles, about one-fifth of all persons arrested for drunkenness accounted for two-thirds of the total number of arrests for that offense. Pittman, "Public Intoxication" 1.

[12] The number of alcoholism arrests in a given community, it must be remembered, depends largely on police policies. In New York City, arrests are limited to actual instances of disorderly conduct. Consequently, New York City, with a population of almost 8 million, has averaged 30,000 drunk arrests in recent years. Los Angeles, with a population of 2.5 million, has nearly 100,000 arrests yearly. Murtagh, "Arrests for Public Intoxication," in President's Commission on Law

Probably no other area of drug abuse exists where the role of a drug as a precipitating factor in dangerous behavior is so clear.[13] This is especially obvious in terms of traffic fatalities. New York City records show that of all motorists killed in 1957, 55 percent were under the influence of alcohol. Fatalities among pedestrians frequently reflect similar evidence. Of each year's 40,000 American traffic fatalities and the million more who suffer painful and crippling injuries, it is estimated that about one-half could be saved if those intoxicated could be prevented from driving.[14]

The direct relationship between alcohol's effects and criminal behavior has long been suspected. Alcohol, though itself a depressant rather than a stimulant, acts to relieve the inhibitory control mechanisms.[15] Consequently, those under the influence of alcohol frequently become aggressive, assaultive, or comatose.[16] (By contrast, under the influence of opiates, the addict's primary needs, anxieties, and conflicts are relieved or eliminated.)[17] Forty percent to fifty percent of those incarcerated in penal institutions in the United States have had serious drinking problems.[18] A pilot study conducted in June 1954, in the State Prison at Raiford, Florida, reported that 66 percent of the inmates admitted in June were to some degree under the influence of alcohol when they committed the crimes for which they were imprisoned.[19] Not surprisingly, surveys of alcoholic felons report a preponderance of crimes of violence and comparatively few skilled offenses.[20] Professor Wolfgang's study of homicides committed in

---

Enforcement and the Administration of Justice, *Task Force Report: Drunkenness* 65. In 1965 Washington, D.C., reported nearly 45,000 drunkenness arrests. St. Louis, Missouri, with an almost equal population, reported 2,445 such arrests. *Ibid.* 2–3.

[13] Blum, "Mind-Altering Drugs and Dangerous Behavior: Alcohol," *Ibid.* 29, 41.

[14] Heise, "Drinking and Driving," 167 *J.A.M.A.* 1499 (1958).

[15] Wortis, "Alcoholism," in *Textbook on Medicine* 1730 (Cecil-Loeb ed. 1963).

[16] Isbell *et al.,* "An Experimental Study of the Etiology of 'Rum Fits' and Delirium Tremens," 16 *Q. J. Stud. Alcohol* 1–37 (1957).

[17] A. Wilkes, *Opiates and Opiate Antagonists: A Review of Their Mechanism of Action in Relation to Clinical Problems,* Public Health Monograph No. 52 (1958).

[18] Guze *et al.,* "Psychiatric Illness and Crime, with Particular Reference to Alcoholism: A Study of 223 Criminals," 134 *J. Nerv. and Mental Disease* 512–15 (1962).

[19] A later study of the prison's total population established that 38.7 percent of all the inmates were drinking or drunk at the time they committed their last offense. Grigsby, "The Raiford Study: Alcohol and Crime," 54 *J. Crim. L.C. & P.S.* 296, 305 (1963).

[20] Clark, Hannigan, and Hart, "Alcoholism, A Parole Problem: A Statistical Study of 100 Male Felons Paroled from Sing-Sing Prison to the New York Area

Philadelphia in the 1948–58 period concluded that in nearly two-thirds of the cases the offender or the victim or both had been drinking immediately prior to the slaying.[21]

Alcoholics are suicide prone. Psychiatrist Karl Menninger has considered alcoholism itself a form of "chronic suicide," implying that the drinker's exposure to toxic effects and social degradation is a willful even though unconscious effort at self-destruction.[22] The suicide rate of male alcoholics admitted for treatment in a London psychiatric hospital is reported to be 86 times higher than the rate for men in the same age groups in the general London population.[23] Likewise, a Scandinavian study of male alcoholics revealed that 7 percent kill themselves within five years of their release from hospital treatment. A study in St. Louis revealed that of 119 suicides whose histories were available 26 percent had a record of chronic alcoholism.[24]

Yet to be accurately tallied are the losses to industry and business through alcoholic absenteeism (estimated at $2 billion annually),[25] the cost of medical services for alcoholics, and the numerous other derivative social burdens of alcoholic unemployment—such as the costs of family support and child care. The toll of alcoholism is apparently taken in the next generation as well. A Swedish survey comparing school performance of children from alcoholic and from non-alcoholic families revealed that 48 percent of the first group were rated as problem children by their teachers, compared with only 10 percent of the second group.[26]

THE ALCOHOLIC AND THE LAW

The law has never displayed a tolerant view toward alcoholic excess, though in early English common law drunkenness was not in itself a criminal offense.[27] Blackstone, for example, classed it as an offense against God and religion.[28] Judged to be a sin and within the

---

During 1962," in 6 *Current Projects in the Prevention, Control and Treatment of Crime and Delinquency* 353 (1964–65).

[21] M. E. Wolfgang, *Patterns of Criminal Homicide* (1958).

[22] Blum, "Mind-Altering Drugs and Dangerous Behavior: Alcohol."

[23] Kessel and Walton, *Alcoholism* 104, Kessel and Grossman, "Suicide in Alcoholics," *Brit. Med. J.* 1672 (December 23, 1961).

[24] Kessel and Walton, *Alcoholism* 165.

[25] 112 *Cong. Rec.* 6973 (remarks of Representative Kupferman, 1966).

[26] Kessel and Walton, *Alcoholism* 118.

[27] Moser v. Fulk, 74 S.E.2d 729 (N.C. 1953).

[28] 4 *Blackstone Commentaries* 41, 64 (1765).

church's realm, drunkenness was punished by the ecclesiastical courts. Only when a drunk created a public nuisance was he punished under the jurisdiction of the law courts.

As early as 1606, however, public intoxication was made a statutory offense in England.[29] Subsequently, even in the absence of specific state laws, public drunkenness has been recognized in the United States as a common law crime.[30] In some New England jurisdictions, the early statutes provided that a person arrested for drunkenness could be compelled to disclose where and from whom the alcohol was obtained so that the source also might be appropriately punished.[31] Several states recognized not only the crime of "public drunkenness" but established the separate crime of being a "common drunkard," encompassing persons for whom public drunkenness had become a habit.[32] Some jurisdictions, on the other hand, have no laws prohibiting drunkenness but resort instead to disorderly conduct statutes as a means of controlling those who are drunk in public.[33]

To constitute the offense of public drunkenness, it is usually sufficient that the accused has lost normal bodily and mental control. Intoxication in some states, however, must be manifested by a boisterous or indecent condition or action or by profane language.[34] Likewise, the offense must usually be committed in a public place, defined as a place where the public has a right to go and be,[35] so that, ordi-

---

[29] Jac. I c. 5, §2 (1606). The language of this law is revealing of the mores and concerns of the time: "AN ACT FOR REPRESSING THE ODIOUS AND LOATHSOME SIN OF DRUNKENNESS: WHEREAS, The loathsome and odious sin of drunkenness is of late grown into common use within this realm, being the root and foundation of many other enormous sins, as bloodshed, stabbing, murder, swearing, fornication, adultery, and such like, the great dishonor of God, and of our nation, the overthrow of many good arts and manual trades, the disabling of divers workmen, and the general impoverishing of many good subjects, abusively wasting the good creatures of God: II. Be it therefore enacted . . . That all and every person or persons, which shall be drunk, . . . shall for every such offense forfeit and lose five shillings, . . . to be paid . . . to the hands of the churchwardens . . . (3) and if the offender or offenders be not able to pay . . . shall be committed to the stocks for every offense, there to remain by the space of six hours."

[30] Cf. Inman v. State (Tenn.), 259 S.W.2d 531 (1953).

[31] Corpus Juris, "Drunkards" §40 (1920); cf. in re Irish, 64 Vt. 376, 25 A. 435 (1892).

[32] Corpus Juris, "Drunkards" §41. Cf. City of Cleveland v. Davey, 120 N.E.2d 454 (1954), which upheld a statute providing that no person shall be found in a state of intoxication; the place of intoxication was of no importance.

[33] Murtagh, "Arrests for Public Intoxication" 1–7.

[34] Ala. Crim. Code §14–120 (1958); Ga. Code Ann. §58–608 (1965).

[35] Corpus Juris, "Drunkards" §§9, 15.

narily, the law does not interfere with intoxication in a private residence unless disorderly conduct accompanies that condition.

Criminal penalties for public drunkenness or disorderly conduct vary from jurisdiction to jurisdiction and from one judge to another. In many jurisdictions an arrested person will be released directly from the police station upon posting a collateral of $10 to $20 which may be forfeited in lieu of an appearance before the court. Nearly half of those arrested in the District of Columbia during 1965 were so released.[36] Those coming before the courts may be fined or may receive a suspended sentence for the first offense, while subsequent offenses usually result in jail sentences ranging from two days to six months.[37]

After the advent of the automobile and the recognition of its hazards, a new crime came into being: driving under the influence of alcohol.[38] The penalty for drunken driving is much more severe than for public intoxication, ranging up to imprisonment for one year in addition to possible permanent loss of driving privileges and heavy fines.[39] Most states have enacted "negligent homicide" or "reckless homicide" statutes, with penalties of up to five years of imprisonment, which are applicable when death is caused by the negligent driving of a motor vehicle, including driving while intoxicated.[40] The strict penalties under these offenses, however, remain too infrequently exercised. Indeed, the police and the courts have much more thoroughly cleared the streets of pedestrian alcoholics than the public roads of drunken drivers.

Of special interest is the alcoholic's or highly intoxicated person's

---

[36] President's Commission on Crime in the District of Columbia, *Report* 477 (1966).

[37] President's Commission on Law Enforcement and the Administration of Justice, *Task Force Report: Drunkenness* 3. Sentences still remain usually light. *See* the Oklahoma case of Rothrock v. State, 206 P.2d 1009 (1949), which reversed a 30-day jail sentence on the ground of severity because the evidence showed no public disturbance. The conviction resulted in a fine of $10 plus costs.

[38] *See, e.g.,* D.C. Code Ann. §40–609 (1967).

[39] *Ibid.* §40–609(d).

[40] *Ill. Crim. Code* §9–3(b) and (c); *Ore. Rev. Stat.* §163.040(2). Some earlier cases resulted in the involuntary manslaughter conviction of drunken drivers. People v. Townsend, 214 Mich. 267, 183 N.W. 177 (1921). But juries were usually reluctant to convict drivers of manslaughter since "in common understanding manslaughter acts deal with brutal killings by a debased type of individual, whereas the motorist is generally a reputable citizen, and the wrong committed by him which brought someone to his death finds its counterpart in the driving of many others." State v. Whahn, 204 Or. 84, 282 P.2d 675 (1955). The new statutory offenses were designed to lessen the severity of the offense and thus to make convictions easier.

responsibility for other types of criminal conduct: assault, larceny, robbery, or murder. The recent case of Daniel Allen Frank is illustrative of the questions being raised.[41] Frank, known also as "Chippy Bean," was convicted of rape by a Maryland jury and was sentenced to 15 years imprisonment. There was ample evidence to show that Frank had engaged in sexual intercourse against the will of the female involved; there was also evidence that he was highly intoxicated at the time. Appealing his conviction, Frank argued that the jurors should have been instructed that they could consider the fact of his intoxication a possible negation of the criminal intent required for conviction. The Maryland Court of Special Appeals found against Frank, saying that it has been "universally recognized that voluntary drunkenness is generally not a defense to crime."[42]

Since drunkenness has been viewed both as voluntarily induced and as socially reprehensible, the courts have not been willing to accept it as a defense to criminal conduct in the same manner that insanity has been accepted.[43] Furthermore, the courts have held that intoxication does not involve the same degree of loss of rationality as does insanity, and, consequently, they have ruled that alcoholism does not justify the offender's relief from criminal responsibility.[44] Responding to the challenge that alcoholism is a disease like insanity, and that those suffering from it should be equally recognized as ill and exempt from criminal responsibility, most courts and writers declare that the community's safety requires preservation of the traditional rule denying the insanity defense to those voluntarily intoxicated. If intoxication were accepted as a defense, "[e]very murderer would drink to

[41] Frank v. State, 6 Md. App. 332 (1968).

[42] *Ibid.* 334.

[43] "It is a well settled law . . . that voluntary drunkenness is not a defense to crime. A man who puts himself in a position to have no control over his actions must be held to intend the consequences. The safety of the community requires this rule. Intoxication is so easily counterfeited, and, when real, is so often resorted to as a means of nerving a man up to the commission of some deliberate act, and withal it is so inexcusable in itself, that the law has never recognized it as an excuse for crime." People v. Guillett, 343 Mich. 1, 69 N.W.2d 140, 141 (1955).

[44] It must be remembered that not all cases of insanity but only those falling within certain prescribed criteria (e.g., the M'Naghten, Durham, ALI tests), have been recognized as affecting criminal responsibility. Alcoholism has not been found to comply with these requirements. In Flannagan v. People, 86 N.Y. 554 (1881), for example, the court held that alcoholics know the difference between right and wrong and therefore fail to come within the M'Naghten criteria. *See* the cases in Hall, "Intoxication and Criminal Responsibility," 57 *Harv. L. Rev.* 1045 (1944).

shelter intended guilt. There never could be a conviction for homicide if drunkenness should avoid responsibility. As it is, some of the most premeditated homicides are committed under the stimulus of liquor."[45]

As early as 1603, Lord Coke asserted that those deviants, such as the drunkard, who voluntarily deprived themselves of their reason should not be heard to claim incapacity as a defense in a civil or criminal action. Indeed, the fact that by their own act they had limited their ability to reason should constitute an aggravation of the offense.[46]

While criminal law adheres to the principle that intentional or negligent drunkenness does not absolve one of crime,[47] involuntary intoxication is universally accepted as a defense to criminal charges.[48] Increasingly, nonetheless, the state courts are allowing evidence of drunkenness to show the absence of the specific mental state required for such crimes as first-degree murder, larceny, burglary, attempt to commit rape, and attempt to commit murder.[49] In homicide cases, for example, evidence of intoxication can demonstrate the absence of premeditation and deliberation required for first-degree murder and thus may serve to reduce the charge to second-degree murder or manslaughter. Similarly, intoxication may be introduced to show that a person accused of larceny lacked the specific intent to steal.[50] But, generally, intoxication will not serve as a defense in most misdemeanors and felonies, such as rape, manslaughter, or assault, where the mere general intent to do the prohibited act suffices for convic-

[45] Lloyd, "Insanity: Forms and Medico-legal Relations," in *Medical Jurisprudence* 237 (F. Wharton and E. Stickney eds. 1882–84). "All that the crafty criminal would require for a well-planned murder, would be a revolver in one hand to commit the deed, and a quart of intoxicating liquor in the other with which to build his excusable defense." State v. Arsenault, 152 Me. 121, 124 A.2d 741, 746 (1956).

[46] Beverly's Case, 76 Eng. Rep. 1118 (K.B. 1603).

[47] In one unique exception, the New Hampshire Supreme Court suggested in 1869 that if alcoholism were proved a disease and a murder were shown to be its product, the defendant would not be criminally responsible. State v. Pike, 49 N.H. 399. See, generally, Hutt, "The Recent Court Decisions on Alcoholism," in President's Commission on Law Enforcement and the Administration of Justice, *Task Force Report: Drunkenness* 109, 110.

[48] 4 *Blackstone Commentaries* 24, 25; Martin v. State 31 Ala. App. 334, 17 S.2d 427 (1944).

[49] 22 *C.J.S. Criminal Law* §§65–72 (1961); Bishop v. United States, 107 F.2d 297 (D.C. Cir. 1939).

[50] For intoxication as a defense to attempted burglary see Bullock v. State, 195 Miss. 340, 15 S.2d 285 (1943), and as a defense to assault with intent to commit rape see Whitten v. State, 115 Ala. 72, 22 So. 483 (1897).

tion.[51] Consequently, it is accurate to conclude that drunkenness neither aggravates, excuses, extenuates, nor mitigates most crimes.[52]

While the general relief of alcoholics from criminal responsibility is not usually favored, there has been growing discontent with regard to the utility of the criminal law in controlling the public drunk. The enforcement of the criminal laws which provide punishment for public intoxication is further attacked for being overly selective and in practice favoring the affluent. The president's crime commission reported recently:

> The police do not arrest everyone who is under the influence of alcohol. Sometimes they help the inebriate home. It is when he appears to have no home or family ties that he is most likely to be arrested and taken to the local jail. Drunkenness arrest practices vary from place to place.... In fact, the number of arrests in a city may be related less to the amount of public drunkenness than to police policy.

> If the [arrested] offender can afford bail, he usually obtains release after he sobers up. In many jurisdictions an offender is permitted to forfeit bail routinely by not appearing in court. Thus, if the arrested person has the few dollars required, he can avoid prosecution; if he has no money, as is usually the case, he must appear in court.[53]

The indigent drunk is thus usually kept overnight in the "tank" of the local jail, a special cell which may hold 50 to 200 inmates. Rarely is medical care provided. Offenders are brought before a judge the morning after and are passed through the court system with extraordinary haste. It is not unusual for them to appear before the judge in groups of 15 or 20, and seldom will one find procedural due process safeguards applied in these cases. The right to be confronted by the accuser, the opportunity for cross-examination, and the privilege against self-incrimination are totally disregarded.[54] Counsel is not

[51] Frank a/k/a Bean v. State, 6 Md. App. 332 (1968). Some jurisdictions have not accepted this distinction between crimes requiring specific intent and those requiring general intent and have permitted evidence of intoxication in neither. State v. Garrett, 391 S.W.2d 235 (Mo. 1965); Kincaid v. State, 150 Texas Crim. 45, 198 S.W.2d 899 (1946).

[52] Beims, "The Law's Approach to Alcohol Addiction: Satisfactory?" 8 *Washburn L. J.* 59, 64 (1968).

[53] President's Commission on Law Enforcement and the Administration of Justice, *Task Force Report: Drunkenness* 1, 73.

[54] *Ibid.* 3; Foote, "Vagrancy-Type Law and Its Administration," 104 *U. Pa. L. Rev.* 603 (1956).

afforded by the court and rarely is a retained attorney present for the accused.[55]

After court appearance, the offender with a previous record will usually be sent to a short-term penal institution, which is perpetually overcrowded. (Nearly half of the misdemeanants in this country's jails and workhouses are drunkenness offenders.) After a brief stay, the inmate will find himself dumped back into his usual surroundings.[56]

THE MEDICAL NATURE OF ALCOHOLISM

Civilization has always been burdened by those who indulged excessively in alcohol, either sporadically, or regularly in response to a chronic condition. Historically, alcoholic indulgence was ascribed to weak individual constitutions and concomitant moral weakness. With the advent of the behavioral sciences, new reasons for man's excessive and habitual drinking were advanced and the characterization of alcoholism as a disease rather than a moral shortcoming became more common. As multidisciplinary research into the nature and causes of alcoholism was undertaken, new facts evolved.

Alcoholics, in the first instance, are users of alcohol, which is a form of food. Obviously, not all users of alcohol are alcoholics. As much of a distinction should be drawn between the abstaining teetotaler and the moderate social drinker, as between the latter and the alcoholic, who may be either an excessive drinker or a chronic alcoholic. Alcoholics are persons addicted to alcohol. As such, they are unable to cease drinking spontaneously. Although alcoholics may go for several months without a drink, they usually cannot maintain their abstinence permanently without outside support. In addition, alcoholics will generally suffer from withdrawal symptoms when their drinking is halted. These symptoms often consist of serious, though brief, physical or mental disturbances, described as even more dangerous than the manifestations of morphine withdrawal.[57] Chronic alcoholism is evidenced by the most severe stage of physical and

[55] Recent experimental programs demonstrated a sharp drop in convictions when counsel was assigned to inebriates. In March 1965, in the absence of counsel, there were only 325 acquittals out of 1,590 arraignments in New York City. In March 1966, presence of counsel brought about 1,280 acquittals out of 1,326 arraignments. Murtagh, "Comments," 16 *Inventory* 13, 4 (N.C. Rehabilitation Program, July–September 1966); *New York Times*, April 23, 1966, p. 14.

[56] District of Columbia, Commission on Prisons, Probation, and Parole, *Report* 110 (1957).

[57] World Health Organization, Expert Committee on Alcohol and Alcoholism, *Report* 6–7, 11 Technical Report Series, no. 94 (1955); Johnson, "The Alcoholic

mental deterioration, in which the effects of alcohol persist even when the alcoholic is not drinking.[58]

Two basic components are required to produce an alcoholic—the intoxicant and the person. The intoxicant is ethyl alcohol, a chemical compound of carbon, hydrogen, and oxygen. Pure ethyl alcohol is a colorless, almost odorless liquid that gives a burning sensation when imbibed due to its dehydrating effect upon human tissues. Most of the alcohol consumed by humans comes from a fermentation of sugars which are naturally found in such plants as barley, grapes, apples, and potatoes. The natural alcoholic concentration of a fermented liquid is often increased by distillation. Coloring or flavoring is also commonly added.[59] Unlike most foods, however, alcohol is absorbed into the bloodstream immediately without digestion and therefore passes rapidly into the tissues and fluids of the body. The interval between a drink and its physical or mental effect usually depends upon the amount and type of other food present in the stomach at the time. When the alcohol reaches the brain, the principal effects are upon the nervous system, lessening its inhibitory controls and generally reducing its activities. After the alcoholic content of the blood reaches 0.3 percent, muscular coordination, speech, and vision become markedly disturbed and the thought processes become confused. Finally, at 0.5 percent the drinker loses consciousness, a fortunate reaction, for more alcohol could well be fatal.[60]

Analysis of the intoxicant is much easier than analysis of the drinker. Few generalizations can be made about him, his socioeconomic background, or his personality.[61] It is known that the ratio in the United States of male to female alcoholics is six to one, though almost as many women as men drink.[62] The accepted customs of the society or subculture strongly influence the attitude toward alcohol. Some investigators have believed that inherited metabolic patterns result in nutritional deficiencies that in turn give rise to a craving for

---

Withdrawal Syndromes," *Q. J. Stud. Alcohol*, supp. no. 1, p. 66 (November 1961).

[58] World Health Organization, Committee on Alcohol, *Report* 17.

[59] R. G. McCarthy, *Drinking and Intoxication* 8 (1959).

[60] Coleman, *Abnormal Psychology* 399.

[61] Pittman reports the typical chronic alcoholic to be middle aged, often of English, Irish, or Negro ancestry, educationally disadvantaged, of lower-class background, and with no or poor marital experience. Pittman, "Public Intoxication" 11–13.

[62] Popham, "Some Social and Cultural Aspects of Alcoholism," 4 *Can. Psych. A. J.* 222, 225 (1959); Robinson, "Parents Seek Ways to Prevent Alcoholism," 3 *Alcoholism* 9, 10 (1955). In some Scandinavian countries the rate of male to female alcoholics is as high as twenty-three to one; in England it is only two to one. Popham, "Aspects of Alcoholism."

alcohol.[63] Others have claimed that the normal expectancy of alcoholism is significantly higher among children of alcoholic parents than among the general population.[64] As to personality characteristics, it has been noted that the drinkers often have a less than average tolerance for the anxieties caused by frustration and criticism.[65] "Alcohol," it has been observed, "does not make people do things better, it makes them less ashamed of doing them badly."[66] Despite all of these observations, in the final analysis it still appears that "why one person in a setting favorable to alcoholism remains untouched while a second succumbs, and why others in similar situations develop ulcers of the stomach or become schizophrenic, cannot be explained."[67]

Contrary to popular belief, alcohol is quite clearly a physical depressant in all quantities. While psychologically it may stimulate sexual desire by breaking down inhibitions, its effect upon male potency is adverse. Several consistent reaction patterns have been reported with regard to the average drinker's social behavior; some become sad, others sleepy, while still others become suspicious, irritable, and pugnacious. The great majority of excessive drinkers, however, become euphoric and experience a sense of well-being, sociability, and temporary adequacy.[68]

What precisely happens between the initial and moderately pleasant experience with alcohol and the final complete subjection to alcoholic addiction is little known. Even though the etiology of alcoholism is not completely understood, increasingly the suggestion is made that it can best be understood as a disease.[69] Others have insisted that the alcoholic condition is a nutritional deficiency or a somatic or psycho-

---

[63] They suggest also that once the original deficiency is met, the body develops an increased craving. R. J. Williams, *Nutrition and Alcoholism* (1951) and *Alcoholism: The Nutritional Approach* (1959).

[64] Myerson and Mayer, "Origins, Treatment and Destiny of Skid-Row Alcoholic Men," 19 *S.C. L. Rev.* 332, 340 (1967).

[65] Kessel and Walton, *Alcoholism* 56–80.

[66] *Encyclopedia Britannica*, s.v. "Alcoholism."

[67] *Ibid*. But as in the case of the drug addict, the one personality factor common to all alcoholics is their social deviance. Hill, Haertzen, and Davis, "An MMPI Factor Analytic Study of Alcoholics, Narcotic Addicts and Criminals," 23 *Q. J. Stud. Alcohol* 411–33 (1962).

[68] Coleman, *Abnormal Psychology* 400.

[69] Jellinek, the acknowledged authority on the problems of alcoholics, divided alcoholism into four classes, alpha to epsilon, the characteristics of which range from a pure psychological dependence upon alcohol as a relief for bodily or emotional pain to a progressive stage at which withdrawal symptoms, a need for increasing dosage, and adaptive cell metabolism are manifested. E. M. Jellinek, *The Disease Concept of Alcoholism* (1960).

somatic illness;[70] many others consider it primarily a psychiatric problem.[71] Regardless of the specific orientation, it is clear that alcohol alone does not account for alcoholism. Coleman has excellently summed up the social process from initial use to total dependence:

> ... it is well to repeat that alcohol is a rapidly acting solvent of unpleasant reality, is easily obtainable and to a large extent socially acceptable. Consequently it is not surprising that for some individuals its use becomes the predominant reaction pattern for relieving tension. Then, as the individual relies more and more upon alcohol for tension reduction, other adjustive techniques may drop out from lack of use so that alcohol becomes increasingly significant in his life. In a general sense, the individual has become psychologically dependent on alcohol, and during a period of severe stress he may cross the boundary line from excessive symptomatic drinking to chronic alcoholism.[72]

On the average, it has been noted, it takes some fifteen years for men to move from the stage of regular or heavy use of alcohol to addiction; for women the process requires eleven to twelve years.[73] It is fruitless to point the accusing finger at one particular circumstance or element as the cause of alcoholism; rather, it is more likely a sum of all of the individual's physical, psychological, and social environments. Before reaching the final stage, the future alcoholic is likely to pass through several developmental levels. Beginning with drinking that is confined to conventional social situations (the pre-alcoholic symptomatic phase), the drinker may soon become increasingly susceptible to alcohol (the prodromal stage), then go on to a stage in which overall control over drinking is substantially lessened (the crucial phase) and finally reach the chronic phase in which all control over drinking is lost. Alcohol having become the dominant and only force in the victim's life, he goes on "benders" for days and weeks on end and will drink anything, including rubbing alcohol, if regular alcoholic beverages are unavailable.[74]

It is obvious that neither medicine nor law need be overly concerned with an individual arrested for boisterous behavior after a New Year's party, a wedding, or a wake. Occasional and moderate drinking is not a grave social problem. Concern commences once

---

[70] Keller and Efron, "The Prevalence of Alcoholism," 16 *Q. J. Stud. Alcohol* 619 (1955).

[71] Coleman, *Abnormal Psychology* 404.

[72] *Ibid.* 405.

[73] S. J. Holmes, *Chemical Comforts and Man* 25 (1964).

[74] Jellinek, "Phases of Alcohol Addiction," 13 *Q. J. Stud. Alcohol* 673 (1952).

alcohol turns from a moderate flavoring for human life and action into a substitute for them, for it is at that stage that the alcoholic's conflict with existing social values erupts. He is unable to carry on with his social duties: often he constitutes a public spectacle and poses hazards to himself and others, and his family becomes a public burden. Significantly, a great majority of alcoholics who come into repeated contact with the law live on "skid row," divorced from the society around them.[75] They are usually homeless, penniless, and beset with acute personal problems.[76]

As these facts concerning alcoholism and the alcoholic became apparent, many commentators recognized the limited utility of fines and short-term jail sentences imposed by the traditional criminal process.[77] Although punishment for intoxication may deter some voluntary drinkers from excessive use, it is ineffectual with respect to the chronic drinker because it disregards his already contracted condition. Indeed, punishing the alcoholic for his lack of self-control over drinking often drives him deeper into drink,[78] and the whole criminal law process becomes a "deviancy reinforcement cycle."[79] Critically observed, punishing an alcoholic may amount to little more than punishing a sick person in order to deter others from contracting his illness.[80] Past critics have referred to criminal sanctions for alcoholism as the "revolving door" approach, likening the criminal system to the medieval treatment of the insane, when "treatment for mental patients was limited to punishment" on the theory that they were "possessed by an evil spirit that could be driven out by beating or other abuses."[81] Today, it is asserted, society is partly to blame for the alcoholic's becoming sick; yet society—unable to provide a suitable method for his

[75] Canadian studies indicate that the skid-row alcoholic is not typical. Most alcoholics are never involved with the law; one-half of all alcoholics are fully employed; a third are partly employed; a sixth are not in the labor force; two-thirds are between the ages of 30 and 54. Alexander, "The Criminal Responsibility of Alcoholics and Drug Addicts," 31 *Sask. B. R.* 71, 77–78 (1966).

[76] President's Commission on Law Enforcement and the Administration of Justice, *Task Force Report: Drunkenness* 1.

[77] Pittman, "Public Intoxication" 7.

[78] M. A. Block, *Alcoholism: Its Facets and Phases* 60, 135 (1965); Rubington, "The Chronic Drunkenness Offender," 315 *Annals of the American Academy of Political and Social Sciences* 65, 67 (1958).

[79] Once a man gains a reputation as a deviant, the likelihood of additional encounters with the police is increased. Lovald and Stub, "The Revolving Door: Reactions of Chronic Drunkenness Offenders to Court Sanctions," 59 *J. Crim. L.C. & P.S.* 525 (1968). These authors also found fines more effective than jail sentences in deterring drunkenness recidivism.

[80] Coburn, "*Driver* to *Easter* to *Powell*: Recognition of the Defense of Involuntary Intoxication?" 22 *Rutgers L. Rev.* 103, 125 (1967).

[81] Block, *Alcoholism* 60.

cure—persists in punishing him for his conduct.[82] Recognizing the
futility of the "street-jail-street-jail" process, through which pass two
million arrested alcoholics a year, America finally undertook in the
early part of this century a search for nonpenal remedies and programs for the treatment of alcoholics.[83]

THERAPY FOR THE ALCOHOLIC

At present, 26 states have noncriminal procedures for the hospitalization of seriously disturbed alcoholics.[84] These civil commitment
procedures, often part of laws pertaining generally to mental patients,[85] are created by statute, even though they are attributed to the
state's ancient *parens patriae* powers.[86] Under the noncriminal procedures, an alcoholic can be institutionalized either through his own

[82] Coburn, *"Driver* to *Easter* to *Powell"* 129.

[83] *See, e.g.,* Leavitt v. City of Morris, 117 N.W. 393 (Minn. 1908); *ex parte*
Schwarting, 108 N.W. 125 (Neb. 1906); J. B. Robitscher, *Pursuit of Agreement:
Psychiatry and the Law* 180 (1966); D. J. Pittman and C. W. Gordon, *Revolving
Door* 140–46 (1958).

[84] The relevant state laws, with the year of their enactment, are: *Ark. Stat. Ann.*
§§83–701 to 717 (1955); *Conn. Gen. Stat. Ann.* §17–155a to j (1961); *Ga.
Code Ann.* §§88–401 to 412 (1964); *Ind. Ann. Stat.* §§22–1501 to 1513
(1957); *Kan. Stat. Ann.* §§74–4401 to 4413 (1953); *Ky. Rev. Stat.* §222.020
to 195 (1960); *Me. Rev. Stat. Ann.* tit. 22, §§1351–55 (1954); *Mass. Gen.
Laws* §123.80 (1962); *Minn. Stat.* §§144.81–84 (1957), §§14.831–34 (1967), and
§253A.03–07 (1967); *Miss. Code Ann.* §§436–01 to 12 (1950); *Mont. Rev. Code
Ann.* §§38–701 to 711 (1911); *Nev. Rev. Stat.* §§433.250–90 (1967); *N.H. Rev.
Stat. Ann.* §§172.1–14 (1967); *N.M. Stat. Ann.* §§46–12–1 to 13 (1949), §46–12.7
(1967); *N.Y. Mental Hygiene Law* §§3301–09 (1965); *N.C. Gen. Stat.* §122.7.1
(1961), §§122.35.13–17 (1967), §122.65.6–9 (1967); *N.D. Cent. Code*
§§23–17.1–01 to 07 (1965), §54–01–19, subd. 4 (1963), §§54–38–01 to 09
(1965); *Pa. Stat.* tit. 50, §§2101–13 (1953); *R.I. Gen. Laws Ann.* §11–45–1
(1962), §§40–12–1 to 23 (1951); *Tenn. Code Ann.* §§33–801 to 811 (1963);
Tex. Rev. Civ. Stat. art. 5561c (1953, 1967); *Vt. Stat. Ann.* tit. 18, §§8401–62
(1967); *Va. Code Ann.* §§18.1–200.1 (1966) and §§32.378.1–4 (1966); *W. Va.
Code Ann.* §27–6–1 to 5 (1965); *Wis. Stat.* §51.09 (1935, 1963) and §51.25 (1963);
Wyo. Stat. Ann. §25–32 (1899). *See also The Mentally Disabled and the Law*
87–88 (F. T. Lindman and D. M. McIntyre eds. 1961).

[85] *Ex parte* Hinkle, 196 P. 1035 (Idaho 1921). "From time immemorial the
state has found it necessary . . . to confine dipsomaniacs and inebriates, for similar
reasons that require the confinement of the insane, because these conditions are
only another form of insanity." *Ibid.* 1037.

[86] Here, as in the other areas of mental illness, there is no uniform statutory
definition of the degree of inebriation sufficient to justify commitment. Some of
the statutes merely use the terms "alcoholic," "dipsomaniac," and "habitual drunkard" without any definition. The Virginia requirement for commitment is that a
person be "inebriate" and not be in confinement on a criminal charge. *Va. Code*,
§37–61.1(a) (Supp. 1966). Another test applied in Virginia is that the person,
through the use of alcoholic liquors, "has become dangerous to the public or himself or unable to care for himself or his property or his family." *Ibid.* §37–1(14).

voluntary application or as a result of an involuntary commitment order.[87] The commitment period is usually indeterminate and conditioned upon the achievement of a cure. Since alcoholic commitments are described as civil and therapeutic, they are not considered punishment. Through these involuntary commitments the power of the state is used to force confinement and treatment for those who have become so addicted to alcohol as to endanger either their own or the public welfare and safety.

Although civil commitment laws were conceived as tools for social progress in the treatment of alcoholism, their accomplishments have been limited. Frequently, the same institutions served as the depositories for both the mentally ill and the alcoholics.[88] Inadequate treatment facilities have made civil commitment therapeutic in designation but not in fact.[89] The State of New York, with an estimated alcoholic population of 700,000, until recently operated only two alcoholic treatment units with a total of 130 beds.[90]

The Maryland test is less specific and provides for the commitment of the "drunkard" as any person who has acquired the habit of using spirituous, malt, or fermented liquors, cocaine, or other narcotics to "such a degree as to deprive him of reasonable self-control." *Md. Code Ann.* art. 16, §48 (Repl. vol. 1966). While these statutes were obviously intended for the chronic cases of alcoholism, this intent is not always clearly stated by the law. Some states use the term "habitual" for this purpose. Others, such as Kansas, make five convictions for intoxication the requisite standard for commitment. *Kan. Stat. Ann.* §74–4401 (1964). North Carolina, on the other hand, requires that the alcoholic condition be of at least one year's standing. *N.C. Gen. Stat.* §35–1 (1966).

[87] Nearly one-half of the alcoholic patients are admitted on a voluntary rather than a compulsory basis. Plaut, "Developing Community Services" 121.

[88] Peter B. Hutt, an attorney closely connected with recent legal developments in the area of alcoholism, expressed the alcoholic's response to long-term involuntary treatment: "From their viewpoint, lengthy incarceration in a health facility has the same degrading effect on the derelicts as incarceration in jail. Both rob the inebriate of any willingness to attempt to find his way out of his present situation in life, and make him more passively dependent upon institutionalization." Hutt, "Modern Trends in Handling the Chronic Court Offender: The Challenge to the Courts," 19 *S.C. L. Rev.* 305, 318 (1967).

[89] One "treatment" center was recently described as consisting of a single dormitory, with a small yard surrounded by a high fence. The patients did not work and had very little opportunity for exercise or recreation. Patients were given very little medical attention. One patient testified that during his 31-day stay at the center he saw a psychiatrist once—for 5 minutes. District of Columbia v. Walters, Crim. Action #18150-66 (D.C. Ct. of Gen. Sess.) filed 8/16/66.

[90] 112 *Cong. Rec.* 6973 (remarks of Representative Kupferman, 1966). A survey conducted a few years ago showed that only 3 percent of the resident population of the state mental institutions was admitted with a diagnosis of alcoholism. This hospitalization rate accounts for one out of every 300 estimated alcoholics. The others either go unattended or else are still being processed through the criminal system. Robitscher, *Pursuit of Agreement* 183; Plaut, "Developing Community Services" 121.

In the United States today, whether an alcoholic is to be tolerated, civilly committed, or subjected to criminal sanctions is neither objectively nor scientifically determined. The alcoholic's social background, his economic means, the facilities available in the particular community, local policies, and sheer happenstance will all play an important role in determining whether he will be ignored, will seek and receive voluntary treatment, or will be made subject to involuntary sanctions. This inconsistency is not restricted to the United States alone. A recent commentary states:

> Whether an alcoholic is viewed as a medical or as a social problem will profoundly affect the future course of his disorder. Where the alcoholic is dealt with by the courts he is likely to spend time in jail in an atmosphere that is both custodial and punitive, not directed towards his rehabilitation. Where medical treatment is available and doctors are prepared to accept responsibility for the management of his condition, the institution to which the alcoholic is admitted is more likely to be a hospital. The measures adopted then will be therapeutic, designed to foster his self-respect and sustain his resolve to overcome his disability. Today, in Britain each method is applied and the disposal generally depends not upon the individual's needs but on the relatively trivial circumstance that brings him to the notice of one or the other service.[91]

THE *DRIVER* AND *EASTER* REVOLUTIONS

The concept of alcoholism as a disease was first espoused 164 years ago.[92] The turn-of-the-century laws providing for the civil commitment of alcoholics to mental institutions are further evidence of this trend. But in America, the dramatic turn toward the therapeutic control of alcoholic addiction was taken through two decisions of United States courts of appeals in early 1966. The first decision was in the case of *Driver* v. *Hinnant*,[93] rendered by the Court of Appeals for the Fourth Circuit. The effect of this decision extends to Virginia, West Virginia, North Carolina, South Carolina, and Maryland. The *Driver* case was followed by *Easter* v. *District of Columbia*,[94] which specifically concerns Washington.

At the time of what was to be his precedent-setting conviction for

[91] Kessel and Walton, *Alcoholism* 22.
[92] T. Trotter, *An Essay, Medical, Philosophical, and Chemical, on Drukeness and Its Effects on the Human Body* (1804).
[93] 356 F.2d 761 (4th Cir. 1966).
[94] 361 F.2d 50 (D.C. Cir. 1966).

public intoxication, Driver, a resident of North Carolina, was 59 years old. He had been convicted for the same offense more than 200 times over thirty-five years and had been incarcerated for alcoholism for nearly two-thirds of his life. The North Carolina law punished first and second offenses for alcoholism by a fine not exceeding $100 or imprisonment for not more than 60 days. The third and subsequent violations within a twelve-month period were treated as misdemeanors, subject to stricter penalties.[95] Being more than a three-time repeater, Driver was sentenced to imprisonment for two years.

Driver's defense was grounded on the Eighth Amendment to the Constitution, prohibiting cruel and unusual punishment. Driver argued that chronic alcoholism is a disease which destroyed the power of his will; since his public intoxication was not an act of his volition, his punishment violated the constitutional prohibition. After a series of appeals through the state courts, the Federal Fourth Circuit Court of Appeals upheld this defense.[96]

The court reviewed the medical literature regarding alcoholism and agreed that the chronic alcoholic does not drink voluntarily, even "though undoubtedly he did so originally."[97] The alcoholic, consequently, is not chargeable with either a *mens rea* (criminal intention) or an *actus reus* (criminal act)—the combination of which is traditionally required to establish criminal responsibility.[98] Distinguishing between the mere excessive drinker (whom the court considered a voluntary agent) and the chronic alcoholic, the court held that the latter is devoid of "evil intent" or "a consciousness of wrongdoing," thus lacking a *mens rea*. Furthermore, the alcoholic's presence in public, said the court, "is not his act, for he did not will it," meaning that the *actus reus* was lacking also. Concluding that the state "cannot stamp . . . [a] chronic alcoholic as a criminal . . . ," the *Driver* court, in essence, followed in the footsteps of *Robinson* (the drug addiction case)[100] by holding that the constitutional prohibition of cruel and unusual punishment prevented a state from punishing an involuntary symptom (public intoxication) of the alcoholic disease.

To exempt a drunkard from the penalties of the criminal law, the

[95] *See N.C. Gen. Stat.* §§14-334 and 14-335.

[96] Driver v. Hinnant, 356 F.2d 761 (4th Cir. 1966).

[97] *Ibid.* 765.

[98] G. L. Williams, *Criminal Law* 374–75 (1953).

[99] Driver v. Hinnant, 356 F.2d 374–75 (4th Cir. 1966). Four of the judges in this case relied upon the constitutional protection against cruel and unusual punishment. The whole panel of eight agreed, however, that criminality was barred by the common law principle that one is not responsible for nonvoluntary conduct.

[100] Robinson v. California, 370 U.S. 660 (1962).

Driver test requires medical testimony to the effect that the accused is not merely a steady or spree drinker. His condition must be shown to be chronic and involuntary. The court also hastened to state that its decision does not relieve an alcoholic of liability for criminal activities other than public intoxication. As expressed by the Court: "[O]ur excusal . . . is confined exclusively to those acts on his part which are compulsive as symptomatic of the disease. With respect to other behavior—not characteristic of confirmed chronic alcoholism—he would be judged as would any person not so afflicted."[101]

The conclusions and self-imposed limitations reached by the court do not precisely reflect the purest of logic. The requirement of chronic alcoholism, as distinguished from excessive drinking, draws a very fine line, as one Maryland judge put it, "between those alcoholics who can't control themselves and those drunks who won't."[102] The distinction also appears to put a prize upon the attainment of the chronic condition. Since the court asserts that the excessive drinker continues to possess volition and freedom of choice, which make him subject to criminal sanctions, is not the decision (at least in theory) an encouragement for the excessive drinker to go one step beyond? Neither is there clarity in the demarcation between excused conduct and what is unexcused. In decreeing the excusal of public intoxication by chronic alcoholics, the court cites the absence of a "consciousness of wrongdoing" on the offender's part. If this is to be the standard, it should also apply to other offensive conduct where such "consciousness" is absent. But, the court abandoned the standard in midstream and, addressing itself to criminal acts other than public intoxication, it avowed excusal of only those acts which are "symptomatic of the disease." The latter standard relies less on the individual's lack of evil intent than upon the direct causal relationship between alcoholism and the prohibited conduct; it is thus reminiscent of the "product" test under the *Durham* insanity formula.[103] What then is to be the final criterion for excusal: the absence of a *mens rea*—a "consciousness of wrongdoing"; the loss of volition; or an act symptomatic or causally connected to chronic alcoholism?[104]

101 *Ibid.*
102 "Alcoholism and the Law," *Washington Star*, January 28, 1966, p. A12.
103 Durham v. United States, 214 F.2d 862 (D.C. Cir. 1954). "The rule . . . is simply that an accused is not criminally responsible if his unlawful act was the product of mental disease or mental defect." *Ibid.* 874–75.
104 It has been broadly asserted, however, that once the defense of alcoholism is recognized by the courts, it would, like insanity, be available as a defense for any criminal activity "caused by it." Hutt, "Recent Court Decisions on Alcoholism 111, n. 23.

If chronic alcoholics languishing on street corners are not to be treated as criminals, what is the proper measure for protecting both the addict and the public against alcoholic excesses? The *Driver* court does not overlook this question. "Of course," said the court, "the alcohol-diseased may by law be kept out of public sight."[105] The state cannot stamp a chronic alcoholic charged with public intoxication a criminal, but there is nothing in the new judicial revolution to preclude "appropriate detention . . . [of the alcoholic] for treatment and rehabilitation so long as he is not marked a criminal."[106]

This conclusion of the *Driver* case was endorsed in substance a few months later by the United States Court of Appeals for the District of Columbia in the case of DeWitt Easter, another chronic alcoholic with 70 previous intoxication arrests.[107]

Both the *Driver* and *Easter* decisions in essence call for the partial divestment of criminal justice in the alcoholism arena and its replacement with a therapeutic *parens patriae* system. Despite strong support for this revolutionary summons in the president's 1967 crime commission,[108] the response in the states subject to these new judicial decisions has not been uniform.

The most dramatic development took place in the District of Columbia. Public intoxication, obviously, did not suddenly end in the District. Faced with its manifestations, the police continued apprehending alcoholics as before and holding them in jail for two or three days until sufficiently detoxified to face the courts.[109] It was at this stage that the impact of the new law was heavily felt. In the past, the courts would often sentence alcoholics for 60 to 90 days at the District of Columbia Workhouse, the term serving both as a drying-out time and reorientation device. Under the *Easter* formula, chronic alcoholics were no longer to be treated as criminals and were to be separated from the regular run of excessive drinkers. It was soon discovered,

[105] Driver v. Hinnant, 356 F.2d 764 (4th Cir. 1966).

[106] *Ibid.* 765. Compulsory civil commitment to a rehabilitative program has been held constitutional, even though the committed person is subject to criminal sanctions for refusing to cooperate in the program. *In re* De La O, 52 Cal.2d 128, 378 P.2d 793, *cert. denied*, 374 U.S. 856 (1963).

[107] Easter v. District of Columbia, 361 F.2d 50 (D.C. Cir. 1966). The *Easter* decision relied in rationale upon the existence of District of Columbia laws calling for the medical treatment of alcoholics and also upon the chronic alcoholic's lack of necessary *mens rea* (criminal intent) in being publicly drunk. Four of the eight judges also subscribed to the Eighth Amendment reasoning in the *Driver* case.

[108] President's Commission on Law Enforcement and the Administration of Justice, *Task Force Report: Drunkenness* 5.

[109] "Death Ends Alcoholics Freedom," *Washington Post*, June 4, 1966, p. A2.

however, that medical services for making the necessary distinction were lacking, and that some judges were simply releasing all those charged with public drunkenness on the presumption that all were chronic alcoholics. Many of those released began panhandling money for another drink as soon as they were on the street.[110] Even as diagnostic facilities were developed, adequate treatment facilities were not available. Thus, upon a finding of chronic alcoholism, the courts still were faced with the question of whether to release the alcoholic altogether, to order him to receive outpatient care, or to commit him to the limited facilities for treatment.

Alcoholics in the District of Columbia and in two-thirds of the states, as previously noted, may be civilly committed to institutional care. To further the therapeutic aim, Congress in 1947 adopted an alcoholic rehabilitation law for the District of Columbia.[111] Judges of the Court of General Sessions were permitted to suspend any minor criminal case (the court's jurisdiction is limited to misdemeanors) if the evidence indicated that the defendant was a chronic alcoholic. After a preliminary hearing, such a defendant was to be committed to a special clinic for diagnosis and treatment. Within 90 days, the clinic director was to recommend whether the patient be released conditionally and under supervision, be further hospitalized for treatment, or be returned to court for trial on the original charge. For 19 years, however, little use was made of this law. The only noncriminal approach to alcoholism was through civil commitment to St. Elizabeths Hospital, and this was limited to alcoholics not charged with criminal offenses.

After *Easter*, what would happen to the District of Columbia's chronic alcoholics who could no longer be sentenced to jail or to the workhouse on charges of public intoxication? Sending large numbers of alcoholics to St. Elizabeths Hospital, which serves the mentally ill, would have upset the hospital's operations. As a solution, one of the facilities of the Department of Corrections was transferred to the Public Health Department for the accommodation and treatment of alcoholics found publicly intoxicated. Under the 1947 law, an alcoholic may be committed to this facility.[112] At the expiration of the 90-day detention period, he must be discharged, unless additional treatment is recommended and approved by the court. But without proper accommodations, the chronic alcoholic need not be committed at all.

---

[110] "Police Say Drunks Fare Better in Jail," *ibid.*, June 10, 1966, p. C2.
[111] "Rehabilitation of Alcoholics," *D.C. Code* §24–501 *et seq.* (1967).
[112] *Ibid.* §24–504.

Under the *Easter* decision, "commitment for treatment is not mandatory. In the judge's discretion the accused may be released. But he may not be punished."[113]

Like all revolutions, the *Easter* revolution achieved no immediate salvation. The recent report of the President's Commission on Crime in the District of Columbia reached the conclusion that: "Since *Easter* there has been, in fact, a marked deterioration in the health of the city's derelict alcoholics—a condition which goes unheeded only by a callous disregard for human life."[114] Treatment facilities remained limited and unsatisfactory. "Medical attention was minimal; prison uniforms were simply exchanged for hospital smocks. Indeed, normal conditions at the workhouse for regular prisoners appeared superior to those for alcoholic 'patients.' "[115] Only the very serious cases could be given this inpatient care; most others were directed to receive outpatient treatment in a clinic. But "[p]atients committed to the clinic did not appear for subsequent treatment and were re-arrested with great frequency."[116]

Are the District of Columbia and similar programs destined for success? What is actually accomplished or lost by the transition from the criminal treatment to a therapeutic emphasis? It is much too early for meaningful answers. There are those who seriously doubt the value of rehabilitating the typical skid-row alcoholic. For him the new program may be a promise without hope. According to the previous Director of the Department of Corrections in the District of Columbia:

> In the early 1950s, the Department of Health joined forces with us in an attempt to develop a better treatment program. We put the alcoholics in a special unit in the D. C. Workhouse which was staffed by Health Department personnel. The project for rehabilitating intoxication offenders was abandoned, however, when research evaluation revealed the disappointing results. Recent studies have indicated that if alcoholism can be caught in its early stages, there is a 50–70% chance of a cure. However, such estimates deal with the middle class alcoholic. A more accurate expectation in the case of poor, skid-row inhabitants would be 5%. These are the men with whom our Department must cope.[117]

[113] Easter v. District of Columbia, 361 F.2d 50, 53 (D.C. Cir. 1966).
[114] President's Commission on Crime in the District of Columbia, *Report* 491.
[115] *Ibid.* 489.
[116] *Ibid.* 490.
[117] Sard, "Chronic Alcoholism: What Can Be Done?" *Washington Post* (Potomac Magazine), July 24, 1966, p. 8.

Judging from the present state of medicine and the paucity of existing facilities, it appears that only a small number of alcoholics can be helped by short-term hospitalization or by the alternative outpatient treatment. For the great number of chronic alcoholics, these changes may seem a mere continuation of society's harassment, now under a therapeutic instead of criminal aegis.

The overall impact of the *Driver* and *Easter* revolution is lessened by the fact that the occasional and the excessive drinkers, as distinguished from the chronic, remain subject to criminal sanctions. Similarly, the chronic alcoholic is not relieved from prosecution for disorderly conduct or offenses other than public intoxication. Moreover, until one is judged to be a chronic alcoholic, the police will continue to arrest him and the prosecuting attorney will continue to prosecute him even if the charge is only public intoxication. Even those adjudicated as chronic alcoholics continue to be apprehended by the police and are kept in jail overnight for detoxification until it is determined whether they are on the list of adjudicated chronic alcoholics.[118] At that time, although they cannot be subjected to criminal sanctions, a decision must be made whether release, outpatient treatment, or hospitalization is most fitting.[119] At the institution or clinic, there is nothing to guarantee that the treatment will be effective or that it will even be forthcoming. In fact, the majority of chronic alcoholics will return to alcohol and the old (albeit therapeutic instead of criminal) revolving door treatment. Society, it seems, often discovers the shortest route for a return to the status quo.

Whereas the District of Columbia went through the appearance of a revolution, with results that might nevertheless constitute merely a change of labels, the adjoining states barely responded to the Federal Court decision applicable to them. Reports from Virginia indicate no reduction in the number of convictions for drunkenness. Most Virginia

---

[118] In the District of Columbia, when a person not previously adjudged a chronic alcoholic is arrested for public intoxication, the public health nurse will review his arrest record. If the record shows a high number of drunkenness arrests the nurse will interview him. Sometimes psychiatric social workers may be called in. The court usually acts upon the recommendation of the nurse or social worker in finding chronic alcoholism. Hutt, "The Chronic Court Offender" 331.

[119] In the first year after the *Easter* decision, 4,382 individuals were adjudged chronic alcoholics in the District of Columbia. The D.C. Crime Commission estimated there were 6,000 derelict chronic inebriates in the District and well over 50,000 chronic alcoholics in all walks of life in a population of under 900,000. At the time of the *Easter* decision there were less than fifty beds and a small outpatient clinic for the treatment of alcoholics. One year later there were 550 beds, still too few to deal with the staggering number of alcoholics. *Ibid.* 321.

judges do not seek out the chronic alcoholic.[120] Since very few offenders brought before the bench for public intoxication have defense attorneys, most are not aware of this defense; others may be reluctant to admit to being a chronic alcoholic. Several Virginia judges further expressed the belief that the states should not be burdened with the noncriminal treatment of alcoholics "unless they show a desire to be cured."[121]

MUCH TOO FAR ON TOO LITTLE KNOWLEDGE

The time was 1968, two years after *Driver* and *Easter*. The stage was set before the United States Supreme Court. The court had agreed to decide whether Texas, consistent with the traditional standards of criminal law and the constitutional prohibition of cruel and unusual punishment, could punish Leroy Powell for public intoxication.[122] Powell, working at a tavern shining shoes and making about $12 a week, admitted that all his earnings were used to buy wine, that although he had a family he did not contribute to its support, that he drank wine every day, got drunk about once a week, and then usually went to sleep, mostly in public places such as sidewalks. Powell's latest conviction for public intoxication was one in a string of approximately 100 dating back to 1949. The issue was whether the court would nationalize the geographical enclaves of divestment established by the *Driver* and *Easter* decisions. Also in the balance lay a possible expansion or construction of *Robinson* v. *California*,[123] which underpins this area of the divestment of criminal justice. On the one hand was the pronouncement of *Robinson* that criminal sanctions could not be inflicted on one charged with a mere status where its possessor lacked the volitional power of extrication. On the other was the fact that Powell's offense was one step beyond that involved in *Robinson*. Robinson was punished for a pure status, drug addiction, as distinguished from an act causally related to that status, such as

[120] Most District of Columbia judges hold the view, however, that the court has the duty to inject this issue on its own motion. District of Columbia v. Walters et al., Crim. No. D.C. 18150, D.C. Ct. of Gen. Sess., p. 3 (reprinted in 112 *Cong. Rec.* 22716, September 22, 1966). See analogous cases of mental illness: Whalem v. United States, 346 F.2d 812 (D.C. Cir. 1965); Pate v. Robinson, 383 U.S. 375 (1966).
[121] "Virginia Courts Are Still Treating Drunkenness as a Crime," *Washington Post*, August 8, 1966, p. B1.
[122] Powell v. Texas, 392 U.S. 514 (1968).
[123] 370 U.S. 660 (1962).

drug possession, use, or sale; Powell was convicted not for his status, alcoholic addiction, but, rather, for his presence in an intoxicated condition in a public place.

In the face of the complex nature of alcoholism and its myriad social and legal ramifications, no majority in the Supreme Court could agree on both the disposition of the case and the rationale. Five justices (the Chief Justice, Marshall, Black, Harlan, and White) in three separate opinions agreed that the conviction should be affirmed. But this disposition is devoid of clear meaning since four dissenting justices (Fortas, Douglas, Brennan, and Stewart), joined again by Justice White, also reasoned that the crime of public intoxication committed by a chronic alcoholic could not be criminally punished if the offender lacked control to prevent his presence in public.[124] The apparent reason for this curious inversion between the disposition and the rationale was Justice White's refusal to adopt the lower court's finding, accepted by the four dissenting justices, that because Powell was a chronic alcoholic, he was also unable to choose the sites of his intoxication, thus making his public presence involuntary. As stated by Justice White:

> The trial court said that Powell was a chronic alcoholic with a compulsion not only to drink to excess but also to frequent public places when intoxicated. Nothing in the record before the trial court supports the latter conclusion, which is contrary to common sense and to common knowledge.... For these reasons, I cannot say that the chronic who proves his disease and a compulsion to drink is shielded from conviction when he has knowingly failed to take feasible precautions against commiting a criminal act, here the act of going to or remaining in a public place. On such facts the alcoholic is like a person with smallpox, who could be convicted for being on the street but not for being ill, or like the epileptic, punishable for driving a car but not for his disease.[125]

Some commentators ignore the decisional outcome and find in the dissenters' rationale, which was supported by a majority of the court, an affirmation of the *Driver* and *Easter* philosophies, whose scope may now be asserted to stretch across the country. The more cautious are

[124] Writing for the minority, Justice Fortas pointed out that the medical profession generally agrees that chronic alcoholics suffer from a disease, that the offense charged in the instant case is one of condition and is closely allied to the status involved in *Robinson*, that this condition (regardless of how it originated) is one which the defendant has no capacity to change or avoid and that criminal punishment for such condition would therefore constitute a violation of the constitutional prohibition. 392 U.S. 554–70.

[125] Powell v. Texas, 392 U.S. 514, 549–50 (1968) (footnotes omitted).

likely to find in this decision, with its unusual grasp of both the legal and social issues involved, an indication of the Supreme Court's conviction that alcoholism controls should be left alone for state experimentation, instead of being made to conform to a national formula.

For the time being, at any rate, the *Driver* and *Easter* decisions remain binding only in their respective jurisdictions. In other areas either traditional criminal process or new therapeutic measures remain a local option. Had the Supreme Court decision in *Powell* gone the other way, both the "one-horse town" as well as the complex metropolis either would have had to treat therapeutically the involuntary public drunk or permit him to remain beyond the pale of punishment. Moreover, if public intoxication were to be exempted from criminal penalties, further pressure might have mounted to exempt chronic alcoholics from other alcohol-connected offenses and possibly from all criminal responsibility.[126] Such developments the court was not willing to introduce, given the present limits of medical knowledge. In their reluctance to overturn Powell's conviction, the majority of the court exhibited concern about further diminution of the role of criminal sanctions as deterrents for alcohol-connected deviations and further expressed their doubts about the wisdom of substituting a therapeutic model for the criminal one in the face of inadequate treatment facilities.

The court pointed out the newness, uncertainty, and lack of unanimity regarding the disease concept of alcoholism.[127] Noting that alcoholism has many definitions and that various disciplines have asserted their special competence with regard to it, the court stressed that labeling it a disease means merely that the medical profession recognizes it as such and is willing to attempt treating those who have drinking problems.[128]

---

[126] Amsterdam, "Federal Constitutional Restrictions on Crimes of Status, Crimes of General Obnoxiousness, Crimes of Displeasing Police Officers, and the Like," 3 *Crim. L. Bull.* 205, 235–36 (1967).

[127] Whether or not alcoholism is a disease may be critical to the propriety of its punishment. Medical dictionaries have defined addiction as "habituation" or "being given up to some habit." *Stedman's Medical Dictionary* 26 (21st ed. 1966); *Dorland's Medical Dictionary* 31 (24th ed. 1965). Yet a habit is not necessarily a disease and "[a]lthough a disease might excuse one from criminal responsibility, a bad habit would not." Kirbens, "Chronic Alcohol Addiction and Criminal Responsibility, 54 *A.B.A.J.* 877 (1968).

[128] Pointing out that the "disease concept of alcoholism" means primarily that "alcoholism is caused and maintained by something other than the moral fault of the alcoholic, something that, to a greater or lesser extent depending upon the physiological or psychological makeup and history of the individual, cannot be controlled by him," the dissenting justices insisted that the deficiency of medical,

The uncertainty of the causal relation between alcoholism and behavior, as well as the effect of punishment upon the behavior of alcoholics, was of further concern to the court: How much volition does the alcoholic retain, and can punishment deter him? The testimony of the defense psychiatrist on behalf of Powell was that the act of taking the first drink was a "voluntary exercise" but that this exercise of will by a chronic alcoholic was under the "exceedingly strong influence" of a "compulsion" (though the compulsion was not "completely overpowering"). This terminology the court found of little meaning in determining a chronic alcoholic's volition. It considered significant Powell's admission, under cross-examination, that he had had only one drink on the morning of the trial and that he had been able to stop drinking in order to keep from getting intoxicated prior to his court appearance. Clearly, then, Powell was able to restrain his drinking; could he also have prevented his public exposure when drunk?

To permit alcoholism as a defense to prohibited conduct, the Supreme Court majority felt, an accused would have to demonstrate a complete lack of fault, by proving both an "inability to abstain" from drinking in the first place and a total "loss of control" over his conduct once he had commenced to drink.[129] These requisites were not met in Powell's case. To free from criminal sanctions behavior that, as in the present case, may at least in part be volitional would, in the majority opinion, go "much too far on the basis of too little knowledge."[130] If Leroy Powell may not be convicted of public intoxication, concluded the court, it is difficult to see how a state can convict an individual for murder, if that individual suffers from a "compulsion" to kill.[131] Voicing a need for continued reliance upon criminal sanctions, Justices Black and Harlan similarly pointed out in their con-

---

diagnostic, and therapeutic knowledge should not deter the court from substituting a therapeutic process for the ineffective penal one. 392 U.S. 514, 560–61.

[129] The dissenters felt that the voluntariness of the alcoholic's initial exposure to alcohol should not matter; the only question regarding the propriety of punishment should be his present ability to extricate himself. *Ibid.* 565–68. It is interesting to note, in this connection, the reports of recent experiments conducted with alcoholics in England. "The results . . . do not bear out the established view that one drink of alcohol necessarily precipitates a hitherto abstinent 'loss-of-control' drinker into a drinking bout. . . . Psychological and environmental factors may be more important influences in initiating 'loss-of-control' drinking." Merry, "The 'Loss of Control' Myth," 1 *Lancet* 1257 (1966).

[130] 392 U.S. 514, 521 (1968).

[131] *Ibid.* 534.

curring opinion[132] that the punishment of alcoholics can serve several deterrent sanctions: by giving the potential alcoholic an incentive to control his drinking, and by strengthening the chronic drinker's incentive to control the frequency and location of his alcoholic bouts.

In their unwillingness to abdicate the roles of free will and personal responsibility and in their concomitant resort to punishment for the control of alcoholism, the Supreme Court's majority also relied in great part upon the realities of the therapeutic model. Pointing to the fact that the criminal law usually imposes upon the alcoholic a short jail term only, assuring his needed detoxication in the process, the promises of indeterminate therapeutic civil commitment remain much too ambiguous and even threatening; the court concluded, therefore, that before the present system is condemned across the board, a clear promise of a better alternative must be demonstrated.[133]

THE DIRECTION OF THE FUTURE

A change of labels alone does not produce a true revolution. The classification of alcoholism as an illness is not likely, by itself, to produce salvation.[134] Unless tested rehabilitation programs are developed and effectively utilized, alcohol-connected crimes will continue, public and private drunkenness will continue, police burdens for removing the alcoholic from the streets will continue, civil commitments or community clinic referrals for ineffective treatment will continue, and so will unemployment, child neglect, vehicular homicide, and all other derivative manifestations of alcoholic irresponsibility.

Illustrative of the continuing inadequacies that plague the incoming therapeutic state is a recent newspaper account of DeWitt Easter's demise:

> DeWitt Easter, the 62-year-old skid-row drunk whose name is attached to a landmark court case that changed the way alco-

---

[132] *Ibid.* 538–39.

[133] *Ibid.* 530. For similar conclusions *see* the decision of the Supreme Court of Washington in Seattle v. Hill, 435 P.2d 692 (1967).

[134] Federal Judge J. Skelly Wright, in a recent dissent, dealt with the question of whether America was prepared for a transition from a criminal to a therapeutic model in the alcoholism arena. "The question is whether society recognizes that the behavior pattern in question is caused by the diseased determinants and not free will. If so, there should be no criminal responsibility. In determining societal recognition, four areas should be explored: (1) medical opinion, (2) the existence of treatment methods and facilities, (3) legal opinion, and (4) governmental recognition (legislative, executive and judicial)." Salzman v. United States, 405 F.2d 358, 366 (D.C. Cir. 1968).

holics are treated in Washington, died yesterday in D.C. General Hospital.

He died of massive complications that followed second- and third-degree burns he suffered in a bed fire Nov. 11 while a patient at George Washington University Hospital. He was later transferred to D.C. General.

Mr. Easter, who had been arrested more than 70 times since he became an alcoholic 30 years ago, had been a patient in the city's hospitals and rehabilitation facilities almost constantly since the U.S. Court of Appeals for the District ruled in his case on March 31, 1966, that alcoholism must be treated as an illness, not a crime.

A frail plasterer with steady, steel-blue eyes, Mr. Easter recognized the importance of the court's ruling. But he could not stop drinking. His latest hospitalization came after a two-month drinking spree.[135]

The growing recognition that the traditional treatment of alcoholics has been without success will probably result in a continuing national transition from criminal repression to therapeutic programs. Even in the face of the *Powell* failure to make the therapeutic model applicable nationwide, the divestment process will undoubtedly grow through legislation and state court decisions to encompass several of the minor offenses directly connected with the alcoholic status, such as public intoxication, vagrancy, and disorderly conduct.[136]

For more serious crimes, the speed with which the therapeutic model may be accepted as a substitute for penal measures will depend on what is offered in its name. Underlying much of the past public suspicion and judicial unwillingness to expand the application of the insanity defense in criminal law has been the fear that the offender would be totally exempted from both criminal and therapeutic controls. There is a similar apprehension that, with the elimination of criminal punishment, the alcoholic will also successfully resist therapeutic measures.[137] There is the further public and legal conviction that,

---

[135] "Figure in Key D.C. Case on Alcoholism Is Dead," *Washington Post*, December 5, 1967, p. B1.

[136] Pennsylvania has authorized the commitment of an alcoholic found guilty of any crime except murder in lieu of a criminal sentence if such commitment will not be "injurious to the interests of society." Treatment and confinement may extend up to one year. 50 Pa. Stat. 2105(b) (1954).

[137] Fuzzy thinking regarding the issue of criminal responsibility of alcoholics generally is illustrated by some post-*Easter* and *Driver* comments. Peter Hutt would permit alcoholism as a defense to all criminal charges causally connected to drunkenness but urges at the same time that no alcoholic be compelled to undergo treatment once the acute state of drunkenness has ceased. What this

unlike insanity, alcoholism is voluntarily induced and therefore reflects at least partial fault upon those who contract it or act under its influence.[138] The conviction that the alcoholic is not totally devoid of volition,[139] combined with the fear that elimination of his criminal culpability will adversely affect society's ability to foster and rely upon individual self-restraint, requires demonstrating that the substitution of therapeutic for penal measures will not jeopardize the public safety.

At present, we lack both sufficient scientific data and facilities for charting comprehensive nation-wide programs for the treatment of alcoholism.[140] With scientific advances, the therapeutic promise is likely to increase. Along with this promise, an increasing trend away from criminal sanctions and toward compulsory "cures" will also become evident. Says one rehabilitation expert: "Is there any 'bad way' to bring a person to his senses? Is there any bad way to help a per-

---

means is that the alcoholic who committed a crime while intoxicated could assert his defense and, as soon as he sobered up, be free from any criminal or civil sanctions, possibly to go again through the same cycle. Hutt, "Recent Court Decisions on Alcoholism" 111–18.

[138] In most crimes, criminal responsibility requires both the doing of a prohibited act (*actus reus*) and the presence of a wrongful intent or guilty mind (*mens rea*). Obviously, many criminal acts are committed by alcoholics under such state of intoxication as to raise doubts about the extent of the offender's control over his act or about his capacity to possess the requisite intent. In such cases, however, courts have found, perhaps fictitiously, the necessary act and guilty mind in the circumstance that the accused drank the alcohol voluntarily. Alexander, "Criminal Responsibility" 71, 86.

[139] It is a traditional criminal law precept that an act is not punishable if it is done involuntarily. This is nowadays described as the defense of automatism, referring to an act which is done by the muscles without any control by the mind, such as spasm or convulsion, or an act done by a person who is not conscious of what he is doing, such as an act done while sleep-walking. Edwards, "Automatism and Criminal Responsibility," 21 *Mod. L. Rev.* 375 (1958); Cross, "Reflections on Bratty's Case," 78 *L. Q. Rev.* 236 (1968).

[140] Many of those arguing for the exemption of the alcoholic from criminal sanctions similarly urge his exemption from therapeutic controls. "The vast majority of alcoholics do not suffer from severe mental illness. For these people, involuntary treatment is not appropriate.... The unfortunate plight of the derelict inebriate cannot lead us to deprive him of his liberty on humanitarian grounds any more than it would lead us to deprive him of his liberty on criminal grounds. The former is as unconstitutional as the latter." Hutt, "The Chronic Court Offender" 305, 320, 321. For a more balanced public safety approach *see* Kirbens, "Chronic Alcohol Addiction" 877. "The concomitant to an acquittal for serious crime by reason of involuntary alcoholism should be a mandatory civil commitment. The alcoholic murderer may be no less dangerous to society than the homicidal lunatic, and he should not be allowed to have his cake and eat it too. A due process approach to alcoholism should recognize the legal sanctity of the offender's psyche and at the same time safeguard the security of the community." *Ibid.* 882.

son accept the fact that he has problems? There is usually no hesitancy ... to insist that a reluctant person take treatment for venereal disease or tuberculosis. Yet, there often is a hesitancy about enforcing treatment upon alcoholics."[141] This approach clearly poses for alcoholism the very questions of individual liberty and "due process" which we have detailed with regard to other deviants. Should an alcoholic be allowed to assert: "I am satisfied with my private euphoria and do not wish to be cured," or "I am sufficiently deprived of volition not to be sent to jail, yet not so ill as to be denied the right to refuse treatment"? How far advanced must an alcoholic's condition be before society may assume the right to treat him against his will?

The question of compulsion is compounded by scientific evidence suggesting that alcoholic rehabilitation cannot be compulsorily achieved.[142] "[T]he possibility of arrestability in the individual case ... ," reported one commentator, "seems to rest primarily on the degree of motivation present or potentially present in the patient. If the alcoholic is not motivated to have help, he cannot be helped."[143] While some studies indicate a rate of 25 percent or better success in public institutions using fairly elaborate psychotherapy, one therapist reported only a 7 percent estimate of success with a group of involuntary court commitments which included a large number of "hobos and psychopaths."[144] If this is the case, then involuntary commitment for asserted treatment may serve primarily as a tool of social defense, to shelter the public from alcoholics, rather than as a therapeutic vehicle.

The compromise between public order and welfare on one hand and individual liberty and nonconformity on the other is not easily attainable. Unsolicited public intervention, whether designated punishment or therapy, will be objectionable to many alcoholics; similarly,

[141] Soden, "Constructive Coercion and Group Counseling in the Rehabilitation of Alcoholics," 30 *Fed. Prob.* 56–57 (1966).

[142] There is recent evidence, however, that voluntary participation is not essential. E. M. Blum and R. H. Blum, *Alcoholism: Modern Psychological Approaches to Treatment* (1967). Plaut also notes: "Evidence is accumulating that changes in the organization, operation, and treatment philosophy of an agency can have a substantial effect on its ability to work with the supposedly unmotivated patient." Plaut, *Alcohol Problems* 81. Regarding the issue of motivation generally, *see* Pitman and Sterne, "Concept of Motivation: Sources of Institutional and Professional Blockage in the Treatment of Alcoholics," 26 *Q. J. Stud. Alcohol* 41 (1965).

[143] Pfeffer, "The Natural History of Alcoholism," in *Alcoholism as a Medical Problem* 75 (H. D. Krause ed. 1956).

[144] *Alcohol Addiction and Chronic Alcoholism* 74–76 (E. M. Jellineck ed. 1942).

they may prefer not to seek voluntary aid. Since indiscriminate and at times lengthy commitments, even in the name of therapy, clearly constitute a dangerous social solution, how then are needed services to be offered and the hazards of compulsion minimized?

The recent National Crime Commission provides us with few meaningful guidelines regarding the compulsory treatment of alcoholics. Concluding that public drunkenness alone should not be a criminal offense, the commission nevertheless recognized the need for the removal of alcoholics from the streets to detoxication centers. The commission expressed a preference for the operation of such centers under the civil authority of the public health facilities, but it concluded also that release should follow sobriety.[145] After the inebriate becomes sober, "the decision to continue treatment should be left to the individual."[146]

The District of Columbia Crime Commission produced a more elaborate formula.[147] Its two-track system provides a noncriminal process for publicly intoxicated persons who are not disorderly and a criminal process for those charged with disorderly conduct or more serious offenses.[148]

Neither the national nor the District of Columbia Crime Commission came to grips, however, with the question of nonvoluntary treatment for alcoholics. Both agreed on the public right to provide the alcoholic with short-term "drying out" care. But how is continuing medical care to be provided to the unwilling patient beyond that point? And if treatment is substituted for the criminal process, what is to be the limit on the duration of such treatment and what is to be done with offenders not responding to it? Similarly unanswered by these commissions is the question of the alcoholic charged with offenses more serious than disorderly conduct. Should he be prison- or therapy-bound?

The solutions will depend upon a rational analysis of the alcoholic

[145] President's Commission on Law Enforcement and the Administration of Justice, *Task Force Report: Drunkenness* 4.

[146] *Ibid.* 5.

[147] President's Commission on Crime in the District of Columbia, *Report.*

[148] The docile inebriate found at large and unable to take care of himself will be taken to noncriminal "drying out" facilities for a medical examination and short-term care for three to four days. Subsequent to this emergency care, those deemed chronic cases are to be channeled into further voluntary medical treatment programs. Only for the severely debilitated alcoholics in this group is involuntary civil commitment suggested. Alcoholics charged with disorderly conduct, on the other hand, would continue to be processed through the criminal system. After arrest for the criminal offense, a medical examination and emer-

problem and the alcoholic community. The occasional drinker needs to be differentiated from the chronic alcoholic. A distinction must also be drawn between the debilitated elderly alcoholic who cannot be treated and who requires shelter or other public welfare assistance, and the acute alcoholic who is likely to benefit from a concentrated therapeutic program. Similarly, the public drunk who merely offends the community's esthetic sensitivities should be distinguished from the one whose drinking practices cause a direct and grave public hazard—through drunken driving or more aggressive crimes.

To encourage societal order and stability, the social or occasional drinker, as distinguished from the chronic, must continue to be controlled by means of the criminal process in those cases where his offense justifies social intervention. Since extensive therapy is not appropriate for the nonchronic drinker, the rewards and punishments of criminal justice remain necessary tools. For the nonchronic drinker whose transgressions are minor, such as public intoxication, society's noninterference is appropriate; readily accessible shelters for overnight relief are all that is required. For most chronic cases who are similarly docile and whose main requirement is public welfare, compulsory measures should likewise be eliminated and voluntary provisions made for drying out facilities and residential community shelters. Only for the more dangerous chronic alcoholic will compulsory detention and treatment be necessary as tools of social defense, once criminal sanctions are eliminated. But even as the penal model is replaced with therapy, the criteria for social intervention and the duration of the therapeutic sanction should be carefully controlled by law.[149] No compulsory commitment should be permitted without a demonstrated and serious public threat, nor should the term of therapy be unrestricted.

Clearly, the precise limits upon compulsion in the service of the

---

gency care will be provided. If the offender is a chronic alcoholic, efforts will be made to direct him to a treatment program and the criminal charges will be dropped. For the nonchronic alcoholic, criminal proceedings will be utilized, including the current practice permitting offenders to forfeit posted collateral instead of going to court. *Ibid.* 495.

[149] One recent commentator would limit compulsory or involuntary treatment to three instances only: first, in situations where the alcoholic is not mentally competent to make a rational decision regarding treatment; second, in situations of extremely debilitated alcoholics found on the street and requiring emergency care; third, in cases where the alcoholic directly and substantially endangers the safety of others. Hutt, "Recent Court Decisions on Alcoholism" 117. Hutt argues against broad compulsory commitment practices on the grounds that: (1) involuntary commitment will not be necessary once adequate therapy is made available;

therapeutic state will continue in great part undefined. The time is not yet ripe for a comprehensive answer. The continuing growth of therapeutic programs will, it is hoped, provide the testing grounds for developing the necessary substantive and procedural law and the requisite balance between individual liberty and public welfare. To expedite such healthy growth, it is imperative, however, that the processes of the therapeutic state not be conducted in darkness and that opportunities be provided for proper legal challenge and testing. Adequate judicial scrutiny, including the right to counsel, are important components of such development.[150]

As we become increasingly concerned about the limits of public compulsion, whether in the name of the criminal process or under the therapeutic label, it appears that future solutions must rely heavily upon voluntary public welfare facilities for the skid-row and other chronic alcoholics and upon treatment methods which do not require total institutionalization.

A realistic and pluralistic society must recognize, furthermore, that unless it is willing to pay the price for total conformity, it must learn to tolerate its deviants. This is particularly true with regard to those deviants who pose no immediate and direct threat to the public safety. Burdening the criminal process with two million public intoxication cases a year is not only an overextension of the police function but is also wasteful, economically as well as socially.[151]

---

(2) constitutional safeguards allow the chronic alcoholic, as much as any other ill person, to choose or reject medical treatment; (3) compulsory treatment is unethical from a purely medical viewpoint; (4) since the facilities for mass commitment of alcoholics are lacking, society should first improve the treatment offered to voluntary patients. *Ibid.* 117–18. For similar views in the mental illness area *see* Note, "Civil Commitment of the Mentally Ill: Theories and Procedures," 79 *Harv. L. Rev.* 1288, 1290–91 (1966).

[150] The President's Commission on Crime in the District of Columbia recommended counsel only for drunkenness offenders who are subject to penal sanctions. It is evident that this protection is equally desirable in involuntary therapeutic commitments. *Report*, 500.

[151] Fenster v. Leary, 20 N.Y.2d 309, 229 N.E.2d 426 (1967), held the New York vagrancy statute unconstitutional on the ground that it was an overreaching of the police power. "[T]oday the only persons arrested and prosecuted as common law vagrants are alcoholic derelicts and other unfortunates, whose only crime, if any, is against themselves, and whose main offense usually consists in ... disturbing by their presence the sensitivities of residents of nicer parts of the community." *Ibid.* 315–16. See Murtagh, "Status Offenses and Due Process of Law," 36 *Fordham L. Rev.* 51 (1967). For an early case which challenged the state's power to punish the status of being a "common drunk" *see* State v. Ryan, 36 N.W. 823 (Wis. 1888).

Greater promise rests with pre-addictive, community-based prevention programs and with education that leads toward voluntary therapy. Outpatient clinics and halfway houses, permitting the alcoholic patient a partial participation in society, must replace the neglect and the isolation centers of the past. Training the alcoholic for a new and useful social function in the outside world, while allowing him to lean back upon the security provided by the outpatient clinic or the halfway house, may make treatment more desirable to persons who previously saw in it only an involuntary and useless social sanction.[152] Unless the outside world is made more welcome for the isolated, uprooted, demoralized, and educationally disadvantaged alcoholic, why should he want to return to it?[153]

[152] For a survey of suggested treatment innovations *see* Pittman, "Public Intoxication" 17–22.

[153] The most serious shortcoming of the past institutional treatment of alcoholics was the almost total absence of aftercare and follow-up activities. Plaut, "Developing Community Services" 125.

7

STERILIZATION AND OTHER Modifications of MAN

So among the experiments that may be tried on man those that
can only harm are forbidden, those that are innocent are
permissible, and those that may do good are obligatory.—Dr. Claude
Bernard, quoted in Lasagna, "Ethics of Human Testing,"
Washington Post, February 27, 1968, p. A18

It would be strange if it could not call upon those who already
sap the strength of the state for these lesser sacrifices, often not
felt to be such by those concerned, in order to prevent our
being swamped with incompetence. It is better for all the world, if
instead of waiting to execute degenerate offspring for crime,
or to let them starve for their imbecility, society can prevent those
who are manifestly unfit from continuing their kind.—Holmes,
J., in Buck v. Bell, 274 U.S. 200, 207 (1927)

The power to sterilize   may have subtle, far-reaching and
devastating effects. In evil or reckless hands it can cause races
or types which are inimical to the dominant group to wither and
disappear.—Douglas, J., in Skinner v. Oklahoma, 317 U.S. 535,
541 (1942)

THOSE WHO SAP THE STRENGTH OF THE STATE

An inmate in a state mental institution is classified a chronic schizophrenic requiring long-term hospitalization. The hospital has a policy of open wards, and the patient's appeal to female inmates creates an apprehension of undesired liaisons. May the hospital administrator order the inmate's sterilization?

After many years of institutional care and training, a mentally retarded female is being considered for release from a special state school. She has demonstrated an ability to work and live at large. Conceivably, she could even marry. Her retardation, however, appears hereditary; moreover, she would most likely be unable to assume the heavy burden of parenthood. Does the state have the right to sterilize her prior to release?

A mother petitions a court to have her eighteen-year-old feebleminded daughter committed to a state institution. The mother alleges that the daughter, who has an I.Q. of 36, is unable to care for her year-old illegitimate child. Furthermore, she has been promiscuous with a number of men since the birth of the child. There are no vacancies in the state's institution for the feebleminded. Does the court have the power to order the sterilization of the promiscuous daughter, to prevent the birth of more children?

A father is criminally charged for not supporting his illegitimate minor children. Although he fails to provide for the mother and his children, he returns from time to time to father more children. Does a court have the power to suspend the errant father's jail sentence on the condition that he submit to a sterilization operation?

The mother of two illegitimate children has been on the public welfare rolls for a long time. Should the continuation of welfare payments to her be conditioned upon her submitting to sterilization?

Today, the general public and even the practicing bar may consider involuntary sterilization as of historical interest only, believing that sterilization finally vanished in the collapse of Nazism's racist empire.[1] Yet sterilization remains an operative institution in America. Twenty-three American states authorize compulsory sterilization by

---

[1] The German sterilization law, which went into effect in July 1934, was proposed and considered several years before the Nazi regime. It provided: "Those hereditarily sick may be made unfruitful [sterilized] through surgical intervention when, following the experience of medical science, it may be expected with great probability that their offspring may suffer severe physical or mental inherited damage.

"The hereditarily sick, in the sense of this law, is a person who suffers from one of the following diseases: Inborn feeblemindedness, schizophrenia, circular

law. Others practice it without specific legislative authority. Several would permit sterilization under most of the situations outlined above.[2]

But sterilization, both for protecting the unfit individual against undue burdens and for guarding the state against the sapping of its reserves, poses policy questions beyond those in the examples above. For accepting sterilization's philosophical justification and social utility can have many far-reaching implications for the expansion of governmental powers and controls over the citizen of the therapeutic state.

How is the therapeutic state to exert its powers over deviants? Northern Europe in the Middle Ages used the "Ship of Fools" to discard the insane.[3] In the later, more affluent therapeutic state of the eighteenth and nineteenth centuries, commitment to institutions, patterned after monastic and penal models, was the primary tool.

The institutions protected the public from the deviant and sheltered the deviant from the public. This quarantine, accompanied by religious ministerings, was hoped to have rehabilitative effect. In the nineteenth and twentieth centuries, more elaborate and sophisticated programs to rehabilitate deviants through education, vocational training, psychiatric services, and surgical and drug therapy have found their way into the institutional enclaves. One of the more radical programs has been sterilization.

Sterilization has probably been the most drastic sanction employed under the power of *parens patriae*.[4] The result of its imposition is as

---

insanity, hereditary epilepsy, hereditary Huntington's chorea, hereditary blindness, hereditary deafness, severe hereditary physical deformity. Further, those may be made unfruitful who suffer from severe alcoholism." Peter, "Germany's Sterilization Program," *Amer. J. Pub. Health* 187–91 (March 1934). As a concession to the Catholic Church, the law provided that persons need not be operated on if they were kept in institutions without cost to the state. The official point of view of the Third Reich was that, in spite of those who would deny the state the right to interfere with the personal freedom of man, sterilization was based on deep humanitarianism. It is better to prevent widespread misery, which is transmitted by those inflicted with hereditary disabilities, than to pity the unfortunates and to burden the community with them. *The Nazi Primer: Official Handbook For Schooling Hitler Youth*, ch. 4 (H. L. Childs trans. 1938).

[2] *In re* Simpson, 180 N.E.2d 206 (Ohio S.Ct. 1962); *in re* Andrada, 33 U.S. Law Week 3278 (1965), *cert. denied*, 380 U.S. 953 (1965). For a recent case dealing with the sterilization of institutionalized defectives prior to their release to the community *see in re* Cavitt, 157 N.W.2d 171 (1968); Cavitt v. Nebraska, Docket 54, October Term, 1969, United States Supreme Court.

[3] M. Foucault, *Madness and Civilization* 7 (1965).

[4] Sterilization has also been utilized as a tool of the criminal law. Several states permit the compulsory sterilization of sexual and other "hereditary" offenders. O'Hara and Sanks, "Eugenic Sterilization," 45 *Geo. L. J.* 20, 34, 42 (1956).

determinative of procreation as capital punishment is of life, or frontal lobotomy is of creative mental capacity. Together with execution and lobotomy, sterilization shares a finality not contemplated by commitment to institutions. Yet sterilization may be distinguished from any other sanction or tool of social control by its promised long-range prophylactic effects.

Sterilization promises not only to keep the rapist from producing an unwanted and stigmatized issue but guarantees against impregnation of the mentally and socially unfit female who is likely to perpetuate her kind. It can insure the welfare state against a crushing burden of support for the children of the economically irresponsible. It has been hailed as a comprehensive tool for genetic and social selection, a means for perpetuating socially acceptable behavior and repressing future generations of deviants.

Sterilization can stand as a symbol for the surgical, biological, and chemical tools that will become increasingly available to the state as it endeavors to eradicate deviation and to modify man by means other than old-fashioned incarceration. The history of sterilization will therefore be useful in examining two of the most critical questions raised by the therapeutic state: What degree of deviation should justify state intervention? What limits should be imposed upon the nature, type, and content of the sanctions exercised under the *parens patriae* powers?

THE NEW THERAPIES

Testifying before a Congressional committee in 1966, Professor D. N. Michael described new potentials for electronic and computer control of deviants:

> It is not impossible to imagine that parolees will check in and be monitored by transmitters embedded in their flesh, reporting their whereabouts in code and automatically as they pass receiving stations (perhaps like fireboxes) systematically deployed over the country as part of one computer-monitored network. We may well reach the point where it will be permissible to allow some emotionally ill people the freedom of the streets, providing they are effectively "defused" through chemical agents. The task, then, for the computer-linked sensors would be to telemeter, not their emotional state, but simply the sufficiency of concentration of the chemical agent to insure an acceptable emotional state.[5]

[5] U.S. Congress, House, Committee on Government Operations, *Hearings before a Subcommittee*, 89th Cong., 2d sess., pp. 184–93 (D. N. Michael, "Speculations

More recently, Harvard researcher Ralph K. Schwitzgebel proposed a complex electronic surveillance and rehabilitation system as a new alternative to the incarceration of chronic recidivists.[6] It would permit not only the monitoring of their locations but also the regulation of specific offending behaviors in the community. A parole officer could easily send a signal to the deviant asking him to call in. Signals could also be used to reward or warn a deviant regarding certain types of behavior. "Thus, for example, if a parolee who had previously been very inconsistent in his work patterns was at work on time he might be sent a signal from the parole officer that meant, 'You're doing well,' or that he would receive a bonus. On the other hand, if it appeared that the parolee was in a high crime-rate area at 2 o'clock in the morning, he might be sent a signal reminding him to return home."[7]

The past chapters have dealt with the major classes of deviants and the manner in which society has undertaken to treat them in the name of therapy. By and large, the most widely used tool of the therapeutic state to this day has been commitment to a "total institution" for confinement and treatment for a period deemed necessary to effect a cure. This indeterminate commitment has been a major source of abuse by the therapeutic state and a major object of criticism in this book. We have suggested that some committed persons should be completely relieved of compulsory societal intervention, and that others could be adequately treated in their everyday milieu; and we have emphasized that, for most, institutional treatment may be worthless without followup care in a normal environment. Many other commentators have similarly criticized the institutional model of treatment, and the therapists themselves are often dissatisfied with the limitations that the institutional environment places both on patients and on treatment opportunities.

Given an increasing disaffection with indeterminate commitment as the primary tool of therapy for deviants, new methods of controlling human behavior have been discovered. Hormone injections can alter the intensity of sexual drives and modify the response to sexual stimuli. Drugs that act on the brain and central nervous system to modulate moods and alter states of consciousness are in use in many

on the Relations of the Computer to Individual Freedom and the Right to Privacy . . .," July 26, 27, and 28, 1966).

[6] Schwitzgebel, "Issues in the Use of an Electronic Rehabilitation System with Chronic Recidivists," 3 *Law Soc. Rev.* 597 (1969).

[7] *Ibid.* 603.

mental institutions. Psychosurgical techniques have advanced in recent years beyond the early lobotomies. Brain stimulation by electronic impulses through implanted electrodes has proved capable of modifying human behavior. Some electronic techniques leave overall patterns of personality and behavior intact while eliciting specific desired responses by selective stimulation of pleasure or pain centers, using miniaturized devices permanently implanted and remotely operated. Psychopharmacology and neurosurgery have generated a process for implanting areas of the brain with cannulae of drugs, which slowly release their contents for long-term control without need for continuous medications.[8]

As present means for diagnosing and correcting abnormalities in a person's genetic code are becoming more sophisticated, geneticists propose to manipulate the human embryo or ovum in order to improve the offspring or at least preselect it to better fit social demands.[9] Psychiatrists, clinical psychologists, and other behavioral experts are experimenting with environmental conditioning techniques in order to modify objectionable social manifestations. Others have claimed to be able to predict future antisocial conduct on the basis of prepubertal performance.[10] Similarly, genetic screening of all male babies to identify those with the XYY syndrome—and therefore possible propensity to violence—has begun in selected areas.[11]

A Reuters dispatch from Shrewsbury, England, carries the proposal of a British psychiatrist that compulsive speeders be "cured" by electric shock treatment. According to Dr. John Barker of the Shelton Hospital, treatment would start with a film of a driver exceeding 70 miles per hour past speed limit signs. In the consulting room, the patient would recognize himself in the film breaking the law and would receive shock up to 70 volts through a strap attached to his wrists. "It simply boils down to associating excessive speed with discomfort and pain," Dr. Barker is reported to have said.[12]

---

[8] Quarton, "Deliberate Efforts to Control Human Behavior and Modify Personality," 96 *Daedalus* 837, 841–45 (1967).

[9] J. Rostand, *Can Man Be Modified?* (S. Griffin trans. 1959); G. R. Taylor, *The Biological Time Bomb* (1968).

[10] S. and E. Glueck, *Family Environment and Delinquency* (1962); Glueck, "Spotting Potential Delinquents: Can It Be Done?" 20 *Fed. Prob.* 7 (1956). For a critique of prognostic techniques *see U.N. International Review of Criminal Policy*, no. 7–8, pp. 29–30 (1955).

[11] Walzer, Breau, and Smith, "A Chromosome Survey of 2400 Normal Newborn Infants," 74 *J. Pediatrics* 438 (1969).

[12] "Shocks Proposed to Cure Speeders," *Washington Post*, January 9, 1967, p. A7.

With the aid of computers and newly developed experimental methods of monitoring human conduct and response through internal changes in chemistry and sophisticated miniature electronic seurveillance devices, the general control technique could easily be made ambulatory and perhaps much more sensitive to behavior patterns deemed offensive or detrimental by society. A man might be sensed working himself into a rage and about to assault another individual. A brain electrode could be activated to divert his aggression to some harmless end, or an implanted drug could be released to calm his hostility.

In their formulation, these new therapeutic solutions for social control could have great public appeal. They can be related to the humanistic desire for therapy and improvement that has marked the growth of the *parens patriae* power, and they offer social controls and improvements without dreary institutions and with ostensible freedom. No chains—only conditioning.

Yet these very elements of appeal give rise to dangers unknown in the old penal system or in the present incarnation of the therapeutic state. Today's forms of punishment or therapy, both of which rely heavily upon involuntary confinement, are subject to some legal and social controls, however weak and inadequate. The specter of depriving a man of his liberty for a substantial period has caused society to hedge the power of the penal system with limitations. This same specter of incarceration has also been the generating force behind many of the criticisms of the operation and goals of the therapeutic state. But with the rise of techniques that allow the deviant to remain at large in society, this major point of confrontation between the *parens patriae* power and the rights of individuals will tend to be less visible. With it may disappear many of the objections to the further expansion of the power of the therapeutic state—possibly even into minor areas of deviation (such as traffic control) which to date have not seriously been affected by the shift from the penal system to the rehabilitative ideal.

The application of the new therapies to unborn generations evokes a less emotional reaction than do proposals for treatment of a living person. In addition, parents confronted with the scientific prediction that their son or daughter (unborn or not) will become a burden or danger to society unless certain treatments are undertaken early in life would probably be less opposed to therapy than would the deviant mature adult. As British social worker Eileen Younghusband observed with great insight: "Undoubtedly many people would prefer to be punished rather than improved. They want above all things the kind of punishment which will enable them to get it over and done with and to be free to go on with all their fundamental weaknesses unfaced."[13] However, when it is someone else being labeled "deviant," therapeutic improvement becomes easier to accept. With the introduction of treatments to modify personality at a very early age, the parent, weighed down with considerations of social responsibility, personal repugnance to the projected deviation, and genuine loving concern for the welfare of the child, is less likely to challenge the opinion of the therapists, and the individual may be modified before he ever has an opportunity to object.

Another danger posed by the newer therapies arises from the fact that they are difficult to resist. One of the major criticisms of institutional treatment is that the prison-like atmosphere of many institutions generates resistance by the patient. In the usual case, the patient is able to refuse to be cured. He may remain addicted, alcoholic, delinquent, or antisocial, and refuse to submit to therapy. With the new therapies, however, resistance becomes impossible. Since the new treatments affect the basic chemistry and response mechanisms, as well as altering fundamental personality characteristics, the power to resist their operation is stripped away.

The degree to which these new treatment methods will tempt society to undertake comprehensive programs for the suppression of deviation is yet another problem. Every therapeutic program which society has heretofore attempted has been motivated not only by the individual's need for protection but also by considerations of social defense. In the future, amid increasing manifestations of a permissive and at times an anarchistic society, the defenders of the order will be tempted to extend the new therapies to all who show the potential for asocial or antisocial behavior. This means that a broader range of persons may become candidates for therapy for conduct now considered only mischievousness. With the new ease of implementation and ostensibly mild incursion into an individual's everyday affairs, these new therapies would be as hard to oppose philosophically as a compulsory vaccination against smallpox is today.

Although the advancements of science present new dangers from the overexercise of the therapeutic powers, some nonincarcerative treatments for deviance have been with us for many years. Utilized

[13] Younghusband, "The Dilemma of the Juvenile Court," 33 *Soc. Serv. Rev.* 17 (1959).

mainly in the institutional setting, shock treatment, lobotomy, and sterilization possess many of the attributes of the new therapies. In charting a course for the control of these new powers, a review of society's curbs on the older treatments will be helpful.

THE OLD THERAPIES

Lobotomy and Shock Treatment

In 1890, Dr. G. Burkhardt, a Swiss psychiatrist, began to remove portions of patients' brains. He believed that mental troubles had their seats in various parts of the brain and that by surgically removing the affected area, sick and dangerous individuals would be transformed into persons harmless to society and themselves. He was reported to be successful in his goal but was forced to discontinue his operations because of ethical pressures from his colleagues. In 1935 two Portuguese physicians, Moniz and Lima, performed the first prefrontal lobotomy. They were led to this treatment by evidence that certain mental abnormalities were linked to physical damage and disease of the frontal lobes of the brain. The patient's behavior was changed as a result of the operation, which consisted of removing a small round portion of skull bone near the temple and severing the connection between the frontal lobes of the brain and the mid-brain by inserting a knife into the white matter of the brain and twisting it. In 1936 Walter Freeman and James W. Watts introduced the operation into the United States.[14]

Although the operation met with some early criticism and resistance from the medical profession, the successes of Freeman and Watts soon made the treatment acceptable. Freeman and Watts had through lobotomy changed irritable, uncooperative, unclean, and helpless chronic schizophrenics into quiet, clean, cooperative, and self-sufficient patients, some of whom could be sent home as employable. These successes generated a search for other uses for prefrontal lobotomy, and for a time the operation was an accepted treatment for the early stages of schizophrenia, manic depression, and even neurosis.[15]

The treatment's frequent side effects, however, prevented its becoming a routine treatment. From Dr. Freeman's records of 624

[14] Goldstein, "Prefrontal Lobotomy: Analysis and Warning," 182 *Sci. Amer.* 41 (1950).
[15] *Ibid.*

lobotomies, he reported 24 fatalities (3.6%), and 321 (51.5%) patients with undesirable side effects such as partial paralysis, loss of bladder control, and convulsions.[16] The introduction of new surgical techniques reduced these figures to more tolerable levels. The transorbital lobotomy, in which an icepick-like instrument inserted into the brain through the eye socket is used to cut the frontal lobes, had a fatality rate of only 1.7 percent and an undesirable side effect rate of 5.2 percent. In addition, the number of patients who experienced undesirable behavioral complications (such as indolence, excessive profanity, and sexual irregularities) from the transorbital lobotomy was only one-tenth that of the prefrontal lobotomy. With these developments, lobotomy's acceptance by the medical profession spread. In fact, swift use of the operation on new patients was urged because statistics showed that the chance of favorable results was doubled when the mental patient had been in the hospital less than six months.[17]

In the early fifties, however, the old and lingering doubts concerning lobotomies were given substance. Research disclosed that the operation destroyed the capacity to form abstract thoughts[18] and robbed the individual of ambition, conscience, and planning abilities. The lobotomized person could react quickly to stimuli but was unable to reflect before reacting on the wisdom or effects of his response.[19] With these developments, psychiatrists began to use lobotomies with much more restraint. It remains a rarely used treatment—a last resort for extremely dangerous and incorrigible patients. Its use to relieve the custodial burdens of the mental hospital staffs is acknowledged,[20] but the introduction of drugs for much the same purpose has further diminished lobotomy's use as a palliative.[21]

Shock treatment, like lobotomy, may convert violent patients into quiet, subdued ones, and is therefore used in the treatment of manic-depressive psychoses. Although it may quiet a patient in the manic phase of this illness, it is also, and commonly, used to relieve the deep depression experienced by some patients. Brought to this country from Italy by Dr. Lothar Kalinowski, the therapy consists of applying various amounts of electricity, under general anesthesia, to cause muscular contractions. Occasional deaths have been reported from

---

[16] "Looking Backward at Lobotomy," 61 *Time* 46 (June 22, 1953).
[17] *Ibid.*
[18] Goldstein, "Prefrontal Lobotomy."
[19] A. C. Guyton, *Function of the Human Body* (1964).
[20] Quarton, "Efforts to Control Human Behavior" 837, 848.
[21] *Ibid.*

the treatment, generally from heart failure during or soon after treatment. In addition, the severe convulsions that occur during the treatment can cause fractures of bones and loss of teeth.[22]

Although shock treatment is widely applied, doubts about its curative powers persist. There seems to be little relation between shock treatment and the period of hospitalization, and there is evidence of a high rate of relapse among patients released after shock treatments. It has been asserted that shock is merely a palliative treatment and is used as much for the relief of the staff as for the patient's benefit.[23] Sometimes shock treatments are administered in view of other patients, perhaps as a general deterrent.[24]

Safeguards

Despite the severe implications of psychosurgery and shock treatment, few safeguards protect the individual from inadvisable use. State laws usually make no reference to these treatments; generally, they have been controlled only by the discretion of the doctor or staff of the confining hospital. In practice, hospitals often require the consent of the patient before drastic psychosurgery can be performed, but the value of consent by a patient previously determined to be mentally incompetent is at best suspect. Nor can the patient's best interest be served by conditioning the treatment upon family consent, since the relatives are quite often willing to abide by medical recommendation as long as they are relieved of the burdens of caring for the patient. Illinois specifically provides that consent of the mental patient is not necessary to perform a lobotomy.[25] Ohio[26] and Oklahoma[27] provide that notice of the operation be given to the patient's relatives, except in emergency cases, but in Ohio the hospital does not have to obtain their consent.[28] In a few states the administrative regulations of the department of health or of the state mental hospital require that consent be obtained from someone prior

[22] *Ibid. See also* Quinley v. Cooke, 183 Tenn. 428, 192 S.W.2d 992 (1946); Farber v. Olkon, 246 P.2d 710 (Cal. App. Ct. 1952), *aff'd.* 40 Cal.2d 503, 254 P.2d 520 (1953); Johnston v. Rodis, 151 F.Supp. 345 (D.D.C. 1957).

[23] I. Belknap, *Human Problems in a State Mental Hospital* 191–95 (1956).

[24] *The Mentally Disabled and the Law* 149 (F. T. Lindman and D. M. McIntyre eds. 1961).

[25] *Ill. Ann. Stat.* §91 1/2–5–18 (1956).

[26] *Ohio Rev. Code Ann.* §5123.03 (Baldwin 1958).

[27] *Okla. Stat.* §43A–96 (1957 Supp.).

[28] 1 *Vt. Atty. Gen. Rep.* 209 (1945).

to brain surgery,[29] but the preponderant medical opinion has been that obtaining consent, while a recommended practice, should not interfere with the prescribed treatment. The state, as *parens patriae*, has obligated itself to provide the necessary care and treatment for the patient, the argument runs; this treatment should be dictated by expertise and experience and should not be governed by what the patient or his relatives consider to be his best interest. Other than the limited requirements for notice or consent, as contained in a few statutes or administrative regulations, there is no means by which to challenge the medical decision.

There is even less protection against the possible abuse of shock treatment. The existing statutory pronouncements on the subject are directed toward protecting the administering physician against suits for damages due to physical injury resulting from the therapy.[30] The only legal pronouncement touching on the questions of permissibility of shock treatment is a 1948 opinion of the Attorney General of Pennsylvania, who concluded that the administration of the treatment should be left to the sound discretion of the superintendents of the state mental hospital unencumbered by any legal requirements of consent from either the patient or others.[31]

Sterilization

Programs for the control of human birth and life are of ancient origin. Initially they were negatively conceived—to prevent real or imagined ills. Euripides, in the *Trojan Women*, relates that when the Acaeans conquered Troy, both the adult warriors and the infantile claimant to the vanquished throne were killed in order to squelch any future spirit of rebellion. Similarly, the tragic story of Oedipus was derived from his father's decision to send the new-born child away to his death, in order to prevent the realization of the Delphic oracle's prediction of patricide.[32] The Bible reports the ancient Pharaoh's alarm at the increase in the numbers of the Israelites who had migrated to Egypt—lest "when there falleth out any war, they join also unto our enemies."[33] Pharaoh's Egypt thus provides the first historical report of

[29] *See, e.g.,* Kentucky, Department of Mental Health, *Policies and Procedures,* Reg. 2–2 (1958).

[30] *Mentally Disabled and the Law* 150 (Lindman and McIntyre eds.).

[31] "Shock Therapy in State Hospitals," 64 *Pa. D. & C.* 14 (1948); 97 *Pa. L. Rev.* 436 (1949).

[32] Sophocles, *Oedipus Rex.*

[33] Exod. 1:10.

a comprehensive national policy directed against the progeny of a suspect minority: "Every son that is born ye shall cast into the river, and every daughter ye shall save."[34]

Even the first concept of procreation controls as positive tools for race improvement had been recognized in ancient time. Plato pleaded for the planned improvement of mankind. "The principle has been already laid down," he reports, "that the best of either sex should be united with the best as often, and the inferior with the inferior, as seldom as possible; and that they should rear the offspring of the one sort of union but not of the other, if the flock is to be maintained in first-rate condition."[35]

It was modern science, however, that gave society both a well-reasoned motive and a humane procedure for the control of procreation. The motive was provided by those who preached that the laws of heredity should be adapted to the improvement of the human population; the procedure was the development of new "civilized" techniques of birth control. The infanticide measures utilized by the ancients had been discarded as inhuman. Castration, the most direct method of limiting reproduction in males, was equally drastic, for it involved removal of the testicles, with the result that the patient's sexual desires were reduced. He was incapable of participating in the sexual act and additionally suffered undesirable changes in his secondary sex characteristics, such as voice, whiskers, and physical appearance.

The more modern methods of sterilization are directed only at the prevention of procreation and do not materially affect either sexual desire or ability to participate in the sex act.[36] Both male sterilization (vasectomy—developed in the United States in 1895), and female sterilization (salpingectomy[37]—developed in France at about the same time), can be performed easily and safely under proper surgical conditions, although the female operation is considered "major surgery."

[34] Exod. 1:22.

[35] Plato, *The Republic*, ch. 5, p. 459 (B. Jowett trans. 1901).

[36] The most extensive study on the sexual and psychological effects of sterilization indicates that the operation often produced exhilarating or at least no depressive effects on sexual activities in about 95 percent of the cases studied. Koya, "Sterilization in Japan," 8 *Eugenics Q.* 135, 139 (1961); 2 *Excerpta Criminologica* 735, 735 (1962).

[37] Vasectomy involves the cutting of the vas deferens, the tube connecting the testes with the urinary canal, thus preventing the sperm from thereafter passing into the urinary canal. Salpingectomy involves the opening of the abdominal cavity and the cutting of fallopian tubes to prevent the uniting of sperm and egg. Note, "Elective Sterilization," 113 *U. Pa. L. Rev.* 415–16 (1965).

With the development of these procedures, "the advocacy of wide-spread sterilization was no longer a movement without a method."[38]

EUGENIC STERILIZATION

The eugenic movement spearheaded the modern use of sterilization. Coined by Sir Francis Galton in 1885, the term eugenics (from the Greek "well born") describes a social program derived from the earlier scientific studies of Charles Darwin and Gregory Mendel. Darwin's work showed that species could change markedly over many generations, while Mendel's experiments with plants and insects demonstrated the transmitability of simple characteristics from parent to offspring according to discoverable mathematical patterns. The merger and extension of these discoveries into the human arena gave rise to the eugenic theory that complex traits in human beings were hereditary and could be selectively bred.[39] In essence, the philosophy of the eugenic movement can be summarized as follows:

> The word eugenics is used to cover any proposals or plans for the improvement of the racial qualities of human beings.... They differ fundamentally from other projects ... in that they are concerned with the improvement of the human material and not of the surroundings. But they are not alternative to those projects. Improvement of the surroundings should go on at the same time. ... Human history is largely the story of attempts by man to bring his destiny under control. But if he wishes to bring his destiny under control he must turn his attention to the control of human material as well as to the control of human surroundings. He must attempt to govern his own racial evolution.[40]

Scientific and popular literature at the turn of the century attempted to document the hereditary factors involved in pauperism and crime. The most famous of these studies are those of the Jukes family, the tribe of Ishmael, the Nan family, and the Kallikak family.[41] The

[38] O'Hara and Sanks, "Eugenic Sterilization" 20.

[39] F. Galton, *Inquiries into Human Faculty* 17 (1908).

[40] *Encyclopedia Britannica* (1955 ed.) s.v. "Eugenics"; A. M. Carr-Saunders, *Eugenics* (1926).

[41] R. L. Dugdale, *The Jukes: A Study in Crime, Pauperism, Disease and Heredity* (1877); A. H. Estabrook, *The Jukes in 1915* (1916); McCulloch, "The Tribe of Ishmael: A Study in Social Degradation," in *Proceedings of the Fifteenth National Conference of Charities and Correction* (1888); Estabrook and Davenport, *The Nan Family: A Study in Cacogenics* (1912); H. Goddard, *The Kallikak Family* (1912).

writings strove to substantiate the applicability of the Mendelian laws
to human beings. In the footsteps of these studies came several reports emphasizing the role of defective mentality in crime and pauperism. A few highlights from these reports illustrate views of some of
the leading early eugenicists. Charles Goring, the English penal authority, concluded that "the one vital mental constitutional factor in
the etiology of crime is defective intelligence."[42] Dr. Walter E. Fernald, Medical Superintendent of the Massachusetts School for the
Feebleminded, asserted: "Every feeble-minded person, especially
the high-grade imbecile, is a potential criminal, needing only the
proper environment and opportunity for the development and expression of his criminal tendencies. The unrecognized imbecile is the most
dangerous element in the community. There are many crimes committed by imbeciles [the mentally deficient] for every one committed
by an insane person [the mentally ill]."[43] The implications of this
evidence and a plea for social controls are clearly contained in a report to the Governor of Kansas in 1919: "All the feeble-minded lack
self-control. . . . Their immoral tendencies and lack of self-control make
the birth rate among them unusually high. . . . We know that the
social evil is fed from the ranks of feeble-minded women, and that
feeble-minded men and women spread venereal disease. . . . Their tendencies to pauperism and crime would seem to be sufficient grounds to
justify the claim that the feeble-minded are a menace to society."[44]
Sterilization seemed a simple and natural long-range answer to the
dangers posed by the feebleminded and other defectives. By not allowing the defectives to renew themselves, society would soon be rid of
them.

Contributing Factors

Although the greatest impetus for sterilization laws was eugenics,
other considerations affected the legislators who drafted these statutes.
The environmentalists, though by and large discounting the claims of
the eugenicists, nevertheless lent their support to sterilization proposals, for they saw benefits in sterilization independent of any biological theories. In limiting the procreation of socially undesirable

---

[42] *The English Convict: A Statistical Study* 263 (C. Goring ed. 1913).
[43] Fernald, "The Burden of Feeble-Mindedness" 23–24 *Medical Communications of the Massachusetts Medical Society* 4–7 (1912).
[44] Commission on Provision for the Feeble-minded
[44] Kansas, Governor's Commission on Provision for the Feeble-minded, *Report
on the Kallikaks of Kansas* 6–14 (1919).

elements, society would be reducing the numbers of children born to and raised in socioeconomically unfit homes which generated criminals and antisocial behavior. According to environmentalist theory, this would in turn lead to a reduction in crime and delinquency.

Throughout this period, "social eugenics" was couched in language that subordinated it to hereditary eugenics, and the social arguments were largely used in scientific circles to bolster the standard eugenic proposals. Speaking to the proposition in 1936, Dr. Himes asserted:

> It is becoming increasingly clear that we shall never make a frontal attack on social inadequacy until we recognize that family stocks differ in genetic endowment, and hence in potentialities of their offspring; further, that even if heredity has no influence whatever on social inadequacy, defectives do not make good parents. Therefore, they should not reproduce for social as well as biological reasons.[45]

Thus, if "social inadequacy," not genetic pollution, is the reason for sterilization, the "defectives" who are to be sterilized need no longer be subject to hereditary mental deficiencies but only to social deficiencies. Philosophically, therefore, social eugenics hinges upon any substandard *socioeconomic* condition that might cause an individual's children to be burdensome or dangerous to society. In this context the root meaning of *eugenic*—"well born"—appears especially ironic.

The last factor which influenced the adoption of sterilization laws was therapeutic and humane. Females who could conceive but who would suffer physical injury or emotional trauma either from bearing the child or from the burdens of parenthood should through sterilization be saved from such distress. Although sometimes voluntary, such sterilization could be compelled if the individual were so mentally disoriented as to be unable to exercise her own judgment in the matter.

The sterilization programs that sprang from these origins were not generally considered penal in nature. Like many of the other experiments of the fledgling therapeutic state discussed previously, they were postulated as improvements rather than punishments.

Criteria and Procedures

Sterilization was informally practiced in several state institutions for the feebleminded even before such operations were authorized by

[45] Himes, "Some Inferences from History," *Birth Control Rev.* 1 (November 1936).

law.[46] In 1897, the Michigan legislature defeated the first sterilization bill, and the governor of Pennsylvania vetoed a similar act in 1905. In 1907, Indiana enacted the first statute authorizing sterilization[47] and providing for a committee of experts to examine the inmates of certain designated institutions. It vested these experts with broad discretion:

> If, in the judgment of this committee of experts and the board of managers, procreation is inadvisable and there is not probability of improvement of the mental condition of the inmate, it shall be lawful for the surgeons to perform such operation for the prevention of procreation as shall be declared safest and most effective.[48]

Although the Indiana sterilization statute was later held unconstitutional as a violation of procedural due process[49] and a similar fate befell several other sterilization laws,[50] the definitive policy toward eugenic sterilization was finally set in 1927 in the Supreme Court decision of *Buck* v. *Bell*.[51]

Following *Buck* v. *Bell*, 20 additional states enacted sterilization statutes, most of which were patterned after the constitutionally sanctioned procedure.[52] A total of 31 states and the Commonwealth of Puerto Rico have had sterilization laws at one time or another. No new eugenic sterilization statutes have been added since 1937, when 28 states[53] had such laws, and in fact 2 of these have since dropped them, leaving 26 states with involuntary sterilization laws.[54]

---

[46] E. Gosney and P. Popenoe, *Sterilization for Human Betterment* 184 (1929); A. Deutsch, *The Mentally Ill in America* 370 (1949). Many of these operations were allegedly for "curative" rather than eugenic reasons. Among the curative reasons given was "persistent masturbation." M. W. Barr, *Mental Defectives* 196 (1904). In the late 1930s, the superintendent of the Kansas Industrial School for Girls had 62 inmates sterilized on the grounds of "insubordination." Oglesby, "What Has Happened to Kansas' Sterilization Laws?," 2 *Kan. L. Rev.* 174, 176–77 (1953).

[47] *Ind. Acts of 1907*, ch. 215. For the historical background *see* Deutsch, *Mentally Ill in America* 355–70.

[48] *Ind. Acts of 1907*, ch. 215.

[49] Williams v. State, 190 Ind. 526, 131 N.E. 2 (1921).

[50] Smith v. Board of Examiners of Feebleminded, 85 N.J.L. 46, 88 A 963 (1913); Haynes v. Lapeer Circuit Judge, 201 Mich. 138, 166 N.W. 938 (1918); *in re* Thomson, 100 Misc. 20, 109 N.Y. Supp. 638 (1918), *aff'd*. Osborn v. Thomson, 185 App. Div. 902, 171 N.Y.S. 1094 (1918).

[51] Buck v. Bell, 274 U.S. 200 (1927).

[52] Note, "Human Sterilization," 35 *Iowa L. Rev.* 251, 253 (1950).

[53] Note, "Sterilization Laws—Their Constitutionality—Their Social and Scientific Bases," 17 *B. U. L. Rev.* 246, 260 (1937).

[54] Kansas and North Dakota have repealed their laws; New York, New Jersey, and Washington failed to re-enact their sterilization laws after they were declared unconstitutional on procedural grounds. The states which have sterilization

The original sterilization laws were typically true to the eugenic arguments and were therefore made applicable to three classes of individuals: the mentally ill, the mentally deficient, and the epileptic. This pattern is still carried today in most sterilization statutes. The mentally deficient are subject to sterilization in all the states that authorize the operation. Similarly, the mentally ill are subject to sterilization in all these states except Alabama and Nebraska. Fourteen states continue to extend their statutes to epileptics.[55] Eleven states authorize the eugenic sterilization of "hereditary" criminals[56] and seven states permit the sterilization of sex offenders, "degenerates," "moral degenerates," and syphilitics for somewhat tenuous eugenic reasons.[57] The broadest criteria appear to be contained in the Oregon statute which covers "all persons who are feebleminded, insane, epileptic, habitual criminals, incurable syphilitics, moral degenerates or sexual perverts, and who are, or . . . will likely become, a menace to society."[58]

The statutes currently in force reveal that the benefits of social eugenics were not lost upon latter-day legislators.[59] Of the 26 states authorizing sterilization, only 6 use purely biological considerations as the justification for the operation. Twelve states base the operation on a determination that a person's offspring will face inherent social inadequacies, while the remaining states cite the patient's therapeutic needs or other social factors. Although a few states demand a positive finding that the operation will benefit the patient mentally, morally, or physically, most simply call for a determination that his

statutes presently on their books are Alabama, Arizona, California, Connecticut, Delaware, Georgia, Idaho, Indiana, Iowa, Maine, Michigan, Minnesota, Mississippi, Montana, Nebraska, New Hampshire, North Carolina, Oklahoma, Oregon, South Carolina, South Dakota, Utah, Vermont, Virginia, West Virginia, and Wisconsin. Ferster, "Eliminating the Unfit—Is Sterilization the Answer?" 27 *Ohio St. L. J.* 591, 596 (1966).

[55] These states are Arizona, Delaware, Idaho, Indiana, Mississippi, Montana, New Hampshire, North Carolina, Oklahoma, Oregon, South Carolina, Utah, Virginia, and West Virginia.

[56] California, Connecticut, Delaware, Georgia, Idaho, Iowa, Michigan, Oklahoma, Oregon, Utah, Wisconsin.

[57] California, Georgia, Idaho, Iowa, Michigan, North Dakota, and Oregon. Paul, "State Eugenic Sterilization Laws in American Thought and Practice" 221 (unpublished manuscript at Walter Reed Army Institute of Research, 1965). *See also Mentally Disabled and the Law* 183, 185 (Lindman and McIntyre eds.).

[58] *Ore. Rev. Stat.* §436.030. The Oregon law also authorizes the sterilization of any person convicted of the crime of rape, incest, sodomy, or contributing to the sexual delinquency of a minor. *Ibid.* §§436.040 and 167.040.

[59] "Sterilization is being increasingly applied on social and economic rather than eugenic grounds." H. I. Clarke, *Social Legislation* 197 (1940).

procreating is "deemed inadvisable." Some states invoke the operation upon such grounds as the advancement of the public good; the probability that the patient's offspring will become a menace or a ward of the state; the patient's inability to perform the duties of parenthood; or the fact that the patient is eligible for parole or discharge.[60] Despite the breadth and vagueness of these criteria, some protection to the public is provided by the common restriction that the operation may be performed only on inmates of state mental institutions, a holdover from the early eugenic sterilization days. Only 9 states authorize the sterilization of noninstitutionalized persons.[61]

Sterilization laws also differ with regard to the requirements for patient or family consent. The statutes of Connecticut, Michigan, Minnesota, and Vermont[62] require the consent of the patient or guardian as a precondition of sterilization. By administrative order, sterilization in California is performed only with the consent of the patient or guardian.[63] All others authorize the operation notwithstanding the lack of consent of either the patient or his guardian. Three states, Iowa, Oregon, and Wisconsin,[64] permit sterilization on both voluntary and involuntary bases.

The power to authorize an involuntary sterilization has traditionally been vested not in the courts but in various specially designated public agencies. In some of the 26 states this agency is the State Board of Medical Examiners; in others, the State Board of Mental Health; and in others, ad hoc commissions comprised of the superintendent of the institution in which the patient is confined and one or two surgeons or psychiatrists.[65]

In the majority of the 26 states, the involuntary sterilization procedure commences when the superintendent of the confining institution files an application to have the operation performed. Five states permit applications to originate with physicians, relatives, sheriffs, and public welfare commissioners. Similarly, it is these people who must apply for the sterilization of noninstitutionalized patients.[66]

[60] *Mentally Disabled and the Law* 185 (Lindman and McIntyre eds.).

[61] Delaware, Idaho, Iowa, Michigan, North Carolina, Oregon, South Dakota, Utah, and Vermont. For a comprehensive survey of the various state statutes *see* Forster, "Eliminating the Unfit" 596–97.

[62] *Conn. Gen. Stat. Ann.* §17–19 (1965); *Mich. Stat. Ann.* §14.481 *et seq.* (1965); *Minn. Stat. Ann.* §256.07 *et seq.* (1959); *Vt. Stat. Ann.* §18.3201 *et seq.* (1959).

[63] *Cal. D.M.H. Policy and Operations Manual* §3520.2.

[64] *Iowa Code Ann.* §145 *et seq.* (1966); *Ore. Rev. Stat.* §436.010 *et seq.* (1965); *Wis. Stat. Ann.* §46.12 (1957).

[65] *Mentally Disabled and the Law* 185 (Lindman and McIntyre eds.).

[66] *Ibid.*; *see also* Table VI, pp. 192–97, *ibid.*

Since the proceeding is deemed nonpenal in nature,[67] the patient is not usually allowed to invoke the safeguards available in the criminal process. Several states make no provision for a hearing before the agency that passes upon the sterilization application. While most states do provide for a hearing, the patient is not generally entitled to legal counsel. Nor do all the states require that the patient, his next of kin, or guardian be given notice that an application has been filed. Frequently, when notice to the patient's next of kin or his guardian is required, the patient himself need not be notified.[68]

All but three states permit an appeal to the courts from the deci sion of the sterilization tribunal. Two of the states (Idaho and Iowa) provide for an automatic judicial review in all cases where the operation would be involuntary. Fourteen states also grant the patient the right to be represented by counsel upon an appeal. Seven states provide for the appointment of an attorney if the patient does not have one.[69]

Despite the fact that sterilization laws were enacted after the development of the modern sterilization techniques, which control fertility without affecting the ability to participate in the sexual act, several states fail to specify or to limit techniques to be used. Four of the states which authorize involuntary sterilization use the term "asexualization," which has ordinarily been interpreted to mean castration.[70] Michigan includes X-ray treatment as a possible technique; Iowa specifically bars the use of castration; nine other states fail to deal with the question.[71]

THE CONSTITUTIONALITY OF STERILIZATION

The Substantive Attack

Since the advent of eugenic sterilization laws in the United States, many state and federal courts have considered the constitutionality of

[67] Buck v. Bell, 274 U.S. 200, 207 (1927); *in re* Main, 162 Okla. 65, 19 P.2d 153, 155 (1933).

[68] *Mentally Disabled and the Law* 185 (Lindman and McIntyre eds.); Ferster, "Eliminating the Unfit" 628–33.

[69] Ferster, "Eliminating the Unfit" 628–29.

[70] California, North Carolina, Oregon, and Utah. Paul, "State Eugenic Sterilization Laws" 222a. In Kansas, which recently repealed its law, a total of 229 castrations were reported by the State Training School at Winfield in the period from 1923 to 1940. *Ibid.* 629.

[71] Alabama, Delaware, Iowa, Nebraska, North Carolina, Oregon, South Dakota, Washington, and Wisconsin. *Ibid.* 222.

both the substance and the procedures of this experiment in social control. The substantive challenges have employed a variety of arguments against sterilization laws: that they violate due process; that they constitute cruel and unusual punishment; that they constitute a bill of attainder; and that they deny equal protection of the laws to affected individuals. The attacks have not in general been successful.

The Fourteenth Amendment to the United States Constitution requires that no person shall be deprived of life, liberty, or property without due process of law. This is a two-pronged guarantee containing both substantive and procedural safeguards. As a standard, due process is not easily definable since constitutional law is like a progressive science: adapting old words to express answers to modern needs. Justice Cardozo defined due process as those practices "implicit in the concept of ordered liberty"[72] and those practices "so rooted in the traditions and conscience of our people as to be ranked as fundamental."[73] Justice Frankfurter described the test for ascertaining whether a given practice complies with due process as "an evaluation based on a disinterested inquiry pursued in the spirit of science, on a balanced order of facts exactly and fairly stated, on the detached consideration of conflicting claims . . . on a judgment not *ad hoc* and episodic but duly mindful of reconciling the needs both of continuity and of change in a progressive society."[74] The substantive requirement of due process means societal fairness at a given point in time. It requires a logical and fair connection between the stated purpose of the law and the measures employed for its attainment and it presupposes a valid governmental interest in prohibiting or regulating the subject matter of the law.

Eugenic sterilization laws have been attacked as violating all the standards included under substantive due process. First, critics have argued that the laws are unfair to those to whom they are applied. Given the other methods of limiting procreation (segregation of sexes, contraceptives) and the means of caring for the offspring of mentally defective or socially unfit parents (whether or not the children are themselves defective or unfit), the irrevocable sterilization of individuals is grossly inconsistent with the concept of fairness contained in the due process clause. Second, neither the biological nor social eugenicists have demonstrated the actual capacity of sterilization to accomplish the goal of eugenic theory—the improvement of

---

[72] Palko v. Connecticut, 302 U.S. 319, 325 (1937).
[73] Snyder v. Massachusetts, 291 U.S. 97, 105 (1934).
[74] Rochin v. California, 342 U.S. 165, 172 (1952).

man and society. The clumsy sterilization laws that now exist are so pragmatically unrelated to the professed goals of such laws that they violate the requirement that a logical connection exist between the stated purpose of the laws and the means for its attainment. Lastly, there are some who argue that regardless of the scientific certainty of eugenic success or the alternative means of caring for offspring of unfit parents and controlling procreation, the state is never justified in invading an individual's bodily integrity and depriving him of his fundamental power to procreate—that is, that sterilization exceeds any valid state interest.[75]

In 1927, however, Justice Holmes, speaking for the United States Supreme Court in *Buck* v. *Bell*,[76] laid these due process objections to rest and upheld sterilization as falling within the permissible constitutional dimensions. Carrie Buck was committed to a Virginia mental institution as mentally deficient. Both her mother and her own illegitimate daughter were similarly feebleminded. Under the state's procedure for effecting sterilization,[77] it was determined that the best interest of the patient and society would be served if Miss Buck were infertile. The Supreme Court addressed itself to the substantive issue of whether the state had the power to order the sterilization of an individual for eugenic purposes. The state's interest in the maintenance of the quality of the species, Holmes held, was superior to any individual's power of procreation. Without evaluating the scientific evidence, the court stated that it could not, as a matter of law, override the determination of the legislature that certain conditions are hereditary and inimical to the public welfare, nor could it override the determination of the Virginia Supreme Court of Appeals that the petitioner possessed those inimical characteristics. The oft-quoted rationale is summarized by Justice Holmes:

> In view of the general declarations of the legislature and the specific findings of the Court, obviously we cannot say as a matter of law that the grounds do not exist, and if they exist they justify the result. We have seen more than once that the public welfare may call upon the best citizens for their lives. It would be strange if it could not call upon those who already sap the strength of the

[75] Morris and Breithaupt, "Compulsory Sterilization of Criminals—Perversion in the Law," 15 *Syracuse L. Rev.* 738, 741 (1964); Gest, "Eugenic Sterilization: Justice Holmes vs. Natural Law," 23 *Temp. L. Q.* 306, 308 (1950); Berns, "Buck v. Bell: The Sterilization Decision and Its Effect on Public Policy" 26 (unpublished thesis in the University of Chicago Library 1951).

[76] 274 U.S. 200 (1927).

[77] *Va. Laws of 1924,* ch. 394.

State for these lesser sacrifices, often not felt to be such by those concerned, in order to prevent our being swamped with incompetence. It is better for all the world, if instead of waiting to execute degenerate offspring for crime, or to let them starve for their imbecility, society can prevent those who are manifestly unfit from continuing their kind. The principle that sustains compulsory vaccination is broad enough to cover cutting the Fallopian Tubes. . . . Three generations of imbeciles are enough.[78]

Although later critics, unconvinced by Holmes' analogies, continue to press for reconsideration of this decision, *Buck* v. *Bell* remains as the binding legal authority regarding the fundamental constitutionality of sterilization as a state power. This early case has so pervasively influenced the field that none of the later decisions have considered the scientific validity of the eugenicists' claims, relying instead on the court's decision that this question is within the sole province of the legislatures.[79] Therefore, while the substantive due process arguments may still carry moral force and appeal, they have not yet swayed the courts.

The argument that involuntary sterilization constitutes "cruel and unusual punishment"[80] has been similarly unfruitful. The courts have avoided the constitutional confrontation by characterizing the insane and feebleminded as noncriminals and the operation as nonpunitive. Since sterilization is designed for social improvement and not punishment, the courts hold, it is not subject to the limitations imposed upon criminal punishment. By this semantic device, courts have also sustained the sterilization of convicted criminals if the purpose behind the practice was allegedly eugenic rather than punitive.[81] Only two courts (both federal) have held that the operation is unconstitutionally cruel punishment of criminal offenders.[82] One of these reasoned that the result of the operation would "follow the man during the balance of his life. The physical suffering may not be so great, but that is not the only test of cruel punishment; the humiliation, the degradation, the mental suffering are always present and known by all the public, and will follow him wheresoever he may go. This be-

[78] Buck v. Bell, 274 U.S. 200, 207 (1927).

[79] *Mentally Disabled and the Law* 188 (Lindman and McIntyre eds.).

[80] U.S. *Const.*, amend. VIII: "Excessive bail shall not be required, nor excessive fines imposed, nor cruel and unusual punishments inflicted."

[81] State v. Troutman, 50 Idaho 673, 299 P. 668 (1931); *in re* Main, 162 Okla. 65, 19 P.2d 153 (1933).

[82] Davis v. Berry, 216 F. 413 (S.D. Iowa 1914); Mickle v. Henrichs, 262 F. 687 (D. Nev. 1918).

longs to the Dark Ages."[83] Because of *Buck* v. *Bell*, however, these decisions no longer have any effect.

The same federal court which held that sterilization was cruel and unusual punishment has also been the only tribunal in America to invalidate the practice as a violation of the constitutional prohibition against bills of attainder—legislation which imposes summary punishment upon named or identifiable individuals without the benefit of a judicial inquiry in each case.[84] The question arose when a twice-convicted felon was confronted with a mandatory vasectomy. After noting that all twice-convicted felons would be subject to sterilization without a public hearing, without judicial process, and without medical discretion, the court concluded: "One of the rights of every man of sound mind is to enter into the marriage relation. Such is one of his civil rights, and deprivation or suspension of any civil right for past conduct is punishment for such conduct, and this fulfills the definition of a bill of attainder, because a bill of attainder is a legislative act which inflicts punishment without a jury trial."[85] Most courts, however, answer this argument by holding that sterilization is nonpunitive and therefore cannot form the basis for a bill of attainder.

The weight of legal authority also holds that sterilization does not constitute a denial of equal protection of law as guaranteed by the Fourteenth Amendment.[86] Attacks on that ground have been predicated upon the limitation of sterilization in many statutes to institutionalized patients only, thus leaving unaffected uninstitutionalized persons with similar disorders. Such a discrimination against institutionalized persons can have no rational basis, since the whereabouts of a mental defective is not related to his eugenic defect; if anything, the noninstitutionalized defective is more dangerous to the race from a genetic point of view because of his wider social contacts, general liberty of movement, and unsupervised behavior. Since the differentiation between institutionalized and noninstitutionalized patients is unrelated to the stated purpose of the law, it violates the equal protection clause, which states that the legislative designation of classes to which any given law becomes applicable must have a reasonable foundation.

[83] 216 F., 416.
[84] *U.S. Const.*, art. I, §9: "No Bill of Attainder or ex post facto law shall be passed."
[85] Davis v. Berry, 216 F. 413, 419 (S.D. Iowa 1914).
[86] Smith v. Command, 231 Mich. 409, 204 N.W. 140 (1925); Buck v. Bell, 274 U.S. 200 (1927).

Provisions in various state laws for the sterilization of criminals have been attacked on the grounds that they unreasonably distinguish between closely related classes of criminals for whom the eugenic arguments for sterilization are equally persuasive. These attacks had been upheld in only a small number of state cases where the courts agreed that the sterilization programs affected only a segment of those who should properly come under them according to the stated purposes of the statutes.[87] However, Justice Holmes, again in the seminal decision of *Buck* v. *Bell*, repudiated these conclusions, stating that "the law does all that is needed when it does all it can, indicates a policy, applies it to all within the lines, and seeks to bring within the lines all similarly situated so far and so fast as its means allow."[88]

On the question of equal protection, the most important decision was made by the United States Supreme Court in *Skinner* v. *Oklahoma*.[89] Skinner had been convicted once of chicken stealing and twice of armed robbery. He was ordered sterilized under the Oklahoma law authorizing sterilization of habitual criminals. Taking notice that the Oklahoma statute exempted various offenses, including embezzlement, violation of prohibition laws, and political offenses, from the sterilization sanction, the Supreme Court held the law unconstitutional. Larceny and embezzlement are intrinsically similar, the court said, and when the law "lays an unequal hand on those who have committed intrinsically the same quality of offense and sterilizes one and not the other, it has made as invidious a discrimination as if it had selected a particular race or nationality for oppressive treatment."[90] Although the court in *Skinner* displayed a discomfort regarding the fundamental propriety of sterilization, society's power to utilize it has not been disestablished.

The Procedural Attack

The constitutional validity of a sterilization program hinges not only on the substantive propriety of the operation but also on the fairness of the procedures which lead to the operation. A person's

---

[87] Osborn v. Thomson, 103 Misc. 23, 169 N.Y.S. 638 (Sup. Ct.), *aff'd.* 185 App. Div. 902, 171 N.Y.S. 1094 (1918); Haynes v. Lapeer Circuit Judge, 201 Mich. 138, 166 N.W. 938 (1918); Smith v. Board of Examiners of Feeble-minded, 85 N.J.L. 46, 88 A. 963 (1913).

[88] Buck v. Bell, 274 U.S. 200, 208 (1927).

[89] 316 U.S. 535 (1942).

[90] *Ibid.* 541.

rights and privileges must not be affected except in accordance with certain minimum standards of procedure.

The Supreme Court has never determined the minimum procedural standards for sterilization. In criminal proceedings, the court has long held that due process demands adherence to definite requirements. Among these are the accused's right to counsel,[91] his right to adequate notice of charges,[92] his right to a public trial, and the opportunity to be heard in his defense.[93] Since a sterilization proceeding is nonpenal in nature,[94] however, these requirements of criminal justice are generally held to be unnecessary.

The Supreme Court did comment broadly on the Virginia procedure in *Buck* v. *Bell.* "There can be no doubt that so far as procedure is concerned the rights of the patient are most carefully considered ... there is no doubt that in that respect ... [he] ... has had due process of law."[95] The Virginia form could well serve, therefore, as a starting point in determining the standards which must be attained. This procedure, as described in *Buck* v. *Bell,* can be summarized as follows:

(1) *Commencement*—The superintendent of the institution in which the patient is committed files a petition, accompanied by affidavit, stating the facts which led to his conclusion that the welfare of society would be enhanced if the individual were sterilized.

(2) *Hearing Agency*—A special board receives the superintendent's petition and holds a hearing on the matter. All evidence and findings of the board must be reduced to writing.

(3) *Notice*—Notice of the petition and of the hearing are to be given to the individual and to his guardian. If there is no guardian, the superintendent must have one appointed by the county court.

(4) *Hearing*—The individual may attend the hearing if he or his guardian so desire.

(5) *Appeal*—If sterilization is ordered by the board, the inmate or his guardian may appeal the decision to the county court. The

---

[91] Powell v. Alabama, 287 U.S. 45 (1932); Gideon v. Wainwright, 372 U.S. 335 (1963).

[92] Powell v. Alabama, 287 U.S. 45 (1932).

[93] *In re* Oliver, 333 U.S. 257 (1948).

[94] Buck v. Bell, 274 U.S. 200, 207 (1927); *in re* Main, 162 Okla. 65, 19 P.2d 153, 155 (1933). This nonpenal character precludes the application of the Eighth Amendment's prohibition against cruel and unusual punishment because the constitutional inhibition has reference only to penal sanctions.

[95] 274 U.S. 200, 207 (1927).

court may review the order of the board upon its record and may hear any other admissible evidence. The court may revise, affirm, or reverse the order. An appeal from the county court may also be taken to the Supreme Court of Appeals, but unlike the appeal from the board's decision, granting this appeal is discretionary with the Supreme Court.[96]

The Supreme Court's decision that the Virginia procedures satisfied due process requirements has been supplemented by several state decisions. A North Carolina case held that the sterilization of a mentally defective person without notice or hearing violated due process requirements.[97] An Indiana decision invalidated a sterilization order where the inmate was not accorded an opportunity to cross-examine the experts who decided upon the operation, or to controvert their decision that he was within the applicable statutory class.[98] The Washington Supreme Court voided a procedure which did not afford the patient an opportunity for notice and a hearing but instead provided an opportunity for appeal from the sterilization board to the courts.[99] Conflicting opinions have been rendered on the patient's right to both an administrative hearing and a judicial appeal. Kansas has held that the right to appeal was not essential if notice and a hearing before the administrative tribunal were granted.[100] The Alabama Supreme Court, however, has held that both an administrative hearing and a subsequent right to judicial review were essential.[101]

Comparing the procedures of many of the existing sterilization statutes with the Virginia process (as approved by the United States Supreme Court), it is apparent that several of the prevailing procedures offer substantially less protection and therefore might not meet the minimum requisites of due process. The Delaware sterilization statute,[102] for example, does not provide for a hearing, nor does it provide for a complete *de novo* judicial determination of the sterilization order. Twenty-five persons were sterilized under the procedure in 1963 and Delaware is the only state which has shown a significant increase in the number of sterilizations performed per year.[103]

[96] *Ibid*, 206.
[97] Brewer v. Valk, 204 N.C. 186, 167 S.E. 638 (1933); *but see* Garcia v. State Dept. of Institutions, 36 Cal. App. 2d 152, 97 P.2d 264 (Dist. Ct. App. 1939).
[98] Williams v. Smith, 190 Ind. 526, 131 N.E. 2 (1921).
[99] *In re* Hendrickson, 12 Wash. 2d 600, 123 P.2d 322 (1942).
[100] State *ex rel.* Smith v. Schaffer, 126 Kan. 607, 270 P. 604 (1928).
[101] *In re* Opinion of the Justices, 230 Ala. 543, 162 So. 123 (1935).
[102] *Del. Code Ann.* tit. 16, §5701 (1953).
[103] Ferster, "Eliminating the Unfit" 591, 633, app. C, pt. 2.

The practice in many states of giving notice of the impending operation only to the inmate is similarly inadequate. The purpose of a notice requirement is to apprise the person that his rights may be curtailed for a specific reason at a designated future hearing and to allow him time to prepare and present his defense. Service of such notice on the institutionalized patient alone is obviously inadequate, for generally he will be incapable of comprehending the nature and consequences of the hearing. To safeguard the patient's rights, it is essential to have counsel or a guardian appointed to protect his interests.

Concern with the inadequacies of present procedural safeguards was expressed by the Task Force on Law of the President's Panel on Mental Retardation: "The procedures by which selection for sterilization is made vary widely. In practice, great discretion is placed in the superintendent of the institution. Legal protections for the patient range from the slightest to a very careful system of judicial review. In view of the general irreversibility of sterilization, no laxity in protecting the retarded can be allowed."[104]

The implementation procedures of the sterilization statutes which seek to buttress their legality by requiring the consent of the patient, his parent, or his representative should also be carefully scrutinized. The "voluntariness" of such consents cannot always be accepted at face value.[105] It is questionable whether consent merely by some member of the family should be sufficient authorization. The American Bar Foundation, in its report on the rights of the mentally ill, commented as follows:

> The value of consent by an incompetent patient is highly questionable. If the patient is incompetent, should consent be given by a relative? It is possible that relatives may simply ratify the hospital's advice without realizing that further investigation may show the hospital's opinion to be unjustified. There are of course many patients who are competent. However, one wonders how "voluntary" the consent actually is if the patient believes that release from the hospital is dependent upon his consent to the operation. There is little doubt that the patient would be better protected if an attorney participated in all sterilization proceed-

[104] President's Panel on Mental Retardation, *Report of the Task Force on Law* 23 (1963).

[105] The meaning of voluntariness may require careful evaluation in the face of the 1942 reports from the San Quentin Prison that the prison surgeon vasectomized over 628 inmates at their own request. Smith, "Constitutional Law: Validity of Statute Providing for Sterilization of Habitual Criminals," 30 *Calif. L. Rev.* 189, 191 n. 17 (1942).

ings. The lack of representation by counsel is undoubtedly a partial explanation for the infrequency of legal contests in the scrilization area.[106]

THE RECORD OF STERILIZATION IN AMERICA

In the heyday of the eugenic movement, a model law was proposed which would have extended sterilization to inebriates, drug addicts, the tuberculous, the leprous, the blind, the deaf, the crippled, those with chronic and infectious diseases, homeless paupers, tramps, and ne'er-do-wells.[107] Fortunately, no American legislature embraced eugenics to this extent. Neither did the courts. Although there are in this country millions of institutionalized and noninstitutionalized mentally ill, mentally deficient, and epileptic patients, as well as various groups of sexual and "hereditary" offenders who could be subjected to sterilization, probably fewer than 70,000 persons have been involuntarily sterilized since the turn of the century. By comparison, when the German sterilization law came into force in July 1934, an estimated 400,000 persons were subject to its provisions, and it is estimated that within a year 150,000 of these had been sterilized.[108] A fear of similar zealousness did exist in many American circles. Justice Douglas appropriately warned that "the power to sterilize may have subtle, far-reaching and devastating effects. In evil and reckless hands it can cause races or types which are inimical to the dominant group to wither and disappear."[109]

In practice, the number of involuntary sterilizations has declined in recent years.[110] The immediate cause for this decline is that eleven states appear to have permitted their sterilization laws to become completely dormant, having reported (as of 1966) no operations for several years,[111] while eight other states make little use of their

[106] *Mentally Disabled and the Law* 190 (Lindman and McIntyre eds.).
[107] H. H. Laughlin, *Eugenic Sterilization in the United States* 446–47 (1922).
[108] Kapp, "Legal and Medical Aspects of Eugenic Sterilization in Germany," *Amer. Sociol. Rev.* 761–77 (October 1936).
[109] Skinner v. Oklahoma, 316 U.S. 535, 541 (1942).
[110] From 1907 to 1964, an estimated total of 63,678 persons have been sterilized under the various statutes. Of these, 24,716 were males and 38,962 females. The deceleration of the rate of sterilization is illustrated by comparing the total of 11,555 persons who were sterilized in the eight years between 1928 and 1935 with the 5,390 sterilizations which occurred in the nine-year period from 1956 to 1964. In 1963 there were only 467 sterilizations compared to 1,638 in 1943. Bligh, "Sterilization and Mental Retardation," 51 *A.B.A.J.* 1059 (1965).
[111] Alabama, Arizona, Kansas, Montana, Oklahoma, West Virginia, Minnesota, New Hampshire, North Dakota, Utah, and Vermont. Ferster, "Eliminating the Unit" 633, app. C, pt. 2.

sterilization procedures, each reporting fewer than half a dozen operations a year. Of the 467 operations performed in 1963, more than half occurred in North Carolina (240), with Virginia (30), Michigan (33), Iowa (30), Delaware (25), Oregon (23), and California (17) being the other major contributors to the total.[112]

The basic cause for the decline in the number of sterilizations, however, is scientific disaffection with the operation, in part predicated upon challenges to the eugenic movement and its fundamental premises: that modern scientific advances have facilitated the survival of the unfit and that, in the absence of social prophylactics, the procreation and propagation of the mentally unfit will become a threat to the existence of the race.[113] In 1943 Dr. Abraham Myerson discounted the threat of inundation by the feebleminded and those with other inherited disorders, citing several countervailing forces:[114] low marriage rates among those suffering from the serious and transmittable mental diseases due to their unattractiveness to the population at large; a lower sexual drive in the mentally disordered compared with the population at large; a higher divorce rate among those afflicted with mental disease because of personality and temperamental inadequacies; a poorer general health record of those with mental disease and a concomitantly higher death rate; and a lower birth rate among the mentally ill and the mentally deficient. (See however, the reference to Slovenko on p. 329 below.) Dr. Myerson stated that the apparent increase in mental deficiency during recent decades can be explained by the fact that mental defectives are more noticeable in a modern industrialized society than in a pastoral environment. "A feebleminded shepherd would not be particularly noticed, but a moron trying to operate machinery would show his defectiveness quickly."[115] More than thirty years ago, the American Neurological Association's Committee for the Investigation of Eugenic Sterilization, after careful study, found no evidence of an increase in mental illness or mental deficiency resulting in "biological deterioration of the race."[116]

[112] Human Betterment Association for Voluntary Sterilization, Inc. of America, reported in *ibid.* 591, 633.

[113] American Neurological Association, Committee for the Investigation of Eugenic Sterilization, *Eugenic Sterilization* 24–25 (1936); Cook, "Eugenics or Euthenics," 37 *Ill. L. Rev.* 287 (1943).

[114] Myerson, "Certain Medical and Legal Phases of Eugenic Sterilization," 52 *Yale L. J.* 627 (1943).

[115] *Ibid.* 628.

[116] American Neurological Association, *Eugenic Sterilization* 56, cited in Ferster, "Eliminating the Unfit" 602.

Criticism has also been directed at the eugenicists' emphasis upon heredity. Heredity, the critics assert, should not be overstated as a factor in mental illness, mental deficiency, or epilepsy. Admitting that genetically determined characteristics probably contribute to mental illness "in an infinitely subtle and complex manner," the experts nevertheless conclude that "the causal responsibility of heredity has not been fixed with any certainty."[117] Considering the current lack of knowledge of the etiology of the two major mental diseases, schizophrenia and manic-depressive psychosis, the claim that the foundation of mental illness is hereditary remains precarious. With regard to mental retardation, it is observed that in "some instances inheritance may be a primary factor, but to conclude, in general, that heredity is primarily responsible for most cases . . . would be to go far beyond the available evidence."[118] The American Bar Foundation has commented that "while there is sufficient evidence to show that mentally deficient persons have more subnormal children than do persons of normal intelligence, it is also recognized that, in addition to the hereditary factor, there are other causes for mental deficiency, including birth injuries and thyroid deficiency."[119] Also questionable is the ancient belief that epilepsy is inheritable. Geneticists have shown that some but not all forms of the disease are inherited. Once it was incurable and completely debilitating, but advances in medical treatment now afford a normal life to 80 percent of all epileptics.[120]

Sterilization has also been challenged on the ground of its inefficacy. Even if the scientific evidence of hereditary defects were conclusive, an effective program of social controls must nevertheless rely on our ability to identify the groups which carry these dangerous hereditary genes. Yet it has been estimated that 89 percent of all mental deficiency is transmitted by those not so afflicted themselves.[121] These outwardly normal carriers cannot be readily identified or segregated by means of existing medical science. Consequently, even if all known defectives could be sterilized, there would be only an 11 percent reduction of mental deficiency in the subsequent generation. Mental

---

[117] R. J. Plunkett and J. E. Gordon, *Epidemiology and Mental Illness* 30 (1960); *see also* South Dakota Medical Association, Mental Health Committee, *Explanation of Proposed S. D. Mental Health Act* 9 (1959). For a review of other critical writings *see* Ferster, "Eliminating the Unfit" 603.

[118] M. Hutt and R. Gibby, *The Mentally Retarded Child* 219 (1958).

[119] *Mentally Disabled and the Law* 186 (Lindman and McIntyre eds.).

[120] R. L. Barrow and H. D. Fabing, *Epilepsy and the Law,* 2, 7–8 (1966); *Mentally Disabled and the Law* 187 (Lindman and McIntyre eds.).

[121] Deutsch, *Mentally Ill in America* 373, 374.

deficiency could not be significantly diminished through such limited procedures alone.

Should it ever be possible to identify all carriers of mental defects, the enormity of the required sterilization program would be socially unbearable. Because of the nature of heredity, recessive as well as dominant traits may be carried on to future generations. Since as many as 89 percent of all feebleminded children come from normal parents,[122] a truly comprehensive and effective program of social selection and sterilization would assume intolerable magnitudes and would involve the sterilization "not only of persons who themselves are mentally deficient . . . but also of carriers of defectiveness who are phenotypically normal. It has been estimated that the normal carriers are from ten to thirty times more numerous than the affected persons. This would involve the sterilization of . . . at least 10% of the population."[123]

If such a program could be carried out, however, some critics of eugenics argue that the result could well be a backfiring disaster, eliminating along with the undesirable traits some elements of mankind's genetic bank essential to its survival. "We have come to recognize that the balance of a race is dependent upon the contributions which all types of individuals . . . make as a composite heterogeneous mass to what we call normalcy. The genes that are transmitted from people who are retarded in their intelligence may be just as important and valid towards the future fertility of the race as those of the community which is highly intelligent."[124]

As sterilization for genetic reasons has gradually waned in promise, "social eugenics" has similarly lost its appeal. The sterilization of those social or environmentally unfit for parenthood has been criticized as a crass and selfish program of public control thinly disguised as a therapeutic and scientific endeavor,[125] a selective process of control over the poor and socioeconomically disadvantaged, and a cheap way to eliminate society's stepchildren. Such programs are especially re-

[122] Fisher, "Elimination of Mental Defect," *J. Heredity* 529 (1927); Note, "Human Sterilization" 251, 254.

[123] Wallin, "Mental Deficiency," *J. Clinical Psychology* 153 (1956).

[124] Dr. David Thomas, in Paul, "State Eugenic Sterilization Laws" 201–2.

[125] "In my 20 years of psychiatric work with thousands of children and their parents, I have seen percentally at least as many 'intelligent' adults unfit to rear their offspring as I have seen such 'feebleminded' adults. I have . . . come to the conclusion that to a large extent independent of the I.Q., fitness for parenthood is determined by emotional involvements and relationships." L. Kanner, *A Miniature Textbook of Feeblemindedness* 4–5 (1949).

pugnant in America's present state of affluence. No such drastic curtailment of one's procreative power is justified, the critics say, until
"all reasonable attempts at improving the environment and rehabilitation of the disabled" have failed or until "food and air shortages . . .
become so severe that there might not be enough to bear the burden
of any further growth in population."[126]

Yet despite the disaffection with sterilization, scientific support for
such programs continues to appear. In early 1967, a National Institutes of Health scientist reported new evidence that heredity plays an
important role in causing schizophrenia, the nation's major psychosis,
affecting about 1 percent of the population. According to Dr. David
Rosenthal, a child with two schizophrenic parents is 35 times more
likely to become schizophrenic than a child with two normal parents.
While agreeing that environment may influence the fate of children,
he nevertheless felt that "a jump of this magnitude almost certainly
reflects a genetic factor."[127] Nearly concurrently, Professor Slovenko
reasserted the parental inadequacy of the mentally unfit:

> Mentally defective persons, and the severely mentally ill, have
> more children than the average. They are usually poor individuals,
> with little sense of responsibility and with the ability to do little
> more than procreate. They may not know what they are doing
> and they may not enjoy their children. Sexual promiscuity and a
> high rate of illegitimate pregnancies among defective females are
> well-known facts. Such behavior is not due to increase in sexual
> drives, but rather to lack of judgment, impulsiveness, suggesti-
> bility, and inability to resist victimization.[128]

The proponents of selective and carefully supervised sterilization
emphasize its apparent advantages. They stress that sterilization may
often be a preferable substitute for indeterminate institutionalization,
that mentally defective inmates might be entitled to release and
possibly even marriage if the burdens of pregnancy and child-rearing
could be removed.[129]

Where eugenic surgical sterilization is not practiced because the
medical staff believes that the law does not allow it, or because

---

[126] Forster, "Eliminating the Unfit" 000.

[127] *Washington Post*, March 22, 1967, p. 43.

[128] Slovenko, "A Panoramic View," in *Sexual Behavior and the Law* 102 (R.
Slovenko ed. 1965). The reference to the feebleminded who produce large
families is apparently directed to the morons and borderline groups, since idiots
and many imbeciles are sterile. H. I. Clarke, *Social Legislation* 185 (1940).

[129] An interesting analysis of interviews with mentally retarded patients who
had been sterilized prior to discharge is reported by Sabagh and Edgerton, "Steri-

they do not approve of it because of medical, social or religious beliefs, there may be a question of whether patients who are involuntarily institutionalized for life would be discharged if surgical sterilization were performed; therefore, the issue then becomes the question of whether the eugenic sterilization is being accomplished by institutionalization, that is by segregation, rather than by surgery.[130]

The control of procreation through sterilization differs only in technique from the state laws which seek to prevent undesired births by prohibiting the marriage of mentally retarded or defective persons.[131] Indeed, sterilization may be a less drastic sanction, for it would permit these persons to partake more fully of the normal experiences of life.[132]

This is the ostensible philosophy behind the most recent legal development in the area of sterilization. In states lacking specific sterilization laws or in instances not covered by law, some courts have proceeded to authorize the operation on a nonprotested basis; that is, a court will order sterilization if approved by a parent or guardian or if the patient himself agrees to it as an alternative to a criminal sentence or civil commitment. Some Ohio probate courts, for example, have recently exercised this power as part of their overall supervision over the mentally retarded, ordering sterilization of such persons who could not be institutionalized for lack of space.[133] In a recent case, the

---

lized Mental Defectives Look at Eugenic Sterilization," 9 *Eugenics Q.* 212 (1962). The authors emphasize the need to study the role of sterilization in hindering or facilitating the adjustment in the community.

[130] Birnbaum, "Eugenic Sterilization," 175 *J.A.M.A.* 951 (1961).

[131] W. M. Gallichan, *The Sterilization of the Unfit* 94 (1929). Some eighteen states prohibit such marriages: Iowa, Pennsylvania, South Dakota, Delaware, Indiana, Kansas, Maine, Minnesota, Missouri, Montana, New Hampshire, New Jersey, North Carolina, North Dakota, Vermont, Virginia, Washington, and Wisconsin. Bass, "Marriage for the Mentally Deficient," 2 *Mental Retardation* 198, 202 (1964). Another researcher reports that by the mid-30s some 41 states prohibited marriage of the insane and feebleminded, 17 prohibited marriage of epileptics, and 4 barred drunkards from marriage. Paul, "State Eugenic Sterilization Laws" 155.

[132] "The sole purpose of the laws denying marriage for the retarded appears to be the prevention of the birth of children to those who are unable to care for them, or to prevent the transmission of the defect in cases of hereditary mental deficiency. More liberal laws could accomplish this same purpose by allowing the retarded to marry if they had been sterilized." Bass, "Marriage" 202. "There is no difference between compulsory sterilization and compulsory segregation. The latter quite effectively takes away sexual freedom and destroys procreation." J. Fletcher, *Morals and Medicine* 168 (1960).

[133] *See, e.g.*, *in re* Simpson, 180 N.E.2d 206 (Ohio S.Ct. 1962); Note, "Sterilization of Mental Defectives," 61 *Mich. L. Rev.* 1359 (1963).

mother of two unmarried female retardees, 19 and 22 years old, found her daughters pregnant and asked the doctors to protect them against future pregnancies through sterilization. Uncertain of the legal issues involved, the doctors sought judicial assistance. Upon the mother's affidavit asserting the daughters' feeblemindedness and granting her consent to sterilization and a court hearing (in which a psychologist reported I.Q.'s of 35 and 44 for the daughters), the judge authorized the operation. Noting that the state school for the mentally retarded was filled, the judge concluded:

> Due to their physical attractiveness and considering their mental capacity and further considering the medical testimony these girls would in all probability continue to be promiscuous and likely to again become pregnant. There is still the probability that such offspring would be mentally deficient and become public charges the same as the two young mothers are at the present time. This would present an additional burden upon the mother, State and County Welfare Departments, where support payments have of necessity been reduced due to lack of funds.[134]

While the opinion speaks first to the therapeutic considerations for sterilizing the sisters, it is significant that the "additional burden upon the State and County Welfare Departments" in times of fiscal stress weighs equally heavy in the judge's decision to authorize the operation.

In California, judges have offered convicted individuals lower sentences and probation on condition that they submit to sterilization. Most of these individuals are on welfare or are drawing aid for dependent illegitimate children. The first of these was *in re* Andrada,[135] where a man convicted of nonsupport was placed on probation after consenting to a vasectomy, consenting to marry the woman with whom he was currently living, and agreeing to contribute partially to the support of his four welfare-receiving children by another woman. In *People* v. *Tapia*,[136] the female defendant and her male accomplice were convicted of welfare fraud. They were given reduced sentences and placed on probation after submitting to sterilization.

In May 1966, Mrs. Nancy Hernandez was convicted of being in a

---

[134] Quoted in Paul, "State Eugenic Sterilization Laws" 597A; *see also* Gavnor, "Mansflied Supports Sisters' Sterilization, *Akron Beacon-Journal*, February 20, 1966, p. A1.

[135] 33 U.S. Law Week 3278 (1965), *cert. denied* 380 U.S. 953 (1965).

[136] Record Case no. 73313, Santa Barbara Sup. Ct., July 7, 1965.

place where marijuana was in use—a misdemeanor. She was given a suspended sentence and placed on probation upon condition that she be sterilized. When she refused to go through with the operation, the judge revoked her probation and sentenced her to jail. Mrs. Hernandez was the mother of two children and received welfare for one of them—an illegitimate child—and herself. In the judge's opinion, Mrs. Hernandez was a proper subject for sterilization because of "her propensity to lead an immoral life," and because she was "in danger of continuing to live a dissolute life and to be endangering the health, safety and lives of her minor children."[137] The Superior Court of Santa Barbara County, on appeal, vacated the sentence and remanded Mrs. Hernandez into the custody of her probation officer under the terms of the earlier order with the notable exception of the sterilization requirement, holding that such a condition to probation was beyond the power of the court and therefore void.[138]

The courts are not alone in looking to sterilization as a cure for rising welfare costs. Recent proposals in four state legislatures have in one way or another attempted to make sterilization a prerequisite to welfare payments for mothers of illegitimate children,[139] and similar suggestions have been made by public officials in three others.[140] Recently, about 20 percent of the persons interviewed in a Gallup Poll indicated that women who receive aid for dependent children and continue to bear illegitimate children should be sterilized.[141]

These court decisions, legislative proposals, and popular sentiments are in no way connected with previous human selection theories— hereditary or environmental. They are clearly motivated by immediate fiscal considerations, not by hopes for an improved populace sometime in the future. The feeling seems to be that three generations of welfare recipients is enough. Significantly, the prevalence of sterilization in the past has shown itself related not only to scientific fashion, but also to fluctuating economic situations. The Depression, for example, brought on a rapid increase in the rate of sterilization in Kan-

[137] *Washington Post*, May 25, 1966, p. A9.

[138] *In re* Hernandez, Record Case no. 76757, Santa Barbara Sup. Ct., June 8, 1966, *contra*, People v. Blankenship, 16 Cal. App. 2d 68, 61 P.2d 352 (1936). *See also* California, Legislature, Assembly, Interim Committee on Judicial System and Judicial Process, *Preliminary Report of the Subcommittee on Sex Crimes* 52 (Sacramento, 1950); K. M. Bowman, *Sexual Deviation Research* 70 (Report to California Assembly, March 1952).

[139] Delaware, Maryland, Mississippi, and North Carolina. Paul, "The Return of Punitive Sterilization Proposals," 3 *Law & Soc. Rev.* 77 (1968).

[140] *Ibid.* They are Georgia, Illinois, and Iowa.

[141] *Washington Post*, January 27, 1965, p. A2.

sas. Nearly 2,000 operations were reported in the decade 1932–42, compared with a mere trickle before that.[142] It now seems that as we pass through a period of ballooning social welfare costs, at least some authorities may seek to invoke sterilization as a means of weathering the crisis.

THE LESSONS OF THE OLD THERAPIES

How compatible are sterilization, shock therapy, and lobotomy with current views of ordered liberty and fundamental fairness? What needs or conditions of a progressive society justify these drastic therapies? Should society be permitted to utilize sterilization in order to

prevent the entrance into our society of offspring who because of the hereditary or environmental effects of the parents' mental disorders will be too socially inadequate to be able to stay out of a penal institution; too socially inadequate to be able to earn a minimum livelihood so as not to be a burden upon the state; too socially inadequate to be able to conform to the publicly proclaimed sex mores that are often not followed in private life; or, too socially inadequate to be able to achieve some other goal of our culture?[143]

Should lobotomy and shock therapy be approved as a means for guaranteeing tranquility and order?

What is clearly needed is a rational and fair line against societal excesses,[144] remembering that in a pluralistic society such as the United States variation and contrasts must be promoted rather than suppressed. Seeking to draw a line against undue interference with the individual in the names of predicted antisociality and social defense, Professor Slovenko suggests:

Whether a disorder or disturbance is the produce of nature or nurture, the application of statistics to the individual case is hazardous, especially when the statistics leave much to be desired. . . . Sterilization should not be employed as a means of racial improvement, but only for individual medical reasons, as for example, in the case of a woman for whom further pregnancy would prove dangerous. As a general statement, it might be said

[142] Paul, "State Eugenic Sterilization Laws" 620, 627.

[143] Birnbaum, "Eugenic Sterilization" 951, 965.

[144] "Eugenics for general improvement does not mean trust the state or any other authority with some arbitrary power for deciding what are good and what are bad hereditary qualities." J. S. Huxley, *Evolution in Action* 133–34 (1957).

that physical illness should be the only consideration for sterilization.[145]

The preventive eugenic scheme of sterilization was upheld by the
Supreme Court in 1927 as within the ambit of the state's police
power.[146] In view of this dispositive holding of the Supreme Court,
any present contention to the contrary would be academic, unless the
court could be swayed to the position that what was recognized as
acceptable within the boundaries of ordered liberty in 1927 is no
longer tolerable today. It is a reasonable conclusion that, unless it is
demonstrated that no eugenic and social benefits will flow from
sterilization, the states cannot be denied their power to employ
sterilization for the advancement of eugenic selection. At present, the
evidence relied upon in *Buck* v. *Bell* remains strong. Although the
primacy of heredity in human character has been seriously attacked
in recent years, no responsible investigators reject heredity as at least
a partial cause in most mental and behavioral disorders.

Less clear and certain is the justification for sterilization where lack
of fitness for parenthood is due to social rather than genetic inadequacies. In essence, sterilization as a eugenic tool has been hitherto
justified primarily upon biological predictability. But reliance upon
such biological predictability as a premise for social action furnishes
little support for the use of sterilization where the parental stock is
lacking not biologically but in social or economic resources. Medical
and psychiatric evidence demonstrates that where the parental deprivation is more environmental than biological, predictability of the
progeny's social unfitness becomes much more speculative. Environmental enrichment, for both parent and child, seems preferable to
sterilization.

Probably the most compelling claim for involuntary sterilization is
the patient's therapeutic need. The therapeutic state has long substituted its judgment for that of the mentally unfit. Certainly, sterilization as a protection against therapeutically hazardous pregnancies by
mentally ill mothers cannot be viewed as less socially justified than
institutional incarceration. Even so, therapeutic sterilization must be
guardedly used lest it become a guise for other motivations.

Most questionable is the harnessing of sterilization in the service of
morality and the public purse. In a society of expanding public wel-

---

[145] Slovenko, "A Panoramic View" 103–4.
[146] Buck v. Bell, 274 U.S. 200 (1927).

fare, where guaranteed income is seriously debated, and racial integration is actively encouraged by sanctions of law, a program which will permanently deprive the poor, the promiscuous, or certain racial groups[147] of the power to procreate stands little chance of constitutional endorsement. In all likelihood, the suggestions in this direction represent little more than a passing middle-class resentment against the burdens of an increasingly socialized national order.

In the final analysis, sterilization will probably retain a limited role in the nonpenal scheme of the *parens patriae* state. But it is apparent that newer and possibly less drastic techniques are causing its continued decline.[148]

Similarly, but for different reasons, lobotomy and shock therapy will not become more widely used in the future. The therapeutic value of these techniques has been subjected to scientific scrutiny and found wanting. Moreover, moral questions involving their use are likely to confine them to the institution where they can be utilized without offending the public's conscience. However, it is equally likely that, as with sterilization, other more acceptable means will be found to accomplish results heretofore possible only through these treatments. It is with these new programs that society must be wary.

The American experience with lobotomy, shock therapy, and sterilization clearly demonstrates that the nonincarcerative therapies are subject to the same abuse and errors as various forms of confinement. They too suffer from overzealousness and a lack of substantive criteria and procedural safeguards. They too can be used for ends never envisioned by their creators. Sterilization can be used not to improve the race of man but simply to preserve the taxpayer's good offices toward the politician. These measures once received the praise of the scientific community as the panacea of social and mental ills, only to be recognized after closer inspection as being of limited use, and sometimes definitely undesirable. But after how many had been lobotomized, shocked, or sterilized? This is the fault not only of those who performed the operations but of the general failure to pro-

[147] While proof is absent, assertions are not lacking regarding the potential use of sterilization against Negroes. *See* Morrison, "Illegitimacy, Sterilization and Racism—A North Carolina Case History," 39 *Soc. Serv. Rev.* 1 (1965); Windle, "Factors in the Passage of Sterilization Legislation: The Case of Virginia," 29 *Pub. Opinion Q.* 306 (1965); Student Nonviolent Coordinating Committee, *Genocide in Mississippi* (1964).

[148] American Medical Association, Committee on Human Reproduction, "The Control of Fertility," 194 *J.A.M.A.* 462, 469 (1965).

vide a meaningful standard by which the wisdom and social justification for those operations could be measured. How does one count the
cost of our laxity: in years? in dollars? personalities? children?

It would be simple if we could say that all present nonincarcerative
treatments should be abolished and no more instituted. But this solution is unsatisfactory, for it precludes the continuation of the very real
contributions that science has heretofore bestowed upon man and
society. What is needed for the future is not repression but a legislative and administrative sophistication sadly lacking in the past.

The abuses of the existing programs must be eradicated, but the
real danger lies in the new therapies. Our past record with nonincarcerative treatments is such that we dare not allow any of the new
treatments to become generally endorsed as welfare measures or
social controls until more is known about them. Specifically, we must
be satisfied that the motive behind them is truly therapeutic and unlikely to be perverted; we must be satisfied that the means of application are not broader than necessary; we must be satisfied that the
therapy will be effective; and we must know the side effects of the
treatment so that we can judge whether the cost of the therapy is
worth the benefits to be derived.

The question of motive must be answered not only in the context
of contemporary thinking but also in terms of future uses. Before any
new program is made generally applicable, it must be clear that the
proposed treatment does not exceed what is necessary to effect the
goals set by society. No broad programs should be endorsed on
grounds that the therapists need the flexibility to accomplish their
task effectively. There is too much opportunity for abuse to sanction
such a gamble.

The treatment program must be shown to be capable of accomplishing the announced goals prior to implementation. Without this
assurance, the program may become an intervention into peoples'
lives and liberties for no acceptable purpose. The individual will have
been sacrificed, and society will have gained nothing.

Before any tampering is done with an individual's bodily or personality structure, the undesirable side effects of such interference
must be well known and properly weighed. No treatment should be
compelled unless the patient can be assured that he will not be injured or adversely affected beyond the extent necessary to accomplish
the therapeutic goal.

How can we guarantee that these requirements will be imposed
upon any new therapeutic nonincarcerative programs? How can we

guarantee that future administrators, seeking to implement their own goals, will not pervert these programs, broaden their scope and application, and ignore their detrimental aspects? It would be well if our legislators were as creative in the formation of safeguards as the scientists are in generating new programs and treatments, but they are not. Science has outstripped the legislative disciplines. We must therefore seek some comprehensive methods for maintaining liberty in the therapeutic state.

THE FUTURE OF HUMAN MODIFICATION

To what degree can the therapeutic state invade a person's bodily and personal integrity?[149] The limits imposed on the criminal process do not now exist in the therapeutic realm. But the development of applicable boundaries cannot be long overlooked. More than 25 years ago, Justice Jackson clearly warned that "there are limits to the extent to which a legislatively represented majority may conduct biological experiments at the expense of the dignity and personality and natural power of the minority."[150] Where are these limits to be drawn and by whom? A possible suggestion for the limits upon the powers of the therapeutic state may lie in the words of the Ninth Amendment to the United States Constitution: "The enumeration in the Constitution, of certain rights, shall not be construed to deny or disparage others retained by the people." Is there not inherent in this language a limitation upon the state's power to modify man?

[149] The potential for the social modification of man is only hinted at by the practice of sterilization. Recent chemical and biological research into the mysteries of DNA and the genetic code raises much more complex questions regarding the need for future legal controls. A popular assessment of the social implications of new scientific discoveries appeared in *Life*: "There is simply no calculating at this point the amount of benefit man might gain medically through his mastery of the genetic code. This mastery will not only permit him to improve the lot of individuals. By manipulating the DNA in human eggs and sperm cells, he may be able to correct genetic defects and thus save countless future generations from illness and premature death. Most scientists regard this potential as a mixed blessing, however, for if man can manipulate the genes of all humankind in this fashion, it means he can decide what characteristics he deems desirable in future generations and simply write the genetic messages into DNA.... The DNA molecule has been called the 'atom' of life. When man succeeds in harnessing *this* atom, the problems raised by the harnessing of the uranium atom will look simple indeed. As they contemplate the golden opportunities the new powers will give man, scientists also stop to think about the opportunities for the abuses of these powers—and, when they do, their thoughts sometimes make them shudder." "DNA's Code: Key to All Life," *Life* 70, 90 (October 4, 1963); *see also* I. Asimov, *The Genetic Code* (1962).

[150] Skinner v. Oklahoma, 316 U.S. 535, 546 (1942) (Jackson, J., concurring).

It is doubtful in the face of contradictory scientific evidence and the current social climate, that the state legislatures will seek to disturb the precarious legislative balance of sterilization by adding to it broader aims and powers of human modification. At the same time, in an age which extols the merits of birth control and psychochemistry, it would be anachronistic to deny society the power to control procreation and human modification altogether. Yet if eugenic considerations can supply lawful justifications for the State's exercise of this drastic sanction, should social or environmental considerations be accorded any less weight? How much evidence of a compelling public need and how clear a prediction of social evil should be the prerequisites for preventive social action?

If legislatures remain cautious, the authority for social experiments in human modification will rest with the administrative level, even though it is highly undesirable for drastic state power over procreation or other human modification to be invoked by experts and administrators without prior legislative deliberation and enactment. The future battles for the modification of man will therefore undoubtedly be fought in the judicial arena. There the due process requirements of the Fourteenth Amendment and the residual rights provisions of the Ninth Amendment are likely to provide the general frames of reference for creation of the appropriate balance between man and society.

If the individual's right to be left alone is to be protected, the searchlight of public scrutiny must be focused upon this long-ignored power to modify man. The traditional Anglo-American tools of judicial process and review provide some of the most effective means for scrutiny known in any social system. Applied to sterilization and other man-modifying programs, judicial review should aid in the development of the new legal standards for the therapeutic state. Here, as in the other realms covered in this book, the opportunity for frequent and open adversary judicial testing is the first line of defense against tyranny, zeal, and neglect, whether legislative, judicial, or administrative. Here, as in the other areas, the right to a day in court is an indispensable element for the healthy growth of the therapeutic state.

American experience with sterilization, shock therapy, and lobotomy demonstrates the difficulty in drawing a clear line between what the therapeutic state does *for* its wards and what it does *to* them. The distinction between the patient's therapeutic need and society's desire for defense is often confused. The old therapies also illustrate the problems inherent in any social program predicated upon a scientific theory, the validity of which has not been established in practice.[151] The great promise of eugenics to transform the race of man into a race of supermen and to rid society of dangerous deviants has proved empty. In part the failure is due to scientific invalidity; in greater part it is due to the fact that social misgivings deterred the theory's full implementation. Lobotomy was the tranquilizer of the furiously mad, but at the cost of various higher mental abilities. The lessons are very pertinent.

Adoption of a skeptical attitude is especially necessary in view of the claims being made for new techniques of mind and behavior control. Before new drastic methods are drafted for use in maintaining social order, they must be shown to comport with the acceptable aims of a pluralistic and individualistic society. In addition, to prevent the perversion of the powers granted under these programs, procedural safeguards must be vouchsafed in advance of their adoption. The lesson learned from experience demands nothing less.

[151] "The legal career of sterilization is thus a useful example, first, of the law too quickly adopting a popularized scientific promise without exposing it to adequate scrutiny, and second, of the law's consequent difficulty in keeping abreast of the revisions of scientific hypotheses." Kalvern, "A Special Corner of Civil Liberties: A Legal View," 31 *N.Y. U. L. Rev.* 1157, 1233–34 (1956).

8

The Therapeutic Ideal: The Evils of Unchecked Power

If we work out a system of making penal treatment fit the crime, we risk losing sight of the individual delinquent in pursuit of system. If we look only at the individual delinquent, we risk losing system in pursuit of individual treatment and lose the objectivity which is demanded when we are constraining the individual by the force of politically organized society. It comes down to the reconciling of the general security with the individual life, which as I have said, is a fundamental problem of the whole legal order.—R. Pound, "The Rise of Socialized Criminal Justice" (1942), in *Roscoe Pound and Criminal Justice* 186–87 (S. Glueck ed. 1965)

It gives us a nice warm feeling to talk about treating people rather than punishing offenses; but do not let us delude ourselves about it. It is comparatively easy, straightforward, precise, and measurable to punish offenses—an eye for an eye and a tooth for a tooth—whereas to understand and treat persons presupposes that we do in fact know how to diagnose and treat them and that we have the necessary facilities available. This is not a valid assumption.—Younghusband, "The Dilemma of the Juvenile Court," 33 *Soc. Serv. Rev.* 11 (1959)

... it may well be that the status of [involuntary] patient is half the disease.—B. Korn, quoted in Platt, "The Child Savers" 322 (1966)

DEVIATION AND THE THERAPEUTIC STATE

"The history of man," says Erich Kahler, "could very well be written as a history of the alienation of man."[1] Technological progress and material affluence have not made our families more cohesive, our streets safer, or the bonds of our social organization stronger. Despite the growing benefits of economic prosperity, the expansion of public welfare, and the strides toward social and racial equality, the United States suffers from many acute manifestations of social pathology.[2] Increasingly, the remedies of the therapeutic state rather than the traditional tools of the criminal process are being proposed as the more effective cures for these ills.

Crimes of violence against person and property are multiplying. Reported murders rose 50 percent, rapes 84 percent, and aggravated assaults 86 percent from 1960 to 1968.[3] Lesser crimes have grown at equal rates. In 1968 a total of more than 5.5 million arrests were reported, an increase of nearly 20 percent over 1960;[4] of those, nearly 1.5 million arrests were for drunkenness alone, over 300,000 for drunken driving, and some 600,000 for disorderly conduct. Nearly 100,000 persons were arrested for vagrancy (lacking a home and visible means of support), and another 100,000 were arrested for curfew and loitering law violations.[5]

Nor should criminal behavior be looked upon as the only manifestation of social pathology in the United States. Only a segment of the population's deviant behavior has traditionally been subject to the control of the criminal law. Many other forms of conduct that may adversely affect the public interest are tolerated or left to informal condemnation. Divorce rates are on the increase—nearly half a million divorces were reported in 1965. While the marriage rate has decreased since the turn of the century, the yearly divorce rate has grown from 1 per 1,000 population in 1915 to 2 in 1940 and to 2.7 in 1967.[6] Similarly revealing are the statistics of illegitimacy. More than 318,000 illegitimate children were born in America in 1967. From a 1940 figure of 7.1 illegitimate births per 1,000 unmarried women (between

---

[1] *The Tower and the Abyss* 43 (1956).

[2] For a decade-old study of social pathology in Great Britain *see* B. Wootton, *Social Science and Social Pathology* (1959).

[3] FBI, *Uniform Crime Reports for the United States* 8–11 (1969).

[4] *Ibid.* 33.

[5] *Ibid.* 110–11.

[6] U.S. Bureau of the Census, *Statistical Abstract of the United States* 47 (1969).

the ages of 15 and 44), the rate increased to 24.0 illegitimate births in 1967.[7] With the family structure so disrupted, it is not surprising that delinquency cases in the juvenile courts have increased from 10.5 cases per 1,000 juveniles in 1940 to 16.1 in 1950, 32.1 in 1960, and to 44.3 in 1967.[8] Arrests of juveniles under 18 years of age similarly increased by more than 100 percent from 1960 to 1968.[9]

Not all those who have been or may be described as deviants have come within the scope of the present study. We have not dealt with criminal deviation—that is, behavior which remains subject to traditional police and penal sanctions. Nor have we mentioned the types of deviation that may result in informal social control and condemnation, through family, school, church, or peer-group action. Hippies, Yippies, and nonworking coupon-clipping millionaires are excluded, as are bachelors, multidivorced persons, and most mothers of illegitimate children, even though each is certain to be looked upon with disdain by one social group or another. Our focus has been on the rapidly expanding group of deviates who are viewed as sufficiently dangerous or debilitated to be publicly controlled but who in growing numbers are being taken out of the criminal realm and placed under the controls of the therapeutic state.

The initial shift from penal to therapeutic controls, which we described as the divestment of criminal justice, has occurred primarily in areas where the offenders or deviants were considered either mentally abnormal (the mentally ill, the psychopaths, and, to a degree, alcoholics and drug addicts) or else chronologically immature (the juvenile delinquents). A combination of considerations made the *parens patriae* or therapeutic approach both more appealing and more relevant in the treatment of these groups. The growth of deterministic theories, both hereditary and environmental, with regard to human behavior made the classical criminal law seem irrelevant and futile. The moral standards of criminal responsibility (evidenced by the requirement of *mens rea*—a guilty mind or a consciousness of wrongdoing) seemed clearly inapplicable to offenders incapable of criminal intent.[10] Criminal sanctions, furthermore, appeared medically inappropriate and constitutionally improper for offenders who were

---

[7] *Ibid.* 50.

[8] *Ibid.* 151.

[9] FBI, *Uniform Crime Reports* 112 (1969).

[10] "To begin with, a punishment must involve an unpleasantness imposed upon a person in virtue of the fact that he is believed to have done some blameworthy action for which he was responsible when he acted. A treatment, on the other hand, need not involve an unpleasantness (although it may, as in the case of the

more ill than evil.[11] Finally, therapeutic controls (including the medically oriented indeterminate commitment) which were designed to fit the particular needs of the offender seemed to offer both a more personalized and more effective system of prevention and rehabilitation than the classical criminal law's insistence upon a punishment that fits the crime.

In a dramatic portrayal, Anthony Platt of the University of Chicago described the advent of the juvenile process:

> The child savers depicted delinquents as irresponsible and incapable of free choice, and as victims of uncontrollable forces.... With this emphasis upon predetermined as opposed to volitional conduct, there was an accompanying tendency to regard delinquents as psychologically incapacitated and therefore not responsible. As a consequence ... juvenile court judges were cast in the role of physicians whose task it was to diagnose social diseases and to recommend appropriate remedies.[12]

From time to time, the continuing dissatisfaction with the meager societal successes in controlling deviation is likely to produce demands for a return to the old-fashioned retributive criminal sanctions.[13] More often, though, this dissatisfaction is likely to be channeled into even greater efforts toward newer therapeutic programs, reputed to be more humane, scientific, and efficacious. The breadth of this dramatic change in orientation has been characterized by British writer and social reformer, Lady Barbara Wootton:

> Indeed, thanks to this development, it would seem that in the course of a couple of centuries some wheels have nearly come full circle. In the eighteenth century no clear distinction was drawn between the mentally afflicted and the criminal. Lunatics were treated more or less as criminals. In Paris the principal eighteenth century institutions for the care of the insane—the Biceth and the Salpetriere—were indifferently known as hospitals

---

tuberculosis victim); and assessments of responsibility and blameworthiness are simply irrelevant." Wasserstrom, "Why Punish the Guilty?" *Princeton Alumni Weekly*, March 17, 1964, p. 26.

[11] The Eighth Amendment to the Constitution prohibits cruel and unusual punishment and the courts have held that punishing for an illness violates the constitutional intent. *Cf.* Robinson v. California, 370 U.S. 660 (1962); Driver v. Hinnant, 356 F.2d 761 (4th Cir. 1966); Easter v. District of Columbia, 361 F.2d 50 (D.C. Cir. 1966).

[12] Platt, "The Child Savers" 300 (1966).

[13] *See, e.g.*, "Who Commits the Crimes?" *U.S. News & World Report*, May 8, 1967.

or as prisons. Today, for quite different reasons, the distinction between the two classes has once more become confused; but, instead of treating the lunatics as criminals, we now regard many criminals as lunatics, or at any rate as mentally disordered.[14]

The therapeutic state's recent history reveals, however, that the divestment of criminal justice and the concurrent therapeutic expansion have not always arisen, as they did in the case of insane and youthful offenders, from religious and humanitarian considerations or from a sense of wardship toward the disadvantaged. With regard to psychopaths, drug addicts, and the diverse candidates for sterilization, shock therapy, and lobotomy, divestment has not served primarily as a means for the removal of criminal stigmas from offenders who are not fully responsible for their actions. Instead, the *parens patriae* model has become a pragmatic tool for accomplishing under therapeutic auspices what could not be done at all in the criminal realm. Divestment has thus increasingly served as the vehicle for bringing into the American scene the social defense formulas advanced by the late nineteenth-century positive criminologists: the substitution of the indeterminate commitment that "fits the criminal" for the inadequate determinate sentence that merely "fits the crime"; orienting the process of sanctions toward the offender's total personal deficiency rather than toward the manifestations of the particular offense; placing greater emphasis upon who the deviate *is* and what his propensities are than upon his *overt* and antisocial past *act*; granting greater discretion to the treatment and correctional arms of the state, often represented by social and behavioral scientists, in formulating programs that might more effectively curb and modify deviant behavior.

Soon, however, society may be willing to extend further the divestment process and to exempt from criminal sanctions offenders for whom therapeutic treatments have never before been postulated. A test program recently instituted by the Manhattan Criminal Court will, for example, secure jobs or job training for selected defendants in criminal cases which will not be prosecuted. These defendants, neither juveniles nor mentally affected offenders, come from deprived socioeconomic backgrounds. In announcing the plan, Mayor John V. Lindsay described it as a bold experiment in rehabilitating "persons forced into crime by *economic* or *social pressures*."[15]

[14] Wootton, *Social Science and Social Pathology* 203.
[15] King, "Job, Not Jail, Due Under Plan Here," *New York Times*, May 14, 1967, p. 43 (emphasis added).

The divestment of criminal law is thus assuming dramatically new proportions. The earlier growth of the therapeutic state was very heavily endowed with psychological and psychiatric implications. When the mentally ill, the mentally defective, the juveniles, the psychopaths, the drug addicts, and the alcoholics were taken out of the penal process, it was on the premise that these classes were deprived of volition because of their innate mental deficiencies, and therefore could be and needed to be distinguished from the "normal" or "sane" offenders. To those from the sociologically or environmentally inclined disciplines, the therapeutic state was a symbol of medicine's usurpation of an area which required the contributions of more than a single discipline.[16] They were distressed at the therapeutic state's orientation, seeing it as a victory of nature over nurture, personality over culture, and eugenics over euthenics. Referring thus to recent efforts to excuse males having an XYY chromosomal irregularity from criminal responsibility, Leon S. Minckler of the Virginia Polytechnic Institute wrote:

> There is strong evidence that a tendency toward more aggressive or other types of behavior may be inherited in the normal way; that is, through genes. Suppose it is established that certain genes do predispose people toward forms of criminal behavior. Then will these people be excused as not being responsible for their acts? Does this mean that only behavior attributed to environment would be considered as responsible acts in the legal sense? Then who would decide between people responsible for their acts and people not responsible?[17]

Slowly, however, the balance has been shifting from the emphasis upon hereditary and constitutional factors. With increasing attention directed to poverty, the environmental disciplines are gaining increasing importance in the social plans for the explanation and control of deviation. It is to be expected, therefore, that environment, like mental defects in the past, will increasingly be suggested by determinists as a main cause for deviation and deviants. Indeed, environmental justifications of criminality have recently found increased acceptance as an explanation for the high crime rate among urban minority groups. Responding to a criticism that responsible Negro leaders stood mute during a Baltimore civil disturbance, a Maryland NAACP

---

[16] Wootton, *Social Science and Social Pathology*, esp. ch. 7.
[17] Minckler, "Chromosomes and Criminals," *Science* March 14, 1969.

leader asserted: "The laws and the system have turned our children into criminals and looters."[18] Explaining the reason for a resolution adopted by a Negro group which labeled the killing of a white police officer as "justifiable homicide," the Democratic National Committeeman for the District of Columbia stated: "The white policeman . . . does not sympathize with the black and acts towards him as he has been conditioned by the society. The black man, in turn, is conditioned to expect police to use their guns and suppression. He thus acts as he has been conditioned to act and defends himself."[19]

Projects like the Manhattan court's experimental program with economically and socially deprived offenders are but pilot steps toward the expansion of the therapeutic *parens patriae* model from the mentally to the socially disadvantaged.[20] These developments well illustrate the societal preference for new therapeutic programs and may be, in fact, foretelling the demise of criminal justice as the principal tool of social control in the not too distant future.

THE KINGDOM OF THERAPY

The transition in social controls from a penal to a therapeutic emphasis[21] is closely associated with our increased emphasis on the total public welfare. In societies less concerned with the comprehensive planning of the individual's role and his well-being, criminal sanctions were considered more or less adequate tools, for they guaranteed that the majority of the populace would remain undisturbed in the pursuit of life and property, while the small group of offenders would be drastically and effectively exercised.[22] Incidentally, it was also hoped that such removal would provide the opportunity and conditions for the offender's penitence and reformation.

---

[18] "Agnew Raps Negro Leaders for Their Pre-Riot Silence," *Washington Post,* April 12, 1968, p. A1.

[19] "Black Front Calls Killing of Policeman Justifiable," *Washington Post,* July 5, 1968, pp. A1, A4.

[20] Brakel and South, "Diversion from the Criminal Process in the Rural Community," 7 *Amer. Crim. L. Q.* 122 (1969).

[21] For an interesting summary of the variations in societal reactions to crime (including the movement from "purely punitive" to "purely non-punitive") *see* Cressy, "Crime," in *Contemporary Social Problems* 66–69 (R. K. Merton and R. A. Nisbet eds. 1961).

[22] A major concern in the nineteenth century was to hold down these dangerous classes. H. A. Fregier, *Des Classes Dangereuses de la Population dans les Grandes Villes,* 2 vols. (1840); H. Mayhew, 4 *London Labour and the London Poor* (1861–62).

Our new affluence, our new moral and social consciousness, and indeed the new powers of the social masses, who produce the largest numbers of offenders, have created a society no longer satisfied with this form of social control. No longer can the bad boys be sent permanently out of the room. For one thing, there are too many of them.[23] The suspicion has grown, moreover, that the offenders are no more evil than other members of society. The new expectation, therefore, is that offenders will not be banished forever but will be quickly reformed, transformed, and returned to society.

So effective has been the incursion of the therapeutic state into the old penal system that less than half of the American population may now be subject to the sanctions of criminal law. Not only have the juvenile delinquents and the mentally ill (including various other types accommodated under these labels) been transferred from the penal arena into the realm of social welfare and therapy; the psychopath, the alcoholic, the drug addict, and the economically disadvantaged are being accorded a similar treatment.

The transition from a penal model to a therapeutic model not only suits the new social requirements of greater humaneness but meets many of the objectives of the social and behavioral sciences regarding the reformation of social behavior. The therapeutic model appears to offer both a frame of reference and tools that may have greater effectiveness in the reformation of proved deviants. Ours is increasingly becoming a society that views punishment as a primitive and vindictive tool and is therefore loath to punish;[24] the therapeutic emphasis that brings a humanizing influence to the criminal process well suits the mood of the times. This influence, which manifests a striving for the improvement of the deviant's personal and social health, is clearly preferable to the earlier brutal and retributive methods of the penal process.

The therapeutic concept may also have a direct and important bearing upon the deviant's responses to the social sanction. One of the serious criticisms directed against the criminal process is the adverse effect of its "branding" technique.[25] Once a person is designated a criminal, the machinery of the "self-fulfilling prophecy" is put into

[23] A recent projection indicates that 29 percent of all men and 7 percent of all women in England and Wales will be convicted of an indictable offense if the present crime rate continues. L. Radzinowicz, *Ideology and Crime* 62 (1966).

[24] A. S. Goldstein, *The Insanity Defense* 7 (1967).

[25] S. Shoham, *Crime and Social Deviation* 12–13 (1966); F. Tannenbaum, *Crime and the Community* (1938); H. S. Becker, *Outsiders: Studies in the Sociology of Deviance* (1963).

motion.[26] Danish psychiatrist George Stürup has for years stressed the theory of double-expectancy, describing the evil circle in which the offender continues to perform in the character and manner which he believes society expects of him. The criminal process thus reinforces criminal conduct. Conversely, the offender who is tagged as inadequate, ill, or unfortunate is likely, it is argued, to respond favorably to the perception of a more positive social climate in which ill and underprivileged people are expected to improve and recover.

The increasing movement toward the therapeutic state raises fundamental public policy questions. The benevolent philosophy of the *parens patriae* process, noted Anthony Platt, "often disguises the fact that the offender is regarded as a 'non-person' who is immature, unworldly, and incapable of making effective decisions with regard to his own welfare and future."[27] Will this indiscriminate therapeutic emphasis, which totally bypasses the question of personal responsibility and guilt, act to erode the concept of free will and personal restraint, qualities upon which we have long relied as tools of social control?[28] As claimed by Oxford law professor A. L. Goodhart, "a community which is too ready to forgive the wrongdoer may end up by condoning the crime."[29]

What effect may the differences in emphasis have upon the social sanctioning process and upon the deviant's receptiveness to reform? In modern times the criminal process has served—or been expected to serve—a dual purpose: to discourage the transgressor from committing other crimes (specific deterrence) and also to prevent other people from following his example (general deterrence). Looking to criminal sanctions as a deterrent, we presume that we can pursue both objectives simultaneously, in that the unpleasant consequences of wrongdoing will dissuade both present and potential offenders.[30] The therapeutic model, by its very character, promises less. While criminal justice emphasized blameworthiness and personal guilt, the therapeutic state emphasizes physical, mental, and social shortcomings. The criminal process relies upon the imposition of unpleasantness,

---

[26] Merton, "The Self-fulfilling Prophecy," 8 *Antioch Rev.* 194 (1948).

[27] Platt, "The Child Savers" 318.

[28] Nineteenth-century French sociologist Gabriel Tarde maintained that guilt must be retained as "a dogma that was socially necessary, though scientifically untenable." *See* Radzinowicz, *Ideology and Crime* 110.

[29] *English Law and Moral Law* 92–93 (1953).

[30] For some critical questioning of the effectiveness of general deterrence in the criminal process *see* Radzinowicz, *Ideology and Crime* 121; and J. Andenaes, "General Prevention—Illusion or Reality," 43 *J. Crim. L.C. & P.S.* 176, 197 (1952).

the therapeutic model upon the deviant's reconditioning by treatment. Thus, although treatment might be more effective than punishment in rehabilitating the proved offender, the therapeutic model fails to offer the specter of deterrence to potential deviants. "Whereas lenient and sympathetic handling may be most efficacious in bringing an offender to see the error of his ways, the effect of this upon other people may well be to foster the belief that they can get away with it," warned Lady Wootton.[31]

The classical system of criminal justice is thoroughly confined, through both philosophical standards and precepts of constitutional law (such as "punishment that fits the crime," and the requisites of "the equal protection of the laws"), to patterns of action and limitations upon its power that could not easily be ignored. The welfare and therapeutic system, with its nonpenal aims and without such rigorous limitations, permits much freer experimentation with social engineering.[32] Awareness of this freedom originally manifested itself in the treatment of the mentally ill. Within the *parens patriae* and therapeutic framework, sterilization, frontal lobotomy, shock therapy, and indeterminate commitments[33] have been tolerated—experiments which would have been questionable within the more strict confines of the criminal system, limited as it is by the Eighth and Fourteenth Amendment safeguards against cruel and unusual punishment and the requirements of due process.[34] In fact, recent apologists for the psychopathy laws seek their justification not in scientific evidence of the validity of the psychopathic classification but in a pragmatic consideration: that under the mantle of such classification and the purportedly noncriminal auspices of *parens patriae*, society will be permitted experimental programs that otherwise might not be tolerated.[35]

THE FUTURE THERAPEUTIC IDEAL?

There is today a growing body of knowledge of how man behaves, what factors compose his character and personality, and what experiences affect his development. The application of a treatment here, a requirement there, a different environment or family structure,

---

[31] Wootton, *Social Science and Social Pathology* 253.

[32] *Ibid.* 254, 267.

[33] On the general evolution toward indeterminate sentences *see* J. Jimenez de Asua, *La Sentencia Indeterminada* 19–22, 205 (1947). This has been one of the major tenets of the positivist social defense movement, commencing with Raffaele Garofalo and Enrico Ferri. *See* Radzinowicz, *Ideology and Crime* 53–55.

[34] *Mentally Disabled and the Law* 310 (F. T. Lindman and D. M. McIntyre eds. 1961).

[35] P. H. Gebhard *et al., Sex Offenders* 867 (1965).

specially ordered education, or economic placement can significantly change the course of an individual's life. Whether these approaches will come within the ambit of the therapeutic power and be imposed is difficult to say. What is clear is that there is no bar to such compulsion under the present construction of the therapeutic power. What prevents the state, under the therapeutic aegis, from compelling changes in the education, job training, residence, or marital condition of one whose present circumstances indicate that he will become harmful to society? In this context it is well to remember that we already compel the education of children to a certain age and require treatment for numerous other classes deemed immature or otherwise mentally or socially deficient. Cannot such broader exercise of power by the state be considered a treatment for ignorant persons who would be less productive members of society without it? As society becomes increasingly specialized and sophisticated, deviance becomes more and more objectionable since the other parts of society are hindered by the defects of the deviant. In this context almost any deviation can become dangerous and therefore require treatment.

With the ability to monitor and alter human behavior comes the power to remake society into a deviant-free, crime-free, and smoothly ordered community. Before this feat can be accomplished, however, certain premises and conditions of everyday life will have to be changed. Some controls will be relaxed, others will be substituted.

Under a future therapeutic ideal, police and criminal process might be abandoned. The environment would be manipulated and controlled. Preventive measures would be taken to render any antisocial action impossible. There would be perhaps a perpetual monitoring instead of policing of every individual's behavior. In this way, antisocial activity would be detected and prevented before harm could result. When one demonstrated antisocial tendencies, he would not be subject to a criminal trial but rather would be medically diagnosed and treated so that the behavior would not recur. Complete histories of individuals would be kept from birth to death, to generate the statistical knowledge necessary to sound diagnosis and to provide the necessary feedback to measure the efficacy of treatment. Secrets would be taboo, privacy unheard of, resistance to the new controls pathological. Man's innermost thoughts would have to be open to complete scrutiny if the preventive model were to be successful.[36]

[36] P. Landon, *Behavior Control* (1969).

Seen in this light, it is clear that our traditional notions of privacy would be swept away by the adoption of therapeutic controls as the primary tool of social defense. Similarly, our traditional constitutional safeguards against governmental invasion of privacy would have to be compromised. What would be the effect of such constant scrutiny on a man's outlook and personal makeup?

Recently, a man was placed on the moon. Man has already lived and worked for extended periods at great depths in the sea. Plans are being made for the establishment of a space station where men would live and work in orbit around the earth. In these hostile environments, it is essential that the men involved be under constant environmental, physical, and mental surveillance, for one error or miscalculation could endanger not only the individual but the entire miniature society. The men who are involved in this work must be able not only to cope with the hostile environment but literally to thrive under the constant watchfulness of some controlling authority. That men are undertaking such tasks under such constant scrutiny suggests—although the analogy is not exact—that man might adapt himself to live under the conditions of total surveillance that must prevail in a therapeutic society.[37]

The therapeutic ideal thus presents society with a choice. Do we want to abandon our privacy and diversity, and the constitutional safeguards thereof, for a world in which there is maximum security from physical harm and where there are no deviant persons to offend our sensibilities? Or do we want to preserve the traditional ideals at the risk of crime and untoward behavior by part of the populace?

More than once society has changed its societal ideals, and the individual in society has had to change and adapt to the new ideal or suffer the consequences. Once the ideal was to be religious, and the heretic was burned if he did not repent and embrace orthodoxy. Once the ideal was a classless society, and the aristocrat was beheaded for his birth. In the future it could well be that the ideal will be to be social, orderly, cooperative, productive, and above all "normal," and the eccentric and asocial as well as the overtly antisocial will be treated unless they conform to this model. We could well be at the crossroads of such an alteration of social ideal, and to find comfort in the notion that the therapeutic state is merely a creature of science fiction is to hasten the day when it rises to its fullest fruition.

[37] In a telecast from Apollo 10, Ground Control at Houston used the epigram "Big Brother Is Watching" to describe its source of information about the space craft. One of the astronauts replied, "And we're glad he is!"

THE FEAR OF THERAPEUTIC TYRANNY

Writing recently to the editor of the *New York Times Magazine*, one reader envisioned an antidote for inhumanity:

> I have come to believe that man cannot hope to solve the problems of our world, so many of which are due to our own nature, without some consciously contrived antidote to our anti-social, antihuman proclivities.... But why not research a truly harmless and agreeable, but not incapacitating, drug which every human being on earth should take, and every infant with its mother's milk, perhaps only one time in his life, as certain immunization drugs are administered? Such a drug, with mildly tranquilizing effects, might completely eliminate greed and acquisitiveness, fear and suspicion, chauvinism and fanaticism, hatred and hostility, and put us "on" to the truth that life can be beautiful, people can be good, kind, loving, generous, and even capable of turning the other cheek and doing unto others as we would have others do unto us.[38]

On the surface, measures of therapeutic control have much to recommend them. They disclaim the ugly retributive aims of traditional penology and profess a humanistic desire for a cure and improvement. They talk not in terms of the mystical and ambiguous concepts of moral or religious guilt but in the scientific language of abnormality, deviant behavior, and social change. Finally, they offer as major tools of social control not dungeons but hospitals, not chains but psychological conditioning, drugs, and surgery. It is under these very auspices that involuntary sterilization, lobotomy, and the indeterminate incarceration of various classes of deviants arose in this country.

Even the most devoted exponents of the therapeutic state, however, do not view the new system as being without a need for limitations. All are in agreement that individuality and diversity are desirable assets of society which must be preserved. Indeed, it is generally admitted that great care must be exercised in defining the criteria and the procedures whereby people are selected for therapeutic controls, since here, unlike in other welfare areas, we are often dealing with unwilling recipients. As Eileen Younghusband has observed with great insight, many people would undoubtedly prefer to be punished rather than improved, so as to be free to go on with all

---

[38] Reynolds, "An Antidote for Inhumanity?" *New York Times Magazine*, November 9, 1969, p. 14.

their fundamental weaknesses unchanged.[39] How, therefore, is the therapy recipient to be selected? On the basis of medical testimony, scientific testing, past social behavior, prediction tables, or other criteria? What procedural safeguards should accompany this selection process? Who will guarantee that the therapeutic measures will not exceed certain societal limitations—assuring, for example, that the shock therapy, in the case of the speeder treated by Dr. Barker in Shrewsbury, England, will be permitted only to cure speeding in excess of 70 miles per hour but not to eliminate the desire to drive altogether? Finally, which types of deviation are to be cured and which should society agree to tolerate? Says Professor Norval Morris of the University of Chicago:

The rehabilitative ideal is seen to impart unfettered discretion. Whereas the treaters seem convinced of the benevolence of their treatment methods, those being treated take a different view, and we, the observers, share their doubts. The jailer in a white coat and with a doctorate remains a jailer—but with larger power over his fellows.[40]

To those suspicious of the divestment of criminal justice and its replacement by unfettered therapeutic controls, the new trend suggests unimagined horrors. They fear that granting the therapeutic state the power of compulsion for the promotion of greater mental and social health among deviants poses a new threat of social paternalism. To support this contention they point out that in the therapeutic literature, the concept of adjustment (to family life, acceptable sex practices, and work stability, for example) is particularly prominent. But adjustment clearly means adjustment to a particular culture or to a particular set of institutions, whether good or evil.[41]

"Many of us do indeed rejoice," says Barbara Wootton, "that psychotherapists are more often concerned with bringing about the adjustment of murderers and rapists to a gentler way of life, than

[39] Younghusband, "The Dilemma of the Juvenile Court," 33 *Soc. Serv. Rev.* 17 (1959).

[40] Morris, "Impediments to Penal Reform," 33 *U. Chicago L. Rev.* 627, 637 (1966).

[41] "To conceive adjustment and maladjustment in medical terms is in effect to identify health with the ability to come to terms with ... [a given] culture or ... [given] institutions—be they totalitarian methods of government, the dingy culture of an urban slum, the contemporary English law of marriage, or what ... [has] elsewhere ... [been] called the standards of an 'acquisitive, competitive, hierarchical, envious' society." Wootton, *Social Science and Social Pathology* 218.

with the adjustment of deviant liberals to a Nazi or similar regime."[42] Since the standard of mental health (unlike physical health) is not a scientific but a value judgment,[43] the question persists: How can we protect individualism and the diversity of democracy against an excessive zeal to realize the therapeutic ideal?

The problem has been dramatically illustrated in a recent English case involving a 21-year-old ice-cream salesman, Eric Edward Wills, charged with larceny and obtaining property under false pretenses. Sent to a Lancashire mental hospital for observation, Wills was diagnosed as a compulsive gambler and psychopath. Attributing his legal difficulties to gambling, the medical report recommended that his brain be operated on, in the hope that the leucotomy operation would cure him of his compulsion. The magistrate, heeding the medical report, ordered that he be committed and operated upon under the 1959 Mental Health Act. The decision caused widespread alarm. The press raised the question whether Parliament in the 1959 act vested too much power in psychiatrists to decide the fate of the criminally accused. Added the *Sunday Times*: "And is the drastic measure of operating on a man's brain an appropriate remedy for what respected pundits have called a national psychosis?"[44] Especially significant were the comments of a spokesman for Gamblers Anonymous, a self-help British organization: "Compulsive gambling is sometimes caused by mental illness, but in and of itself it is not evidence of mental abnormality, any more than any other deviant behavior. It's terribly phoney ... to think you can control gambling—an extremely complex thing—by cutting people's brains."[45] In the face of this adverse public reaction, the magistrate rescinded his order.

The most vocal American spokesman against therapeutic tyranny has been Dr. Thomas Szasz. A leading psychiatrist concerned with the indiscriminate expansion of the mental illness concept as a justification for social compulsion, Dr. Szasz is also alarmed by the concurrent casting of the psychiatrist in the role of the jailer-custodian. He has therefore set out to demonstrate how in modern society moral standards have declined in social pre-eminence, "how health values have usurped the place of moral values," and how "social engineering" has arrived "disguised as mental health."[46] Describing the hazards to liberty contained in this transformation, Dr. Szasz asserts:

---

[42] *Ibid.* 221.
[43] J. W. Eaton and R. J. Weil, *Culture and Mental Disorders* 27, 189 (1955).
[44] *The Sunday Times,* April 21, 1968, p. 5.
[45] *Ibid.*
[46] T. S. Szasz, *Law, Liberty and Psychiatry* 2, 4 (1963).

I am opposed to coercive methods in the mental health field. . . .
The redefinition of moral values as health values will now appear
in a new light. If people believe that health values justify coercion, but that moral and political values do not, those who wish
to coerce others will tend to enlarge the category of health
values at the expense of the category of moral values. We are
already far along this road.[47]

While Dr. Szasz properly fears that the substitution of health values
for moral and political values will be used to justify coercion where
it was not previously tolerated or where it should no longer be permitted in our social order, he has overlooked the therapeutic state's
positive effects—humanizing health values have been replacing penal
values in areas where coercion was once the rule.

Campaigning against the tyranny of health and welfare, the new
critics find themselves cast, in some eyes, not in the role of libertarians, but in the robes of archconservatives—in conflict with those
who have long committed themselves to the proposition that crime
and deviation are more of an illness than an evil and that treatment
is a far superior tool of social control and conformity than are condemnation and retribution. Suspicious of societal compulsion, whether
exercised for political or welfare reasons, these critics, strangely, are
often confused with the enemies of fluoridation and "big government." By voicing doubts as to whether modern psychiatry possesses
the necessary knowledge to control society's present ills, any more
than the seventeenth-century church had the adequate means of control over witchcraft, the doubters finally become cast in an antiscientific role. (While Dr. Szasz opposes the power assumed by the
therapeutic state partly because in his opinion the therapeutic disciplines lack the technical skills for the discharge of such powers, it
is this writer's fear that the therapeutic state, although lacking the
necessary social restraints, already possesses a disturbing number of
skills for the modification of man.)

Unfortunately, the arguments of the opponents of the indiscriminate
parens patriae and "therapy" movements are often dismissed by the
enthusiastic supporters of the therapeutic state. The critiques therefore fail to contribute to a more balanced appraisal of the merits and
evils of therapeutic controls. It is ironic, however, that the stand
which today is viewed as antiprogressive and antiscientific is a direct
descendant of a great liberal lineage.

When the modern capitalistic and individualistic state was emerging from the restraints of feudal society, the question of the state's role was also hotly debated. Medieval society was built on elaborate systems of social organization which controlled religion, government, family, and the economy. Freedom from such controls and an opportunity for maximum individual expression, as long as it remained compatible with social survival, was the banner of eighteenth-century liberalism. Nothing expresses this aim more clearly than Mill's often-quoted words:

> The principle is, that the sole end for which mankind are warranted, individually or collectively, in interfering with the liberty of action of any of their number is self-protection. That the only purpose for which power can be rightfully exercised over any member of a civilized community, against his will, is to prevent harm to others. His own good, either physical or moral, is not a sufficient warrant. He cannot rightfully be compelled to do or forbear because it will be better for him to do so, because it will make him happier, because, in the opinions of others, to do so would be wise, or even right. These are good reasons for remonstrating with him or reasoning with him, or persuading him, or entreating him, but not for compelling him, or visiting him with an evil in case he do otherwise. To justify that, the conduct from which it is desired to deter him must be calculated to produce evil to some one else.[48]

Does not this admonition against the *restraints inherent in feudalism* and authoritarian regimes become relevant in today's social order, where government planning and public welfare once more may be producing the tightly knit, constrictive forms of social organization absent since feudal times? Do not Mill's fears assume especially threatening proportions in the face of society's acquisition of new tools for the control and modification of individualism offered by modern science? In the interests of a pluralistic society, should we not limit the exercise of the therapeutic power to situations of clear social danger?

PUBLIC SAFETY, MORALS, WELFARE, AND HEALTH

In attempting to predict the future scope and types of social controls over individual behavior, it is instructive to reflect upon the historical role of the state in the pursuit of safety, morals, welfare, and

[48] J. S. Mill, *On Liberty* 11–12 (1930).

health. The early medieval state, out of which the present criminal and therapeutic processes grew, manifested little direct supervision over deviant behavior. Behavior which was overtly dangerous to the safety of others, including typical present-day criminal offenses such as homicide, rape, and robbery, was usually left to the revenge or other sanctions of the offended person and his family. Due to the strong influence of the church, ecclesiastic laws and courts had control over those types of behavior, such as intoxication, adultery, and witchcraft, which were viewed as offensive to Christian morality. The distribution of welfare benefits and regulations regarding the recipients was not a state responsibility but the function of the feudal landlords, churches, or persons of good will. And state regulations regarding behavior offensive to the public health long remained negligible.

It was only in twelfth-century England that responsibility for the imposition of sanctions for criminal behavior became a state function.[49] As the state's assumption of this responsibility broadened in scope, behavior which was previously proscribed or regulated by the church, feudal master, or family became the subject of the sovereign's criminal laws. Being derived from these diverse strains, the criminal law's responsibility was naturally viewed by the traditional common law scholars and judges as extending not only to behavior which directly threatened public safety but also to conduct adverse to public morals, welfare, and health.[50]

Especially with the rapid incursion of the state into public welfare functions at the beginning of the seventeenth century, increased criminal sanctions against offensive (as distinct from dangerous) persons, such as vagrants, idlers, and vagabonds, came about as a means for reducing demands on the public purse. Critically viewed, the entire state welfare program introduced under the 1601 Elizabethan Poor Laws could well be viewed as a lesser form of criminal sanction.[51] The state at that time drew few distinctions among persons who troubled it. Behavior was either socially acceptable or not. In seventeenth- and eighteenth-century England it thus made little difference whether the individual was convicted of a crime or was found to be a pauper. In either case he was objectionable to the larger community and as a consequence was subjected to the coercion of the legal process. The results of the coercion may have been somewhat different, depending on whether he was an active (criminal) or

[49] T. F. T. Plucknett, *A Concise History of the Common Law* 426 (1956).

[50] People v. Munoz, 211 N.Y.S. 146, 172 N.E.2d 535, 539 (1961).

[51] S. and B. Webb, *English Poor Law History: The Old Poor Law* (1927).

passive (pauper) threat to society, but viewed by today's standards the treatment of the poor was punishment. They were confined to institutions, forced to labor in workhouses, and contracted out to private consumers of labor. In addition, the poor were expected to undergo reformative change in order to correct their pauperism.

In a very real sense, there was a fairly uniform system of social controls operating prior to the end of the eighteenth century over all those disagreeable to society. (The lack of formal procedures and criteria under the early common law also helped to make distinguishing between criminals and paupers difficult.) But this simple and uniform approach to deviance was finally disrupted through the conceptualization of criminal law by the classical criminologists.[52] The emphasis upon carefully and antedelictually defined crimes and punishments placed limits on the state's power to interfere with an individual's life. The state was recognized as potentially inimical to individual liberty, and safeguards were guaranteed against abuses of its power. Crimes were now to be delineated and adjudicated under strict procedures. Limits were set upon the degree to which the state under the criminal law could force its way upon a person's property or liberty. The effect of these developments appeared to separate the criminal from the pauper and to free the latter from the compulsion of legal process.

While classical criminal law was emerging, important changes were also occurring in the delivery and nature of the state's welfare service. Special institutions for various types of welfare recipients, such as the mentally ill and the juveniles, were coming into being and aid for the needy was beginning to be channeled not only through confining institutions but also through state services in the community. Two distinct schemes of social controls were thus generated by the ascendancy of classical criminology: the criminal model and the welfare model. Under the first an overt act which is attributed to the offender's evil will must be proved before the state may interfere with his life. Under the welfare model, however, no act need be proved against an individual. Destitution and the requirement of welfare are the only considerations. Moreover, under the criminal model the state's role is compulsory; under the welfare model its services are supposedly voluntarily delivered.

Despite this bifurcation of controls, a full separation never did occur. Soon it became obvious that significant numbers of those who

[52] C. B. Beccaria, *On Crimes and Punishments* (J. A. Paolucci trans. 1880).

were allegedly welfare beneficiaries continued to be subjected to compulsory controls. Borrowing from the earlier practices of private and church welfare, under which aid was often conditioned upon the recipient's response to the grantor's needs through work, reformation, or restitution, the welfare state adopted as its guiding philosophy the view that as a donor it had the power and right to impose conditions upon its grant of services to the needy. These conditions, intended as a rehabilitative effort, were assumed, however, to be at the welfare recipient's consent and therefore different from the compulsory intervention of criminal law. The welfare state, moreover, viewed the needy as people whose socioeconomic afflictions were at least partially due to their own moral and mortal shortcomings and who were not therefore entitled to benefits from the state's benevolence without demonstrating their own efforts toward reformation. The imposition of various requirements and standards upon the welfare recipient was viewed as necessary to prevent his further corruption and to encourage a change from his evil ways.

While the welfare process was thus engaging in compulsory corrections, the penal process continued to handle persons who were primarily in need of welfare rather than compulsion. Groups whose major offense was the lack of economic resources were accordingly being processed through the criminal rather than the welfare system. Manifesting a preference for the stick rather than the carrot, the state continued to prosecute the idler and vagrant for failing to secure employment and a residence, instead of offering them the welfare tools required for a new life.

To confuse further the state's respective roles in the criminal and welfare arenas, positive criminology arose in the second half of the nineteenth century,[53] and soon thereafter its direct issue, the therapeutic state, saw light. Under the new doctrines, the criminal law's emphasis upon the overt act was deemed no longer appropriate and attention was shifted to the conditions or statuses that might be potential threats to society. Seeing the seed of future crime in personality aberrations and in socioeconomic want, the therapeutic state felt entitled to intervene in circumstances where a *state of dangerousness* had been demonstrated. No longer was there a need to wait for the actual criminal act before social intervention could be exercised. Moreover, disclaiming penal aims and professing a commitment to personal rehabilitation, the positivists did not consider themselves

[53] E. Ferri, *Criminal Sociology* (Kelly and Lisle trans. 1917).

bound by the classicists' requirements that the punishment be proportionate to the crime, insisting instead that the rehabilitative ideal was limited only by the deviant's need.

Totally obscured in these developments was the identity of the underpinnings of the new therapeutic state. For Enrico Ferri and his disciples, positive criminology derived its justifications from the needs of social defense—the emphasis was clearly upon social protection. In the American setting the mushrooming therapeutic state claimed its ancestry in *parens patriae* and welfare considerations, stressing the need to protect and serve those incapable of piloting their own destinies. Consequently, while the welfare state based its regulations over the aid recipient upon his alleged consent, and the criminal law grounded its intervention upon the offender's evil will, the therapeutic state derived justification from the chain of the deviant's own incompetence. In reality, however, the new therapeutic state has from the beginning contained mixed strains of both social defense and individual welfare, carrying out programs of confinement and compulsory therapy which could not be justified by considerations other than those of social defense, yet relying upon its manifested dedication to welfare in order to combat criticisms of its disregard for the traditional safeguards of the criminal process.

Only the past two decades have seen a growing movement in America toward a rational reassessment of social controls, whether founded in consideration of public safety, morality, welfare, or health. Within the criminal model there has been evident a concern with overcriminalization and pressure for a retrenchment of the criminal process. Serious questions have been raised regarding the propriety of the criminal law's function outside the area of public safety, when it branches out to serve the less immediate needs of public morals, health, and welfare. Both legal and popular literature have questioned, for example, whether criminal sanctions have a fitting role in the regulation of morality, such as homosexuality or prostitution, where the offensive behavior produces no victim other than the offender himself.[54] Similarly questioned in literature as well as in the courts is the criminal law's place in the promotion of public health through the prohibition of substances, such as alcohol, tobacco, or marijuana, which affect mainly the user rather than society.[55] The movement to curtail the incursion of the criminal process into welfare

[54] Great Britain, Home Office of the Scottish Home Department, Committee on Homosexual Offenses and Prostitution, *Wolfenden Report* (1957); E. M. Schur, *Crimes Without Victims* (1965).

[55] H. Packer, *The Limits of Criminal Sanctions* (1968).

functions has been aided also by an increasing number of successful court cases challenging the validity of criminal vagrancy laws punishing offenders who are charged with nothing more than economic want.[56]

Concurrent with the new limitations upon the criminal model, the welfare recipient's guarantees against unwarranted governmental incursions have been gaining equal attention. Protections have grown within the welfare model against invasions of privacy in the form of home inspections, work requirements, prohibitions against a man being in the house, and regulations affecting additional pregnancies.[57] Increasingly, the welfare recipient is moving from a position of near criminality and bare tolerance to a position of right. Increasingly, the government's power to condition its welfare grant upon behavioral modifications is being drastically limited.

In this climate of curtailed social intervention under both the criminal and welfare models, the therapeutic state remains unfazed by the increasing demand for reduced governmental controls. Given the current public prestige of the psychological and psychiatric disciplines, the portrayal of the mentally ill, the juvenile, the psychopath, the drug addict, and alcoholic as helpless, therapy-requiring individuals is quite generally accepted. The public has been prepared to view the subject of the therapeutic state as somebody "different," rarely considering the possibility that deviance could easily be broadened to encompass many unsuspecting candidates.

Yet, while the humanitarians continue to relish the nonpenal manifestations of the therapeutic state, the pragmatists of law and order seek to exploit the stern realities of its social controls. And while those subject to the sanctions of the criminal process or the restraints imposed under the welfare model now find increasing protections against governmental excesses, these liberalizing benefits have not been generally available to the beneficiaries of the therapeutic model. The nonpenal aims and the deviant's mental aberration continue to be asserted in opposition to the granting of procedural and substantive safeguards to the beneficiaries of therapy; and the therapeutic state's preventative ideal similarly militates against strict substantive standards limiting state intervention. As a result the therapeutic model

---

[56] Fenster v. Leary, 20 N.Y.2d 309, 229 N.E.2d 426 (1967); Alegata v. Commonwealth, 353 Mass. 287, 231 N.E.2d 201 (1967).

[57] Burrus and Fessler, "Constitutional Due Process Hearing Requirements in the Administration of Public Assistance: The District of Columbia Experience," 16 *Amer. U. L. Rev.* 199 (1967); Reich, "Individual Rights and Social Welfare: The Emerging Legal Issues," 74 *Yale L. J.* 1245 (1965).

now offers the only system of social control unlimited in potential applications, for by its very aims the therapeutic state is required to look beyond the question of past misconduct and into those factors of morals, welfare, and health which might produce a present or future *state of dangerousness.*

AN AUDIT FOR THE THERAPEUTIC STATE

One fundamental safeguard for liberty contained in the United States Constitution is the assurance that a person may not be deprived of life, liberty, or property without due process of law.[58] The constitutional protection of due process, as traditionally defined, is twofold: first, the criteria advanced to justify governmental interference must be reasonably related to society's needs and unambiguously stated so as to give concerned persons a fair notice of society's proscriptions; second, fair procedures must be utilized to ascertain the relevant facts supporting governmental intervention.[59] While the Constitution contains several other guarantees for individual liberty, most are directed specifically against the abuses of the criminal process; but the due process requirement also stands guard against the tyranny of the therapeutic state.

In its second century, the American experiment under the therapeutic model is clearly at a crossroad. While some of its manifestations have been compared to the infamous Star Chamber proceedings, the pressure for yet more comprehensive therapeutic controls has not diminished. To help define a course of future development, it now becomes critical to seek in the therapeutic state's previous performance an index of congenital weaknesses as well as potential strengths. Particularly important in this search is the determination of how well individualism has fared in the face of pressures for societal conformity, and how adequate the procedural protections afforded to unwilling beneficiaries of the therapeutic state have been against unreasonable governmental intervention.

Uncertain and Unjust Criteria

Throughout the development of the therapeutic experiment, criteria of judgment have usually been ambiguously defined. Humanitarian

---

[58] *U.S. Const.*, amend. V and amend. XIV.
[59] Remington, "Due Process in Juvenile Proceedings," 11 *Wayne L. Rev.* 688, 691 (1965).

considerations of health and welfare, combined with a preventive impulse, have frequently resulted in societal intervention before a public danger was clearly demonstrated. A California physician thus justified involuntary commitment to a mental asylum on the grounds that the patient in question had paranoid delusions and feelings of persecution, that there was a "reasonable" possibility that he would seek redress for his persecution, and that the physician "had no assurance that such redress would be of an orderly or lawful type."[60] In a Georgia case a young woman was similarly committed on the basis of evidence that she had taken to sitting by the roadside at night, had joined the Jehovah's Witnesses, and had spent many days away from home, knocking on strange doors and "going into houses of all sorts of people."[61]

In the face of such imprecise standards, medical expertise was looked to for protection against abuse.[62] Since mental asylums were designated medical institutions and were run by professionals, it was convenient to assume that there was little fear that persons not suffering from mental illness would be committed or retained. But this assumed *entente* between medicine and law, under which strict legal criteria and procedures have not been stressed, produced many examples of gross inequity, including commitments on the ground of mere social nonconformity, the confinement of those who required voluntary assistance only, and the inclusion of epilepsy among the mental disorders which justify indeterminate commitment.[63]

Worse yet, vague standards bringing together in one institute diverse groups of social misfits have contributed to the perpetuation of old-fashioned mental institutions as multipurpose human depositories. In these total institutions—not unlike prisons—effective treatment has no atmosphere in which to flourish, and security considerations often have dominated therapeutic ones. Banishment to these asylums, while relieving the community of direct contact with mental problems, has long postponed the development of community-based therapeutic programs.

[60] Brock v. Southern Pacific Co., 195 P.2d 66, 76–77 (Calif. 1958).

[61] Paul v. Longino, 28 S.E.2d 286, 289 (Ga. 1943).

[62] For criticism of psychiatric diagnoses *see* Scheff, "Decision Rules, Types of Error, and Their Consequences in Medical Diagnosis," 8 *Behav. Sci.* 97 (1963); Scheff, "The Societal Reaction to Deviance: Ascriptive Elements in the Psychiatric Screening of Mental Patients in a Midwestern State," 11 *Soc. Prob.* 401 (1964); Scheff, "Social Conditions for Relationality: How Urban and Rural Courts Deal with the Mentally Ill," 7 *Amer. Behav. Sci.* 21 (1964).

[63] See Chapter 2.

In the case of the juvenile, the criteria for state intervention have similarly moved away from the certainties and the imminent-danger requirements of the criminal law toward more shadowy determinations based on each family's resources and expectations, as well as on each community's and juvenile court's gauge of tolerance. Frequently, the criteria for social intervention and compulsion rest heavily on the deviant's socioeconomic background and resources. Those who can demonstrate the availability and means for noninstitutional care are frequently relieved of therapeutic compulsion and allowed to pursue their own solutions.

The lack of fair and reasonable criteria for social intervention is especially evident in the psychopathy laws. Particularly objectionable in this arbitrary grouping is the emphasis upon the sexual offender as a member of an allegedly homogeneous group and the attribution of equal significance to relatively harmless and dangerous types of conduct. Consequently, while society is developing an increasing tolerance of deviant sexual behavior between consenting adults (and new behavioral surveys report a growing degree of deviance which challenges the traditional assumptions of normalcy),[64] those practicing such deviations can still be subjected, as psychopaths, to indeterminate incarceration and "rehabilitative" therapy.

Most social controls, such as indeterminate commitments, are often induced by a fear of an evident social danger; sterilization, on the other hand, is motivated by much more remote considerations. It is not today's or tomorrow's hazards that motivate this societal program, but rather the fear of a yet unconceived generation that, because of its mental inadequacy or birth into an improper environment, may become a social or economic burden. Sterilization is therefore a particularly significant illustration of the therapeutic zeal, not only because of the radical nature of the social sanction employed, but also because of the comparatively remote nature of the potential harm.[65]

Sterilization, in most states, has been limited to inmates of mental institutions—in order not to overly offend public sensitivities. Due to this restriction, however, the program never seriously sought to make

[64] A. C. Kinsey *et al.*, "Concepts of Normalcy and Abnormalcy in Sexual Behavior," in *Psychosexual Development in Health and Disease* 28 (Hoch and Zubin eds. 1949).

[65] *See, e.g.*, Holmes' oft-quoted "clear and present" test in Schenck v. United States, 249 U.S. 47, 52; 39 S.Ct. 247 (1919).

a significant impact upon the perpetuation of mental illness or deficiency; for if this drastic measure is scientifically, legally, and socially defensible, those at large who manifest similar defects and who have a greater opportunity to procreate should require the operation even more urgently than those who are confined. By so confining itself to those least vocal and least protected in the population, sterilization has clearly demonstrated its discriminatory and nonscientific motivations.

Most recently, the therapeutic promise has centered on alcoholism and drug addiction. Even here the therapeutic programs have been generating concern because of uncertain criteria and ill-defined social aims. While *Robinson* v. *California*[66] and the recent *Driver* and *Easter* decisions[67] have ordained that a person may not be punished for the status of drug addiction or chronic public intoxication, no limits have been imposed upon the therapeutic sanctions which may be applied to the addict and the drunk. Since society's past willingness to forego punishment has often been conditioned upon the imposition of even tighter controls through therapy, there is a need to limit the duration and severity of the therapy that might be visited upon alcoholics and addicts relieved of criminal punishment.[68]

As one surveys criteria utilized by society in the enforcement of the therapeutic programs, one is struck by their unusually diverse origins in public safety, morality, health, and welfare. Especially significant is the manner in which these criteria permit societal controls based on an individual's status rather than on his actions. In the criminal realm, American society is increasingly restricting societal interference to situations of clear and present danger; the therapeutic trend, however, is to prevent such danger from arising through earlier societal intervention. Clearly, the more society departs from the old standard of the overt act and the more it permits the compulsory control of a vague condition of status,[69] the more the doors to

[66] 370 U.S. 660 (1962).

[67] Driver v. Hinnant, 356 F.2d 761 (4th Cir. 1966); Easter v. District of Columbia, 361 F.2d 50 (D.C. Cir. 1966).

[68] The argument against compulsory treatment gains force from the strong evidence denigrating the efficacy of therapy in the case of uncooperative alcoholics and drug addicts. Since certain types of deviants are more responsive to treatment when it is carried out in an environment devoid of physical restraint, it is questionable whether involuntary commitment by the therapeutic state should be encouraged in these instances. Secretariat of the First U.N. Congress on the Prevention of Crime and Treatment of Offenders, *Report* 76 (Geneva, 1955).

[69] Robinson v. California, 370 U.S. 660, 666, 667 (1962).

potential abuses of power and to assaults upon individual diversity
are opened.[70]

The Absence of Procedural Safeguards

The desire to differentiate between the criminal and therapeutic
models, to remove thereby the stigma of criminality from the latter,
and to find means for a personalized, earlier, and more scientific
identification of those requiring therapeutic intervention, was long
thought to require dispensing with formal, adversary, and judicial
procedures. Describing the juvenile court as a "laboratory of human
behavior" where the judge's task is to "get the whole truth about a
child" in the same way that a "physician searches for every detail
that bears on the condition of a patient,"[71] the reformers saw traditional judicial proceedings as a burden. The strong movement against
traditional formalism in therapeutic proceedings has been further
supported by both legal[72] and nonlegal[73] authorities who stressed the
traumatic effect of the formal process upon the potential patient and
the lack of necessity for formalism when society is acting not to punish but to cure.

The influence of this philosophy has resulted in the erosion in the
therapeutic area of the procedural standards first developed in the
criminal law and often applicable throughout the civil law process
as well. The defendant's traditional rights to a hearing and adequate
notice of such hearing, the right of cross-examination, the protection against self-incrimination, and the rights to counsel, bail, and
trial by jury were generally not made available under the purportedly
noncriminal therapeutic auspices. Concluding paternalistically that
"a child's case is not a legal case,"[74] the operants of the therapeutic
state decreed that any suggestion of the old-fashioned criminal
trial should be avoided and that in the newer process, where the

---

[70] See, for comparison, the criterion of the state of danger, or l'état dangereux,
as utilized by the social defense movement. Loudet, "Le Diagnostic de l'État Dangereux," in Proceedings of the Second International Congress of Criminology 12
(1950).

[71] Van Waters, "The Socialization of Juvenile Court Procedure," 13 J. Crim.
L. 61, 69 (1922).

[72] M. S. Guttmacher and H. Weihofen, Psychiatry and the Law 295 (1952).

[73] Group for the Advancement of Psychiatry, Commitment Procedures, Report
no. 4, April 1949.

[74] Henderson, "Juvenile Courts: Problems of Administration," 13 Charities
340–41 (1905).

emphasis was to be upon purely educational and rehabilitative principles, the child required no legal representation.

The decline of procedural safeguards, however, has not been uniform in all the *parens patriae* areas. In the juvenile process the power to remove a delinquent from parental custody and to commit him to institutional care remains vested in the courts. At the very least this guarantees the *parens patriae* beneficiary some kind of hearing and possibly an opportunity to appeal. On the other hand, in nearly half of the states, commitment to mental institutions can be accomplished through the action of an administrative tribunal or on the basis of a medical certification by private physicians, without the benefit of any hearing.

Similarly, the determination of psychopathy is often made informally. At times, the procedure consists of nothing more than a medical examination and a written report to the court: the defendant often has no opportunity to be heard or to challenge the medical conclusions. Sterilization orders are even less restricted by procedural requisites. The authority to make such orders is typically vested in a medical board, often composed of those who administer the very institution from which the request for sterilization originates. Procedural safeguards are minimal; right to counsel is rarely accorded; notice to the patient (the very one who has previously been institutionalized because of mental illness or defect) is often considered sufficient to alert him of the impending operation. Thus a meaningful opportunity to challenge the conclusions of the medical experts is totally lacking. Moreover, for lobotomy operations no decision by an independent and unbiased tribunal is required, and the therapist is totally free to act at his own discretion.

The absence of procedural safeguards in the therapeutic state has not gone totally unprotested. Legal scholars have argued that historical due process and fundamental fairness are being denied; administrative law experts have observed that the safeguards in these therapeutic proceedings have fallen far below the standards required by administrative tribunals or in civil cases which involve only property rights. In an oft-quoted dissenting opinion regarding due process in the juvenile court, Pennsylvania's Justice Musmanno[75] urged that, despite the allegedly nonpenal aims of the court, procedural propriety was mandatory in determining the fact upon which the court's very

[75] *In re* Holmes, 379 Pa. 599, 109 A.2d 523, 528–37 (1954), *cert. denied*, 348 U.S. 973 (1955).

jurisdiction was premised. For a long time these were cries in a wilderness.

Few were willing to admit that in the *parens patriae* areas it is as essential as in other legal forums that an orderly and fair process be followed to determine whether the legal criteria for the exercise of therapeutic controls indeed exist in a given case. Moreover, the demonstrated laxity of criteria in the therapeutic realms require even greater than usual emphasis on fair procedures to help decide, for example, whether a given juvenile committed the acts that would denominate him a delinquent, whether the mentally ill person is actually dangerous to himself or others, whether the alleged psychopath does indeed have a record of past violations and in fact demonstrates a propensity for further crime, and whether procreation by the patient for whom sterilization is requested is likely to produce defective children.

Not only are procedural safeguards necessary to guarantee that the exercise of therapeutic powers conforms to legally established criteria, but they have the added function, in a highly routinized and mechanical society, of furnishing the affected individual an opportunity to question whether the asserted disposition in a given case is indeed the most appropriate social answer. For example, is commitment to a mental institution necessary, or will a less drastic mental care program suffice? Need the juvenile be sent to reform school, or are more appropriate facilities available? Should the alcoholic be civilly committed, or will other social resources supply a better disposition? Procedural safeguards in the therapeutic state are required, therefore, not primarily as a protection against scheming relatives or overzealous public officials, but rather as a protection against public haste, neglect, and negligence.

Orderly and fair judicial proceedings are necessary not only to safeguard individual liberty but to produce a salutary effect on the affected individuals. In contrast to the usual harried proceeding, geared solely to the individual's speedy placement under the therapeutic aegis, a meaningful involvement and an honest attempt at empathy between the committed individual and the committing tribunal may well facilitate the beneficient ends of the therapeutic process. Written with reference to the juvenile process, the following comment applies equally to other *parens patriae* proceedings:

> . . . it is vital that young people should feel that all the circumstances are being fairly, unhurriedly, and impartially heard. . . .

They should not only be allowed to say what they want to say but should also be helped to do so, in order that they may begin to experience understanding by the court, even though at the same time they are held to account for what has happened if the case is found proved. . . . Most of those who come before courts are anxious, confused, hostile, and sometimes aggressive. . . . One of the most effective ways to decrease this anxiety, hostility and confusion is by the greatest possible orderliness, calm and courtesy in the manner in which the proceedings are conducted. . . . This courtesy and manifest desire to understand is also related to the necessity for the courts to strengthen rather than to destroy a sense of responsibility. This sense of responsibility is obviously weak in many young offenders, but if they are to be held accountable then the court should try to involve them in thinking . . . about what each can do to help remedy the situation. . . . a wise court will nearly always try to involve the offender and his parents in its decision, so that they may know the reasons on which they are based, and if possible take part in making them and agree to them.[76]

THE EVILS OF UNCHECKED POWER

The willingness of the United States to give the operants of the therapeutic state too much power lies at the heart of the problems outlined in the earlier chapters. Had it not been for the relaxation of the restrictions limiting the operations of the criminal law, the abuses which run throughout the therapeutic programs could not have occurred so easily. Words spoken regarding the administrative process of government have equal application to society's exercise of therapeutic sanctions: "The principle whose soundness has been confirmed by both earlier and recent experience is the principle of check. We have gone far beyond Montesquieu. We have learned that danger of tyranny or injustice lurks in unchecked power, not in blended power."[77]

Without exception, the therapeutic programs violate this cardinal principle by allowing unchecked control of their standards and policies to repose in the hands of those who administer them. Legislators rarely provide for an independent review of the operation of the

---

[76] Younghusband, "Dilemma of the Juvenile Court" 10, 19. Typical of the contrary approach is State *ex rel.* Sweezer v. Gree, 360 Mo. 1249 S.W.2d 897 (1950): "[T]his Act is but a civil inquiry to determine a status. It is curative and remedial in nature instead of punitive." *Ibid.* 900.

[77] K. C. Davis, *Administrative Law Treatise* 74 (1958).

therapeutic programs. Where they have attempted to condition the exercise of power (for example, insisting on the element of dangerousness as a criterion for a civil commitment for mental illness), the courts have been all too willing to accept the therapist's mimeographed affidavit stating that the conditions have been met, without independently testing the validity of the attestation.

More specifically, the error of our legislatures lies in the establishment of therapeutic programs without sufficient attention to the fundamental question of how they are to be used. Ignored are possibilities that overzealous administrators may use the broad therapeutic powers to excess. Similarly, the element of social defense rarely enters the discussion of therapeutic programs and consequently the problem of an overreliance on therapy as a tool of social defense is never reached. With these questions unplumbed, the general concept of the scientist as a seeker of truth and a trusted servant of mankind allows legislators and judges to abdicate comfortably to the expertise of the therapist in setting the criteria, procedures, and limits of the therapeutic programs. The results are the common denominators of the therapeutic programs: criteria that are vague and broad; procedures that are irregular and meaningless; and compulsory treatments of dubious merit or incarceration without any treatment at all.

In each facet of the therapeutic state, the criteria for the invocation of state power is not written in precise and definite language but rather in vague and amorphous phrases which often mean less to the therapist than they do to the lay population. Who really knows or can describe the degree or kind of mental illness or defect that will subject an individual to compulsory commitment? What behavior will subject a juvenile to the "individualized" treatment of that program? Psychopathy is a word held in disrepute by psychiatrists, and sterilization, shock therapy, and lobotomy are subject to scarcely any criteria at all.

Even where relatively definitive criteria exist, as for narcotics addiction and juvenile criminal activity, legislators as well as therapists have chosen to broaden these criteria beyond their application. Thus persons who may be in danger of becoming narcotics addicts and juveniles who are associating with gamblers, idlers, and others of ill repute are subject to treatment. The intent behind these criteria (or absence thereof) was to provide the widest possible latitude to programs that were largely experimental; it was believed that the nonpenal motives behind the legislation, coupled with the benevolent attitudes of the therapist, would obviate any abuses of these powers. Clearly this has not been so.

Bowing to the desires and ostensible good-faith opinions of the experts, the law forsook its role as the censor of the exercise of state power and left the therapists to devise their own means for bringing the therapeutic power to bear. Although legislators abetted this process by establishing special and informal administrative procedures for the therapists and appending no safeguards thereto, the absence of procedural safeguards in the therapeutic realm is equally the fault of the courts. They have withheld constitutional protections from putative patients on the basis that the proceedings were noncriminal, and have uncritically accepted the testimony and opinions of doctors, social workers, and others charged with the therapeutic mission. By abridging the individual's right to object and by neglecting to scrutinize the state's requests to exercise therapeutic power, the courts have placed the therapist outside societal controls. The specific abuses resulting from judicial abdication have been chronicled in previous chapters, but general procedural irregularity has allowed individuals to be classified as mentally ill, delinquent, psychopathic, eugenic, or a euthenic threat, and to be compelled to undergo therapy without an adequate opportunity to object, challenge, or offer alternative remedies. Lack of procedural standards has also permitted the therapeutic powers to be invoked for clearly nontherapeutic purposes, especially in the case of psychopathy and sterilization.

Our legal institutions, both judicial and legislative, have also been loath to oversee the actual treatments used under the therapeutic aegis. There has been little effort or inclination to set substantive limits to the application of the therapeutic power, largely because of an understandable reluctance to second-guess the expertise of the therapist in his own field. In fact, given the reverence of the legislatures and the courts for the diagnostic opinions and treatment skills of the therapists, it is no wonder that their day-to-day operations have escaped general scrutiny. The therapists thus became total masters of empires they did not seek in the first place and for whose administration they were never granted the proper supports and tools. Frequently, the true powers of the therapeutic state finally devolved upon custodial staffs, and considerations of custodial security often took precedence over individual treatment. As a result of this unconcern and abdication, human beings have languished in institutions which can do nothing for them and have been subjected to drastic invasions of mental and bodily integrity, all in the name of therapy.

Liberty in the Therapeutic State: Reducing the Dominance of the Savers

Experience should teach us to be most on our guard to protect liberty when the government's purposes are beneficient. Men born to freedom are naturally alert to repel invasion of their liberty by evil-minded rulers. The greatest dangers to liberty lurk in insidious encroachment by men of zeal, well-meaning but without understanding—Brandeis, J., dissenting in Olmstead v. United States, 277 U.S. 438, 479 (1928)

If salvation is not sought voluntarily and cooperatively, it merely increases the passivity of those who are saved and increases the dominance of the savers.—Platt, "The Child Savers" 328 (1966)

THE BALANCE OF TWO MODELS: PENAL AND THERAPEUTIC

Until recently, it has not been possible to view the therapeutic state as an integrated model in which comparative assessments and analogies could aid in the overall plans for either growth or restraint. Each area has been a separate experiment, the experiments nevertheless possessing a common ancestor—orthodox criminal law. Each came into being through the same process—an expropriation of areas from that common ancestor. And each has been nurtured with a similar mixture of humanism, deterministic philosophies, and social-defense aims. It is not surprising, therefore, that these once separate enclaves of social experimentation share many common attributes, praised as well as lamented, which now can be subsumed under a common nomenclature, the therapeutic state, denoting its humanizing and rehabilitative yet involuntary emphasis.

The product of the continuing process of divestment has been a dual system of institutional models, utilized mostly alternatively but at times concurrently in dealing with those who deviate from society's norms. Neither the penal nor the therapeutic model is pure; rather, each is imbued with certain attributes of the other. Most significantly, the rehabilitative ideal, a hallmark of the therapeutic processes, has had a revolutionary impact on the complexion of orthodox criminal law.

The introduction of probation, parole, psychological counseling, halfway houses, and other correctional innovations into the criminal law has already produced the demise of purely retributive criminal sanctions. Reformation and rehabilitation are no longer mere serendipitous boons of incarceration in the criminal process. They are its goals, although retribution, incapacitation, and deterrence have not been discarded. Since the aims and the tools of both the criminal law and the therapeutic state are not always dissimilar, solutions offered under these diverse tracts are often unexpectedly similar. The narcotics addict convicted for possession or use of the drug, or even convicted of a more serious offense, might receive the same treatment as the addict who is civilly committed for treatment under the therapeutic program. Likewise, the sexual offender criminally convicted for an overt act could receive the same psychiatric help as one committed for sexual-psychopathic therapy. On the other hand, both could receive the same "nonhelp" where the modes of treatment have not been developed or where the newer techniques are not employed.

What then distinguishes the therapeutic state from today's criminal law? Philosophically, the difference lies in the concept of free will and personal responsibility, the existence of which is denied by the therapeutic state but is still affirmed in the criminal law. Since this concept has historically been at the center of our theory of criminal intervention and sanctions, it cannot, and probably will not, be easily ejected. Although the concept of free will as a justification for punishment in criminal justice has been flexible, which permitted the rehabilition goal to stand alongside retribution and deterrence, the absence of this concept deprives the therapeutic state of a justification for using sanctions designed to deter or incapacitate. At the same time, the criminal law superstructure, consisting of definitions of fixed overt offenses matched by incarceration or fines geared to the severity of the acts (thus making the punishment proportionate to the crime), could not support a total shift to the rehabilitative ideal (requiring a treatment that fits the deviant). The need for therapy clearly does not depend on the nature of the offense, which, in classical criminal law, measures the sanctions through which the offender may be reformed. The criminal law must continue to respond primarily to the offense, while the therapeutic state seeks to meet the needs of the offender.

These inherent philosophical constrictions, aside from constitutional restrictions upon penal sanctions, will continue to prevent any accommodation of the therapeutic state within the current framework of criminal justice. Although limited reformation can, admittedly, be accomplished within the criminal process, the total rehabilitative ideal would suffocate in that atmosphere. The functioning of the therapeutic state is dependent upon an atmosphere which de-emphasizes the overt act and permits the needs of the offender to dictate the length of his confinement and the measure of his treatment.

The inability of classical criminal law to secure order and tranquility in present-day society guarantees that the desire for new social experimentation, combining the spread of the deterministic philosophies and sciences, will further expand the horizons of the therapeutic state. The expansion will in part be motivated by the same sense of paternalism, humaneness, and moral sensitivity that has contributed to society's past willingness to exempt certain deviants from the criminal process. In significant part, however, the growth of the therapeutic state will continue to be an accommodation to the desire for more effective and stricter measures of social defense.

THE BEST OF BOTH WORLDS: PROCEDURAL REFORM

During most of the 120 years of this nation's therapeutic experiment (beginning with the construction of special institutions for the mentally ill), no thorough legislative or judicial review of either its concepts or its operations has been undertaken. Little by little, however, the procedural and then the substantive questions of the therapeutic state have been gaining attention in the last several years.

Until the last decade the Supreme Court of the United States only

twice trod along the fringes of this developing area. Both decisions—
Buck v. *Bell*,[1] upholding the use of involuntary sterilization for the
mentally deficient, and *Pearson* v. *Probate Court*,[2] sanctioning the
commitment of sexual psychopaths—offer little insight into the broader
issues of the therapeutic state.[3] In all that time the court never
heard a case dealing with mental commitment, juvenile delinquency,
drug addiction, or alcoholism. It is not certain whether the absence
of searching judicial opinion, either by the nation's Supreme Court or
by the state courts, stemmed from lack of awareness and opportunity,
was part of the traditional neglect accorded in our society to personal
as contrasted with property rights, or was motivated by a conscious
effort not to "rock" the new experimental therapeutic programs.

But by the end of the fifties, a host of legal writers began detailed
and critical reviews of the juvenile process.[4] In 1955 the American
Bar Association authorized a comprehensive study of the rights of the
mentally ill.[5] In 1960 the United States Senate Subcommittee on Constitutional Rights, under the chairmanship of Senator Sam Ervin, held
extensive hearings concerning the rights of the mentally ill;[6] and in
1963, Dr. Thomas Szasz expressed the alarm of the therapist at the
uncurtailed power society has vested in him and others of his profession.[7]

These developments were followed by the Supreme Court's entry
into the arena. In 1962 the court rendered the *Robinson* decision,
which held that drug addiction (as distinguished from the possession,
use, and sale of drugs) is an illness and therefore not punishable
under the sanctions of criminal law.[8] In 1965 the Supreme Court for
the first time in its history undertook to review the juvenile court

---

[1] Buck v. Bell, 274 U.S. 200 (1927); *see also* Skinner v. Oklahoma, 316 U.S.
535 (1942).

[2] Minnesota *ex rel.* Pearson v. Probate Court, 309 U.S. 270 (1940).

[3] But *see* Skinner v. Oklahoma, 316 U.S. 535 (1942) (concurring opinion of
Jackson, J.).

[4] Paulsen, "Fairness to the Juvenile Offender," 41 *Minn. L. Rev.* 547 (1957);
Antieau, "Constitutional Rights in Juvenile Courts," 46 *Cornell L. Q.* 387 (1961);
Beemsterboer, "The Juvenile Court—Benevolence in the Star Chamber," 50 *J.
Crim. L.C. & P.S.* 464 (1960); F. A. Allen, *The Borderland of Criminal Justice*
(1964).

[5] This study, originally planned and directed by this author, produced *The Mentally Disabled and the Law* (F. T. Lindman and D. M. McIntyre eds. 1961).

[6] U.S. Congress, Senate, Committee on the Judiciary, Subcommittee on Constitutional Rights, *Hearings on Constitutional Rights of the Mentally Ill*, 87th Cong.,
1st sess., 1961, pts. 1 and 2.

[7] *Law, Liberty and Psychiatry* (1963), followed later by *Psychiatric Justice*
(1965).

[8] Robinson v. California, 370 U.S. 660 (1962).

process. The court first made a preliminary reference to procedural safeguards in the *Kent* case.[9] It next decided to hear *in re* Gault,[10] where a juvenile's right to a whole range of procedural safeguards was at issue. The lengthy decision rendered in May of 1967 in the *Gault* case clearly established the principle that the humane ends of therapeutic treatment do not justify short-circuiting a juvenile's constitutional rights. The right to counsel, the right to confront one's accusers, the right to remain silent, and the right to timely notice of the charges were all extended into the juvenile proceeding.[11]

Just as significant to the guaranty of procedural safeguards in the therapeutic state is another 1967 Supreme Court decision, one almost totally overlooked by legal and medical commentators. *Specht* v. *Patterson*[12] deals with the procedures by which a habitual criminal offender may be sentenced to an indeterminate prison term under Colorado's Sex Offender Act, paralleling the civil commitment of habitual sexual offenders under the psychopathy laws. Holding that Specht's conviction for a crime was not alone sufficient to bring him within the criteria of the habitual sex offender law, the court ordained that he must be accorded procedural safeguards and, through them, an opportunity to challenge the experts' decision that he was a habitual offender requiring indeterminate commitment. "These commitment proceedings whether denominated civil or criminal are subject both to the Equal Protection Clause of the 14th Amendment ... and to the Due Process Clause,"[13] the court concluded.

Thus the circle is being closed. After three-quarters of a century of juvenile courts and their special procedures, the experiment is beginning to receive its overdue public review. Slowly, judicial scrutiny is spreading throughout the therapeutic realm. The synthesis of *Gault-Specht* amounts to a *parens patriae* process with procedural safeguards.

Referring to the inadequacy of procedural safeguards in the juvenile process, Justice Fortas noted in the *Kent* case:

While there can be no doubt of the original laudable purpose of juvenile courts, studies and critiques in recent years raise serious questions as to whether actual performance measures well enough against theoretical purpose to make tolerable the immunity of

[9] Kent v. United States, 383 U.S. 541, 556 (1966).
[10] *In re* Gault, 387 U.S. 1 (1967).
[11] *Ibid.*
[12] Specht v. Patterson, 386 U.S. 605 (1967).
[13] *Ibid.* 4341.

the process from the reach of constitutional guaranties applicable to adults. There is much evidence that some juvenile courts, including that of the District of Columbia, lack the personnel, facilities and techniques to perform adequately as representatives of the State in a *parens patriae* capacity, at least with respect to children charged with law violations. There is evidence, in fact, that there may be grounds for concern that the child receives the worst of both worlds: that he gets neither the protection accorded to adults nor the solicitous care and regenerative treatment postulated for children.[14]

The question raised by Justice Fortas is equally applicable to most of the other therapeutic *parens patriae* programs; whether the regenerative treatment postulated for the recipients of these programs justifies a dispensation of traditional safeguards requires serious consideration. Notably, however, both the *Kent* and *Gault* courts shied away from the deeper philosophical problem implied: whether the dispensation of constitutional safeguards could be tolerated even if the therapeutic program's actual performance measured well in relation to its postulations. Instead the court undertook to resolve the problem on the basis of realities, predicating an answer which determines the need for legal safeguards not on the basis of asserted theory and goals but upon demonstrated practice and achievements. Since the court pointedly cited the lack of personnel, facilities, and techniques necessary to assure the state's proper discharge of the *parens patriae* role, the inescapable conclusion follows that continued vigilance and a re-adoption of many of the safeguards traditional in the criminal process are required. In the 1967 *Gault* case,[15] the court therefore specifically extended to children in the juvenile court several of the safeguards contained in the Bill of Rights.

To some observers, saddling the *parens patriae* programs with due process requirements may appear overly encumbering. To others it appears only as a reasonable guaranty of justice in an affluent civilized state. Moreover, therapy and rehabilitative treatments have not been shown to be impaired where due process rights have been observed.[16]

[14] Kent v. United States, 383 U.S. 541, 555–56 (1966).

[15] *In re* Gault, 387 U.S. 1 (1967).

[16] It was advocated by this author before the Supreme Court in the *Gault* case that: (1) the procedural safeguards contained in the adversary system of justice remain the best guaranty of the necessary balance between societal and individual interests; (2) the absence of full-fledged judicial scrutiny deprives the individual of needed protection and removes from society an important protective device against overzealous, scientifically ill-founded, and promise-without-fulfillment social programs; (3) depriving juveniles of legal safeguards available to

Although only applicable to juvenile courts, the *Gault* principle that therapeutic goals do not justify dispensing with procedural safeguards will undoubtedly give momentum to a reassessment and a re-establishment of procedural guarantees in other therapeutic realms. If the legislatures and courts continue to assert and, more important, to support the nonpenal aims of the *parens patriae* state while recognizing the necessity for more effective procedural safeguards, then the recipients of therapeutic sanctions will cease to be the victims of both worlds and may become the beneficiaries of the best that can be offered: a system of social controls that is fair and not retributive. This will happen when courts recognize that no system of social sanctions (whether designated criminal, civil, *parens patriae*, therapeutic, or otherwise) which possesses the power to deprive a person of his freedom, to separate him from his family, or to interfere with his bodily integrity, can be exempt from the checks and balances to which we long ago committed ourselves through the Constitution. Indeed, one of the major permanent contributions of the therapeutic experiment to America may be the demonstration that we cannot allow the development and existence of two systems of social control, one conforming with traditional legal safeguards and the other expert-dominated and extra-legal.

CURBING THE CONGLOMERATE THERAPEUTIC STATE: REFORM OF CRITERIA

The hazard of society prematurely, hastily, and arbitrarily designating a given behavior as deviant, abnormal, and socially hazardous, and thus requiring protracted and drastic therapy, cannot be realistically alleviated through the institution of procedural safeguards alone. To guard against abuses of substantive due process, the criteria for social intervention must be constantly tested for reasonableness and certainty, must be modernized to comport with the latest scientific knowledge, and must be made responsive to democracy's commitment to pluralism and diversity.

To define better the proper criteria for the therapeutic state, realistic appraisal must be made both of its manifest aims and its

---

adults not only is objectionable from a constitutional viewpoint but tends also to affect adversely their development toward responsible citizenship; (4) while the institution of additional safeguards in the *parens patriae* programs will require more personnel and expenditure of time, these are the expected costs of American justice. Brief of American Parents Committee, 8, 9 (Nicholas N. Kittrie, counsel), *in re* Gault, October Term, 1966, no. 116, United States Supreme Court.

actual past performance. In this connection it is imperative to minimize the confusion over the therapeutic state's role in securing public safety, promoting morality, dispensing public welfare, and advancing individual health. Frequently, as we have previously noted, the therapeutic state has served all four functions without careful distinction.

Running throughout society's *parens patriae* programs is an ambivalence regarding the justification for compulsory treatments. On the one hand, public sanctions are generally presumed to be derived from the need to protect society. On the other, the therapeutic state has adopted criteria which permit the state to invoke the compulsory therapeutic power in order to benefit the individual.

Who is to be the proper arbiter of individual well being? Under Mill's thesis, in a free and pluralistic society it must be the individual himself. Unless he presents a threat to others, society has no obligation or right to interfere with his condition. Yet under the therapeutic thesis, the individual is subject to societal standards of morals, health, and welfare. If he deviates from conventional standards, the state has the authority to intervene and rehabilitate him. Seen from this perspective, the therapeutic power is the successor to earlier enforcers of conformity and compulsory reformation—ecclesiastical orthodoxy and the poor laws.

By claiming a primary loyalty to individual welfare rather than to social defense, the therapeutic state has been able to assert its humanitarian precepts as justification for its reforming zeal. Too often, however, the welfare and health components of the therapeutic power have served as subterfuge for circumventing traditional limitations against excesses of state power, and the conglomerate nature of the therapeutic power has helped to give rise to the many abuses documented throughout this book. The containment of therapeutic excesses is not possible without first discarding the composite nature of the therapeutic power. A separation must be accomplished between its health-welfare-morality role and its social-defense role.

Welfare and health should be voluntarily offered to those who seek to alter their lives. Compulsory rehabilitation, on the other hand, must be restricted to those who pose a clear social threat and hazard. Furthermore, the threat and hazard must be to others and not to oneself. In need of repetition is Mill's admonition that one may not be compelled to do or forbear merely because the majority believes that it will be better for him to do so, or that to do so would be right, or wise, or moral. Let society increasingly offer attractive welfare, treatment, shelter, and educational services to those who do not comport with the majority's morals and mores, but let it not compel acceptance or attendance.

Applicable throughout the therapeutic state are the recommendations of the President's Panel on Mental Retardation: "We would minimize intervention by the law insofar as possible. The courts should be regarded as residual resource, if not a last recourse.... We would minimize mandatory requirements whenever voluntary compliance can be obtained ... the richer and better the services available ... the less need there is of coercive intervention to provide care."[17]

Drawing the distinction between the social-defense and the public-welfare purposes of the therapeutic state and limiting compulsory therapy to situations which present a grave social hazard would thus serve two important functions. First, it would crystalize the social-defense role of the therapeutic power and point up the need for safeguards against excesses when compulsion is used. Second, it would lead to an increased realization of the need for innovative voluntary programs under the welfare wing of the therapeutic power; such offering of early treatment might substantially lower the incidence of dangerous behavior requiring compulsory intervention.

Limiting compulsory therapy to purposes of social defense only raises the further question of how to determine when an individual poses a threat sufficiently dangerous to justify the use of the state's power. That is, at what point does society become empowered to act in its own defense against the liberty of the individual?

Restraints for Dangerousness?

We have previously distinguished the model of social controls represented by the therapeutic state from the model represented by the criminal process. Criminal justice is primarily an instrument of crime management: it proscribes certain acts that are designated crimes and utilizes penal sanctions as deterrent devices. The criminal process is thus constructed as an overt act-deterrence model. The therapeutic state, on the other hand, is usually thought of as an instrument of crime prediction and prevention: it defines a certain human status or condition as potentially hazardous to the social order and sets out to prevent the occurrence of the danger by rehabilitating or reforming those subject to the adverse conditions. The therapeutic state is therefore built as a status-prevention model.

[17] President's Panel on Mental Retardation, *Report of the Task Force on Law* 17 (1963).

In the criminal realm, the law has increasingly elected to resort to interference with individual freedom only in cases where the individual has actually demonstrated his capacity to harm society. A long tradition has produced in the criminal law substantive standards, such as the constitutional prohibition against bills of attainder and *ex post facto* laws, in order to limit the power of the state over individuals whose status is suspect but who have caused no actual harm. In the common law tradition a criminal offense required not only a socially dangerous state of mind (*mens rea*) but also the commission of a prohibited act (*actus reus*). Indeed, to guard against the potential for abuse inherent in the early crime of conspiracy, the common law subsequently added the requirement of an overt act toward the accomplishment of the plot—in order to prevent punishment for thought only.

Under the therapeutic model of social controls these protections appear to be antiquated and irrelevant. Since the ideal is to treat the status of an individual, all that is needed is a proper diagnosis of the status. At that point, to wait for an overt act before commencing treatment is a senseless waste of time and resources.

Obviously, therefore, the reasonableness of state intervention under the therapeutic aegis is a function of the immediacy and degree of the social danger posed by the status to be controlled and of the accuracy of the diagnostic technique. In other words, the propriety of intervention based on status must be directly related to the correlation between the status and resultant dangerous behavior. Unless this correlation is very high, society is not justified in imposing treatment upon all who suffer from that condition in order to restrain some who will commit dangerous acts in some future time. Not only must there be a high correlation between status and degree of dangerousness, but the harmful activity must not be remote in time. It must be demonstrated, therefore, that intervention is essential to prevent the harmful behavior and that neither voluntary therapy nor other supervening factors are likely to terminate the existing threat to society.

The reasonableness of therapeutic intervention for social defense based upon status is also conditioned by the effectiveness of the treatments proposed to alter the status and prevent the harmful conduct. If the treatment is not 100 percent effective in preventing harmful acts, there are some persons whose lives will have been interfered with for no demonstrable social benefit. Many alcoholics and narcotics addicts may thus be subjected to long periods of restrictive therapy which will not result in any social gain in terms of preventing future harmful behavior. In this light, preventive interference with a deviant who would not have committed any dangerous future act results in a price totally out of proportion with the social benefits.

We cannot now know whether the therapeutic state's improved predictive techniques will solve most of the problems inherent in the attempt to utilize an individual's status as a justification for intervening in the name of social defense. Perhaps the new tools of diagnosis, increased surveillance of individual behavior, compilation of knowledge about genetic predispositions, and the effects of environment will eventually enable scientists to unerringly predict harmful behavior. Similarly, treatment programs may improve the cure rates to a reasonable level. Today, however, it remains plain that the correlation between status and degree of dangerousness is uncertain. Similarly, treatment efforts are so sadly lacking in success that intervention based on status yields too small a profit to society when compared with the personal cost to the nonharmful member of the group controlled for its status. If we are to correct the abuses documented in this book and to avoid new errors, it is essential that the therapeutic state discard the status criteria and restrain its power unless prompted by an overt act.

Interestingly, this suggestion has been voiced in other quarters. There is a strong parallel between the status criteria of the therapeutic state and *l'état dangereux* (the state of dangerousness) or *pericolosita* propounded by Enrico Ferri and the positivist movement of earlier times. It is significant that many European authorities have recently stressed that *l'état dangereux* can very rarely be diagnosed with reasonable certainty before an actual offense has been committed. They have recommended, therefore, that *l'état dangereux* be abandoned as a consideration for compulsory preventive measures prior to criminal behavior and be retained only for postdelictual dispositions and the prevention of recidivism.[18]

Utilization of the overt act as the test of social dangerousness and therapeutic intervention does not militate against the humanitarian and philosophical advances underlying the therapeutic model of social controls. Unlike the criminal process, which must insist upon punishment once guilt is determined, the *parens patriae* power would not have to be invoked after a harmful act has been committed if the therapists could satisfy themselves that the individual posed no further threat to society. Therapeutic treatment (and any accompanying un-

[18] De Greeff, "Le Probleme de l'État Dangereux," in *Proceedings of the Third International Congress of Criminology* 332 (1953).

pleasantness) would only be resorted to if the individual was found to constitute a continuing threat to society.

Compulsory and Cooperative Therapies

If we accept Mill's criterion for the exercise of societal intervention—the prevention of harm to others—and further agree that an overt act is necessary before the state can interfere with individual liberty, there remains the question of what type of harm must be suffered by society before the state is justified to impose therapeutic controls for its defense. In a post–World War II study of deviation, an eminent German criminologist included among those requiring control and treatment a group that he classified as "fanatic psychopaths," consisting of "offenders from political conviction," as well as "incurably litigious persons" and those who refuse military service.[19] Clearly, an offense to individual safety is more severe than an offense to morals or aesthetics, and the invocation of treatment must reasonably correspond to the nature of the danger posed. But in our world of population pressures and close social interaction, precisely when does deviant conduct cease to be eccentric, or amusing, or harmful only to oneself and begin to produce evil of sufficient magnitude to call for intervention and control? Should the state act against a man if alcoholism, neurosis, or laziness reduces his earning capacity and injures the well-being of his family? Should a conscientious objector who harms the public by refusing to carry his military burden be subject to social sanction? Should the homosexual, who limits his practices to consenting partners, be forcibly institutionalized or otherwise treated?

Since the therapeutic state was primarily based on individual welfare, not social defense, society much too often has been willing to apply compulsory therapy to individuals whose conduct was not sufficiently harmful to warrant criminal punishment. Oftentimes, therefore, the therapeutic state has become the receiving ground for past mistakes of criminal law, when society finally repents of its error but is not yet willing to tolerate the offensive activity, even though it is not particularly harmful. Many of the activities of the mentally ill which result in commitment are of this ilk. Similarly, this is the direction that the movement for treating alcoholics is taking. In addition, once the therapeutic model is established, it is particularly easy for

[19] F. Exner, *Kriminologie* 188 (1949).

it to accommodate within its sanctions forms of behavior which other-wise would be left unsanctioned by the criminal law. This was the history of the "juvenile offenses" following the advent of the juvenile court system in America. By this process, the therapeutic state brings compulsory power to bear upon activity which may be morally and aesthetically objectionable but is not directly dangerous to others.

Several of the deviations and deviants subjected to the therapeutic sanctions pose only a remote threat to the social order; for the most part these deviants and their conditions are only morally objection-able to the majority of the populace. The roaming insane, the volun-tary adult sex deviant, the juvenile who refuses parental supervision, the habitual drinker who fails to hold a steady employment—all might be objectionable to the general morality, yet the degree and im-mediacy of their social threat do not clearly justify intervention by the state.

The therapeutic state, therefore, must be protected against becom-ing the last refuge of unjust social compulsion in the name of moral-ity, welfare, and health.[20] In setting out to define the scope and criteria of the state's therapeutic intervention, caution must be exer-cised lest, in our preoccupation with the new and benevolent labels, we set out to sanction therapeutically that which does not need legal controls. In other words, when no justification is available for state controls, even therapeutic controls, if compulsory, must be viewed as excessive. Our legislatures must determine what types of social be-havior or status will justify intervention by the state's sanctioning power, whether designated criminal or therapeutic. But once public support no longer exists for criminal sanctions regarding a given be-havior, it will not do to bring that conduct under the compulsory therapeutic realm. To members of the Mattachine Society, which urges the right of the adult homosexual to engage in his behavior with consenting adult partners, substitution of the criminal process by involuntary therapeutic treatment is not a desired accomplishment but an insidious threat. Similarly, if the ungovernability of juveniles should properly be left to parental rather than state control, subject-ing youth to the therapeutic rather than the criminal process will not redeem this unnecessary societal intervention. Extreme care must be

[20] Younghusband, "The Dilemma of the Juvenile Court," 33 *Soc. Serv. Rev.* 10, 12 (1959). *See*, generally, P. Devlin, "The Enforcement of Morals" (Mac-cabaian Lecture, British Academy, 1959); Hart, "Immorality and Treason," *Listener*, July 30, 1959, p. 162; Rostow, "The Enforcement of Morals," 16 *Cambridge L. J.* 174 (1960).

taken, therefore, in order that concepts of mental health and adjustment to group norms not be utilized to establish conformity where the
public safety does not demand it.

Many of those customarily brought within the therapeutic realm
are there not primarily because of their potential social threat but
because of the absence of other and more fitting community resources.
For the elderly patient suffering from senile dementia, the mentally
retarded, the neglected child, and the skid-row alcoholic, the therapeutic state is not as much an instrument for reformation as a public
welfare service. For them the therapeutic state provides the only
place to go. Yet when social service is so dispensed, inequity and
repression result from the fact that the candidates for therapeutic
sanctions are often selected not by reason of their social dangerousness but because of their poverty or helplessness.[21]

The conglomerate role of the therapeutic state as a guardian of
social defense, an enforcer of compulsory reformation, a promoter of
morality, and a dispenser of welfare and health has seriously diminished its rehabilitative potential and successes. The utilization of compulsory institutions instead of voluntary, community-based facilities
undermines the rehabilitative function of the therapist since the penal
milieu which so often accompanies compulsory therapeutic programs
is detrimental to effective treatment. An unwilling and uncooperative
patient, furthermore, makes true therapy very difficult, and better
results could almost certainly be obtained through attractive voluntary programs, totally divorced from social compulsion.

In large part, the therapeutic state remains to this day the successor to the poor laws. Within its realms we seek to accommodate many
of today's socially and economically deprived—the New Poor, who
remain closely akin to the populations subject to England's and
America's seventeenth-century poor law programs.[22] The therapeutic
state has relied heavily upon institutionalization. Yet effective social
programs require increasing specialization, as well as community-
based facilities. Specialization has produced the modern mental clinics
out of medieval prisons; modern public welfare has replaced the
contracting out of the disadvantaged to the highest bidder. Similarly,
the composite role of the therapeutic state must be relinquished and
a separation accomplished: its welfare and health functions should
be voluntarily offered to those who seek them, and the social-defense

---

[21] Allen, *The Borderland of Criminal Justice* 7.
[22] S. and B. Webb, *English Poor Law History* (1927); *idem, English Poor Law
Policy* (1963).

responsibilities should be involuntarily imposed only in clear instances of social threat and hazard. More specifically, if those who require welfare, health, shelter, or education were to be offered these services freely within the community, compulsory treatment under the therapeutic aegis would be less common.[23]

THE LIMITS OF THERAPY

The hazards of societal zeal in prescribing therapeutic programs will not be totally assuaged, however, through the reassessment of criteria and the introduction of procedural safeguards. One can foresee more drastic methods of modifying deviation through psychiatric, electrophysiological, or biological manipulations, of which sterilization, lobotomy, and shock are only the primitive precursors. Dr. Jose Delgado of Yale's School of Medicine believes that current researchers support the distasteful conclusion that motion, emotion, and behavior can be directed by electrical forces and that humans can be controlled like robots by push buttons."[24] Commenting on recent research demonstrating that newly developed drugs can improve the learning capacity in mice specifically bred for their stupidity, Dr. David Krech of the University of California at Berkeley states: "Here we have a 'chemical memory pill' which not only improves memory and learning, but which can serve to make all mice equal when God—or genetics—has created them unequal! It's most pregnant with social implications, and promises and foreboding for the future."[25] Is there any limit on the powers of society to modify its deviant members? How much experimentation should be allowed in the involuntary therapeutic programs?

A cogent commentary on this therapeutic hazard has been written by law professor Richard Wasserstrom:

> Treatments, no less than punishments, are capable of giving rise to serious moral problems. If, for instance, a person can be treated effectively only by performing a prefrontal lobotomy or

[23] This is not to suggest that the voluntary dispensing of welfare is totally free of due process encroachments. "The welfare state, in providing a multiplicity of new expectations, nevertheless established additional points of conflict by the use of administrative techniques; these new forms of administration in the hands of regulators and managers make the role of the individual more dependent upon the rule of law to assure fairness and justice." Becker, "Social Reality and Planning Illusions: Some Observations on the Need for a Legal Philosophy of Group Interests," 13 *Rutgers L. Rev.* 588, 589 (1959); Jones, "The Rule of Law and the Welfare State," 58 *Colum. L. Rev.* 143, 156 (1958).

[24] Krech, "Controlling the Mind Controllers," 32 *Think* 5 (1966).

[25] Perlman, "The Search for the Memory Molecule," *New York Times Magazine*, pp. 8, 34; *The Sunday Times*, July 7, 1968, sec. 6.

by altering in some other more sophisticated fashion his basic personality or identity, it might well be that punishment would have the virtue (and it is no small one) of leaving the individual intact. Imprisonment may be a poor way to induce a person to behave differently in the future, but imprisonment may, nonetheless, permit him to remain the same person throughout. In short, treatments as well as punishments may involve serious interferences with the most significant moral claims an individual can assert. Like punishments, treatments of the type contemplated will doubtless be imposed without the actor's consent. The substitution of treatment for punishment could never, therefore, absolve us from involvement in that difficult but inavoidable task of assessing and resolving the competing claims of society and the individual.[26]

In the criminal process, which relies on defined crimes and personal responsibility, the Eighth Amendment protection against cruel and unusual punishment provides a scale against which the crime, the offender's culpability, and the resultant public sanction can be measured. When the Bill of Rights was adopted, our system of criminal justice was heavily weighted by retributive and deterrent considerations. Even so, the framers felt compelled to limit the state's retributive and deterrent zeal. Mere effectiveness will not justify the imposition of a punishment, for certain punishments may be objectionable either because of their method or because of their disproportionate severity. The therapeutic state disclaims penal aims and asserts, therefore, freedom from limitations upon punishment. Moreover, by ignoring or at least bypassing personal culpability and guilt, the therapeutic state finds itself with no measuring stick by which to determine the propriety of its sanctions, other than effectiveness. Says Barbara Wootton:

> Only when ... [the presumption of responsibility] is removed can science pursue unhindered its morally neutral task of designing ... the method of achieving a prescribed aim that is most likely to be effective; but whether that instrument be hydrogen bomb, hangman's noose or analyst's couch, the demonstration of effectiveness is not, and cannot be, by itself a command to use.[27]

Yet already in 1942, concurring in the sterilization case of *Skinner* v. *Oklahoma*,[28] Justice Jackson warned that there may be limits to the

---

[26] Wasserstrom, "Why Punish the Guilty?" *Princeton Alumni Magazine*, March 17, 1964, pp. 25, 29–30.

[27] B. Wootton, *Social Science and Social Pathology* 254 (1959).

[28] Skinner v. Oklahoma, 316 U.S. 535 (1942).

extent to which a majority may conduct biological experiments at the expense of the dignity, personality, and natural power of the minority. Since that statement, the therapeutic skills of the state have grown, and the number of tools for the modification of man has increased. The time has come to recognize that therapeutic excesses, like penal excesses, need be and can be curbed.

> A system of treatment need not be attended by these defects. Within such a system certain treatments might be deemed impermissible for the same reasons that some punishments are presently proscribed. Modes of undesirable but untreatable behavior might be tolerated just because the alternatives were less desirable still.[29]

Can outer limits of tolerance, similar to those placed upon the criminal process by the Eighth Amendment prohibition against cruel and unusual punishment, thus be imposed upon the exercise of the therapeutic powers?

The Right to Bodily and Personal Integrity

Currently there are no absolute limits on the exercise of the therapeutic power. Thus, while the power to alter totally and irrevocably the individual's state of consciousness is coming within the grasp of the therapist, no limits have been set to its exercise.

The awesome moral problem of these treatments is confused by the fact that the individuals so treated may in most cases be incapable of objecting to the treatment after it has occurred. In his altered state, the patient is pleasant and happy; he has no recollection of his prior condition and is therefore incapable of asserting any objections he might have to the treatment, be they physical, philosophical, or recalcitrant. The new personality is reformed and even somewhat artificial, almost as if a new soul had been transplanted into an old body.

But where has the old "soul" or personality gone with its hangups, tensions, prejudices, bias, problems, dreams, talents, and individuality? Has it not in a very real way been executed? Is the death of the body the only criteria for the destruction of a man? Does not the personality of man need protection as much as the life of man?

How can we protect the personality of a man from the incursions of therapeutic power? Heretofore, all of our objections to the workings of the therapeutic state have been resolved by resorting to our tradi-

---

[29] Wasserstrom, "Why Punish the Guilty?" 30.

tional requirements of fair criteria and fair procedures as safeguards against abuse of the state's power. Yet these safeguards offer no protection against drastic therapeutic measures, no protection against the execution of the personality. A new right is needed—the right to personal and bodily integrity. It is a right that has constitutional dimensions. However, the chances of creating a totally new right, without a grounding in existing constitutional doctrine, are slim at best. The odds are much more favorable to an expansion of one or more of our traditional constitutional doctrines to include the right to personal and bodily integrity, much the same as freedom of association and the right to privacy, to which the Constitution does not specifically allude, were forged.[30]

Almost immediately the language of the Fourth Amendment springs to mind: "The right of the people to be secure in their persons . . . against unreasonable searches and seizures, shall not be violated." Although in the past this amendment has been mainly used to protect persons suspected of crimes from overzealous police activity, the wording of the amendment seems to be fortuitously directed at the very problem under discussion. While there might be some conceptual difficulty with the search and seizure of a personality, it should be recalled that recently the United States Supreme Court held that something as abstract as a conversation could be searched and seized through the use of electronic surveillance and recording devices.[31] Is it any stranger to conceive of a person's mind being searched by drugs or other therapy and his personality being seized and controlled or replaced?

Yet the protections of the Fourth Amendment are not unqualified; the search and seizure is not unreasonable if it is supported by probable cause. In the past this meant probable cause to believe that the searched person had committed a crime. In the future this might mean probable cause for believing that the individual has a particular condition and is in need of treatment. Consequently, the Fourth Amendment does not appear to be the repository of an unqualified right to safety from personality intervention.

The Fifth Amendment privilege against self-incrimination, if its application solely to criminal cases could be overcome, may hold some element of the right to personality. It should certainly prohibit the searching examination of a person's character and personality to deter-

[30] United States v. Robel, 389 U.S. 258 (1967); Griswold v. Connecticut, 381 U.S. 479 (1965).
[31] Katz v. United States, 389 U.S. 347 (1967).

mine if he is suffering from some disorder which needs treatment. However, it will not provide any protection from the extinction of the individual personality if all the elements of due process are complied with.

Together, however, the Fourth and Fifth Amendments, peripherally joined by the First and Third Amendments, already have been conceptually merged to form the right of privacy.[32] This right is new and yet untested in its scope, but it does create a zone or field of individual life and activity into which the state may not enter. This zone certainly guarantees against the state's interference with the internal thoughts and emotions of an individual. Therefore, it should also be sufficient to prohibit the state from invading the personality and altering it, for to do so would be to tamper with the internal thoughts and feelings protected by the right to privacy.

Under the traditional criminal process, the Eighth Amendment's protection against cruel and unusual punishment provided the measure beyond which society could not interfere with a man's body or life in the name of social control. The protection stood for the principle that, no matter how effective a particular punishment might be, there were boundaries of human dignity and humanity which could not be transgressed.

Although the ramifications of this protection have not been extensively examined by the Supreme Court,[33] the protection embodies two standards which may be applied to test the constitutionality of a punishment. First, by its nature and quality, is the punishment *per se* contrary to the accepted standards of civilized decency in our society?[34] Second, is the punishment as imposed for a given crime unacceptable in either its excessiveness or its inappropriateness to the particular offense?[35]

These basic precepts seem to provide a direction for development

[32] Griswold v. Connecticut, 381 U.S. 479 (1965).

[33] Trop v. Dulles, 356 U.S. 86 (1958).

[34] Thus flaying, pillarying, and quartering would today be cruel and unusual *per se*. Also, imprisonment in irons at hard and painful labor would be declared excessively cruel. Weems v. United States, 217 U.S. 349 (1910).

[35] Imprisonment in irons at hard and painful labor was declared to be unusual punishment when it was imposed for the crime of falsifying public records. *Ibid.* 346. In Robinson v. California, 370 U.S. 660 (1962), ninety days imprisonment for the "crime" of being addicted to narcotics was declared to be cruel and unusual punishment, not because ninety days imprisonment was cruel *per se* or excessive, but because it was inappropriate to the "crime" of having a disease condition. "Even one day in prison would be a cruel and unusual punishment for the 'crime' of having a common cold." *Ibid.* 667.

of the right which would equally restrict the power of the therapeutic state. Certain treatments that would alter the physical or psychological structure of an individual to the point of permanently depriving him of certain physical powers or basic personality traits might be prohibited as *per se* unreasonable treatments. Treatments that would leave the individual intact, but would require lengthy terms of treatment, close surveillance, submission to indignities, etc., could be prohibited as excessive or inappropriate when measured against the danger posed by the untreated individual.

Before the Eighth Amendment could be expanded to reach such results, however, the distinction between punishment and treatment would have to be abolished. This could be accomplished by reading punishment in a much broader sense to include any interference, however motivated, by the state in the life of the individual for the greater good of the community. Presumably, this is the intended effect of punishment, and at the time the amendment was penned, no other form of interference had been conceived. Thus to hold that the Eighth Amendment places limits on the nature and effects of treatments that may be employed under the therapeutic power would be in the best tradition of constitutional application.

The New Ninth Amendment

If the Eighth Amendment's protections are withheld from the patient because he is not undergoing punishment, the final possible repository of the right to personality is the Ninth Amendment. Its language is broad, sweeping, and vague: "The enumeration in the Constitution, of certain rights, shall not be construed to deny or disparage others retained by the people." No one knows what rights the framers of the Constitution had in mind when this clause was added to the Bill of Rights. Yet the framers of the amendment obviously conceived of a residuum of rights, some type of natural rights, above and beyond those specifically listed in the Constitution, which continued to be vested in the people. What rights are here spoken of: the right to privacy? the right to be different and be left alone? the right to the preservation of one's dignity, personality, and natural power? the right to remain psychologically and physically intact? the right not to be experimented with?

Unfortunately, the Ninth Amendment has not been the subject of much judicial interpretation defining and implementing its protections.[36] The most authoritative construction of the Ninth Amendment occurred in 1965 in *Griswold* v. *Connecticut*.[37] In that case, the petitioner, a Planned Parenthood counselor, had been convicted of aiding and abetting a married couple in the use of a contraceptive device in violation of Connecticut law. Although reversing the conviction on the grounds that the statute was unconstitutional, the justices were not of one mind as to what portion of the Constitution was offended. No fewer than four opinions set forth various grounds ranging from infringement of the due process clause of the Fourteenth Amendment alone to the infringement of one of the unenumerated rights guaranteed to the people by the Ninth Amendment (Justices Goldberg, Warren, Brennan). Justices Douglas and Clark also rested their conclusion on the Ninth Amendment, but in concert with the First, Third, Fourth, Fifth, as applied through the Fourteenth Amendment, and without more than passing reference to the Ninth.

In discussing the relevance of the Ninth Amendment to the case, Justice Goldberg argued that the Ninth Amendment had a purpose and must be read as such. He found that marital privacy was a fundamental right in our society and should therefore be protected from infringement by the state. Although the right to marital privacy was nowhere mentioned in the Constitution, this is no major obstacle since the Ninth Amendment clearly states that not all the rights retained by the people are iterated in the Constitution and that their absence from the written Constitution should not be construed as silent authorization for the government to disregard and infringe upon them. Pointing out that if we grant government the power to interfere in the marital relationship through the prohibition of contraception, the state would be equally free to order the sterilization of those who fathered a designated number of children. Justice Goldberg sought a comprehensive constitutional prohibition against such invasion. The rights spoken of in the Ninth Amendment, he concluded, are those which emanate from the total constitutional scheme and are so rooted in the collective conscience and traditions of the people as to be fundamental to our social structure.

Surely the right to live one's life free from bodily and psychological alteration is basic to our scheme of society. The ability to remain as you are is clearly a right suggested by the general pattern of the Bill of Rights. The First Amendment prohibitions against state invasion of religious freedom and interference with the free transmission

[36] B. B. Patterson, *The Forgotten Ninth Amendment* (1955); Kelsey, "The Ninth Amendment to the Federal Constitution," 11 *Ind. L. J.* 309 (1936).
[37] 381 U.S. 479 (1965).

of ideas demonstrate that a man's thoughts, mind, conscience, and psychological processes are not to be manipulated or coerced by the state. Furthermore, the Eighth Amendment indicates that there are limits of human dignity beyond which the state cannot go in defending itself against the most heinous of offenders. Thus, even under a narrow construction of the Ninth Amendment, room can be found for the right to personality and bodily integrity.

Perhaps the question should not be what the past use of the Ninth Amendment has been, but whether it has any import for us today. If the framers of the Constitution could have foreseen the therapeutic power, would they not have made some provision to protect individual dignity and integrity? Should we not have the wisdom to react to new dangers using the broadsword they gave us in the Ninth Amendment?

Seeking to define the future limits of therapy, one might outlaw certain surgical, chemical, or psychological techniques altogether, or at least insist that the measure of treatment be proportionate to the severity and social hazard of the deviation.[38] Speaking with regard to classical criminal law, the German philosopher Immanuel Kant stressed that "punishment can never be imposed merely for the purpose of securing some extrinsic good, either for the criminal himself or for civil society; it must in all cases be imposed (and can only be imposed) because the individual upon whom it is inflicted has committed an offense.... The right of retaliation ... properly understood ... is the only principle which ... can definitely guide a public tribunal as to both the quality and quantity of just punishment."[39] One could insist that therapeutic controls should be similarly measured.

One might attempt to delineate personality characteristics that would be immune from alteration. Or one might approach the solution altogether differently. Since the therapeutic state claims for itself a parental role, emphasizing the individual's salvation and well-being over the public's retributive and protective urge, perhaps the propriety of therapy should depend on whether the treatment is constituted for the patient as an end in himself rather than as a means

[38] *See*, in this connection, the writings of Norval Morris, whose concern for the abuses of the therapeutic Ideal led him to propose a ceiling upon therapeutic sanctions: that no power should be exercised over a criminal's life in excess of that which would be taken in the absence of therapeutic considerations. This ceiling does not help us, however, with regard to those areas of the *parens patriae* state in which no criminal law equivalent exists, such as commitments to mental institutions, the treatment of children charged not with criminality but with delinquency, etc. Morris, "Impediments to Penal Reform," 33 *U. Chicago L. Rev.* 627, 638 (1966).

[39] Quoted in J. Heath, *Eighteenth Century Penal Theory* 272 (1963).

to broader social aims. It is wrong, it has been insisted, to use a person simply as a means to benefit others. What this means is that the aim of treatment should be the patient's own self-fulfillment, not his greater service to or conformity with societal imperatives for the benefit of society. But could we secure a synthesis of the diverse concepts of man's role in the universe, and a consensus among the diverse insights into the sociopsychological makeup of the human nature,[40] which would be necessary for such self-fulfillments? There is a challenge.

Only the future will substantively define the scope of the individual's right not to be altered. Under the criminal process, in an admittedly retributive society, the Eighth Amendment provided a measure for punishment, but little attention has been given in the past to the limits upon the therapeutic process. In tomorrow's manipulative yet assertedly benevolent therapeutic state, the Ninth Amendment should undoubtedly be used in order to furnish a new scale for measuring the type and scope of justified state "treatment."[41]

Such limitations on the therapeutic power may indeed hinder the "cure" of many patients. But what kind of a cure is sought by treatments which seek only to preserve the external shell of the treated? Since the therapeutic power seeks justification in the name of therapy and humanity, what reasonable objection could be raised against protections against the very destruction of the essence of humanness? Should we not be willing to accept these limitations to preserve human variation and pluralism in the same way that we have been willing to accept limitations on the exercise of the police power in order to preserve liberty at the expense of more crime, delinquency, and offensive behavior?

THE RIGHT TO TREATMENT:
PARENS PATRIAE'S CONTRIBUTION

While it appears axiomatic that *parens patriae's* humanizing influence and rehabilitative emphasis would achieve better results than

[40] For general sources on the proposition that the human person has inalienable rights which cannot be forfeited to the state *see* E. S. Corwin, *The Higher Law Background of American Constitutional Law* (1955); J. W. Gogh, *Fundamental Law in English Constitutional History* (1955); J. Maritain, *Man and the State* (1951); *Origins of the Natural Law Tradition* (A. L. Harding ed. 1954); Hassett, "Freedom and Order Before God: A Catholic View," in *Readings in Legal Method* (B. Shartel and B. J. George, Jr., eds. 1962).

[41] On the question of the state's right to inflict sanctions which destroy a man's faculties, mutilate his organs, or violate his human dignity *see* J. V. Sullivan, *The Morality of Mercy Killing* 33–38 (1950).

the brutalizing and retributive penal system, it must nevertheless be admitted that surprisingly little evidence is today available as to the actual effectiveness of the sanctions employed by the therapeutic state. "Clear evidence what reformative measures do in fact reform would be very welcome," concluded Barbara Wootton.[42]

In part, at least, the reform effort has been hindered by reliance upon institutions and machinery which differ in name only from those long discredited in the penal process. The therapeutic transformation was not a change in contents; it often was merely a change of labels, described in German as an *etickettenschwindel* ("labeling fraud"). The therapeutic state continued to rely heavily upon total institutions, where all of the patient's needs are met in one confining setting, neglecting community-based activities. Security needs of the institutions took precedence over their reformative work, and personnel shortages resulted in custodial rather than rehabilitative emphasis. In another connection, Professor Radzinowicz of Cambridge University observed that legal classifications have made little difference to the way offenders have actually been dealt with; the realities usually depend "on the general social climate and the available resources."[43]

The therapeutic state, although disclaiming all retributive goals, has neglected to recognize that "treatment" cannot be looked to as a uniform and all-encompassing tool for the modification of man. Punishment has come to include treatment. Can treatment also include punishment? What precisely is meant and done in the name of treatment is not easily ascertainable, for different disciplines continue to stress religious reformation, education, vocational training, surgery, individual therapy, environmental adjustment, or social reform. Much remains to be learned about the means and effects of treatment.

What then is the actual accomplishment of the therapeutic state? Professing at times to cure what is incurable, undertaking in other instances to treat on a one-to-one ratio what requires epidemiological approaches, emphasizing psychological factors while ignoring environmental dynamics, and all along failing to provide adequate supportive therapeutic facilities, society has under the therapeutic mantle assumed too much power without enough knowledge or resources.[44]

Yet, in the final analysis, it must be admitted that a carefully guarded *parens patriae* system has many advantages over the retribution-oriented criminal process. How well could one argue against enlightened societal programs which seek, in George Bernard Shaw's

---

[42] Wootton, *Social Science and Social Pathology* 335.
[43] L. Radzinowicz, *Ideology and Crime* 110 (1966).
[44] Younghusband, "The Dilemma of the Juvenile Court" 10, 20.

words, to substitute rehabilitation for injury? At the very least, the therapeutic programs help set a humanizing climate of new social expectations and aims. Under modern medicine, the ill are increasingly expected to become well; no longer is the hospital, as in grandfather's day, viewed simply as a place to die. Rehabilitation finds a more promising setting and climate in a hospital than in prison. The change in climate, it is hoped, would be followed by a well-conceived programming of social resources for the accomplishment of the new aims. But the shift from a terminology and standards of criminal law to a terminology and standards of therapy and *parens patriae* is important not only as a declaration of a new public policy. It could also be instrumental in translating the theory into reality through our system of checks and balances.

Under the traditional criminal formula, society is the wronged party. It owes nothing to the guilty party, and his rehabilitation remains an incidental accomplishment of the penal sanction. Under the *parens patriae* formula, the concept of personal guilt is bypassed, if not totally discarded, and much more weight is given the offender's shortcomings and needs. Society accordingly cannot shrug off its responsibility for treatment, since it is inherent in the very exercise of this social sanction. The growing legal recognition of this premise is evident in the fact that throughout the entire history of criminal sanctions, that system has never been subjected to the same searching scrutiny of its social justification and effectiveness as therapeutic sanctions are currently undergoing.

Judicial scrutiny of the actual workings of therapeutic sanctions is a new development. In the vanguard of this trend is the 1953 case of *Miller* v. *Overholser*,[45] in the District of Columbia. Miller was committed as a sexual psychopath after being charged with both sodomy and taking indecent liberties with a child. After commitment to Saint Elizabeths Hospital, he filed a petition for writ of habeas corpus on the ground that he was being confined with the criminally insane and receiving no treatment. In reversing the lower court, which refused to investigate the conditions of Miller's confinement, the Court of Appeals commented:

Both the intent and the terms of the statute are for the commitment of these persons to a hospital for remedial treatment. They

[45] Miller v. Overholser, 206 F.2d 415 (D.C. Cir., 1953). *See also* White v. Reid, 125 F. Supp. 647 (D.D.C. 1954), but *cf.* People v. La Burt, 218 N.Y.S.2d 739 (1961).

are denominated "patients." They are not confined for violation of law. . . . We are here considering an indefinite commitment, justifiable only upon a theory of therapeutic treatment.[46]

Two 1966 decisions of the United States Court of Appeals for the District of Columbia embody most dramatically the growing trend toward therapeutic review. In *Lake* v. *Cameron*,[47] the appellant challenged the need for her confinement as an insane person at Saint Elizabeths Hospital. The evidence indicated that Catherine Lake was found "wandering about" by a policeman. Sixty years old, she was shown to be senile and unable to care for herself adequately. The Court of Appeals did not blithely assume the propriety of the mental commitment order. It noted instead that the medical testimony merely indicated Mrs. Lake's need for "attention" rather than constant supervision. The case was therefore remanded to the District Court for an inquiry into "other alternative courses of treatment."[48] In making this referral, the appellate court pointed out that both Mrs. Lake and the public might be sufficiently protected if she were required to carry an identification card on her person so that she could be taken home if found wandering. Other alternatives to commitment suggested by the court were foster care, community health services, or some form of private care.

The other decision, similarly recognizing the need for a critical review of the therapeutic state's promise of treatment, was *Rouse* v. *Cameron*.[49] Having been found not guilty, by reason of insanity, of carrying a deadly weapon, Charles Rouse was summarily committed to Saint Elizabeths Hospital for treatment of his mental condition. The crime of carrying a deadly weapon is a misdemeanor punishable by a maximum sentence of one year. Rouse's therapeutic commitment, on the other hand, was noncriminal in nature and continued for three years before he filed a habeas corpus petition. Rouse challenged his continued detention on the ground that he was receiving no treatment. The Court of Appeals held that the goal of the commitment of one found not guilty by reason of insanity was both the recovery of the patient from his illness and the protection of society.

[46] Miller v. Overholser, 206 F.2d 415, 418–19 (D.C. Cir., 1953). The court also rejected the argument that the judiciary has no power to correct evils in institutional administration.

[47] 364 F.2d 657 (1966).

[48] *Ibid.* 661.

[49] 373 F.2d 451 (1966). *See also* Millard v. Cameron, 373 F.2d 468 (D.C. Cir. 1966); Tribby v. Cameron, 379 F.2d 104 (D.C. Cir. 1967).

Relying specifically upon a statute providing that any person committed to a mental hospital "shall . . . be entitled to medical and psychiatric care and treatment,"[50] the court concluded that one committed to a mental hospital has a right to treatment which the courts will enforce.

The outlines may not be clear yet, but a new right has been born under the therapeutic state. The offender under the criminal law had no positive rights, merely a guarantee against abuse: a protection against excessive fines and cruel and unusual punishments.[51] In the therapeutic realm a new concept of due process is growing. This concept is founded upon a concurrency between the exercise of social power and the assumption of social responsibility.[52] Its implication is that effective treatment must be the *quid pro quo* for society's right to exercise its *parens patriae* controls.[53] Whether specifically recognized by statutory enactments or generally derived from the constitutional requirements of "due process," the right to treatment is here. To some, the formulation of this concept, which curtails the state's therapeutic power through legal supervision, may sound like a call for undue judicial and legal interference with medical and therapeutic prerogatives.[54] To others, this development is a mere annunciation that this nation's fundamental tool for the promotion of national aims and the protection of individual rights—the system of checks and balances—is finally reaching into the dark corners of the institutions

[50] *D.C. Code Ann.* §21–562 (Supp. V, 1966). The Rouse opinion noted that ten states recognize by statute the right to treatment. 373 F.2d 454 and n. 21 (1966).

[51] *U.S. Const.*, amend. VIII: "Excessive bail shall not be required nor excessive fines imposed, nor cruel and unusual punishments inflicted." Justice Brennan has commented with regard to the judicial supervision of criminal justice: "Let me remind you, furthermore, that the judge is not finished with the accused after conviction and sentence. . . . There appear to be situations where even a federal judge may exercise some influence over the administration of correctional institutions . . . for example, a federal district judge held a hearing on charges by certain Utah convicts that their institutional treatment constituted cruel and unusual punishment."

[52] Birnbaum, "The Right to Treatment," 46 *A.B.A.J.* 499 (1960). For recent surveys *see* "Civil Restraints, Mental Illness, and the Right to Treatment," 77 *Yale L. J.* 87 (1967); "The Right to Treatment, A Symposium," 57 *Geo. L. J.* 673 (1969).

[53] Similarly, prisoners sentenced to indeterminate terms for treatment reasons in Denmark have a "next friend" appointed for them and are given easy access to the courts in order to seek release from custody if the treatment purposes either have been fulfilled or are not being carried out. Morris, "Impediments to Penal Reform," 627, 644.

[54] The American Psychiatric Association recently contended: "The definition of treatment and the appraisal of its adequacy are matters for medical determina-

entrusted with the thankless role of storing, curing, and rehabilitating those who deviate from society's norms.[55]

As we resort in the future to the right to treatment as a means of compelling the state to keep its promise of rehabilitation, we must remember, however, that the overriding reason for subjecting a person to either punishment or treatment is social defense. Persons are removed from social intercourse basically as a quarantine measure. Until this fact is admitted, the right to treatment and all the other grand principles of the therapeutic state will be compromised. If strictly interpreted to mean that unless the state can guarantee an individual treatment that will enable him to re-enter society it has no right to keep him in quarantine, then the right to treatment will be diluted into a meaningless principle. As long as the therapeutic state grounds its claim of intervention and power upon needs of individual welfare, the individual who cannot be treated because of lack of treatment or facilities must be released if the right is to be faithfully applied. Yet as long as an individual remains dangerous, there is no way that society will tolerate his release, and if the right to treatment is insisted upon, those passing upon his confinement must take such a broad view of what constitutes treatment as to turn the new right into an old lie.

Here again, as with all its other cardinal principles, the therapeutic state has suffered to some degree or another from the duplicity and disingenuousness of the practice of social defense in the name of humanity and individualized justice. What is needed, under the social defense function of the therapeutic state, is a clear understanding of individual accountability to society, of the nature of quarantine for those charged with dangerous acts, and the reservation of institutional incarceration to those who pose an immediate danger to society. The standards of dangerousness which will justify continued confinement for those charged with dangerous acts must be clear and subject to the scrutiny of judicial determination, with full enjoyment of constitu-

---

tion." "A Position Statement on the Question of Adequacy of Treatment," 123 *Amer. J. Psychiatry* 1458 (1967).

[55] As to the judicial function in this area *see* Tribby v. Cameron, 379 F.2d 104, 105 (1967): "We do not suggest that the court should or can decide what particular treatment this patient requires. The court's function here resembles ours when we review agency action. We do not decide whether the agency has made the best decision, but only make sure that it has made a permissible and reasonable decision in view of the relevant information and within a broad range of discretion." *See also* Kittrie, "Can the Right to Treatment Remedy the Ills of the Juvenile Process?" 57 *Geo. L. J.* 848 (1969).

tional rights by the allegedly dangerous individual. Until we face the issue of the therapeutic state's right to confine even when it cannot treat and develop and implement standards and procedures for such admittedly social-defense measures, we will find progress past the deficiencies of the criminal model of social controls either strewn with new dangers to individual liberty or else totally unacceptable to meet the needs of social defense.

THE THERAPEUTIC BILL OF RIGHTS

Criticism and self-knowledge are revolutionizing the tenets of the therapeutic state, and therapists no longer flatly assert or believe that long-term confinements are tools necessary to achieve the rehabilitative ideal. Short-term treatment accompanied by probationary return to the community, halfway houses, ambulatory treatment, and voluntary treatment are the new and preferred social tools. The excommunicating institutional walls that used to encircle the therapeutic state are being torn down.

Obviously, the more reliance is placed upon voluntary therapy and the more use is made of short-term community treatment, the less the opportunities for abuse and the less the need to burden the therapists with complex procedural and judicial safeguards. Yet new therapies create added potentials for abuse of liberty not hitherto realized: scientific infringements upon the human personality far exceeding the societal controls possible under the old therapeutic state.

The total abolition of social compulsion in the *parens patriae* realm will always remain a utopian dream. To expect the delinquent juvenile, the mentally ill patient, the recidivist offender, the drug addict, and the alcoholic always to concur in the social judgment and willingly to submit to programs of treatment is unrealistic. And as long as compulsion continues, safeguards remain necessary.

The dangers which stem from the therapeutic movement, however, are not that its administrators are perverse or that the system represents an insidious undermining of our social structure. Rather, its deficiencies are those of any overworked, zealous, and philosophically uncertain movement. Those who administer the therapeutic programs are usually, by their own description, unable to provide the treatments necessary to effect the cures intended because they lack the manpower and capital required to do the job. Thus persons who should be receiving treatment are allowed to languish. Since the programs are fairly new, there exists a tendency on the part of their proponents and society in general to resolve doubts in favor of the therapeutic system, partly because the programs should be given a fair chance, partly because the lay community is reluctant to interfere in a distinctly expert field, and partly because there is a belief that therapists are benignly motivated and will watch over the interests of their charges who therefore need no other protections.

The greatest danger, however, results from the shaky philosophical underpinnings of our therapeutic programs. While their origins in humanism and paternalism are avowed, their third parent, utilitarian determinism, is rarely recognized. The fact that the therapeutic programs serve the public's interest of social defense is often masked by pointing to the barbarian alternative of punishing those who are unable to control their behavior. Left out of the discussion altogether, or involved only as a side benefit, is the social-defense argument which was the foundation of the early proponents of the therapeutic order. In this fashion, the features of the therapeutic state which would militate against the individual are disguised by an emphasis on the humane advantages of the therapeutic state over the criminal process. The danger thus exists that in the implementation of the rehabilitative ideal, the social-defense role will gain ascendency, leaving the individual with little or no protection from the powers of the therapeutic state.

These are factors which have caused the injustices discussed in the previous chapters. Unless rectified, these deficiencies will lead to one of two results, neither desirable. If the therapeutic state continues to grow unrestrained, the injustices will grow with it. More and more persons will find themselves subject to compulsory treatment for the well-being of society in general with little or no protections offered against error, abuse, oversights, or untoward infringements of privacy. At that time we would truly be near the Brave New World. Alternatively, a reaction against therapeutic sanctions may set in, causing a complete and utter scrapping of the new order of social controls. Since every therapeutic program today has some measure of social defense as a motive, it would be quite easy to characterize the entire therapeutic state as a subterfuge for effecting social controls without guaranteeing constitutionally protected rights. The easy answer then would be to apply the entire constitutional Bill of Rights to any and all compulsions by the state congruent to their application in criminal proceedings. According to those who administer the therapeutic system, treatment under such restrictions would be next to impossible. Thus, under this alternative, the benefits offered by the therapeutic state would be forever put out of reach.

What is therefore needed is a body of principles which will operate to protect the fundamental rights and liberties of individuals from the present deficiencies of the therapeutic state and to insulate the system from sharpening criticism, while at the same time leaving the therapists sufficient free play in their functions to achieve their nobler goals.

Since each therapeutic program will have differing patients, goals, and methods of treatment, it is not possible to suggest detailed and specific remedies which will apply to all. Yet some general principles could be combined under a proposed Therapeutic Bill of Rights:

1. *No person shall be compelled to undergo treatment except for the defense of society.* The therapeutic state must be separated into its two major model components: (a) the welfare offerings which are successors to the old poor laws, and (b) the social-defense preventive measures which have replaced the criminal process. The first model should be essentially voluntary and informal. Brought under it will be the neglected child as contrasted with the delinquent child, the docile public drunk as contrasted with the dangerous alcoholic, the senile mental patient as contrasted with the threatening maniac. The second model, continuing in great part to be involuntary and limited to those who have committed crimes or who pose a clear and present danger to themselves or others, must be carefully circumscribed with regard to both criteria and procedures.

2. *Man's innate right to remain free of excessive forms of human modification shall be inviolable.* A new body of laws must be developed within the framework of the Constitution in order to guard against the therapeutic state and its possible zeal in carrying out compulsory societal experiments.

3. *No social sanctions may be invoked unless the person subjected to treatment has demonstrated a clear and present danger through truly harmful behavior which is immediately forthcoming or has already occurred.* Generally an overt act should be required. For those who are so incompetent, lacking in lucidity, or immature in age that they cannot be left at large, even though not publicly dangerous, greater emphasis must be placed upon voluntary welfare services in a community setting in lieu of total institutionalization.

4. *No person shall be subjected to involuntary incarceration or treatment on the basis of a finding of a general condition or status alone. Nor shall the mere conviction of a crime or a finding of not guilty by reason of insanity suffice to have a person automatically committed or treated.* This is necessary to protect against the dangers of vague and uncertain criteria and the undue expansion of such

designations as "mental illness," "psychopathy," "alcoholism," "addiction," and "juvenile delinquency," and to guarantee that all subjected to compulsory controls be accorded equal rights.

5. *No social sanctions, whether designated criminal, civil, or therapeutic, may be invoked in the absence of the previous right to a judicial or other independent hearing, appointed counsel, and an opportunity to confront those testifying about one's past conduct or therapeutic needs.* While it may not be necessary or desirable to follow the mandates of the constitutional Bill of Rights fully, they can be used as guides for deciding what rights must be required. The drafting of acceptable procedures will require a great deal of imagination. The legal profession and the therapists must together work to implement procedures that will serve both the humanistic goals of the *parens patriae* while protecting the individual from the dangers to freedom inherent in the social-defense goals of the therapeutic state. Due to the alleged diminished mental capacity of those coming under the therapeutic controls, the deviant's right to counsel should be absolute; under no circumstances should he be asked or allowed to waive such right.

6. *Dual interference by both the criminal and the therapeutic process is prohibited.* The double-barreled approach presently in effect in the narcotics and psychopathy arenas offends the philosophies of both the criminal law and the therapeutic state. Furthermore, it subjects one to a tribute in terms of time spent under compulsory sanction that is often out of proportion to the offensive behavior. The state should be entitled to either criminal or therapeutic controls in a given case. The insistence upon both reveals an incredible disregard for individual liberty and dignity.

7. *An involuntary patient shall have the right to receive treatment.* If no treatment is available, then any restraint must be justified solely upon the danger the individual represents to society. A separate hearing with full constitutional safeguards should be accorded on the question of dangerousness. Unless it is likely that the individual will beyond a reasonable doubt be harmful, he should be released. Persons retained for their dangerousness alone should be detained in special institutions. Our therapeutic centers must cease being the repositories of highly dangerous, untreatable offenders.

Some further steps must be taken, however, in order to guarantee that the treatment received by an involuntary patient be genuine. Perhaps commitment under therapeutic programs should not be indeterminate, but should be limited to a specific term based on medical estimates of the time required for cure. If this time is considered reasonable by the committing court, it shall establish a treatment review date based on the prognosis. If the term is excessive when judged by the nature of the dangerous act committed and compared with the corresponding penal term for the same act, the committing court may establish its own review date. If the patient is not released by the review date, the therapists shall have the burden of showing cause why the individual should continue treatment. Interim amendments to the treatment plan and revision of the review date may be obtained through the committing court. In addition, boards of visitors, consisting of medical, social, behavioral, and legal specialists, should be appointed in every state. These boards would make regular institutional visits to assess the continuing need and efficacy of the treatment of individuals. The boards would also have the obligation to evaluate periodically the treatment facilities and report their findings to the public and responsible public officials. Furthermore, the Department of Public Welfare of each state should keep a full centralized record on all involuntarily committed persons, which should be open for inspection by attorneys and other interested persons.

8. *Any compulsory treatment must be the least required reasonably to protect society.* No person should be subjected to full-time institutionalization or other drastic controls if lesser measures—in the form of voluntary welfare, probation, half-way houses, and so forth—are adequate to protect society while providing the necessary treatment.

9. *All committed persons should have direct access to appointed counsel and the right, without any interference, to petition the courts for relief.* To make this right meaningful, a responsible member of the community, including members of the bar, should be appointed as the next friend for every committed patient. Such a plan would act as a check against institutional abuses, increase community-wide awareness of institutional problems, and provide a liaison between the patient and the legal process.

10. *Those submitting to voluntary treatment should be guaranteed that they will not be subsequently transferred to a compulsory program through administrative action.* All involuntary patients must be accorded the same substantive and procedural safeguards. Such assurance should encourage the seeking of voluntary treatment.

So circumscribed, in order to prevent its excesses, the therapeutic state seems destined to replace the traditional criminal process.

The advent of the therapeutic state and its growth will undoubtedly continue unaffected by the new assertions of philosophers, social administrators, and some psychiatrists that "our society cannot afford to redefine crime as illness."[56] Writing in 1967, psychiatrist Seymour Halleck would reverse the divestment process in order to "foster a greater sense of responsibility throughout our society." He argues that we should "designate as criminals any persons who were proven to have committed a criminal act" and concludes that an "offender should not be released from his responsibility to society just because he is mentally ill."[57] Yale law professor Abraham S. Goldstein similarly concluded that "even if we have misgivings about blaming a particular individual, because he has been shaped long ago by forces he may no longer be able to resist, the concept of 'blame' may be necessary."[58]

Those urging the revitalization of the criminal model believe that it could best serve society's need for preserving order. They stress that under the traditional criminal model, founded on the concept of free will and personal guilt, the offender is conceived as a mature member of society who remains responsible to society even when he is gravely disturbed. This concept of individual maturity and responsibility is viewed as critical for the encouragement of desirable individual behavior. It is further urged that criminal responsibility and punishment have an important social function as constitutive elements in the "symbolism of morality."[59] "The ultimate justification of any punishment," writes Lord Denning, "is not that it is a deterrent but that it is an emphatic denunciation by the community of a crime."[60] In this fashion, crime and punishment periodically provide society with morality plays or rituals which serve to uphold institutionalized values.

While the value of guilt and of the ritual of punishment cannot be readily dismissed, it is nevertheless ironic and anachronistic that late nineteenth-century determinism and its denial of the criminal model should be currently followed by a movement re-emphasizing the requirement of individual guilt and indeed seeking to curtail the therapeutic experiment in the name of a growing concern for social controls.

---

[56] S. L. Halleck, *Psychiatry and the Dilemmas of Crime* 348 (1967). See, on the other hand, K. Menninger, *The Crime of Punishment* 254 (1969). "... according to the prevalent understanding of the words, crime is not a disease. Neither is it an illness, although I think it *should* be!"

[57] *Ibid.* 341.

[58] A. S. Goldstein, *The Insanity Defense* 224 (1967).

[59] Platt, "The Child Savers" 310 (1966).

[60] Great Britain, Royal Commission on Capital Punishment, *Final Report* 53 (1949–53).

But this concern is not new. Enrico Ferri, the leader of ninteenth-century positive criminology, addressed himself to the question of whether society can operate without reliance upon the twin institutions of personal guilt and free will. "If moral culpability is to be ignored, how can we hold man responsible?" Ferri asked. Yet he soon concluded that the answer to this "terrible question" was simple: "Man's acts may be imputed to him and, hence, he is responsible for them because he lives in society."[61] What this means is that society is entitled to require conformity with societal rules and to impose social controls upon those who offend its safety without the need to rely upon the religious-moralistic adjudication of guilt.

Accountability to society need not be intertwined with either personal guilt or with a condition of illness. We do not and should not have to predicate the protection of society upon either guilt or treatability. Merely the fact that an individual has harmed and will continue to harm society is enough to justify intervention. It has always been so and will continue to be so. We should, however, recognize this social reality and hedge societal controls with full safeguards so that the liberty of the individual will not be unduly compromised.

The mistakes of the past in both the criminal and therapeutic models of social controls can be tied to the failure to recognize this principle. By relying on guilt and punishment, the criminal law has refused to deal with those incapable of forming *mens rea* (for whatever reason), even though they pose great danger. The therapeutic state is consequently saddled with the task of quarantining under the guise of treatment those who are unpunished. This compromises the therapeutic process and renders the therapeutic state open to abuses. If, instead of guilt, society was to rely upon social accountability for dangerous conduct, the quarantine could be effected, the individual would be freed from moral approbation, and the therapists could be freed from untreatable patients. The modern answer of Greenland[62] is quite similar: it recognizes the offender's social accountability and the state's right to control him (for therapy if available and for social defense if therapy is lacking) without concerning itself with the question of free will or personal guilt.[63] Such emphasis upon social accountability, well illustrated by the fact that the divestment of criminal justice in our midst has not resulted in a void but in an alternative

---

[61] E. Ferri, *Criminal Sociology* 347, 361–62 (Kelly and Lisle trans. 1951).

[62] V. Goldschmidt, "The Greenland Criminal Code and Its Sociological Background," 1 *Acta Sociologica* 217 (1956).

[63] A similar provision was incorporated in the 1921 draft of the Italian penal code prepared by Ferri. Relazione sul Progetto Preliminare di Codice Penale Italiano (Libro I) (Ministero della Giustizia, Rome, 1921), art. 18, pp. 43–46.

system of therapeutic controls, should continue to guarantee against individual irresponsibility in the therapeutic state. At the same time, the therapeutic state's concept of the deviant as a patient in need of a positive change (personal or environmental) continues to provide a much more effective model for behavioral change than is supplied by the criminal process' concept of the criminal as one who requires negative sanctions. There is a world of difference between the therapeutic conclusion that "you have done a terrible thing and must change before you resume your role in society" and the criminal law's pronouncement that "you are a terrible person and must be punished."[64] As long as the criminal model continues to condemn the offender, it gives up much of the hope of treating him; yet the therapeutic state, as long as it remains careful not to condone the deviant's act, need not relinquish the right or hope of changing him. Because of these conceptual differences, the therapeutic state will be better able to resort to positive reinforcements as tools of individual change while the criminal process remains heavily committed to the negative specter only.

Progress toward the replacement of the criminal process (classically founded upon religious and moral grounds) by the therapeutic state (whose deterministic orientation, while amoral[65] and existentialist,[66] reflects also the pragmatism of social defense) is now in its second century. Despite recent agitations a reversal is not in view.[67] For a long time to come, both the system of criminal justice and the therapeutic state are likely to coexist as dual modes of social control. Increasingly, however, the therapeutic state will receive those offenders and deviates with whom society is willing to experiment through newer programs of rehabilitation and therapy. The therapeutic state is therefore likely to show the road toward more effective treatment techniques.

Sometime, in an uncertain future, both modes are destined to merge into a unified system of social sanctions where individual guilt will be relatively irrelevant[68] and each offender and deviant will be

---

[64] Sachar, "Behavioral Science and Criminal Law," *Sci. Amer.*, November, 1963, p. 5.

[65] See E. Durkheim's concept of the new morality in *Images of Man* 477 (C. W. Mills ed. 1960).

[66] A. Camus, *The Plague* 107 (Penguin Books, 1960).

[67] Wootton, *Social Science and Social Pathology* 251.

[68] ". . . We must renounce the philosophy of punishment, the obsolete, vengeful penal attitude. In its place we should seek a comprehensive, constructive social attitude—therapeutic in some instances, restraining in some instances, but preventive in its total social impact." Menninger, *The Crime of Punishment* 280. Such a new system, which would dispense with the requirement of guilt, would, by

directed toward the treatment—or waiver thereof if he is no longer
offensive—most responsive to his inadequacies. Looking toward that
time, but recognizing the hazards already inherent in the therapeutic
state, this book has tried to suggest the need for fundamental safeguards in the *parens patriae* realm. These suggestions, it is hoped,
should help guarantee man's right to be different and to be left alone,
even in the face of society's asserted benevolence.

THE CHANGING TRENDS

In its formative years, the therapeutic state has heavily and uncritically relied upon what appeared to be scientific criteria and discretion. Often it has been satisfied to relinquish control over the need
and type of therapeutic sanctions to the experts and administrators.
Slowly the trend is changing. It is, in fact, a sign of maturity for the
therapeutic experiment that we finally dare test its precepts in our
judicial forums. The tests will inevitably produce the strength, stability, and fairness of blended power. Clearly this is not an easy task;
it is, however, a worthy one. The late Alexander Pekelis of the New
School of Social Research called for it years back:

> Social scientists are with us for good, and are going to remain in
> the very midst of government. It is true that some experts, or
> some specialized agencies or even a specialized court, may de-
> velop a new father complex, beaming the eternal human quest
> for objective certainty on the power of technicians. To prevent
> this result is one of the main tasks of an intelligent judicial re-
> view. Judges may and should become acquainted with the various
> non-legal disciplines. But because of the variety of these disci-
> plines, and of the variety of their judicial tasks, they will always
> remain intelligent *laymen*, as far as these disciplines are con-
> cerned. And intelligent lay control of technical administrative
> activity seems the best defense against the tyranny of experts.[69]

---

necessity, have to be constructed on a nonpenal model. Under the requirements of
due process in the traditional criminal law, convictions usually require a finding
of *mens rea*, or guilty mind. Within the criminal process it is therefore impossible
to dispense with the question of personal guilt. Previous attempts to eliminate the
requirements of *mens rea* as well as the insanity defense in the criminal law have
been unsuccessful. Goldstein, *The Insanity Defense* 222–24; State v. Strasburg,
110 P. 1020 (Wash. 1910); Sinclair v. State, 132 S. 581 (Miss. 1931). Only the
transition to the noncriminal model of the therapeutic state has permitted the
utilization of social sanctions without the consideration of personal guilt. On the
general function of "guilt" in Anglo-American law see Mueller, "On Common
Law Mens Rea," 42 *Minn. L. Rev.* 1043 (1958).
  [69] A. Pekelis, *Law and Social Action* 39 (1950).

Ill-defined, multipurposed, and expert-reliant throughout much of its history, the therapeutic state is slowly being fitted into more carefully delineated molds. As one reviews the developments across the horizon of the therapeutic state, it soon becomes clear that throughout this realm legal scrutiny is the tool which is increasingly being utilized both for the preservation of individual liberty and for the necessary audit of societal fulfillment vis-à-vis the therapeutic promise.

Society's growing reliance upon judicial review of the scientific promise is particular to the American scene. On the Continent and in our own common law mother, the United Kingdom, similar therapeutic treatment programs have often been relegated to administrative and professional supervision and responsibility. As Britain's 1959 Mental Commitment Act well illustrates, there is greater reliance there upon medical and institutional responsibility (albeit subject to subsequent judicial review) than in the United States, where greater emphasis is placed upon judicial and adversary safeguards, usually prior to the exercise of the therapeutic controls.[70] Possibly, there may be greater faith and credit accorded to the professional experts in Europe, a faith derived from a long history of medieval guilds and the subsequent organization of tight professionalism. Just as possibly, however, the United States may have a much greater commitment to the role of the judicial process as the keeper of the public conscience and the guardian of individual rights.[71] Whatever the reason, it clearly appears that our commitment to adversary procedural safeguards is such that we cannot expect to see, even in the *parens patriae* area, a diminution of these procedures and a shift to less formal proceedings for many years to come.

The movement toward more effective legal checks upon the therapeutic state and its processes may not only help guarantee greater measures of treatment but can also contribute to the growing departure from the sterility of institutional detentions and to the concurrent drive to expand community-based treatment programs. The therapeutic state has long emphasized the behavioral or "personality" over the environmental or "cultural." The behaviorists, often trained in medicine, have tended to equate mental illness and social deviation

---

[70] *See, e.g.*, the District of Columbia 1964 Ervin Act, Pub. L. No. 88–597.

[71] Pekelis, "The Case for a Jurisprudence of Welfare," in *Law and Social Action* 1, 39. "Jurisprudence of welfare is no answer to the problems of our time. In fact, it is no answer at all, but rather a mode of inquiry. It is an invitation to learn, a suggestion as to how questions should be asked, a call for the growth of a systematic participation of the judiciary—burdened with responsibility and stripped of its pontifical robes—in the travail of society." *Ibid.* 40.

with physical disease and have sought to treat their patients in total institutions resembling medical hospitals. To the environmentalists the treatment of a social deviation through isolation in an artificial setting has always been questionable.[72] Yet throughout the major portion of its history the therapeutic state has displayed an unwavering loyalty to institutional commitments.

But just as there has recently been a new willingness to make the benefits of the therapeutic model available not only to the mentally but also to the socially and economically deprived, so there has been a growing willingness to utilize environmentally weighed, community-based treatment side by side with the behaviorally oriented institutional therapy. There are currently many indications of the search for a better accommodation between the behavioral emphasis upon "nature" and the environmental reliance upon "nurture" and of the formation of a more effective joint effort on behalf of the rehabilitative ideal. Such an effort is essential for the widespread accomplishment of our new preventive and therapeutic aims and for the security of social order. A therapeutic state which relies heavily upon individual therapy in an institutional setting will never be able to cope with the increasing numbers of human deviants and deviations. Only heavy reliance upon greater tolerance, upon reforms in our social environment, and upon voluntary treatment within the community setting can guarantee the benefits of the therapeutic state to the masses who may require them.

[72] S. Shoham, *Crime and Social Deviation* 147 (1966).

Bibliography

Abrahamsen, David. *Who Are The Guilty?* New York: Rinehart, 1952.
Alexander. "Constitutional Rights in Juvenile Court." *Justice for the Child.* Edited by M. K. Rosenheim. New York: Free Press of Glencoe, 1962.
——. "The Criminal Responsibility of Alcoholics and Drug Addicts in Canada." 31 *Sask. B. Rev.* 71, 1966.
Alexander and Szasz. "Mental Illness as an Excuse for Civil Wrongs." 43 *Notre Dame Lawyer* 24, 1967.
Alexander, Franz Gabriel, and Staub, Hugo. *The Criminal, the Judge and the Public.* Translated by Gregory Zilboorg. Rev. ed. Glencoe, Ill.: Free Press, 1956.
Algase. "The Right to a Fair Trial in Juvenile Court." 3 *J. Fam. L.* 292, 1963.
Allen, Carleton Kemp. *The Queen's Peace.* London: Stevens, 1953.
Allen, Francis A. *The Borderland of Criminal Justice: Essays in Law and Criminology.* Chicago: U. of Chicago Press, 1964.
——. "The Borderland of Criminal Law: Problems of Socializing Criminal Justice." 32 *Soc. Serv. Rev.* 107, 1958.
——. "The Juvenile Courts and the Limits of Juvenile Justice." 11 *Wayne L. Rev.* 676, 1965.
American Law Institute. *Model Penal Code.* Draft no. 4, 1955.
American Medical Association, Committee on Human Reproduction. "The Control of Fertility." 194 *J.A.M.A.* 462, 1965.

————, Council on Mental Health. "Reports on Narcotic Addiction." 165 *J.A.M.A.* 1968, 1957.

American Neurological Association, Committee for the Investigation of Eugenic Sterilization. *Eugenic Sterilization.* New York: Macmillan, 1936.

American Psychiatric Association. "A Position Statement on the Question of Adequacy of Treatment." 123 *Amer. J. Psychiatry* 1458, 1967.

————. *Psychiatry Glossary.* Washington: American Psychiatric Association, 1957.

————, Committee on Nomenclature and Statistics. *Mental Disorders: Diagnostic and Statistical Manual.* Washington, 1952.

American Psychiatric Association and National Association for Mental Health. *Fifteen Indices.* Washington: American Psychiatric Association, 1964.

Amsterdam. "Federal Constitutional Restrictions on Crimes of Status, Crimes of General Obnoxiousness, Crimes of Displeasing Police Officers and the Like." 3 *Crim. L. Bull.* 205, 1967.

Andenaes. "General Prevention—Illusion or Reality." 43 *J. Crim. L.C. & P.S.* 176, 1952.

Antieau. "Constitutional Rights in Juvenile Courts." 46 *Cornell L. Q.* 387, 1961.

Arens. "Due Process and the Rights of the Mentally Ill: The Strange Case of Frederick Lynch." 13 *Catholic U. L. Rev.* 3, 1964.

Arieff and Rotman. "Psychopathic Personality." 39 *J. Crim. L.C. & P.S.* 158, 1948.

Aronowitz. "Civil Commitment of Narcotic Addicts." 67 *Colum. L. Rev.* 405, 1967.

————. "Civil Commitment of Narcotic Addicts and Sentencing for Narcotic Drug Offenses." President's Commission on Law Enforcement and the Administration of Justice, *Task Force Report: Narcotics and Drug Abuse.* Washington, 1967.

Asimov, Isaac. *The Genetic Code.* New York: Orion Press, 1962.

Association of the Bar of the City of New York, Special Committee to Study Commitment Procedures. *Mental Illness and Due Process.* Ithaca, N.Y.: Cornell U. Press, 1962.

Attenborough, Frederick Levi, ed. and trans. *The Laws of the Earliest English Kings.* Cambridge: At the University Press, 1922.

Axelrod. "Negro and White Institutionalized Delinquents." 57 *Amer. J. Sociol.* 569, 1952.

Baker. "Procedure of the Boston Juvenile Court." 24 *Survey* 649, 1910.

Bailey. "The Case for the Voluntary Outpatient Method of Handling Narcotic Addiction." 31 *F.R.D.* 53, 1962.

Ball. "Two Patterns of Narcotic Drug Addiction in the United States." 56 *J. Crim. L.C. & P.S.* 203, 1965.

Ballagh, James Curtis. *White Servitude in the Colony of Virginia.* Baltimore: The Johns Hopkins Press, 1895.

Bar, Karl Ludwig von. *A History of Continental Criminal Law.* Boston: Little, Brown, 1916.

Barnes, Harry Elmer. *A History of the Penal, Reformatory and Correctional Institutions of New Jersey*. Trenton, N.J.: MacCrellish & Quigley Co., 1918.

Barr, Martin W. *Mental Defectives: Their History, Treatment, and Training*. Philadelphia: Blakiston's Sons, 1904.

Barrow, Roscoe L., and Fabing, Howard D. *Epilepsy and the Law*. 2d ed. rev. New York: Hoeber Medical Division, Harper & Row, 1966.

Bass. "Marriage for the Mentally Deficient." 2 *Mental Retardation* 198, 1964.

Beccaria, Cesare Bonesana di. *On Crimes and Punishments*. Translated by J. A. Paolucci. London, 1880.

———. *An Essay on Crime and Punishments*. Translated by Edward D. Ingraham. Philadelphia: Nicklin, 1819.

Beck, Bertram M. *Five States: A Study of the Youth Authority Program as Promulgated by the American Law Institute*. Philadelphia: American Law Institute, 1951.

Becker. "Social Reality and Planning Illusions: Some Observations on the Need for a Legal Philosophy of Group Interests." 13 *Rutgers L. Rev.* 588, 1959.

Becker, Howard Saul. *Outsiders: Studies in the Sociology of Deviance*. New York: Free Press of Glencoe, 1963.

Beemsterboer. "The Juvenile Court—Benevolence in the Star Chamber." 50 *J. Crim. L.C. & P.S.* 464, 1960.

Beims. "The Law's Approach to Alcohol Addiction: Satisfactory?" 8 *Washburn L. J.* 59, 1968.

Belknap, Ivan. *Human Problems of a State Mental Hospital*. New York: Blakiston Division, McGraw-Hill, 1956.

Bentham, Jeremy. *An Introduction to the Principles of Morals and Legislation*. Oxford: Clarendon Press, 1907.

Bergan. "The Sentencing Power in Criminal Cases." 13 *Albany L. Rev* 1, 1949.

Berliner. "The Helping Process in a Hospital for Narcotics Addicts." 26 *Fed. Prob.* 57, 1962.

Berman, Harold Joseph, ed. *Soviet Criminal Law and Procedure*. Translated by Harold J. Berman and James W. Spindler. Cambridge: Harvard U. Press, 1966.

Biggs, John. *The Guilty Mind: Psychiatry and the Law of Homicide*. Baltimore: The Johns Hopkins Press, 1967.

Bingham, Joseph. *Antiquities of the Christian Church*. London: W. Straker, 1843–45.

Birnbaum. "Eugenic Sterilization." 175 *J.A.M.A.* 951, 1961.

———. "Primum Non Nocere: How to Treat the Criminal Psychopath." 52 *J.A.M.A.* 69, 1969.

———. "The Right to Treatment." 46 *A.B.A.J.* 499, 1960.

Blackstone, William. *Commentaries*. London: W. Straham, 1783.

Blanton, Wyndham Bolling. *Medicine in Virginia in the Seventeenth Century*. Richmond: William Byrd Press, 1930.

Bleicher. "Compulsory Community Care for the Mentally Ill." 16 *Clev.-Mar. L. Rev.* 93, 1967.

Bligh. "Sterilization and Mental Retardation." 51 *A.B.A.J.* 1059, 1965.

Block, Marvin A. *Alcoholism: Its Facets and Phases.* New York: John Day Co., 1965.

Blum. "Drugs, Dangerous Behavior, and Social Policy." President's Commission on Law Enforcement and the Administration of Justice, *Task Force Report: Narcotics and Drug Abuse.* Washington, 1967.

———. "Mind-Altering Drugs and Dangerous Behavior: Dangerous Drugs." President's Commission on Law Enforcement and the Administration of Justice, *Task Force Report: Narcotics and Drug Abuse.* Washington, 1967.

———. "Mind-Altering Drugs and Dangerous Behavior: Narcotics." President's Commission on Law Enforcement and the Administration of Justice, *Task Force Report: Narcotics and Drug Abuse.* Washington, 1967.

Blum, Eva Maria, and Richard, H. *Alcoholism: Modern Psychological Approaches to Treatment.* San Francisco: Jossey-Bass, 1967.

Bonger, William Adrian. *Criminology and Economic Conditions.* Translated by Henry P. Horton. Boston: Little, Brown, 1916.

Bowman and Engle. "Sexual Psychopath Laws." *Sexual Behavior and the Law.* Edited by Ralph Slovenko. Springfield, Ill.: Thomas, 1965.

Brakel and South. "Diversion from the Criminal Process in the Rural Community." 7 *Amer. Crim. L. Q.* 122, 1969.

Briggs and Wirt. "Prediction." *Juvenile Delinquency.* Edited by Herbert C. Quay. Princeton: Van Nostrand, 1965.

Brown, Thorvald T. "Narcotics and Nalline: Six Years of Testing." 27 *Fed. Prob.* 27, 1963.

———. *The Enigma of Drug Addiction.* Springfield, Ill.: Thomas, 1961.

Burrick. "An Analysis of the Illinois Sexually Dangerous Act." 59 *J. Crim. L.C. & P.S.* 254, 1968.

Burrus and Fessler. "Constitutional Due Process Hearing Requirements in the Administration of Public Assistance: The District of Columbia Experience." 16 *Amer. U. L. Rev.* 199, 1967.

Caldwell. "Constitutional Psychopathic State." 3 *J. Crim. Psychopath.* 171, 1941.

California, Department of Mental Hygiene. *Policy and Operations Manual* §3520.2.

———, Governor's Special Study Commission on Juvenile Justice. *A Study of the Administration of Juvenile Justice in California.* Sacramento, 1960.

———, Langley Porter Neuropsychiatric Institute. *California Sexual Deviation Research.* Sacramento: Assembly of the State of California, 1953.

———, Legislature, Assembly, Interim Committee on Judicial System and Judicial Process. *Preliminary Report of the Subcommittee on Sex Crimes.* Sacramento, 1950.

Capen, Edward Warren. *Historical Development of the Poor Law of Connecticut.* New York, 1905.

Caplan, Gerald. *Principles of Preventive Psychiatry.* New York: Basic Books, 1964.

Carr-Saunders, Alexander Morris. *Eugenics*. London: William & Norgate, 1926.

Carter, Harry William. *A Short Account of Some Principal Hospitals*. London: Underwood, 1819.

Chafee, Zechariah. *Free Speech in the United States*. Cambridge: Harvard U. Press, 1946.

Chafetz, Morris E., and Demone, Harold W. *Alcoholism and Society*. New York: Oxford U. Press, 1962.

Chassaigne, André. *Des Lettres de Cachet Sous L'Ancien Régime*. Paris: A. Rousseau, 1903.

Cheatham, Elliott E. *Cases and Materials on the Legal Profession*. 2d ed. Brooklyn, N.Y.: Foundation Press, 1955.

Chein. "The Use of Narcotics as a Personal and Social Problem." *Narcotics*. Edited by Daniel M. Wilner and Gene G. Kassebaum. New York: Blakiston Division, McGraw-Hill, 1965.

Chess. "The Social Factors in Delinquency." 23 *Amer. J. Orthopsychiatry* 5, 1953.

Chicago, Citizens Committee of the Family Court. *Bulletin No. 4*. April 1965.

———, Police Department, Youth Division. *Annual Report*. 1964.

Childs, Harwood Lawrence, trans. *The Nazi Primer: Official Handbook for Schooling Hitler Youth*. New York: Harper & Bros., 1938.

"Civil Restraints, Mental Illness and the Right to Treatment." 77 *Yale L. J.* 87, 1967.

Clark, Hannigan, and Hart. "Alcoholism, a Parole Problem: A Statistical Study of 100 Male Felons Paroled from Sing Sing Prison to the New York Area during 1962." *Current Projects in the Prevention, Control and Treatment of Crime and Delinquency*. Vol. 6, U.S. Pub. Health Serv. Pub. No. 1292, 1964–65.

Clark, William Lawrence, and Marshall, William Lawrence. *A Treatise on the Law of Crimes*. 6th ed. rev. Chicago: Callaghan, 1958.

Clarke, Helen Isabel. *Social Legislation*. New York: Appleton-Century Co., 1940.

Cleckley, Hervey Milton. *The Mask of Sanity*. 2d ed. St. Louis: Mosby, 1950.

Cobban, Alfred. *In Search of Humanity: The Role of Enlightenment in Modern History*. London: Cape, 1960.

Cobean. "New Kansas Philosophy about Care or Treatment of the Mentally Ill." 6 *Washburn L. J.* 448, 1967.

Coburn. "*Driver* to *Easter* to *Powell*: Recognition of the Defense of Involuntary Intoxication?" 22 *Rutgers L. Rev.* 103, 1967.

Cohen. "The Function of the Attorney and the Commitment of the Mentally Ill." 44 *Tex. L. Rev.* 424, 1966.

Cohen and Kozol. "Evaluation for Parole at a Sex Offender Treatment Center." 30 *Fed. Prob.* 50, 1966.

Cole. "Report on the Treatment of Drug Addiction." President's Commission on Law Enforcement and the Administration of Justice, *Task Force Report: Narcotics and Drug Abuse*. Washington, 1967.

Coleman, James Covington. *Abnormal Psychology and Modern Life*. 2d ed. Chicago: Scott, Foresman, 1956.

Comment. "Civil Insanity in the Law of Alabama." 18 *Ala. L. Rev.* 340,
    1966.
————. "Commitment of the Narcotic Addict Convicted of Crime." 32
    Albany L. Rev. 360, 1968.
————. "Compulsory Commitment of Narcotic Addicts in New York
    State." 43 *N.Y.U. L. Rev.* 1172, 1968.
————. "Criteria for Commitment under the Wisconsin Sex Crimes
    Act." 1967 *Wis. L. Rev.* 980.
————. "Hospitalization of the Mentally Disabled in Pennsylvania: The
    Mental Health Retardation Act of 1966." 71 *Dick. L. Rev.* 300, 1967.
————. "Hospitalization of the Mentally Ill in Utah: A Practical and
    Legal Analysis." 1966 *Utah L. Rev.* 223.
————. "Incarceration of the Mentally Ill—New York's New Law." 17
    Syracuse L. Rev. 671, 1966.
————. "Liberty and Required Mental Health Treatment." 114 *U. Pa.
    L. Rev.* 1067, 1965.
————. "Sexual Psychopathy—A Legal Labyrinth of Medicine, Moral
    and Mythology," 36 *Neb. L. Rev.* 320, 1957.
————. "Three Controversial Aspects of New Illinois Mental Health
    Legislation." 47 *Nw. U. L. Rev.* 100, 1952.
————. "Veto of Illinois Mental Health Bill." 36 *Ill. L. Rev.* 747, 1942.
Cong. Rec. Daily eds., 1962 and 1966.
Connecticut. *Public Records of the Colony of Connecticut.* Hartford, 1759.
Cook. "Eugenics or Euthenics." 37 *Illinois L. Rev.* 287, 1943.
Corwin, Edwin Samuel. *The Higher Law Background of American Consti-
    tutional Law.* Ithaca, N.Y.: Great Seal, 1955.
Council of State Governments. *The Mental Health Programs of the Forty-
    Eight States.* Chicago, 1950.
————, Interstate Clearinghouse on Mental Health. *Action in the States in
    the Fields of Mental Health, Mental Retardation and Related Areas.*
    Chicago, 1963.
Cressy. "Crime." *Contemporary Social Problems.* Edited by R. K. Merton
    and R. A. Nisbet. New York: Harcourt, Brace & World, 1961.
Cross. "Reflections on Bratty's Case." 78 *L. Q. Rev.* 236, 1968.
Curran. "Hospitalization of the Mentally Ill." 31 *N.C. L. Rev.* 274, 1953.
————. "Massachusetts Drug Addiction Act: Legislative History and Com-
    parative Analysis." 1 *Harv. J. Legis.* 89, 1964.

Davis, Kenneth Culp. *Administrative Law Treatise.* St. Paul, Minn.: West
    Pub. Co., 1958.
De Asua, J. Jimenez. *La Sentencia Indeterminada.* 2d ed. Buenos Aires,
    1947.
De Greeff. "Le Probleme de l'État Dangereaux." *Proceedings of the Third
    International Congress of Criminology.* Paris, 1953.
Deutsch, Albert. *The Mentally Ill in America.* Garden City, N.Y.: Double-
    day, 1937.
————. *The Mentally Ill in America.* 2d ed., rev. and enl. New York: Co-
    lumbia U. Press, 1949.

Devlin, Patrick. "The Enforcement of Morals." *Criminal Law and its Process.* Edited by Monrad G. Paulsen and Sanford H. Kadish. Boston: Little, Brown, 1962.
————. *The Enforcement of Morals.* London: British Academy Proceedings, 1959.
Diana. "The Rights of Juvenile Delinquents: An Appraisal of Juvenile Court Procedures." 47 *J. Crim. L.C. & P.S.* 561, 1956–57.
Diskind. "New Horizons in The Treatment of Narcotics Addiction." 24 *Fed. Prob.* 56, 1960.
Diskind and Klonsky. "A Second Look at The New York State Parole Drug Experiment." 28 *Fed. Prob.* 34, 1964.
District of Columbia, Commission on Prisons, Probation, and Parole. *Prisons, Probation, and Parole in the District of Columbia.* Washington, 1957.
"DNA's Code: Key to All Life." *Life,* October 4, 1963, p. 70.
Dole and Nyswander. "A Medical Treatment for Diacetylmorphine (Heroin) Addiction." 193 *J.A.M.A.* 646, 1965.
Douglas, David C. *English Historical Documents.* London: Eyre & Spottiswoode, 1955.
Drake, Francis Samuel. *Town of Roxbury.* Roxbury, 1878.
Dubarry, Armand. *LeBrigandage en Italie.* Paris, 1875
Duffy, Clinton T., and Hirshberg, Albert. *Sex and Crime.* Garden City, N.Y.: Doubleday, 1965.
Dugdale, Richard Louis. *The Jukes: A Study in Crime, Pauperism, Disease and Heredity.* 3d ed. rev. New York: Putnam, 1877.
Dunham. "The Juvenile Court: Contradictory Orientation in Processing Offenders." 23 *Law & Contemp. Prob.* 508, 1958.
Dunham, H. Warren, and Weinberg, S. Kirson. *The Culture of the State Mental Hospital.* Detroit: Wayne State U. Press, 1960.
Durvall, Lock, and Brill. "Follow-up Study of Narcotic Drug Addicts Five Years After Hospitalization." 78 *Pub. Health Rep.* 185, 1963.

Eaton, Joseph W., and Weil, Robert J. *Culture and Mental Disorders.* Glencoe, Ill.: Free Press, 1955.
Eddy, Halbach, Isbell, and Seevers. "Drug Dependence: Its Significance and Characteristics." 32 *Bull. World Health Org.* 724, 1965.
Edwards. "Automatism and Criminal Responsibility." 21 *Mod. L. Rev.* 375, 1958.
Eichorn. "Delinquency and the Educational System." *Juvenile Delinquency.* Edited by Herbert C. Quay. Princeton: Van Nostrand, 1965.
Eldridge, William Butler. *Narcotics and the Law.* New York: American Bar Foundation, 1962.
Elson. "Juvenile Courts and Due Process." *Justice for the Child.* Edited by M. K. Rosenheim. New York: Free Press of Glencoe, 1962.
Esmein, Adhémar. *A History of Continental Criminal Procedure, with Special Reference to France.* Boston: Little, Brown, 1914.
Estabrook, Arthur Howard. *The Jukes in 1915.* Washington: Carnegie Institution, 1916.

Estabrook and Davenport. *The Nan Family: A Study in Cacogenics.*
Memoir no. 2. New York: Eugenics Record Office, 1912.

Exner, Franz. *Kriminologie.* 3d ed. Berlin: Springer Verlag, 1949.

Ferdinand. "Some Inherent Limitations in Rehabilitating Juvenile Delinquents in Training Schools." 31 *Fed. Prob.* 30, 1967.

Fernald. "The Burden of Feeble-Mindedness." 23–24 *Medical Communications of the Massachusetts Medical Society* 4, 1912.

Ferrero, Gina Lombroso. *Criminal Man According to the Classification of
Cesare Lombroso.* New York: Putnam, 1911.

Ferri, Enrico. *Criminal Sociology.* Translated by Joseph I. Kelly and John
Lisle. Edited by William W. Smithers. Boston: Little, Brown, 1917.

———. *The Positive School of Criminology.* Translated by Ernest Unter-
mann. Chicago: C. H. Kerr & Co., 1906.

Ferster. "Eliminating the Unfit—Is Sterilization The Answer?" 27 *Ohio St.
L. J.* 591, 1966.

Fine, Benjamin. *1,000,000 Delinquents.* Cleveland: World Pub. Co., 1955.

Finestone. "Narcotics and Criminality." 22 *Law & Contemp. Prob.* 69, 1957.

Fisher. "Elimination of Mental Defect." 1927 *J. Heredity* 529.

Fletcher, Joseph Francis. *Morals and Medicine.* Boston: Beacon Press, 1960.

Flexner. "The Juvenile Court as a Social Institution." 23 *Survey* 607, 1909.

Foote. "Vagrancy—Type Law and Its Administration." 104 *U. Pa. L. Rev.*
603, 1956.

Fortas. "Implications of Durham's Case." 113 *Amer. J. Psychiatry* 577, 1957.

Foucault, Michel. *Madness and Civilization.* Translated by Richard Howard. New York: Pantheon Books, 1965.

Foulkes. "Compensating Victims of Violence." 52 *A.B.A.J.* 237, 1966.

Fradkin. "Disposition Dilemmas of American Juvenile Courts." *Justice for
The Child.* Edited by M. K. Rosenheim. New York: Free Press of
Glencoe, 1962.

Frankel. "Narcotic Addiction, Criminal Responsibility and Civil Commitment." 1966 *Utah L. Rev.* 581.

Frégier, Honoré Antoine. *Des Classes Dangereuses de la Population dans
les Grande Villes.* Paris: Baillière, 1840.

Frisbie. "Treated Sex Offenders Who Reverted to Sexually Deviant Behavior." 29 *Fed. Prob.* 52, 1965.

Fuller, Lon Luvois. *The Morality of Law.* New Haven: Yale U. Press, 1964.

Funck-Bretano. "Les Lettres de cachet d'apres des Documents Inedits."
Revue des Deux Mondes, 1892.

Gainfort. "How Texas is Reforming Its Mental Hospitals." *Reporter,* November
29, 1956, p. 18.

Gallichan, Walter Matthew. *The Sterilization of the Unfit.* London: T. W.
Laurie, 1929.

Galton, Francis. *Inquiries Into Human Faculty.* New York: Dutton & Co.,
1908.

Gebhard, Paul H. *Sex Offenders: An Analysis of Types.* New York: Harper
& Row, 1965.

George Washington University, Center for Behavioral Science. *Biographical
Data Survey of Juvenile Court Judges.* Washington, 1964.

Gest. "Eugenic Sterilization: Justice Holmes vs. Natural Law." 23 *Temp. L. Q.* 306, 1950.

Gillin, John Lewis. *Poverty and Dependency.* Rev. ed. New York: Century, 1926.

Glueck. "Indeterminate Sentence and Parole in the Federal System." 21 *B. U. L. Rev.* 20, 1941.

———. "Spotting Potential Delinquents: Can It Be Done?" 20 *Fed. Prob.* 7, 1956.

———. "Toward Improving the Identification of Delinquents." 53 *J. Crim. L.C. & P.S.* 164, 1964.

Glueck, Sheldon and Eleanor. *Family Environment and Delinquency.* Boston: Houghton Mifflin, 1962.

———. *Predicting Delinquency and Crime.* Cambridge: Harvard U. Press, 1959.

———. *Unraveling Juvenile Delinquency.* New York: Commonwealth Fund, 1950.

Goddard, Henry Herbert. *Human Efficiency and Levels of Intelligence.* Princeton: Princeton U. Press, 1920.

———. *The Kallikak Family: A Study in the Heredity of Feeblemindedness.* New York: Macmillan, 1912.

Goldschmidt. "The Greenland Criminal Code and Its Sociological Background." 1 *Acta Sociologica* 217, 1956.

Goldstein. "Prefrontal Lobotomy: Analysis and Warning." 182 *Sci. Amer.* 41, 1950.

Goldstein, Abraham S. *The Insanity Defense.* New Haven: Yale U. Press, 1967.

Goodhart, Arthur Lehman. *English Law and Moral Law.* London: Stevens, 1953.

Goring, Charles Buckman, ed. *The English Convict: A Statistical Study.* London: Darling & Son, 1913.

Gosney, Ezra Seymour, and Popenoe, Paul. *Sterilization for Human Betterment.* New York: Macmillan, 1929.

Gough, John Wiedhofft. *Fundamental Law in English Constitutional History.* Oxford: Clarendon Press, 1955.

Great Britain, Home Office of the Scottish Home Department, Committee on Homosexual Offenses and Prostitution. *Wolfenden Report.* London, 1957.

———, Royal Commission on Capital Punishment. *Final Report.* London, 1949–53.

———, Royal Commission on the Law Relating to Mental Illness and Mental Deficiency. *Report.* London, 1957.

Greenblatt, Milton, Levinson, Daniel J., and Williams, Richard H. *The Patient and the Mental Hospital.* Glencoe, Ill.: Free Press, 1957.

Grigsby. "The Raiford Study: Alcohol and Crime." 54 *J. Crim. L.C. & P.S.* 296, 1963.

Group for the Advanacement of Psychiatry. *Commitment Procedures.* Report no. 4, April 1949.

———, Committee on Forensic Psychiatry. *Psychiatrically Deviated Sex Offenders.* Report no. 9, February 1950.

Grunhut. "Juvenile Delinquents Under Punitive Detention." 5 *Brit. J. Delinq.* 191, 1955.

Grygier. "The Concept of The 'State of Delinquency' and Its Consequences for Treatment of Young Offenders." 11 *Wayne L. Rev.* 627, 1965.

————. "The Concept of 'The State of Delinquency'—An Obituary." 18 *J. Legal Educ.* 131, 1966.

Guttmacher. "The Psychiatric Approach to Crime and Correction." 23 *Law & Contemp. Prob.* 633, 1958.

Guttmacher and Weihofen. "Sex Offenses." 43 *J. Crim. L.C. & P.S.*, 153, 1952.

Guttmacher, Manfred Schanfarber, and Henry Weihofen. *Psychiatry and the Law.* New York: Norton, 1952.

Guyton, Arthur C. *Function of the Human Body.* Philadelphia: Saunders, 1964.

Guze *et al.* "Psychiatric Illness and Crime, with Particular Reference to Alcoholism: A Study of 233 Criminals." 134 *J. Nerv. and Mental Disease* 512, 1966.

Hacker and Frym. "A Sexual Psychopath Act in Practice: A Critical Discussion." 43 *Calif. L. Rev.* 766, 1955.

Haines. "Gault and the District of Columbia." 17 *Amer. U. L. Rev.* 153, 1968.

Hakeem. "A Critique of the Psychiatric Approach to Crime and Delinquency." 23 *Law & Contemp. Prob.* 650, 1958.

Hall. "Responsibility and Law: In Defense of the M'Naghten Rules." 42 *A.B.A.J.* 917, 1956.

————. "Intoxication and Criminal Responsibility." 57 *Harv. L. Rev.* 1045, 1944.

Halleck, Seymour L. *Psychiatry and the Dilemmas of Crime.* New York: Harper & Row, 1967.

Halliday, Sir Andrew. *A General View of the Present State of Lunatics and Lunatic Asylums.* London: Underwood, 1828.

Hamon. "The Illusion of Free Will." 13 *Univ. Magazine*, 1899.

Handler. "The Juvenile Court and The Adversary System: Problems of Function and Form." 1965 *Wis. L. Rev.* 7.

Harding, Arthur Leon, ed. *Origins of the Natural Law Tradition.* Dallas: Southern Methodist U. Press, 1954.

Hart. "Immorality and Treason." *Listener*, July 15, 1956, p. 162.

Hassett. "Freedom and Order Before God: A Catholic View." *Readings in Legal Method.* Edited by Burke Shartel and B. J. George, Jr. Ann Arbor, Mich.: Overbeck Co., 1962.

Havinghurst. "Dealing with Problem Youth." *Exceptional Children.* Edited by James F. Magary and John R. Eicharn. New York: Holt, Rinehart & Winston, 1960.

Hayek, Friedrick A. *The Road to Serfdom.* Chicago: U. of Chicago Press, 1956.

Heath, James. *Eighteenth Century Penal Theory.* London: Oxford U. Press, 1963.

Hegland. "Unauthorized Rendition of Lifesaving Medical Treatment." 53 *Calif. L. Rev.* 860, 1965.

Heise. "Drinking and Driving." 167 *J.A.M.A.* 1499, 1958.

Henderson. "Juvenile Courts: Problems of Administration." 13 *Charities* 340, 1905.

Henderson, David Kennedy, and Batchelor, Ivor R. C. *Textbook of Psychiatry.* 9th ed. rev. New York: Oxford U. Press, 1962.

Henderson, David Kennedy, and Gillespie, R. D. *Textbook of Psychiatry.* 7th ed. New York: Oxford U. Press, 1950.

Hill, Haertzen, and Davis. "An MMPI Factor Analytic Study of Alcoholics, Narcotic Addicts and Criminals." 23 *Q. J. Stud. Alcohol* 411, 1962.

Himes. "Some Inferences from History." *Birth Control Rev.*, November 1936.

Hobbes, Thomas. *The Leviathan.* Introduction by Michael Oakeshott. Oxford: Blackwell, 1946.

Hollingshead, August de Belmont, and Redlich, Frederick C. *Social Class and Mental Illness.* New York: Wiley, 1958.

Holmes, S. J. "Medical Profession Seen as Leader in Combatting Narcotics Addiction," *Papers on Drugs.* Ontario: Alcoholism and Drug Addiction Research Foundation, 1962.

Holton. "Prevention of Delinquency through Legal Counseling: A Proposal for Improved Juvenile Representation." 68 *Colum. L. Rev.* 1080, 1968.

Howard, John. *The State of Prison in England and Wales, with Preliminary Observations, and an Account of Some Foreign Prisons.* London: Cadell & Conant, 1780.

Howe. "An Alternative Solution to the Narcotics Problem." 22 *Law & Contemp. Prob.* 132, 1957.

Hutt. "Modern Trends in Handling the Chronic Court Offender: The Challenge to the Courts." 19 *S.C. L. Rev.* 305, 1967.

———. "The Recent Court Decision on Alcoholism." President's Commission on Law Enforcement and the Administration of Justice, *Task Force Report: Drunkenness.* Washington, 1967.

Hutt, Max L., and Gibbey, Robert Gwyn. *The Mentally Retarded Child.* Boston: Allyn & Bacon, 1958.

Huxley, Aldoux Leonard. *The Doors of Perception.* London: Chatto & Windus, 1954.

Huxley, Julian Sorell. *Evolution in Action.* New York: Harper, 1953.

Illinois, Commission on Sex Offenders. *Report by the Sixty-eighth General Assembly of the State of Illinois.* Springfield, 1953.

Irving. "Juvenile Justice—One Year Later." 8 *J. Fam. L.* 1, 1968.

Isbell. "Medical Aspects of Opiate Addiction." *Narcotic Addiction.* Edited by John A. O'Donnel and John C. Ball. New York: Harper & Row, 1966.

———. "Meeting a Growing Menace—Drug Addiction." 50 *Merck Report* 4, 1951.

——— et al. "An Experimental Study of The Eitology of 'Rum Fits' and Delirium Tremens." 16 *Q. J. Stud. Alcohol* 1, 1957.

Ives, George. *A History of Penal Methods.* London: S. Paul & Co., 1914.

Jellinek. "Phases of Alcohol Addiction." 13 *Q. J. Stud. Alcohol* 673, 1952.

Jellinek, Elvin Morton. *The Disease Concept of Alcoholism*. New Haven: Hillhouse Press, 1960.

————, ed. *Alcohol Addiction and Chronic Alcoholism*. New Haven: Yale U. Press, 1942.

Johnson. "The Alcoholic Withdrawal Syndromes." 1 *Q. J. Stud. Alcohol* supp. 66, 1961.

Joint Committee of the American Bar Association and the American Medical Association on Narcotic Drugs. *Drug Addiction: Crime or Disease? Final Report*. Bloomington: Indiana U. Press, 1961.

Jolowicz, Herbert Felix. *Historical Introduction to the Study of Roman Law*. Cambridge: At the University Press, 1939.

Jones. "The Rule of Law and The Welfare State." 58 *Colum. L. Rev.* 143, 1958.

Jones, Kathleen. *Lunacy, Law, and Conscience*. London: Routledge & Kegan Paul, 1955.

Kadish. "A Case Study in the Signification of Procedural Due Process." 9 *West. Pol. Q.* 93, 1956.

Kahler, Erich. *The Tower and the Abyss*. New York: G. Braziller, 1957.

Kahn, Alfred J. *A Court for Children*. New York: Columbia U. Press, 1953.

Kalvern. "A Special Corner of Civil Liberties: A Legal View." 31 *N.Y.U. L. Rev.* 1157, 1956.

Kanner, Leo. *A Miniature Textbook of Feeblemindedness*. New York: Child Care Publications, 1949.

Kansas, Governor's Commission on Provision for the Feeble-Minded. *Report on the Kallikaks of Kansas*. Topeka, 1919.

————, Legislative Council. *Survey of Psychiatric Facilities in Kansas*. Pub. no. 143. Topeka, 1946.

Kapp. "Legal and Medical Aspects of Eugenic Sterilization in Germany." *Amer. Sociol. Rev.* 761, October 1936.

Keller and Efron. "The Prevalence of Alcoholism." 16 *Q. J. Stud. Alcohol* 619, 1955.

Kelsey. "The Ninth Amendment to the Federal Constitution." 11 *Ind. L. J.* 309, 1936.

Kentucky, Department of Mental Health. *Policies and Procedures*. 1958.

Kessel and Grossman. "Suicide in Alcoholics." *Brit. Med. J.*, December 23, 1961, p. 1672.

Kessel, Neil, and Walton, Henry. *Alcoholism*. Baltimore: Penguin Books, 1965.

Ketcham. "Guidelines from Gault: Revolutionary Requirements and Reappraisal." 53 *Va. L. Rev.* 1700, 1967.

————. "Legal Rennaissance in Juvenile Court." 60 *Nw. U. L. Rev.* 590, 1965.

————. "Summer College for Juvenile Court Judges." 51 *J. Amer. Jud. Soc.* 330, 1968.

————. "The Unfilled Promise of The Juvenile Court." *Justice for the Child*. Edited by M. K. Rosenheim. New York: Free Press of Glencoe, 1962.

————. "What Happened to Whittington." 37 *Geo. Wash. L. Rev.* 324, 1968.

Keve. "Administration of Juvenile Court Services." *Justice for the Child.* Edited by M. K. Rosenheim. New York: Free Press of Glencoe, 1962.

Kinsey, Alfred C., *et al.* "Concepts of Normality and Abnormality in Sexual Behavior." *Psychosexual Development in Health and Disease.* Edited by Hoch and Zubin. New York: Grune & Stratton, 1949.

Kirbens. "Chronic Alcohol Addiction and Criminal Responsibility." 54 *A.B.A.J.* 877, 1968.

Kittrie. "Can the Right to Treatment Remedy the Ills of the Juvenile Process?" 57 *Geo. L. J.* 848, 1969.

Koestler, Arthur, and Rolph, C. H. *Hanged by the Neck.* Baltimore: Penguin Books, 1961.

Kolb, Lawrence. *Drug Addiction: A Medical Problem.* Springfield, Ill.: Thomas, 1962.

Kolb and Himelsbach. "Clinical Studies of Drug Addiction, III: A Critical Review of Withdrawal Treatments with Method of Evaluating Abstinence Syndrome." 94 *Amer. J. Psychiatry* 759, 1938.

Koya. "Sterilization in Japan." 8 *Eugenics Q.* 135, 1961.

Kozel. "The Criminally Dangerous Sex Offender." 275 *N. Eng. J. Med.* 81, 1966.

Krech. "Controlling the Mind Controllers." 32 *Think* 5, 1966.

Krueger, Mommsen, Schoel, and Kroll, eds. *Corpus Juris Civilis.* Vols. I and II. Berolini: Wiedmannos, 1893–1920.

Kuh. "A Prosecutor's Thoughts Concerning Addiction." 52 *J. Crim. L.C. & P.S.* 321, 1961.

Kutner. "The Illusion of Due Process in Commitment Proceedings." 57 *Nw. U. L. Rev.* 383, 1962.

Lambard, William. *Eirenarcha: Or of the Office of the Justice of Peace.* London, 1582.

Landon, Perry. *Behavior Control.* New York: Harper & Row, 1969.

Lang. "President's Commission Task Force Report on Narcotics and Drug Abuse: A Critique of Apologia." 43 *Notre Dame Lawyer* 847, 1968.

Lange, Johannes. *Crime and Destiny.* New York: C. Boni, 1930.

Larimore. "Medical Views on the Narcotics Problem." 31 *F.R.D.* 53, 1961.

Laughlin, Harry Hamilton. *Eugenic Sterilization in the United States.* Chicago: Psychopathic Lab., Municipal Court of Chicago, 1922.

Lea, Henry Charles. *History of the Inquisition in the Middle Ages.* New York: Harbor Press, 1955.

Lindesmith, Alfred Ray. *The Addict and the Law.* Bloomington: Indiana U. Press, 1965.

Lindman, Frank T., and McIntyre, Donald M., eds. *The Mentally Disabled and the Law.* Chicago: U. of Chicago Press, 1961.

Lloyd. "Insanity: Forms and Medico-legal Relations." *Medical Jurisprudence.* 4th ed. Edited by Francis Wharton and Edward Stickney. Philadelphia: Kay & Bro., 1882–84.

Logan and Kleeman. "Berlin Report: Juvenile Delinquency Before the Wall and Afterward." 1963 *Wash. U. L. Q.* 296.

"Looking Backward at Lobotomy." *Time*, June 22, 1953, p. 46.

Lopez-Rey. "Present Approaches to the Problem of Juvenile Delinquency." 23 *Fed. Prob.* 24, 1959.

Lou, Herbert H. *Juvenile Courts in the United States.* London: Oxford U. Press, 1927.

Loudet. "Le Diagnostic de l'État Dangereux." *Proceedings of the Second International Congress of Criminology.* Paris, 1950.

Lovald and Stub. "The Revolving Door: Reactions of Chronic Drunkenness Offenders to Court Sanctions." 59 *J. Crim. L.C. & P.S.* 525, 1968.

Lubove, Roy. *The Professional Altruist: The Emergence of Social Work as a Career, 1880–1930.* Cambridge: Harvard U. Press, 1965.

Ludwig. "Rationale of Responsibility for Young Offenders." 29 *Neb. L. Rev.* 521, 1950.

Ludwig and Levine. "Patterns of Hallucinogenic Drug Abuse." 191 *J.A.M.A.* 29, 1965.

Lukas. "Crime Prevention: A Confusion in Goal." *Contemporary Correction.* Edited by Paul Wilbur Tappan. New York: McGraw-Hill, 1951.

Lynch. "The California Narcotic Addict Rehabilitation Law." 12 *N.Y. L. F.* 369, 1966.

McCarthy, Raymond Gerald. *Drinking and Intoxication.* New Haven: Yale Center of Alcohol Studies, 1959.

MacCormick. "The Community and the Correctional Process." 27 *Focus* 88, 1948.

McCulloch. "The Tribe of Ishmael: A Study in Social Degradation." *Proceedings of the Fifteenth National Conference of Charities and Correction.* Buffalo, 1888.

MacDonald. "Alcoholism and Drug Addiction." 21 *Ohio St. L. J.* 96, 1960.

McDonald. "The Prompt Diagnosis of Psychopathic Personality." 122 *Amer. J. Psychiatry* 48, 1966.

Mack. "The Juvenile Court." 23 *Harv. L. Rev.* 104, 1909.

Mackay, Thomas. *A History of the English Poor Law.* New York: Putnam's Sons, 1899.

McMahon. "The Working Class Psychiatric Patient." *Mental Health of the Poor.* Edited by Frank Riessman, Jerome Cohen, and Arthur Pearl. New York: Free Press of Glencoe, 1964.

MacMillan. "Community Treatment of Mental Illness." *Lancet*, July 26, 1958.

Maddox. "Hospital Management of the Narcotic Addict." *Narcotics.* Edited by Daniel M. Wilner and Gene G. Kasselbaum. New York: Blakiston Division, McGraw-Hill, 1965.

Madox, Thomas. *History and Antiquities of the Exchequer.* London, 1769.

Maglio. "The Citizenship Training Program of the Boston Juvenile Court." *The Problem of Delinquency.* Edited by Sheldon Glueck. Boston: Houghton Mifflin, 1959.

Maine, Henry James Sumner. *Ancient Law.* London: Oxford U. Press, 1931.

Marinello, Berkson, Edwards, and Bannerman. "A Study of the XYY Syndrome in Tall Men and Juvenile Delinquents." 208 *J.A.M.A.* 321, 1969.

Maritain, Jacques. *Man and the State.* Chicago: U. of Chicago Press, 1951.

Marshall, Nathaniel. *Penitential Discipline of the Primitive Church.* Oxford: J. H. Parker, 1844.

Marx, Karl. *The Poverty of Philosophy.* Moscow, 1935.

Maryland, Commission to Study and Re-evaluate Patuxent Institution. *Report.* Baltimore, 1961.

————, Department of Mental Hygiene. *Statistics Newsletter.* August 10, 1965.

————, Legislative Council, Research Division. *An Intermediate Sentence Law for Defective Delinquents.* Research Report No. 29. Baltimore, 1950.

Maurer, David W., and Vogel, Victor H. *Narcotics and Narcotic Addiction* Springfield, Ill.: Thomas, 1954.

Mayhew, Henry. *London Labour and the London Poor.* London, 1861–62.

Menninger, Karl. *The Crime of Punishment.* New York: Viking, 1969.

Merck. *Manual of Diagnosis and Therapy.* Edited by C. E. Lyght. 9th and 11th eds. New Jersey: Merck & Co., 1956, 1966.

Merry. "The 'Loss of Control' Myth." 1 *Lancet* 1257, 1966.

Merton. "The Self-fulfilling Prophecy." 8 *Antioch Rev.* 194, 1948.

Merton, Robert King. *Social Theory and Social Structure.* Rev. and enl. ed. Glencoe, Ill.: Free Press, 1957.

Merton, Robert K., and Nisbet, Robert A., eds. *Contemporary Social Problems.* New York: Harcourt, Brace & World, 1961.

Michigan, Governor's Study Commission on Sex Deviates. *Report.* Lansing, 1951.

Mihm. "A Re-examination of the Validity of our Sex Psychopath Statutes in the Light of Recent Appeal Cases and Experience." 44 *J. Crim. L.C. & P.S.* 716, 1954.

Miles, Arthur Parker. *Introduction to Public Welfare.* Boston: D.C. Heath, 1949.

Mill, John Stuart. *On Liberty.* London: Watts & Co., Thinker's Library, 1930.

Mills, C. Wright, ed. *Images of Man.* New York: Braziller, 1960.

Minckler. "Chromosomes and Criminals." *Science,* March 14, 1969.

Modlin and Montes. "Narcotics Addiction in Physicians." 121 *Amer. J. Psychiatry* 358, 1964.

Moneschesi. "Prediction of Criminal Behavior." *Encyclopedia of Criminology.* Edited by Vernon C. Branham and Samual B. Kutash. New York: Philosophical Library, 1949.

Morris. "Impediments to Penal Reform." 33 *U. Chicago L. Rev.* 627, 1966.

Morris and Breithaupt. "Compulsory Sterilization of Criminals—Perversion in the Law." 15 *Syracuse L. Rev.* 738, 1964.

Morrison. "Illegitimacy, Sterilization and Racism—A North Carolina Case History." 39 *Soc. Serv. Rev.* 1, 1965.

Moylan. "Comments on the Juvenile Court." 25 *Md. L. Rev.* 310, 1965.

————. "Comments" (N.C. Rehabilitation Program). 16 *Inventory* 13, 1966.
————. "Status Offenses and Due Process of Law." 36 *Fordham L. Rev.*
    51, 1967.
Mueller. "On Common Law Mens Rea." 42 *Minn. L. Rev.* 1043, 1958.
Myerson. "Certain Medical and Legal Phases of Eugenic Sterilization." 52
    Yale L. J. 627, 1943.
Myerson and Mayer. "Origins, Treatment and Destiny of Skidrow Alco-
    holic Men." 19 *S.C. L. Rev.* 332, 1967.

National Committee Against Mental Illness. *What Are the Facts About
    Mental Illness?* Washington, 1964.
National Council for Civil Liberties. *Submissions to the Minister of Health
    on the Recommendation of the Royal Commission on the Law Relat-
    ing to Mental Illness and Mental Deficiency.* London, 1957.
National Council on Crime and Delinquency, Advisory Council of Judges
    Procedure and Evidence in the Juvenile Court. New York, 1962.
————. "Transfer of Cases between Juvenile and Criminal Courts—A Policy
    Statement." *Crime and Delinquency,* 8, no. 1, 1962.
New Jersey, Commission on the Habitual Sex Offender. *The Habitual Sex
    Offender.* Trenton, 1950.
New York City, Police Department, Statistical and Recorder Bureau. *Statis-
    tical Report of Narcotics Arrests and Arrests of Narcotics Users.* 1964,
    1965.
New York State, Department of Mental Hygiene. *Report to the N.Y. Nar-
    cotic Addiction Control Commission.* 112 *Cong. Rec.* 26579. Daily
    ed., October 6, 1966.
————, Division of Parole. *Final Report on an Experiment in the Super-
    vision of Paroled Offenders Addicted to Narcotic Drugs.* Albany,
    1960.
Nice, Richard W., ed. *Criminal Psychology.* New York: Philosophical Li-
    brary, 1962.
Nicholas. "History, Philosophy, and Procedures of Juvenile Courts." 1
    J. Fam. L. 151, 1961.
Nietzshe, Friedrich Wilhelm. *The Twilight of the Idols.* Translated by
    A. M. Ludovici. New York: Macmillan, 1911.
Note. 30 *Calif. L. Rev.* 189, 1942.
————. "Civil Commitment of the Mentally Ill: Theories and Procedures."
    79 *Harv. L. Rev.* 1288, 1966.
————. "Civil Commitment of Narcotic Addicts." 76 *Yale L. J.* 1160, 1967.
————. "Commitment of the Mentally Ill—Superior Court of Los Angeles
    County." 36 *S. Calif. L. Rev.* 109, 1962.
————. "Compulsory Commitment of Narcotic Addicts in New York State."
    43 *N.Y.U. L. Rev.* 1172, 1968.
————. "District of Columbia Juvenile Delinquency Proceedings: Appre-
    hension to Disposition." 49 *Geo. L. J.* 322, 1960.
————. "Elective Sterilization." 113 *U. Pa. L. Rev.* 415, 1965.
————. "Human Sterilization." 35 *Iowa L. Rev.* 251, 1950.
————. "Juvenile Delinquents: The Police, State Courts and Individualized

Justice." 79 *Harv. L. Rev.* 775, 1966.
————. "The *Parens Patriae* Theory and Its Effect on the Constitutional Limits of Juvenile Court Powers." 27 *U. Pitt. L. Rev.* 894, 1966.
————. "The Plight of the Sexual Psychopath: A Legislative Blunder and Judicial Acquiescence." 41 *Notre Dame Lawyer* 527, 1966.
————. " 'Psychopathic Personality' and 'Sexual Deviation': Medical Terms or Legal Catch-alls: Analysis of the Status of Homosexual Alien." 40 *Temp. L. Q.* 328, 1967.
————. "State Statute to Provide Compensation for Innocent Victims of Violent Crimes." 4 *Harv. J. Legis.* 127, 1966.
————. "Sterilization Laws—Their Constitutionality—Their Social and Scientific Bases." 17 *B. U. L. Rev.* 246, 1937.
————. "Sterilization of Mental Defectives." 61 *Mich. L. Rev.* 1359, 1963.
————. "Three Controversial Aspects of New Illinois Mental Health Legislation." 47 *Nw. U. L. Rev.* 100, 1952–53.
————. "The XYY Chromosome." 57 *Geo. L. J.* 892, 1969.

O'Callaghan, Edmund Bailey. *Documents Relative to the Colonial History of the State of New York.* New York, 1853–87.
O'Donnell. "The Lexington Program for Narcotic Addicts." 26 *Fed. Prob.* 55, 1962.
Oglesby. "What Has Happened to Kansas' Sterilization Laws." 2 *Kan. L. Rev.* 174, 1953.
O'Hara and Sanks. "Eugenic Sterilization." 45 *Geo. L. J.* 20, 1956.
Overholser. "The Voluntary Admission Law: Certain Legal and Psychiatric Aspects." 3 *Amer. J. Psychiatry* 475, 1924.
Ozarin and Brown. "New Directions in Community Mental Health Programs." 35 *Amer. J. Orthopsychiatry* 10, 1965.

Packer, Herbert L. *The Limits of Criminal Sanctions.* Stanford, Calif.: Stanford U. Press, 1968.
Patterson, Bennett B. *The Forgotten Ninth Amendment.* Indianapolis: Bobbs-Merrill, 1955.
Paul. "The Return of Punitive Sterilization Proposals." 3 *Law & Soc. Rev.* 77, 1968.
Paulsen. "The Delinquency, Neglect and Dependency Jurisdiction of the Juvenile Court." *Justice for the Child.* Edited by M. K. Rosenheim, New York: Free Press of Glencoe, 1962.
————. "The Expanding Horizons of Legal Services—II." 67 *W. Va. L. Rev.* 267, 1965.
————. "Fairness to the Juvenile Offender." 41 *Minn. L. Rev.* 547, 1957.
————. "The Juvenile Court and the Whole of the Law." 11 *Wayne L. Rev.* 597, 1965.
Pekelis, Alexander. *Law and Social Action.* Ithaca, N.Y.: Cornell U. Press, 1950.
Perkins, Rollin M. *Criminal Law.* Brooklyn, N.Y.: Foundation Press, 1957.
Perlman, "Reporting Juvenile Delinquency." 3 *J. Nat. Prob. & Parole Assoc.* 243, 1957.

————. "The Search for the Memory Molecule." *New York Times Magazine*, July 7, 1968, p. 8.

Peter. "Germany's Sterilization Program." 24 *Amer. J. Pub. Health* 187, 1934.

Pfeffer. "The Natural History of Alcoholism." *Alcoholism as a Medical Problem*. Edited by H. D. Krause. New York: Hoeber-Harper, 1956.

Phillipson, Colemen. *Three Criminal Law Reformers*. New York: Dutton & Co., 1923.

Pittman. "Public Intoxication and the Alcoholic Offender in American Society." President's Commission on Law Enforcement and the Administration of Justice, *Task Force Report: Drunkenness*. Washington, 1967.

Pittman and Sterne. "Concept of Motivation: Sources of Institutional and Professional Blockage in the Treatment of Alcoholics." 26 *Q. J. Stud. Alcohol* 41, 1965.

Pittman, David Joshua, and Gordon, C. Wayne. *Revolving Door*. Glencoe, Ill.: Free Press, 1958.

Plato, *The Republic*. Translated by B. Jowett. New York: Colonial Press, 1901.

Platt, "The Child Savers." Ph.D. dissertation, University of California, 1966.

Plaut. "Some Major Issues in Developing Community Services for Persons with Drinking Problems." President's Commission on Law Enforcement and the Administration of Justice, *Task Force Report: Drunkenness*. Washington, 1967.

Plaut, Thomas F. A. *Alcohol Problems: A Report to the Nation*. New York: Oxford U. Press, 1967.

Ploscowe, Morris. *Sex and the Law*. New York: Prentice-Hall, 1951.

Plucknett, Theodore Frank Thomas. *A Concise History of the Common Law*. Boston: Little, Brown, 1956.

Plunkett, Richard J., and Gordon, John E. *Epidemiology and Mental Illness*. New York: Basic Books, 1960.

Popham. "Some Social and Cultural Aspects of Alcoholism." 4 *Can. Psych. A. J.* 222, 1959.

Pound. "The Rise of Socialized Criminal Justice" *Roscoe Pound and Criminal Justice*. Edited by Sheldon Glueck. Dobbs Ferry, N.Y.: Oceana, 1965.

Quarton. "Deliberate Efforts to Control Human Behavior and Modify Personality." 96 *Daedalus* 837, 1967.

Radzinowicz, Leon. *Ideology and Crime*. London: Heinemann Educ. Books, 1966.

Reade, Charles. *Hard Cash*. London: S. Low, 1863.

"Recent Cases." 97 *U. Pa. L. Rev.* 436, 1949.

Reeves, John. *History of the English Law*. London, 1814–29.

Reifen. "The Implications of Laws and Procedures in the Juvenile Court in Israel." 3 *Brit. J. Crim.* 130, 1962.

Reich. "Individual Rights and Social Welfare: The Emerging Legal Issues." 74 *Yale L. J.* 1245, 1965.

Remington. "Due Process in Juvenile Proceedings." 11 *Wayne L. Rev.* 688, 1965.

Reynolds. "An Antidote for Inhumanity?" Letters to *New York Times Magazine*, November 9, 1969.

Rhodes. "Delinquency and Community Action." *Juvenile Delinquency*. Edited by Herbert C. Quay. Princeton: Van Nostrand, 1965.

"The Right to Treatment: A Symposium." 57 *Geo. L. J.* 673, 1969.

Robinson. "Institution for Defective Delinquents." 24 *J. Crim. L.C. & P.S.* 352, 1933.

———. "Parents Seek Ways to Prevent Alcoholism." 3 *Alcoholism* 9, 1955.

Robitscher, Jonas B. *Pursuit of Agreement: Psychiatry and the Law*. Philadelphia: Lippincott, 1966.

Roche, Philip Q. *The Criminal Mind: A Study of Communications between the Criminal Law and Psychiatry*. New York: Grove Press, 1958.

Roche Laboratories. *Aspects of Alcoholism*. Philadelphia: Lippincott, 1963.

Rock, Daniel. *The Church of Our Fathers*. London: C. Dolman, 1903.

Rosenheim. "Perennial Problems in the Juvenile Court." *Justice for the Child*. Edited by M. K. Rosenheim. New York: Free Press of Glencoe, 1962.

Rostand, Jean. *Can Man Be Modified?* Translated by Jonathan Griffin. New York: Basic Books, 1959.

Rostow, Eugene V. "The Enforcement of Morals." 16 *Cambridge L. J.* 174, 1960.

Rubin. "Protecting the Child in the Juvenile Court." 43 *J. Crim. L.C. & P.S.* 425, 1952.

Rubin, Ted., and Smith, Jack F. *The Future of the Juvenile Court*. Washington: Joint Commission on Correctional Manpower and Training, 1968.

Rubington, Earl. "The Chronic Drunkenness Offender." 315 *Annals of the American Academy of Political and Social Sciences* 65, 1958.

Sabagh and Edgerton. "Sterilized Mental Defectives Look at Eugenic Sterilization." 9 *Eugenics Q.* 212, 1962.

Sachar. "Behavioral Science and Criminal Law." *Sci. Amer.*, November, 1963, p. 5.

Sadoff. "Sexually Deviated Offenders." 40 *Temp. L. Q.* 305, 1967.

Saleilles, Raymond. *The Individualization of Punishment*. Translated by R. S. Jastrow. Boston: Little, Brown, 1911.

Samuels. "Compensation for Criminal Injuries in Britain." 17 *U. Toronto L. J.* 20, 1967.

———. "A Visit to Narco." *New York Times Magazine*, April 10, 1966.

Scheff. "Decision Rules, Types of Error, and Their Consequences in Medical Diagnosis." 8 *Behav. Sci.* 97, 1963.

———. "Social Conditions for Rationality: How Urban and Rural Courts Deal with the Mentally Ill." 7 *Amer. Behav. Sci.* 21, 1964.

———. "The Societal Reaction to Deviance: Ascriptive Elements in the Psychiatric Screening of Mental Patients in a Midwestern State." 11 *Soc. Prob.* 401, 1964.

Scheff, Thomas J. *Being Mentally Ill: A Sociological Theory.* Chicago: Aldine, 1966.

Schreiber. "How Effective Are Services for the Treatment of Delinquents?" *Juvenile Delinquency.* Edited by Herbert C. Quay. Princeton: Van Nostrand, 1965.

Schuessler and Cressey. "Personality Characteristics of Criminals." 55 *Amer. J. Sociol.* 476, 1950.

Schur, Edwin M. *Crimes without Victims: Deviant Behavior and Public Policy.* Englewood Cliffs, N.J.: Prentice-Hall, 1965.

Schwitzgebel. "Issues in the Use of an Electronic Rehabilition System with Chronic Recidivists." 3 *Law & Soc. Rev.* 597, 1969.

Scofield, Cora Louise. *Court of Star Chamber.* Chicago: U. of Chicago Press, 1900.

Selinger. "Criminal Hygiene," 10 *Fed. Prob.* 16, 1946.

Shelford, Leonard. *A Practical Treatise on the Law Concerning Lunatics, Idiots, and Persons of Unsound Mind.* Vol. 2. London: S. Sweet, 1833.

Shelly and Bassin. "Daytop Lodge: Halfway House for Drug Addicts." 28 *Fed. Prob.* 46, 1964.

Sheridan. "Double Jeopardy and Waiver in Juvenile Delinquency Proceedings." 23 *Fed. Prob.* 43, 1959.

———. "Juveniles Who Commit Noncriminal Acts: Why Treat in Correctional Systems?" 31 *Fed. Prob.* 26, 1967.

"Shock Therapy in State Hospitals." 97 *U. Pa. L. Rev.* 436, 1949.

Shoham, Shlomo. *Crime and Social Deviation.* Chicago: H. Regnery Co., 1966.

Silving, Helen. *Constituent Elements of Crime.* Springfield, Ill.: Thomas, 1967.

Sloane. "The Juvenile Court: An Uneasy Partnership of Law and Social Work." 5 *J. Fam. L.* 170, 1965.

Slovenko. "A Panoramic View." *Sexual Behavior and the Law.* Edited by Ralph Slovenko. Springfield, Ill.: Thomas, 1965.

Smith. "Constitutional Law: Validity of Statute Providing for Sterilization of Habitual Criminals," 30 *Calif. L. Rev.* 189, 1942.

Soden. "Constructive Coercion and Group Counseling in the Rehabilitation of Alcoholics." 30 *Fed. Prob.* 56, 1966.

South Dakota Medical Association, Mental Health Committee. *Explanation of Proposed S. D. Mental Health Act.* 1959.

Spencer and Grygier. "The Probation Hostel in England." *The Problem of Delinquency.* Edited by Sheldon Glueck. Boston: Houghton Mifflin, 1959.

"Standard Juvenile Court Act—Text and Commentary." 5 *J. Nat. Prob. & Parole Assoc.* 351, 1959.

Starrs. "A Sense of Irony in Southern Juvenile Courts." 1 *Harv. Civ. Lib.— Civ. Rights L. Rev.* 129, 1966.

Stephen, James Fitzjames. *A History of the Criminal Law of England.* 6th ed., vol. 1. London: Macmillan, 1883.

Strauss, Anselm L. *Psychiatric Ideologies and Institutions.* New York: Free Press of Glencoe, 1964.

Street, Vinter and Perron. *Organization for Treatment.* New York: Free Press of Glencoe, 1966.

Student Nonviolent Coordinating Committee. *Genocide in Mississippi.* Atlanta, 1964.

Studt. "The Client's Image." *Justice for the Child.* Edited by M. K. Rosenheim. New York: Free Press of Glencoe, 1962.

Stürup. "Sex Offenses: The Scandinavian Experiences." 25 *Law & Contemp. Prob.* 361, 1960.

Stürup, G. *A Situation Approach to Behavior Disorders.* Leeds Symposium on Behavior Disorders, March 1965.

Sullivan, Joseph Vincent. *The Morality of Mercy Killings.* Westminster, Md.: Newman Press, 1950.

Sussman, Frederick B. *Law of Juvenile Delinquency.* 2d ed. rev. Dobbs Ferry, N.Y.: Oceana, 1959.

Sutherland, Edwin Hardin, and Cressey, Donald R. *Principles of Criminology.* 5th ed. rev. Philadelphia: Lippincott, 1955.

"Symposium: Compensation to Victims of Crimes of Personal Violence—An Examination of the Scope of the Problem." 50 *Minn. L. Rev.* 211, 1965.

Szasz. "Whither Psychiatry." 33 *Soc. Res.* 439, 1966.

Szasz, Thomas Stephen. *Law, Liberty and Psychiatry: An Inquiry into the Social Uses of Mental Health Practices.* New York: Macmillan, 1963.

————. *Psychiatric Justice.* New York: Macmillan, 1965.

Tannenbaum, Frank. *Crime and the Community.* Boston: Ginn & Co., 1938.

Tappan. "Approach to Children with Problems." *Justice for the Child.* Edited by M. K. Rosenheim. New York: Free Press of Glencoe, 1962.

————. "Objectives and Methods in Corrections." *Contemporary Correction.* Edited by Paul Wilbur Tappan. New York: McGraw-Hill, 1951.

————. "Sentence for Sex Criminals." 42 *J. Crim. L.C. & P.S.* 332, 1951.

————. "Some Myths About the Sex Offender." 19 *Fed. Prob.* 7, 1955.

Tappan, Paul Wilbur. *Crime, Justice, and Correction.* New York: McGraw-Hill, 1960.

————. *Juvenile Delinquency.* New York: McGraw-Hill, 1949.

Tarde, Gabriel de. *Penal Philosophy.* Translated by Rapelje Howell. Boston: Little, Brown, 1912.

Taylor, Gordon Rattray. *The Biological Time Bomb.* London: Thames & Hudson, 1968.

Teeters, Negley King, and Reinemann, John Otto. *The Challenge of Delinquency: Causation Treatment and Prevention of Juvenile Delinquency.* Englewood Cliffs, N.J.: Prentice-Hall, 1950.

Terry, Charles Edward, and Pellens, Mildred. *The Opium Problem.* New York, 1925.

Theobald, Robert, ed. *The Guaranteed Income: Next Step in Economic Evolution?* Garden City, N.Y.: Doubleday, 1966.

Toch, Hans, ed. *Legal and Criminal Psychology.* New York: Holt, Rinehart & Winston, 1961.

Trotter, Thomas. *An Essay, Medical, Philosophical, and Chemical, on*

Drunkenness and its Effects on the Human Body. 2d ed. London, 1804.

Tylor, Edward Burnett. *Primitive Culture*. Vol. 2. New York: Brentano, 1924.

U.N., Congress on the Prevention of Crime and the Treatment of Offenders. *Report*. New York: Department of Economic and Social Affairs, 1955.

———, Department of Economic and Social Affairs. *International Review of Criminal Policy*, no. 7–8, 1955.

———, Economic and Social Council, Commission on Narcotic Drugs. *Summary of Annual Reports of Governments Relation to Opium and Other Dangerous Drugs*. E/NR 1961/Summary.

U.S., Bureau of the Census. *Current Population Reports, Population Estimates*. Series p–25, no. 321, November 30, 1965.

———. *Statistical Abstract of the United States*. Washington, 1960, 1966, 1968, 1969.

U.S., Commission on Civil Rights. *Report*. Washington, 1965.

U.S., Congress, House, Appropriations Committee. *Subcommittee Hearings on Treasury Appropriations for 1967*. 89th Cong., 2d sess. 1966.

———. *Narcotic Drug Rehabilitation*. H. Rep. 1486. 89th Cong., 2d sess., 1966.

———, Committee on Government Operations. *Hearings before a Subcommittee*. 89th Cong., 2d sess., 1966, pp. 184–93 (D. N. Michael, "Speculations on the Relation of the Computer to Individual Freedom and the Right to Privacy . . . ," July 26–28, 1966).

———, Ways and Means Committee. *Hearings on Taxation of Marihuana*. 75th Cong., 1st sess., 1937.

U.S., Congress, Senate, Committee on Government Operations, Permanent Subcommittee on Investigations. *Hearings*. 88th Cong., 2d sess., 1964.

———, Committee on the Judiciary, Subcommittee on Constitutional Rights. *Hearings*. 88th Cong., 1st sess., 1963.

———. *Hearings on Constitutional Rights of the Mentally Ill*. 87th Cong., 1st sess., 1961, pts. 1 and 2.

———, Subcommittee on Criminal Laws and Procedures. *Hearings on S. 2191*. 89th Cong., 2d sess., 1966.

———, Subcommittee on Improvements in the Federal Criminal Code. *The Causes, Treatment, and Rehabilitation of Drug Addicts*. S. Rep. 1850. 84th Cong., 1st sess., 1955.

———, Labor and Public Welfare Committee. *Report No. 294*. 90th Cong., 1st sess., 1967.

———, Subcommittee to Investigate Juvenile Delinquency. *Report No. 1664*. 89th Cong., 2d sess., 1966.

U.S., Department of Health, Education, and Welfare. *Alcohol and Alcoholism*. Washington, 1968.

———. *Patients in Mental Institutions*, pt. 2. Washington, 1965.

———, Children's Bureau. *1937 Juvenile Court Statistics*. Statistical Series, no. 83. Washington, 1965.

————. *Standards for Juvenile and Family Courts.* Pub. no. 437. Washington, 1966.

————. *Statistics on Public Institutions for Delinquent Children: 1964.* Statistical Series, no. 81. Washington, 1965.

————, National Clearinghouse for Mental Health Information. *Patients in Mental Institutions 1964: State and County Mental Hospitals,* pt. 2. Public Health Service Pub. no. 1452. Washington, 1966.

————, National Institute of Mental Health. *Patients in Mental Institutions,* pt. 2, "Public Hospitals for Mentally Ill." Public Health Service Pub. no. 483. Washington, 1952.

————, Federal Security Agency. *A Draft Act Governing Hospitalization of the Mentally Ill.* Public Health Service Pub. no. 51. Washington, 1950.

————, Office of Program Analysis, Committee on Juvenile Delinquency, *Programs and Services in the Field of Juvenile Delinquency.* Washington, 1958.

U.S., Federal Bureau of Investigation. *Uniform Crime Reports for the United States.* Washington, 1965, 1968, 1969.

U.S., President's Advisory Commission on Narcotics and Drug Abuse. *Final Report.* Washington, 1963.

U.S., President's Commission on Crime in the District of Columbia. *Report.* Washington, 1966.

U.S., President's Commission on Law Enforcement and the Administration of Justice. *The Challenge of Crime in a Free Society.* Washington, 1967.

————. *Task Force Report: Drunkenness.* Washington, 1967.

U.S., President's Panel on Mental Retardation. *Report of the Task Force on Law,* Washington, 1963.

U.S., Treasury Department. *Annual Report of the Secretary of the Treasury, 1966.* Washington, 1967.

————, Bureau of Narcotics. *Traffic in Opium and Other Dangerous Drugs.* Washington, 1965.

Vaillant and Rasor. "The Role of Compulsory Supervision in the Treatment of Addiction." 30 *Fed. Prob.* 53, 1966.

Van Waters. "The Socialization of Juvenile Court Procedure." 13 *J. Crim. L.* 61, 1922.

Vedder, Clyde Bennett. *Juvenile Offenders.* Springfield, Ill.: Thomas, 1963.

1 *Vermont Attorney General Report* 209, 1945.

Walzer, Breau, and Smith. "A Chromosome Survey of 2400 Normal Newborn Infants." 74 *J. Pediatrics* 438, 1969.

Wasserstrom. "Why Punish the Guilty?" *Princeton Alumni Weekly,* March 17, 1964, p. 25.

Webb, Sidney and Beatrice. *English Poor Law History: The Old Poor Law.* Vol. 1. London: Longmans, Green, 1927.

————. *English Poor Law Policy.* Hamden, Conn.: Archon Books, 1963.

————. *English Prisons Under Local Government.* London: Longmans, Green, 1922.

Westbrook. "*Mens Rea* in the Juvenile Court." 5 *J. Fam. L.* 121, 1965.

Westermarek, Edvard Alexander. *The Origin and Development of Moral Ideas*. New York: Macmillan, 1906–8.

Wheeler, Stanton, and Cottrell, Leonard S. *Juvenile Delinquency: Its Prevention and Control*. New York: Russell Sage Foundation, 1966.

"Who Commits the Crimes?" *U.S. News & World Report*, May 18, 1967.

Wickenden, Elizabeth. "Memorandum. Poverty and the Law: The Constitutional Rights of Assistance Recipients." National Social Welfare Assembly, March 25, 1965.

Wilkes, Abraham. "Opiates and Opiate Antagonists: A Review of Their Mechanism of Action in Relation to Clinical Problems." Public Health Monograph No. 52, 1958.

Williams. "Sex Offenses: The British Experience." 25 *Law & Contemp. Prob.* 334, 1960.

Williams, Glanville Llewelyn. *Criminal Law: The General Part*. London: Stevens, 1953.

Williams, Roger John. *Alcoholism: The Nutritional Approach*. Austin: U. of Texas Press, 1959.

——. *Nutrition and Alcoholism*. Norman: U. of Oklahoma Press, 1951.

Windle. "Factors in the Passage of Sterilization Legislation: The Case of Virginia." 29 *Pub. Opinion Q.* 306, 1965.

Wines, Enoch Cobb. *State of Prisons and Child-saving Institutions in the Civilized World*. Cambridge: J. Wilson & Sons, 1880.

Winick. "Marihuana Use by Young People." *Drug Addiction in Youth*. Edited by Ernest Harmes. New York: Pergamon Press, 1965.

——. "Narcotic Addiction and Its Treatment." 22 *Law & Contemp. Prob.* 9, 1956.

Wirt and Briggs. "The Meaning of Delinquency." *Juvenile Delinquency*. Edited by Herbert C. Quay. Princeton: Van Nostrand, 1965.

Wolfgang, Marvin E. *Patterns of Criminal Homicide*. Philadelphia: U. of Pennsylvania Press, 1958.

Wootton, Barbara. *Social Science and Social Pathology*. London: Allen & Unwin, 1959.

World Health Organization. *Hospitalization of Mental Patients*. Geneva, 1955.

——. Technical Report Series, no. 21, 1950.

——. Expert Committee on Alcohol and Alcoholism. *Report*. Technical Report Series, no. 94, 1955.

——, Expert Committee on Mental Health, Alcoholism Subcommittee. *First Report*. Technical Report Series, no. 42, 1951.

——. *Second Report*. Technical Report Series, no. 48, 1952.

Wortis. "Alcoholism." *Textbook on Medicine*. Edited by Cecil-Loeb, 11th ed. Philadelphia: Saunders, 1963.

Yablonsky. "The Anti-Criminal Society: Synanon." 26 *Fed. Prob.* 50, 1962.

——. "The Role of Law and Social Science in the Juvenile Court." 53 *J. Crim. L.C. & P.S.* 426, 1962.

Younghusband. "Dilemma of the Juvenile Court." 33 *Soc. Serv. Rev.* 10, 1959.

Index

and the therapeutic state, 362–
66. *See also* Due process
Sussman, F. B., on delinquency,
119
Sutherland, Edwin H., 25
Sweezer, Allen T., 200
Szasz, Thomas, 46, 88, 97, 354–
55, 375

Tahbel, *in re*, 145
Therapeutic Bill of Rights, 402–4
Therapeutic ideal, 5
Therapeutic proceedings, 38
Therapeutic programs: for alcoholics and addicts, 213–14; public ambivalence toward, 175, 214
Therapeutic sanctions: and crime
prevention, 8; to fit the offender,
37; judicial review of, 396–98;
questionable success of, 394–95;
and social accountability, 406–7
Therapeutic state: abuses resulting
from conglomerate nature of,
378–79; benefit of humanizing
climate of, 395; characteristics
of, 39–44; compared to the criminal process, 348–49, 373–74;
and compulsory treatment, 42–
44; and the concept of social defense, 42; and crime prediction
and prevention, 380; critics of
the unlimited, 352–56; dangers
of, 400–401; and degree of social
danger initiating, 380–83; early
development of, 356–62; erosion
of personal responsibility in, 46;
function of, 3; historical attitude
of, toward deviants, 299; incarceration under, 6–7; its emphasis on the individual deviant,
347–48; its emphasis on treatment and rehabilitation, 40; judicial review as limitation of,
408–9; and *mens rea*, 40; and
the parallel penal system, 372–
73; and the *parens patriae*
power, 41; potential of the unlimited, 349–51, 401; and the
problem of compulsory therapy,

383–86; recent theoretical
changes in, 400; and the right to
individual integrity, 388–91; and
the right to treatment, 398–400;
and social defense, 47, 399–400;
unchecked by legal institutions,
369–71; an involuntary system of
controls, 175. *See also* Due process; Procedural safeguards; Substantive safeguards
Therapy: failure of the old forms
of, 338–39; and genetics, 302;
limitations needed for, 386–98;
medical control of behavior,
301–2; new forms of, 300–305;
old forms of, 305–10; personality
modification of the young, 303–
4; standards needed for nonincarcerative, 335–37; and the
suppression of deviation, 304.
See also Lobotomy; Rehabilitation; Shock treatment; Sterilization
Third United Nations Congress on
Crime and the Treatment of Offenders (1965), 45
Treatment, the right to, 164, 254,
398–400

Uniform Narcotic Drug Act, 227,
228
United States Bureau of Narcotics,
258
United States Constitution: and
due process, 362; First Amendment, 390, 392; Third Amendment, 390, 392; Fourth Amendment, 4, 389, 390; Fifth Amendment, 4, 136, 185, 202, 389, 390,
392; Sixth Amendment, 4; Seventh Amendment, 90; Eighth
Amendment, 4, 35, 36, 202, 239,
279, 349, 387, 390, 391, 393,
394; Ninth Amendment, 337,
391–94; Fourteenth Amendment,
4, 70, 90, 141, 206, 208, 239,
320, 349, 392
United States Supreme Court: on
the burden of proof in juvenile

Some other books published by Penguin
are described on the following pages.

Edited by Stanley Cohen

IMAGES OF DEVIANCE

Seven prominent sociologists look at behavior that deviates from society's rules. The subjects considered range from hooliganism and marihuana smoking to suicide and industrial espionage. In all of these, the parts played by the press, television, and the police are evaluated. The writers focus especially on the attitudes of society towards deviants, and they take full account of the change from a punitive to a therapeutic approach. Their conclusions are not unanimous in every detail, but each of them is concerned with the criteria by which behavior is considered deviant and with the standing of the deviant in society. Stanley Cohen is a lecturer in sociology at the University of Durham.

Derek Wright

THE PSYCHOLOGY OF MORAL BEHAVIOR

An introduction to the psychological study of moral behavior. This clearly written survey closely examines such subjects as resistance to temptation, the psychological effects of wrong-doing, the influence of adult behavior on behavior in children, delinquency, altruism, moral insight and ideology, different types of character, religion and education. Derek Wright, of the Department of Psychology at the University of Leicester, stresses the difficulty of discussing morality without being biased by personal beliefs. Yet he succeeds in bringing this book to its conclusion with flawless objectivity.

Ted Honderich

PUNISHMENT
The Supposed Justifications

A look at arguments for and against the practice
of punishment. Should we punish? If so, should
all offenders be punished? How severe should
penalties be? Should we, as many urge, abandon
punishment and rely on treatment instead? Finding traditional views indefensible, Ted Honderich
gives fresh answers to these and other important
questions. He also assesses contemporary combi-
nations and variants of the traditional doctrines,
presents a new argument about the reality behind
punishment theories, and makes imposing suggestions as to the best that can be said in punishment's favor. The final chapter considers the
question of what behavior should lie beyond the
reach of the law. Ted Honderich teaches philosophy at University College in London.

PELICAN BOOKS

THE RIGHT TO BE DIFFERENT

Nicholas N. Kittrie is Professor of Criminal and Comparative Law at The American University and Director of the Institute for Studies in Justice and Social Behavior. He has done research at universities in England, Poland, Germany, Israel, and Egypt. Previously counsel to the Judiciary Committee of the United States Senate, Dr. Kittrie is the author of *The Mentally Disabled and the Law* and was instrumental in bringing the *In re Gault* case before the United States Supreme Court.